CATHOLIC
MORAL
THEOLOGY
& SOCIAL
ETHICS

CATHOLIC MORAL THEOLOGY

& SOCIAL ETHICS

A NEW METHOD

CHRISTINA A. ASTORGA

ORBIS BOOKS

Maryknoll, New York 10545

ORBIS BOOKS
Maryknoll, New York 10545

Fathers and Brothers
MARYKNOLL.

Founded in 1970, Orbis Books endeavors to publish works that enlighten the mind, nourish the spirit, and challenge the conscience. The publishing arm of the Maryknoll Fathers and Brothers, Orbis seeks to explore the global dimensions of the Christian faith and mission, to invite dialogue with diverse cultures and religious traditions, and to serve the cause of reconciliation and peace. The books published reflect the views of their authors and do not represent the official position of the Maryknoll Society. To learn more about Maryknoll and Orbis Books, please visit our website at www.maryknollsociety.org.

Library of Congress Cataloging-in-Publication Data

Astorga, Christina A.
   Catholic moral theology and social ethics : a new method / by Christina A. Astorga.
      pages cm
   Includes bibliographical references and index.
   ISBN 978-1-62698-054-9 (pbk.)
      1. Christian ethics—Catholic authors. I. Title.
   BJ1249.A79 2013
   241'.042—dc23
                                                    2013022792

Dad and Mom
Gilbert, Joseph, Cely, and Tonette—
This one is for you
with love

Contents

Part II
NORM

Part III
CHOICE

Preface

What is the precise relationship between moral theology and social ethics? James Keenan calls moral theology "the constant . . . the overarching concept about the Church's search for the moral response to Christ." Today some might prefer to use *theological ethics,* but this is only a difference in name, not in content and substance. Moral theology or theological ethics is the "common umbrella under which we find multiple areas of investigation: social ethics, fundamental morals, bioethics, sexual ethics, church ethics, political ethics, etc."[1] This book is specifically about the directions Catholic moral theology has taken since after Vatican II and the impact of these directions on the shifts in its vision, content, and method as a field of inquiry. The specific goal of the book is to bring these new directions in Catholic moral theology and their accompanying shifts to bear on social ethics, particularly in creating a new method for decision making in conflict situations relative to social issues and problems. The singular pursuit of the book is that this new method in social ethics draws from the heart of the Christian faith, in line with Catholic moral theology.

Catholic moral theology has been in a concentrated state of renewal and transition for some fifty years since the close of Vatican II, considered to be the most important event in the history of the modern church. It inaugurated changes that brought about countless shifts in theology. Vatican II pointed to the need for renewal in all areas of theology but noted a particular urgency for the rethinking of moral theology.

The rethinking that took place in moral theology resulted in a decisive break with the traditional manual approach, the authoritative approach followed since the Council of Trent. These manuals originated from the need for an educated clergy, trained particularly for hearing confessions. With this particular focus an alliance was naturally formed between moral theology and canon law as "sister

---

[1] James F. Keenan, *A History of Catholic Moral Theology in the Twentieth Century: From Confessing Sins to Liberating Consciences* (New York: Concilium, 2010), 5, 6.

sciences."[2] This gave moral theology a legalistic and juridical character, as canon law held a dominant influence on its vision and approach.

Over the past decades numerous efforts have been made to respond to the call for renewal in moral theology. The renewal reconnects moral theology with other theological sources, the most primary of which is scripture. Moral theology has been taken out of its autonomous place and developed in relation with the whole theological discipline, drawing from the riches of scriptural studies, systematic theology, spiritual theology, and pastoral theology, while facing the challenges posed by inculturation, interreligious dialogue, feminism, and global ethics.

At the heart of the renewal is a vision of moral theology that is concerned not only with laws, acts, rules, or obligation, but also with the formation of virtue and character. With this shift of focus, the dimensions of affectivity and spirituality ceased to be peripheral to moral theology, and were brought to its core. The shift of focus, however, did not eliminate the importance of norms, rules, and principles. The moral situation is much more subtle and complex than can be grasped by any one approach. In the particularities of life, the world of politics and ideologies, business, economics, indeed in the entire arena of human engagements, there is a need for norms in dealing with conflict situations. A balance of vision ethics and normative ethics is necessary for moral theology to respond to all the facets of human life, as required by the imperatives of acting morally in complex human situations. This integral and balanced approach shows that in Christian morality there is not just something of the scientist at work, there is also the artist, the believer, and the mystic.[3]

Richard McCormick writes that "the problem of elaborating a satisfying value system within the totality of Christian realities remains one of the most important unfinished tasks in the field of Christian morality."[4] McCormick's challenge of the unfinished task has been on my mind for a long time, especially since he and I spoke about it when I had the privilege of meeting him for the first time in person at the University of Notre Dame only a few months before he passed away. I took up his challenge as the vision of my work in the field. In view of this challenge and Vatican II's call for the renewal of moral

---

[2] Timothy E. O'Connell, *Principles for a Catholic Morality*, rev. ed. (New York: Harper San Francisco, 1990), 19.

[3] Daniel C. Maguire, *The Moral Choice* (Garden City, NY: Doubleday, 1978), 112.

[4] Richard A. McCormick, *Notes on Moral Theology 1965 through 1980* (Washington, DC: University Press of America, 1980), 295.

theology, I conceived this book along the lines of vision ethics and normative ethics, of the reconnection of moral theology with the primary sources of the faith within an ecclesial context, and of the place of reason, imagination, affectivity, and spirituality in relation to morality, particularly in making choices in conflict situations. In the flourishing current literature in the field the unique and distinctive contribution of this book is its use of the paradigm of vision, norm, and choice in applying in one coherent whole the various directions that have developed in the field of Catholic moral theology in view of a holistic theo-ethical method for addressing conflict situations in social ethics.

Conflict situations are circumstances in which all goods cannot be protected at the same time. The realization of one value is inevitably and regretfully at the cost of another. There are many conflict situations that involve social issues which have been subjects of heated contention, like the public policies regarding abortion, immigration, healthcare reform, gay marriage, and more. In the past, different areas of ethics were separated. Social ethics was distinguished from, for example, sexual ethics and bioethics. Today, the lines between the personal and the social in ethical questions and issues have been blurred. Lisa Sowle Cahill writes that "all ethics is social ethics."[5] All ethical issues have a social dimension, and thus social ethics includes sexual ethics as well as bioethical issues. The separation of the private and public arenas of moral discourse has resulted in the failure to see the social roots of so-called personal problems and to identify the larger issues that impinge on these problems. This book proposes a method for social ethics that addresses conflict situations in all areas of ethics.

The Introduction presents the directions taken toward the renewal of Catholic moral theology over the decades since the closing of Vatican II in 1965. I develop the patterns of renewal using the framework of three themes: (1) recovering the depth of moral theology; (2) building bridges: the task of integration; and (3) facing the challenge of polarity, diversity, and commonality. Based on these patterns I discern the shifts in the vision, content, and method of post–Vatican II Catholic moral theology. The Introduction lays the groundwork of the entire book.

Bernhard Häring describes the pursuit of reform and renewal of moral theology in the following way: "Moral theology, as I understand it, is not concerned first with decision making and discrete acts. Its

---

[5] Lisa Sowle Cahill, "Feminism and Christian Ethics," in *Freeing Theology: The Essentials of Theology in Feminist Perspective*, ed. Catherine Mowry LaCugna, 211–34 (San Francisco: Harper, 1993), 218.

basic task and purpose is to gain the right vision, to assess the main perspectives, and to present those truths and values which should bear upon decisions to be taken before God."[6] To realize this pursuit that Häring describes, I propose using the paradigm of vision, norm, and choice for a new method for social ethics.

Our moral vision is intertwined with the kind of person that we are. We see the world in a particular way because we are particular sorts of persons. Moral vision provides the perspective that influences the disposition, intention, and affectivity that move persons to be and act in a certain way. We do not go from rules and norms to choice; rather, we choose because of who we are and what we envision life to be. The sources of moral vision in our Christian faith context are culture, religion, scriptures, and systematic theology. I show how these sources shape our moral vision in the three chapters of Part 1.

Chapter 1 shows how culture and its dynamics with religion shape our moral vision. The way we are, as influenced by culture and religion, enters into the way we choose, act, and behave morally. Taking the perspective of Paul Tillich, culture is a form of expression of religion, and religion is the substance of culture.[7] The dynamics of culture and religion have a bearing on moral vision. The way people image themselves, what they do with their lives, and how they choose and act are within the influence of their culture (a particular way of being human) within the horizons of their experience of the divine, in their quest for transcendent and ultimate meaning (religion). I use the Filipino People Power Revolution of 1986 to illustrate the dynamics of culture and religion and its bearing on moral vision—the moral vision that was the source of the revolution's totally nonviolent spirit and power as a people toppled a regime without one single shot of a gun.

We are as the stories of our lives are. The use of scriptural stories that bring the reader into an encounter with the scriptural text and its world of character, events, and meaning is the theme of the second chapter. Engaging reason and imagination, it enables the reader to penetrate into the inner reality of scripture. I choose narrative criticism as my hermeneutical lens for scriptural interpretation because of its potential to bring the reader into touch with the life and vitality of scripture as a story. One major lacuna of narrative criticism, however, as is the case with historical criticism and also with cultural criticism, is the engagement with flesh-and-blood readers who significantly

---

[6] Bernhard Häring, *Free and Faithful in Christ: Moral Theology for Clergy and Laity* (New York: Seabury, 1978), 6.

[7] Paul Tillich, *What Is Religion* (New York: Harper and Row, 1969), 73.

contribute to the meaning of the text. This lacuna is filled in by contextual biblical pedagogy—a reading of scripture from the eyes of the disenfranchised, a feminist reading of scripture, and a reading with a global optic. What I finally propose is an integral biblical pedagogy, which makes use of the tools of various pedagogies across the entire spectrum of biblical criticism for a full and rich reading and interpretation of scripture with reference to the use of narrative criticism.

At the heart of the call of renewal of Vatican II to moral theology is to be a genuine theological science of the Christian faith. Moral theology is not to be taught only as a system of abstract truths, ideals, and principles, which degenerates all too easily into an impersonal and minimalist ethics, but as one that is not only deeply rooted in scripture but also infused with the truths of the faith. Drawing from the contemporary discourse in systematic theology, I develop a theological anthropology on the basis of the doctrines of the faith, insofar as they define a Christian conception of human existence. In defining this conception I take a tripartite stance in the third chapter. From the breadth and richness of the doctrines of faith, three fundamental realities are unraveled and enter into our narrative of who God is and who the human person is: the primacy of love, the primacy of grace, and the primacy of community.

I use the framework of these three primacies to present a broad synthesis of the doctrines of the faith. Under the primacy of love I take up the doctrines of creation, Trinity, and Jesus Christ. Under the primacy of grace I develop the tension of grace and sin, the supernatural existential and original sin, that is, the ambiguity that cuts into the very depths of the person in the face of the eschatological hope that is the ultimate word of soteriology. Under the primacy of community I present the church as the locus of community and also the common destiny shared by the whole of humankind, the earth, and the entire cosmos. In relating systematic theology and moral theology I discuss the Christian moral vision that is shaped by the primacies of love, grace, and community.

Part 2 is centered on the notion of norm. The necessary function of moral norms is mediating the moral vision in the peculiarities and complexities of human choices and acts. Their binding force lies in the moral vision they mediate and make explicit. Moral norms are the repository of the accumulated communal and ecclesial experience of values. As such, they are necessary points of reference and criteria for determining what is right regarding complex human problems and social issues. Catholic social teaching constitutes a substantial body of norms on social questions and issues.

I propose an ethical framework for the study and analysis of Catholic social teaching for an ordered, substantive, and effective reading of its voluminous documents. The proposed framework consists of the following: historical context, principles/norms of judgment, directives for action, and critical excursus. The *historical context* shows how a social encyclical was shaped by the social, economic, political, and cultural realities of its own time. *Principles/norms of judgment* refers to the moral criteria that govern ethical judgment on specific issues that are addressed. *Directives for action* refer to the call to moral praxis by an encyclical. *Critical excursus* refers to an assessment of the relevance of a social teaching, of its prophetic message or narrow view, and of its radical vision or limited horizons as it is engaged with the social issues of our times.

This framework reconfigures the matter of the encyclicals without losing their substance. It rearranges the content according to an order that makes reading less dense and dry and that reappropriates the language to evoke interest that opens to critical thought and inquiry while remaining faithful to its essence. The goal is to give serious readers of Catholic social teaching greater access to its texts, which summaries or excerpts cannot give and which could not replace the academic experience of coming into contact with the full texts. To illustrate the use of the proposed framework, I apply it in the study and analysis of selected encyclicals, showing both change and continuity of the social tradition: *Rerum Novarum* is a classic text; *Mater et Magistra* represents Catholic social thought in transition; *Octogesima Adveniens,* on the eightieth anniversary of *Rerum Novarum,* represents a post-conciliar Catholic social teaching; *Centesimus Annus* is the centenary encyclical for *Rerum Novarum.* The development of these four selected encyclicals using the proposed ethical framework constitutes the four chapters of Part 2.

In Part 3, centered on choice, I show how moral vision and norm are realized in the actual choices one makes. Apart from the choice, vision and norm lose their essence in the existential and practical order. Moral vision and norm are incarnated in the specific choice, directed by reason and principles, influenced by values and virtues, and inspired by spirituality. In developing an ethical methodology for decision making in conflict situations, I integrate the ethics of holistic reasoning and virtue ethics in Chapter 8. I use *ethics of holistic reasoning* instead of *proportionalism,* because the latter suggests to some a "dissenting view" relative to the instructions of *Veritatis Splendor.* What I attempt to do is draw from the specific elements of proportionalism and demonstrate how it represented a general move in moral theology to see norms and decisions in a more holistic and contextual way, a distinctive strength of the method that I believe has been lost in the heat of the polemics. This perspective is much needed when dealing with complex situations, especially those in which life and death are on the line. Using the term *ethics of holistic reasoning* instead of *proportionalism* highlights what the method is at its core.

I present the approaches of the ethics of holistic reasoning and virtue ethics in their best and truest light as they provide a moral compass amid the complexities of being moral. While the ethics of holistic reasoning has no causal relationship with virtue ethics, it preceded it in its turn to the subject in relation to the act. Virtue ethics, however, is not only concerned with moral being, but it is also engaged in moral doing, for being and doing are intrinsically related. The profound connection between the ethics of holistic reasoning and virtue ethics lies in the virtuous person whose calculus of values is human and Christian. The significance of integrating the ethics of holistic reasoning and virtue ethics is the development of an ethical methodology that fills in the gaps in a purely virtue-centered approach and also in a purely principle-centered approach. Integrating the ethics of holistic reasoning and virtue ethics to achieve a comprehensive account of being moral in conflict situations is an effort to break new ground and move forward the ongoing discourse in the field.

I offer four considerations for an integrated ethical methodology for conflict situations: primacy of context—thinking with stories; a larger framework for thinking with stories; systematic moral analysis and discernment; and judgment and decision.

Primacy of context is based on the premise that no moral theory can be adequate if it does not take into account the narrative of our experience. *Thinking with and through stories,* we establish the human context of moral situations. The narrative of the moral experience is critical for moral reasoning because it is necessary to establish the context, the human locus of moral objectivity. All moral reasoning begins with, is shaped by, and determined by context. Without the human context, moral reasoning exists in a vacuum. The stories may be personal, of a community, or of a people; the more plural, the richer, so multiple voices and competing perspectives are heard in difficult conflict situations. A good ethicist is a good narrativist, because thinking with stories is itself theoretically robust. It requires critical and empathetic skills to cut through the rich fabric of narratives to understand the intelligibility and coherence of people's lives as deeply rooted in their cultures and religions, even in their brokenness and fragmentation.

A larger framework for thinking with stories reflects a need to put "thinking with stories" within a larger frame of reference beyond the experiential. All pertinent data and information regarding the issue contained in the story must be gathered to provide a larger frame for study and analysis of the context. These data and information are drawn from social science, behavioral science, empirical science, and any other field of study or research that is relevant to the said issue or problem. While putting "thinking with stories" in a larger context is necessary, James Gustafson warns against the lack of critical engagement with the presuppositions and biases of empirical sources; he warns too against the facile move from the "is" to the "ought" in developing norms.[8] Charles Curran respects the value of science and technology but stresses that there is no perfect identity between what is human and what is empirical.[9] Ethicists must engage in critical discernment and judgment regarding the use of sources when putting the moral situation within broader realms of investigation.

Systematic moral analysis and discernment make up the third part of the proposed integrated ethical methodology; I call it *reflective equilibrium* because it involves the weighing and balancing of virtues, values, rules, and principles in the process of moral reasoning in conflict situations. Both virtue ethics and ethics of holistic reasoning are necessary in the reflective equilibrium to arrive at a decision that is truly human and Christian. One asks what virtues are demanded of the moral agent in the concrete human situation he or she is in. Virtues can conflict in human situations, and it takes prudence to discern which takes priority over competing allegiances when one asks questions of identity and purpose: Who am I? What ought I to be? What kind of people are we? What kind of community or nation are we? The questions of identity and purpose enter deeply into the choice or action one decides upon.

The ethics of holistic reasoning provide an ethical framework for moral discernment and judgment by asking reality-seeking questions: *What? Why?* Is the value sought greater than or at least equal to the value sacrificed? *How? What else?* Is there no other way to realize this value in the here and now with the least possible harm? *What it?* Will the means used to protect this value not undermine it in the long run? These questions represent the integral approach of the ethics of holistic reasoning as it inquires about all aspects of moral judgment. In asking

---

[8] James Gustafson, *Theology and Christian Ethics* (Philadelphia: Pilgrim Press, 1974), 222, 228.

[9] Charles E. Curran, *Critical Concerns in Moral Theology* (Notre Dame, IN: University of Notre Dame Press, 1984), 105–6, 108.

these questions moral agents are called to engage in a true discernment not only of what they are seeking to do, but more primarily of who they are, for the weighing and balancing of values is grounded in the integrity of one's person and character. And this is where virtue ethics and ethics of holistic reasoning profoundly connect. It is the virtuous person or community of virtuous persons whose calculus of values is human and Christian. The discernment of virtues must be brought to bear in determining through prudential judgment the priority of values in difficult conflict situations.

Judgment and decision form the final moment of the moral reasoning process. One makes a judgment based on the results of the moral analysis, as shaped by the concrete narrative of the ethical situation. One makes a moral decision founded on this judgment. While the integral ethical methodology proposed is virtue oriented and principle directed, it remains on the level of discursive reasoning. There is need for moral reasoning to draw from the depth of illumination of prayer and spiritual discernment.

Discernment is the distinctive contribution of Ignatius's *Spiritual Exercises* in the fundamental engagement of persons in spiritual decision making. Making moral decisions is a lifelong challenge. Confronted by moral dilemmas in conflict situations, persons ask the most basic question: What is the right thing to do? Such situations range from the intimate issues of personal morality to the larger contexts of social issues involving global questions of war, politics, and economics. Collective decisions are made on issues of broad import, where a variety of individuals participate as members of society in the shaping of such decisions as moral agents based on their conscientious discernment.

Any treatment of the writings of Ignatius must be cognizant of the cultural context in which they were shaped and the worldview that underlies them. Commentaries on Ignatian discernment are sharply divided on fundamentals, especially on the interpretation of the three Ignatian modes of discernment, with many appropriating them through the new hermeneutical lens of contemporary theology and philosophy. My attempt at an appropriation of Ignatian discernment in Chapter 9 is an effort to make accessible the inner logic of Ignatian discernment in a language that can be understood by men and women of our times.

I end the book with the integration of vision, norm, and choice, the goal of the entire book. I premise this integration on the primal necessity of the formation of the moral agent, for moral decision making is neither a matter of technique or skill nor merely a rationalistic and analytical approach. At the center of decision making are moral agents in community. It is their formation in vision and norm that directs, influences, and shapes their choice.

Bernhard Häring has written of a visional way of deciding morally. Richard McCormick, however, criticized a stress on vision that neglects the place of moral deliberation. His position is in consonance with the early revisionists of moral theology whose turn to the foundations in moral theology did not make them abandon the necessity for providing guidance for decision making in concrete situations. In the final chapter I present a review of the ethical methodology proposed for decision making in conflict situations and show how vision and norm are integrated in this methodology. This involves, in particular, showing how virtues and principles are understood within the framework of religion, culture, scripture, systematic theology, and Catholic social teaching. Moral agents who have been formed in Christian moral vision and norm bring a quality and depth to their understanding of virtues and principles as they strive to meet the imperatives of virtue ethics and ethics of holistic reasoning in dealing with conflict situations. In the actual decision making, moral agents formed in moral vision and moral norm are not operating in a moral vacuum. They bring a specific Christian ethos to bear as they understand virtues and principles as shaped by culture and religion, scriptures, and systematic theology (moral vision) and as grounded in Catholic social teaching (moral norm).

Finally, I demonstrate the confluence of reason, affectivity, and spirituality through the integration of the entire ethical methodology as proposed and the modes of Ignatian discernment. The ethical methodology that engages discursive reasoning can be integrated into the third mode of Ignatian discernment, in which one gathers all facts and pieces of evidence, thinks through pros and cons, mulls over the alternative decisions, and ponders the various options and their possible consequences. In this discernment affectivity is the criterion, and the love of Christ is the focus. As one wrestles with one's feelings regarding the choice made using the exercise of reason, one focuses on Christ and asks: Lord, what are you asking of me? What is your loving desire? What does it mean to love and to follow you? When reason is bathed in the waters of affectivity and spirituality, it is purified and cleansed and comes to its full illumination.

The significance and relevance of this book are in its fundamental insight that Christian morality engages the whole person. In this light it offers a holistic and integral approach, drawing from the vast wisdom of the Christian faith tradition, as enshrined in culture and religion, scripture, doctrines of the faith, Catholic social teaching, ethics of holistic reasoning, virtue ethics, and Ignatian spirituality. Rather than a moral theology reduced to a marginal science, whose task is seen from the narrow lens of canon law and casuistry, this book offers a moral theology with a grand view that inspires and governs Christian human existence, drawn from the entire theological enterprise as exemplified and applied in a method for conflict situations in social ethics.

Acknowledgments

This book was long in the making. It took a journey parallel to my personal journey. I wrote chapters at different times of my life, and later on I wove them together using the overarching framework of vision, norm, and choice. I began in 2003,. when I was a fellow at the Jesuit Institute of Boston College. I thank the Jesuit Institute and its director, T. Frank Kennedy, SJ, for honoring me with the distinction of being one of the two fellows of the Institute. As a fellow I had an unlimited access to the unimaginable wealth of resources for scholarship at Boston College. I also had the rare privilege of presenting my work to renowned scholars in the field of ethics and religious education: Lisa Sowle Cahill, David Hollenbach, SJ, James Keenan, SJ, Edward Vacek, SJ, Thomas Massaro, SJ, and Thomas Groome. Meeting in person and engaging in academic conversation with these scholars of stature, to whose work I make references in my footnotes, was an experience beyond compare. But even more precious were the warm personal friendships that were forged and that have endured through the years.

When I received another fellowship from Woodstock Theological Center at Georgetown University in 2004, I continued to work on the book I envisioned. I presented the fruit of my research to the international fellows: the late Bishop F. Claver, SJ, Sr. Margaret Scott, aci, Dr. Anthony Savari Raj, and Dr. Donna Orsuto. Thomas Schubeck, SJ, who was working on his own book, also participated in the presentations and discussions. These academic events, along with personal encounters, left us with warm memories of the Woodstock experience.

Having access to the vast and historic Woodstock library at Georgetown, one of the most notable Catholic theological libraries in scope and breadth, as well as to the Georgetown University library, was awe inspiring. Woodstock Theological Center, however, is closing after forty years of tradition and service. In gratitude to the center and its director, Gasper Lo Biondo, SJ, its board of directors, and its staff, I offer my book as part of its rich history and legacy in research and publications that have advanced the church's understanding of the role of faith in public life.

After my back-to-back fellowships, everything came to a standstill. Life took over, so to speak. As I was faced with the lingering illness of family members and the increasing demands of work, I lost my space for research and writing entirely. It was only in 2011, when my life took an unexpected turn, that I was able to reclaim this space. Fordham University, through the recommendation of Dr. Terrence Tilley, chair of the Theology Department, appointed me a visiting research scholar.

With full access to the world-class Fordham library, I was able to do extensive research work on the book, updating all the previous work, writing new chapters, and finally bringing the entire book project to completion. I thank Fordham University, particularly Dr. Benjamin Cooker, associate vice president, and Dr. Terrence Tilley, for this once in a lifetime academic experience.

It takes an "entire village" to complete a book project. Lisa Cahill considered my concept and encouraged me to pursue it. She also took time to read the longest chapter of the book, the foundational chapter that grounds it in the shifts of vision, content, and method of Catholic moral theology. And she helped firm up the conceptual base of the book. I thank her not only for sharing her renowned academic expertise, but for having walked with me throughout my entire career journey in the United States, in its ups and downs, with her unfailing support and friendship. Here where it really matters, Lisa is loved, valued, and cherished by many.

Tom Massaro read the entire section on Catholic social teaching and expertly evaluated it, using the best resources in the field. I relied on Ed Vacek's profound and brilliant insight into ethical methodologies for my chapter "Ethics of Holistic Reasoning and Virtue Ethics: Proposing an Ethical Methodology for Conflict Situations." To have them as my colleagues in the field and as my personal friends makes me look forward to Catholic Theological Society of America (CTSA) and Society of Christian Ethics (SCE) conferences, not only for professional growth, but for renewal of bonds.

I was privileged to have two scriptural scholars of stature to read critically my chapter on scripture. Daniel Harrington, SJ, read the chapter in its initial development of scripture and moral vision, where I proposed the use of narrative criticism as a method that engages reason and imagination, enabling the reader to penetrate into the inner reality of scripture in view of its moral vision. Daniel Kendall, SJ, read the later development of the chapter, in which I proposed an integral biblical pedagogy that makes use of the tools of the various pedagogies across the entire spectrum of biblical criticism for a full and rich reading and interpretation of scripture, considering that every method depends on other methods to fill in its lacunae. He recommended two excellent documents that gave support to the direction of the entire chapter. I am thankful that I could depend on their expertise for a critical and creative use of scripture in moral theology.

Roger Haight, SJ, with his deep and broad knowledge of theology and spirituality, was an invaluable critical reader. He generously invested time reading the entire book with scholarly care. When I asked Charles Curran and Bryan Massingale to be among the reviewers of the completed book, I asked two of the most renowned and respected scholars in social ethics. What a special grace indeed to belong to a true community of scholars. I thank all my colleagues in the field for their incalculable support, and beyond that, for their abiding friendship.

I thank Joseph L. Roche, SJ, my professor and mentor at Loyola School of Theology, for my training and formation in theology. A systematic theologian of formidable stature, both loved and feared, his enduring legacy is his singular work for the first national catechism of the Philippines and the Formation Institute for Religion Educators (FIRE), which he founded. The integrated approach of this book is a fruit of my many years of collaborative work with Fr. Roche, whose expertise goes beyond systematic theology, as he envisioned a theology that is holistic and relevant, making sense of the faith for the lives of women and men. I am grateful to him more deeply than words can express.

Considering the broad reach of the book, I asked two of my closest friends who are outside of the field of ethics to read the manuscript. Maureen O'Brien, chair of the Theology Department of Duquesne University, raised some critical questions on the overview of the entire book project and subjected some parts of the book to her sharp editorial eye. Randy Bustamante of the School of Theology and Ministry of Boston College also went through some chapters. He also read these chapters through the prism of style and showed how style and substance are wedded for greater impact on the reader. I thank Maureen and Randy for their invaluable recommendations and for being there to cheer me on from the sidelines as I ran to the finish line.

Robert Ellsberg, publisher of Orbis Books, waited for this book project to see the light of day according to its own time. I thank him for never giving up on me and for keeping an abiding faith in me as a writer and scholar. Working with James Keane as the editor of my book gave me a greater appreciation for what editors do, which is to give the work a second or third critical eye so that it might reach its zenith. I thank Orbis Books for including me in its distinguished line of scholars and authors.

The writing of this book would have not been possible without my family, a wellspring of support. Beth and Phil not only opened their home in New York, but they also opened their hearts and gave me the support I needed to finish. Simon, their Havanese pet, was my tension buster. I never understood why people fall in love with their dogs until I fell in love with Simon. No words are enough to thank Beth, Phil, and Simon for being there for me when the going was toughest and for giving me their unqualified care. I thank my sister Terry, who encouraged me to keep writing, and who together with my brother-in-law Vergs faithfully accompanied me in my endeavor with daily prayers. I am grateful to Ralph and Tom, who drove from New York to Pittsburgh and back to help me move on to a new season in my life. I thank my sisters, Jean, Marnie, and Baby, my brothers-in-law, Tony, Cesar, and Jes, and all my nieces and nephews in the Philippines, in the States, and in other parts of the world, whom I feel deeply connected with even from afar, and in whose unfailing love I find the reason to keep going.

In my career journey in the United States, there have been many turns of seasons. But at every turn, there have been gifts of friendship and solidarity. When I moved from New York to Spokane, Washington to assume my new academic position in Gonzaga University, a small community of Filipinos immediately embraced me as their own, like they have always known me. Vic, Eva, and their son Joseph, Fred and Flor, helped me cope with the extreme challenge of settling down in a new place, while I was working on the final editing of my book. For the surprise of grace they are for me, my heart is full of gratitude.

I dedicate my book to Mom and Dad, to Gilbert, Joseph, Cely, and Tonette, whose passing away have left a deep absence in my life, but whose names I now forever engrave on my book with love.

Introduction

Patterns of Renewal
in Post–Vatican II Moral Theology

At the heart of moral theology is the foundational search for the way to live the upright life of Christian discipleship. This Introduction presents the directions of moral theology since Vatican II, as shown in its shifts of vision, content, and method. These shifts are brought to bear on a new method in social ethics in addressing conflict situations involving social issues and problems.

Vatican II (1962–65) broke new ground and created radical shifts of horizons in the extent, range, and depth of subjects that it addressed, as well as in the overall vision, orientation, and direction it gave to the church in a new era of world history. Here was a church with a vital and robust spirit (in stark contrast to the church in the age of modernism), placing its stakes on the line as it engaged with the world, its explorations and achievements, and its anxieties and hopes. Here was a church building bridges with the world and also building bridges within itself in a spirit of renewal and transformation. Looking outside in and looking inside out, the church of Vatican II gave birth to new visions, challenged old systems, and created new structures. It envisioned new responses to the demands of the faith in a growing and changing world.

In the renewal of theology particular focus was given to moral theology:

Special attention needs to be given to the improvement of moral theology. Its scientific exposition should be nourished more by the teaching of Scripture, and it should throw light on the exalted nature of the calling of the faithful in Christ, and on their obligation to produce fruit in love for the life of the world. (*Decree on Priestly Formation* [OT], no. 16)[1]

---

[1] All official church documents are available on the vatican.va website. Quotations from these documents will have paragraph numbers given in the text.

This special attention given to moral theology was not due to its pre-eminence over other disciplines of theology, but due to its diminishment as a science of faith over time.

The council required above all that moral theology and other theological disciplines be renewed in the mysteries of the faith and be rooted in scripture, the "soul of theology." Theology must not be taught as a system of abstract truths, ideals, and principles, but as one that is so infused with the truths of the faith that it enlivens, nourishes, and transforms life in the spirit. The council defined in clearest terms its vision of moral theology as a genuine theological science of the Christian faith in moral life, stating that scientific exposition of moral theology must be nourished more fully by faith so that it may shed light upon the nobility of the vocation of the faithful in Christ to bring forth fruit in charity for the life of the world.

Initiators of Reform in Moral Theology

A study of the past yields an appreciation of the shape that moral theology has taken in the present and will take in the future. The spirit of reform of moral theology engendered by Vatican II was not entirely a new spirit. There had been earlier reformers in moral theology who had forged this spirit in their time. The work of Odom Lottin (1880–1965) carved the landscape of reform that was seen throughout the twentieth century. He was a sharp critic of the focus on the moral manuals on sin and canon law taking over moral theology, with its stress on external acts rather than on the internal life. Overtaken by canon law, moral theology lost its moorings in dogmatic theology and its roots in scripture. Moreover, by its narrow vision of morality as merely avoiding wrongful external acts, it lost not only its larger purpose, to pursue the Christian vocation, but also its intrinsic connection with ascetical and mystical theology.[2] In Lottin's view the terrible decline into which moral theology fell after Thomas Aquinas was due to the disconnection of moral theology from the entire theological system: "It separated itself from its living sources, scripture and dogmatics; it amputated the limbs of ascetical and mystical theology; it introduced a number of canonical questions which sought no solution in biblical texts; and it became much more interested in sin than in virtue."[3]

---

[2] Odom Lottin, *Morale Fondamentale* (Belgium: Tournai, 1954), 23–25.

[3] Odom Lottin, *Au Coeur de la Morale Chrétienne* (Tournai: Declees, 1957), 6.

Noting that after the Scholastics, the moralists were fixated on sin, Lottin envisioned a moral theology deeply rooted in its virtuous ends, both natural and supernatural. He wrote that "the true grandeur of being human resides in morality, because one's moral life is one's own self manifesto, the fruit of one's personality."[4] He saw formation of conscience is foundational to the moral life.[5] This is not the pathology of conscience in the moral manuals, but the virtue-centered formation of conscience developed by learning what prudence means. Turning to prudence, he viewed moral life as the capacity of persons to find within themselves, their community, church tradition, and the scriptures the foundation of their discernment of moral objectivity.[6] The notion of moral objectivity raised a question: Is right determined by the authority of clerics or ethicists or by the individual Christian's prudential judgment? This question is critical, as it challenges one's whole view of moral theology, leading ethicists like Josef Fuchs into the revisionist school. Lottin's turn to the person, to virtues, and to prudence was the foundation of the reform movement.[7]

While Lottin envisioned a moral theology that was rooted in scripture, developed from dogmatic theology, and embedded in spiritual theology, it was three others who actually developed a moral theology in relation to these other theological disciplines—Fritz Tillmann (1874–1953), Gérard Gilleman (1910–2002), and Bernhard Häring (1912–98). Tillmann's scientific career as a biblical scholar came to an end because he was the editor of a commentary on the New Testament that included an essay by Friedrich Wilhelm Maier that upheld the then-controversial two-source theory concerning the Synoptic Gospels, a theory that is accepted today by almost everyone. Both Tillmann and Maier were given the option of changing theological disciplines. Maier did not take the offer and became instead a prison chaplain. Tillmann decided to change fields and became a top moral theologian. This change was providential in the shaping of moral theology.[8] James Keenan writes:

---

[4] Odin Lottin, *Aux Sources de Notre grandeur Morale* (Louvain: Abbaye du Mont César, 1946), 20.

[5] See Lottin, in *Morale Fondamentale*, 297–339.

[6] See ibid., 341-470, esp. 363-69, 448-52.

[7] James F. Keenan, *A History of Catholic Moral Theology in the Twentieth Century: From Confessing Sins to Liberating Consciences* (New York: Concilium, 2010), 43.

[8] Ibid., 60–61.

Catholic moral theology could not make the much-needed and extraordinarily urgent turn to the Bible if it did not have within its guild a superb scripture scholar. One can hardly imagine a moral theologian credibly developing a biblically based moral theology. Tillmann's exile from the land of exegesis and his finding safety and sanctuary in the field of moral theology became itself the fundamental occasion for realizing one of the most significant developments in twentieth-century Roman Catholic moral theology.[9]

He found virtue as the bridge between moral theology and scripture, with charity at the heart of his ethics; these are profoundly connected to the call to discipleship—the following of Christ, the essence of living a Christian moral life.[10]

The work of Gérard Gilleman continued the project of Tillmann. "In the love command, Tillmann gave a deep directionality to the material agenda of Catholic moral theology; in the idea of discipleship, he gave Christians a moral identity, and in the use of scriptures, he gave us a 'new' text. What Tillmann's project needed was an ascetical theology to animate the disciple. Gilleman answered that need by advocating for a charity-inspirited spiritual tendency."[11] Like Lottin and Tillmann, Gilleman criticized the moral manuals. He wrote that law rather than love was the dominant theme of the manuals, and that moral theology was bereft of the inner spiritual impulse, losing its moorings in dogmatic theology.[12]

Gilleman's distinctive contribution is a deeply affective and spiritual foundation for moral theology founded on charity. The focus is not on external actions but on the interior disposition of the heart that seeks union with God, neighbor, and self, which charity strives to attain. His work on the primacy of charity became arguably the most important single work in moral theology in the twentieth century. That moral truth is realized in the "right realization of the human person called by charity to be a member of the community of the disciples of Christ becomes the foundational shift in moral theology in the twentieth century." Moral theology and ascetical theology come to unity in the primacy of charity, and in this unity, a person strives to live morally by seeking to be in communion with God who is *agape,* which bears

---

[9] Ibid., 61.

[10] Ibid., 69.

[11] Ibid., 75.

[12] Gérard Gilleman, *The Primacy of Charity in Moral Theology* (Westminster, MD: Newman, 1959), xxx.

fruit in one's acts of justice, temperance, fortitude, and prudence in relation to others in community.[13]

In the 1950s many Catholic moral theologians continued teaching moral theology in line with the constricted vision of the manuals as an aid for the priest confessors, while others followed the innovative spirit of the revisionists, who were pursuing a more positive, more interior, and more integrated moral theology. Richard McCormick, who was among the more notable revisionists, criticized the manuals as "all too often one-sidedly confession oriented, magisterium-dominated, canon law-related, sin-centered, and seminary-controlled." Furthermore, the theological anthropology at its base shows "the agent as solitary decision maker."[14] Bernhard Häring described the pursuit of the reformers: "Moral theology, as I understand it, is not concerned first with decision making and discrete acts. Its basic task and purpose is to gain the right vision, to assess the main perspectives, and to present those truths and values which should bear upon decisions to be taken before God."[15]

The turn of the moral theologians to the foundations in moral theology, however, did not mean abandoning the necessity of offering moral guidance for moral decision making in concrete situations. Rather than the narrow and pithy judgments the manualists had offered, they followed what Häring proposed—a more visional way of acting morally.[16] This means that we do not go from a law, principle, or norm to a choice. We envision first our entire stance to the problem or issue from the perspective of truths and values which inspire and influence our decisions and choices. The task of moral theologians, then, is not only to provide answers to cases but also to inspire moral vision for action.

In 1954 Häring published in German the sixteen-hundred-page magisterial three-volume *Das Gesertz Christi* (English: *The Law of Christ: Moral Theology for Priests and Laity*), which is considered his landmark contribution. The vision of the book is decisively clear as articulated in its foreword: "The principle, the norm, the center, and the goal of Christian moral theology is Christ."[17] As Keenan writes:

---

[13] Keenan, *A History of Catholic Moral Theology in the Twentieth Century,* 72, 59, 70, 74, quotation at 70.

[14] Richard A. McCormick, "Moral Theology 1940–1989: An Overview," *Theological Studies* 50/1 (1989): 3, 22.

[15] Bernhard Häring, *Free and Faithful in Christ: Moral Theology for Clergy and Laity* (New York: Seabury, 1978), 6.

[16] Keenan, *A History of Catholic Moral Theology in the Twentieth Century,* 83–84.

[17] Bernhard Häring, *The Law of Christ* (Paramus, NJ: Newman, 1954), vii.

"Each word was central: Christ is the principle, the foundation, the source, the wellspring of moral theology; Christ is the norm, indeed a positive norm, a norm about being, a norm about persons as disciples; Christ, not the human, is the center; and Christ is the goal, for charity is union with God for ever."[18]

Studying at Tübingen brought Häring into contact with the re-formers (Lottin, Tillmann, Mersch, and Gilleman). He appropriated the contributions of these reformers and drew insights from three other theologians (Johannes Stelzenberger, Gustav Ermecke, and Theodor Steinbüchel). "Haring's work represents a certain com-ing together of 40 years of variety of attempts to resituate moral theology as a theological enterprise deeply connected to dogmatic (Lottin, Mersch, Stelzenberger, Ermecke), biblical (Tillmann and Steinbüchel), and ascetical (Gilleman) theology." It was now upon Häring to do a synthesis of fundamental moral theology, rooted in scripture, grounded in dogma, and founded on spirituality, and at the same time to provide new modes of normative guidance for right moral conduct.[19]

The Law of Christ provided the solid foundation for the claims of the revisionists. The works of the fathers of revisionism as appropri-ated by Häring have become contemporary moral theology. There was no need to make anew a case for revisionism. Vatican II validated the revisionists' work in the *Decree on Priestly Formation*, whose two-sentence statement on moral theology has become "a kind of terse manifesto of the revisionists' agenda."[20] At the council Häring served on pre-conciliar and conciliar commissions and was the secretary of the editorial committee that drafted the *Pastoral Constitution on the Church in the Modern World (Gaudium et Spes)* [GS]. Charles Curran spoke of Häring as "quasi-father" of that document.[21] The influence of Häring must have been the reason why Joseph Selling, in a recent collection of essays from Leuven University, *Vatican II and Its Legacy,* sees in *Gaudium et Spes* the foundational outline for fundamental moral theology.[22]

---

[18] Keenan, *A History of Catholic Moral Theology in the Twentieth Century*, 88.

[19] Ibid., 90–91.

[20] Ibid., 95.

[21] Charles E. Curran, "Bernhard Häring: A Moral Theologian Whose Soul Matched His Scholarship," *National Catholic Reporter* 34 (July 17, 1998), 11.

[22] Joseph A. Selling, "*Gaudium et Spes:* A Manifesto for Contemporary Moral Theology," in *Vatican II and Its Legacy,* ed. Mathijs Lamberigts and Leo Kenis (Leuven: Leuven University, 2002), 145–62.

Publishing an extraordinary number of books that address a broad spectrum of moral themes and issues, Charles Curran is one of the world's most notable moral theologians and is highly esteemed by his colleagues in the field. He served as president of the Catholic Theological Society of America in 1969–70, was the first Roman Catholic elected president of the Society of Christian Ethics (1971–72), and was the first recipient of the John Courtney Murray Award. He credits Bernard Häring with having the most important influence on his moral theology. Inspired by Häring's vision, Curran holds that "moral theology should deal with the fullness of the Christian life and the call to holiness, and not just with the sinfulness of particular acts." After he was declared by the Congregation for the Doctrine of the Faith as no longer suitable or eligible to exercise the function of a professor of Catholic theology on July 25, 1986, because he dissented from the Ordinary Magisterium regarding sexual and marital issues, Curran published *Faithful Dissent*, which attempts to give both the historical record and interpretation of the controversy of the decision of the Congregation for the Doctrine of the Faith over his case. Calling it a "teaching moment," he offers his insights on five issues that were at the base of his dismissal as a Catholic theologian, issues that remain critical challenges to the church of our times: the role of the theologian; public theological dissent from some non-infallible hierarchical church teachings; the Christian faithful and dissent; justice and fairness of the process; and academic freedom, theology, and Catholic institutions of higher learning.[23] Vatican II brought in winds of change, but whether they were enough to address some seemingly intransigent problems remained to be seen.

The direct reference of Vatican II to moral theology may have been brief, but it was full of significance, as gleaned from all the council's other declarations that have implications on Christian morality. Through many years after this major event in the life of the church, moral theology has taken the road of renewal, attempting to realize the full implications of the vision of Vatican II. There is no one comprehensive moral theology today that has realized the ideal of moral theology in the light of the council's vision, but there are elements in the many and various attempts at renewal. As John Mahoney vividly describes the radical challenge and demand of creating this ideal moral theology: "It was not simply a matter of tuning the engine and tightening the steering of moral theology, but of a thorough systematic

---

[23] Charles E. Curran, *Faithful Dissent* (Kansas City, MO: Sheed and Ward, 1986), 8, 50–74, quotation at 8.

overhaul of the whole vehicle and sending it off into quite new and (for it) uncharted areas of modern living."[24]

An emerging generation of Catholic moral theologians has distinguished itself from those who were immersed in the Catholic subculture before Vatican II and those who were called to go beyond this subculture by Vatican II to engage deeply with the world. This Post–Vatican II generation, which is behind the New Wine, New Wineskins project,[25] feels no need to engage with the world; it is immersed in the world, but unlike those who had a Catholic subculture that gave them a point of reference, a center from which to come, these theologians consider themselves as standing on loose ground in terms of their Catholic identity and thus see the need to root themselves in the Catholic locus. They "exhibit a turn from the world toward the church in search of wisdom. Once nourished by this wisdom, they then turn back toward the world in witness and service."[26] John Dunne calls this a practice of "passing over and coming back."[27] According to this approach, "one takes stock of one's own standpoint, then 'passes over' through sympathetic understanding to the standpoint of another person, culture, or religion, searching for resonances or conflicts with one's own experience, then 'comes back' to one's own life with an enriched understanding."[28]

The members of this generation recognized the attractions and seductions of the pluralistic world in which they live, and they saw the need for a Catholic framework of meaning within which they

[24] John Mahoney, *The Making of Moral Theology: A Study of the Roman Catholic Tradition* (Oxford: Clarendon, 1987), 307.

[25] This is the project of a group of young intellectuals who reflect on their work in the discipline of moral theology as a vocation in service of the church and the academy. Institutionally supported by the University of Notre Dame, the group has been meeting annually since 2002 and presenting their work addressing key issues in Catholic moral theology. Their work was published in *New Wine, New Wineskins: A Next Generation Reflects on Key Issues in Catholic Moral Theology*, ed. William C. Mattison III (Lanham, MD: Rowman and Littlefield, 2005). The book presents Catholic moral theologians who care about spiritual formation and ecclesial roots as they strive to do Catholic moral theology from the heart of the church.

[26] See David Cloutier and William C. Mattison III, "Introduction," in Mattison, *New Wine, New Wineskin*, 1–5, quotation at 5.

[27] John S. Dunne, *The Way of All the Earth: Experiments in Truth and Religion* (New York: Macmillan, 1972), ix, 53.

[28] The quotation is William Collinge's encapsulation of John Dunne's approach, cited in *Gathered for the Journey: Moral Theology in Catholic Perspectives*, ed. David Matzko McCarthy and M. Therese Lysaught (Grand Rapids, MI: Eerdmans, 2007), 6.

could negotiate and navigate this world. As shown in the articles written by the thirteen outstanding young scholars in *Gathered for the Journey,* their main goal is do moral theology from a distinctively Catholic locus, drawing on the wealth of its traditions and bringing it to bear on contemporary issues with fresh perspectives and with an impact on Christian life, where men and women face concrete quandaries of Christian living today.[29] They strive to do Catholic moral theology from the heart of the church, drawing on the faith tradition but critiquing it too, as shown in essays on the theology of body of John Paul II by David Cloutier[30] and William Mattison III.[31] And they bring this tradition to bear on day-to-day life, for example, in David Matzko McCarthy's *The Good Life: Genuine Christianity of the Middle Class,*[32] which challenges men and women to live the gospel in their homes, in their neighborhoods, and in their cultures.

This study of the patterns of renewal of post–Vatican II moral theology, the era to which this generation belongs, presents renewed moral theology through a specific Catholic lens. I present in broad outlines the directions taken toward renewal in moral theology over the past four decades after the closing of Vatican II in 1965. The objective is to see the patterns of renewal as reflected in the scholarship in the field. I propose to present these patterns under three headings: recovering the depth of moral theology; building bridges—the task of integration; and facing the challenges of polarity, diversity, and commonality.

Based on these three patterns of renewal I present in the conclusion of the chapter the shifts in vision, content, and method in post–Vatican II moral theology relative to that of moral theology of times past. What I mean by *vision* is the overarching outlook of what moral theology is all about, rooted in a self-understanding of its thrust as a discipline; *content* refers to the subject matter that moral theology takes up in its expositions, discourses, and debates; and *method* is the approach taken in relation to theory and reality and their dialectics,

---

[29] See McCarthy and Lysaught, *Gathered for the Journey,* 1–19.

[30] David Cloutier, "Heaven Is a Place on Earth? Analyzing the Popularity of Pope John Paul II's Theology of the Body," in *Sexuality and the US Catholic Church: Crisis and Renewal,* ed. Lisa Sowle Cahill, John Garvey, and T. Frank Kennedy, 18–31 (New York: Crossroad, 2006).

[31] William C. Mattison III, "'When they rise from the dead, they neither marry nor are given to marriage': Marriage and Sexuality, Eschatology, and the Nuptial Meaning of the Body in Pope Paul II's Theology of the Body," in Cahill, Garvey, and Kennedy, *Sexuality and the US Catholic Church,* 32–51.

[32] David Matzko McCarthy, *The Good Life: Genuine Christianity for the Middle Class* (Grand Rapids, MI: Brazos, 2004).

involving a structure of thinking, critiquing, valuing, judging, and deciding.

Recovering the Depth of Moral Theology

If there is one thing that Vatican II has done for moral theology, it is the recovery of its depth. If not deeply rooted, moral theology would fail to rise to its true nature and purpose as a theological discipline. Its sphere would be narrow and constricted, bereft of the expanse, breadth, and richness of the Christian faith. Since the close of Vatican II moral theology has been recovering its depth by establishing itself as a genuine theological discipline by being re-rooted in scripture, centered in Christ, and relocated in relation to the entire discipline of theology, in particular to systematic theology and spiritual theology. A turn to the subject in theological anthropology has also contributed to recovering the depth of moral theology as shown in the notion of fundamental commitment, a key concept that has brought about shifts in the understanding of freedom, conscience, and sin.

Scripture as Source of Moral Theology

Scripture, the word of God, is the privileged but not the exclusive source of knowing the divine will and intentions for human living to inform and shape Christian moral life. But just how scripture does this is a difficult and complex matter. There remains a wide diversity in the ways in which theologians use scripture in the field of Christian morality. Both Protestant ethics and Catholic moral theology continue to grapple with the question of methodology.[33] The end goal is to develop a more biblically centered morality, but there is no single approach to this goal.

The basic reason for this situation is the very nature of ethical materials in scripture. Scripture's language is not that of a scientific ethical treatise but rather of literature—imaginative, parabolic, symbolic. Its meaning comes at different levels. More story than history, more wisdom than law, scripture must be interpreted in the context of its profuse and bewildering use of literary forms and genres, in narratives, parables, sayings, paradoxes, apocalyptic literature. Because its logic is

---

[33] See Charles E. Curran and Richard A. McCormick, eds., *Readings in Moral Theology*, no. 4, *The Use of Scripture in Moral Theology* (New York: Paulist Press, 1984).

elusive and often paradoxical, it is difficult to pin down its normative authority in clear, exact, and unequivocal terms.[34]

Ethics is not monolithic. Neither is scripture. There is a richness and complexity to scripture in the diversity of its canonical texts, the wealth of its literary forms, and the pluralism of its historical-critical contexts. This makes any facile appeal to scripture naive. Any approach to scripture that is not attentive to the diversity and development of morality in scripture is bound to encounter problems. Moreover, the cultural distance between biblical times and the present era brings into question how normatively significant scripture is for contemporary moral questions and issues. To determine the meaning of the text in its original context and also its meaning for today requires serious work in exegesis and hermeneutics.

The exegetical task seeks to determine what the text meant in its original setting. Because the scriptural texts are expressions of a historical and communal faith, they are bound by the language and cultural categories of their times. The exegete opens the world of the texts, of their socio-cultural-political horizons, of their variety of literary genres. The cultural conditioning of scripture must be considered for a better appreciation of its moral imperatives. In view of this, "careful exegetical work is the crucial first step leading to the satisfactory fulfillment of the other tasks in using scripture in moral theology."[35]

The late nineteenth and early twentieth centuries saw the rise of a historical-critical exegetical approach to scripture. It was primarily concerned with the questions of sources, authorship, and literary forms in its attempts to determine the literal sense of scripture.[36] The turn to literary criticism, with its appropriation of secular

---

[34] Vincent MacNamara, *Love, Law, and Christian Life: Basic Attitudes of Christian Morality* (Wilmington, DE: Michael Glazier, 1988), 54.

[35] Richard Gula, *Reason Informed by Faith: Foundations of Catholic Morality* (New York: Paulist Press, 1989), 168. Michael Cahill, in "The History of Exegesis and Our Theological Future," concludes that "the historic-critical method need not be repudiated while postmodernism promotes a pluralist perspective. . . . The essential thing is that the discipline of biblical studies be both inclusively historical and no less critical" (*Theological Studies* 61/2 [2000]: 347). See also Marie Ann Mayeski, who argues that systematic theologians need to join the exegetes and those who are investigating the history of exegesis. The insertion of the discipline of systematic theology is profitable regarding the question of method in the use of scripture ("Catholic Theology and the History of Exegesis," *Theological Studies* 62/1 [2001]: 140–53).

[36] Scriptural texts cannot be transposed directly to the contemporary scene without attention to the theo-historical context of the text. The biblical teachings on marriage and homosexuality are two instances.

literary-critical theories ranging from structuralism (focus on formal structure of the text, without attention to the author or reader) and to deconstructionism (readers' reading of meanings in the text is limitless) has challenged the claims of the historical-critical method both to objectivity and hegemony of meaning tied to the literal sense of scripture.[37]

When social history and sociology gained prominence in the 1970s, there was a turn to the community, which prompted new studies concerning the social world of scripture and the use of social-scientific methods for such studies. Social history studies the specific social conditions, organizations, history, or world view of a given community in antiquity,[38] while sociology and anthropology, using models, investigate the way a human society is organized and functions within such a community.[39] As a form of contextual criticism, the social-scientific approach studies the text as it stands in relation to the environment, for example, the political, economic, and cultural patterns of Israel and Palestine that shaped the biblical writings. As Christian communities today wrestle with the contemporary world, they turn to examples of biblical communities engaging their own contexts as analogically usable for present times.[40]

The turn to the community has also invited attention to the social location of the readers. According to the social locations of the texts, liberation theologians and feminist theologians renewed the challenge regarding the claims of objective methods of interpretation and engaged in a hermeneutics of suspicion relative to the ideological biases of such methods. They have argued that there are no self-interpreting texts and no objective method of interpretation. They consciously pursue a hermeneutics from the standpoint of justice and liberation.[41]

---

[37] Allen Verhey, "Scripture and Ethics: Practices, Performance, and Prescription," in *Christian Ethics: Problems and Prospects,* ed. Lisa Sowle Cahill and James F. Childress, 18–44 (Cleveland: Pilgrim Press, 1996), 22.

[38] See Jonathan Z. Smith, "The Social Description of Early Christianity," *Religious Studies Review* 1 (1975): 19–25.

[39] See Bruce J. Malina, *Christian Origins and Cultural Anthropology: Practical Models for Biblical Interpretation* (Atlanta: John Knox, 1986).

[40] Lisa Cahill refers to the "*hermeneutics* of social embodiment," which "investigates the pattern of interaction between biblical narratives and their generating environment, and then seeks appropriate recapitulation of such patterns in the contemporary church. . . . Not all social interactions indicated by texts historically understood are ones we necessarily want to replicate. Hence, the notion of analogy may be helpful" ("The New Testament and Ethics: Communities of Social Change," *Interpretation* (December 1990): 389.

[41] The tension between the biblical text and women is rooted in the scriptural presentation of humanity, which not only raises the male as normative but also

Although the historical-critical or even social-scientific exegetical method is criticized, both can be used without granting them the monopoly or hegemony of interpretation.

The reluctance to move from what scripture meant in the past to what it means today, especially in the area of ethics and morality, is due largely to the complexity and difficulty involved in the move. This is the task faced by hermeneutics. Its goal is to build a bridge between the world of the text in antiquity and the world of the contemporary reader. The process of doing so must be grounded in faith, for one is not dealing only with a historical artifact but a sacred text that mediates the divine self-communication. The hermeneutical task is done by one who is inwardly Christian and whose worldview is nourished by the symbols and stories of the Christian faith. Only with this faith vision can one discern the presuppositions or biases underlying the moral attitudes, values, and precepts of an earlier age and determine which are truly normative.[42] To move from scripture to contemporary normative reflection, hermeneutics engages the principles of analogy, critical distance, and surplus of meanings, in order to move toward "fusion of horizons" relative to shared meanings or to "divergence of horizons" relative to critical disagreements.[43]

The hermeneutical task requires not only a critical examination of the presuppositions of the text but also a critical assessment of the presuppositions we bring to the text, as it is opened to our world of meaning. George Montague stresses the necessity for the Christian community to protect the word from the arbitrariness of the readers' self-projection. It is in the environment of a community that is striving

---

diminishes women as inferior, subject to men by divine design, and designated primarily responsible for sin in the world. Feminist biblical scholarship charges that scripture is deeply embedded in patriarchy. See Sandra Schneiders, "The Bible and Feminism," in *Freeing Theology: The Essentials of Theology in Feminist Perspective,* ed. Catherine Mowry La Cugna, 31–57 (San Francisco: Harper Collins, 1993), esp. 34.

[42] Vincent MacNamara, *Faith and Ethics: Recent Roman Catholicism* (Dublin: Gill and Macmillan, 1985), 87–88. Hermeneutics, briefly, is interpreting the text so that the "past may become alive and illumine our present with new possibilities for personal and social transformation" (Walter Wink, *The Bible in Transformation: Toward a Paradigm for Biblical Study* [Philadelphia: Fortress Press, 1973], 2.

[43] Sandra Schneiders, in particular, uses these hermeneutical processes to overcome the hegemony of the meaning given to the text by releasing it to new readers and new contexts and creating liberating and transforming meanings, particularly for women. See "Feminist Ideology Criticism and Biblical Hermeneutics," *Biblical Theology Bulletin* 19/1 (1989): 3–10. See also Agnes Brazal, "Feminist Ideological Critique: The Bible and the Community," *MST Review* 2/2 (1999): 97–117.

to live the gospel that one finds a corrective and supportive matrix for hearing and reading the word. The objective is not only information but transformation.[44]

Together with the exegetical and hermeneutical tasks is the methodological task that one should engage in as "what scripture meant" moves to "what it means today," and as scripture is used in relation to the formation of character or to concrete moral judgment. Distinguishing the use of scripture as "illuminative" or "prescriptive" is helpful in determining the kind of direction we can expect to get from scripture and in learning what way it bears on our judgment. Scripture as illuminative shapes and influences the perspectives and horizons of the person making a judgment but does not determine or prescribe the specific content of the moral judgment. Scripture in this sense provides images that awaken moral awareness and sensitivity, but it does not provide concrete directions for one's action. On the other hand, scripture as prescriptive provides moral precepts and rules for action and behavior.[45]

Rooting moral theology in scripture should not lead to the exaltation of scripture for the negation of tradition, experience, and reason. Every coherent and adequate Christian morality draws in an integral way from scripture, tradition, experience, and reason. This is easier stated, however, than practiced. In an ethical judgment the critical question remains: how to discern among the different sources. At best the following principle must be upheld in dealing with the sources of Christian ethics and morality: "The sources are not independent variables in the theological or ethical equation; they mutually condition and mutually critique each other."[46]

---

[44] George T. Montague, "Hermeneutics and the Teaching of Scripture," *Catholic Biblical Quarterly* 41/1 (January 1979): 11.

[45] *Illuminative* or *paranetic* ethics deals with the foundations of morality, its overall orientation, and the deep intentional and dispositional level; to this belong moral attitudes, values, and ideals. *Prescriptive* or *normative* ethics deals with concrete actions and behavior. To this category belong moral rules and precepts. This distinction is possible theoretically, but in the order of concrete choices and decisions of individuals, these two dimensions of ethics interrelate and interact. Attitudes, values, and ideals "enter" into the concrete action, qualifying, modifying, and grounding it. See Hans Schürmann and Philip Delhaye, "The Actual Impact of the Moral Norms of the New Testament: Report from the International Theological Commission," in Curran and McCormick, *Readings in Moral Theology*, 78–104, at 84.

[46] David Hollenbach, "Fundamental Theology and the Christian Moral Life," in *Faithful Witness: Foundations of Theology for Today's Church*, ed. Leo J. O'Donovan and T. Howland Sanks, 167–84 (New York: Crossroad, 1989), 182.

Centrality of Christ

For centuries Catholic clergy were trained and formed through the manuals of moral theology. Largely based on natural law that cuts through all levels of human knowing and experience, the manuals operated on common practical reason without any reference to Jesus Christ and the Gospels. Since Vatican II moral theologians have been attending to the question of the centrality of Jesus Christ as the norm and paradigm of Christian morality. And recent research on the historical Jesus, which has turned to history, literary criticism, and the social sciences to discover his identity and meaning, accounts for the focused christological interest in contemporary theological discourse.[47]

This recent research on the historical Jesus is important not only for what it reveals about the ethical, social, and political significance of Jesus and the early Christian movement in the first-century context, but also for its implications on the present christological discourse. The current state of this discourse is at best dynamic and open ended, with the pluralism of models it presents for understanding the person of Jesus Christ, human and divine, his mediatorship of salvation, and his place and significance relative to all other religious traditions.

To recognize and believe Jesus as the Christ (Messiah) "requires what the prophets had called *teshuva,* a fundamental 'turning' or conversion in thinking and identity. . . . Jesus redefines what it is to be Messiah, just as the concept Messiah redefines Jesus' identity."[48] To understand Jesus as Christ is to link Jesus to God, as "God's anointed one," and to claim at the minimum that "God's saving and liberating power is manifest in Jesus"[49] or at the maximum that Jesus not only is a manifestation of God's power but is himself divine.[50]

---

[47] The 1994 convention of the Catholic Theological Society of America addressed the theme of Jesus for the first time in its fifty-year history. See *Christology: Memory, Inquiry, Practice*, ed. Anne Clifford and Anthony J. Godzieba (Maryknoll, NY: Orbis Books, 2003), which contains the papers presented at the convention. These papers focused on two questions: Who is Jesus Christ? Why is he significant?

[48] Robert Masson, "The Clash of Christological Symbols: A Care for Metaphoric," in ibid., 73. Masson states that "a univocal and literal reading in that sense—a reading that does not negotiate the entailed shifts in fields of meanings—will mistake the logic of predication."

[49] Marinus de Jonge, "Christ," in *The Anchor Bible Dictionary*, ed. David Noel Freedman (New York: Doubleday, 1992), 1:921.

[50] See John P. Galvin, "Jesus Christ," in *Systematic Theology: Roman Catholic Perspectives,* ed. Francis Schüssler Fiorenza and John P. Galvin, vol. 1 (Minneapolis: Fortress Press, 1991), 251–324; William P. Loewe, "Chalcedon, Council of," in *The New Dictionary of Theology*, ed. Joseph A. Komonchak, Mary Collins, and

Roger Haight holds that "the formal divinity of Christ is a constant, the object of development, but that this divinity will be understood and affirmed in new ways."[51] He, like a number of other theologians who are engaged in the current christological discourse, proposes new ways of understanding the faith claims about Jesus's divinity, seeking to avoid a monophysitism[52] that compromises his integral humanity and a high Christocentrism that undermines the dialogue with other religious traditions.[53]

Moral theology focuses on the moral significance of Jesus Christ for Christians today. Thus it is wise to heed Jon Sobrino's assertion: "Even after faith in Christ, the New Testament goes back to Jesus, and has to go back to Jesus, precisely to safeguard true faith in Christ."[54] Sobrino focuses on Jesus from the conviction that "whenever, in the course of history, Christians have sought to reinvest Christ with his totality, they have returned to Jesus of Nazareth."[55] Sobrino does not break the bond between the exalted Christ and Jesus of Nazareth, and he asserts that any christological claim that Jesus is Christ must have the Jesus of history as its referent and ground. The original experience that forms the foundation for the belief that Jesus is Christ is Jesus, not abstracted from his person, but Jesus who lived in history. As Haight puts it, "In Jesus, God assumes every aspect of human existence, so

---

Dermot Lane (Wilmington, DE: Michael Glazier, 1987), 177–78; and Elizabeth A. Johnson, *Consider Jesus: Waves of Renewal in Christology* (New York: Crossroad, 1993).

[51] Roger Haight, "The Future of Christology: Expanding Horizons, Religious Pluralism, and the Divinity of Jesus," in Clifford and Godzieba, *Christology*, 56. See also idem, *Jesus Symbol of God* (Maryknoll, NY: Orbis Books, 1999).

[52] Even in its dialectical language the doctrine of Chalcedon, in exalting the divinity of Jesus in order to assert that God alone saves, has reduced his humanity to mere instrument of the *Logos*, one without its own *esse* and individuality, and thus suggests he is not an integral human being. It is good, as Rahner reminds us, that even though we have the doctrine of two natures, we are really monophysites in practice because we understand the doctrine such that the human nature of Jesus has become a mitigated reality. It does not define integrally his person or ontological reality ("The Position of Christology in the Church Between Exegesis and Dogmatics," *Theological Investigations*, vol. 11, *Confrontations*, trans. David Bourke, 185–214 [New York: Seabury Press, 1974], 198).

[53] Christology must be contextualized in a postmodern world, where there is multiplicity of cultures, beliefs, and religions. In this context Christology must cease to be on the level of high Christocentrism if it is to speak to other voices and if it is to respect the fact and necessity of pluralism.

[54] Jon Sobrino, *Jesus the Liberator: A Historical Theological View*, trans. Paul Burns and Francis McDonagh (Maryknoll, NY: Orbis Books, 1993), 38–39.

[55] Jon Sobrino, *Spirituality of Liberation Toward Political Holiness* (Maryknoll, NY: Orbis Books, 1988), 130.

that it is healed, cleansed, cured, and saved. . . . God has saved by assuming a human being and thus the human race as such as God's own."[56] This is the Jesus of history, whose cross was the ultimate sign of the seriousness and radicality of his life so utterly given for others, in fidelity to his mission and to the will of God. He died as he lived, for he believed and loved fully unto death.

If moral theology is centered on Jesus Christ, then it claims that the Jesus Christ story is normative for Christian moral living as its concrete universal. William Spohn explains how this story is normative as a concrete universal: "The story is concrete because it has a particular shape in a definite time and place. It is universal because that shape and the moral dispositions engendered by the story are morally relevant in every situation in the Christian's life."[57] Through faithful imagination, the Jesus story becomes paradigmatic for Christian moral life. The Christian is called to discipleship—to follow Jesus. This does not mean to imitate Jesus but to follow him by way of analogical paradigmatic imagination, which is the "ability to see one thing as another, to recognize the similarities between the world of biblical imagery and that of ordinary experience."[58] What Garrett Green says about scripture also applies to Jesus: "The Scriptures are not something to look *at* but rather look *through*, lenses that focus what we see into an intelligible pattern."[59] The Jesus story is normative in the shaping of Christian moral life in the way one perceives reality, who one is and seeks to become, and in how one should be engaged and disposed to act.[60] In Jesus is a new way of seeing, a new norm for thinking, a new ground for forgiving, a new reason for loving, and a new context for acting in this world.

Christian morality presupposes that commitment to Jesus shapes our total stance to the fundamental meaning and direction that human life ought to take. Living in him and for him sets life in one particular direction, one singular vision. At the heart of Christian moral life

---

[56] Haight, *Jesus Symbol of God*, 239.

[57] William C. Spohn, "Jesus and Christian Ethics," *Theological Studies* 56/1 (1995): 101–2.

[58] Ibid., 103.

[59] Garrett Green, *Imagining God: Theology and the Religious Imagination* (San Francisco: Harper and Row, 1989), 107.

[60] "The concrete universal of Jesus guides three phases of Christian moral experience: perception, motivation, and identity. This is so, because it indicates which particular features of our situation are religiously and morally significant; how we are to act, even when what we should do is unclear, and who we are to become as a people, and as individuals" (Spohn, "Jesus and Christian Ethics," 102–3).

rooted in the mystery of Jesus Christ is a call to live a life in the spirit
of the Paschal Mystery—the way of life through death, of glory in
suffering, and freedom in self-surrender. There is mystery here—deep
and unfathomable. Only in the context of faith can we can make sense
out of the contradictions of the vision of life that is God's in Jesus.

The Integration of Dogmatic Theology and Moral Theology

In the days of the great theological *summas,* dogmatic theology
and moral theology were presented as one single discipline. Dogmatic
theology embraced both "theoretical" and "practical" dogmas; moral
theology dealt with the practical details of Christian behavior in application of the theological principles that dogmatic theology lay down.
The inner connectedness of dogmatic theology and moral theology is
seen from the point of view of dogmatic theology in relation to moral
theology, and vice versa. But when moral theology was focused on the
training of the Catholic clergy as confessors, which was largely based
on the study of casuistry and the law, it was wrenched from its inner
connectedness with sacred scriptures, dogmatic theology, and spiritual
theology and became more closely linked with canon law.[61]

To rediscover its true theological character and depth, moral theology must once again seek its intrinsic relatedness with dogmatic
theology. History has shown that when moral theology becomes
excessively autonomous, it concentrates one-sidedly on the moral act
as a single action and neglects the total meaning of human persons
as moral agents in their fundamental relationship with God and with
others. The real depth of moral theology can be understood only
when its presuppositions on freedom, conscience, sin, and moral law
are understood in the context of who the human person is in the light
of faith—a theological anthropology based on the great Christian
mysteries.

The truths of the Christian faith give a particular view of what it
means to be human and of the basic attitudes and dispositions a Christian ought to have toward the world. According to Charles Curran,
the five Christian mysteries of creation, sin, incarnation-redemption,
grace, and eternal destiny are the constitutive elements of a Christian
perspective, horizon, and stance.[62] They articulate the fundamental

---

[61] Charles E. Curran, *Toward an American Catholic Moral Theology* (Notre
Dame, IN: University of Notre Dame Press, 1987), 3–5.

[62] Charles E. Curran, "The Stance of Moral Theology," in *Directions in Fundamental Moral Theology* (Notre Dame, IN: University of Notre Dame Press, 1985),
29–62.

truths underlying human meaning, dignity, and destiny. In the same line of thought Richard McCormick writes that the full Christian experience provides the refinement of sensitivity to natural values.[63] The Christian perspective opens the depths of meaning to moral reasoning. A value judgment that is not within the faith horizon of meaning might otherwise be determined solely by sheer empiricism. When decision making is separated from the framework of faith, it could become merely a rationalistic and sterile ethics.[64] McCormick writes:

> The Christian story tells us the ultimate meaning of ourselves and the world. In doing so, it tells us the kind of people we ought to be, the goods we ought to pursue, the dangers we ought to avoid, the kind of world we ought to seek. It provides the backdrop or framework that ought to shape our individual decisions. When decision making is separated from this framework, it loses its perspective. It becomes a merely rationalistic and sterile ethics subject to distortions of self-interested perspectives and cultural fads, a kind of contracted etiquette with no relation to the ultimate meaning of persons.[65]

Recognizing the rich tradition behind him as a Catholic moral theologian, McCormick stressed the place of religious faith in the ethical task. He held that there was a place for an approach for problems by those who are thoroughly stamped by and unabashedly proud of a historic religious faith.[66] He stressed the fact that any moral theology that is to be truly Christian must take full account of the full Christian mystery of creation, sin, incarnation, redemption, and resurrection. The Paschal Mystery lies at the center of the Christian understanding of frustration, suffering, tragedy, and ultimately death.[67] Underscoring the Christian perspectives on moral life, he writes that the "sifting and sorting of experience by use of preference-principles must be done in an atmosphere highly charged with Christian intentionalities such as the cruciform spirit of Christian life, resurrection, destiny, the eschatological kingdom, the following of the poor, and the humble

---

[63] Richard A. McCormick, *Notes on Moral Theology: 1965 Through 1980* (Washington, DC: Catholic University of America Press, 1981), 82.

[64] Ibid., 63.

[65] Richard A. McCormick, *Health and Medicine in the Catholic Tradition: Tradition in Transition* (New York: Crossroad, 1984), 50.

[66] Richard A. McCormick, *How Brave a New World? Dilemmas in Bioethics* (Washington, DC: Georgetown University, 1981), ix.

[67] McCormick, *Notes on Moral Theology: 1965 Through 1980*, 295.

Christ."[68] McCormick, however, concluded that it is precisely the relations of these Christian intentionalities to morality that remains an unfinished theological task. He states, "The problem of elaborating a satisfying value system within the totality of Christian realities remains one of the most important unfinished tasks in the field of Christian morality."[69]

Anthropology of Fundamental Commitment

Fundamental commitment is the key concept that has radically altered moral theology, with its enormous repercussions on basic moral concepts and realities: freedom, conscience, sin, virtue, and confession, to mention a few. At the base of this key concept is Rahner's theological anthropology, which envisions the person whose being is characterized by depth and complexity. The human person is construed in various layers. In the words of Rahner, the human person is a "many-layered being . . . constructed as it were in layers, starting at an interior core and becoming more and more external."[70] At the center lies our core freedom, where we stand in absolute openness before God. There at the core we define ourselves as either a lover or a sinner in our fundamental yes or no to God. Engaged in the self-determination of the person as a whole in the face of God's total demand is our fundamental capacity for making a final and irrevocable choice to be someone, to be a particular kind of person.[71]

Josef Fuchs, the primary proponent of the idea of fundamental commitment (or fundamental freedom), distinguishes it from free acts to choose this or that object. He holds that fundamental commitment is "more than any particular action or actions and more than the sum of them; it underlies them, permeates them, and goes beyond them, without ever being actually one of them."[72] Fundamental commitment, however, is actualized and validated through free acts, insofar as these acts summon our full disposal as persons to God and to others. This

---

[68] Ibid., 370.

[69] McCormick, *Notes on Moral Theology*, 295.

[70] Karl Rahner, "Some Thoughts on Good Intention," *Theological Investigations*, vol. 3, *The Theology of the Spiritual Life*, trans. Karl-H. and Boniface Kruger, 105-28 (Baltimore: Helicon, 1967), 113.

[71] See Ronald Modras, "The Implications of Rahner's Anthropology for Fundamental Moral Theology," *Horizons* 12 (1985): 74.

[72] Josef Fuchs, "Basic Freedom and Morality," in *Introduction to Christian Ethics: A Reader*, ed. Ronald P. Hamel and Kenneth R. Himes, 187–98 (New York: Paulist Press, 1989), 188.

implies that in the peripheral concentric circles we may do certain acts that do not engage us from the core, and thus freedom as fundamental commitment is not involved. Viewed from the anthropology of fundamental commitment, moral life is a dynamic growth process, the gradual self-actualization of the person as a moral being.[73]

This understanding of moral life has implications on the traditional understanding of sin, particularly mortal sin. If mortal sin is understood in terms of fundamental commitment, which is the radical disposal of our entire life before God, a mechanistic understanding of sin that sees the rapid transition from sin to grace cannot be held—if we commit a morally evil act on Friday sufficient to condemn us, then we convert to the love of God on Saturday, and then fall again into mortal evil during the following week. And if mortal sin involves us in our definitive self-determination as sinners before God, it is not tenable to assert that this is realized in one isolated singular act, unless it is seen as the culmination of a whole process. The traditional understanding of the conditions of mortal sin as grave matter, involving full knowledge and full consent, understood only within the framework of discrete free acts with their particular objects, cannot hold up under the impact of the encompassing notion of fundamental commitment. In understanding these conditions there is a turn to persons as moral subjects whose acts are signs of an engagement or lack of engagement of their fundamental commitment, which determines the gravity of the matter, the depth of knowledge, and the extent of consent.

In treating the material gravity of matter from the perspective of fundamental commitment, the exterior action is not a yardstick but a sign of the greater or smaller depth of one's interior decision. It is truly a sign, and only one sign.[74] It can become evident that there may be cases in which an external action that is generally and rightly considered as a matter of mortal sin may not be so, and a wrong choice in a small matter may be a mortal sin, not only because one has scorned God's law but also because a person may have decided the whole direction of his or her life in that choice, as a culmination of a whole life pattern. McCormick writes, "Fundamental option enters to explain the existence and gravity of personal *sin*, which cannot be

---

[73] See Josef Fuchs, *Human Values and Christian Morality* (Dublin: Gill and Macmillan, 1970), 92–111. See also Mark E. Graham, "Rethinking Morality's Relationship to Salvation: Josef Fuchs, SJ, on Moral Goodness," *Theological Studies* 64/4 (2003): 750–72.

[74] Josef Fuchs, "Basic Freedom and Morality," 195.

simply be equated with the gravity of matter."[75] Fuchs elaborates on the meaning of sin in terms of the disposition of self:

> A sin is not so much an individual act about a particular object. It is much more a disposition of myself as a person, not merely one single act. True, sin involves an individual act about a particular object, but far more important is the realization that in sin I bring about a certain self-realization. Here we find the central reality in sin; it is much deeper than simply introducing moral disorder into this world. In every moral act, a person tries much more to realize himself as whole, as a person, than to realize a particular act. . . . Therefore, if in a sinful moral act a person is realizing not only one particular act but himself as a person, then in this moral act this person is realizing his personal relationship to his ultimate end, and therefore to God. . . . There is a major distinction between these two liberties: the particular liberty to make a choice between one good or another and the fundamental liberty that makes it possible for me to dispose of myself as a whole, as a person. With this fundamental liberty I am not only committing a sin, an act, but I am also making *myself a sinner*.[76]

Full knowledge involves not only a conceptual knowledge but also an evaluative knowledge, which has been built upon and reinforced from a moral pattern or habit that has been in opposition to the good. Full consent does not refer only to how free or not free a person was in making his or her decision. It refers to the basic freedom that engages a person at his or her core. Whether a sin is mortal or venial, the question posed is this: In this sin, is the person fully engaged as a person? Is the person disposing all that he or she is before God and others?

Objections to this notion have been raised in church teachings, particularly in *Veritatis Splendor* (1993), which warned against reducing mortal sin to an act of fundamental option, for "mortal sin exists also when a person knowingly and willingly, for whatever reason chooses something gravely disordered" (no. 70). But what does "knowingly and willingly" mean? If it refers to freedom of choice only, then that is not accepted by most theologians, for mortal sin is synonymous with the engagement of fundamental freedom. The radical turning away

---

[75] Richard A. McCormick, *The Critical Calling: Reflections on Moral Dilemmas Since Vatican II* (Washington, DC: Georgetown University Press, 1989), 186–87.

[76] Josef Fuchs, "Sin and Conversion," in Hamel and Himes, *Introduction to Christian Ethics*, 206–7.

from God, which results in the loss of charity, must be a self-disposition and not merely freedom of choice that is only engaged in relation to this or that particular object.[77] While one must consider the warnings of the church regarding possible abuses and misunderstandings that can be engendered by the notion of fundamental commitment, resulting in the trivialization of sin, diminishment of a sense of sin, or undercutting the objective nature of the act, still there is no other concept that has envisaged the true depth of the person and that of the moral act. The anthropology at its base is "realistic and consoling, challenging and inspiring."[78] It resonates with how people experience themselves not only in their depth and complexity, in their brokenness and vulnerability, but also in their grace and strength.

Building Bridges: The Task of Integration

The manuals had reduced moral theology to a preoccupation with sin, and this had constricted its vision and methodology. The post–Vatican II efforts at renewal of moral theology have taken the path of a more integrated and holistic approach. Bridges have been built between positions; false dualisms and reductionisms have been addressed; and lacunae have been filled in. The renewal efforts are demonstrated in the integration of the realms of the visional and normative, cognitive and affective, ethical and spiritual, personal and social.

Visional and Normative: Ethics of Being and Ethics of Doing

Since the Enlightenment moral thinking has focused on discrete and specific acts and their governing rules and principles, without attention to questions of virtue, character, and vision, whereas the manualists departed from Aristotle and Aquinas in their treatment of theological and moral virtues as more constitutive of the bases of moral obligation than the very content and dynamics of moral living. Revisionists working on the norms of proportionate reasoning were criticized for being taken up with discursive moral reasoning relative to particular acts, and some suggested that the question of virtues, character, and motivation was not within their frame of thought. To correct the seeming imbalance in view of Christian morality, attention has been given to the primacy of character and vision, and focus

---

[77] McCormick, *The Critical Calling*, 182.
[78] Ibid., 175.

has been redirected to virtue ethics, which shifts the preoccupation with moral action to a concern for the character of the moral agent. The project of integration, however, challenges any direction in moral theology that emphasizes either the visional or normative. Both are necessary because persons as moral agents are involved in situations where character, vision, reason, and judgment are all involved.

Reacting to the concentration on moral reasoning as the hallmark of moral life, Stanley Hauerwas and Craig Dykstra are among those who have made a strong case for the primacy of character and vision. Dykstra, for example, contends that "our decisions and choices root themselves not in rules, principles, and formal operations but in our vision of reality."[79] Stanley Hauerwas develops the key themes of vision, narrative, and Christian character in his writings. He claims that his work stems from his dissatisfaction with the language of rationality and objectivity, and overconcentration on individual acts as the dominant form construing moral life. He contends that there is a need for a greater focus on the agent and his or her vision.[80] Vision in Hauerwas's thought is related to character, a key concept of his thought. In *Character and Christian Life* Hauerwas concludes that Christian ethics is best understood as an ethics of character, and only when the notion of character is the interpretative key to moral experience can its richness and complexity be plumbed.[81] Character constitutes the distinctiveness of the self. "Nothing about my being is more 'me' than my character. Character is the basic aspect of our existence. It is the mode of the formation of our 'I,' for it is character that provides the content of the 'I.'"[82] Hauerwas concludes that Christian ethics is best understood as an ethics of character. He refers to character as the moral determination of the self's unity and integrity. The formation of character and vision is within the context of a storied society, and for the Christian, the church is the locus of God's story in Jesus Christ. Christians are demanded to be faithful as a people whose true destiny is found in God's story.[83]

---

[79] Craig Dykstra, *Vision and Character: A Christian Educator's Alternative to Kohlberg* (New York: Paulist Press, 1981), 28.

[80] Stanley Hauerwas, "Obligation and Virtue Once More," *Journal of Religious Ethics* 3 (Spring 1975): 29.

[81] Stanley Hauerwas, *Character and Christian Life: A Study in Theological Ethics* (San Antonio: Trinity University, 1975), 7–8.

[82] Ibid., 203.

[83] Stanley Hauerwas, "The Gesture of a Truthful Story," *Theology Today* 42 (July 1985): 182.

Dykstra develops what he calls visional ethics, which has significant points of congruence with Hauerwas's character and vision. For visional ethics, action follows vision, and vision depends on character.[84] Dykstra stresses that actions are not mere rational products of rational principles but are expressions of character and vision. In the same line of thought as Hauerwas, Dykstra develops his work around the themes of character, vision, and narrative.

This focus on character and vision has led to the return of virtue ethics. In 1981, Alasdair MacIntyre published *After Virtue*, considered to be the most influential book to that date on the topic.[85] Placing the moral agent and not the moral act at the center of ethical discourse distinguishes virtue ethics from other schools of moral thought. With moral agency as the focus, MacIntyre proposes three questions that must guide moral reasoning: Who am I? Who ought I become? How ought I get there? These basic questions place virtues at the center of the moral enterprise. Virtue ethics filled the lacunae in moral theology and posed a corrective to the reductionism in its methodology, that is, an overstress on rules and principles.

Many books have been written on virtue ethics, but the work of William C. Mattison III, a leading voice among young Catholic moral theologians, provides a solid introduction to Catholic moral theology that draws deeply from virtue ethics. Challenging college students to wrestle with fundamental questions—for example, why be moral?— Mattison lays out the role of virtue in the good life, presents its inner logic, and then applies it in case studies on issues like premarital sex and euthanasia. Although written primarily from a Catholic perspective, drawing from Thomas Aquinas's *Summa Theologiae*, it makes serious scholarship accessible for thoughtful engagement and dialogue in a wide audience of Christian academics and believers.[86]

While virtue ethics is of paramount importance, it is not without problems or objections. One problem is the nature of virtues as dispositional; as such, they elude public scrutiny and therefore fall short of the public accountability that morality requires.[87] As dispositions, virtues rely on feelings and intuitions, and unless governed by rules

---

[84] Dykstra, *Vision and Character*, 59.

[85] Alasdair MacIntyre, *After Virtue: A Study in Moral Theory*, 2nd ed. (Notre Dame, IN: University of Notre Dame Press, 1984).

[86] William C. Mattison III, *Introducing Moral Theology: True Happiness and the Virtues* (Grand Rapids, MI: Brazos, 2008).

[87] This problem is pointed out in William C. Spohn, "The Return of Virtue Ethics," *Theological Studies* 53/1 (1992): 63–64.

and consequences, they remain vague and impractical. They point to how and why a person should act, but they do not illuminate what a person should do, especially in complex conflict situations. Thus, some ethicists, like philosopher William Frankena and moral theologian Bruno Schüller, do not regard virtue ethics as an independent method of moral reasoning but as only an auxiliary to other existing methods. They claim that principles and rules direct, while virtues merely enable us to perform what the principles command.[88] Martha Nussbaum takes a contrary position, arguing that virtues are used precisely to judge moral conduct, and in fact principles and rules derive their content from virtues and are grounded in them.[89] In the same vein, Gregory Trianosky argues that virtues are indispensable for applying rules and determining what to do when no rules apply. In the first case, rules must be applied and conflicts among rules must be resolved. "But the rules themselves do not tell us how to apply them in specific situations, let alone how to apply them well, or indeed when to excuse people for failing to comply with them."[90] Since much of right conduct cannot be codified in rules or principles, and moral situations are too complex and principles are too general, it is a person of wisdom and prudence along with a basic sense of moral rightness who can best make the practical moral judgments.

Richard A. McCormick criticized the reduction of moral thought and life to either moral vision or moral deliberation. Rather than putting stress on one or the other of these two dimensions, there is a need, he says, to integrate them. Otherwise moral thought and life will increasingly become sectarian, mere exhortation, or unbiblical rationalism. He notes that those who emphasize vision and character often do not engage in moral justification with regard to concrete moral problems, or if they do, their moral justification often lacks a critical and well-grounded basis.[91] The integration of virtue ethics and normative ethics is best stated by Jean Porter: "True moral rectitude is necessarily grounded in the orientation of the whole personality

---

[88] See William Frankena, "Conversations with Carney and Hauerwas," *Journal of Religious Ethics* 3 (Spring 1975): 45–62; idem, "Ethics of Love Conceived as an Ethics of Virtue," *Journal of Religious Ethics* 1 (Fall 1973): 21–36; and Bruno Schüller, *Die Begründung sittlicher Urteil* (Düsseldorf: Patmos, 1980).

[89] Martha Nussbaum, *The Fragility of Goodness: Luck and Ethics in Greek Tragedy and Philosophy* (New York: Cambridge University, 1986), 299.

[90] Gregory Trianosky, "What Is Virtue Ethics All About?" *American Philosophical Quarterly* 27 (October 1990): 342.

[91] Richard A. McCormick, "Notes on Moral Theology: 1980," *Theological Studies* 42/1 (March 1981): 95–96.

that charity creates; and yet charity cannot be exercised, or even exist, unless moral rules generated by right reason are observed."[92] Stating the necessary relation of virtues to rules and principles does not, however, tell us precisely how virtues are to be related to rules and consequences.

Affectivity, Spirituality, and Ethics

Recent discussions in moral theology have focused on the importance of emotions and affectivity for moral wisdom, as they are necessarily integral to thinking and valuing that go into moral judgment and decision making. Correlated with the relationship of emotions and morality is the relationship of ethics and spirituality, insofar as spirituality consists of holy affections that have a bearing on the moral agent's identity, perception, and motivation. Taking a more specific dimension in the discussion of spirituality and ethics is the relation of worship and morality, as worship is seen as the formative ground of morality and the matrix of communal moral life. Also within this relation of ethics and spirituality is the specific issue of the place of religion in political life.

In stressing the rational component of moral choice and behavior, Christian ethics in the past tended to neglect the place of affectivity in the total moral process. Emotions are often seen as negative factors in morality, as thwarting rational actions. Emotions and passions are perceived as getting in the way of clear and objective moral judgment, or leading one to irrational and disruptive behavior. In recent years ethics has become less suspicious of the role of emotions in moral experience and more attentive to the possibility that they are a positive resource in moral life. Recent discussions have illumined the interplay of reason and emotions, with emotions considered as having an intelligence of their own. If properly understood and deployed, and if maturely integrated and exercised, emotions have real wisdom that guides thinking, valuing, and decision making for truly moral living.[93] The underscoring of emotions and affectivity in moral experience is a necessary corrective to theories that emphasize critical and disciplined

---

[92] Jean Porter, "*De Ordine Caritatis*: Charity, Friendship, and Justice in Thomas Aquinas' *Summa Theologiae*," in *The Thomist* 53/2 (1989): 213.

[93] William Cosgrove, "Our Emotional Life," *The Furrow* 49/5 (May 1998): 270-76. See also, Carlo Leget, "Martha Nussbaum and Thomas Aquinas on the Emotions," *Theological Studies* 64/3 (2003): 558–81; and Peter Black, "The Broken Wings of Eros: Christian Ethics and the Denial of Desire," *Theological Studies* 64/1 (2003): 106–26.

analysis of moral principles to the practical exclusion of other dimensions or aspects that come into play in moral thought and life. An excessive stress on moral reasoning can lead to what Daniel Maguire terms the "intellectualistic fallacy" in ethical deliberation. By this he means an "analytical and rationalistic approach that assumes that morality that becomes intelligible in the same way that mathematics and logic do." Maguire argues that moral knowledge is born in the awe and affectivity that characterizes foundational moral experience. This, he says, is not the conclusion of a syllogism, even though it can be supported by human reasoning.[94]

There is a correlation between emotions and morality, and also between spirituality and morality. True religion, writes Jonathan Edwards, consists of holy affections.[95] In his exploration of the connections between spirituality and ethics, William Spohn begins by pointing out the distinction between morality and ethics as analogous to the distinction between lived spirituality and reflective spirituality.[96] The relation of morality and spirituality to ethics and reflective spirituality is a rich and broad area of study, both promising and problematic, as spirituality as a discipline is still in flux, and the variety of spiritualities is enormous. Spohn proposes that perception, motivation, and identity are "three regions of moral experience where the concerns and practices of spirituality are supplementing, if not supplanting, formal ethical approaches."[97] Perception concerns what we pay attention to, which influences what we value; the resources for our attentiveness are derived from spirituality or from morality or ethics. Motivation is found in the dispositions of the heart, which are shaped by spiritual practices; these dispositions guide and direct actions. Identity refers to one's sense of self, to which spirituality brings a depth of meaning and a source of transformation.[98]

Love, Human and Divine by Edward Vacek is in the tradition of Gérard Gilleman, who wrote that "the very soul of moral life is expressed in the fundamental law of love." And yet, as Gilleman himself noted, "love does not obviously appear to be reflected in our classical

---

[94] Daniel C. Maguire, "Ratio Practica and Intellectual Fallacy," *Journal of Religious Ethics* 10 (Spring 1982): 22–39, quotation at 27.

[95] See John Smith et al., *A Jonathan Edwards Reader* (New Haven, CT: Yale University Press, 1959), 93–124.

[96] William C. Spohn, "Spirituality and Ethics: Exploring the Connections," *Theological Studies* 58/1 (1997): 111–12.

[97] Ibid., 114.

[98] Ibid., 115–22.

treatises."[99] Garth Hallett comments, "Strange as this assertion may sound after nearly two millennia of Christian emphasis on agape, the Christian norm of neighbor-love offers relatively virgin territory for inquiry."[100] Enda McDonagh notes that none of the great theologians "have given it the central, architectonic place one might expect. . . . In moral theology [love] received a very skimpy treatment."[101] Stanley Hauerwas, however, takes a contrary position; he directly attacks the very centrality of love in ethics. "If Christianity is primarily an ethic of love I think that is clearly wrong and ought to be given up."[102] Vacek's goal for his work, the central idea of which is that God's love and our love for God create and form a community, is to provide a distinctively *theological* foundation for Christian ethics.[103] He accomplished this in a masterful fashion, integrating affectivity, spirituality, and ethics.

In *Racial Justice and the Catholic Church* Bryan Massingale asserts that race remains a significant lens through which we see the world and reality. The reality of unconscious racism, Massingale notes, explains its insidious tenacity. "Race functions as a largely unconscious or preconscious frame of perception, developed through cultural conditioning and instilled by socialization."[104] For this reason, Massingale criticizes approaches that presume rational analysis, hard work, and tenacious determination are sufficient to address the problem of racism. Such overly practical and technical approaches cannot contend with the depth and tenacity of racism.[105] He writes: "Racism engages us viscerally. This makes racial injustice, on its deepest levels, impervious to rational appeals and cognitive strategies. . . . Racism numbs us to the reality of injustice and makes us calloused and hardened to its manifold harms. Logic alone seldom compels action in the face of indifference."[106]

---

[99] Gérard Gilleman, *The Primacy of Charity in Moral Theology* (Westminster, MD: Newman, 1959), xxi.

[100] Garth Hallett, *Christian Neighbor-Love* (Washington, DC: Georgetown University Press, 1989), vii.

[101] Enda McDonagh, "Love," in Komonchak, Collins, and Lane, *The New Dictionary of Theology*, 602.

[102] Stanley Hauerwas, "Love's Not All You Need," *Cross Currents* 22 (Summer-Fall 1972): 172.

[103] Edward Collins Vacek, *Love, Human and Divine: The Heart of Christian Ethics* (Washington, DC: Georgetown University Press, 1994), xv–xvi.

[104] Bryan N. Massingale, *Racial Justice and the Catholic Church* (Maryknoll, NY: Orbis Books, 2010), 8, quotation at 26.

[105] Ibid., 104.

[106] Ibid., 104–5.

Another kind of response is needed, one that transcends the limits of logic and reason—a response of lament, "cries of anguish and outrage, groans of deep pain and grief, utterances of profound protest and righteous indignation over injustice, wails of mourning and sorrow in the face of unbearable suffering."[107] Lament as an emotionally laden protest in the face of injustice and suffering constitutes a principal part of Israel's prayer and our faith heritage. It provides a language that disrupts the "way things are" and interrupts what is "apparently normal in a skewed racialized culture and identity."[108] Honest lament gives rise to compassion. The Greek word used in the context of Jesus being moved with compassion is *splanchnizesesthai*, which "connotes a visceral response of profound feeling and strong emotion; it emanates from one's bowels or guts."[109] It is this profound and visceral emotion that could lead one to penitence instead of being the cause of the grief and suffering of others; it could move one to cross the social boundaries as one is stirred from one's deepest humanity in the face of human agony and need.[110] "Compassion overrides social, cultural, racial, economic, and religious boundaries."[111]

Compassion is thoroughly studied by Maureen O'Connell in *Compassion: Loving Our Neighbor in an Age of Globalization*. The central thesis of her book is that privileged Christians need to reexamine the virtue of compassion exemplified by the Samaritan on the road to Jericho in the face of massive suffering in the globalized world and the radical inequality that leaves many in the roadside ditches while others live in scandalous affluence.[112] One of the main authors she used was Martha Nussbaum, who holds the centrality of emotion in moral reasoning and development. O'Connell takes Nussbaum's stance that emotions and reason are not diametrically opposed. In fact, emotions are "intelligent responses to perceptions of value" that cannot be "sidelined" from ethical theories precisely because they are involved in judgments about and appraisals of flourishing.[113] More specifically, "emotions are not just the fuel that powers the psychological mechanism of a reasoning creature, they

---

[107] Ibid., 105.
[108] Ibid., 110.
[109] Ibid., 114.
[110] Massingale, *Racial Justice and the Catholic Church*, 113–14.
[111] Maureen H. O'Connell, *Compassion: Loving Our Neighbor in an Age of Globalization* (Maryknoll, NY: Orbis Books, 2009), 70.
[112] Ibid.
[113] Ibid., 101.

are parts, highly complex and messy parts, of this creature's reasoning itself."[114]

Politics and Religion

Within this relation of ethics and spirituality is the specific issue of the place of religion in political life, a topic of vigorous discussion and debate. This debate has been most intense when it touches on urgent practical issues. As Charles Curran notes, David Hollenbach's *The Global Face of Public Faith* shows that no one has a better grasp than Hollenbach of the critical issues involved in the role of church and religion in a pluralistic society from the perspective of the contemporary debate and in the light of Catholic tradition.[115]

Hollenbach states that it is best to step back and situate the debate in practical issues (for example, public policy on abortion, economic justice for the poor, sex education, health services in relation to the AIDS crisis, and military response to terrorism) to bring to light the theoretical context within which to consider these issues. He emphasizes the value of exploring the theoretical grounding of the public role of religion in a democratic and pluralistic society.[116]

The general positions in the debate show conflicting views of religion. One position holds that religion is private, having no place in the public discourse; the other position argues that religion is interconnected with all of human life as the bearer of humanity's deepest convictions about the human good. If it is reduced to a private role, common life will lack the liberating power and depth of religion.[117] Martha Nussbaum holds that we need a vision of the good life arising from myths and stories that engage our collective imagination beyond our private enclaves. To the degree that this engagement is present in civil society, it will have political impact.[118] Though Nussbaum's writing makes no particular comment on religious truth claims, Hollenbach, who holds that religion should be given a greater public

---

[114] Martha C. Nussbaum, *Upheavals of Thought: The Intelligence of Emotions* (Cambridge: Cambridge University Press, 2001), 2, 3.

[115] David Hollenbach, *The Global Face of Public Faith: Politics, Human Rights, and Christian Faith* (Washington, DC: Georgetown University Press, 2003), back cover.

[116] Ibid., 99.

[117] See David Hollenbach, "Religion and Political Life," *Theological Studies* 57/1 (1991): 87–106.

[118] Martha Nussbaum, "Aristotelian Social Democracy," in *Liberalism and the Good*, ed. Bruce Douglass, Gerald M. Mara, and Henry S. Richardson, 203–52 (New York: Routledge, 1990), 217.

space, concurs with her that religious and metaphysical beliefs can make important contributions to a social understanding of the genuine human good.[119]

Hollenbach's position is in line with that of Michael Perry and Robin Lovin, which is opposed to the liberal democratic stance with secularist implications held by Richard Rorty (which pushes it to a radical edge) or by John Rawls (who takes a more moderate position).[120] Rorty's radical historicism rejects any transcultural norms of morality as embodied in religious traditions. He maintains that, according to Hollenback, "notions such as transcendent human dignity and human rights cannot be invoked to stand in judgment of particular historical traditions from outside these traditions." His radical historicism leads directly to the privatization of religious and philosophical matters.[121]

Rawls, says Hollenbach, does not reject religion and how it shapes people's conceptions of a good life, but he holds that in a pluralistic democratic society such religious conceptions influencing one's political views must be argued in the public arena in a way that they are at least reasonable for others to accept.[122] Both John Courtney Murray and the documents of Vatican II would support Rawls's position, which is a later revision of his earlier position, which seemed to suggest that because a religiously pluralistic society does not have a consensus about religious convictions, such convictions cannot be engaged in a public discourse which shapes communal life.[123]

Hollenbach notes that Kent Greenawalt addresses the tension between the principle that government and law have secular purposes and the principle that citizens are free to influence public policies with their freely held convictions, even when these are religious. Greenawalt, says Hollenbach, maintains that citizens who rely on religious convictions on social issues should not appeal to these convictions in the public forum in a pluralist context. They are not prohibited from standing by their religious convictions, which they can engage in with those who share their faith, but all religious talk should be kept out of public square.[124] Robin Lovin concludes that in the end "Greenawalt's argument is not a case for the public relevance of religious reasons, but

[119] Hollenbach, "Religion and Political Life," 106.
[120] Hollenbach, *The Global Face of Public Faith*, 100.
[121] Ibid., 104, 105, quotation at 104.
[122] Ibid., 108.
[123] Ibid., 108–9.
[124] Ibid., 111–12.

for the public acceptance of individual choices that rest on religious reasons."[125] Religion, therefore, remains a privatized affair. Greenawalt continues to uphold a central tenet of the liberal theory.

Many others fundamentally oppose the privatization of religion and its marginalization in the public discourse on social issues. Michael Perry, a Roman Catholic deeply rooted in the alliance of faith and reason, holds that "questions of human good, in particular deep questions of what it means to be authentically human—are too fundamental, and the answers to them too determinative of one's politics, to be marginalized and privatized." When public political discourse is cut off from religion, he contends, it is cut off from some of the richest resources for thinking about the human: "the resources of the great religious traditions."[126] Robin Lovin pursues the same line of argument as Perry while deepening it with a theological content and language. Identifying three reasons people bring the language of faith to bear on public choices as "proclamation," "conversion," and articulation," Hollenbach explains how Lovin views religion as challenging secular discourse with an alternative vision; transforming the terms of this discourse with the premises of faith; and enriching and enlarging the vision of good from a secularist perspective.[127] Hollenbach's assertion for a public role for religion is eloquently articulated in the following:

> Religious convictions are potentially explosive when confined to small spaces. And rightly so. They are, after all, about God. And beliefs about God entail convictions about the whole of human life, not simply a small compartment of it. Whether one professes the *shema* of Israel ("Hear, O Israel: the Lord our God is one God"), the Christian *credo* ("We believe in one God, the Father Almighty, creator of heaven and earth"), or the Muslim *shahadah* ("There is no God but God"), private religion is theologically self-contradictory. Because religion is about the ultimate good of the whole of human life, it will be untrue to itself if it accepts the private niche to which liberal theory would assign it.[128]

---

[125] Robin W. Lovin, "Perry, Naturalism, and Religion in Public," *Tulane Law Review* 63 (1989): 1521.

[126] Michael J. Perry, *Morality, Politics, and Law: A Bicentennial Essay* (New York: Oxford University Press, 1988), 182, 183.

[127] See Hollenbach, *The Global Face of Public Faith*, 115–16.

[128] Ibid., 118.

Personal and Social Ethics

While it was convenient in the past to classify different areas of ethics, distinguishing social ethics from sexual ethics and bioethics, the lines of distinction between what is personal and social in ethical questions and issues have been blurred. In a real sense all ethical issues have a social dimension, and thus social ethics include sexual issues as well as bioethical issues. The dualism of personal and social morality is a false one. Lisa Cahill writes, "All ethics is social ethics."[129] Cahill demonstrates this principle in the field of bioethics in her groundbreaking book *Theological Bioethics*. Cahill proposes that justice concerns must be integral to bioethics. The advocacy for healthcare justice concerns, however, has been challenged by public debates that see bioethical issues through the narrow prism of protection of embryos and fetuses, a perspective that has been supported by many Catholic bishops in recent years in their priority for the rights of the unborn over healthcare reform.[130] The primary thrust of Cahill's argument is that bioethics in the twenty-first century, in the context of globalization, must in every case be social ethics not only in theory but in action/praxis. This is not to deny the personal and individual dimension of moral decision making, but there is no decision that is separated from its social context.[131]

Cahill points out that a new item on the agenda of both theology and public bioethics is a critical examination of the connection between individual choices and social practices. The goal is to show how practices that marginalize the poor and favor the privileged have an impact on global health patterns and resources. This has global consequences on individuals and communities. The language of the common good, inclusion, distributive justice, and solidarity must be infused into the ethical narrative of bioethics. But Cahill argues that theological bioethics is not just about talk; it is about action. It must go beyond decrying injustice, beyond taking a prophetic stance; it must envision a more egalitarian and solidaristic future. She writes: "Theological bioethics must critically reflect on, make normative judgments about, theoretically account for, and ultimately take part in a global social network of mobilization for change."[132] Quoting Schillebeeckx, she

---

[129] Lisa Sowle Cahill, "Feminism and Christian Ethics," in Mowry La Cugna, *Freeing Theology*, 218.

[130] Lisa Sowle Cahill, *Theological Bioethics: Participation, Justice, Change* (Washington, DC: Georgetown University Press, 2005), 1.

[131] Ibid., 2–3.

[132] Ibid., 3.

emphasizes the linking of theology to Christian practices if theology is to be of value: "Theology is valueless, whether it is progressive or conservative, as soon as it loses contact with the empirical basis of the praxis of believers."[133]

This dualism of personal and social is particularly eroded by feminist ethical thought in its singular motto: The personal is political. This reiterates that any personal choice is a social act. It has social reverberations within a network of relationships, regardless of the size and extent of such a network. What is highlighted here is a general movement in Christian ethics to view what is personal in relation to its social context and location, integrating the personal with the social and communal. In feminist thought, for instance, issues involving women are critically seen in the light of their roots in patriarchy and all its ramifications in the order of the social, cultural, economic, and political.[134] The necessary integration of the personal and social ethics poses a critique to the two-voice hypothesis of Carol Gilligan and to the privatization of moral problems like violence in homes and families. What cannot be stressed enough is the need to locate ethical problems in broader and larger social contexts, and to view them in their social roots, beyond individual and personal causes. The stress on the social brings into focus the impact of liberation theology on the shifts in the vision and methodology in moral theology.

Reversing the dualism of what is personal and social to a more integral and holistic view of ethics is particularly evidenced in the discussions on ethics of justice and caring. The two-voice hypothesis expressed in Gilligan's *In a Different Voice* suggests that in relation to moral issues and problems, women favor a caring-responsibility approach while men prefer a justice-rights approach.[135] This two-voice taxonomy claims that the difference in preference has its roots in the fact that boys learn autonomy from the crisis of separation from the mother, while girls develop a greater appreciation for caring from

---

[133] Edward Schillebeeckx, *The Schillebeeckx Reader,* ed. Robert Schreiter (Edinburgh, UK: T and T Clark, 1984), 118. This passage was originally published in 1971.

[134] Ibid., 218–19.

[135] See Carol Gilligan, *In a Different Voice: Psychological Theory and Women's Development* (Cambridge, MA: Harvard University Press, 1983). Gilligan's work was in protest to Lawrence Kohlberg, whose method denigrated women's responses to moral dilemmas. See Lawrence Kohlberg, *The Philosophy of Moral Development: Moral Stages and the Idea of Justice* (San Francisco: Harper and Row, 1981). For Kohlberg's response to Gilligan and other critics, see Lawrence Kohlberg, *The Psychology of Moral Development: The Nature and Validity of Moral Stages* (San Francisco: Harper and Row, 1984).

continuing attachment to their mothers.[136] These development patterns make women more inclined to intimacy over separation, while men are more driven to individuality over attachment. This view is criticized for its overreliance on psychological explanations, ignoring the cultural and political forces that have confined women to attachment roles. One key criticism of the two-voice hypothesis is the reductionism that results from viewing moral reality as approached from either the caring perspective or the justice perspective. Justice cannot be defined apart from care nor care apart from justice.[137] Giving a different view, Sidney Callahan writes that moral reasoning does not reveal any sex reasoning. Men and women, girls and boys, do not reason differently, and women are as principled and justice oriented as men. Class, race, age, and power status play a more significant influence on moral perspective than gender.[138]

The separation of the private and public arenas of moral discourse has resulted in the failure to see the social roots of so-called personal problems and to identify the larger issues that impinge on these problems. This separation of the private and public, personal and social, is particularly clear in the way violence in homes and families is kept largely behind the closed doors of marital or family relations. The privatization of family life in general isolates it from the wider network of social relationships—the economic, political, and social systems upon which the family is dependent and that play a crucial role in its formation. The family is and should be the center of mutuality and commitment, the locus of intimacy and emotional expression, necessary for it to be the school of fundamental human values. It is, however, also an arena of social conflict, where the kinds of dilemmas experienced by marital partners are linked with the issues of justice and empowerment in the wider society.[139] The direction that has been taken in the ethical search for a more integral and holistic approach to moral problems is to view them in their social roots, beyond the

---

[136] See Lilian B. Rubin, *Intimate Strangers: Men and Women Together* (New York: Harper and Row, 1984), 46–64.

[137] Owen Flanagan, *Varieties of Moral Personality: Ethics and Psychological Realism* (Cambridge, MA: Harvard University Press, 1991), 209, 240–41.

[138] Sidney Cornelia Callahan, *In Good Conscience: Reason and Emotion in Moral Decision Making* (San Francisco: Harper San Francisco, 1991), 196.

[139] See Sarah Bentley, "Bringing Justice Home: The Challenge of the Battered Women's Movement for Christian Social Ethics," in *Violence Against Women and Children: A Christian Theological Sourcebook*, ed. Carol J. Adams and Marie M. Fortune (New York: Continuum, 1995), 151–71. The best single history of the battered women's movement is Susan Schechter, *Women and Male Violence* (Boston: South End Press, 1982).

personal causes, and to see a much broader view of these problems within society with its cultural values, its economic and legal systems, and its structures of power.

Another book by Lisa Cahill, *Family*, offers a fresh social ethics perspective on family from the Christian perspective. While the family is a place where the bonds of kinship, affection, and faithfulness are deeply rooted, its members must also go beyond their inner circle of relations and be agents of social transformation. Christian concepts of family must place it in this larger social context. As vehicles of social justice, families participate in the common good of society. Cahill, who has been addressing the issue of patriarchy from her North American middle-class context, now sees it in a more global and intercultural framework. She has become increasingly aware of how deeply entrenched patriarchy is, and how women worldwide, who are often defined in terms of childbearing roles and primarily seen as fulfilling male needs, have little or no independent access to economic and social resources. The feminization of poverty renders women among the "poorest of the poor" in a world where power and greed combine to devastate those who are most vulnerable in society. From a social justice perspective, she particularly addresses the social situations of families in relation to the debate about welfare reform. Paying careful attention to race and class, she offers her moral wisdom on the issues this debate raises. Her position is that the moral revival of the family as the foundation of society requires a just redistribution of society's goods and resources.[140]

Julie Hanlon Rubio, in *A Christian Theology of Marriage and Family*, takes the same perspective as Lisa Cahill in addressing the question of the calling and vocation of Christian families in contemporary society. Weaving together theology and social science and drawing from her own experience as a wife and mother, Rubio presents the ideals of marital and parental commitment while confronting the reality of marital problems and divorce in the face of the larger demands of family ethics and social justice. While deeply invested in children and family, she is also strongly committed to women's equality.[141]

---

[140] Lisa Sowle Cahill, *Family: A Christian Social Perspective* (Minneapolis: Fortress Press, 2000), ix–xiv. Cahill writes that the following books make arguments in some way similar to hers: Barend A. de Vries, *Champions of the Poor: The Economic Consequences of Judeo-Christian Values* (Washington, DC: Georgetown University Press, 1998); Michael G. Lawler, *Family: American and Christian* (Chicago: Loyola University, 1998); and Stephen G. Post, *More Lasting Unions: Christianity, the Family, and Society* (Grand Rapids, MI: Eerdmans, 2000).

[141] Julie Hanlon Rubio, *A Christian Theology of Marriage and Family* (New York: Paulist Press, 2003).

Concerning the necessity of locating the social roots of moral problems, Richard McCormick hails the emergence of liberation theology as one of the significant developments over the past half-century and one that has left a lasting impact on moral theology. He cites three ways in which liberation theology has influenced moral theology. First, it has replaced a separatist worldview, which divides reality into profane and sacred, with one that views the world as the arena of grace where Christ's redemptive work embraces every dimension of human existence. Second, it has put active participation in creating a just order at the center of the church's mission. And third, it has stressed the primacy of social concerns in any engagement in the moral-spiritual life and in the conception of moral theology, over and against the cult of individualism that seems to reign in Western industrialized democracies.[142] There has been a continuing discourse on the impact of liberation theology on morality. Thomas Schubeck lays out the issues in liberation theology that have been recently discussed in theological literature and concludes with a discussion of the kind of ethics that liberation theology is.[143] These issues include its thrust, the preferential option for the poor; its vision, the "church of the poor"; and its method, the dialectic of theory and praxis. The interest in this theology has permeated all branches of Christian theology from biblical studies to systematics and ethics.[144] The preferential option for the poor, considered the "linchpin of liberation theology and its ethics," has become a focus of controversy. Donal Dorr calls it "the most controversial religious term since the Reformers' cry, 'salvation through faith alone.'"[145] Schubeck's article summarizes four points that opponents of the term *option for the poor* raise. First, they charge that the preferential option for the poor contradicts the universal love of God, by the focus on the poor as privileged recipients of God's love and as

---

[142] Richard A. McCormick, *Corrective Vision: Explorations in Moral Theology* (Kansas City, MO: Sheed and Ward, 1994), 14. While some theologians concur that liberation theology has influenced moral thinking in important and lasting ways, others have questioned such an assertion and all else in relation to liberation theology in general. Offering a balanced view is Arthur F. McGovern, *Liberation Theology and Its Critics: Toward an Assessment* (Maryknoll, NY: Orbis Books, 1989).

[143] Thomas L. Schubeck, "Ethics and Liberation Theology," *Theological Studies* 56/1 (1995): 107–22.

[144] For the broad content and sources of contemporary discussions on liberation theology, see Peter C. Phan, "Method in Liberation Theologies," *Theological Studies* 61/1 (2000), 40–63.

[145] Donal Dorr, *Option for the Poor: A Hundred Years of Vatican Social Teaching* (Maryknoll, NY: Orbis Books, 1992), 1.

the primary mediators of divine salvation. This perspective suggests a marginalization of the rich in the total divine scheme.[146] Second, they claim that liberation ethics, by using the preferential option for the poor as its foundational principle, has made moral thinking partial and thus has negated its own ethical ground.[147] Third, liberation theology is criticized for advocating the use of Marxist theory and analysis, with the poor pitted against the rich.[148] Fourth, they have questioned the epistemological privilege given to the poor, by their sheer social location, insofar as the nature and dynamics of dominant systems and structures in society.[149]

In "Proper and Improper Partiality and the Preferential Option for the Poor," Stephen Pope argues that the preferential option for the poor constitutes a form of partiality, but far from being morally pernicious, this partiality is morally justified, and indeed, required. To show partiality as justifiable, he contrasts it with that which is unjustifiable. Justifiable partiality is seen in divine preference of care for the needy, in the passion for the cause of the poor, and in the moral commitment to the priority of the poorest and most vulnerable within an ordering of social priorities. Rather than fostering exclusivism, justifiable partiality promotes inclusivism as it creates opportunities for the deprived, so that all parts will be able someday to participate fully in the whole. In contrast, unjustifiable forms of partiality include a threefold bias: cognitive bias that ideologizes the truth; moral bias that determines human worth as determined by class membership; and religious bias that holds that God arbitrarily favors some social classes over others.[150]

---

[146] Robert Benne, "The Preferential Option for the Poor and American Public Policy," in *The Preferential Option for the Poor*, ed. Richard John Neuhaus, 53–71 (Grand Rapids, MI: Eerdmans, 1988), 54; and Gordon Graham, *The Idea of Christian Charity: A Critique of Some Contemporary Conceptions* (Notre Dame, IN: University of Notre Dame Press, 1990), 116–18.

[147] For the discussion of impartiality vs. partiality, see Alan Gewirth, "Ethical Universalism and Particularism," *Journal of Philosophy* 85 (1988): 283–302; and R. M. Hare, *Moral Thinking* (Oxford: Clarendon, 1981). For a discussion on the limits of impartiality, see James Rachels, *The Elements of Moral Philosophy*, 2nd ed. (New York: McGraw-Hill, 1993), 9–13; Margaret Urban Walker, "Partial Consideration," *Ethics* 101 (1991): 758–74. On challenging impartialist theories, see Lawrence A. Blum, *Moral Perception and Particularity* (New York: Cambridge University Press, 1994).

[148] See, for example, Michael Novak, *Will It Liberate? Questions for Liberation Theology* (New York: Paulist Press, 1986), 108–9.

[149] Ibid., 151.

[150] Stephen J. Pope, "Proper and Improper Partiality and the Preferential Option for the Poor," *Theological Studies* 54/2 (1993): 264–65.

What is critical in understanding the preferential option for the poor is that this preference is due to need and not to merit. The poor are not upheld as morally superior by virtue of their special virtues.[151] But as divine care for the most needy is stressed, it must not compromise an unwavering commitment to fairness. Pope asserts that a harmonious balance of special concern and fairness, both of which are important aspects of justice, must be maintained. "Both must be held together in a complementary and mutually-correcting account of preferential option."[152]

Facing the Challenges of Plurality, Polarity, and Commonality

Charting new grounds and vistas beyond the world of the manuals in the shifting cultures and worldviews of contemporary times, moral theology has entered the murky waters of plurality, polarity, and commonality. Discussed here are three main topics: first, plurality in understanding natural law, the return of casuistry as a method of moral reasoning, and the polarity of double effect and proportionate reasoning; second, emergence of feminism; and third, the challenge of common morality or global ethics.

Plurality in Ethical Methodology

The firestorm that greeted Pope Paul VI's *Humanae Vitae* in July 1968 has profoundly influenced the discipline of moral theology, particularly the area of normative ethics. It has brought the classicist understanding of natural law into a critical light. The hopeful prediction of *Humanae Vitae*—that its ethical view founded on its natural law reasoning would be widely or even universally accepted—did not prove to be so. On the contrary, its teaching set off wave after wave of protest. The official Catholic version of the natural law in *Humanae Vitae* is based on the essential unchanging human nature of the person, bounded by the bodily dimensions of human existence. It is an understanding of "natural law that offers a way to think morally about the bodily dimensions of human existence. It calls on men and women to cognizance of the limitations imposed upon us by our physical and animal nature, and it suggests that no lasting

---

[151] Ibid., 266.
[152] Ibid., 267. See *The Option for the Poor in Christian Theology*, ed. Daniel G. Groody (Notre Dame, IN: University of Notre Dame Press, 2007).

individual happiness or social peace can be attained unless those limits are acknowledged."[153]

This strain of the natural law tradition (according to nature), in contrast to that which locates the essence of the person in his or her exercise of will and intellect (according to reason), has been criticized as physicalist and reductionist. It presents, however, an understanding of natural law that offers moral certainty, clarity, and unambiguity, bound as it is by the "givens" in nature. By this understanding, since the nature of human genitalia is to reproduce, the use of the genitals for something other than procreation is a violation of the natural law. These unchanging laws of nature are seen as the manifestations of the divine will of the Creator. On the other hand, the notion of natural law that gives importance to reason and human experience, consonant with what is distinctive of the person as a rational and historical being, is criticized as too dependent on the shifting nature of human experiences and circumstances.[154]

Many theologians came to reject the basic claim that there is an unchanging human nature from which moral norms are derived. In this light traditional Catholic sexual ethics became increasingly problematic and the natural law reasoning grounding this ethic was brought into serious question.[155] Both Karl Rahner and Bernard Lonergan objected to a view of human nature that was "static" or "classical."[156] The ways in which our human nature is historically conditioned reveal how unfounded are the moral conclusions drawn from what are considered permanent structures of that nature. Catholic scholars like Richard McCormick and Charles Curran equated natural law with the deliverances of moral reason. "From the viewpoint of moral theology

---

[153] Jean Porter, "The Natural Law and the Specificity of Christian Morality," in *Method and Catholic Moral Theology: The Ongoing Reconstruction*, ed. Todd A. Salzman, 209–29 (Omaha, NE: Creighton University, 1999), 215.

[154] See Richard M. Gula, *Reason Informed by Faith: Foundations of Catholic Morality* (New York: Paulist Press, 1989), 220–49.

[155] Jean Porter, *Natural and Divine Law: Reclaiming the Tradition for Christian Ethics* (Grand Rapids, MI: Eerdmans, 1999), 30.

[156] For Rahner's reformulation of the natural law, see James E. Bresnahan, "An Ethics of Faith," in *A World of Grace: An Introduction to the Themes and Foundations of Karl Rahner's Theology*, ed. Leo J. O'Donovan, 169–84 (New York: Seabury, 1980). For a good review and assessment of Lonergan's work on the natural law, see Michael J. Himes, "The Human Person in Contemporary Theology: From Human Nature to Authentic Subjectivity," in Hamel and Himes, *Introduction to Christian Ethics*, 49–62.

or Christian ethics anyone who admits human reason as a source of moral wisdom adopts a natural law perspective."[157]

The line of interpretation in the "new natural law" theory developed by Grisez and Finnis departs from the older Catholic version of natural law in that it denies that what is moral may be defined by the givens of nature. Their theory posits that persons as rational agents seek to obtain something that attracts them because it is a good. Moral norms must be derived from reason alone, that is, from purely rational intuitions of the basic goods that are self-evidently such, "which provide the fundamental reasons for all action, and which cannot be rationally rejected through direct actions."[158] According to Grisez and Finnis the eight basic human goods are (1) human life (including health and procreation), (2) knowledge and aesthetic appreciation, (3) skilled performances of all kinds, (4) self-integration, (5) authenticity/practical reasonableness, (6) justice and friendship, (7) religion/holiness, and (8) marriage.[159] Jean Porter sees that while the theory of Grisez and Finnis departs from the older Catholic version of natural law, it remains committed to defending the traditional theory of morality.[160] "Even the traditional Catholic prohibition of the use of contraceptives is interpreted by them as a sin against life, which represents the same stance of will as is present in murder, rather than as a violation of the natural processes of sexuality."[161]

Jean Porter holds that the theory of "pure reason" is no more promising than "pure nature" as a basis for a theory of morality. We cannot claim that a moral theory grounded in reason provides us with a clear alternative.[162] Until recently, most Christian theologians and ethicists have been reluctant to address the question of the moral significance of human nature. Associating this topic with premodern accounts of natural law, they found it deeply problematic. Yet, in Porter's view,

---

[157] Charles E. Curran and Richard A. McCormick, eds., *Readings in Moral Theology*, no. 7, *Natural Law and Theology* (New York: Paulist Press, 1991), 1.

[158] Jean Porter, *Nature as Reason: A Thomistic Theory of the Natural Law* (Grand Rapids, MI: Eerdmans, 2005), 127.

[159] This list (with the exception of marriage, which was added later) is taken from Germain Grisez, *The Way of the Lord Jesus*, no. 1, *Christian Moral Principles* (Chicago: Franciscan Herald Press, 1983), 124.

[160] See Porter, "The Natural Law and the Specificity of Christian Morality," 215–22; and idem, "'Direct' and 'Indirect' in Grisez's Moral Theory," *Theological Studies* 57/4 (1996): 611–32.

[161] Porter, *Natural and Divine Law*, 93. See also Germain Grisez, Joseph Boyle, and William May, "Every Marital Act Ought to Be Open to New Life: Towards a Clearer Understanding," *The Thomist* 52/3 (July 1988): 365–426.

[162] Porter, *Nature as Reason*, 131.

so long as Christian theologians avoid talking about the moral significance of human nature (rather than just "pure nature" or "pure reason"), both theological ethics and the wider social discourse will be impoverished.[163] Problems in biomedical and sexual ethics make this discussion necessary. Besides, not engaging in this discussion prevents theologians from bringing a distinctively theological perspective to bear on the recent work on the biological roots of morality. Studies occasioned by developments in natural sciences (sociobiology) and evolutionary psychology are open to the natural as a source of normative moral guidance. Retrieving the insights of the older natural law theory, in seeing natural processes as having moral significance, they retain the insight of the older natural law theory but avoid its tendency to absolutism.[164]

Evolutionary psychology is premised on the continuity between what we think of as moral practices and the behavior of at least the higher animals.[165] Ethologist Frans de Waal lists some human abilities that are recognizable in other animals: attachment; empathy; adjustment to and special care for the disabled; internalization of "prescriptive social rules"; concepts of giving, trading, and revenge; tendencies toward peacemaking and social maintenance; and the practice of negotiation.[166] The recent upsurge of interest in the biological roots of human behavior and in the related question of the moral standing of animals has led philosophers to question the sharp line that has been drawn between a human morality grounded in autonomy and reason and instinctual, nonrational animal behavior.[167] As a result, a growing number of Christian ethicists have pursued the question of the moral significance of human nature, and this pursuit has not been confined to Catholic scholars. Reformed Church theologian James Gustafson is one of the most influential voices in these discussions. In his view

---

[163] Porter, *Natural and Divine Law,* 27.

[164] Porter, "The Natural Law and the Specificity of Christian Morality," 222–24. See also Stephen J. Pope, "Descriptive and Normative Uses of Evolutionary Theory," in Cahill and Childress, *Christian Ethics,* 166–82.

[165] For a good summary and assessment of the relevant literature, see Stephen J. Pope, *The Evolution of Altruism and the Ordering of Love* (Washington, DC: Georgetown University Press, 1994), 99–127; and Galen Strawson, "In Deepest Sympathy: Toward a Natural History of Virtue," *Times Literary Supplement* (November 29, 1996), 3–4.

[166] Frans de Waal, *Good Natured: The Origins of Right and Wrong in Humans and Other Animals* (Cambridge, MA: Harvard University Press, 1996).

[167] See Mary Midgley, *Beast and Man: The Roots of Human Nature* (New York: Meridian, 1978); and idem, *The Ethical Primate: Humans, Freedom and Morality* (London: Routledge, 1994).

the Catholic commitment to natural law ethics has maintained the importance of nature as a theological category. He writes: "If God is in any sense controlling or ordering nature—from the creation of the universe to its prospective demise, from the simplest forms of life to the complexity of the human organism—how can theological ethics avoid nature?"[168]

In the study of the natural law the body has come up for much attention in recent philosophical and theological work, and the relevance of the body to moral judgment has always been stressed in the traditional Catholic teaching. This has led to its being criticized as tending toward physicalism, particularly in defining sexual norms. The church teaching "tends to revert to a sacralization of physical processes whenever sex is the moral issue."[169] Lisa Sowle Cahill writes that ethics always has to do with the body, since it is dealing with human action that is embodied. The current interest in the body is largely on the affirmation of the body as constitutive of personhood and the specific context or nexus around which social relations and values are built.[170]

Jean Porter's *Natural and Divine Law* "represents an extraordinarily important intervention into this current discussion."[171] Her careful scholarship helps us understand and appreciate natural law as it emerged and developed in the medieval age, and how a retrieval and renewal could move our contemporary discussion forward. The Scholastic concept of the natural law brings together three traditional loci for moral reflection: nature, reason, and scripture.[172] Porter attempts to show the points of contact between the Scholastic conception of natural law and contemporary thought. Scholastic writings on the relationship between the pre-rational aspects of our nature and rationality bring to mind the recent scientific and philosophical studies on the relationship between animal behavior and human morality. Contrary, however, to the accusation that the Scholastics derive moral norms directly from the observation of animal behavior, they interpret human morality as the distinctively human expression of the ways of

---

[168] James Gustafson, "Nature: Its Status in Theological Ethics," *Logos* E (1982): 8.

[169] Richard A. McCormick, "Some Early Reactions to *Veritatis Splendor*," *Theological Studies* 55/3 (1994): 492.

[170] Lisa Sowle Cahill, *Sex, Gender, and Christian Ethics* (Cambridge: Cambridge University Press, 1996), 76.

[171] Nicholas Wolterstorff, "Foreword," in Porter, *Natural and Divine Law*, 11.

[172] Porter, *Natural and Divine Law*, 51.

behaving that are found generally common throughout the animal kingdom.[173]

A second point of contact between the Scholastic authors and those who work in the field of theological ethics is that the Scholastic concept of natural law is a theological concept, not purely a philosophical construct. But while contemporary theology sees natural law and scripture as sources of moral knowledge which are mutually complementary, supplementary, and also mutually corrective, the connection between the Scholastic concept of natural law and scripture is more substantive. For the Scholastics the scriptural grounding of the natural law identifies and defines what is normative of human nature.[174]

For many contemporary readers the Scholastic emphasis on the rational character of the natural law corresponds to their understanding of natural law. The use of reason is what is distinctively human. This seems particularly to be the common ground between the theory of Finnis and Grisez and that of their Scholastic forebears, but while in one sense this is true, it cannot be pressed too far. There is a fundamental difference between the new natural law of Finnis and Grisez and the Scholastic concept of the natural law. Sharing in the modern view that a line is drawn between the rational and pre-rational, the former hold that moral norms must be derived from reason alone, that is, from pure rational intuition. No Scholastic would interpret reason as autonomous and separate from pre-rational aspects of human nature. Essential continuity is presupposed between what is natural and what is rational, since nature is itself an intelligible expression of divine reason. "In particular, the pre-rational components of human nature have their own intelligible structures, in virtue of which they provide starting points and parameters for the exercise of practical reason."[175]

In *Nature as Reason* Porter draws from her earlier exposition and analysis of Scholastic thought to construct an original Thomistic theory of natural law. She holds that Aquinas's account of the natural law cannot be fully understood outside the context of his forebears, nor is its significance for contemporary times fully apparent apart from this context. She develops her own account of natural law that uses Aquinas's analysis as its fundamental theoretical structure but is not a straightforward presentation of Aquinas's own views.[176] It is not possible to detail Porter's account fully here, but it suffices to say that

---

[173] Ibid., 52.
[174] Ibid., 52.
[175] Ibid., 93.
[176] Porter, *Nature as Reason*, 46–47.

she combines an understanding of natural law that is unapologetically theological and yet takes seriously the Aristotelian naturalism of Aquinas's natural law theory, and therefore avoids being sectarian. While reason is its distinctively human component, it veers away from the sterility of pure rationalism.

Porter's account of natural law is premised on Aquinas's dictum that the natural law represents the rational creature's distinctive way of participating in the eternal law (*ST* I–II 91.2). It is the creature's way of attaining the final end, which is union with God, the first principle and final end of all created existence. This end can only be attained through the process of rational choices, informed by some grasp of what that end might be. The use of reason, however, is not autonomous or self-legislating; it is grounded in the natural inclinations that stem from one's created nature, and the teleological orientation of the creature as a whole, rather than that of particular inclinations, much less of particular organs.[177] Porter writes: "The cornerstone of a Thomistic theory of the natural law will be an account of happiness, understood as the final end and ultimate perfection of the human creature."[178] This end is attained through basic inclinations that are directed toward virtue, making a life of virtue naturally desirable, admirable, and satisfying.[179]

Once again we see the Scholastic continuity of the pre-rational and the rational dimensions of natural law. "Nature as nature" informs and directs "nature as reason." "Reason takes its starting points from inclinations which are not simply blind surges of desire, but intelligibly structured orientations towards goods connatural to the human creature, and it is informed through a process of ongoing reflection on those intelligibilities."[180] For Aquinas, it is not reason operating by itself that leads to action. While it is true that reason takes its starting point from first principles (for example, "good is to be sought and done, and evil is to be avoided" [I–II 94.2]), by themselves principles do not lead to action until they are engaged by desires, which move one into reflection and action.[181] Daniel Westberg points out that this rules out any interpretation of right practical reason as understood in Kantian self-legislating reason:

---

[177] Ibid., 321–22.
[178] Ibid., 322.
[179] Ibid., 323.
[180] Ibid., 262.
[181] Ibid., 249.

Movement towards perfection or completion of a being's nature is described by Thomas as attraction to the good. Moral goodness is established in judgment about actions, but the motivation is attraction, not a sense of duty. Thus the term prudence signals a rejection of a Kantian view of morality based on duty and opposed to inclination.[182]

Porter's account of natural law is holistic, taking human persons in their totality, in their profound connection with the rest of creation, with union with God as their ultimate end, which they realize through rational choices directed by their basic inclinations toward virtue, which is desire and attraction to the good, the foundation of a truly happy life.

Cynthia Crysdale also makes a significant contribution to the ongoing discussion on natural law. A key insight of her position is that an understanding of the natural law need not be circumscribed by either of the two strains in the tradition, one emphasizing the givens of the body and the other human rationality and freedom. She proposes a view that undercuts the nature vs. reason debate in our understanding of natural law and the dualism that results from such an understanding. Applying "emergent probability" (defined by Lonergan as a worldview that incorporates both the regularities explained by classical laws and the probabilities explained by statistical laws) to the understanding of natural law, she concludes that such an understanding must be rooted in the nature of the person as conditioned by his or her bodily existence and as progressively shaped by his or her freedom and consciousness. This is a view of the person evolving through the interaction of both the recurrence and creativity built into his or her nature as an embodied being and a free and rational being.[183]

For the retrieval of a truer understanding of the natural law that overcomes essentialism, James Keenan argues for an interdisciplinary approach to understanding nature and its role in moral reasoning. He writes:

Nature is no longer understood as the pure object that we engage and examine, as something distant and apart from the human

---

[182] Daniel Westberg, *Right Practical Reason: Aristotle, Action, and Prudence in Aquinas* (Oxford: Clarendon, 1994), 4.

[183] Cynthia S. W. Crysdale, "Revisioning Natural Law: From the Classicist Paradigm to Emergent Probability," *Theological Studies* 56/3 (1995): 464–84.

being. Nature is not seen as an object as it was in essentialism; rather, nature is a complex and unfolding system whose finality, development, and ways of interacting are grasped only partially—though not arbitrarily—by human insight.[184]

This interdisciplinary understanding of nature integrates humanity and nature, so that the better we understand ourselves, the better we understand nature. Our capacity for understanding is dependent on human reason and its reflection on experience. And if experience is the base of our continuing understanding of ourselves, as assisted by evolving data from contemporary sciences, then our understanding is partial, relative, and open to revision.[185] Experience is a fluid concept, and as Cristina Traina observes: "Experience is perhaps both the most-cited factor and wildest variable in debates over methods and questions in ethics."[186]

From this perspective on natural law, the interpretation of natural law norms, in contrast to classical essentialism, is an ongoing process. "Ethical norms are not properties of nature but the results of interpretation by nature."[187] In a real sense, then, we are constantly realizing the natural law; norms change and develop as interdisciplinary investigations disclose fresh discoveries about our humanity and the direction to our fuller human flourishing. And there is a contextual understanding of core natural law norms that gives them a different texture and spirit, even as they hold abiding values of inclusiveness, equality, and solidarity that constitute a common moral vision.

Polarities in Moral Reasoning

In "The Return of Casuistry" James Keenan reintroduces casuistry as a method of moral reasoning in resolving moral dilemmas. A difference is drawn between geometric casuistry (direct application of abstract principles) and taxonomic casuistry (comparison and analysis of cases against a paradigm case). Keenan points out that the priority of cases

---

[184] Keenan, *A History of Catholic Moral Theology in the Twentieth Century*, 174–75.

[185] Ibid., 175.

[186] Cristina Traina, "Papal Ideals, Marital Realities: One View from the Ground," in *Sexual Diversity and Catholicism: Toward the Development of Moral Theology*, ed. Patricia Beattie Jung, 269–88 (Collegeville, MN: Liturgical Press, 2001), 270.

[187] Wilhelm Korff, "Nature or Reason as the Criterion for the Universality of Moral Judgments," Concilium 150, *Christian Ethics: Uniformity, Universality, Pluralism*, ed. Jacques Pohier and Dietmar Mieth, 82–88 (New York: Seabury Press, 1981), 86.

over principles is the subject of some discussion in ethics today. Here, a sheer application of abstract principles is avoided and a more case-based approach is taken, where cases are studied against paradigm cases to bring to light subtleties, differences, and nuances of moral reasoning as circumstances are revealed, maxims are unearthed, and biases are exposed. Today's casuistry insists on the concrete over and against the abstract—a "casuistry with a face" that deals with persons in their contexts. This is held, however, without denying the place and value of principles, as principles and cases are engaged dialectically, in a relation of mutual critique and modification. This turn to the subject stresses the context-dependence of ethical issues.

Keenan says that because it is context dependent, casuistry is simply a rhetorical and reasoning method. It is content free, and it takes a particular shape in a particular context, as the moral reasoning of those engaged in the casuistic process is influenced by their long-held beliefs, their view of circumstances, and their grasp of existing principles.[188] As Stanley Hauerwas writes: "Casuistry is the mode of reflection a community employs to test imaginatively the often unnoticed and unacknowledged implications of its narrative commitments."[189] Keenan stresses that those who engage in casuistry must ask questions not only about the intentionality of the action but more important about character—who they are and who they ought to become by the casuistry they employ in reaching their decisions. The question of virtue and character provides the horizon of meaning against which casuistry is engaged to reach answers to a human problem. Otherwise, he points out, one might just as well seek answers from a *ouija* board. In the return of casuistry the enduring claims of the past are challenged by the fresh directions in the present.

Polarities in moral reasoning are sharply illumined in the points of divergence between the principle of double effect and the principle of proportionate reasoning. This divergence was highlighted when *Veritatis Splendor* singled out so-called theories of proportionalism and consequentialism as recent developments that are incompatible with revelation, because such theories justify morally wrongful acts by a good intention and thus deny the existence of intrinsically evil acts (nos. 71–83). *Veritatis Splendor* elicited a broad range of reactions, and it set in motion waves of protests from key proponents of proportionalism because of what they perceived as a gross misrepresentation

---

[188] See James F. Keenan, "The Return of Casuistry," *Theological Studies* 57/1 (1996): 123–39.

[189] Stanley Hauerwas, "Casuistry as a Narrative Art," *Interpretation* 37 (1993): 381.

of their ethical position. The misunderstanding stems from a difference of understanding of what precisely defines an act as morally right or wrong, and this comes down to a difference of ethical methodology.

It is helpful at the outset to establish that there is in fact no monolithic consequentialist or proportionalist position, inasmuch as there are significant differences that individual theologians bring to their analyses.[190] The emergence of proportionalism is not seen as a radical break from adherence to the historic principle of double effect but as a continuity or development of it within a new ethical framework and language. In a seminal article that began the movement now known as proportionalism, Peter Knauer places double effect at the heart of moral analysis—the fundamental principle of all morality. He writes: "Every human act brings evil effects with it. The choice of a value always means concretely that there is denial of another value which must be given as a price in exchange."[191] Christopher Kaczor asserts that proportionalism, if it ever was a development of Catholic moral tradition, is better understood as an extension of neo-Scholastic Jesuit manuals than as a recovery of Aquinas.[192] Knauer and those who follow him presented a revisionist version of the four criteria of the double effect. There is, however, no monolithic view of the revised version among the revisionists, but rather a range of views, with specific nuances here and there.

The continuing discourse and debate among ethicists regarding double effect and proportionate reason revolve around proportionalist revisions of the four criteria or conditions of double effect and their

---

[190] Richard A. McCormick's writings on proportionalist theory, for instance, might be classified as representing a teleological model of ethical argumentation. This model holds that a particular way of acting is ethically right or wrong based in part on consequences it produces. But there are significant differences among theologians within this "teleological school" of moral thinking. For example, an extreme teleology has been made popular by Joseph Fletcher in his situation ethics. Sometimes called utilitarianism or consequentialism, this form of absolute teleology counts only consequences. It is described as the ethical attitude that seeks to produce the greatest good for the greatest number. McCormick's writings, on the other hand, represent a middle position described as mixed teleology, which differs from strict consequentialism insofar as it regards moral obligation as arising from the way in which the good or evil is achieved by the moral agent and from elements other than consequences. See Bruno Schüller, "Various Types of Grounding for Ethical Norms," in *Readings in Moral Theology*, no. 1, *Moral Norms and Catholic Traditions,* ed. Charles E. Curran and Richard A. McCormick, 184–98 (New York: Paulist Press, 1979).

[191] Peter Knauer, "The Hermeneutical Function of the Principle of Double Effect," in Curran and McCormick, *Readings in Moral Theology,* 1:1.

[192] See Christopher Kaczor, "Double Effect Reasoning from Jean Pierre Gury to Peter Knauer," *Theological Studies* 59/2 (1998): 297–316.

implications on the resolution of moral dilemmas in bioethics, sexual ethics, and social ethics. Several critical responses arose to revisions, such as the introduction of the premoral concept to overcome the problematic concept of intrinsic evil, which holds that no intention or circumstance can possibly redeem the wrongness of an object; it is so clearly, unalterably wrong that it could never be considered a right action. Fuchs held that no sufficient moral judgment can be made until the full complexity of an object, the end or intention, and circumstances are adequately considered. And yet even prior to final moral judgment, certain realities have a claim on us, and Fuchs referred to them as pre-moral evil.[193]

Moralists like Servais Pinckaers and John Connery held that the centrality of the moral object had been diminished, and that reductionism and relativism had taken over moral absolutes.[194] Some moralists criticized proportionalism as an act-oriented method. Others raised the question whether proportionalism, like other methods of contemporary reasoning, created a false dichotomy between the agent and the action.[195] Joseph Selling took up the critique, defending proportionalism as a holistic and integrated method.[196] Frederick Carney maintains that a utilitarian calculus is at the heart the teleological method of proportionalism.[197] Germain Grisez holds that proportionalism is altogether unworkable and is "dangerous nonsense" because it is founded on the weighing of values that are incommensurable.[198] McCormick, in responding to Grisez, points to situations of conflicted values where it is necessary to cause harm as we go about doing good. In such situations weighing of values is a moral imperative.[199]

---

[193] See Josef Fuchs, "The Absoluteness of Moral Terms," in *Proportionalism: For and Against*, ed. Christopher Kaczor, 60–99 (Milwaukee, WI: Marquette University, 2000), 83–86.

[194] Keenan, *A History of Catholic Moral Theology in the Twentieth Century*, 157.

[195] See Brian V. Johnstone, "Objectivism, Basic Human Goods, and Proportionalism," *Studia Moralia* 43 (2005): 97–126.

[196] See Joseph A. Selling, "Distinct But Not Separate: The Subject-Object Relation in Contemporary Moral Theology," *Studia Moralia* 44 (2006): 15–40. See also Brian Johnstone, "The Subject Object Relation in Contemporary Moral Theology: A Reply to Joseph A. Selling," *Studia Moralia* 44 (2006): 41–62.

[197] See Frederick Carney, "On McCormick and Teleological Morality," *Journal of Religious Ethics* 6 (Spring 1978): 81–107.

[198] See Germain Grisez and Joseph M. Boyle Jr., *Life and Death with Liberty and Justice: A Contribution to the Euthanasia Debate* (Notre Dame, IN: University of Notre Dame Press, 1979), 349–51.

[199] Richard A. McCormick, "Does Religious Faith Add to Ethical Perception?" in Hamel and Himes, *Introduction to Christian Ethics*, 142.

Whichever position one takes, in the engagement of either double effect or proportionate reason the human social contexts of problems must be considered. Principles must not be treated as abstract and ahistorical universal norms unrelated to the concrete situations of moral agents, who live in relational and social contexts. Morality refers not only to universal laws but also to moral subjects and the personal and social realities that surround them.

Emergence of Feminism

With the emergence of feminism, theological thought entered a whole new era. Through almost four decades after its emergence, its impact has profoundly challenged and changed theological thinking in all the areas of specialization: biblical studies, systematic theology, moral theology, spirituality, and sacramentology. It has produced a vast body of literature that ranges across all these theological specialties and beyond. Feminism opened the theological enterprise to the reality of diversity and pluralism as it broke the boundaries of a consistently male theology. What follows is a discussion of the vision and method of feminist ethics, including the multiplicity of women's experience and its normativity, the basis and rationale of which have been challenged. The overall framework of feminist methodology of critique, retrieval, and (re)construction is presented and applied in relation to some issues like embodiment, the two-natures theory, role expectations of men and women in family and society, ethical dilemmas of abortion, reproductive technologies, and environmental ethics.

Feminism has influenced moral theology and ethics at a fundamental level by shaping its worldview and determining its method. First, the definition of Sandra Schneiders underlines the concerns of feminism, "a comprehensive ideology, which is rooted in women's experience of sexual oppression, engages in a critique of patriarchy as an essentially dysfunctional system, embraces an alternative vision for humanity and for the earth, and actively seeks to bring this vision to realization."[200] Anne Patrick, in the same line of thought, has defined feminist stance as the fundamental belief that men and women are equal and a commitment to reforming society, including religious society. It also means deconstruction of the entire thought system that

---

[200] Sandra M. Schneiders, *Beyond Patching: Faith and Feminism in the Catholic Church* (New York: Paulist Press, 2004), 15.

gives legitimacy to the social order that promotes the unjust relationship between man and woman.[201] Lisa Sowle Cahill writes that "virtually by definition, feminist theology is 'moral' theology or ethics. It emerges from a practical situation of injustice and aims at social and political change."[202] This may be true of contemporary theology in general in its focus on praxis governed by "ethical-political-criteria" of validity,[203] but it is true in a special way of feminist and other liberation theologies. The primary tasks of feminist ethics are defined by the demands of equality and justice and the pursuit of reform for more egalitarian social arrangements relative to gender relations, with women's experience as the critical point of reference.

The multiplicity and normativity of women's experience, however, has been a topic of discourse and debate. Gloria Schaab uses the image of the kaleidoscope, with "its symmetrical patterns from fragments of various materials, illuminated by a source of light," to illustrate vividly the diversity of approaches, variety of sources, and the complexity of norms relative to women's experience.[204] She uses the term "women's experiences" in the plural rather than in the singular to signify a particularity of women's experiences that does not allow universalization or generalization. This is to give voice to the experiences of women in their different contexts beyond the white North American experience; to include black Americans, Latin Americans, Asians, and numerous other groups representing various designations of theology, such as womanist and mujerista; and to recognize a variety of particularities based on social locations as defined by racial, ethnic, cultural, and religious affiliations and sensitivities.[205] The normativity of the experiences of women has also been subjected to debate. If the feminist experience is to be considered normative, on what grounds can this stance be accepted? On what basis is the validation of this stance argued? Is it an assumption to be accepted as true by the sheer assertion of the epistemological privilege of its

[201] See Anne Patrick, "Authority, Women, and Church: Reconsidering the Relationship," in *Empowering Authority: The Charism of Episcopacy and Primacy in the Church Today*, ed. Patrick Howell and Gary Chamberlain, 17–33 (Kansas City: Sheed and Ward, 1990).
[202] Lisa Sowle Cahill, "Feminist Ethics," *Theological Studies* 51/1 (1990): 50.
[203] David Tracy, "The Uneasy Alliance Reconceived: Catholic Theological Method, Modernity, and Postmodernity," *Theological Studies* 50/3 (1989): 569.
[204] Gloria L. Schaab, "Feminist Theological Methodology: Toward a Kaleidoscopic Model," *Theological Studies* 62/2 (2001): 342.
[205] Ibid., 348.

proponents? What possibilities of objectivity and verification can there be for the feminists' claims?

Some feminist thinkers have argued for the objectivity and verification of their claims on the basis of truth, founded in commitment and practice. As Carol Christ writes: "It is more true that women's contributions to the human community have been and are as important as men's than to believe in the opposite."[206] The perspectival nature of all truth does not necessarily lead to relativism. Rather, it stimulates a dialogue of perspectives in which the validity and verification of one perspective are proven to have more grounding than in the other, on the basis of what David Tracy calls "political-ethical criteria." One verifies the truthfulness of a claim by its pragmatic consequences on personal lives and communities. For instance, the "turn to the oppressed" and to the "otherness in all who are oppressed" in the spirit of inclusion and hospitality, which marks the advocacy of feminist theology, rooted as it is in the experience of women as victims of oppression themselves, claims a truth grounded in what practical reason sees as liberative of human action for persons and communities.[207] Elisabeth Schüssler Fiorenza asserts that "all theology, knowingly or not, is by definition always engaged for or against the oppressed."[208] And Schaab states, "It takes its position of advocacy either to uphold or to challenge the power relationships in the community from whom its articulations are derived and to whom its articulations are addressed."[209] Generally speaking, feminists are aware of the perspectival character of assertions about religious truth and moral order, and thus they are attentive to their historical contextualizations. They see the necessity of a constant dialectic of the ethical criterion they use with theological and philosophical sources, communal religious traditions, broad social consequences, and the consequences for women's lives.

The overall framework of feminist methodologies includes three basic elements: critique, retrieval, and (re)construction. "The fundamental tasks of these elements are to analyze inherited oppressions, through a deconstruction of texts and formulations, to search for women's alternative wisdom and suppressed history, and to risk new

---

[206] Carol P. Christ, "Embodied Thinking: Reflections on Feminist Theological Method," *Journal of Feminist Studies in Religion* 5/1 (1989): 13.

[207] Anne Patrick, "The Linguistic Turn and Moral Theology," *Proceedings of the Catholic Theological Society of America* 42 (Louisville, KY: Bellarmine College, 1987), 56.

[208] Elisabeth Schüssler Fiorenza, *Bread Not Stone: The Challenge of Feminist Biblical Interpretation* (Boston: Beacon, 1984), 26.

[209] Schaab, "Feminist Theological Methodology," 347.

interpretations in conversation with women's lives."[210] Space here does
not permit an in-depth treatment of the issues, but some salient themes
are revisited that have been at the locus of discourse in feminist ethics
and have yielded voluminous writings.

One important theme is that of embodiment. Feminist theology
reacts against theories that link woman to body and nature simply
because dualistic and reductionist anthropology (represented by the
two-natures theory) identifies men with mind and soul and women
with body.[211] The two-natures theory grounds the gender roles assigned to men in the public sphere, where rationality is engaged, and
those assigned to women in the private domestic sphere of the home,
where affectivity is primary. But, as Elizabeth Johnson points out,
"with what right are compassionate love, reverence, and nurturing
predicated as primordially feminine characteristics, rather than human
ones? Why are strength, sovereignty, and rationality exclusive to the
masculine?"[212] She further writes: "Could it not be, as Ruether formu-
lates the fundamental question, that the very concept of the 'feminine'
is a creation out of patriarchy, an ideal projected onto women by men
and vigorously defended because it functions so well to keep men in
positions of power and women out of public roles?"[213] Feminist ethics, criticizing the two-natures theory, upholds the common human
nature of man and woman that warrants similar moral treatment of
them and avoids the division of men and women into different spheres
of dominance and submission. It asserts that the fundamental social
roles and duties of men and women are the same.[214]

Feminists emphasize the cultural nuance of embodiment and its
social character. While menstruation, pregnancy, childbirth, and
motherhood might constitute what is distinctively female embodiment,
they are mediated by culture.[215] In oppressed cultures embodiment of

[210] Ibid., 357. "The term reconstruction implies that a particular feminist
theological effort is directed toward the change or transformation of an existing
interpretation or construct."

[211] Susan A. Ross, "Feminist Theology: A Review of Literature: The Physical and
Social Context for Feminist Theology and Spirituality," *Theological Studies* 56/2
(1995): 330–31.

[212] See Elizabeth A. Johnson, "The Incomprehensibility of God and the Image
of God Male and Female," *Theological Studies* 45/3 (1984): 456.

[213] Ibid. Johnson refers here to Rosemary Radford Ruether, "The Female Nature
of God: God as Father?" *Concilium* 143 (New York: Seabury Press, 1981), 66.

[214] Cahill, "Feminism and Christian Ethics," 216.

[215] See Anne E. Carr and Elisabeth Schüssler Fiorenza, eds., *Motherhood: Experience, Institution, Theology* (Edinburgh: T. and T. Clark, 1989); idem, *The
Special Nature of Women?* (London: SCM, 1991); Susan R. Bordo, *Unbearable*

women means vulnerability to control, exploitation, and violence.[216]
For example, Hispanic women often do not align with feminist views
of equality in an individualist sense, perhaps because this is perceived
as lessening the importance of the ties of women to their families and
children.[217] Embodiment provides the context for social and relational values, living in harmony and autonomy, with interdependence
and reciprocity, and the recovery of a sense of the intrinsically good
against instrumental relationships. Embodiment demands the building of social relations of respect, equality, and mutuality. Lisa Sowle
Cahill summarizes the project and task of Christian feminists relative
to embodiment:

> In re-examining human experience as male and female, they
> focus on its embodied and its social character; they extend the
> moral meaning of embodiedness beyond sex-based gender roles;
> they challenge historical constructions of gender as oppressive to
> women, as culturally biased, and as not demanded by natural sex
> differences; and they critically combine both Christian resources
> and philosophical and social analysis to guide their transforma-
> tive vision of more co-operative and egalitarian communities.[218]

Feminist ethics poses a critique to specific role expectations of men
and women in family and society, which have their origin in lopsided
gender relations. Women are seen as more religious, spiritual, and
moral, and theirs is the call and vocation to sacrifice themselves for
husband and children. Christian feminist ethics maintains the ideal of
self-sacrifice but applies it evenly to women and men in a relationship
of mutuality and reciprocity, which deepens and enriches the relational
dimensions of love.[219] In what Anne Patrick calls the patriarchal paradigm for virtue, women are expected to excel in charity and chastity
while men are trained to think in terms of justice and rights, when in

---

Weight: Feminism, Western Culture, and the Body (Berkeley and Los Angeles:
University of California Press, 2003); Herbert Anderson, Edward Foley, Bonnie
Miller-McClemore, and Robert Schreiter, eds., *Mutuality Matters: Family, Faith,
and Just Love* (Lanham, MD: Rowman and Littlefield, 2004); and Lisa Sowle
Cahill, *Family: A Christian Social Perspective* (Minneapolis: Fortress Press, 2000).

[216] See, for example, Delores Williams, "A Womanist Perspective on Sin," in *A
Troubling in My Soul: Womanist Perspectives on Evil and Suffering*, ed. Emilie
M. Townes, 130–49 (Maryknoll, NY: Orbis Books, 1993).

[217] See, for example, Ada Maria Isasi-Díaz, *En La Lucha = In the Struggle:
Elaborating a Mujerista Theology* (Minneapolis: Fortress Press, 2004).

[218] Cahill, "Feminist Ethics," 56.

[219] Cahill, "Feminism and Christian Ethics," 216–17.

fact all Christians are expected to be kind, chaste, just, and humble.[220] This anthropological dualism results in rigid stereotyping of human characteristics as predominantly masculine or feminine.

The question of women's maternal role as a focus of feminist discourse has provoked the thesis that the subordination of women is not based on "innate" human characteristics but is reproduced through the institution of mothering. The pernicious effects of the two-natures doctrine are most visible in the rigid stereotyping in gender roles in marriage and parenthood, within the web of the social, cultural, and religious institutions that are patriarchal. The anthropology of the papal encyclical *Mulieris Dignitatem* further promotes the two-natures theme that marginalizes men from the home and family and diminishes the role and vocation of women in public life.

A culturally nuanced understanding of sexuality, embodiment, and marriage is crucial in assessing a number of moral dilemmas around abortion and reproductive technologies. Viewing sexual and family ethics within social conditions and consequences, many Catholic authors resist a narrow and single ethical criterion as morally decisive in the question of abortion, whether that stresses the "right to life" of the fetus or the abortion rights or free choice of women.[221] Discussions of reproductive technologies consider the interrelation of embodiment, family, and technology, raising issues of technological alienation of conception, commercialization of women's reproduction, exploitation of poor women, instrumentalization of childbirth, and more.[222]

Similarly, the concern for justice and right relationships that extends into every dimension of life is the same concern brought to the relationship of human beings to the nonhuman world. Ecofeminism poses a critique of the hierarchical relations of domination and submission that have devastating consequences for women and for the earth. Discussions are directed toward a new understanding of creation doctrine that reformulates and reenvisions the relationship between God and humanity, among human beings, and between humans and the nonhuman world.[223]

---

[220] Anne Patrick, "Narrative and the Social Dynamics of Virtue," in *Changing Values and Virtues,* ed. Dietmar Mieth and Jacques Pohier, Concilium 191 (Edinburgh: T. and T. Clark, 1987), 72.

[221] Cahill, "Feminist Ethics," 62.

[222] Ibid., 63.

[223] For example, see Rosemary Radford Ruether, *Gaia and God: An Ecofeminist Theology of Earth Healing* (San Francisco: Harper, 1992), 15–58; Sallie McFague, *The Body of God: An Ecological Theology* (Minneapolis: Fortress Press, 1993).

Toward a Global Ethics

Prospects for a Common Morality, edited by Gene Outka and John Reeder, has brought major positions taken in debates over common morality from a broad diversity of perspectives to the table since its publication in 1993.[224] This question of common morality is even more pressing in the face of global pluralism. Some scholars promote the reality and validity of common morality or global ethics; others hold that if a global ethics is promulgated, it can only be platitudinous and bereft of real content; and still others propose a revised concept of common morality or common good that is more based on praxis. I do not attempt a comprehensive bibliographic survey of these positions but will take representatives of each position for a sufficient appreciation of the discussions that have been undertaken.

Hans Küng, known for his work in interreligious dialogue both in his writing and his active engagements, was behind the *Document Toward a Global Ethics,* which was passed by the Parliament of the World's Religions in its meeting in Chicago, September 4, 1993, with 115 religions represented among more than 6,500 delegates.[225] As Küng explains, in this declaration people of different religious backgrounds have come to a consensus of minimum ethical directives that were already affirmed in their traditions. Such a minimal ethics is absolutely necessary for human survival; it is not directed against anyone but invites all men and women of good will to live according to its principles.[226] The most fundamental principle stated is that every human being must be treated humanely. This is followed by four irrevocable directives: commitment to a culture of nonviolence and respect; commitment to a culture of solidarity and a just economic order; commitment to a culture of tolerance and a life of truthfulness; and commitment to a culture of equal rights and partnerships between men and women.[227] When asked why this declaration was necessary, Küng said that "without morality, without universally binding ethical norms, indeed without global standards, the nations are in danger of maneuvering themselves into a crisis which can ultimately lead

---

[224] Gene Outka and John P. Reeder, eds., *Prospects for a Common Morality* (Princeton, NJ: Princeton University Press, 1993).

[225] For the text of the document, see Hans Küng, ed., *Yes to a Global Ethic* (New York: Continuum, 1996), 7–26. The document is also available online on the parliamentofreligions.org website.

[226] Ibid., 2.

[227] See Küng, *Yes to a Global Ethic,* 7–26.

to national collapse, i.e., to economic ruin, social disintegration, and political catastrophe."[228]

There are others who hold the same view but with varying rationales. Alan Gewirth specifies human rights as the basis for a common morality that claims a normativity on the meta-ethical universal level; these rights protect the interests all persons have in common.[229] David Little, arguing from the same basis of rights, says that they possess cross-cultural validity. Rights protect something of indispensable importance, which is neither earned nor achieved but is "natural" to us and must not be disallowed by virtue of race, creed, ethnic origin, or gender, for human rights are claimable by all.[230]

A fundamental criticism of consensus statements, such as the Parliament of World Religions document, is that they remain on the level of abstract generalities. Küng himself comments that while the stated principles of global ethics are good, "some will object that they are still far too general."[231] Annette C. Baier writes, "Lists of universal rights, if they are both to cohere and to receive anything like general assent, must be so vague as to be virtually empty."[232] Jean Porter echoes Baier's position:

> The claim that all moral traditions share a fundamental core which amounts to a universally valid morality, appears to me to be defensible only if the core in question is described at such a high level of generality as to be virtually empty, and even then, it is difficult to arrive at a statement of principles that would be universally accepted.[233]

Noting that questions were raised regarding the equal place given to men and women, the question of nonviolence, and the character

---

[228] Hans Küng, "The History, Significance, and Method of the Declaration Toward a Global Ethic," in *A Global Ethic: The Declaration of the Parliament of the World's Religions*, ed. Hans Küng (New York: Continuum, 1998), 26.

[229] See Alan Gewirth, "Common Morality and the Community of Rights," in Outka and Reeder, *Prospects for a Common Morality*, 29–52.

[230] See David Little, "The Nature and Basis of Human Rights," in Outka and Reeder, *Prospects for a Common Morality*, 73–92.

[231] Hans Küng, *Global Responsibility: In Search of a New Ethics* (New York: Crossroad, 1991), 63. See also Hans Küng and Helmut Schmidt, *A Global Ethic and Global Responsibilities: Two Declarations* (London: SCM, 1998).

[232] Annette C. Baier, "Claims, Rights, Responsibilities," in Outka and Reeder, *Prospects for a Common Morality*, 152.

[233] Jean Porter, "The Search for a Global Ethic," *Theological Studies* 62/1 (2001): 121.

of the document as too Western, Porter holds that consensus among representatives of different traditions is impossible. What is necessary is an approach with modest goals pursued with the spirit of humility. A universal ethic may not be reached, but perhaps it may not be needed to develop a basis for a workable moral consensus on a wide range of issues.[234]

Arguing against Alan Gewirth's justification of human rights, Alasdair MacIntyre holds that one cannot find an objective basis for rights in general facts about human beings. Beliefs in human rights are "one with belief in witches and in unicorns."[235] Sharon Welch, working from a Foucauldian perspective, suggests that Western notions of equality are creations of a dominant gender and class that mask oppression.[236] In the same vein Margaret Farley recognizes that the notion of a universal morality has marginalized particular groups and masked differences. From a feminist perspective she sees two major obstacles to universal morality: the feminist emphasis on particularity, and the lack of commonality even in women's experiences. Despite these obstacles she believes in common features of human experience that are recognizable by diverse cultures. She cites the capacity for human suffering and joy as intrinsic to being human, in spite of differences in gender, class, race, and culture. Farley's position is representative of those critical of the Enlightenment's understanding of universal morality, but it is also representative of those seeking a new way of viewing common morality. She questions whether all efforts to identify commonalities nullify differences, with the contingent mistaken for the essential. She attempts to strike a balance between those who claim that universal or common morality is an illusion and those who hold that a universal morality is determined by a dominant class and thus marginalizes others and masks differences.[237]

Lisa Sowle Cahill writes that the Catholic "common good" paradigm, relying on nature, reason, and universal law, has come to be seen as an Enlightenment relic, naively isolated from cultural pluralism, economic globalization, and competing philosophical and theological interpretations of the human condition, especially interpretations projected from other cultural situations. She remarks that these challenges

---

[234] Ibid.

[235] MacIntyre, *After Virtue*, 69. Gewirth replies in "Rights and Virtues," *Review of Metaphysics* 38/4 (June 1985): 739–62.

[236] Sharon D. Welch, *Communities of Resistance and Solidarity: A Feminist Theology of Liberation* (Maryknoll, NY: Orbis Books, 1985).

[237] See Margaret A. Farley, "Feminism and Universal Morality," in Outka and Reeder, *Prospects for a Common Morality*, 170–90.

possibly invalidate the very question of universal ethics or a normative common good. Perhaps it is no longer even the right question to ask.

Cahill proposes a revised concept of the common good by bringing to bear on global ethics some aspects of Aquinas's view of practical reason, especially in its historical contextuality and its interdependence on moral virtue. Aquinas's moral theory is useful in breaking the impasse between the historicity of reason and the universality that global ethics demands by a praxis-based interpretation of moral objectivity and reasonableness. For Aquinas, moral reason is practical reason perfected by the virtue of prudence, whose chief purpose is to attain truthful action, not speculative truth. Moral truth as practical truth is a truth of action, and moral truth understood in the realm of action is realized inductively, experientially, and interactively in the actual engagement of concrete human problems and projects. Taking this Thomistic view of practical truth in relation to global ethics, Cahill writes that "the possibility of global ethics, then, should not be pondered in the realm of abstract or deductive reason alone, but through engagement with practical political affairs. . . . The criterion of global truth must be a network of global experiences and practices that also provide its content."[238] One sees here a search for a global ethics that is beyond its theoretical focus, stressing its experiential and contextual focus as different cultural and religious traditions engage in moral conflict and agreement on concrete issues in a long and difficult inductive process toward a convergent ethics, where common values, principles, and meanings are shared in a transcultural and global realm.

Two important books on this topic are *Ethics and World Religions: Cross-Cultural Case Studies*, edited by Regina Wolfe and Christine E. Gudorf, and *Explorations in Global Ethics: Comparative Religious Ethics and Interreligious Dialogue*, edited by Sumner Twiss and Bruce Grelle. These represent the current direction the search for global ethics has taken in the realm of praxis and pragmatic negotiations. As stated by Twiss and Grelle in their introduction, the overriding purpose is to bring the discipline of comparative religious ethics into constructive collaboration with the community of interreligious dialogue, where interreligious dialogue offers a practical, praxis-based orientation to comparative religious ethics, and comparative religious ethics offers critical tools and methods for more effective practical work in interreligious dialogue. The collaboration is seen as yielding a vision

---

[238] Lisa Sowle Cahill, "Toward Global Ethics," *Theological Studies* 63/2 (2002): 335.

for ethical inquiry and discourse in a pluralistic world, which takes a hermeneutical-critical-practical approach in the "quest for cross-cultural understanding and the fusion of diverse moral and religious horizons."[239]

Taking the praxis-based approach, Wolfe and Gudorf focus on how religions respond to practical, real-life dilemmas. In their use of true-to-life cases the discourse grapples with distinctions and differences in the face of complex issues and the existence of conflicts in moral values. In these attempts to arrive at shared values a genuine appreciation of legitimate diversity is necessary and moral pluralism must not be mistaken for moral chaos.[240] Using the same praxis-based discourse, Daniel C. Maguire has treated the questions of contraception and abortion from the perspective of an interreligious dialogue. His conclusions, based on his study of the ten world religions—Roman Catholicism, Hinduism, Buddhism, Taoism, Confucianism, Judaism, Islam, Protestant Christianity, Native American traditions, and native African religions—show the religions' positive views on sexual pleasure and their flexibility on birth control, and even abortion, in the face of conflicts and challenges in an imperfect world.[241]

Since 1965 *Concilium*, in its six linguistic editions, has fostered international discourse in ethics. Richard McCormick made his "Moral Notes" at *Theological Studies* a forum for international ethical discourse that continues today after more than forty years. And, in *Catholic Ethicists on HIV/AIDS Prevention*, thirty-four ethicists from more than twenty-five countries worked together for the first international project on a globalized threat. The development of regional indigenous faculties of theology across the world made cross-cultural discourse necessary.[242]

When four hundred moral theologians gathered in July 2006 in Padova, Italy, for the first international conference on Catholic theological ethics, made possible by the extraordinary vision and leadership of James Keenan, cross-cultural discourse reached a new high point. The issues with which the participants engaged reflected

---

[239] Sumner Twiss and Bruce Grelle, eds., *Explorations in Global Ethics: Comparative Interreligious Dialogue* (Boulder, CO: Westview Press, 2000), 1–6; see also Regina Wolfe and Christine E. Gudorf, eds., *Ethics and World Religions: Cross-Cultural Case Studies* (Maryknoll, NY: Orbis Books, 1999).

[240] Wolfe and Gudorf, *Ethics and World Religions*, 1–19.

[241] Daniel C. Maguire, *Sacred Choices: The Right to Contraception and Abortion in Ten World Religions* (Minneapolis: Fortress Press, 2001).

[242] Keenan, *A History of Catholic Moral Theology in the Twentieth Century*, 216.

the human problems in their contexts: chronic poverty, structural inequalities, violence, and environmental destruction. The theological insights that were born of this international meeting were shaped by the different global contexts. The conference papers, published in English, Spanish, Italian, Portuguese, Filipino, and Indian editions, show the expanse of the cross-cultural discourse. More cross-cultural collaboration followed the Padova meeting. *Calling for Justice Throughout the World: Catholic Women Theologians on the HIV/ AIDS Pandemic* brought together twenty-five women theologians and ethicists from around the globe to address the social justice issues regarding the prevention of HIV/AIDS and care for its victims.[243] There was a meeting in Manila in August 2008 of East Asian moralists, and the second international conference was held at Trento, Italy, in July 2010.

A review of the scholarship in theological ethics across the globe shows great diversity but also a common vision in terms of core truths and values. The plural voices of scholars of color, scholars from the South, indigenous scholars, and women scholars are addressing the critical issues of our times. Keenan cites the theological frameworks within which ethicists contextualize their work: "The Europeans developed an autonomous ethics, the Latin Americans liberation theology, the Africans a liberative inculturation approach, the Asians a liberative inculturation with interreligious dialogue, and the North Americans the Catholic social tradition in any number of contexts."[244] They bring their own traditions as they enter into cross-cultural conversations and interconnect with a global church.

Shifts in Vision, Content, and Method

The extent, breadth, and depth of the work done in moral theology to approximate the ideal that Vatican II set for it are shown in the various discourses and debates in moral theology regarding wide-ranging issues and concerns. At the heart of this ideal is a call for moral theology to be true to its theological core and to be a genuine science of faith that engages the culture of its own times with its own questions and problems. While it must keep its coherent Christian

---

[243] Mary Jo Iozzio, Mary M. Doyle, Elsie M. Miranda, eds., *Calling for Justice Throughout the World: Catholic Women Theologians on the HIV/AIDS Pandemic* (New York: Continuum, 2008).

[244] Keenan, *A History of Catholic Moral Theology in the Twentieth Century,* 220.

identity, it must also speak a language that is intelligible to the world in which it finds itself.

Using a framework of three themes—recovering the depth of moral theology; building bridges; and facing the challenge of polarity, diversity, and commonality—one discerns the shifts in the vision, content, and method of post–Vatican II moral theology. At the heart of the renewal is a vision of moral theology that is concerned not only about laws and rules but also about the formation of virtue and character, as signaled by the return of virtue ethics. The anthropology behind this vision of moral theology is the person integrally and adequately considered. This anthropology is at the base of the *fundamental commitment*, a key concept in contemporary moral theology, which sees persons in their depths as moral subjects. With this shift of focus the dimensions of affectivity and spirituality have ceased to be peripheral to moral theology. The shift of focus, however, has not eliminated the place of norms, rules, and principles, for the balance of visional ethics and normative ethics is necessary for moral theology to respond to the demands of a complex world. This integral and balanced approach shows that in Christian morality there is not just something of the scientist at work, but there is also the artist, the believer, and the mystic.[245]

The vision of moral theology has also broadened beyond the individual and personal. The line between the personal and the social has been sharply marked in the past, distinguishing social ethics from bioethics and sexual ethics. This dualism of personal and social morality, however, has been debunked, with the claim that all ethics is social ethics. Any personal choice is a social act; any issue that affects individuals has a social context. The separation of private and public arenas of moral discourse has resulted in the failure to address the social roots of problems and to contextualize them within the larger issues. Social justice themes of inclusion, distributive justice, common good, solidarity, and the preferential option for the poor now enter into the narrative of bioethics, sexual/gender ethics, and family ethics, where the focus before was very much personal and interpersonal. When the social is brought into the analysis of ethical problems, the dimensions of class and power are unraveled, and when the global stretches the understanding of social, the reach goes intercultural and interreligious, bringing in a richness and a complexity that must be navigated.

---

[245] Daniel C. Maguire, *The Moral Choice* (Garden City, NY: Doubleday, 1978), 112.

Moral theology is reconnected with the disciplines of theology, the most primary of these being scripture, with its centeredness in Christ, which brings us to a larger view of Christian moral life beyond merely the avoidance of sin. Sin, however, is a fact of the human condition. Neither preoccupied with sin nor diminishing the reality of sin, moral theology has reoriented the focus of sin from the act alone by relating the act to the actor, the moral agent. It has also shifted the understanding of sin from the narrow stress on individual offenses to a wider view of sin as social. Moral theology has been taken out of its autonomous place and put in relation with the whole of theology, drawing from the riches of systematic theology, liberation theology, spiritual theology, and pastoral theology. It has engaged with the challenges of inculturation, interreligious dialogue, feminism, and global ethics, which have opened it to new modes of thought, different contexts of valuing, and various orientations of critique.

In this wider perspective religion takes a central part. Rather than private, religion must be brought into the public arena; rather than apologizing for it, its force for social transformation must be contended with. As the bearer of humanity's deepest convictions about the human good, religion cannot be privatized without impoverishing the public moral discourse. Our lives are deeply interconnected as we search for meaning through the path of religion, in which our conscience is formed, both personal and social. Religion challenges the value system informed by market ethics, where human beings are held as essentially autonomous agents whose fulfillment lies in maximizing their self-interest in the pursuit of acquisition and consumption. Religion calls for community and solidarity, the most fundamental qualities for a life to be fully and richly lived. In dealing with problems in all fields of ethics, religion provides the transcendental framework of values that informs human judgments and decisions.

Feminism has brought a critical stance to issues regarding gender roles, family and social values, cultural sensitivities, and moral dilemmas. It has profoundly challenged and changed theological thinking and has opened the theological enterprise to diversity and pluralism as it put an end to a dominant male theology. Feminist ethics in particular aims at the change of structures and systems that legitimate inequality between men and women. This social thrust of feminist ethics is the thrust of contemporary moral theology in general, which rejects the preoccupation with the self and with the individual that marked the moral manuals. With the influence of liberation theology, it has adopted an integral approach in which the personal and the social are not separated, as moral problems are viewed in both their personal causes and social roots, and with justice (and the preferential option for the poor) as the abiding criterion.

Moral theology as a science of faith must engage in reasoned understanding of moral truths and principles in view of adequately examined data and facts. The shift in method is shown in its inductive and praxis-based approach, which is context sensitive, open to diversity, and tolerant of polarities. It is from this stance that the ethical methods used in the past are reconstructed. For instance, casuistry, which was the key method in the manuals of moral theology, is now used with a strong dependence on context and praxis. Avoiding a direct and deductive application of abstract principles, casuistry can be not only case based but also subject oriented, as it is concerned not only with the intentionality of actions but also with the character and virtue of the one engaged in the casuistic process.

The method one uses in moral theology depends on one's concept of natural law, the understanding of which has been in flux, from natural law "according to nature" to natural law "according to reason." But the current conversation has unraveled the notion that a sharp demarcation line is not to be drawn between the two strains of natural law. There are attempts to integrate both, and studies on the biological roots of morality show that what is natural can be a source of moral guidance, and that while the use of reason is distinctively human, it is not self-legislating as an autonomous faculty. It takes as starting points inclinations that are not simply blind surges of desire, but which are oriented toward virtue and are realized by rational choices. The dualism between nature and reason is undercut, as we come to a more holistic and integral understanding of ourselves as conditioned by our bodily existence and as progressively shaped by our freedom and consciousness. Our body is constitutive of our person, and we evolve through the interaction of the givens in our embodied existence and the possibilities we create through our choices as free and rational beings.

The continuing debate between the proponents of deontological and teleological methodologies (as seen in double effect vs. proportionalism) has resulted in revisions of moral criteria and norms, especially for conflict situations. This ongoing discourse involves an evolving understanding of the nature of the human act, grounded as it is in an evolving understanding of nature of the person and of natural law. In the engagement of either double effect or proportionate reason, however, human social contexts must be considered. The principles must not be treated as abstract ahistorical norms that are blind to context. The feminist methodology of critique, retrieval, and (re)construction is strongly praxis based, as it takes women's experiences as its criteria in criticizing patriarchal systems and draws from these experiences the alternative wisdom to *retrieve* and *(re)construct* ethical views and practices, with the objective of transformation and empowerment. The discourse on global ethics shows a moral theology that has explored uncharted grounds at the crossroads of the church and the world, where the search for answers to ethical questions is negotiated in the deep and murky waters of diversity and pluralism of cultures and religions. Yet, it remains a call and challenge that moral theology must speak intelligibly and meaningfully to the world with which it engages and seeks to transform.

From a discipline that was "one-sidedly confession-oriented, magisterium-dominated, canon-law related, sin-centered, and seminary-controlled,"[246] the discipline of moral theology has evolved into what Vatican II envisioned it to be, a science of faith, faithful to its nature as a theological discipline, in the service of the church and of the world. This is a moral theology that has broken out of the confines of the past and has reinserted itself in history, where Christian faith is lived, where the church meets the world. The church of Vatican II ushered in a new era in world history, where the church defines itself as a church in the world, not in flight from the world. And as it is in the world, it inserts itself in its life as the bearer of its joys, hopes, and anxieties. It aspires to be a builder of bridges between cultures and religions and to be the voice of the poor and the oppressed. It is a world church in dialogue with all men and women of good will in search of what is true and good for humankind. The moral theology shaped by this new definition of the church's nature, role, and mission in the world is one that is at the crossroads of the church and the world; there, it spreads and expands to respond to every human issue and problem that touches all, both fascinated and challenged by the realities of diversity and pluralism. This is the moral theology of our time, radically different from the moral theology of the manuals, as it is shaped by the vision and mission of a church in a different age.

---

[246] McCormick, *Corrective Vision*, 3.

PART I

VISION

Our moral vision provides the perspective that influences the dispositions, intention, and affectivity that move us to be and to act in a certain way. Culture and its dynamic relationship with religion shapes our moral vision. The way we are, as influenced by culture and religion, enters into the way we choose, act, and behave morally. The way we image ourselves and what we do with our lives, how we choose and act, is influenced by our culture (a particular way of being human) within the horizons of our experience of the Divine, in our quest for transcendent and ultimate meaning (religion).

We live according to what has been passed on to us from generation to generation. Stories touch us and shape us at our deepest level. The use of scripture for nurturing moral vision presupposes its use as story. We depend on the great formative stories of scripture to disclose to us who we are, what life is all about, and where our final meaning is found. Narrative criticism is rich in its potential to bring us in touch with the life and vitality of scripture as a story. But like any other biblical pedagogy, it is limited, and thus is in need of other pedagogies to fill in its lacunae.

When moral theology is reconnected with the other disciplines of systematic theology, it ceases to be a merely a system of abstract truths, ideals, and principles. It is given a vision, a way of looking at reality, and a way of being and doing. The connection of systematic theology and moral theology is grounded in the theological anthropology that is drawn from the doctrines of the faith, at the heart of which is the mystery of the Divine and human encounter and the common destiny shared by the whole of humankind, the earth, and the entire cosmos, all loved unto fullness, in one divine embrace.

1

Dynamics of Culture, Religion, and Moral Vision

What shapes the moral vision of individuals, of communities, of peoples, and of nations? When culture and religion enter into the shaping of moral vision, something of profound nature and consequence is engaged. This chapter begins by defining the nature of culture and religion, and then shows how they shape moral vision. It engages particularly how religion, which is a primary substance of culture, relates with morality in this shaping of moral vision.

The Meaning of Culture

The concept of culture engages a number of deep and complex realities. From the modern anthropological view, culture is a way of life, a way of being that is peculiar to a people, as expressed in their beliefs, values, attitudes, and worldviews. It refers to the way people construct the character of their lives as groups and societies in particular circumstances and contexts.[1] Culture, however, is not linear and unchanging. It is a dynamic creation of dialogue, conflict, negotiation within multileveled social processes, and interactions. Constituted by beliefs, values, customs, stories, and traditions that form a particular way of being human, culture emerges from historical processes and

---

Originally published in a slightly different form as "Culture, Religion, and Moral Vision: A Theological Discourse on the Filipino People Power Revolution of 1986," in *Theological Studies* 67/3 (2006): 567–601.
    [1] Kathryn Tanner, *Theories of Culture: A New Agenda for Theology* (Minneapolis: Fortress Press, 1997), 33.

continues to evolve as its participants make sense of their experience in changing times and circumstances.[2]

For Kathryn Tanner, who discusses the shift in the study of culture from a modern to a postmodern perspective, the modern view emphasized culture's role in generating social consensus, as people come to a shared experience of values. From the postmodern perspective, this emphasis on consensus appears as an optical illusion. Against the view that cultures are clearly circumscribed, consisting of internally unified beliefs and values that are transmitted as principles of social order, the postmodern view stresses historicity, indeterminacy, fragmentation, and conflict. It rejects the modern tendency of previous students of culture to turn a blind eye to the social conflict and divergence of opinions that mark the struggles of people to make sense of reality, as they either preserve, alter, or revolt against the terms of their world. Tending to intellectualize culture, the modern view ignores the conflicts and the twists and turns of real-life situations and downplays the power dimension in the interpretation of beliefs and values. From a postmodern perspective cultures may have common elements, but rather than being articulated in apodictic terms, they remain vague and unelaborated. This lack of clear and categorical definitions, however, makes dialogue and interactions possible among people who are differently situated. In place of a consensus-driven notion of culture, an idea emerges of one whose meanings are plural and shift according to multivalent circumstances.[3]

Postmodern critics of culture gainsay the cultural stability that anthropologists emphasize. They hold that when cultural forms function as rules directing action, they do not resemble the rules of a game or mathematical formulas that are mechanically applied and executed.[4] Rather, cultural rules are applied with flexibility, creativity, and innovation, according to the complexity of social circumstances. The various ways of responding appropriately to cultural rules depend on the dictates and demands of human situations. People meet in a

---

[2] The modern notion of culture has been criticized for its lack of attention to historical process. Culture viewed as a dehistoricized concept is treated like the facts of nature and "givens" of life, about which human beings can do very little. Treating culture as dehistoricized, however, makes it easier to talk about, to describe its shape, and to understand how it hangs together. See George E. Marcus and Michael M. J. Fisher, *Anthropology as Cultural Critique: An Experimental Moment in the Human Sciences* (Chicago: University of Chicago Press, 1986), 98.

[3] See Tanner, *Theories of Culture*, 38–56.

[4] See Pierre Bordieu, *Outline of a Theory of Practice* (Cambridge: Cambridge University Press, 1977), 1–9.

variety of centers where interactions are multileveled and exchanges are marked by imbalances and inequalities. The interconnections between and among cultures are not static and homogeneous but shifting and pluralistic.[5]

While the postmodern critique is valid at many levels, it can (wrongly) present culture as so shifting, pluralistic, and fragmented as to leave nothing by which to distinguish one culture from another. There may be no clear, a priori homogeneity, but there must be a cultural matrix of historical experiences, values, and beliefs that provides a relative center of engagement and negotiation. Or, to press the point further, there must be some core beliefs and values in a culture that offer reference points for understanding it precisely as a culture, even as it is open to new ways and horizons of meaning. A creative tension of centering and decentering, therefore, is present in the reality of culture.

Ada María Isasi-Diaz, for example, refers to the shared experience of Latinas rather than the sameness of experience. Their shared experience does not define their claim to common identity, or common attributes, or even common situations or experiences, but rather points to their cultural matrix, part of which is the marginality/oppression in which they often live and the way they experience the world because of how others perceive them. This cultural matrix is the common background that directly influences their worldview, and against which their lives unfold, each in his or her own persons and acting in his or her own way.[6] I see in Isasi-Diaz's narrative a nuanced middle position between the modern and postmodern understandings of culture. Without denying a common reality that serves as a relative center of cultural engagement and negotiation, the specificity and concreteness of the historical configurations of individual experiences remain. There is a creative tension between centering and decentering of the cultural experience.

The Meaning of Religion

Religion, like culture, is a complex phenomenon. On the one hand, if one views it only from the socio-anthropological perspective, one can miss its core. On the other hand, if one views it only from

---

[5] Tanner, *Theories of Culture*, 53–56.

[6] Ada Maria Isasi-Diaz, "Creating a Liberating Culture," in *Converging on Culture: Theologians in Dialogue with Cultural Analysis and Criticism*, ed. Delvin Brown, Sheila Greeve Davaney, and Kathryn Tanner, 122–39 (New York: Oxford University Press, 2001), 126–27.

a philosophical-theological perspective, one can neglect its social-contextual constructions. Social anthropology studies religion as a social phenomenon, particularly its impact on society; theology and philosophy inquire into the substance and ground of religion and probe into its transcendental source and origin. Social anthropology describes what is observable about religion as a human and superhuman phenomenon. It describes religion, but it does not ponder the supernatural source and origin of religion. While religion is a social phenomenon embedded in social relations and expressions, it is first of all the experience of the Divine: the a priori love of God at the core of finite existence. Social anthropology observes the effects of the divine experience, but it is an outsider to that experience. Religion is beyond its competence to understand.

Clifford Geertz, a foremost anthropologist of religion whose works have provided the mediating link in the dialogue between social anthropology and theology, makes no claim of competency to speak about the basis of belief. He writes:

> The existence of bafflement, pain, and moral paradox—of The Problem of Meaning—is one of the things that drive men toward the belief in gods, devils, totemic principles, or the spiritual efficacy of cannibalism . . . but it is not the basis upon which those beliefs rest, but rather their most important field of application.[7]

There is, however, a common thread through these socio-anthropological, philosophical, and theological perspectives: the ultimate meaning about which all religions are concerned. This may be termed the human quest for meaning in the face of pointless existence (Geertz);[8] not just any meaning but the ultimate meaning that demands total surrender (Tillich);[9] a quest for meaning that reaches its peak fulfillment by being in love with God (Lonergan);[10] and within that love, the human person as the event of God's self-communication (Rahner).[11]

---

[7] Clifford Geertz, *The Interpretation of Cultures* (New York: Basic Books, 1973), 109.

[8] Ibid., 45–46.

[9] Paul Tillich, *Dynamics of Faith* (New York: Harper and Row, 1958), 1.

[10] Bernard J. F. Lonergan, *Method in Theology* (New York: Herder and Herder, 1972), 105–6.

[11] Karl Rahner, *Foundations of Christian Faith*, trans. William V. Dych (New York: Crossroad, 1984), 127. Rahner defines mysticism as an "ultimate and absolutely radical experience of transcendence in the mystery of God."

Geertz suggests that in religion we seek our answers to the problem of meaning in the face of pointless existence. Chaos threatens to break in on us at the limits of our analytic capacities, moral insight, and powers of endurance. In the face of bafflement, suffering, and intractable ethical paradox, people turn to religion to find meaning.[12] This quest or drive for meaning, Geertz writes, is an imperative in human experience. He writes, "To make sense out of experience, to give it form and order is evidently as real and as pressing as the more familiar biological needs."[13] Geertz is not consciously engaging in theological discourse but trying to understand and interpret human behavior. He sees the dynamic of human meaning as operative in both culture and religion. For him, culture is a complex interplay of symbols expressing meaning, and religion as a cultural system is the expression of the human search for meaning.[14]

In defining religion as the dimension of depth in all reality, Paul Tillich adopted the term *ultimate concern*. Religion or faith, he writes, is the "state of being ultimately concerned."[15] His philosophy of religion as a philosophy of meaning in relation to the Unconditional finds resonance in other voices, such as Abraham Heschel and Robley Edward Whitson. "The concept of the Unconditional is paradoxical"; it is related to all things, and yet is beyond all things; it is not bound to anything, as it stands over and against all things; it is the dynamic reality inherent in all, yet transcending all.[16] Religion as the ultimate and deepest meaning that "shakes the foundations of all things"[17] holds an ecstatic attraction and fascination, for in it the finite finds its rest and fulfillment.[18]

---

[12] Clifford Geertz, "Religion as a Cultural System," in *Anthropological Approaches to the Study of Religion*, ed. Michael Banton (London: Tavistock, 1968), 14. Other relevant works by Geertz include *Myth, Symbol, and Culture* (New York: Norton, 1974); "Impact of the Concept of Culture on the Concept of Man," in *The Interpretation of Cultures: Selected Essays* (New York: Basic Books, 1973), 33–54; and "The Growth of Culture and the Evolution of the Mind," in *Theories of the Mind*, ed. Jordan M. Scher (New York: Free Press, 1962), 713–40.

[13] Geertz, *The Interpretation of Cultures*, 140.

[14] For a collection of commentaries on Geertz's writings, see John H. Morgan, ed., *Understanding Religion and Culture: Anthropological and Theological Perspectives* (Washington, DC: University Press of America, 1979).

[15] Tillich, *Dynamics of Faith*, 1.

[16] James Luther Adams, "Introduction," in Paul Tillich, *What Is Religion?* (New York: Harper and Row, 1969), 15.

[17] Tillich, *What Is Religion?* 163.

[18] Tillich, *Dynamics of Faith*, 15.

Lonergan speaks of the religious experience of being loved by and being in love with God as the highest level of the human intentional consciousness, the peak of the soul, the *apex animae*.[19] "Being in love with God is being in love in an unrestricted fashion. All love is self-surrender, but being in love with God is being in love without limits or qualifications or conditions or reservations. Just as restricted questioning is our capacity for self-transcendence, so being in love in an unrestricted fashion is the proper fulfillment of that capacity."[20] At the apex of religion is the response to the divine initiative of love, which is never ceasing, always giving and loving, deepening and broadening, boundless, unrestricted, unconditioned. In all our human questioning is the question of God, and being in love with God is the ultimate fulfillment of the human capacity for self-transcendence.

Rahner conceives of religion similarly. For him, the origin of religion is the disclosure of Godself as a gracious God gracing the human person. Religion is the prior word God speaks. As hearers of the word, we have an "ear" within us for God's revelation.[21] Our entire being is ordered toward God, with a radical openness *(potential obedientialis)* to God's self-disclosure.[22] To be human is to stand in free love before God, to listen to God's word or to God's silence.[23] This a priori state has its origin in God and is sustained by God: "Everyone, really and radically every person, must be understood as the event of a supernatural self-communication of God."[24]

However deep and intimate the religious experience is, it is not solitary. Religion is communal. Lonergan describes the religious experience as radically personal at the outset, but seeking community in the end. Religion sets itself in a particular context, where it relates with other meanings and values, and there comes to understand itself, but always drawing forth from the power of ultimate concern in the midst of proximate concerns.[25]

---

[19] Lonergan, *Method in Theology*, 107.

[20] Ibid., 105–6.

[21] See Richard J. Beauchesne, "The Spiritual Existential as Desire: Karl Rahner and Emmanuel Levinas, *Église et théologie* 23 (1992): 224.

[22] See Rahner, *Foundations of Christian Faith*, 126–31.

[23] Karl Rahner, *Hearer of the Word: Laying the Foundation for a Philosophy of Religion*, trans. Joseph Donceel, ed. Andrew Tallon (New York: Continuum, 1994), 92.

[24] Rahner, *Foundations of Christian Faith*, 127.

[25] Lonergan, *Method in Theology*, 118.

Rahner speaks of the historical and categorical objectifications of religion. In his theology, religions as social/communal institutions are the a posteriori historicizations of God's transcendent revelation within the framework of the "supernatural existential." They are the historical categorical objectifications of the transcendent supernatural revelation of God. The supernatural existential, therefore, is the root and origin of institutional religions, insofar as religions arose from the originating faith response to the antecedent supernatural revelation of God.[26]

Lonergan speaks of the historical conditionings of the outward word:

> The word, then, is personal. *Cor ad cor loquitur*: love speaks to love, and its speech is powerful. The religious leader, the prophet, the Christ, the apostle, the priest, the preacher announces in signs and symbols what is congruent with the gift of love that God works within us. The word, too, is social: it brings into a single fold the scattered sheep that belong together because at the depth of their hearts they respond to the same mystery of love and awe. The word, finally, is historical. It is meaning outwardly expressed. It has to borrow and adapt a language that more easily speaks of this world than of transcendence. But such languages and contexts vary with time and place to give words changing meanings and statements changing implications.[27]

Before it enters into the world, religion is the prior word of God. The a posteriori word is historically conditioned by the human contexts in which it is uttered, and such contexts vary from place to place, from generation to generation, as religion seeks new words, new expressions, new language.[28]

Theology and socio-anthropology have a common ground for dialogue in the social and contextual expressions of religion. Religion exists because those who believe in it claim to have encountered the Divine in their experience of transcendence and ultimacy. Religion is not the product of social construction but is mediated through social and cultural constructs.[29] While it is a social phenomenon embedded

---

[26] See Rahner, *Foundations of Christian Faith*, 138–61.

[27] Lonergan, *Method in Theology*, 113–14.

[28] Ibid., 112.

[29] For a contrary view, see Émile Durkheim, *The Elementary Forms of the Religious Life*, trans. Joseph Ward Swain (New York: Free Press, 1965), 235ff.

in social relations and expressions, it is first of all the experience of the Divine, the a priori word of God at the core of finite existence, encountered in different and varying human contexts.[30]

Religion, therefore, is a complex, multivalent phenomenon. A basic definition that synthesizes its essential elements is this: Religion is a social and communal phenomenon, grounded in the a priori experience of the Divine in varying intensities and depths, at different levels, and in different modes. In and through all these facets, religion is being grasped by ultimate concern.

The dynamics of culture and religion enter into our moral vision in the sense that they enter into our worldview. I treat here particularly the religious dimension of moral vision, because when religion is related with moral vision, the complex relationship between religion and morality is brought into question. Finally, I focus on this dimension of moral vision to ground my contention that religion as the substance of culture was the liberating force in the Filipino nonviolent struggle for justice and freedom in 1986.[31]

The Meaning of Moral Vision

A worldview is a way of looking at the world in light of the claims or demands reality makes for meaningful human existence. It is a source of presuppositions in thinking, judging, and doing. These presuppositions are the starting points for the ordering and patterning of reality. One's worldview provides the basic model for interpreting reality; that is, it systematizes one's conception of reality. The following story exemplifies different worldviews in action:

A teacher who was a Westerner or trained along Western lines was almost in despair. After a carefully built-up scientific explanation of malaria, its processes, causes, etc., the boys in an Ugandan primary school did not seem to have understood anything. "Why does a man catch malaria?" one boy asked timidly.

---

[30] Paul Knitter speaks of a "frightening and fascinating" journey that a religion, in a world of religious pluralism, has to take with other religions toward the fullness of truth ("Christianity as a Religion: True and Absolute? A Roman Catholic Perspective," in Concilium 136, *What Is Religion? An Inquiry for Christian Theology*, ed. Mircea Eliade, David Tracy, and Marcus Lefebure (New York: Seabury Press, 1980), 19.

[31] Epifanio de los Santos Avenue (EDSA). The People Power Revolution in the Philippines in 1986 is also known as the EDSA Revolution, the Philippine Revolution of 1986, and the Yellow Revolution.

"Because a mosquito, the carrier of the parasite, bites him," replied the teacher, who went on to give the whole explanation again. At this, the class was still unconvinced and solidly behind the daring boy who shouted, "But who sent the mosquito to bite the man?"[32]

The boys are inquiring not from the level of scientific information but from that of the worldview of their cultural beliefs and stories. This brings to mind the Filipino folkloric belief that people must beg pardon of the spirit of a particular outdoor spot where they urinate lest they be harmed by the spirit. Such a belief reflects a worldview that determines one's way of relating to the world.

Peter Henriot narrated the following to illustrate how a worldview peculiar to a culture—in this case the Zambian culture—can explain why people behave the way they do:

> Women by and large work much harder than men—longer hours, double jobs (an outside workplace and work at home). And expectations that this should be accepted as normal are deep in the culture. I commented once to a Zambian man that I was surprised and disturbed to see a largely pregnant woman walking along the road with a small baby on her back and another child clutching her right hand, carrying on her head one piece of luggage and in her left hand another, while her husband walked leisurely behind her carrying only a walking stick. I was told—with almost a straight face—that the man was protecting his wife from the lions they might encounter. The fact that there had been no lions in this particular region for decades did not distract from the cultural imperative that men do not carry their wife's luggage in public, let alone look after children.[33]

The example exemplifies a gender-bound division of labor that may have been justified by past circumstances but that under completely new circumstances cannot be legitimated.[34] Henriot continues with another narrative:

---

[32] Raimundo Pannikar, *Myth, Faith, and Hermeneutics* (New York: Paulist Press, 1979), 322.

[33] Peter Henriot, "Grassroots Analysis: The Emphasis on Culture," in *Liberation Theologies on Shifting Grounds: A Clash of Socio-Economic and Cultural Paradigms*, ed. G. de Schrijver, 333–50 (Leuven: Leuven University Press, 1998), 346.

[34] De Shrijver, *Liberation Theologies on Shifting Grounds*, 420.

I was feeling puzzled why people remained sitting during the reading of the Gospel at Mass. Why did they fail to show respect by standing, the kind of respectful gesture I had grown up with in my own country? I was told by a Zambian that in their culture, respect was shown by taking a lower place when an elder or important person was speaking. One did not show respect by standing but by sitting. I came to appreciate that the value of respect is expressed in different ways in different cultures. This is indeed a simple lesson, but one with profound consequences in efforts to inculturate the faith.[35]

Charles Kraft develops the major functions of worldview as a basic model of reality, which he calls the "central control box." The first function is to explain how and why things have come to be as they are, and how and why they continue or change. If a worldview conditions a people to see the universe as being operated by invisible personal forces beyond their control, they understand and relate to reality differently from those who view this same universe as ruled by the phenomenon of cause and effect of impersonal forces, which can be influenced and even determined by their human agency.[36]

A worldview also has valuing, judging, and validating functions. People reject or accept realities according to their consonance or dissonance with their worldview. A worldview also provides psychological reinforcement, especially in crisis or boundary situations (illness, calamities, death), in life passages (puberty, the coming to womanhood or manhood, marriage), in the changing seasons of sowing and harvesting. Each event is celebrated with a ritual or ceremony providing a sense of security and support for the participants. The worldview also has an integrating function in terms of the way it systematizes and orders people's perception of reality—its premises and presuppositions, its bases and criteria, its limitations and boundaries—into one design, creating a whole way of understanding and interpreting multifarious events. The integrating function of a worldview gives a people a centered and centering vision of a world in the face of conflicts and dissonances.[37]

I understand moral vision in terms of worldview, because we choose and judge according to our perceptions. Morality is deeper

---

[35] Henriot, "Grassroots Analysis," 348.

[36] Charles H. Kraft, *Christianity in Culture* (Maryknoll, NY: Orbis Books, 1999), 53.

[37] Ibid., 54–57.

than choosing. What lies deeper than the choice is the vision or the worldview. How a person sees and responds springs from this depth. We see as we are, and according to our seeing, we act. We see the world in a particular way because we are a particular sort of person. Thus we are inclined to decide in one way or another because of who we are and what we have made of ourselves. Moral vision touches a depth where persons take hold of who they are, where they have set their hearts, how they have integrated and directed their energies, and how deeply they have been moved and influenced by their beliefs and convictions. Our view or vision of the world gives us a perspective that inspires action.

The dynamics of culture and religion constitute the context and ground of moral vision, influencing the beliefs and values a people holds, the stories and traditions that shaped its memories, the relationships and interrelationships it is a part of; and all these are woven and interwoven into the fabric of this people's fundamental relationship with God. Moral vision is deeply connected with a particular way of being human (culture) within the experience of the Divine (religion), which defines one's deepest selfhood and identity. Being moral, therefore, is something of utmost importance and dignity.

Religion and Morality

To speak of religion and its bearing on moral vision, however, is to bring into question the complex relationship between morality and religion. The inescapable claims of fundamental values (such as truth, freedom, justice, and equality) lie at the core of moral existence. There is a transcendent dimension to being moral, in the sense that while it springs from within oneself, it also demands something greater than self. Being moral is experienced as something of utmost importance and dignity, for it is intrinsically bound up with being human.

Why be moral? The answer most commonly given in the past was that one should be moral because God commands it, or that one should be moral out of love of God. But the fact that atheists and nonbelievers who are morally sensitive persons and who live by high moral standards also exist seriously challenges the absolute validity of this position. To say that belief in God is not necessary to be moral or to become aware of moral obligation and demands has a basis in fact. Some may deny God and abandon religion yet still strive to be human and moral. One could even go further and say that some deny

God and religion precisely because of their moral strivings (*Gaudium et Spes* [GS], no. 12).

Nevertheless, morality is still frequently understood and interpreted in the context of religion. Sacred traditions and sacred books have contributed to the strong religious context of morality. Probably the single event that has inscribed the deepest moral images in the minds and hearts of people in Judeo-Christian cultures is the giving of the Ten Commandments to Moses. This event certainly portrays God as the direct source of moral laws and commands imposed by the power of God's authority, with the accompanying threat of divine sanction. An intelligent reading and interpretation of the Ten Commandments episode, however, requires that one distinguish between the religious message and the form and language by which it is communicated. Vincent McNamara writes:

> What the Jews came to realize was that as a people of God, they were to attend to this fundamental strand of human experience. If they were to be God's people, they were to take seriously the horizontal dimension of their lives. Nothing could contribute more powerfully to that insight, nothing could give it greater weight and significance in Jewish minds than to attach morality to Moses, the great prophet, and to regard it as given to him by God as the law for his people. The insight about the significance of morality was important. But we need to distinguish between the reality of the insight and the particularly colorful and impressive way in which it was communicated.[38]

One may speak of God as the source of moral law in the sense that God has created persons and has given them a nature with the capacity to reflect on and respond to the moral thrust in that nature. One should not, however, think of God as the direct and external source of moral commands and obligation imposed on persons, with the threat of divine punishment or with the promise of divine blessings, because morality is grounded in freedom. Only free acts are moral. Thus, any imposition or coercion from an external authority violates the free nature of moral acts. God is not solely an external authority but also is the immediate source of every person's reflective capacity for free moral acts.

It is possible to speak of morality as a human phenomenon with a certain autonomy from religion. The distinction between morality

[38] Vincent McNamara, *Love, Law, and Christian Life: Basic Attitudes of Christian Morality* (Wilmington, DE: Michael Glazier, 1988), 26–27.

and religion, however, does not imply the absence of interrelationship. Both are concerned with the person's ultimate good and value. Thus, although morality makes its own demands, it is ultimately based on the nature of persons in terms of the "should/ought" every person experiences as a being-in-community, which has an intrinsic relation with God as the very source of human nature and its moral thrust. We therefore speak of a *relative* autonomy of morality with respect of religious faith, not an *absolute* autonomy.

For believers, to grasp the total vision of life is not possible without contextualizing it in their relation to God. They perceive morality as situated decisively in their relation to God. Religious faith is not regarded as only one option among other options in life. It is not arranged side by side with other choices. Religious faith is a fundamental choice that engages, shapes, and evaluates the whole of life. As René Latourelle puts it, "The Word of God brings into play our sense of personal existence and our sense of the whole of human existence. Here it is not a question of modifying our prevailing system of values, it is a question of reorienting our whole being. . . . Faith is a decision for God and our whole life ought to pivot on this dramatic decision which involves us even to our innermost aspirations."[39]

Thus religious faith is the all-embracing horizon against which believers look at the whole of life, modifying and qualifying the attitudes, dispositions, values, and aspirations which enter into the very fabric of their concrete choices and decisions. Religious faith brings to morality a depth, intensity, and urgency by situating it in relation to the person's fundamental response to God who calls. What all this suggests is that when we speak of morality, we are confronted with questions that concern human existence as a whole, which must be seen in the general and larger context of the nature and purpose of being human, that is, what the human person was made for.[40]

For morality to develop its sense of responsibility to whatever it is that evokes the obligation to be good, it needs God to complete its inherent drive to become more aware and reflective of realities greater than the one experiencing the obligation. Kant's explanation of morality implies that the moral life can be self-sufficient, because ideally it is based on the only truly good thing, that is, the Good Will. However, Kierkegaard's understanding is closer to the truth of the obligatory nature of morality, because he accounts for the deep urges

---

[39] René Latourelle, "Revelation and Faith: Personal Encounter with God," *Theology Digest* 10 (1962): 237.

[40] Osmond G. Ramberan, "Morality and Religion: An Analytic Approach with Implications for Religious Education," *Religious Education* 72 (1977): 514–27.

of morality to expand the realization of obligations to the point that eventually one knows that to remain moral, one must be committed to something greater than even being good.[41]

Religious belief does not cancel out the value that reason offers in the realm of morality, but it appeals to human beings to see that there is a realm of transcendent values that they have not imagined. That is the way religious faith opens up reason to something greater than what it has envisioned to be the good. It does not subvert it, but it appeals for openness, a widening of horizons, a going in a new direction, seeing a whole new world that one never expected. It is natural, for instance, for one to consider the value of security and possessions. Religious faith widens the horizons of values to include the value of sharing, which is perhaps an even more important value than security and possessions. Religious faith thus challenges individuals to stretch their horizons of meaning, to seek more and become more. To ground morality in religion means to ground it in a vision of the human person as a being grasped by ultimate concern, oriented to the supernatural, and "in love with God," in whom, as Lonergan writes, one's "capacity for moral self-transcendence finds a fulfillment that brings deep peace and joy."[42]

Culture, Religion, and Moral Vision in the Filipino Context

The dynamics of culture and religion were at the base of the moral vision of the Filipino struggle for justice and freedom in the nonviolent People Power Revolution of 1986, which I use here as a case study for the action of religion in culture. But what precisely are the dynamics of culture and religion that enter into the shaping of moral vision? I use Tillich's much-quoted statement that "culture is a form of expression of religion and religion is the substance of culture"[43] to provide an interpretative frame in discussing the dynamics of culture and religion. Using Tillich's framework, one can see the dynamics of culture and religion present in the concrete elements of that extraordinary Filipino event.

---

[41] Dennis Sansom, "Does Morality Need God? A Kierkegaardian Critique of Kant's Moral Philosophy," *Perspectives in Religious Studies* 26/1 (Spring 1999): 17–18.

[42] Lonergan, *Method in Theology,* 122.

[43] Tillich, *What Is Religion?* 73. The relationship between religion and culture is also the central theme of all of Christopher Dawson's writings. See Daniel H. O'Connor, *The Relation Between Religion and Culture According to Christopher Dawson* (Montreal: Librairie Saint-Viateur, 1952).

Culture intersecting with religion in the shaping of moral vision offers rich material for theological reflection. There can be no liberation apart from the beliefs and values of a people, with religion as their deepest source. The struggle against injustice and oppression must be united with a people's consciousness of their cultural rootedness, at the heart of which is their religion. The dynamics of culture and religion and its bearing on moral vision made the Filipino People Power Revolution possible and was the source of its nonviolent spirit.

The following short narrative of the historic event of the People Power Revolution of 1986 sets the background of our study and discourse.

Historical Review of the Filipino Revolution

The story begins in the late 1960s, when the Filipino nation was faced with two crises: first, the one that developed from the student-led protests against the Vietnam War and the founding of a new Communist Party in December 1968; and second, the threat of a Marcos dictatorship that came with allegations of widespread corruption among his family members and cronies. In the face of this threat members of Congress were rapidly polarized, and in the streets a series of violent demonstrations by students, laborers, and peasants began in what came to be known as the First Quarter Storm. On September 22, 1972, Marcos declared martial law.

The imposition of martial law effectively paralyzed all anti-Marcos elements and consolidated the pro-Marcos forces, which controlled the government for the next decade. The threat of arrest, without due process and without warrant, forced the opposition to go underground, and student activists who were radicalized by the futility of their efforts joined the leftist groups. Aboveground the church hierarchy continued an anti-dictatorship movement. The rest of the Filipino people went about their daily lives, unmindful of the national situation, because of their indifference, or fear, or because they were simply ground down by poverty.

In January 1981, Marcos lifted martial law after nine years. Five months later he was elected to another six-year term, his third elected term of office. Two years later Senator Benigno Aquino, Marcos's rival in the political arena, broke his self-imposed exile in the United States and returned to the Philippines. After his plane landed at the Manila International Airport, Aquino, escorted by military men, was shot to death as he descended the stairs of the plane. The last image of him on TV and in newspapers was his bloodied body sprawled on the tarmac. The following week a nation infuriated by his murder spilled into the streets by the millions to form a mammoth funeral procession through the city. The dam of pent-up anger ruptured, and people were awakened to the struggle ahead.

Over the next two years the impact of Aquino's murder and declining social conditions fanned the fires of the protest movement, which crossed ideological lines. The extreme left was at the front line of the organization of workers and the urban poor. In the center left were the urban middle organizers, some university academicians, and the social democratic movement. The center right included the Catholic Church hierarchy, organized business, and conservative social democrats. At the extreme right were those from the old ruling families, dissatisfied military leaders, and the Reform Armed Forces Movement (RAM), a military faction that protested the politicization of the armed forces.

By late 1984, rumors of a possible presidential snap election were already flying, and the divided opposition came together into an alliance that supported the candidacy of Cory Aquino—widow of the slain hero Benigno Aquino—against Marcos. This turn of events marginalized the left, which decided to boycott the elections. The elections, however, were marred by violence and blatant fraud, as Marcos's goons snatched ballot boxes even as volunteers from the National Movement for Free Elections tried to guard the ballots with their bodies. When the Philippine National Assembly proclaimed Marcos the winner, computer technicians from the Commission on Elections staged a walkout to protest the massive election fraud. The Catholic Bishops' Conference of the Philippines (CBCP) declared the election unparalleled in its fraudulent conduct and concluded that a government based on such deceit had no moral basis for its power.

The CBCP declaration was unprecedented. The bishops of a nation had officially condemned its government as morally illegitimate and hence unworthy of allegiance, and had, through its leaders, declared a revolution—even if that word was never used. Unprecedented, too, was the bishops' assertion of independence from the intervention of Rome, which tried to postpone their collective decision to issue their statement until after the Parliament (merely a rubber stamp) had declared Marcos the winner. Rome was in effect telling the CBCP to be silent until President Marcos was proclaimed the duly elected head of state. The CBCP countered Rome by appealing to a principle in *Octogesima Adveniens* that the local church was fully competent to pronounce judgment on local issues. After the CBCP proclamation, the nation saw a clear direction amid its collective fear and confusion. The voices of protest found an authoritative moral basis, and the people were empowered in their moral struggle.

Cory Aquino, in a massive rally in Luneta Park, declared her victory and called for a nationwide civil disobedience to topple Marcos by eroding his economic base. As the call for disobedience mounted, some officers of RAM finalized a plan for a coup d'etat, but this was aborted following a security breach. Instead, the plotters, together with Secretary of Defense Juan Ponce Enrile and General Fidel Ramos, retreated to Camp Aguinaldo along Epifanio de los Santos Avenue (EDSA) and held a televised news conference in which they declared open rebellion against the Marcos regime. Cardinal Sin of Manila broadcast an appeal for people to rally at EDSA to support and protect Enrile and Ramos. In response, some twenty thousand citizens massed outside the camp in the early morning. Even as the first tanks began to move in to crush the rebellion, people continued to pour into EDSA, creating a mammoth barricade around the camp. The crowd swelled to an estimated two million people dressed in yellow, Cory Aquino's signature color, singing songs, praying the Rosary, waving yellow flags, and carrying religious statues. Nearby houses in posh subdivisions opened their kitchens to prepare food for both the soldiers and the crowds; food multiplied, and so did the courage, faith, and hope of the people. People knelt in prayer, threw their bodies in the path of the tanks, offered flowers to the soldiers, and appealed for peace and solidarity. As the crowd continued to grow in size and spirit, the government troops defected in droves to the side of the people.

As military support for Marcos dwindled, US Senator Paul Laxalt, acting on behalf of President Ronald Reagan, told Marcos that the time had come for him to leave. Late in the afternoon of February 25, 1986, the Marcos family fled to Hawaii. As soon as the people heard of their departure, they exploded in euphoria into the streets.[44]

On February 25, 2001, to commemorate the anniversary of the People Power Revolution of 1986, the Alfred Nobel Foundation and the Center for Global Nonviolence conferred upon the Republic of the Philippines the Nobel Peace Prize and the Global Nonviolence Award. Significantly, the award ceremony took place just a few weeks following EDSA 2, in which for the second time in fifteen years Filipinos unleashed People Power to force the resignation of their president, Joseph Ejercito Estrada, whose two and a half years of corrupt and incompetent rule had wrecked the nation's economic and political

---

[44] This historical review is based on the research done by Rowena B. Azada and Ranilo B. Hermida on the background of the EDSA Revolution. See "People Power Revolution: Perspectives from Hannah Arendt and Jürgen Habermas," *Budhi* 5 (2001): 85–149, esp. 104–12.

institutions. In a bloodless and legal transfer of power, Vice President Gloria Macapagal-Arroyo took up the reins of government.

Pierre Marchand, head of the Nobel Peace Prize Laureates Foundation, spoke the following words at the awards ceremony:

> The world salutes the Filipinos for their courage in overthrowing two undesirable presidents. You have given the gift, in a world that only knows force and violence, of effecting radical change without firing a shot. The legacy of People Power would be the Filipino people's gift to other peoples of the world. You were given a national gift. Do not keep it to yourselves. The world will never be the same again if the spirit of EDSA prevails beyond the shores of this tiny archipelago.[45]

The fifteenth anniversary of People Power 1 was significant in that it came eighteen years after the death of Ninoy Aquino, thirty years after the death of Martin Luther King Jr., fifty years after the death of Mahatma Gandhi, and two thousand years after the death of Christ.

Although the second exercise of People Power enhances the revolutionary legacy of the previous demonstration, there are distinctions between the two phenomena, because they arose from different historical contexts and were shaped by different confluences of events and forces. It is not possible, therefore, to study and analyze them as one single phenomenon. However, though the two People Power revolutions are not to be read in the same light, there is a historical continuum that tells the story of a people who took to the streets as the court of last resort to throw off the yoke of abusive and corrupt leadership.

The history of a people that seems to pass from one crisis to another cannot come to a standstill. But it did for a moment, if only to honor the man who was the moral compass and a key figure in the People Power revolts that ousted two presidents. That figure is Cardinal Jaime Sin, who died June 20, 2005. It was fitting to give tribute to a priest and prophet who saw his duty as putting Christ into politics, believing as he did that politics without Christ is the greatest scourge of the nation. Called the divine commander-in-chief for his ability to marshal huge protests, Cardinal Sin did it twice, and with astonishing

---

[45] *Philippine Star,* February 26, 2001. The Nobel Peace Prize Laureates Foundation comprised peace advocates, including Mother Teresa of Calcutta, Nelson Mandela of South Africa, the Dalai Lama of Tibet, Carlos Ximena Belo and Jose Ramos-Horta of East Timor, Mikhail Gorbachev of the Soviet Union, Henry Kissinger of the United States, and Adolfo Perez of Argentina.

grace. "Go to EDSA," he said twice, and in both cases sitting presidents were toppled in a matter of days.

Filipino Culture as a Form of Expression of Religion

Embedded in cultural forms and contexts is the experience of religion, even when its cultural expressions may not be explicitly religious. The holy is a transcendent power made present through symbolic forms without ever becoming identical with any of them. In and through the world of the finite, persons encounter the holy. It is an experience that points beyond itself. Cultural forms and realities are potential symbols of the Divine.[46]

Because religion is incarnated in culture, we must be sensitive and alert to the cultural ethos that gives it shape and form. Religion, as the dimension of depth to all reality, as Tillich observed, is not present only in explicit religious acts and practices.[47] A broader understanding of religion makes one see that reality is not sharply divided into sacred and profane but rather that all reality is potentially sacred. If religion is the depth to all things, then culture, which is pervasive in all life, is the realm of religion.

Cultural exegesis is an interpretative activity that makes explicit what is implicit in culture, unfolding its meaning. It sees a connection with what is going on in the lives of a particular people—their issues, problems, and hopes. Cultural exegesis cannot be undertaken in isolation from what matters to a people, that is, at the locus of human experience where religion addresses them at their depths. In the past, cultural exegesis or analysis was relatively neglected compared to social analysis, which focuses on the structures of economics and politics that are seen at the base of social problems. A shift is now occurring, as it becomes clear that social analysis that ignores cultural dimensions cannot get at the underlying dynamics shaping social movements in various settings.[48] Only when the cultural symbols and values of a people are taken seriously is their creative potential in the

---

[46] R. F. Aldwinckle, "Tillich's Theory of Religious Symbolism," *Canadian Journal of Theology* 10 (April 1964): 111. Tillich explains that symbols open up depths of reality that would otherwise remain hidden, while at the same time they make possible levels of experience from which persons would be excluded but for the power of these symbols. See H. D. McDonald, "The Symbolic Theology of Paul Tillich," *Scottish Journal of Theology* 17 (December 1964): 421–22.

[47] See D. Mackenzie Brown, ed., *Ultimate Concern: Tillich in Dialogue* (New York: Harper and Row, 1965).

[48] See Henriot, "Grassroots Analysis," 338; and José de Mesa, "A Hermeneutics of Appreciation: Approach and Methodology," *MST Review* 4/2 (2000): 23–24.

process of social change unfolded. For sociologist Robert Bellah, the most important social sources are symbolic and cultural, the great collective symbols of social life. The most important social changes are also symbolic and cultural: "We are used to thinking of change in economic and political terms, but it is symbolic change that goes the deepest and lasts the longest."[49]

The hermeneutics of appreciation is a methodology of cultural exegesis that highlights the positive in a culture.[50] It is based on the faith conviction that divine presence graces the life of a people; the theological task is to discern the spiritual qualities and gifts of every people and of every age. As stated in Vatican II's *Ad Gentes*:

> Christ Himself searched the hearts of men and led them to divine light through truly human conversation. So also his disciples, profoundly penetrated by the Spirit of Christ, should know the people among whom they live, and should establish contact with them. Thus they themselves can learn by sincere and patient dialogue what treasures a bountiful God has distributed among the nations of the earth. But at the same time, let them try to illumine these treasures with the light of the gospel, to set them free, and to bring them under the dominion of God their Savior. (no. 11)

If culture, as Tillich states, is a form of expression of religion, we must be alert and sensitive to the depth dimensions of culture. Embedded in culture are expressions of religion, although they may not be explicitly religious. God graces the culture and life of a people and thus in whatever is honorable, just, pure, lovely; in whatever is gracious, religion is mediated and experienced. Any authentic cultural value or experience is an experience of the religious. Religion is understood here as the profound dimension of reality that provokes a sense of depth, transcendence, and ultimacy.

What values at the core of the Filipino culture open it up to the realm of depth, transcendence, and ultimacy, giving a cultural shape and form to the religious experience that the EDSA Revolution of 1986 was to many? I propose three core cultural values: *lakas-ganda* (gracious power), *lakas-awa* (compassionate force), and *lakas-saya* (indomitable joy).

---

[49] As quoted in John Coleman, "The Renewed Covenant: Robert N. Bellah's Vision of Religion and Society," in *Sociology and Human Destiny*, ed. Gregory Baum (New York: Seabury Press, 1980), 89.

[50] See de Mesa, "A Hermeneutics of Appreciation: Approach and Methodology," 6–10.

The Filipino word *lakas* means "strength, might, power, vigor, energy, pull, capacity," while the word for "graciousness," *ganda*, refers to the beautiful, the good, or simply what is ethical or humane. José de Mesa, a lay Filipino theologian, reflects on the meaning of graciousness in the Filipino context:

> Real "beauty" or "goodness" is found in the deepest core of one's personhood, the *loob*. *Loob*, literally the inner self, is where the true worth of a person lies. Authentic graciousness can only be *kagandahang loob*, the graciousness which springs from this personal core. When real, it is said to come from the *loob*. *Bukal sa kalooban* (welling up from the inner self), Filipinos say. The expression suggests that graciousness being outwardly manifested is truly in harmony with the most authentic in the person. The graciousness which orients power, therefore, is that graciousness which comes from within.[51]

Power without graciousness can be arbitrary and manipulative, chaotic and destructive. But without power, graciousness is in vain. The good needs power to be effectual. Without graciousness, power can dehumanize, but without power, graciousness cannot humanize.[52] Only when persons shift their centers of their universe from themselves to others do they show this blend. Similarly, God is not known in Godself. God is known in the divine ways God is graciousness for us.

The EDSA Revolution yielded extraordinary stories that manifested gracious power, and perhaps some could only have happened in the Philippines. A soldier manning a tank told the people to stay so they could hold their fire.[53] Hundreds of thousands of unarmed men, women, and children holding crosses or rosaries formed human barricades around rebel military camps or threw themselves on the roads in front of the tanks. When children gave the Marcos loyalist troops flowers and yellow ribbons, and women hugged and kissed them, the soldiers could not find it in their hearts to open fire. A captain of the Marines explained how it happened that the shock troops failed to attack the crowds that had gathered at EDSA: "We have been given all kinds of training on how to disperse crowds, using truncheons,

---

[51] José de Mesa, "Providence as Power and Graciousness," in *Toward a Theology of People Power*, ed Douglas J. Eldwood, 37–61 (Quezon City: New Day, 1986), 42–43.

[52] Ibid.

[53] Cited in Patricio R. Mamot, *People Power: Profile of Filipino Heroism* (Quezon City: New Day, 1986), 135.

shields, teargas, but we were never trained to face a crowd that was praying, carrying statues and rosaries, and offering smiles, food, and flowers. How could we attack them?"[54] This is gracious power; or a power that was graced.

Another story is told by the chief information officer of the Philippine Air Force, who reported that he overheard radio contact between the Reformist troops in a helicopter and the Marcos loyalists on the ground. He narrated: "Imagine a would-be attacker warning his would-be victims. 'We're coming in! Clear the area!' And those on the ground responding, 'We can't, we can't. Make another turn!' and the helicopters did." With pride tinged with amusement, he commented: "It was a beautiful war."[55] In other words, it was a war that was waged with gracious power.

Bishop Francisco Claver speaks of the compassionate force that played itself out at EDSA and led to the stunning, unprecedented, and thoroughly Filipino People Power Revolution. The blending of power and compassion joins seemingly antagonistic concepts—struggle and peace, conflict and harmony, power and gentleness—each compensating for the faults or limitations of the other and thoroughly infused with faith. Compassionate force finds resonance in the deeply person-oriented Filipino culture. It articulates well what is meant by nonviolent Filipino power. Linguistically, it is thoroughly Filipino; it captures the emotion and spirit of the Filipino soul. Infused by faith, it is a power directed by compassion fundamentally for justice, but also for charity. It is not abusive and self-serving but is used to protect and empower those for whom one has compassion—the weak and the powerless. Precisely because one has power, one is expected to also have compassion for those under one's power, for the weakest and the most helpless. This compassion is the antithesis of the ruthless and violent side of power. It is what made the Filipino soldiers hold their guns and exercise maximum tolerance at EDSA, one of the decisive reasons why People Power remained nonviolent.[56] Again, it was the graciousness in the culture that resonated with the call of nonviolence. In the words of Cardinal

---

[54] As cited in Pedro S. de Achútegui, "Presentation," Miracle of the Philippine Revolution: Interdisciplinary Reflections, symposium organized by the Loyola School of Theology. See *Loyola Papers* 15, ed. Pedro S. de Achútegui, ix–xii (1986), x.

[55] As cited in Mamot, *People Power*, 57.

[56] Francisco F. Claver, "People Power and Value Transformation: Reflections on the February Phenomenon," in Elwood, *Toward a Theology of People Power*, 54–61.

Sin, the spirit of compassionate power at EDSA enabled a "victory without hatred, without the spilling of blood of brothers, without the tears over countless sons and daughters fallen in the battle at the crossfire—but a victory nonetheless."[57]

The strength that comes from the Filipino penchant for song and celebration and a sense of joy even in the most trying times is the cultural basis of the festive and nonviolent People Power. "This sense of joy and humor, characterized by an irreverence bordering on the sublime and possessing a sense of irony which captures the unseen dimension of the event"[58] contributes not only to the Filipino charm but also to the Filipino indomitable spirit. The EDSA Revolution of 1986 is described as a "smiling revolution." It violated all the rules. While militant, it was never sad; it was festive and celebratory.[59] There was nothing grim or stern about it. Even in the most tense moments, dissident soldiers sauntered about the rebel stronghold in Camp Crame with yellow ribbons tied around the barrels of their rifles.[60] The air was festive, as if the people were going out for a big family picnic, with children carried on their fathers' shoulders. At the same time, the people manifested great courage and determination to free themselves from the cruel and oppressive Marcos regime.

This gracious and festive spirit of the revolution is told in many stories. One tells of what happened when the tanks and the armored personnel carriers were unable to attack Camp Crame because they were blocked by the massed bodies of the people. After some negotiations it was agreed that the soldiers would retire to Camp Bonifacio for the night to avoid incidents. As they revved up their engines and began to maneuver out of the field, the people called out to them and bade them farewell, "Goodnight, see you tomorrow."[61] There was also as much eating as there was praying and singing. Life was being created amid death. Joyful celebration took place in the midst of extreme danger and darkness. This is a joy rooted in hope, a hope founded in God.

The Filipino core values at the heart of the EDSA Revolution are imaged in the words of Roger Rosenblatt, a *Time* correspondent:

---

[57] As cited in Mamot, *People Power,* 41.

[58] Conrado de Quiros, "Again the 'Dumb' Masa," *Philippine Daily Inquirer,* April 30, 2001.

[59] Randy David, "What Makes People Power Possible?" *Philippine Daily Inquirer,* February 25, 2001.

[60] See Mamot, *People Power,* 115.

[61] As cited in John J. Carroll, "Looking Beyond EDSA: Part II: Values, Power, and Social Transformation," *Human Society* 43 (1990): 7.

Try not to forget what you saw last week. You say now that it would be impossible to forget: Filipinos armed to the teeth with rosaries and flowers, massing in front of tanks, and the tanks stopping, and some of the soldiers who were the enemy embracing the people and their flowers. Call that revolution? Where were the heads stuck on piles? Where were the torches for the estates of the rich? The rich were in the streets with the poor, a whole country up in flowers.[62]

The Filipino core values manifest the quality and disposition of the Filipino heart and spirit, the Filipino approach to reality as a whole. These values have spiritual or religious roots because they give personal and social relationships a sense of depth, transcendence, and ultimacy, insofar as they pull people out of themselves, and shift their centers from themselves to others, in graciousness, compassion, and joy. These values give shape and form to religion, insofar as religion touches life deeply and profoundly, giving it a transcendental and ultimate meaning. These values were at the base of the nonviolent revolution.

No one has an exclusive claim to the experience of the Divine. It finds its form and expression within one's cultural framework. Thus, the expressions of religion vary as its cultural and historical contexts vary. One encounters the Divine through one's culture. The phenomenon of seeking images, symbols, and language to express and share the experience of the Divine is called the socialization of the experience. Culture and society provide the hermeneutical tools to make this socialization credible and acceptable. There is religion only where the experience of God has become truly incarnate in the culture, history, and life of the people. This must be so if religious experience is to be human and humanly comprehensible.[63]

Popular religion is closely identified with the simple and the deprived, and it is conditioned by their poverty, insecurity, and oppression. They are seen as seeking a simpler and more direct relationship with God beyond the over-intellectualized, cerebral, over-conceptualized dogmatic form of religious practice. Magical, symbolic, and festive, popular religion brings people in contact with a God whom

---

[62] Roger Rosenblatt, "People Power," *Time*, March 10, 1986, available on the time.com website.

[63] The term "socialization of the divine" is used by Orlando Espín, *The Faith of the People: Theological Reflections on Popular Catholicism* (Maryknoll, NY: Orbis Books, 1997), 95.

they image as a God of absolute closeness, within whose orbit of sovereignty everything of weal or woe happens without any distinctions of causality. Arising from their own condition of powerlessness, they view God as one who provides them with access to power against dominant forces.[64]

This empowerment is also embodied in communal celebrations of the different passages of their lives; during these and other important moments they remember and thank Mary and the saints. Through popular devotions people touch the mystery of the Divine in ineffable ways. In their feasting, dancing, and processions, their religion becomes an amalgam of prayer, worship, and social celebrations. This is an example of the way in which religion is always eminently cultural in form, bound up with the totality of other social relationships. "To change an understanding of God and ways of relating to him there must also be change in our understanding of social relations in the same world."[65]

Filipino Faith as the Substance of Filipino Culture

As mentioned earlier, Tillich speaks of religion as the substance of culture.[66] It flows into the content and form of culture. It is from religion that culture derives its essence. Tillich's maxim, however, must be understood with an eye to nuance and diversity of contexts. For example, in secularized northern European cultures, religion sometimes seems barely present. Does this mean that these cultures have lost their substance? How about cultures marked by religious pluralism, as in India? What does religion as the substance of culture mean here? And in the Philippines, where there is a dominant religion of a specific tradition, how is religion as the substance of culture understood?

Religion creates a center around which a culture revolves, so that whatever is vital and essential for the life of society is brought into relation with religion. And this relation does not necessarily take an explicit religious form or language. Business, politics, and economics belong to the sphere of the secular, but they have a religious dimension. They are not ends in themselves, but they participate in an ultimate meaning within the fundamental relationship of the human

---

[64] See Luis Maldonado, "Popular Religion: Its Dimensions, Levels, and Types," in Concilium 4, *Popular Religion*, ed. Norbert Greinacher and Norbert Mette (Edinburgh: T. and T. Clark, 1986), 3–11.

[65] Robert J. Schreiter, *Constructing Local Theologies* (Maryknoll, NY: Orbis Books, 1985), 140.

[66] Tillich, *What Is Religion?* 73.

person, society, and God, and the ethical imperatives of this relationship. Cultures, therefore, have a center of gravity and substance, and
this substance has a religious valence, even if it is not explicitly religious or represented by a particular religion.

Despite the fact that one particular religion does not have to be
identical with the substance of any culture, it can come close to such
a substance, and the ultimacy that attaches to any culture can be
represented by this religion. Such is the case with the Catholic faith
in the Philippines. While technically the Philippines is religiously
pluralistic, it is predominantly Christian and Catholic. The question,
then, is how at the EDSA Revolution did Christianity (as principally
represented by Catholicism) mediate religion as the substance of the
Filipino culture?

According to reports, prior to the revolution a group of sociolo-
gists and political strategists had prepared five possible post-election
scenarios, given the crescendo of political tension and conflict in the
country. None of the scenarios became a reality. What happened in
EDSA was beyond all calculation and projection; it came as a complete surprise. The speculators had missed an essential element: the
Filipino soul and the vibrant religious faith intrinsic to the Filipino
culture. The politburo of the Communist Party of the Philippines had
also prepared a series of post-election scenarios, none of which became a reality either. The authors left out of the equation the people's
religion and discounted it as nothing more than a force of alienation
and oppression. They failed to see that there can be no liberation apart
from the beliefs and values of a people, the deepest source of which
is their religion.[67]

In a Marxist framework popular religion, through its symbolic
structure of evasion and resignation, makes the condition of oppression acceptable or tolerable. This framework has been used to denigrate the place of religion in the task of liberation. Today, however,
that is a minority position. Segundo Galilea speaks of folk religion as
pivotal, arguing that liberation is not possible apart from the beliefs
and values of the people. The struggle against injustice and oppression must be united with the people's consciousness of their cultural
rootedness, at the heart of which is their religion. Popular religion
may have its failings and ambiguities, but a religious experience that
is meaningful to the people is a positive source of empowerment. It
holds the power to shape perspectives and to inspire action—even as

---

[67] Achútegui, "Presentation," x.

a continuing purification of its spurious elements and a strengthening of its liberating dynamism are necessary.[68]

Through the prism of EDSA, we reflect on the religion that was at the base of the entire event, which was for many an experience of the Divine, so astounding that they called it a miracle. At EDSA, the Filipinos were a eucharistic people at the barricades, a people in love with Mary—*pueblo amante de Maria*—and a people bearing a prophetic witness as a church. If there is one image that remains of the EDSA Revolution, it is the image of people sharing food. Though food was limited, no one was left hungry. It was a lived experience of the multiplication of loaves and fishes. As one heartwarming story has it, an old man pulled two pieces of bread from his bag. He took one piece and gave the other to a soldier. Two men on the opposite sides of the revolution broke bread in a fashion that could only be described as eucharistic.[69]

Although Filipinos are deeply divided by social class, ideology, and politics, at EDSA they came together as one eucharistic people. The Eucharist at the barricades gathered the multitudes together in a solemn communal act of prayer at a time of great crisis and danger, pulling together all that was human—the fears, the sorrows, and the hopes. The people were one when they sang and prayed together, one in a way that they had never been, to the point of being willing to die with their arms locked together. Fr. C. G. Arévalo describes one moving experience during those fateful days and nights:

That night after we prayed together, and slept on the street not far from one another, and then when the troops came up from down the valley, we stood beside each other—for the long stretches of time, up to the last anxious hour—and I think we believed we might die together. And what bound us together in those hours was, I guess, our common love for our people and our country. But deeper yet, our common faith. Our belief in the presence of the Lord in our midst during those hours. And for some moments of peace and courage, the presence of our Lady. Someone said to me later. "I knew she was with us. Don't ask me how I know. Simply, I know." Our faith . . . made us one.

---

[68] See Segundo Galilea, "The Theology of Liberation and the Place of Folk Religion," in Eliad, Tracy, and Lefebure, *What Is Religion?* 40–45.

[69] Cited in C. G. Arévalo, "Lagi Nating Tatandaan: Story and Remembering . . . and Story That Is Tradition," in Achútequi, *Loyola Papers,* 30.

. . . Later that night, when things quieted down, a lot of people began drifting away. A time of respite, for some sleep and rest. The seminarians and novices stretched out in their cassocks on the street. I thought God must be looking down on this scene . . . with tenderness. . . . It was the mercy and tenderness of God which alone could make all of us, at that hour, one—one people in a single resolve, sharing a common hope.[70]

Pueblo Amante de Maria—a people in love with Mary; these words express a singular truth about the Filipino people, not just a pious turn of phrase.[71] Their love and devotion for Mary is part of their heritage and of their identity. And it is in this devotion to Mary that one finds the practice of religion taking on popular expressions that make it specifically Filipino, with its local color and pageantry. The various manifestations of popular piety toward Mary appear not only in innumerable churches, chapels, and shrines dedicated to her, but are woven into the ordinary lives of the people, as seen from Filipino religious practices of the past:

Mary marked our communities (so many girls and women at baptism were given her name or her titles). The name and figure of *Mary marked our geography*: so many poblaciones, barrios, towns, were also named after her. *Mary marked our time*: the timetable of all our communities: the oracion, the Angelus and its attendant pieties became the clock of the daily lives of Filipino. The morning started with the entire town praying the rosary, the *Dios te salves* chanted before dawn in every home. Boys went to school, rosaries around their necks, chanting prayers to the Lady. The *Angelus* signaled noon, and beneath the mid-day sun, the town took its break for meal and rest. Work ceased with *oracion* of the evening. And when the day was ending, the *Salve Regina* in the candle-lit church, the leading townfolk dutifully present, gave back the day to God through the hands of her who was the *clemens*, the *pia*, the *dulcis* Virgo Maria.[72]

---

[70] Ibid., 40–41.
[71] C. G. Arevalo, "Bayang Sumisinta kay Maria: Pueblo Amante de Maria," in *Filipino Spiritual Culture, Social Transformation, and Globalization*, ed. José V. Abueva, Arnold Boehme, Ruben F. Balane (Quezon City: Discalced Carmelite Nuns, Monastery of St. Therese, 2003), 42.
[72] Ibid., 46–47.

A familiar sight in Filipino homes, in the rich enclaves or in the slums of the cities, is the holy picture of Mary. Images of her are displayed in buses, jeepneys, and tricycles, in public places, and along the roads—all palpable signs of a people in love with Mary—*ang bayang sumisinta kay Maria*.[73] History points out that Marian devotion has a special role in the rapid conversion of the Philippines to the Catholic faith, and devotion to her was a powerful means of helping the early Filipinos live an intense Christian life.[74] Today, the devotion to Mary has kept and nurtured the Catholic faith of the people.

Given the omnipresence of Mary in the life and tradition of the Filipino, she was undeniably the most visible symbol at EDSA:

> At the various sites where tens of thousands of people converged to wage, for one hundred hours, the revolution of peace and prayer, images of Our Lady were set up in almost every street corner. Rosaries were recited all day long, one after the other, almost without any interruption, as people watched, or knelt in front of armored cars and tanks, or rushed toward descending helicopters and advancing troops.[75]

Many believe that the EDSA Revolution was won due to Mary's intercession in response to the Filipinos' devotion to her. Since the devotion at the heart of Filipino religiosity is the devotion to Mary, no liberation of the Filipino people can be separated from it; it is in this and in the entire expression of their religion that they are what they are as a people. What was regarded as a deadening opiate by a contrary worldview became the motive force and power that galvanized the people into a concerted action and kept that action nonviolent. The place of religion in the Filipino culture signifies strong and clear evidence of religion as the substance of a culture.

The Catholic Church was at the center of the revolution, with Cardinal Sin at the front line. Pastor, patriot, and prophet, Cardinal

---

[73] CBCP, *Ang Mahal na Birhen: Mary in the Philippine Life Today: A Pastoral Letter on the Virgin Mary* (February 2, 1975), no. 14. Filipino Marian popular religiosity is intertwined with Christ and the mysteries of the incarnation and redemption. In this respect, what is true of Latin America is also true of the Philippines. "The fundamental paschal dimension came to us through the devotion to the Blessed Virgin Mary, especially through the recitation of and meditation on the mysteries of the Most Holy Rosary" (quoted in ibid., no. 72; see also nos. 17–19).

[74] Arévalo, "Bayang Sumisinta kay Maria," 47.

[75] Ibid., 49.

Sin stood as the people's beacon of faith and courage. As the custodian of the moral values and of the religious symbols, the Catholic Church was the moral center to which Filipinos gravitated when the nation was in crisis. It was the only social force that could mobilize public opinion and protest against any regime. Claiming allegiance of 84 percent of Filipinos, and with a vast network of communications and services, the church's responsibility in the social order is great. As such, the church in the Philippines holds immense power in the pursuit of justice and freedom for the people.[76]

The relationship between Church and politics had been a burning question within the church in the Philippines from the very first day of Marcos's usurpation of power in September 1972. It was not as if the church, especially the bishops, were suddenly politically alive during the dramatic turn of events at EDSA. Their pastoral letters for fifteen years prior to EDSA showed a progression in the church's teaching role regarding the worsening political situation. It was, however, in the post-election statement of February 1986 that this role reached its zenith, when the bishops declared the Marcos government morally illegitimate and its power without moral basis; the bishops virtually urged the people to rise in protest and revolt against this government.[77] In the estimate of many, the bishops' statement was the pivotal turn in the rapid succession of events, as its prophetic witness gave the revolution a light for all to follow and empowered the people with an invincible moral courage and faith. Under the moral leadership of the Catholic Church the revolution took a radical turn and a clear direction. The lines of the revolution were drawn, and the church was with the people, for the church *is* the people, there at every street, behind every barricade, in front of the tanks—the church as the people of God praying and singing—a vision of communal joy in the face of an impending doom.

The dominant role that Catholic Church played at EDSA mediated the liberating power of religion. When religion's vision of the good is identified with the common good, it holds a power to unify

---

[76] John J. Carroll, "The Church, State, and People Power," *Intersect* 16 (February 2001): 9. Regarding the involvement of the church in politics, Bishop Claver said that it is a good rule of thumb to make a distinction between the political field and the political arena. Clerics have no competence in the political arena where "real" politics, the partisan kind, is played ("The Church in the Political Arena," *Pulso Monograph* 5 [December 1990]: 13).

[77] Francisco F. Claver, "Philippine Church and People Power," *Month* 19 (May 1986): 149–54.

all.[78] At the time of the revolution the Catholic Church was uniquely positioned to become the decisive arbiter of the common good. When religion contributes to the pursuit of the common good and builds solidarity in freedom, it becomes an agent of liberation. As David Hollenbach writes: "Religious beliefs and loyalties are among the factors that energize communities and institutions of civil society, for they give people communal resources, affective motivations, and cognitive reasons for active participation in active public life."[79]

Filipino men and women of different persuasions and affiliations, both believers and nonbelievers involved in the struggle, appropriated Catholic/Christian symbols without necessarily internalizing their content in a formal and explicit way. At the risk of their own lives they heeded Cardinal Sin's call to take to the streets and face the guns and tanks. Religion, in its pursuit of the common good, was a force of unity and liberation at EDSA. People Power is church power when church is truly people, trying to be and to act in living fidelity to the gospel. In the prophetic witness of the church at EDSA, religion was not alien or separated from the Filipinos in their struggle for justice and freedom. This is the church at the barricades, as it should also be at the marketplace, at the railway stations, in the ghettoes, wherever people live and die as they struggle for meaning and purpose as individuals and as a people.

Tillich's maxim must therefore be understood in context, and its meaning must be necessarily nuanced accordingly. Where there are truths and values that are regarded with ultimate concern, religion as the substance of culture is present, even if it does not take an explicitly religious form or language, as in secularized cultures, and even if it is not represented by a particular religious tradition, as in pluralistic religious societies. In the Philippines, which is predominantly Christian and Catholic, religion represents the substance of culture, and this substance elicits explicit expressions that are distinctively Filipino, as seen in the EDSA Revolution. Catholic faith is a force of liberation that gives the Filipino a sense of rootedness, identity, and peoplehood. At EDSA, this dominant religion of a specific tradition drew diverse

---

[78] See David Hollenbach, who writes: "We are not faced with choosing the alternatives of divisive religion on the one hand and the privatization of religion on the other. There is a third option: religious traditions, interpreted properly, have the capacity to contribute to the common good of public life in a way that is compatible with pluralism and freedom" (*The Common Good and Christian Ethics* [New York: Cambridge University Press, 2002], 99).

[79] Ibid., 111.

people to the center of shared humanity and destiny through its vision of the common good.

Dynamics of Filipino Culture, Religion, and Moral Vision

I return to my main contention that the dynamics of culture and religion have a bearing on moral vision, and this vision determines what we are and what we make of our lives, how we choose, and what we do. Moral vision is deeply connected, therefore, with our particular way of being human (culture) within the horizons of our experience of the Divine in our quest for transcendent and ultimate meaning (religion). At EDSA, the moral vision of the people—rooted in their core values as Filipinos and in their experience of religion at the heart of their culture, a force of unity and liberation—was powerfully manifested in their commitment to nonviolence as they placed their lives on the line for freedom and justice. This was a vision of moral courage, self-transcendence, and solidarity.

Schillebeeckx writes that "God reveals himself as the deepest mystery, the heart and the soul of any truly human liberation." He speaks of the mysticism of politics, defining mysticism as an "intense form of experience of God or love of God" and politics as an "intensive form of social commitment." Love of God, which is at the heart of mysticism, enters into the concrete social and political commitment. This is holiness in the political arena (political holiness) that demands the same repentance, self-emptying, suffering, the same dark nights, and utter losing of oneself as in contemplative mysticism.[80]

Moral vision is the moral consciousness of a people needed to sustain their common life together—the vision required if they are to be a people at all. In their common life, people are bound together by strong connections. Hollenbach observes: "They have come together in a *coetus*—the Latin word is cognate to *coitus*, sexual union. Their good is shared in a *communio* or communion. The links among them are formed by their common consent, their consensus, about what is just, right, and good."[81] This common consent, this consensus is born of struggle. This struggle for freedom and justice at the heart of the Filipino People Power inspired extraordinary moral courage. This moral courage was evident in election volunteers who guarded the ballot boxes with their bodies; it was evident in the computer technicians who staged a walkout, at the risk of losing their jobs and even their

---

[80] Edward Schillebeeckx, *Jesus in Our Western Cultures* (London: SCM, 1987), 73, 71–72, 74.

[81] Hollenbach, *The Common Good and Christian Life*, 65–66.

lives, rather than manipulate the election results. For these and many others who faced death, there was often a Gethsemane experience of not wanting to die yet being willing to let go and take extraordinary risks. Witness these accounts:

> As five trucks filled with soldiers were moving towards the barricades, a group of sisters and students ran in the direction of the trucks and then prostrated themselves on the ground and with their hands raised with their rosaries, they waited for their end to come. But the trucks stopped. Another story tells of a group of university students who were given twenty minutes to disperse; the Marines loyal to Marcos were ordered to shoot if they were prevented from attacking the camps. One of the students narrated: "We formed a long line and prayed the rosary. . . . When the tanks came, the soldiers did not molest us. But we were all willing to risk our lives, to die."[82]

The struggle for freedom and justice can only be empowered by a moral vision of genuine self-transcendence. This vision can pull people out of themselves for a greater reality and embolden them to face tanks and put themselves in the line of fire. One cannot be moral unless one is forgetful of self for another, or for others. Being moral takes this paschal meaning: a dying to self that others may live.

Again, only stories can bring us to the reality of the moral vision that impelled people to do what they did for a cause greater than themselves. One striking story from the Philippines concerned a man who drove his Mercedes Benz to the barricades to block the tanks from crossing over to where the people had gathered.[83] It was foolish, one might say, but only self-transcendence for a cause greater than oneself can impel one to be a "fool" for the gospel that confounds the wise and powerful. In a similar story, a man, who, when he heard that a tank assault was coming from the presidential palace and that all might be crushed to death, told his wife to go home so that if he died, someone would be left to care for their children. "Come to think of it," he said, "at that time I realized I was willing to die."[84]

This commitment to nonviolence in the struggle for freedom and justice is only possible in solidarity, for it is from solidarity that the commitment draws much of its life. The vivid images of People Power

---

[82] As cited in Mamot, *People Power*, 115, 130–31.
[83] Cited in Carroll, "Looking Beyond EDSA," 13.
[84] Cited in Mamot, *People Power*, 39.

at EDSA are those of men and women who locked arms with one
another, faced the tanks, and dared to die together. There is no more
eloquent image of solidarity. Suddenly, Filipinos realized their strength
of solidarity. They discovered a power stronger than bullets—their morale and unity in locked arms. Joe Holland calls this the root metaphor
of "social and spiritual creativity of rooted communities networked
in solidarity."[85] In his encyclical *Sollicitudo Rei Socialis,* Pope John
Paul II spoke of solidarity as a "firm and preserving determination to
commit oneself to the common good. . . . It is a commitment to the
good of one's neighbor with the readiness, in the gospel sense, to 'lose
oneself' for the sake of the other" (no. 38).

Solidarity at EDSA meant cutting across all class stratifications and
class barriers. It was incredible to see Filipinos from all socioeconomic
levels forming human barricades and protecting strategic points with
their massed bodies, resolute in their commitment to a singular cause.
The sea of humanity was ordered, directed by the common cause of
nonviolence in the struggle for freedom and justice. As the people
chanted and sang their songs in the battlefield of EDSA, not a single
shot was fired to silence their voices.

The vision of moral courage, self-transcendence, and solidarity at
the base of the Filipino struggle for freedom and justice was made imperative by core Filipino values and by the liberating force of religion
in the Filipino culture. The EDSA People Power of 1986 was, in the
words of Antonio Lambino, a "peaceful, non-violent revolution with
parallels but with no equals. A revolution to which some previous ones
were similar but to which no previous one is identical. A revolution
that could only come from the heart and soul of a nation."[86]

Conclusion

The preceding example of the Filipino People Power Revolution is
consonant with Tillich's insight regarding the dynamics of culture and
religion: culture is a form of expression of religion and religion is the
substance of culture. That culture is a form of expression of religion
means that the experience of religion is given expression through
cultural forms and elements. Tillich's understanding of religion as the
depth dimension of reality opens up the parameters of a transcendent

[85] Joe Holland and Peter Henriot, *Social Analysis: Linking Faith and Justice,*
rev. and enl. ed. (Maryknoll, NY: Orbis Books, 1983), xvii.
[86] Antonio B. Lambino, "Theological Reflection in the Filipino Exodus: August
21, 1983 to February 25, 1986," in Achútequi, *Loyola Papers,* 20.

experience beyond what is explicitly religious and makes all of reality available for the encounter with the Divine. Cultures have a center of gravity and substance, and this has religious valence insofar as it points to realities of ultimate concern that find depths of expressions in different contexts. In the Filipino context, religion as the substance of culture is mediated in expressions that are distinctively Filipino. This was attested in the Filipino People Power Revolution, which was itself steeped in symbols of faith.

The dynamics of culture and religion have a bearing on moral vision. The way people see themselves, and what they do with their lives, and how they choose and act are within the influence of their culture (the core values of which give expression to what is religious) and also within the influence of religion (in which culture draws it depth and substance). This main contention is validated by the EDSA Revolution of 1986, through the expression of People Power, with its deep roots in Filipino cultural values and religiosity. The revolution gave a vision of how, empowered by their innate religiosity, and their cultural rootedness, the Filipinos responded to the cause of justice and freedom in the spirit of nonviolence, founded on moral courage, self-transcendence, and solidarity.

2

Scripture and Moral Vision

Narrative Criticism
and a Proposed Integral Biblical Pedagogy

If moral theology is to be a genuine theological discipline, it must be rooted in scripture. Scripture ought to inform and shape moral theology as a field of study. The place of scripture in moral theology is necessary and essential, but the question of how it is to be realized and by which method opens a whole new discussion with which both Catholic and Protestant moral theologians continue to engage.

The use of scripture can be described as either illuminative or prescriptive. It is illuminative when scripture is used to awaken moral awareness and sensitivity as engendered by a vision of life. It is prescriptive when scripture is used to provide concrete moral precepts and rules for action and behavior. I propose the use of narrative criticism for the illuminative purpose of scripture. This method approaches scripture as a story, bringing the reader into an encounter with the scriptural text and its world of characters, events, and meaning. Engaging reason and imagination, it enables the reader to penetrate into the inner reality of scripture in view of its moral vision.

In this chapter I first offer an overview of different scriptural approaches for the purpose of locating narrative criticism in the spectrum, followed by a presentation of narrative criticism developed in three sections. The first section presents the relation of story and moral vision, because stories shape the way we look at the world. Our lives are ordered around significant stories of our personal and communal history. We are as the stories of our lives are. The focus is on scripture as story, which shows how a literary approach to scripture is used beyond the method of historical criticism and cultural criticism. This approach is rich in its potential for bringing the reader in touch with the life and vitality of scripture. The second section presents the different literary approaches to scripture, one of which is narrative criticism. In the third section the different aspects of narrative criticism—point of view, character, and plot—are discussed.

Following the presentation of the use of narrative criticism is a critical assessment of it in terms of its positive contribution to the field of scriptural interpretation, as well as the objections raised regarding its legitimacy and validity of use.

One major shortcoming of narrative criticism, as is also true of historical criticism and cultural criticism, is the lack of flesh-and-blood readers and their interaction with the text as significantly contributing to its meaning. This absence is filled by contextual biblical pedagogy, the approach presented in the fourth part of the chapter.

What is proposed in the fourth part of the chapter is an integral biblical pedagogy that makes use of the tools of the various pedagogies across the entire spectrum of biblical criticism for a full and rich reading and interpretation of scripture. Engaging with texts as historical, literary, rhetorical, and ideological, and readers as both constructed and as flesh and blood, demands principles that would guide the reading and interpretation of meaning of a text or texts.

The conclusion presents principles to guide a critical and creative engagement with texts and readers using an integral biblical pedagogy with reference to narrative criticism.

An Overview of Scriptural Approaches

The landscape of biblical criticism has radically changed from the mid-1970s when historical criticism—encompassing different methodological approaches or strategies such as literary or source criticism, tradition criticism, form criticism, redaction criticism, and composition criticism—was the dominant type of criticism. Two different approaches in contemporary biblical criticism have emerged since historical criticism was dislodged from its place of dominance, each involving a distinctive mode of discourse. After doing a critique of historical criticism, I briefly present how these approaches evolved and how each represents its own school of thought. In assessing the different scriptural approaches I make reference to *The Interpretation of the Bible in the Church*, presented by the Pontifical Commission to Pope John Paul II on April 23, 1993. In his address during the course of an audience commemorating the centenary of the encyclical of Leo XXIII, *Providentissimus Deus,* and the fiftieth anniversary of the encyclical of Pius XII, *Divino Afflante,* both dedicated to biblical studies, John Paul took note of the spirit of openness in which the new document was conceived. The methods, approaches, and interpretations practiced today in exegesis have been examined, and despite some serious reservations, the valid elements in almost every case were acknowledged for an integral interpretation of the biblical text. The pope also praised the document's balance and moderation. In its interpretation of the Bible, the document called for the harmony of the diachronic (the development of texts or traditions across the passage of time) and the synchronic (the language, composition, narrative structure, and capacity for persuasion) by recognizing the complementarity of both, and their indispensable function for bringing out the truth of the text and for appropriating the biblical message for the modern reader.

Critique of Historical Criticism

Many scriptural narratives are generally recognized as having artistic quality ranking among the foremost literary treasures of the world. But for more than a century biblical scholarship was dominated by historical-critical methods that gave little attention to the literary qualities of the narratives. The historical-critical method has undoubtedly contributed greatly to our knowledge of the world and literature of the scripture. This method, however, could not penetrate into the inner world of the scriptural text and narrative without the aid of literary methods and approaches that treat scripture as narrative.[1]

Historical criticism pursued a wide variety of endeavors: (1) establishing the accuracy of the texts and translations; (2) investigating the cultural and historical milieux in which the text developed; (3) searching for possible sources and analogues of biblical stories that might provide insight into their form and content; (4) determining the religious metaphysics of various sources in scripture that reflect the evolving attitudes of the Hebrew people; (5) seeking the earliest forms of individual stories and how they developed; and (6) explicating biblical theology in terms of faith understanding.[2]

The historical-critical approach is exemplified by the scholarly work done on the birth and youth story of Moses (Ex 1—2). Its focus is on establishing analogies with other ancient Near Eastern heroes' birth stories and the Egyptian background of Moses' name, and investigat-

---

[1] Shimon Bar-Efrat, *Narrative Art in the Bible* (New York: T. and T. Clark, 2004), 9–10.

[2] Kenneth R. R. Gros Louis with James Stokes Ackerman and Thayer S. Warshaw, eds., *Literary Interpretations of Biblical Narratives* (Nashville, TN: Abingdon, 1974), 10.

ing the Egyptian culture and ethos as represented in the pharaoh's court. It employs literary analysis, which identifies different sources providing or editing the text and extrapolates the theologies of these sources that may have influenced the religious viewpoints that developed in the texts. These historical-critical concerns, as identified by Kenneth R. R. Gros Louis, may be necessary and important, but they only serve as "background information" for one who endeavors to interpret the text as a whole.[3] The major limitation of all these approaches, according to Hans Frei, is that they fail to take seriously the narrative character of scriptural accounts.[4] Stories about Moses are not just compilations of miscellaneous data concerning him. The historical-critical method, focusing on the documentary status of the scriptural books, had interpreted not the stories themselves but the historical circumstances behind them.[5]

The historical-critical model approached the biblical text primarily as a means for reconstructing the historical context that it presupposed and addressed. Within this overall historical conception of the text, the focus was on its character as a religious document with a specific theological content and message. The model was profoundly theological in orientation. The meaning of the text resides in the world it represents, in the intention of its original author, or both. The task of contemporary readers, through the proper use of the model's scientific methodologies, was to discover the text's original message addressed to its original audience.[6]

The meaning of the text was regarded as universal and objective, and it could be retrieved if the model's methodology was rigorously applied. But such a task could only be accomplished by an expert critic who, assuming a position of neutrality and impartiality and bringing nothing to the text in the process of interpretation, approximated the

---

[3] Ibid., 10–11.

[4] See Hans W. Frei, *The Eclipse of Biblical Narrative: A Study in Eighteenth and Nineteenth Century Hermeneutics* (New Haven, CT: Yale University Press, 1974).

[5] Mark Allan Powell, *What Is Narrative Criticism?* (Minneapolis: Fortress Press, 1990), 2.

[6] Fernando F. Segovia, *Decolonizing Biblical Studies: A View from the Margins* (Maryknoll, NY: Orbis Books, 2000), 12. For an overview of the historical development of historical criticism, its main figures and concerns, see R. F. Collins, *Introduction to the New Testament* (Garden City, NY: Doubleday, 1983), 41–69; and Peter Stuhlmacher, *Historical Criticism and Theological Interpretation of Scripture: Toward a Hermeneutic of Consent* (Philadelphia: Fortress Press, 1977), 22–60.

meaning of the text and made it available to untrained readers. The text's true meaning could only be retrieved by trained experts who wielded authority and power within a hierarchical system consisting of text-critic-readers.[7]

Historical critics studied texts not as artistic, rhetorical, and ideological constructs in their own right, but as products of a long process of accretion and redaction, rendering their meaning more difficult to retrieve. They were often regarded as problematic and unintelligible, full of *aporias*–textual unevenness, difficulties, or contradictions.[8] Fernando Segovia criticizes the method because by conceptualizing the meaning of the text as residing either in the world represented by it, in the intention of the author, or both, historical criticism was divorced from the presuppositions of the teacher and student, as shaped by their social locations. The methodology was neutral and based on *exegesis*, not *eisegesis*, which is a reading of the text, not a reading into the text. In engaging in *eisegesis* one does not allow the text to speak but inserts one's own words and meaning into the text. This was looked upon not only as intrusive but also as unscholarly, which contaminated the entire process of biblical interpretation. So while the study of the culture and experience underlying the texts was essential for sound biblical scholarship and interpretation, the culture and experience of the readers of the text were looked upon as variables that should not enter into the equation.[9]

This was a pedagogical model based on authority and hierarchy, with emphasis on academic pedigree (who studies under whom), with students and readers dependent on teachers and critics who held the key to the univocal meaning of the text. As such, the method was regarded as highly pyramidal, patriarchal, and authoritative, where the experts were considered to possess the primordial access to the word of God. Segovia criticizes this methodology as "remarkably inbred and thoroughly hegemonic."[10] With a nonexistent dialogue with other critical models and disciplines, historical criticism collapsed from within when its methodological development was no longer able to respond to the evolving shifts in biblical criticism.[11]

---

[7] Segovia, *Decolonizing Biblical Studies*, 14.

[8] Ibid., 13.

[9] Ibid., 15.

[10] Ibid.

[11] For a pointed and spirited defense of historical criticism, see Joseph A. Fitzmyer, "Historical Criticism: Its Role in Biblical Interpretation and Church Life," *Theological Studies* 50/2 (1989): 244–59.

The Pontifical Biblical Commission's *The Interpretation of the Bible in the Church*,[12] presented to Pope John Paul II on April 23, 1993, confirms some of the critique of historical criticism. It states that "the search for the original can lead to putting the word back into the past completely so that it is no longer taken in its actuality. . . . It restricted itself to the task of dissecting and dismantling the text in order to identify the various sources. It did not pay sufficient attention to the final form of the biblical text in and to the message which it conveyed" (Preface, I-A1). And the sterility of its research made access to the living sources of God more difficult, making the Bible a closed book, reserved only for a few specialists (Introduction, A). But given this serious critique, and granting that no approach is self-sufficient, the document still maintains historical method as indispensable in understanding accurately the intention of the authors and editors of the Bible as well as the message they addressed to the first readers (I-A1).

Literary Criticism as an Alternative Approach

From the viewpoint of moral theology and its task of illuminating the power and depth of scripture for moral vision and character, I am of one mind with those who hold that scripture needs to be studied as literature. The need for a more literary approach to the scripture has been called for since William B. Beardslee did so in 1970.[13] Criticizing the sharply historical cast of most biblical scholarship, he proposed that the analysis of biblical forms should not only provide insight into the sources and contexts that influenced these texts but also into the literary meaning and impact of the texts themselves on the reader. This desire for a more literary approach to scripture was born of the recognition of the limitations of an exclusively historical approach. This is not to say that historical criticism has failed or that its methods and goals are invalid, only that something must be done in addition. Scripture needs to be read in a way that it has not been read before. But if it is to be read as literature, a different set of questions in addition to those asked by historical-critical methods must be posed.

To read scripture as story is not to deny that biblical texts grew out of a specific historical and theological context and were designed to satisfy particular needs in those contexts. A literary approach places the biblical writing in a literary frame, emphasizing its universal

---

[12] Pontifical Biblical Commission, *The Interpretation of the Bible in the Church*, *Origins* (January 6, 1994), available on the catholic-resources.org website.

[13] William A. Beardslee, *Literary Criticism of the New Testament* (Philadelphia: Fortress Press, 1970).

signification so as to enable the reader to "create a world and self both affectively and cognitively through interaction with the text."[14]

Attention to the original situation of the text does not abolish the work on scripture as literature. Likewise, to read the text as literature in a more comprehensive way includes a fuller appreciation of its original context. Edgar McKnight writes, "The biblical writers are discovering that it is possible to make sense out of literary criticism, to develop literary approaches to biblical texts which, while not completely objective and scientific, are orderly and rational."[15] The literary approaches that bridge the distance between the ancient texts and the modern reader or critic allow for the integration of the long tradition and wealth of the historical-critical method.

It is worth noting the differences between literary criticism and historical criticism as methods used in scriptural interpretation. Literary criticism focuses on the finished form of the text. The objective of its literary-critical analysis is not to discover how the text has come to be, but to study the text as it now exists in its finished form. It emphasizes the unity of the text as a whole. This differs from the historical-critical methods, which, for instance, view the Gospels as compilations of loosely related pericopes that are studied and analyzed as individual units of tradition. Literary criticism views the Gospels as coherent narratives and its individual units held together as integral parts of a whole story.[16] "A literary approach to the Bible is one that resists the trend of biblical scholarship toward fragmentation."[17] This whole storied text is an end in itself, in the sense that the immediate goal of a literary study is to understand the narrative. The story that is told and the manner in which it is expressed are given full scholarly attention. In contrast, historical criticism treats the text as a means to an end rather than an end in itself. "The 'end' for historical criticism is a reconstruction of something to which the text attests, such as the life and teaching of Jesus, the interests of the early Christians who preserved traditions concerning him, or the concerns of the evangelists and their communities."[18] The difference between the historical-critical methods and the literary approaches is aptly described in terms of the difference between a window and a metaphor:

---

[14] Edgar V. McKnight, *The Bible and the Reader: An Introduction to Literary Criticism* (Philadelphia: Fortress Press, 1985), 11.

[15] Ibid., 11–12.

[16] Powell, *What Is Narrative Criticism?* 7–8.

[17] Kalman P. Bland, "The Rabbinic Method and Literary Criticism," in Gros Louis, *Literary Interpretations of Biblical Narratives*, 36.

[18] Powell, *What Is Narrative Criticism?* 7–8.

Historical criticism regards the text as a window through which the critic hopes to learn something about another time and place. The text, then, stands between the reader and the insight that is sought and may provide the means through which that insight can be obtained. Literary criticism, in contrast, regards the text as a mirror; the critic looks at the text, not through it, and whatever insight is obtained will be found in the encounter of the reader with the text itself.[19]

The difference between treating the text as a window or treating it as a mirror can be stated another way, that is, in terms of the difference between treating the text in its poetic function or its referential function. Literary critics, focusing on the poetic function of the text, are able to appreciate the story of a narrative apart from considering whether it is consonant with history or not. The story world of the narrative is experienced in its totality and is not evaluated in terms of historicity. For the historical critics, elements in the New Testament— God speaking from heaven, miracles, men and women encountering spiritual creatures like devils and angels—prove to be problematic in terms of their referential function, that is, their reference to the real world. The literary critic takes up these elements insofar as they contribute to the story and its impact on the readers.[20] "The art of biblical narrative consists of signals addressed to the sensitive reader. These signals function as agents which stimulate our intellect, our imagination, and our capacity for empathy in order to engage us in a mutual act of literary creation with Scripture itself."[21]

The main focus of the literary-criticism inquiry is no longer on the world behind the text or on the author who conceived it, but rather on the aesthetic or artistic character of the text. As a result, the text as text began to receive an attention it had never been granted before. From the perspective of theory and methodology, the literary paradigm was a liberating step from the hegemony of historical criticism. It opened the way to an enormous diversity of interpretive approaches and a myriad of ways in which to read the meaning of biblical texts. While there is now a focus on the reader and an openness to a plurality of interpretation of text through a rigorous application of proper and scientific methodology, the whole approach is abstracted from the sociocultural location of real authors and readers. The text stands in

---

[19] Ibid., 8.
[20] Ibid.
[21] Bland, "The Rabbinic Method and Literary Criticism," 21.

its own right as a literary and rhetorical product and is interpreted through concepts of *implied author* and *implied reader*, as derived from within the text itself.[22]

The Interpretation of the Bible in the Church states that the new rhetoric of literary-critical approaches is able to "penetrate to the very core of the language of revelation precisely as persuasive religious discourse" (I-B1). A specific form of literary criticism, narrative criticism, offers a method for understanding and communicating the biblical message that corresponds to the form of story, which is well suited to the narrative character of many biblical texts. "It can facilitate the transition, often so difficult, from the meaning of the text in its historical context (the proper object of the historical-critical method) to its significance for the reader of today" (I-B2). However, it also pointed out that the synchronic approach it uses must be supplemented by diachronic studies, and it must also be mindful of the fact that "existential subjective effectiveness of the impact of the word of God in its narrative transmission cannot be considered to be in itself a sufficient indication that its full truth has been adequately grasped" (I-B2). On the other hand, the distinction between real author and the implied author makes the mode of interpretation by this approach more complex (I-B2).

The Emergence of Cultural Criticism

After the dominance of historical criticism was demolished, literary criticism and social-scientific criticism emerged as two different currents that do not often interact or interrelate, even to this day. Cultural criticism or social-scientific criticism, engaged in by its practitioners, turned away from the in-house, largely theological discussion of the discipline to other fields in the humanities, like economics, sociology, and anthropology.[23] This turn to other dialogue partners was also engaged in by literary critics who moved away from the theological moorings of historical criticism toward other fields in the humanities, such as literature and psychology, using various theories like literary theory, psychoanalytic theory, structuralist theory, and rhetorical theory.[24]

With the emergence of cultural criticism, another model of interpretation has entered into the biblical arena, requiring of its adherents a very different type of orientation and application, and

---

[22] Segovia, *Decolonizing Biblical Studies,* 17–22.

[23] Ibid, 22–23.

[24] Ibid., 17.

employing a different analytical apparatus and accompanying vocabulary. Dialogue between historical critics and cultural critics was rare, and yet in terms of location of meaning, the cultural model is closest in spirit to historical criticism. While the text is used as a medium of communication between a sender and receiver, an author and reader, the primary focus of cultural critics is the text as evidence for the time and context of its composition. Unlike historical criticism, cultural criticism does not analyze the historical uniqueness or specificity of the text but rather its sociocultural situation. Such analysis involves questions of social class and conflict as applied across time and cultures, which are addressed from a broad comparative perspective. Questions of social institutions, roles, and behavior, as well as questions of cultural matrix and values, are addressed from a broad comparative perspective.[25]

For cultural critics, the economic, social, or cultural dimensions of the text, rather than its theological or religious character, are their primary interest. The meaning of the text is located in the world "behind" it, retrieved through an analysis of text, author, and readers as they relate to the text's sociocultural context. Whether a reading is synchronic or diachronic is inconsequential for cultural critics. What matters is the proper decoding of the economic, social, or cultural codes contained in the text. The meaning of the texts resides in it as a product of its context.[26]

The dialogue between historical critics and cultural critics proved to be largely nonexistent. For literary critics, the cultural critics were caught in the same stranglehold of historicism as historical critics, with little sense for the character and value of the text as text; for the cultural critics, the literary critics were mired in an aestheticism that was abstract and ahistorical, with a disembodied view of the text as text. But while they made few attempts at joining their methods, their own supporting disciplines were increasingly interrelated and interdependent.[27]

With regard to theory and methodology, the cultural paradigm with which these experts worked was another step away from the domination of historical criticism. It opened the field of biblical criticism to new ways of reading and interpreting the biblical texts. Against the univocal discourse of historical criticism, the emergence

---

[25] Ibid., 24.
[26] Ibid., 25.
[27] Ibid., 23.

of cultural criticism, like that of literary criticism, yielded a number of different discourses, ultimately related but retaining their distinctiveness.[28]

The Interpretation of the Bible in the Church praises cultural criticism, which is basically a sociological approach aimed at enriching and broadening the exegetical enterprise. Knowledge of the sociological data covering the economic, cultural, and religious functioning of the biblical world is indispensable for knowing and understanding the life as actually lived by the early church. It also signaled some of the risks involved in applying the sociological approach to exegesis. The methods used by this approach meet special difficulties when applied to historical societies of a very distant past. "Biblical and extrabiblical texts do not necessarily provide the sort of documentation adequate to give a comprehensive picture of society of the time. Moreover, the sociological method does tend to pay rather more attention to the economic and institutional aspects of human life than to its personal and religious dimensions" (I-D1).

The Use of Narrative Criticism

The use of narrative criticism must first be contextualized in the use of scripture for establishing a moral vision. Following this, we can move to a presentation of the different aspects of narrative criticism as one among other literary approaches to scripture. Last, we can assess narrative criticism in terms of its positive contribution to the field of scriptural interpretation, as well as in terms of the objections raised regarding its legitimacy and validity of use.

Moral Vision and Story: Scripture as Story

While principles and rules are important for moral living, they are not sufficient. People do not live by rules and principles alone; they also are directed and moved by story. Story and principles are complementary. A story without a principle is ineffective; a principle without a story is abstract. Our moral vision is shaped by the stories that have touched our lives, binding our past with the present and opening us to the future. Moral vision is the construal of our self and character formed by the stories of our life.

---

[28] Ibid., 28.

"Metaphors and stories," Hauerwas writes, "suggest how we should see and describe the world—that is, how we should 'look on' ourselves, others, and the world, in ways that rules and principles taken in themselves do not. They do this by providing the narrative accounts of our lives that give coherence."[29] Our moral vision is ordered around significant stories in our lives. We become who we are through the embodiment of our stories in the communities in which we grow up. Stories that have compelling power on us are those that illumine for us the truth of our own existence. There is no "story of stories" that carries a universal point of view unless it bears the mark of a particular history.[30]

The art of storytelling is being revived and is taking its rightful place as a theological method. The distinct interest in story, however, is not new; in fact, it is a return to tradition. The prophets and sages of old preached and taught in stories. Jesus is the great master of story. William Bausch says that "it is story and all related art forms that touch us at our deepest levels and convince us of truth."[31] Anthony Padovano writes that the effect of art is the same as the effect of a story on us: "The artist convinces us of the truth by dealing with us holistically. Artists try to make us feel the truth. Good art gets the truth inside us on a level deeper than the surface of our minds. On this level, truth is irresistible."[32]

Amos Wilder challenges what he calls our "long addiction to the discursive, the rationalistic, and the prosaic." He draws attention to the place of the imagination, which he says is a necessary component of all profound knowing and celebration, the place where any full engagement with life takes place. He criticizes "the stultifying axiom that genuine truth or insight or wisdom must be limited to that which can be stated in discursive prose, in denotative language, stripped as far as possible of all connative suggestion, in clear ideas, in short, in statement or description of a scientific character."[33]

---

[29] Stanley Hauerwas, "Vision, Stories, and Character," in *Hauerwas Reader*, ed. John Berkman and Michael Cartwright, 165–70 (Durham, NC: Duke University Press, 2001), 166.

[30] Stanley Hauerwas, "Character, Narrative, and Growth in the Christian Life," in Berkman and Cartwright, *Hauerwas Reader*, 251.

[31] William J. Bausch, *Storytelling: Imagination and Faith* (Mystic, CT: Twenty-Third Publications, 1984), 11.

[32] Anthony Padovano, "Aesthetic Experience and Redemptive Grace," in *Aesthetic Dimensions of Religious Education*, ed. Gloria Durka and Joanmarie Smith, 3–12 (New York: Paulist Press, 1979), 6.

[33] Amos Niven Wilder, *Theopoetic: Theology and the Religious Imagination* (Philadelphia: Fortress Press, 1976), 1.

The emergence of narrative theology—the theology of story—begins with this critical distancing from what Wilder called an addiction to the discursive. A number of theologians have become interested in the importance of stories. Thomas Driver, among those who believe that theology has in the course of time removed itself too far from its roots in narrative, stresses the importance of imagination. He writes: "Far from merely illustrating truths we already know some other way, the dramatic imagination is the means whereby we get started in any knowledge whatever."[34] William Bausch, who also takes deliberate efforts to modify the undue emphasis placed for so long on the rational and logical in religion, holds that reason should not be pitted against imagination; both must be affirmed, and any overstress on one against the other must be corrected.[35]

The story, whether it is spoken, written, enacted, painted, sculpted, or sung, brings a resonance in us of our past and an echo of our beginnings.[36] We are a storied people who live according to what has been passed on to us from generation to generation. Narrative theology expresses the essence of faith in its original form, not as a text or as a dissertation, but as poetry and story.[37] This is theology that connects us to what we are and dream to be, in places where we meet God in our encounter with one another. Karl Rahner states that "great Christianity and really great poetry have an inner kinship. . . . Great poetry exists where man [sic] radically faces who [he] is."[38]

Stories are a bridge to one's culture, to one's roots. Families, communities, and nations have stories and myths that tell and celebrate who they are. These stories are told and retold so a people can retain its sense of what makes it who it is and hopes to be. A family, community, or a nation without a story is without roots. Though race, culture, and belief can separate us, stories can bind us; they make us see the human condition which we all share and make us recognize the common humanity we share.

The use of scripture for nurturing moral vision presupposes the use of scripture as illuminative. We depend on the great formative stories of scripture to disclose to us who we are, what life is all about, and

---

[34] Tom F. Driver, *Patterns of Grace: Human Experience as Word of God* (Lanham, MD: University Press of America, 1985), xxiii.

[35] Bausch, *Storytelling*, 11.

[36] Ibid., 15.

[37] Ibid., 19.

[38] Karl Rahner, "Poetry and the Christian," in *Theological Investigations*, vol. 4, *More Recent Writings*, trans. Kevin Smyth, 357–67 (Baltimore: Helicon, 1966), 365.

for what we are destined. Stories about creation, exodus, covenant, incarnation, and the death and resurrection of Christ open us to a whole new world of meaning and values. We enter into this world and allow it to challenge and change us. Scripture grounds a particular kind of metaphysics influenced and inspired by faith. It gives us a certain way of looking at the world, one that turns upside down accepted patterns of striving, seeking, and possessing. It tells us about the one thing necessary, about losing and finding our life, taking up the cross, taking no thought for tomorrow, regarding others as better than ourselves, seeking not our rights but those of others, and laying down our life. These stories do not and are not meant to tell us exactly what to do. They are not directives; rather, they describe the thrusts and orientations that our lives must take.

Literary Approaches to Scripture

What is the importance of giving full scholarly attention to the scriptural text as a literary text? Wesley Kort holds that "literary interests do not impose themselves on the religious meaning or theological standing of biblical material. Rather, if there are religious and theological meanings and force in biblical narratives, they derive from and can be traced to the characteristics of narrativity and textuality." It is not, he says, that narrative and text are reduced to mere containers or occasions for religious or theological content and agenda. There is an intrinsic link between the literary and the religious. "If the Bible reveals something about religion and about God, it does so in and through narrativity and textuality. A concept of scripture such as here proposed, therefore, has a literary base before it has a theological consequence."[39]

To study the literary interests in biblical narrative is to encounter a range of methods and approaches. It is not possible here to develop an in-depth development of the methods. For our purpose, we take the categories that Mark Allan Powell develops to cover the broad field that encompasses a vast array of different methodologies of literary approaches to biblical narratives. It is worthwhile to differentiate literary-critical methods that fall under the traditional historical-critical methods of biblical scholarship, which are referential (mimetic) and author-centered modes, unlike the new literary-critical methods used for biblical studies in recent years—structuralism, rhetorical criticism, reader-response criticism, and narrative criticism—which are either

---

[39] Wesley A. Kort, *Story, Text, and Scripture: Literary Interests in Biblical Narrative* (University Park: Pennsylvania State University Press, 1988), 3.

text centered or reader centered.[40] Structuralism seeks to devise a grammar of literature. It holds that the meaning of a text is found within deep structures of the text rather than in the intentions of the author or in the perceptions of the reader. By studying the structures of the text, one comes to understand a biblical work in a way that even the author did not. Rhetorical criticism is a reader-centered approach in which the text is understood from the perspective of those to whom it is directed. It focuses on the means used to achieve a particular effect on the reader. It determines how such an effect is realized, which may be in the types of arguments or proofs that are used, the manner in which the material is arranged and developed, or the style that is employed. It is interested not only in the point that is made but also in the how and why such a point is made. In determining this the rhetorical critic identifies the rhetorical situation of the work's intended audience.[41]

Reader-response criticism is a pragmatic approach to literature that focuses on the role of the reader in determining the meaning of a text. It studies and analyzes how readers perceive literature and the bases on which they create meaning for any given work. It offers different assessments of what goes into the shape of the readers' responses and the extent to which the text itself determines those responses. Some reader-response critics hold the dominance of the reader over the text. This dominance implies that neither literary dynamics nor authorial intention constrain the meaning perceived by the readers. The creation of meaning is found in the readers' subjective perception. The movement known as deconstruction lends support to this specific stance of reader-response criticism.[42] Under the influence of Jacques Derrida, scholars hold that ultimately texts deconstruct themselves into endless labyrinths of possible meanings.[43]

Aspects of Narrative Criticism

Unlike the other approaches, narrative criticism has no counterpart in secular literary scholarship. It has developed within the field of biblical studies and is generally not well known in the secular realm of literary scholarship. Secular critics would probably classify it as a subspecies of the new rhetorical criticism or as a variation on the

---

[40] Powell, *What Is Narrative Criticism?* 12.

[41] Ibid., 14–15.

[42] Ibid., 16–18.

[43] See Robert Detweiler, ed., *Derrida and Biblical Studies*, Semeia 23 (Chico, CA: Scholars Press, 1982).

reader-response movement. It is, however, regarded by biblical scholars as an independent, parallel movement in its own right. The distinction of narrative criticism from the other three approaches is found in its designated readers. Rhetorical criticism is interested in the original readers to whom a work was first addressed, sometimes called *intended readers*. Structuralism points to *competent readers* who can decipher the work's codes. For the reader-response theory proposed by Stanley Fish, *reading communities* are suggested. Narrative criticism generally speaks of *implied readers* who are distinct from historical readers in the same way that the implied author is distinct from the historical author.[44]

Francis Moloney writes that whatever the perspective of a historical flesh-and-blood author may have been, we can only have access to the point of view of the implied author in the text. It may be that the point of view of the real author is mediated through that of the implied author of the text, but at best we can only make conjectures. The historical author of the book, now long since dead, is beyond our knowledge; so are the flesh-and-blood historical first readers. Yet within the text there is a reader addressed by the implied author. As the narrative unfolds, this reader's reactions and responses are shaped by the information and experiences provided by the implied author.[45] The implied reader is the reader constructed and addressed by the implied author on the basis of clues provided by the text itself. The implied author is also constructed by the reader from the text, which serves as the interpretive key to the text. Clues to the anticipated response of the implied reader may exist within the narrative; this is different from the actual responses of real readers, which cannot be predicted. There is a distinction between the reader *in* the text and the reader *of* the text. The real author and the real reader lie outside the parameters of the text. The real author and the real reader are extrinsic to the dynamics in the text relative to the sender, message, and receiver, that is, to the implied author, the narrative, and the implied reader. The concept of an implied reader distinguishes narrative criticism from a purely reader-centered (pragmatic) type of criticism and aligns it more with a text-centered (objective) approach. "Critics speak of a literary construct within the narrative itself, whose responses are totally controlled by the implied author. Such a 'reader' is generally called the implied reader."[46]

[44] Powell, *What Is Narrative Criticism?* 19–21.
[45] Francis J. Moloney, *Sacra Pagina* series, vol. 4, *The Gospel of John*, ed. by Daniel J. Harrington (Collegeville, MN: Liturgical Press, 1998), 16.
[46] Ibid.

The dynamics present in the text between and among its three components have further implications. Narrative criticism, unlike rhetorical criticism, does not need to interpret the work from the perspective of the text's actual, original audience; it is not necessary to know everything that it knew in order to understand the text correctly. The goal of narrative criticism is to read the text with the view of the implied reader, the imaginary person in whom the intention of the text is to be thought of as always reaching its fulfillment. What is called for here is to know everything the text assumes the reader to know and to forget everything that the text does not assume the reader to know. It is important to stress that in narrative criticism, the implied reader is a hypothetical concept; it is actually a principle that sets criteria for interpretation. "It is not necessary to assume that such a person actually existed or ever could exist. To the extent that the implied reader is an idealized abstraction, the goal of reading the text 'as the implied reader' may be somewhat unattainable, but it remains a worthy goal nevertheless."[47]

As its name implies, narrative criticism is concerned with a particular type of literature. A narrative may be defined as any work of literature that tells a story. A story consists of the elements of point of view, characterization, and plot. Point of view is modern to the repertoire of literary criticism; the other two are as old as the art of the story.

Point of View

Let us begin with what critics call point of view, because this has bearing on the characterization and plot of the story. In narrative criticism a central question is how the implied author guides the implied reader in understanding the story. The implied author influences and directs the implied reader to adopt the narrative's evaluative point of view. The evaluative point of view, which is pervasive in narrative criticism, governs the whole stance of the work. It consists of the norms, values, and worldview of the story, providing the standards or criteria of judgment by which the implied reader evaluates the events, characters, and settings that make up the story. Scripture is a narrative world where God's evaluative point of view is accepted by definition as true and right. A point of view that is opposed to God's point of view is wrong and untrue. Satan, who speaks and acts directly in the narratives and works indirectly through agents, is opposed to God's

---

[47] Powell, *What Is Narrative Criticism?* 21.

point of view. The implied reader is directed by the implied author to align with God's point of view and to reject anything that opposes this point of view.

The implied author also guides the implied reader through the use of a narrator—the voice that the implied author uses to tell the story. A classical example is the narrator's voice in the story of Job: "There was once a man in the land of Uz whose name was Job. That man was blameless and upright, one who feared and turned away from evil" (Jb 1:1). This opening statement immediately shapes the way the implied reader responds to the rest of the story. The statement has a strong effect on the implied reader and is accepted without question. In the world of the narrative, unlike that of the real world, there is an implicit contract between the implied author and the implied reader.

The narrator is an integral part of the text, one of its structural components. Without the mediation of the narrator, the implied reader has no access to a true understanding of the character and the events. The implied reader hears and sees through the narrator's eyes and ears. The narrator within the narrative is not identified with the writer as a real person. Thus, knowledge and familiarity of the real author's life and biography are not necessary to understand the narrator, because they do not necessarily hold the same values and attitudes. The narrator and the implied author are rhetorical devices in the narrative itself, and we encounter them only through reading and studying the story.

Narrators as a rhetorical device differ in important ways. In some works the first-person narrator may also be a character in the story. Except for a few instances, the narrators in the Gospels speak in the third person and are not characters in the narratives. Narrators also vary with regard to how much they know and how much they choose to tell. In the Gospels the narrators are very knowledgeable. They report on events that are to happen or that happened in two different places at the same time (for example, Jn 18:12–27), and they declare the inner thoughts and motivations of the characters they describe (Mt 2:3). Their knowledge, however, is limited to the earthly realm. They do not presume to know God's attitude. Whether God is pleased or not pleased, God enters the story and says so (Mt 3:17; 17:5; Mk 1:11; Lk 3:22). The narrators may know the inner thoughts of Jesus but do not make the same claim like Jesus on the thoughts of God. In the Gospel of John, however, such limitations seem to be lessened. The narrator's point of view is aligned with that of Jesus' in a symmetry so close that we cannot always distinguish one from the other. The narrator is able to describe the divine realm, as in the opening of the

Gospel (Jn 1:1–5), and claims to know far more than is told (Jn 20:30; 21:25), and to this extent the implied reader trusts the narrator.[48]

Shimon Bar-Efrat summarizes the possibilities of narrator and narrator modes. There are narrators who know everything about the characters and are ubiquitous; other narrators' knowledge and presence are limited. The former see through solid walls, discover secret corners, and enter into hidden recesses of people's minds, while the latter observe things from the outside and leave the implied reader to glean from his or her observations the inner lives of the characters. There are narrators who break into the story, intruding into the flow of events with their comments and explanations; other narrators tend to be silent, self-effacing, and inconspicuous. The former may address the reader directly, offering interpretations and evaluations of what is happening, while the latter will merely allow the story to unfold. There are also narrators who relate what is happening from a wide lens, offering a panoramic view; others are close to the events and present them as they come, allowing the characters to reveal themselves. Furthermore, there are narrators who watch things unfold from above, hovering over the characters, and others who work from the ground, looking at the events from the viewpoint of one of the characters. There are narrators who take a neutral and objective stance, as reflected in their factual narration, devoid of personal involvement; other narrators take a definitive attitude regarding characters and events, evoking the implied reader's approval or disapproval, acceptance or rejection, praise or censure, and perhaps even identification or abhorrence.[49]

If the implied reader of the Gospels is to believe in the reliability of the narrator, it is because the latter's point of view is in perfect alignment with those of the implied author. As aforementioned, some narrators are more intrusive than others. The narrators in the Gospels are more inconspicuous than intrusive. Their presence usually is so subtle that it almost goes unnoticed, but there are times when they suddenly break into the story and address the reader explicitly, as in Mark 13:14 and John 20:31. Sometimes there is also a person to whom the story is being told, as in Luke-Acts, where the story is being told to someone named Theophilus (Lk 1:3; Acts 1:1) and the implied reader is simply invited to listen in on the telling. The implied reader is given the sense that he or she is a third party to a discourse

---

[48] See ibid., 23–26.
[49] Shimon Bar-Efrat, *Narrative Art in the Bible*, 14–15.

going on between the narrator and the identified reader. The narrator and his or her object are not identified with the implied author and the implied reader; they are created by the implied author as part of the discourse of the narrative through which the story is told and its point of view unfolds.[50]

The implied author uses literary devices to help the implied reader come to the true interpretation and avoid the trap of literalism that some of the characters fall into. Through the use of irony and symbolism, the author guides the implied reader to a location where he or she sees truth in its depth and multiplicity. The literary devices of symbol and irony are related but not the same. They are related "insofar as both involve a detection of multiple meanings. Symbolism, however, implies a recognition that something means more than it initially appears to mean, while irony implies that the true interpretation is actually contrary to the apparent meaning."[51] For instance, the woman's anointing of Jesus (Mk 14:3–9) is symbolic because it signifies far more than the woman's love and affection for Jesus it expresses—the preparation for Jesus' burial. The soldiers' crowning of Jesus with thorns (Mk 15:17), on the other hand, is ironic, for what is intended as insult and ridicule actually is homage to a king who reigns through suffering. His cross is his crown. To understand this use of irony and symbolism may require repeated readings of the narrative.

Character

Characters create the movement of events in a story; they are usually people, but animals and other nonhuman entities can also function as characters, such as the serpent in Genesis and the trees in the Book of Judges. Demons and angels are also part of the drama. Nor are characters limited to individuals, since a group can function as a character in the story, like the crowds in the Gospels. Narrative critics distinguish different kinds of characters on the basis of their traits; either they are flat characters or round characters. Flat characters act in ways that are consistent and predictable; round characters appear in shadows and lights, beyond clear and persistent categories. In the Gospels most of the religious leaders are flat characters whose traits fall into a consistent pattern: proud, hypocritical, and self-righteous. The disciples, on the other hand, are round characters, presented as struggling between faith or unbelief, humility or ambition, fidelity

---

[50] See Powell, *What Is Narrative Criticism?* 26–27.
[51] Ibid., 30.

or cowardice. Jesus is a round character; he acts beyond traditional norms, defies social expectations, and turns things upside down with the radicality of his vision. Unlike the disciples, however, he is always portrayed in a positive light, because he consistently espouses God's point of view. The disciples are shown as struggling, staggering, and failing in embracing this point of view.[52]

Many of the views of a narrative are expressed through the characters, their speech, and their fate. The significance and value of the narrative are conveyed to the implied reader through the characters. They arouse and evoke emotions; the implied reader feels what they feel, celebrates their joys, rejoices in their gladness, grieves at their sorrow, journeys with them in their search, and suffers with them in their fates. As the characters arouse sympathy or provoke revulsion, the implied reader cannot be indifferent to them. The principal devices or techniques used in molding characters in scripture are either direct or indirect. The direct shaping or molding of the characters includes a few details about their outward appearance. In scripture the details of outward appearance are not intended to indicate the characters' inner qualities but are solely used as a means to advance the plot or explain its course. For instance, describing Esau as a hairy man and Jacob as a smooth man (Gn 27:11) are important facts for the plot of that story; Jacob deceived his father to get Esau's blessings by impersonating Esau. In the story of Saul and David, Saul is said to be more than a head taller than any of the other people (1 Sm 9:2), and his height is referenced when he is rejected as king by God in 1 Samuel 16:7: "Do not consider his appearance or his height, for I have rejected him. The Lord does not look at the things man looks at. Man looks at the outward appearance, but the Lord looks at the heart." This affirms that in scripture there is usually no connection between a person's external appearance and internal qualities, but if this appearance is referred to, it holds some significance for the plot. This is seen also in the case of Bathsheba, where in a cursory and undetailed way it is said that she is "very beautiful" (2 Sm 11:2), and also of Tamar, the daughter of David, who is also "beautiful" (2 Sm 13:1). In both cases the beauty of the woman is mentioned solely because it is pivotal to the way events unfolded; it is shown to be the reason for the lascivious behavior of the men that spelled their doom.

Beyond their physical appearance, direct characterization can involve an element of judgment given a voice by the narrator or by one of the characters. What is evident is that the trait noted by the

---

[52] Ibid., 51–55.

narrator is extremely important for the development of the plot and is enfleshed by either the action or speech of the character. We read about Noah: "Noah was a righteous man, blameless among the people of his time, and he walked with God" (Gn 6:9). The men of Sodom are characterized as being "wicked, sinning greatly against the Lord" (Gn 13:13). The sons of Eli are described in these terms: "[They] were wicked men; they had no regard for the Lord" (1 Sm 2:12). Direct characterization takes an absolute validity when it is uttered by God. God says to Noah, "I have found you righteous in this generation" (Gn 7:1). God says to Solomon: "I will give you a wise and discerning heart, so that there will never have been anyone like you, nor will there ever be" (1 Kgs 3:12). God says to Satan: "Have you considered my servant Job? There is no one on earth like him; he is blameless and upright, a man who fears God and shuns evil" (Jb 1:8).

Information can also be given about the inner states of characters by one of the other protagonists. It is difficult, however, to determine if this reflects the implied author's objective view. The implied author can portray any one character through the mouth of another character, but it is not easy to say if the implied author identifies with what is being described about this character. Also, when the information about the inner state of a character is given by another character, this is not to be trusted in the same way that one can trust the direct characterization of the omniscient narrator. Drawing conclusions from external signs, such as speech and behavior, one cannot go beyond subjective interpretation. For instance, it is difficult to believe the words of Joab reflected the true state of David, who was overcome by the death of his son Absalom who plotted to revolt against him: "You love those who hate you and hate those who love you. You have made it clear today that the commanders and their men mean nothing to you. I see that you would be pleased if Absalom were alive today and all of us were dead" (2 Sm 19:6). One can detect the exaggeration in Joab's biting words, most likely in his intention to provoke David, who in his depressed state might completely undermine his rule. Though Joab's words reflect his opinion of the king, objectively they are not an accurate assessment of David.

A different literary device for presenting the inner life of characters is exposing their thoughts, calculations, and intentions. The narrator usually precedes the characters' thoughts by the verb *said* or by a phrase like *he said in his heart* or *thought to himself*, since in ancient times thought was considered to be inner, soundless speech. Some examples illustrate this device: "The Lord smelled the pleasing aroma and said in his heart: 'Never again will I curse the ground because of man, even though every inclination of his heart is evil from childhood. And never again will I destroy all living creatures, as I have done'" (Gn 8:21); "Abraham fell face down; he laughed and said to himself, 'Will a son be born to a man a hundred years old? Will Sarah bear a child at the age of ninety?'" (Gn 17:17); "But David thought to himself, 'One of these days I will be destroyed by the hand of Saul. The best thing I can do is to escape to the land of the Philistines. Then Saul will give up searching for me anywhere in Israel, and I will slip out of his hand'" (1 Sm 27:1).

Apart from the characterizations that involve judgments on the moral aspects of individuals, there are also accounts of their mental traits and other facets of their persons. The narrator tells us that Esau is a skillful hunter, a man of the field, while Jacob is a quiet man, dwelling in tents (Gn 25:27); that Moses is "very humble" (Nm 12:3); that there is not a man among the people of Israel finer than Saul (1 Sm 9:2). The reader also receives information about moods that serves to create the personality of characters in the story. "Why are you downhearted?" Elkanah asks his wife Hannah (1 Sm 1:8). The same applies to the question Jezebel asks her husband: "Why are you so sullen?" (1 Kgs 21:5), and to the question God asks Jonah: "Have you any right to be angry?" (Jon 4:4).

Beyond the direct shaping of characters, there is also indirect shaping, which is found in external features, like speech or actions, that indicate something about the individual's inner state. The implied reader has to interpret these details and to construct the characters' mental and emotional state. This requires robust participation by the implied reader in the narrated events. One classic example of speech is that which contains David's grief over the death of his son Absalom. In 2 Samuel 18:33 David cries out, "O my son Absalom, O Absalom, my son, my son." The repetition of "my son" and the name Absalom that he painfully utters intensifies the pathos of the grief that invades his soul. How could one fathom the heart of a father who, despite what his son had done and would have done to him had things come to pass in his murderous plot, has not ceased calling this wretched son his son? And as if that was not enough, David continues: "If only I had died instead of you" (2 Sm 18:33). This defies all logic, that a father would desire to die in the place of a son who plotted to kill him. It dramatizes the tragic relationship of a father and son, full of conflict and contradiction, beyond any kind of resolution in the end except for the inconceivable final word of the father's love.

Besides speech, an indirect shaping of a character in the story is through the character's actions. We can only hypothesize on his or her motives. The action is functional not only relative to the shaping of character but also to the development of the plot. A great deal is learned about characters in the story from the decisions that they make, because this involves choosing among alternatives, which shows the outcome of their moral and spiritual struggle.[53]

The point of view of the narrative as unfolded by the implied author has a powerful rhetorical effect on the implied reader's view of the characters. The point of view of the story places the implied reader in a privileged position from which to observe and judge characters in the unfolding of the events. Empathy, sympathy, and antipathy describe how the implied reader relates to the characters in the story. Since the implied reader of the Gospel favors the evaluative point of view of God, there is empathy for Jesus because he represents perfectly the one who aligns with this point of view. This empathy is called *idealistic empathy,* because Jesus is the one with whom the implied reader shares a commitment to God's evaluative point of view. With Jesus' disciples the implied reader has what is called *realistic empathy* in the sense that while they too are on the side of God's evaluative point of view, they are conflicted and ambivalent. They struggle to grow in understanding of what following Jesus is all about, but they are either slow in getting it right or fail altogether. The literary concept of sympathy is related to that of empathy but implies a less intense identification. The disciples of Jesus are said to be portrayed more harshly in the Gospel of Mark than in that of Matthew. Thus, though the reader may at times empathize with the disciples in Mark (13:4), such an identification is not in its fullest measure. Though feeling less empathy and more sympathy for the disciples in the Gospel of Mark, the implied reader feels the same way as Jesus does for the disciples, with abiding care for them and faith that they will make it to the mark. Antipathy, feelings of alienation from or disdain for particular characters, is created on the basis of the evaluative point of view in the story. In the Gospel this feeling is directed toward the religious leaders, who are shown as lovers of money who reject the purpose of God for them; they trust in themselves and despise others. In narrative criticism the religious leaders are not evaluated in terms of historical reference but in terms of how they align with or fall short of the worldview of the narrative. As strikingly noted by Mark Alan Powell, the implied reader in Luke's Gospel is actually moved to feel sympathy for the religious leaders instead of intense antipathy, as created in Matthew's narrative. According to narrative criticism this

---

[53] See Bar-Efrat, *Narrative Art in the Bible,* 47–92.

should not be taken as evidence that Luke, the real author, was less anti-Semitic than Matthew. That it is more sympathy than antipathy that the readers of Luke's Gospel have for the religious leaders is due to the fact that Luke has a point to make different from that of Matthew.[54] In Luke, the religious leaders

> contribute to the overall effect of the narrative by demonstrating a tragic response to the protagonist Jesus, who nevertheless refuses to give up hope for them, . . . praying, still, for their forgiveness. The intention of God evident in the ministry of Jesus throughout Luke is not to defeat enemies but to reclaim them. Luke's version of the conflict presents the mission of Christ not as a triumph over evil but as a divine offer of grace, peace, and reconciliation. If Luke sometimes makes the leaders look bad, it is not to highlight the greatness of Christ's victory in defeating them, but the greatness of his mercy in forgiving them. Accordingly, the impact of Luke's story on the implied reader is every bit as profound as Matthew's, but it is a different impact. The lasting images in this story are of Jesus weeping over his enemies' failure to accept the peace he brings (19:41–44) and finally, of Jesus nailed to the cross, praying, still, for their forgiveness.[55]

Plot

"If the characters are the soul of the narrative, the plot is the body. It consists of an organized and orderly system of events, arranged in temporal sequence. . . . The plot of a narrative is constructed as a meaningful chain of interconnected events."[56] "It is a coherent sequence of interrelated events, with a beginning, middle, and end. It is, in other words, a whole or complete action."[57] In the plot events are organized in such a way as to evoke interest and emotional involvement. Not all events, however, are of equal importance. Some events are called kernels or core events; woven together they create the logic of the narrative or story. Others, called satellites, could be deleted without losing the sense of the story.

There is also a distinction between story time and discourse time. Story time refers to the timeline created by the implied author in the

---

[54] Powell, *What Is Narrative Criticism?* 56–58.

[55] Ibid., 67.

[56] Bar-Efrat, *Narrative Art in the Bible*, 93.

[57] Morris A. Inch, *Scripture as Story* (Lanham, MD: University Press of America, 2000), 5.

unfolding of story, while discourse time refers to the order in which the events are described by the narrator. Sometimes the narrator gets out of the sequence of events and talks about an event that is going to happen, or retreats back and tells about an event that had already occurred. For example, in the Gospel of Matthew, the implied reader does not know about the murder of John the Baptist until 14:1–2, when suddenly Herod speculates on whether Jesus might be John raised from the dead. Then, when the narrator enters and describes in some details how Herod had John killed, the implied reader sees that the story is being reported out of exact chronological order, as the narrator was made to do by the implied author, because that was part of the narrative's discourse.[58]

Narrative critics are also interested in the duration and frequency with which events occur in a story. Duration refers to the amount of time the narrator devotes to reporting an event; it may be contrary to the time in the story. For instance, the narrator of Luke's Gospel covers several years of Jesus' life in one sentence: "And the child grew and became strong" (2:40). Alternately, an event may be reported by the narrator in the duration of time in which it must have happened, as shown in a detailed account of actions that may qualify as a scene. There are also instances when story time stops while discourse time continues. The narrator "takes time" to explain something to the implied reader and then picks up the story without leaving the implied reader lost within that space of time; the narrator pauses to explain something for the implied reader's better understanding of the story. A good example of this type of pause is found in Mark 7:3–4, where the narrator brings the story of Jesus' conflict with the Pharisees to a halt to take time to put the account against a background that is necessary for the implied reader's understanding.

In relation to the frequency with which a story treats certain events, there are four possible types: singular narration, where an event that happens once is reported once; repetitive narration, when an event that happens once is reported repeatedly, as illustrated for instance by the three accounts of Paul's conversion at Damascus (Acts 9:1–9; 22:4–16; 26:9–18); multiple-singular narration, which reports repeatedly an event that happens repeatedly, as exemplified in the two accounts of religious leaders asking Jesus for a sign (Mt 12:38–45; 16:1–4); and iterative narration, which reports one single time an event that happens repeatedly, an example of which is found in Luke 22:39, where the narrator tells that Jesus went "as usual to the Mount

---

[58] Powell, *What Is Narrative Criticism?* 36–37.

of Olives." The duration and frequency with which events are referred to in the telling of a story are significant because they may constitute signals for the reader to consider in making sense of the text.[59]

To understand the plot of a narrative, it is also important to consider the elements of causality that link events. Causal relationships among events may be subdivided into categories of possibility, probability, and contingency. Possibility refers to instances when an event makes it possible for another to occur; probability refers to an event that makes the occurrence of another more likely; and contingency refers to an instance as the cause of an event. Establishing causal links in the Gospels responds to the inherent need of the implied reader to make sense of why things happen as they do. We see, for instance, how Jesus' disregard for the Sabbath laws and his claim to be the "Lord of the Sabbath" are causally linked to the plotting of his murder (Mt 12:9–14). Similarly, his teaching caused some people to be amazed by his great authority (Mt 7:28–29; 9:8, 33) and others to reject him (Mt 13:53–58).[60] As a whole, the events of the passion narrative present a "great consummation of purpose toward which the other events in the story are directed."[61] Matthew tells the story of Jesus' ministry of teaching, preaching, and healing in a way that explains why Israel rejected and crucified its Messiah.

At the center of the plot is almost always a conflict. Conflict is broadly defined as "a clash of actions, ideas, desires, or wills."[62] The dynamics of conflict seem to be integral to a narrative, for the movement of a story is not possible without conflict. Conflicts may occur at various levels. There may be a conflict between characters arising from opposition of traits or point of view; it may also come between characters and their setting, as in the struggle against their environment. Conflict may take a social dimension, or it may be expressed in an existential personal context. The theme of conflict runs through the Gospels, as pervasive as it is central. Jesus' encounters with the religious leaders of Israel are conflictual, as are some interactions with his disciples. The Gospels present him subduing demonic forces and the forces of disease and death, and at other times overpowering nature as he stills the storm and walks on water. Beyond his conflicts with external forces, he agonizes and struggles within himself in the face of suffering and death. And in all four Gospels there is the continual

---

[59] Ibid., 38–40.

[60] Ibid., 40–42, 46.

[61] Ibid., 80.

[62] Lawrence Perrine and Thomas R. Arp, *Story and Structure*, 4th ed. (New York: Harcourt, Brace, Jovanovich, 1974), 44.

conflict between truth and untruth, belief and unbelief, between the point of view of God and all other points of view.[63]

We have looked at the elements of order, duration and frequency, causation, and conflict in the plot. Now we study the classical pattern of plot development in the biblical narrative. "The plot line ascends from a calm point of departure through the stage of involvement to the climax of conflict and tension and from there rapidly to the finishing point and tranquility."[64] This line of development is found, among other places, in the narrative of the sacrifice of Isaac (Gn 22). The narrator tells us what is about to happen—God tests Abraham's faith by asking him to sacrifice Isaac, his only son. The narrative gradually brings the plot to the climax; first, Abraham makes preparations for sacrificing his son. He sets out early on the journey to the designated place. As he and Isaac climb the mountain, Isaac asks where the lamb to be sacrificed is. Abraham replies, "God himself will provide the lamb," explicating an unfathomable faith in the God of supreme contradiction. In the discourse of the father and son the tension in the story heightens. When they reach the place, Abraham builds the altar, arranges the wood, binds Isaac, and places him on the wood. The narration is done rapidly and succinctly, as if to lock in and mute all the emotions in the intense human drama of the moment. The narrative reaches its peak when Abraham takes the knife and is about to slay his son, and an angel of the Lord calls Abraham to cease the deathly act. A ram is sacrificed in place of Isaac, and God vows that Abraham be richly blessed. From here the line of plot descends rapidly. Abraham returns to his servants, waiting at the foot of the mountain, and they all journey home. Everything appears to return to ordinary, but as a matter of fact, something extraordinary had occurred. Abraham went through a crucible of fire and came out of it as God's servant, the first among many, the man of faith, the father of all nations.[65]

The healing of the man born blind (Jn 9:1–41) is widely recognized as one of the masterpieces of Johannine storytelling. The story line shows in parallel how the "man born blind sees with increasing clarity and those who claim sight plunge into progressively deepening darkness."[66] The scene begins with Jesus healing the man of his blindness, which becomes the key conflict in the story. Whether the

---

[63] See Powell, *What Is Narrative Criticism?* 42–43.

[64] Bar-Efrat, *Narrative Art in the Bible,* 121.

[65] Ibid., 122.

[66] Charles H. Talbert, *Reading John: A Literary and Theological Commentary on the Fourth Gospel and the Johannine Epistles* (New York: Crossroad, 1992), 158.

healer was from God or was a sinner who healed on the Sabbath and broke the Law is at the heart of the story. The plot builds to the climax through the interrogation scenes: the neighbors interrogate the blind man, the Pharisees interrogated the blind man, the Pharisees interrogated the parents, and the Pharisees interrogated the blind man for the second time. In a bold display of courage the blind man challenged the Pharisees with the evidence of his healing: "I was blind but now I see." That the Pharisees refused to accept the clear fact of his healing shows their unbelief. He held that if Jesus were a sinner, then God would not have listened to him and would have not made possible through him the miracle of restoring his sight. The Pharisees, by focusing on sin, did not see God at work in the miraculous gift of sight. They only saw a sinner. The final action of the Pharisees was what the blind man's parents had feared for themselves: they expelled the young man from the synagogue. Reaching this climactic point of the tension and conflict, the story descends to a tranquil end. Jesus enters the scene. He was present at the beginning of the story and at the end, but it was as if he were present throughout as the focus of the conflict. Jesus encountered the young man twice in the story, and both times the man was an outcast. The first time he was a blind beggar by the roadside. Jesus gave him sight. This second time he was thrown out of the synagogue. More than the gift of sight, Jesus gave him the gift of his person. The response of the man to Jesus' invitation was immediate and without doubt. His faith was the opposite of the rejection of the Pharisees. They refused to believe what they had seen; he believed. When Jesus revealed who he was, the healed man bowed down to worship him.[67]

Most biblical narratives follow this classical pattern; the story line gradually rises to a climax and then descends to its serene conclusion. Some stories, however, include what is called an illusory conclusion. A narrative that has this structural feature does not end after the gradual ascent and the rapid decline. It rises once more to another pinnacle. Only then does it descend to the genuine conclusion. This is exemplified in the story of Job. The tension in the Job narrative comes from the uncertainty about whether Job would pass the trial. The story reaches its peak with the death of all his children. Job's response, founded on his unwavering righteousness, causes a calm turn; he passed the test. At this point, with Job having preserved his

---

[67] See Thomas L. Brodie, *The Gospel According to John: A Literary and Theological Commentary* (New York: Oxford University Press, 1993), 343–57; Moloney, *The Gospel of John*, 290–99; and Barnabas Lindars, *The Gospel of John* (Grand Rapids, MI: Eerdmans, 1981), 341–52.

integrity, the narrative could come to an end. But the plot flares up again in the face of another disaster that overtakes Job, shaking into total disarray what was coming to a resolution in the narrative. Once again Job emerges a victor, but the final tranquility is not attained until the last chapter of the book, when God restores Job's fortunes, double what he has lost.[68]

An illusory conclusion also is found in the narrative of the story of Esau and Jacob. After the conspiracy of Rebecca and Jacob to deceive Isaac has come to fruition, with Jacob getting the desired blessing, the tension in the narrative drops and tranquility reigns. But the narrative does not end; no sooner has Jacob left than Esau enters and the tension and suspense regain their intensity. Tranquility comes only after Jacob departs from home and distance comes between him and Esau. Only after twenty years was complete serenity attained when the two brothers were finally reconciled.[69]

As delineated in the treatment of narrative criticism, the literary devices of point of view, character, and plot, and the literary functions of the implied author, narrator, and implied reader all provide signals in the text for reading the story in a way that its depths and richness may be plumbed for moral vision.

A Critical Appraisal of Narrative Criticism

Reading scripture using the literary principles and devices of narrative criticism has opened new avenues for using scripture in meaningful and effective ways. Any approach to interpreting scripture is not without hermeneutical implications both positive and negative. A critical appraisal of narrative criticism recognizes what it can do and what it cannot do, without pitting it defensively (or offensively) against other methodologies. I explore perspectives of narrative criticism here based primarily on Mark Allan Powell's summation of its benefits and objections to it.

Positive Assessment of Narrative Criticism

Narrative criticism is text focused. It understands scripture on its own terms. It reads and studies scripture itself, not reading and studing about scripture. This is not to say that the social and historical circumstances surrounding the scriptural narrative are of no importance.

---

[68] Bar-Efrat, *Narrative Art in the Bible*, 125.
[69] Ibid., 123.

The method itself requires that one become deeply engaged with the text, be absorbed by its world, with the text serving as its own context and the passages read in the light of the narrative outside its stages of composition or its source strata. It avoids technical questions about the origin or historicity of a text or narrative that have found no real or final resolution among scholars, focusing on the "given," which is the text itself.[70]

Narrative criticism provides an alternative method of interpretation that can serve as a check on traditional methods. For instance, historical critics have often held that Mark's portrayal of the disciples in a negative way was due to the polemical stance he took against the original disciples of Jesus. But narrative critics, while they do not inquire into the historical intentions of a work's real author, claim that the effect of Mark's portrayal as gleaned from the text itself is the opposite—rather than animosity it arouses the reader's sympathy for the disciples. Since historical criticism cannot have a singular claim on a correct and truthful interpretation of scripture, an alternative interpretation offered by narrative criticism opens a viable dialogue on the matter.[71]

It has been said that the historical-critical method took scripture from the common and general reader and put it in the exclusive enclaves of scholars and professional theologians.[72] This critique is based on historical criticism's presupposition that scripture cannot be properly understood without a specialized knowledge of the origin, transmission, and editorial revision of its contents. Brevard Childs remarks: "The danger is acute of losing the biblical text in a mountain of endless historical and philological notes."[73] Students and readers using narrative criticism must know the principles and techniques of literary criticism. But narrative criticism's creation of the implied reader within the text itself frees the interpretation of scripture from knowledge of the origin and sources of scripture in relation to its setting. Narrative criticism offers a method of engaging the text in a way that scripture comes alive, yields a meaning that makes sense, and touches the reader's mind, heart, and imagination. This modifies the claims of scholarship and restates the value of the "plain sense"

---

[70] Powell, *What Is Narrative Criticism?* 85–86.

[71] Ibid., 86–87.

[72] Colin E. Gunton, *Enlightenment and Alienation: An Essay Towards a Trinitarian Theology* (Grand Rapids, MI: Eerdmans, 1985), 111.

[73] Brevard S. Childs, *The New Testament as Canon: An Introduction* (Philadelphia: Fortress Press, 1984), 548.

of scripture.[74] This benefit of narrative criticism, however, should not be overstated to the diminishment of historical criticism as a method. It would be naive to say that the perspective of modern readers is the same as that of the implied readers of the Gospels; Matthew's implied reader, for example, apparently accepts the social institution of slavery (8:9; 10:24–25). This shows that narrative criticism has its limitations and that modern readers of the scriptures who appreciate this method should draw from scholarly work in historical criticism in order to understand the perspective from which a text is to be critically read.[75]

Narrative criticism has made scripture more available to the believing community, in the sense that it focuses more on the intended literary effects of scripture on the readers rather than on its historical references. It treats the texts in a manner that is consistent with the Christian understanding of the canon, in that scripture itself is authoritative rather than the oral traditions or primary sources that stand behind it. Besides its fidelity to the canonical truth of scripture, it also emphasizes the Christian doctrine of the Spirit, which holds that revelation is an event that continues to happen now and is present in the very encounter of the reader with the text of scripture, where the Spirit is active in the process of interpretation.[76] Despite the huge amount of work that historical criticism has produced, "the relationship between the historical consciousness that this method requires and the faith of those on whose behalf it is employed has never been an easy one."[77] As Alan Culpepper puts it: "Historical investigation demands skepticism and offers in the end only a reconstruction of the evidence that is more or less probable."[78] Narrative criticism, by interpreting texts from the point of view of their own implied readers, can offer an interpretation from a faith perspective. Appreciating narrative criticism, however, does not mean invalidating the historical-critical method or denying valid criticism. As Mark Allan Powell puts it, "Employment of narrative criticism as a means of avoiding difficult or controversial issues is a misuse of the methodology. Mature theological reflection demands both appreciation for the faith perspective evident in the

---

[74] "The phrase is roughly equivalent to what Luther meant by 'the literal meaning' of scripture" (Powell, *What Is Narrative Criticism?* 120n6); and Kathryn E. Tanner, "Theology and the Plain Sense," in *Scriptural Authority and Narrative Interpretation*, ed. Garrett Green, 59–78 (Philadelphia: Fortress Press, 1987).

[75] Powell, *What Is Narrative Criticism?* 87–88.

[76] Ibid., 88.

[77] Ibid.

[78] Alan Culpepper, "Story and History in the Gospels," *Review and Expositor* (1984): 467–78, esp. 473.

implied readers of the Gospels and consideration for the skepticism demanded by modern historical consciousness."[79]

Narrative criticism offers potential for bringing scholarship of different persuasions and believing communities together. This is so because the method does not begin with questions of historicity, which are often contentious and in many instances have not reached final resolutions. Thus, without first coming to an agreement on any number of intractable historical issues, scholars and members of believing communities can agree on the literary meaning of the scripture as unfolded in the texts.[80] This coming together might be perceived as avoiding the elephant in the room, but there is a value in being enriched by one another's insights while agreeing to disagree on some critical issues. Other forms of interpretation can also be used, because while narrative criticism holds that the text itself sets parameters for interpretation, it recognizes there may be gaps in the text that cause ambiguity. The presence of these gaps makes it necessary to seek the best interpretation relative to what the implied reader would most likely adopt. Some narrative critics in this instance begin to move in the direction of reader-response criticism, as the ambiguities show that a text can be read in more ways than one. This opens avenues for accepting views of other methods of interpretation.[81]

Narrative criticism also offers fresh interpretations of biblical material for personal and social transformation, as stories have the power to speak in ways that can engage people of all times and places. There is a growing and increasing appreciation of scholars for the power of stories in engaging, challenging, and inspiring the way people perceive themselves and view the world. Perhaps this is so because there is a narrative quality to all of life, and stories have a way of linking us in a profound way to life itself. This is what some suggest that modern biblical scholarship has failed to do, as it has tended to reduce the interaction with scripture to the rational level, robbing the reader of

---

[79] Powell, *What Is Narrative Criticism?* 89.

[80] Tremper Longman, for instance, endorses modern literary study of the Bible while maintaining that the text is also referential—in fact, "inerrant"—in its historical representation. Sallie McFague, on the other hand, favors literary approaches to the Bible because she regards the Bible as authoritative only in that it is a literary class that continues to speak to us. See Tremper Longman III, "Storytellers and Poets in the Bible: Can Literary Artifice Be True?" in *Inerrancy and Hermeneutic: A Tradition, A Challenge, A Debate*, ed. Harvie M. Conn, 137–49 (Grand Rapids, MI: Baker Book House, 1988); Sallie McFague, *Speaking in Parables* (Philadelphia: Fortress Press, 1975); and idem, *Metaphorical Theology: Models of God in Religious Language* (Philadelphia: Fortress Press, 1982).

[81] Powell, *What Is Narrative Criticism?* 89.

the fascinating encounter with the text itself, its beauty, depth, and splendor.[82] "Both historical investigation and doctrinal abstraction reify the biblical stories; they tear the message from its narrative context and force it into categories of thought that can never contain the distinctiveness, fascination, and authenticity of the stories themselves."[83] Narrative criticism brings us, the real and historical readers, to the very source of the life and vitality of faith—the stories of the Bible themselves, remembered, treasured, and interpreted within their narrative form.[84] It is unfortunate when discussion degenerates into debate regarding which should be given primacy—biblical stories or doctrinal abstraction about them. What needs to be stressed is that there is something about stories that cannot be captured in doctrinal formulations. Narrative criticism adds a dimension to biblical studies that is one essential component of the total theological enterprise.[85] Biblical literary criticism is in step with parallel movements in systematic theology and practical theology, which are rediscovering the power of narrative. This direction is represented by story theology, story preaching, and in pastoral care, personal story. Narrative criticism that espouses a story approach to scripture provides avenues for integrating with the story approaches in other theological disciplines.[86]

Negative Assessment of Narrative Criticism

Despite the rich rewards of using narrative criticism, it has provoked some objections concerning the legitimacy and validity of using it for studying scripture, particularly the Gospels, from the literary point of view, and from the perspectives of historical criticism and contextual biblical pedagogy.

Narrative criticism is criticized for imposing on ancient literature concepts drawn from the study of modern literature. This may have a basis, because there are certain elements in modern literary theory that may not be applicable to biblical literature. At the same time, however, there are some conventions of storytelling that are timeless, in that they are inherent in a story, which means that whether ancient or modern, stories consist of events, characters, and settings told from a particular point of view. Ancient literature provides classic examples of conventions and archetypes of storytelling found in the Gospels.

---

[82] Ibid., 90.
[83] Ibid., 90–91.
[84] Culpepper, "Story and History in the Gospels," 471.
[85] Powell, *What Is Narrative Criticism?* 91.
[86] Ibid.

Certainly one cannot assume that biblical writers had knowledge of some modern literary concepts, devices, and terminologies, but for as long as this is considered and remembered, narrative criticism that is consonant with the timeless conventions of storytelling is valid. This is a similar argument to the objection that narrative criticism seeks to interpret the Gospels through methods that were devised for the study of fiction. To the extent, for instance, that genres of novels and gospels share a narrative form, both are subject to narrative analysis. And this is held outside of any evaluation of the integrity and reliability of the historical references of the Gospels.[87]

Narrative criticism is criticized for treating the Gospels as coherent narratives when they are actually collections of disparate materials that were strung together like "pearls on a string." Unrelated elements were juxtaposed in a linear sequence, creating "the impression of narrative," but such an illusion was accidental. This is a position held by proponents of form criticism. Redaction critics, however, have discovered pervasive unifying features that can be found in each of the Gospels, and literary critics have furthered this research by exposing a surprising coherence of narrative elements.[88] Roland Mushat Frye, a scholar of literature, has concluded on the basis of his examination of the four Gospels that each appears to be "a narrative of considerable literary merit, in which diverse materials have been so effectively integrated that each Gospel should be treated as a literary work in its own right."[89] Still, some fault narrative criticism for dismissing too easily the inconsistencies in the Gospels and ignoring the "cracks and crevices" that occur in the Gospels as a result of the disparate materials and sources that are strung together.[90]

Proponents of narrative criticism hold that this critique misses the whole point of its methodology. The validity of the methodology does not presume a narrative unity in the Gospels that must be ascertained on the basis of the analysis of the material content. Rather, it is something that can be assumed. The very form of the narratives of the Gospels is what gives them coherence regardless of the disparate materials that constitute their narrative form. This assumes that the very illusion of a narrative that was apparent even to the form critics is sufficient

---

[87] Ibid., 93–94.

[88] Ibid., 91–92.

[89] Roland Mushat Frye, "A Literary Perspective for the Criticism of the Gospels," in *Jesus and Man's Hope*, ed. Donald G. Miller and Dikran Y. Hadidian, 192–221 (Pittsburgh: Pittsburgh Theological Seminary, 1971), esp. 220n42.

[90] Stephen Moore, "Are the Gospels Unified Narratives?" *SBL* 1987 seminar papers (Atlanta: Scholars Press, 1987), 443–58.

for what is required for narrative criticism. From the perspective of the implied reader, it makes no difference whether the gospel narratives were created from disparate materials, or if they were created intentionally or accidentally. The form of the narrative is a given; it is there, and the reader must treat it as is. Even the inconsistencies are part of the narrative and are facets that are to be interpreted.[91] The discourse on the validity of narrative criticism comes down to one central question: "whether the poetic function of the Gospels in the form that we now have them is a worthwhile subject for investigation. If it is, the somewhat complex processes that led to the composition of the Gospels will not inhibit the undertaking of such research."[92]

Narrative criticism is also criticized as lacking objective criteria for the analysis of texts. This is a critique of literary criticism in general based on the claim of historical criticism that the validity of an interpretation is governed by the authorial intention as determinate of a definitive original meaning of the text.[93] Historical criticism, however, is criticized for this univocal and hegemonic claim based on authorial intention. The fact that narrative criticism proposes that a text can have a multiplicity of meanings makes it a target of this critique of historical criticism. What is held objectionable by proponents of the historical-critical method is the sort of subjective reading that is encouraged by the literary-critical method, as some types of this method are largely centered on the responses of readers to the text. Narrative criticism, while claiming that texts can have multiple meanings, holds that they must be validated by the text itself. Being a text-centered approach, it is bound by the parameters of the text. Thus, while a narrative-critical reading may propose a much broader interpretation of a text beyond that which a historical-critical reading determines, it is not a capricious reading that runs counter to what can reasonably be established in the text. The text exercises a veto power, so to speak, and thus there are certain interpretations that simply cannot be maintained. Narrative criticism evaluates its interpretations according to objective criteria determined by the intention of the text rather than by the intention of the author. The text, of course, includes what narrative criticism calls the implied author, but even this literary device is integral to the text itself. When it comes down to what method is more accessible for evaluation, narrative criticism goes back to the text

---

[91] Powell, *What Is Narrative Criticism?* 92.

[92] Ibid., 93.

[93] Christopher Mark Tuckett, *Reading the New Testament: Methods of Interpretation* (Philadelphia: Fortress Press, 1987), 174–75.

itself as the very basis of its interpretation, a text that is open for any contemporary inquiry or discourse. The traditional historical-critical investigation actually is more conjectural, because no contemporary access to the real authors of the biblical books is possible; thus, any reconstruction of their authors' intentions is bound to be hypothetical.[94]

The most pervasive of the objections to narrative criticism for biblical accounts is that it undermines the historical grounding of the Christian faith in the Gospels by treating them not as testimonies to God's action in history, as reliable records of salvation history, but as literary works having intrinsic worth in and of themselves, apart from any historical accounting of the events they describe.[95] In response to this objection it must be held, first of all, that in using a different method, narrative criticism should be judged according to the nature and integrity of its methods. It is not its goal to establish the legitimacy or lack of legitimacy of the historicity of the events narrated in the Gospels. That is outside of its expertise. Thus, to say that narrative criticism undermines the historical grounding of the Gospels is overstating what narrative criticism can or cannot do. It does not deal with the Gospels in the same way as the historical-critical method does, and the validity of its methods must not be judged against the historical-critical criteria. The critique that narrative criticism is insufficient for the full task of interpretation is a fair assessment, but that is true of any other approach. No one approach is sufficient for the full task of interpretation.

How can narrative criticism work with historical criticism to realize the full task of interpretation? Francis Moloney writes that, given the fact that scripture is historically and culturally conditioned, there is inevitably something "strange" and "foreign" about the text that demands that we wrestle with it. The world behind the text must be respected and studied in order to understand the strange distance of this world and the world in front of the text. And although from the view of narrative criticism, the real historical author and the reader(s) do not play an active role in the events in the narrative, they leave their traces.[96] In this light, narrative criticism must require that modern readers who engage in this method draw from historical-critical scholarship the data that have a bearing on the interpretation of the text. Iser refers to the "reader's repertoire" as that which comprises all the data and information necessary for a full interpretation of the

---

[94] Powell, *What Is Narrative Criticism?* 95–96.

[95] Ibid., 96.

[96] Moloney, *The Gospel of John*, 18, 14.

scriptural work.[97] This may be information regarding the historical world of the story, the social and political realities that lie behind it, and the social and cultural customs implied in the discourse and characterizations. It is possible that narrative criticism, rather than undermining the historicity of the Gospels, may contribute to their historical understanding. Kingsbury has suggested that the story world of the Gospels may prove to be an "index" of the world of the evangelist, and the implied reader may well prove to be an "index" of the real readers for whom the Gospels were originally intended.[98] If the authors of the Gospels were successful, then the intention of the text discerned by narrative criticism may indicate by some reliable index the intention of the author that is sought by historical criticism. For instance, if narrative criticism shows a basic sympathy in the Gospel of Mark toward the disciples, despite their failings, it is likely that it reflects accurately the intention of the real author. From likeliness to certainty is a hermeneutical leap, but not a great one. Thus, rather than a conflictual relationship, one that is symbiotic should exist between the narrative-critical methods and the methods of historical criticism. If the story of Jesus is held by Christians as the very basis of their life of faith, it is not only because it is a meaningful story, but also because it is a story that is also rooted in history. If the meaning of this story is to have a real hold on the minds and hearts of Christians, it must be treated in such a way that it can engage them at a depth, as any story can.[99]

Contextual biblical pedagogy has emerged from an awareness of Christianity as a global religion that has undergone profound shifts in numbers away from the West and toward the two-thirds world, among a plurality of peoples and cultures, and from diverse social locations. A contextual biblical pedagogy has two basic driving forces at its core. First, it takes diversity to heart—diversity in texts, diversity in reading and interpretation, diversity in readers. And second, it brings the voices from the margins fully into the discourse, which challenges the univocal and hegemonic claims of biblical pedagogies of the past. Contextual biblical pedagogy challenges narrative criticism's concept of implied author and implied reader. It is fair to say that in narrative

---

[97] See Wolfgang Iser, *The Implied Reader: Patterns of Communication in Prose Fiction from Bunyan to Beckett* (Baltimore: Johns Hopkins University Press, 1974).

[98] J. D. Kingsbury, "Reflections on the 'Reader' of Matthew's Gospel," *New Testament Studies* 34 (1988): 459.

[99] Powell, *What Is Narrative Criticism?* 97–98.

criticism, the reader remains faceless. Although narrative criticism is open to the concept of a plurality of interpretations, this concept is still circumscribed by the constraints imposed by the text. It does not challenge the text and its ideological stance, as a feminist reading, for instance, would challenge a patriarchal worldview built into the text. Narrative criticism is abstracted from the presuppositions and social locations of actual readers of the text, because its methodology uses a constructed reader within the text itself. In a sense, narrative criticism, like cultural criticism, is subject to the same objections to historical criticism as a biblical pedagogy. All three tend toward a univocal and universal meaning but from different frameworks. All three also represent the period of biblical criticism when a relationship between biblical interpretation and the social location of interpreters and actual readers was nonexistent.

Historical criticism called for the historical contextualization of the text and objectivity on the part of the reader. The univocal meaning of the text located in the author's intention could be retrieved with the use of the right methodological tools, which could turn students and readers, regardless of their sociocultural moorings or theological persuasion, into informed and universal teachers and critics. Narrative criticism, regardless of its use of the concept of a reader-construct, is abstracted from real readers and their presuppositions. While the constraints of the text determine its interpretation, the claim of the text eventually cannot be univocal, as more attention is placed on the possibility of multiple interpretations. And the faceless-reader construct meets the growing challenge of real readers who made claims on the meaning of the text from their own perspectives and social locations.[100] For cultural criticism, which is more akin to historical criticism than literary criticism, the meaning of the text is located primarily in the world behind it, with analysis of text, author, and readers in terms of their participation in this world. Certain distinctions, however, are made regarding the readers behind the model of cultural criticism. Within the socioeconomic approach represented by neo-Marxist criticism, the reader is by no means faceless. Just as the text is considered an ideological product, and thus a site of struggle, so the critic. The task of criticism is not neutral or impartial but ideological to the core. The critical reader is viewed as committed to the side of the oppressed in the struggle for the cause of liberation. Within the sociological approach informed by the sociology of religion, the reader

---

[100] Segovia, *Decolonizing Biblical Studies*, 20–22.

remains faceless—a universal and informed critic taking a position of neutrality and impartiality regarding the text.[101]

It was inevitable that all three biblical methodologies would wrestle with real flesh-and-blood readers who would be determinant in the reenvisioning of biblical critical pedagogy, in the shift of location of meaning of the text, and in the role of presuppositions and worldviews of critics and readers. No one methodology could claim hermeneutical privilege; rather, a meta-theory is needed, a grasp of theory not only within one discipline, but across the disciplinary spectrum.

Toward a Contextual Biblical Theology

While the meaning of the text is located in the text in narrative criticism, and in the author of the text or the world behind the text in historical criticism and cultural criticism, contextual biblical pedagogy locates it in the interchange between text and reader. For the contextual model the reader is not constructed but real. The meaning resides between this reader, socially and historically conditioned, and the text, which is also socially and historically conditioned.[102] The text is not something "out there" with a univocal meaning that cuts across all times and all places; rather, it is to be read and interpreted by a multiplicity of readers and audiences. Since the meaning of the text resides in the interchange between the text and the reader, a text is bereft of meaning without a reader or interpreter. While there are a multiplicity of interpretations, just as there are a multiplicity of readers, this does not create a situation where "anything goes," since readers and interpreters are always engaged in ever-shifting possibilities of meanings in the spirit of critical dialogue.[103]

It is the crucial role taken by flesh-and-blood readers that distinguishes contextual pedagogy so sharply from the other pedagogies. It calls for critical analysis of real readers, who are not seen as neutral or impartial but inextricably positioned in their own social locations, from which they either construct or deconstruct the meaning of a text or texts. These social locations are defined by various constitutive factors of human identity: sexuality and gender; socioeconomic class; race and ethnicity; sociopolitical status and affiliation; socio-educational background and level; socio-religious background and

---

[101] Ibid., 24, 26.

[102] What I call contextual biblical pedagogy, Segovia calls cultural studies. See Segovia, *Decolonizing Biblical Studies*, 42.

[103] Ibid., 45–46.

affiliation; ideological stance. With the emergence of different readers with a multiplicity of voices, contextual biblical pedagogy calls for a complete rethinking and reformulation of biblical pedagogy, discourse, and practice. Unlike the traditional pedagogies, readers are not called to put aside their "faces" and suppress their voices, but on the contrary to allow their faces to show and their voices to be heard, for the Word of God is addressed to them, for their liberation and transformation.[104]

To illustrate how a meaning of a text or texts is interpreted by readers from their social locations, I present examples of how readers defined by their socioeconomic status, their gender, and their race/ethnicity reconstitute the meaning of some selected texts. *The Interpretation of the Bible in the Church* states that the interpretation of a text is influenced by the mindset and worldview of its readers. This brings points of view to the work of interpretation that are "new and responsive to contemporary currents of thought which have not up till now been taken sufficiently into consideration" (I-E). But it warns that bringing these points of view must be done with critical discernment.

Reading from the Eyes of the Disenfranchised

To illustrate a reading of scripture from the eyes of the disenfranchised, we use as an example from Exodus 20:8–10: "Remember the sabbath day, and keep it holy. Six days you shall labor and do all your work. But the seventh day is a sabbath to the Lord your God; you shall not do any work." If we are part of the dominant culture we see that to obey the commandment is good for our spiritual life because we carve a special day of our busy lives to devote to our worship of our God with the faith community. It is also good for our family life, because we reserve a day in a week to deepen our family bonds by spending the day with one another and sharing a meal as family. It is likewise good for our health to find rest for our mind and spirit to renew our strength and energy. Such an interpretation would be a soothing balm to most white, middle-class, or upper-class people.[105]

But how would this text be read through the eyes of the disenfranchised? How would this be preached from the underside of the US economic system? Does working six days a week and resting on the seventh day mean anything to millions who are without work or to those who have to take all the odd jobs they can find, Sunday or not, for their sheer survival? When this text is read from the position

---

[104] Ibid., 46–49.

[105] Miguel A. De La Torre, *Reading the Bible from the Margins* (Maryknoll, NY: Orbis Books, 2002), 6–7.

of economic privilege, we assume that we can take off a day without worry or anxiety about our next meal. That is not the situation of those living at the margins, whose life is a day-to-day struggle.

By listening to the voices of the marginalized and disenfranchised of society, we are confronted by society's vast social inequalities.[106] Could it be that theose who observe this commandment are in fact betraying the God they worship by their complicit participation in an unjust economic system that leaves so many without basic human necessities? Thus, the interpretation of the text is radically changed when it is read from the margins, with the eyes of the disenfranchised. And when reading it from their eyes, those who live lives of economic privilege are called to what true worship of God means. In the words of Amos:

> Alas for you who desire the day of the Lord!
>   Why do you want the day of the Lord?
> It is darkness, not light; . . .
> Is not the day of the Lord darkness, not light,
>   and gloom with no brightness in it?
> I hate, I despise your festivals,
>   and I take no delight in your solemn assemblies.
> Even though you offer me your burnt offerings and
>   grain offerings,
>   I will not accept them;
> and the offerings of well-being of your fatted animals
>   I will not look upon.
> Take away from me the noise of your songs;
>   I will not listen to the melody of your harps.
> But let justice roll down like waters,
>   and righteousness like an ever-flowing stream.
>   (Amos 5:18, 20–24)

The account of the birth of Jesus is also different when read from the eyes of the disenfranchised. Only those who know what it means to live in poverty understand the birth of Jesus in all its realness. The radicalness of the incarnation is that God chose to become poor. Jesus chose to be one among the disenfranchised. He was born, lived, and died in poverty. Our nativity scene has been sanitized. We view the baby Jesus resting comfortably in a crib made of wood while animals look down upon him and kings and shepherds come to worship him.

---

[106] Ibid., 7.

However, based on the stories of Matthew and Luke, Jesus was born in a manger, a wooden box or hole carved out of the cave wall for food for horses and cattle. Mary gave birth to Jesus in the same dirty, smelly place where animals gave birth to their offspring.[107] This reality is not lost on the poor of the earth. It is a reality they live every day. Many have no access to one of the most basic of human needs—clean water. They live in squalid conditions not befitting human beings.

To see Jesus from the social location of the poor is to see him in deep solidarity with the marginalized. He is not only on the side of the poor; he *is* poor. For many who read the Bible from the margins, Jesus' poverty is attested by the sacrifice offered by his parents at his birth. According to Luke, "When the time came for their purification according to the law of Moses, they brought him up to Jerusalem to present him to the Lord. . . . And they offered a sacrifice according to what is stated in the law of the Lord, 'a pair of turtledoves or two young pigeons.'" According to the twelfth chapter of Leviticus, Mary was required to offer a lamb, but she was only able to make the offering of the poor—two turtledoves or two young pigeons.[108]

As an itinerant preacher Jesus lived the life of a poor man. Referring to himself Jesus says, "Foxes have holes, and birds of the air have nests; but the Son of Man has nowhere to lay his head" (Lk 9:58). And referring to himself as the good shepherd, he aligned himself with those without any social status at all. Shepherds live in the wilderness, outside of cities, the centers of culture and civilization. Usually they put their lives on the line for someone else's flock, not their own. Jesus' origins also tell us his social status. He did not come from Jerusalem but from Galilee, whose people were looked down upon as belonging to a low and inferior class—a place from which nothing good can come. This is attested in John 1:46, when Nathaniel, one of Jesus' future disciples, upon learning Jesus was from Nazareth, showed his contempt by saying, "Can anything good come out of Nazareth?" To see the person, life, and mission of Jesus from the margins is to understand the hermeneutical privilege of the poor and disenfranchised. They are in a position to grasp who God is, in God's very essence, as a God of compassionate and merciful solidarity.[109]

Naming this contextual reading a liberationist approach, *The Interpretation of the Bible in the Church* praises it for its undoubted value. Starting from its own sociocultural and political point of view,

---

[107] Ibid., 109.
[108] Ibid.
[109] Ibid., 110.

the liberationist approach interprets scripture in a way that addresses the needs of the people who seek nourishment for their faith and their life. This approach is not focused solely on what the text said in its original context but on the situation of a people here and now. In a situation of oppression the Bible is sought for support through suffering and struggles. It provides the inspiration for authentic Christian praxis, which leads to social transformation through works of justice and love (I-E1).

The foundational beliefs at the base of this liberation approach are that God is the God of the poor, who takes sides on their behalf, and who is at the heart of the struggle to liberate the oppressed. *The Interpretation of the Bible in the Church* states:

> Because the liberation of the oppressed is a communal process, the community of the poor is the privileged addressee of the Bible as word of liberation. Moreover, since the biblical texts were written for communities, it is to communities in the first place that the reading of the Bible has been entrusted. The word of God is fully relevant—above all because of the capacity inherent in the "foundational events" (the exodus from Egypt, the passion and resurrection of Jesus) for finding fresh realization again and again in the course of history. (I-E1)

The "Conclusion" in the same document notes that a singular focus on narrative and prophetic texts which highlight situations of oppression can lead to the neglect of other texts of the Bible. While exegesis should not be neutral, it must also take care not to become one-sided. Certain streams of liberation theology engage in social analysis inspired by materialist doctrines, and use them as a frame of reference for reading the Bible. This is a practice that the document considers very questionable because it involves the Marxist principle of class struggle. The proponents of the liberationist approach must contemplate the coherence of its hermeneutical presuppositions and methods with the faith and the tradition of the church as a whole.

A Feminist Reading of Scripture

The interaction of scripture and the changing thought in our contemporary world has brought about tensions and conflicts, one of the most pervasive of which emerged from feminist consciousness. The sharpest of these is expressed in a critical question on the very nature of scripture as a revelatory text: How can a text that contains so much that is damaging to women function authoritatively in the Christian community as normative of faith and life? Elements of scripture are androcentric (maleness as normative humanity), patriarchal (male domination), and sexist (discriminatory and oppressive of women). This critical question has located a theologically substantive problem, one which must be dealt with honestly and rigorously by the best scholarship possible. Liberationist feminism starts with the assumption that the text is not neutral but is written with a bias, and thus a hermeneutics of suspicion must be employed.[110] The realization of the liberationist message is the freedom of women from patriarchal domination so that they stand as equal partners of men in the transformation of the social order. The starting point and theological framework of liberationist feminism is liberation theology with a clear and explicit advocacy for women. The stance it takes is not reformative but radical, as its hermeneutic is not merely a matter of reinterpretation of the biblical text within a patriarchal framework but a total restructuring of its premises and expressions. The hermeneutical principle that governs its theology of revelation and salvation has the full humanity of women and whatever promotes it as its central norm. This is an empowered and an empowering hermeneutics for women against a long history of patriarchal domination and violence.

The feminist liberationist model envisions the liberation of the oppressed through the transformation of society, a vision that it shares with all liberation theology. But specific to its vision of liberation is its claim that the scriptural text itself must be liberated from its own participation in the oppression of women, the degradation of female sexuality, and the marginalization of women, legitimization of their oppression, and trivialization of their experience.[111] Beyond merely revising the text, the feminist liberationists have constructed an alternative vision of liberation.

---

[110] A variant of the liberationist approach is the hermeneutical-contextual approach of Sandra Schneiders, who sees the experience of oppressed women as a privileged reference point from which to judge what are emancipatory and oppressive interpretations of biblical texts. See, for example, Sandra M. Schneiders, *The Revelatory Text: Interpreting the New Testament as Sacred Scripture*, 2nd ed. (Collegeville, MN: Liturgical Press, 1999), 182; and idem, "Feminist Ideology Criticism and Biblical Hermeneutics," *Biblical Theology Bulletin* 19 (1989): 3–10.

[111] Elisabeth Schüssler Fiorenza radically evaluates the biblical text as a product of patriarchal hermeneutics that has denied the rightful claim of women of their historical and biblical heritage. See *In Memory of Her: A Feminist Theological Reconstruction of Christian Origins* (New York: Crossroad, 1983), 105–54.

The women in the Hebrew Bible were regarded as possessions of men; they existed to fill men's physical, emotional, and sexual needs. They served as vessels to carry the seeds of men. Thus, the ultimate shame for a woman was incapacity to give birth; her highest honor was to give birth to great holy men (not women). The shame of barrenness was worse than death itself.

When women in scripture defy the mores of society by creating an identity for themselves other than what men have prescribed for them, their reputation is destroyed. For example, Mary of Magdala has always been regarded as a prostitute, yet nowhere in the Bible does it say that she was. According to all three Synoptic Gospels (Mt 27:55–56; Mk 15:40–41; Lk 24:10) Mary of Magdala was held as first among Jesus' female disciples. Her role must have been of some primacy (along with other women) to be considered equal to the twelve male apostles.[112] In Luke's Gospel we read:

> Soon afterwards he went on through cities and villages, proclaiming and bringing the good news of the kingdom of God. The twelve were with him, as well as some women who had been cured of evil spirits and infirmities: Mary, called Magdalene, from whom seven demons had gone out, and Joanna, the wife of Herod's steward Chuza, and Susanna, and many others, who provided for them out of their resources. (Lk 8:1–3)

In several apocryphal New Testament writings (for example, the Gospel of Philip), Mary is reported to be an apostle, one who received revelation from the risen Christ. Contrary to 1 Corinthians 15:4–6, which honors Peter as the first witness of the resurrection, Mary of Magdala was the first person to whom the risen Christ appeared and the first person to announce the good news of the resurrection (Mk 16:9–10). In both the biblical text and the early writings of the church her position of leadership was upheld. As the early Christian church reverted to patriarchal structures, however, the leadership role of Mary of Magdala was diminished, to the point that she was eventually discredited as a prostitute.[113]

To do a gender reading of the Gospel, one must read with the same eyes as Jesus, who stood against patriarchy and broke the deeply ingrained social bias against women. In Luke, we are told of incident that involved two of Jesus' disciples, Martha and Mary:

---

[112] De La Torre, *Reading the Bible from the Margins*, 123–24.
[113] Ibid., 124.

Now as they went on their way, he [Jesus] entered a certain village, where a woman named Martha welcomed him into her home. She had a sister named Mary, who sat at the Lord's feet and listened to what he was saying. But Martha was distracted by her many tasks; so she came to him and asked, "Lord, do you not care that my sister has left me to do all the work by myself? Tell her then to help me." But the Lord answered her, "Martha, Martha, you are worried and distracted by many things; there is need of only one thing. Mary has chosen the better part, which will not be taken away from her." (Lk 10:38–42)

Many sermons have been based on this text. The common interpretation is that we must set our priorities right. We should not be taken over by the cares of the world, like Martha, and miss the one thing essential, which is to be with Jesus, like Mary. While this message is uplifting, it misses the radicality of the message—the dismantling of the patriarchal system by Jesus. Jesus' words and actions denounced the bias against women with regards to religious life. Women had no place in religious life; according to tradition it would be better for a Torah to be destroyed than for it to be touched by a woman. Such a profound contempt for women is the reason a pious Jewish man begins his morning prayers by thanking God that he is not a Gentile, a slave, or a woman.

Martha was distracted by her serving duties. The Greek word that is used in the Gospel of Luke is *diakonia*. Nowhere in the account does it tell us that Martha was serving in the kitchen doing "woman's work," which is how it is commonly interpreted. Her duties in serving most likely had something to do with the work and responsibilities of a church deacon, as established in Acts 6:1–6. Luke (who also authored Acts) indicates that Martha must have been among the first, if not *the* first deacon. Martha's preoccupation with serving dealt with her work and responsibilities in her service for the house-church that met at her home, leaving little time to "sit at Jesus' feet."

Mary is also a disciple who serves and proclaims God's message, but she chose to "sit at Jesus' feet." To sit at the feet of someone was a term meaning to be a disciple at the feet of a master teacher, a role reserved for men. For example, in Acts 23:3 we read that Paul was brought up "at the feet of Gamaliel." Is the radicalness of the account that Mary not only touched the Torah but also read and studied it? She and Martha are portrayed as well-known figures of the early church who were beloved by Christ (Jn 11:5). They were not only hearers and servers but also proclaimers of the word. Jesus told Martha that listening to him was better than serving. By affirming these roles for women, Jesus dismantled the patriarchal view of women as belonging only in the home, serving men's needs, particularly being vessels of men's seeds, with no identity other than their subservience to men.[114] A reading of this account from a feminist liberationist stance frees the text from the common reading and interpretation, which fails to capture its transformative power for women.

But even within the context of the feminist liberation movement, there are gaps that need to be filled. While there are common issues in the feminist liberationist movement that bind women, there is a critical view that this movement is profoundly Western, not only in terms of patriarchy, but also in terms of feminism itself. The further evolution of a feminist pedagogical strategy must take into consideration issues of culture, class, ethnicity, and race. K. O'Brien Wicker states that the movement has been colonialist as well, and thus Western women are as implicated as Western men.[115] Beyond the concerns and issues of middle- and upper-class Western women, the feminist liberationist movement must engage in the global issues of women, which are postcolonial in nature.[116]

Feminism remains caught in the Western project of colonization. It must be taken a step further by going beyond a consideration of gender, of woman as woman, to include a consideration of race, ethnicity, and class. Some black feminists, better known as womanists, insist that white feminists have not seriously addressed the dimensions of racism (and classism) within the women's movement. For womanists like Jacquelyn Grant, the identification of black women with Jesus relative to the dismantling of patriarchy, white supremacy, and economic privilege is grounded in imaging Jesus in various ways: Jesus as a co-sufferer, because he took the side of the marginalized of his time and became one among them in their deprivation and suffering; Jesus as an equalizer, because while he took the side of the disenfranchised, he came for all humanity; Jesus as one who upholds and protects freedom not by becoming equal to the oppressor, as womanists claim white feminists are doing, but by liberation from the oppressor and from all forms of oppression; Jesus as the sustainer, a model for the

---

[114] Ibid., 126–27.

[115] See Kathleen O'Brien Wicker, "Teaching Feminist Biblical Studies in a Post-colonial Context," in *Searching the Scriptures*, vol. 1, *A Feminist Introduction*, ed. Elisabeth Schüssler Fiorenza, 367–80 (New York: Crossroad, 1993).

[116] See Laura E. Donaldson, *Decolonizing Feminisms: Race, Gender, and Empire-building* (Chapel Hill: University of North Carolina Press, 1992); and Segovia, *Decolonizing Biblical Studies*, 79n36.

family that has been systematically violated by slavery and its dehumanizing consequences; and Jesus as liberator, because he empowers all those, like black women, who live their lives in a profound quest for liberation.[117]

Section 2, "The Feminist Approach," in *The Interpretation of the Bible in the Church* distinguishes three forms of feminist biblical hermeneutics: radical, neo-orthodox, and critical. The radical form denies the authority of the Bible, maintaining that it was authored by men to perpetuate androcentrism. The neo-orthodox form takes a prophetic stance on the side of the oppressed, and thus also of women, which is adopted as "canon within canon" in order to bring to full illumination whatever in the Bible favors the liberation of women and the protection of their rights. The critical form seeks to rediscover accounts that provide evidence for the egalitarian status and role of women within the life of Jesus and the Pauline churches. These accounts are believed to have been concealed in the writings of the New Testament and buried beneath patriarchy and androcentrism.

Feminist biblical hermeneutics employs two criteria of investigation. The first involves a hermeneutics of suspicion in reading texts because, written from the perspective of victors, their truth is skewed. The second is a sociological bent, and its goal is to reconstruct the history of two different situations of women in the first century, one in the Jewish and Greco-Roman society, and the other in the public life of Jesus and in the Pauline church, where "a community of equals" existed in the spirit of Galatians 3:28. Feminist exegesis, using these two criteria of investigation, has succeeded in illuminating the role of women in the Bible, in Christian origins, and in the church. Because of the work of feminist exegetes, new questions have been put to the biblical texts that seek to unmask and reject commonly accepted interpretations that justify male domination of women.

While *The Interpretation of the Bible in the Church* praises feminist exegesis seeking to transform an androcentric worldview, it also warns that it

> runs the risk of interpreting the biblical texts in a tendentious and thus debatable manner. To establish its positions it must

---

[117] See Jacquelyn Grant, "Womanist Jesus and the Mutual Struggle for Liberation," in *The Recovery of the Black Presence: An Interdisciplinary Exploration,* ed. Randall C. Bailey and Jacquelyn Grant, 125–42 (Nashville, TN: Abingdon Press, 1995); and idem, "Feminist and Womanist Criticism," in *The Postmodern Bible,* ed. Elizabeth A. Castello, Stephen D. Moore, Gary A. Philipps, and Regina M. Schwartz, 225–71 (New Haven, CT: Yale University Press, 1995).

often, for want of something better, have recourse to arguments *ex silentio*. As is well known, this type of argument is generally viewed with much reserve: It can never suffice to establish a conclusion on a solid basis. On the other hand, the attempt made on the basis of fleeting indications in the texts to reconstitute a historical situation which these same texts are considered to have been designed to hide—this does not correspond at all to the work of exegesis properly so called. It entails rejecting the content of the inspired texts in preference for a hypothetical construction, quite different in nature.

Reading Scripture with a Global Optic

At the same time, scholars cannot ignore the changes in the global landscape that have spurred changes in scholarship. Broad geographical shifts have broken the hegemony of the West, as people formerly controlled by the West have found their own voices. These shifts have dramatically changed the demographic constitution of the West as well. According to a 2008 CNN report and based on Census 2000 data, by the year 2050, 54 percent of the population in the United States will be made up of minorities. Hispanic Americans will increase to 30 percent of the population, African Americans to 15 percent, and Asian Americans to 9 percent. (In 2008, they were 15 percent, 14 percent, and 5 percent, respectively.)[118] Because of this, the academic discourse has radically changed, with more and more new faces joining it and reclaiming their voices. It is hard for those who have occupied the center to come to terms with the fact that this center has not only shifted but has actually disintegrated, giving rise to a plurality of voices.

In the field of biblical criticism, which had remained since its inception the preserve of Western males (in particular Western male clerics), there has been the emergence during the last twenty years of those who were considered outsiders. Their presence is opening the discourse to new perspectives and horizons never imagined before: Western women, non-Western theologians and critics; ethnic and racial minorities from non-Western civilizations in the West, who include those of African, Asian, Caribbean, and Latin American descent.[119]

---

[118] "Minorities Expected to Be Majority in 2050," CNN.com/US, August 13, 2008.

[119] See "Reading the Field," *Biblical Interpretation* 1 (1993): 34–114, esp. 67–87. For an essential reference work on the theological contributions of the peoples of Africa, Asia, the Caribbean, Latin America, the Pacific, and the minority and

Biblical criticism, which had already been in serious turmoil as a result of internal, methodological, and theoretical challenges, is now faced with flesh-and-blood readers who question the very character and agenda of biblical criticism, which for so long was determined by the Western claim to scholarly neutrality and objectivity.

From a disciplinary point of view, ethnic and racial minorities in biblical studies have resisted and continue to resist any biblical criticism that claims to be value free and timeless. They see it rather as enmeshed in politics, in both its meanings (politics within the sociopolitical sphere and politics within the realm of ideology). They rise to make their voices heard and take a position against a learned and universal reading of scripture that poses as non-ideological. Holding a contrary position, from the perspective of flesh-and-blood readers, from their own social locations, they insist on a reading of scripture as ideological to its core.[120]

The problem is one not only of different content and modes of discourse but also of sociocultural perception and attitude. At the bottom line, it involves the dynamics of hegemony and colonialism—the relationship between the center and the margins, the dominant group and the subordinate groups, the majority group and the minority groups.

> Ethnic and racial minorities, coming as they do from non-Western cultures, enter not only in an alien context in biblical studies, but also an alienating context, a context where the content and mode of their discourse are not acknowledged, much less accepted or respected, an equal though different or alternative vision of reality. For such individuals, therefore, to pursue biblical studies is to enter further into the world of social stratification set up by the West vis-à-vis "the other."[121]

From the perspective of geopolitical shifts, ethnic and racial minorities are located at a defining moment in history, a time when the long era of Western global domination has begun to draw to a close. There are factors that are contributing to this geopolitical change, including the continuous movement of people into the West through immigration and the high birthrate among ethnic and racial minorities. But along with this geopolitical change is the continuing power and impact of liberation theology in all its various forms, with its clear call for

---

indigenous peoples of the world, see Virginia Fabella and R. S. Sugirtharajah, eds., *Dictionary of Third World Theologies* (Maryknoll, NY: Orbis Books, 2000).

[120] Segovia, *Decolonizing Biblical Studies*, 166–67.

[121] Ibid., 171.

"conscientization"—"for a sense of self-identity, self-consciousness, and self-determination."[122]

Ethnic and racial minorities in biblical studies have increased, and their concerns and interests have expanded. Segovia states:

> I am convinced that the future of biblical studies—like the future of religious and theological studies in general—is a postcolonial, post-Western future, and in that future racial and ethnic minorities will have a fundamental and decisive role to play, whether outside the West or in the trenches in the West. It is a future in which the reading and interpretation of the Bible will be pursued and analyzed from any number of different contexts and perspectives, social locations, agendas, and ideologies.[123]

To illustrate a reading of scripture from the eyes of ethnic and racial minorities, I draw from Miguel A. De La Torre's *Reading the Bible from the Margins*. He writes that the question at the heart of the Gospel, "Who do you say I am?" is answered from one's own social location, from the depths of one's experience, as a Hispanic, as a black American, as an Amerindian, as an Asian, as an African. His entire presentation cannot be taken up here, but his presentation as a Hispanic can be a good representation of a reading of scripture from one's social location.

De La Torre relates in a particular way to the flight of Mary and Joseph from the tyrannical regime of Herod. His own family had to flee to the United States when his father was regarded as a fugitive of the newly installed government in their country. Like Jesus, De La Torre grew up as a political refugee, a victim of circumstances beyond his own comprehension or control. By seeing Jesus as a refugee, the story of Jesus became De La Torre's story as he moved from his social location to the biblical text. Thus, to be asked, "Who do you say that I am?" is to encounter Jesus, as a savior who knows the fears and frustrations of an alien in a land where one is considered outside of those who belong.[124]

Many Latinos/as may not have moved to the United States under the same circumstances as De La Torre. But even those who have lived for hundreds of years on land that would eventually become the United States are regarded as aliens, exiles, and outsiders—people

---

[122] Ibid., 169.
[123] Ibid., 175.
[124] De La Torre, *Reading the Bible from the Margins*, 112–14.

who are at the margins of society. Many of those who come from Mexico and Puerto Rico have found themselves in the United States as a consequence of the quasi-religious ideology of Manifest Destiny. Because of the aggressive territorial expansion of the United States, the people of Puerto Rico and Mexico woke up to find that their borders had moved, making them aliens on their own lands. In other places, like Central America and the Caribbean, territorial invasions and exploitation of natural resources by US corporations were protected by US forces, whose mission usually involved overthrowing the country's legitimate government and to impose a government more willing to protect US trade. With their governments turned into puppet governments, "banana republics," the people of Central America and the Caribbean found themselves under conditions that forced their immigration to the imperial center. They became refugees and aliens in the country responsible for their being there. Even their descendants are seen as foreigners. When asked "Who do you say that I am?" the life stories of these people would shape their answers.

Toward an Integral Biblical Pedagogy

How might narrative criticism be pertinent to a new vision for moral theology? Before I propose the move toward an integral biblical pedagogy, I offer three main conclusions regarding narrative criticism and its use for scripture for moral vision. First, there is a close link between moral vision and story; second, narrative criticism offers the best method for unleashing the power and depth of scripture in shaping moral vision; and third, the use of narrative criticism should be qualified or enriched by other historical and literary approaches and hermeneutical methods.

Moral vision refers to the way we see ourselves in a world of relations, which is largely shaped by the stories that have touched our lives. We are as our stories are; we see reality through the prism of our stories. Our moral vision is ordered around the significant and meaningful stories that are etched deep in our memories. Stories have the power to touch us at our deepest levels. Beyond our personal stories are our collective stories that tell us who we are as a people, as a community, as a nation. These stories are told and retold to enrich and nourish our common vision of what we as a people hold as our most cherished values and hopes. There exists an inner kinship between story and life, between story and vision.

Narrative criticism offers the best method for drawing out the power of story in scripture in shaping moral vision and character.

We are deeply engaged with the text of scripture as we read scripture itself, not about scripture. Attentive to the elements of a story—point of view, character, and plot—we are engaged with the text and absorbed by its world of meaning; in the process we are formed by its moral vision. This way of reading and studying scripture makes it come alive, unleashing its power to inspire and challenging our way of perceiving reality and viewing the world. There is a narrative quality to all of life, and reading scripture as story brings us in touch with the very dynamism of life itself. The encounter with the text engages not only the rational but also the affective and the imaginative parts of our understanding.

Like any other method, however, narrative criticism is incomplete. It is a text-governed pedagogy, and as such it employs the text without any question. By contrast, feminist liberationists, for instance, hold that the text is not neutral, but is written with bias, and thus requires a hermeneutics of suspicion. The text must be critically and creatively engaged in by all other biblical pedagogies with the purpose of exploring more fully the moral vision of the text, particularly as it is addressed to contemporary readers from different social locations.

Proposing an Integral Biblical Pedagogy

The merits and rewards of using narrative criticism should not be exalted to the diminishment of the other approaches and methods. We need a critical and creative integration of the various approaches and methods for scriptural interpretation in view of the formation and shaping of moral vision. In the light of the instructions of the Pontifical Biblical Commission on the need for the complementary use of biblical approaches, I propose an integral biblical pedagogy, which involves the use of various theories across the disciplinary spectrum in interpreting texts.

Narrative criticism is best employed for scriptural stories. But one should begin by researching all data and information provided by historical criticism in order to understand the world behind the text. The social and cultural mores and political realities that are at its base, studied by cultural criticism, contribute further to an enlightened study and interpretation of the text. Those who engage in narrative criticism hold that the original authors and readers of the text do not have a role in understanding the text as a literary text; narrative criticism engages with the world within the text and not the world behind it. But this does not mean that the world behind a text has not left any trace. Any pedagogy, like historical criticism and cultural criticism, that can help in understanding a text, ancient as it is, and thus strange and foreign to contemporary readers, can contribute to the wellspring of knowledge for its study and interpretation.

Likewise, a better appreciation of the craft and beauty of the word of God can contribute to the theological meaning of the text at its core, which is the overriding concern of historical criticism. Historical criticism is profoundly theological in orientation, and it decidedly pursues, beyond its claim to scientific distance, the religious content and message of the texts. And a close study of the text as text may disclose the indexes of the social and cultural realities and also political and ideological forces at play in the text. So rather than a conflictual relationship, these pedagogies are used for an enlightened scriptural study and interpretation.

Given all the data that one could draw from historical criticism and cultural criticism, one engages in understanding the text as a literary text, using the constructs of implied author and implied reader, and understanding the text from the dynamics of point of view, plot, and character. Beyond narrative criticism, and using contextual pedagogy, its meaning is opened up beyond what is circumscribed by the implied author and implied reader. There might be no consonance between the meaning of the text from the viewpoint of the implied author and implied reader and the meaning of the text from the perspective of flesh-and-blood readers, but narrative criticism provides a starting point for a critical discourse between and among different readers through deep engagement with the text as text. Modern readers should read scripture as scripture, not merely read about scripture, as the base of their critical and creative engagement with the text from their social locations.

What results from this critical discourse is a plurality of meanings, which makes the word of God truly a mystery as it is encountered in its inexhaustible depth of meaning. To claim a universal and univocal meaning is to deny the very character of this mystery and to render the word of God monolithic, reserved only for an exclusive group, rather than plural, which is inclusive of all, as it speaks to the heart of our shared humanity in all its richness and diversity.

Principles for Integral Biblical Pedagogy

In using an integral biblical pedagogy the sheer volume of content and subject matter, not only at the level of texts but also at the level of readings and readers of texts, might pose a problem and challenge. Engaging with texts as historical, literary, rhetorical, and ideological, and with flesh-and-blood readers who have their own context and perspective, throws open a wide field that for a long time has been circumscribed by the agenda of deeply entrenched pedagogies. Employing an integral reading and interpretation can result in an explosion of meanings of a text, with each claiming to be as good as the others, ending in what might become a free for all. I propose, thus, three principles to provide a critical framework within which meanings can be negotiated in terms of some hierarchy of preference and priority.

First, priority must be given to the voice of contemporary readers over the voice of historical and rhetorical readers of the text. The text as it is read now is being addressed to contemporary readers. The historical and rhetorical readers are employed only insofar as the profound meaning of scripture can come alive to contemporary readers, inspiring them to reconfigure their lives according to this meaning that touches them in their unique circumstances. The word of God is an ever-renewing word in the encounter between its message and its present reader. While it is also of the past, the word of God is always fresh and new, and the present revelatory event happens in this encounter between the message of scripture and its contemporary reader.

Second, among the competing perspectives of readers, an interpretational privilege exists with reference to the disenfranchised, which is called the hermeneutical privilege of the oppressed. This principle, founded on the broader theme of the preferential option for the poor, is not accepted without contention; it is a subject of critical discourse. The most controversial term in the phrase *preferential option for the poor* is *preferential.* Stephen Pope argues that while it does indeed constitute a form of partiality, far from being morally pernicious, this partiality is morally justified and indeed required. Rather than contracting the universal love of God, the preferential option for the poor in fact expands and deepens it.[125]

To say that God loves the poor because they are poor is true, at least in a very broad sense, but somewhat misleading. It can be taken to mean that God favors the poor over others by virtue of their poverty or their membership in a poor class, which makes partiality a case of simple bias or reverse discrimination. This might be one interpretation of Gregory Baum's claim that "when confronted by conflict between rich and poor (or powerful and powerless, or

---

[125] Stephen J. Pope, "Proper and Improper Partiality and the Preferential Option for the Poor," *Theological Studies* 54/2 (1993): 242.

masters and slaves), then the Gospel demands . . . that [one] side with the oppressed."[126]

Stephen Pope holds that the proper meaning of partiality for the poor is the critical distinction between love and care. Pope makes reference to Toner, who writes about care as "an affirmative affection toward someone precisely as in need."[127] Rather than constituting an alternative to love, care is "only the form love takes when the lover is attentive to the beloved's need."[128] Pope argues his point:

> Because care is proportioned to need, it makes perfect sense to speak of the "preferential option" for the poor as long as "love" is specifically understood under its subcategory of "care" or "caring love." For this reason, the phrase "special care for the needy" seems in some ways more specific and more accurate (if less inspiring) than "preferential option for the poor," "preferential love for the poor," or "love of predilection for the poor." The expression "preferential love" is helpful because it highlights the important truth that for Christians care flows from love rather than from an attitude of *noblesse oblige* or from religious exhibitionism.[129]

An option for the poor in this light is not due to their merit, moral virtue, or superiority of insight but due to their need. The good Samaritan lifted the man lying on the road not because of who the man is, but because of his suffering. One who loves this way comes to a profound understanding of the depth of God's gratuitous and universal love for all—a love that excludes no one—and with a special care for those left at the margins. As the bishops of Puebla stated: "The poor merit preferential attention, whatever may be the moral or personal situation in which they find themselves. Made in the image and likeness of God (Gn 1:26–28) to be his children, this image is dimmed and even defiled. That is why God takes their defense and loves them (Mt 5:45; Jas 2:5)."[130]

---

[126] Gregory Baum, "Liberation Theology and 'the Supernatural,'" *The Ecumenist* 19/6 (September-October 1981): 84.

[127] Jules Toner, *The Experience of Love* (Washington, DC: Corpus Books, 1968), 75.

[128] Ibid., 80.

[129] Pope, "Proper and Improper Partiality and the Preferential Option for the Poor," 258.

[130] Puebla, *The Final Document*, no. 1142, in *Puebla and Beyond: Documentary and Commentary*, ed. John Eagleson and Philip Scharper, trans. John Drury

The preferential option must also be complemented by solidarity with the poor, through which, as the bishops at Medéllin put it, "we shall make their problems and struggles our own."[131] Solidarity grounds the preferential option for the poor in the common humanity that binds us all. And in the light of the principle of the common good, deeply enshrined in Catholic social teaching, the preferential option is not advancing the good of one class over another class but rather giving priority to the most needy and vulnerable so that they may partake of social benefits to which all have a right. For this reason the US National Conference of Catholic Bishops write in *Economic Justice for All* that the "prime purpose of the preferential option is to enable the poor to become active participants in the life of society" (no. 88).

In the light of the proper understanding of the partiality for the poor, reading scripture from the hermeneutical privilege of the poor must not be taken to mean as a "cognitive bias that subordinates truth to ideology, moral bias that regards human worth as a function of class membership, and religious bias that claims that God arbitrarily favors some social classes over others." Rather, this hermeneutical privilege of the oppressed must be seen with an eye turned to "divine preference of care for the needy, human intellectual devotion to the cause of the poor, and moral commitment to the priority of their needs within an ordering of social priorities."[132] This divine preference for the poor and marginalized is embodied and incarnated in the way Jesus lived and loved as witnessed in the Gospels.

Third, scripture is the written testimony of the fullest revelation of God in Christ. The Bible is not the fullest revelation of God; Jesus Christ is. As the testimony of God's revelation, scripture was written by people from within their different social locations. While this multitude of writers spanning centuries all testify to the same mercy and love of God, which reached its fullness in Jesus Christ, their writings reflected the cultural and political ethos of their times. If scripture is the word of God in human words, we do not have an unmediated revelation. Scripture assumes the human mediations of cultural practices, social codes, and political structures, some of which are clearly repudiated in contemporary times. Is the authority of scripture as the basis of faith and ethics diminished or invalidated by the social,

---

(Maryknoll, NY: Orbis Books, 1979), 265.

[131] Medéllin, "On the Poverty of the Church," no. 10, in *Liberation Theology: A Documentary History*, ed. Alfred T. Hennelly (Maryknoll, NY: Orbis Books, 1990), 117–18.

[132] Pope, "Proper and Improper Partiality and the Preferential Option for the Poor," 265.

cultural, and political accretions that accompany its message? The answer is no. But it clearly places greater responsibility on the reader in interpreting scripture.

Men and women of faith must read scripture, then, from the call of Jesus in John 10:10: "I came that they may have life, and have it abundantly." And this life-giving mission must become the lens by which biblical texts are interpreted. Jesus reinterprets the Hebrew scriptures to bring them into line with the gospel message, clearly telling his followers to reject passages that bring subjugation or death to others. Specifically, Jesus says, "You have heard that it was said, 'An eye for an eye and a tooth for a tooth.' But I say to you, Do not resist an evildoer. But if anyone strikes you on the right cheek, turn the other also" (Mt 5:38–39). Jesus calls for the renunciation of a teaching from scripture![133] The same occurs with the teaching on divorce in Deuteronomy. A husband could dismiss his wife simply by serving her with a written bill of divorce (Dt 24:1–2). Matthew 19:3–9 reinterprets such patriarchal passages, which contribute to the marginalization of women.[134]

The entire Bible should be read through the lens of this call to abundant life in John 10:10. As such, any text that advocates the subjugation of one person to another or discrimination against a certain kind of people, or one that protects the interests of the dominant culture to the detriment of others, or that renders women and children as victims, should be repudiated as anti-gospel or anti-scripture. They deny the full life that Jesus has promised for all. There is a connection between the hermeneutical privilege of the oppressed and the life-giving call of John 10:10 as the fundamental interpretative lens. The biblical interpretations from the margins challenge the very system that has locked in both oppressors and oppressed, preventing them from having the abundance of life that Jesus has promised. The oppressors are just as dehumanized as the people they oppress. But for those in the dominant culture to give up their position of advantage goes against the very nature of the concupiscent heart, so those in the margins fight for societal change and transformation through the dismantling of oppressive systems and structures, making possible God's salvation for both oppressors and oppressed.

As *The Interpretation of the Bible in the Church* states, the fullness of life is interpreted in the light of the Paschal Mystery—the life and death of Jesus Christ, who brings a radical newness and, with

---

[133] De La Torre, *Reading the Bible from the Margins*, 52.
[134] See ibid., 91–92.

sovereign authority, gives meaning to the scriptures that is decisive and definitive.

Conclusion

I propose the use of narrative criticism as the best pedagogy to read scripture as scripture, because by using its tools we come in contact with the beauty and craft of the word of God. It evokes scripture's moral vision, in the light of which we could be moved to reconfigure our life. But narrative criticism is limited, as are historical criticism and cultural criticism. In all three pedagogies the meaning of the text is not located in the encounter between the text and flesh-and-blood readers. And in all three, this lack has to be filled in if scripture is to have a transforming claim on the lives of contemporary readers, coming from highly contextualized and perspectival social locations. The geopolitical shifts have disintegrated the center where the dominant culture had once reigned. With the loss of a center, the location of meaning has become plural and multiple, not univocal and universal. This led to the emergence of contextual biblical pedagogy.

Narrative criticism remains valuable in using scripture for moral vision, but it has to wrestle with its own limitations. It has to depend on the tools of other pedagogies across the spectrum of biblical criticism, toward an integral biblical pedagogy. In this pedagogy, narrative criticism draws from historical criticism and cultural criticism a breadth and richness of knowledge and information to bring light to a text that is distant and strange. Although narrative criticism holds that its method of studying the text as literary text stands independent of the world behind it, the text remains a product of its own time; historical criticism and cultural criticism, rather than serving as distractions, in fact contribute to a more enlightened reading and interpretation of the message of the text.

The implied-reader construct of narrative criticism is faceless, but contemporary readers want their faces seen and their voices heard. They constitute the world "in front of" the text. These are diverse readers in a global context, to whom scripture is addressed. Contextual biblical pedagogy opens the reading and interpretation of scripture beyond the pedagogies that preceded it. It has brought biblical criticism to an entirely new place and a whole new level, where its vision can be seen in terms of a scripture that is truly inclusive of all, in a church that is global. Narrative criticism provides the basis for contextual biblical pedagogy; it allows readers to encounter the text as text, and, from there, reconfigure its meaning for their own contexts. But in some instances, using the hermeneutics of suspicion, they question the entire ideological basis of the text and deconstruct it, or even renounce it altogether.

Using narrative criticism within the spectrum of integral biblical pedagogy meets the challenge and demand of biblical criticism, where the past meets the present and within which the future has already taken shape and is determining the entire direction ahead. But amid an explosion of possible readings and interpretations, it must be guided by principles that ensure that the word of God is truly liberative and salvific. The priority of the contemporary reader as the subject of the revelatory event, the hermeneutical privilege of the oppressed as the locus of the scripture's meaning, and the life-giving call of John 10:10 as the basic interpretative lens are the principles that must guide the reading and interpretation of scripture.

3

Systematic Theology from a Feminist, Liberationist, and Global Optic

Grounding Christian Moral Vision

The central task of this chapter is to reconnect systematic theology and moral theology, particularly in terms of Christian moral vision. Moral theology presupposes a moral vision, a way of looking at reality and the world in terms of what is right, true, and virtuous. In moral life people act because of who they are, and who they are is largely shaped by how they see reality and the world. What enters into this seeing is how they view themselves and others as human beings in a web of relationships and interrelationships, the most fundamental and foundational of which is their relationship with God. The primary question I ask is how systematic theology provides the grounding for Christian moral vision. Before this question is addressed, I take up briefly the nature of systematic theology as a science of faith. Francis Schüssler Fiorenza writes that "theology is a fragile discipline in that it is both academic and related to faith. As an academic discipline, theology shares all the scholarly goals of other academic disciplines: it strives for historic exactitude, conceptual rigor, systemic consistency, and interpretive clarity. In its relation to faith, theology shares the fragility of faith itself."[1] In this relation to faith, theology is brought into a realm, different from that of science, at the heart of the mystery of divine and human encounter. The fragility of theology lies in its ambiguity as a science of faith—an ambiguity that it has to endure if it is true to its nature.

---

[1] Francis Schüssler Fiorenza, "Systematic Theology: Task and Methods," in *Systematic Theology: Roman Catholic Perspectives*, 2 vols., ed. by Francis Schüssler Fiorenza and John P. Galvin, 1:3–87 (Minneapolis, MN: Fortress Press, 1991), 5.

The term *theology* includes all the theological disciplines, one of which is systematic theology. Robert Doran holds that for Bernard Lonergan, systematic theology is concerned principally not with the truth of doctrine but with the synthetic understanding of doctrines already affirmed to be true. Doran cites Lonergan's emphasis on the principal function of systematic theology as the "hypothetical, imperfect, analogical, and gradually developing understanding of the mysteries of the faith that are already affirmed on other grounds than systematic argumentation."[2]

The connection of systematic theology and moral theology is grounded in the theological anthropology drawn from the doctrines of the faith, insofar as they define a Christian conception of human existence. The doctrines of the faith teach us about the mystery of being human on the basis of the Christian revelation. Whenever the revelation of God occurs, human existence is brought to a new illumination, for God's disclosure of self reveals the human in its source, origin, and its ultimate destiny. Edward Schillebeeckx writes: "The question of God only has meaning for us human beings in so far as being a human question, it speaks to our humanity; that is, if we then come to realize that the whole issue of man is in the end the issue of God himself [*sic*]."[3] Likewise the mystery of God, in whom the human finds full fulfillment, is unraveled in the disclosure of the human. Drawing from the contemporary discourse in systematic theology I develop a theological anthropology on the basis of the doctrines of the faith. The particular optic I use to integrate the entire discussion is feminist, liberationist, and *global*. When we speak of theological anthropology, there are no generic human beings; there are simply male and female human beings. I take a feminist optic in speaking about God, Christ, and the human being, for only when both woman and man are brought into the discourse on theological anthropology are we speaking truthfully.

Feminism is not a monolithic reality; it is as diverse and varied as its contexts and as the political and philosophical commitments of its practitioners. Unlike Anglo-European women, African American women are discriminated against not only because of their sex but also because of their race and class. They call their struggle womanist, which is derived from the black term *womanish* as opposed to *girlish*, which means outrageous, audacious, courageous, and engaging

---

[2] Robert M. Doran, "Bernard Lonergan and the Functions of Systematic Theology," *Theological Studies* 59/4 (1998): 570.

[3] Edward Schillebeeckx, *Jesus: An Experiment in Christology*, trans. Hubert Hoskins (New York: Seabury Press, 1979), 404.

in willful behavior. Women of Latin American descent also experience oppression due to their ethnicity and class in addition to their gender. They name their struggle *mujerista,* from the Spanish *mujer,* meaning woman, although others prefer the designation Latina or Latina feminist. Women of Africa and Asia, so-called third-world women, are trapped in a web of oppression as they face racism, classicism, colonialism, sexism, and militarism.[4] The contexts of women are diverse, and thus their concerns should not be lumped under one category. However, this chapter is unable to address each specific context. When it refers to the feminist optic relative to the doctrines of the faith, it engages in issues that cut across the diversity of contexts, which may evoke varied levels of resonance in women.

Interlocked with the feminist optic is the liberationist optic. The liberationist optic, when understood in a more general way, includes the feminist optic, for it is seeing the world from the side of all oppressed groups. But to differentiate it from the feminist perspective I use it with reference to a more inclusive group, beyond specifically women, because it refers to all those who are at the margins of society, who are deprived of the most basic of human needs, disenfranchised and disempowered, who cry to the heavens for justice. The recognition of their collective human misery is the context of liberation theology.

Finally, the global optic sees the world as shrinking into one global village. We are all interconnected, largely because of the explosion of communication technology. We can no longer see the world through a narrow prism, because while our lives are interlocked, in the sense that what happens to one of us affects us all, we remain diverse and plural. Aware of and sensitive to particularities of peoples and cultures, and yet with a global worldview, we experience ourselves as many and yet one—one future and one destiny.

I examine the doctrines of the faith from these three optics, but one optic may be more appropriate and relevant than another, depending on the doctrine of faith that is under study. So in certain cases all three are used and in others, only one or two. But in every instance an attempt is made to study a doctrine of the faith from a particular perspective. For there is no truth that is without a context, and no truth is studied without a viewpoint.

Drawing from systematic theology this chapter presents a coherent theological anthropology and its implications for Christian moral vision. It defines our way of being and way of doing as men and women of virtue and integrity. The doctrines of the faith give a particular

---

[4] Ibid., 94–95.

view of what it means to be human and of the basic attitudes and
dispositions a Christian ought to have toward the world. According to Charles Curran, the five Christian doctrines of creation, sin,
incarnation-redemption, grace, and eternal destiny are the constitutive
elements of a Christian perspective, horizon, and stance. They articulate the fundamental truths underlying human meaning, dignity, and
destiny.[5] These five doctrines are used to structure this presentation of
Christian faith. The full Christian experience refines one's sensitivity to
human values; it opens the broader and deeper horizons of meaning
to moral living. A value judgment distanced from the faith horizon of
meaning might otherwise be determined solely by sheer empiricism; it
is turned into a merely rationalistic and sterile ethics.[6]

Doctrines of the Faith

In view of the Christian moral vision, the connection between
systematic theology and moral theology resides in the theological
anthropology developed on the basis of the doctrines of the faith, using the content and discourse of systematic theology. The theological
anthropology of the Christian faith perspective grounds the Christian
moral vision of our way of being and doing as men and women of
virtue and integrity.

The doctrines of the faith open us to the mysteries of God and of
the human person. Theological anthropology focuses on an understanding of the human person in the light of revelation and faith. What
underlies the understanding of the human person from this light is the
faith conviction that the question of who the human person is cannot
be separated from the question of who God is. From the breadth and
richness of the doctrines of the faith, three fundamental realities enter
into our faith narrative of who God is and who the human person
is—the primacy of love, the primacy of grace, and the primacy of community. Using these terms and the reality they represent, I describe the
content of faith taking into consideration the fragility of the mystery
of God and the mystery of the human person.

Under the primacy of love I take up the doctrines of creation, Trinity, and Jesus Christ and show that the one singular thread that runs
through the God narrative of the Christian faith is that God is love,

---

[5] See Charles E. Curran, *Directions in Fundamental Moral Theology* (Notre
Dame, IN: University of Notre Dame Press, 1985), 29–62.

[6] Richard A. McCormick, *Health and Medicine in the Catholic Tradition* (New
York: Crossroad, 1984), 50.

outgoing and outpouring love, the love that draws all to a communion of love. This disclosure of God reveals the human, for if God is the source and origin of humanity, then the foundational truth about persons is that they are made from love, in love, and for love.

Under the primacy of grace I develop the tension of sin and grace, original sin and the supernatural existential—the ambiguity that cuts into the very depths of the person. To be in society is to live in the public square, where one is confronted by the awesome reality of sin in social structures and systems, but it is also to be inspired by the structures of grace in the life-giving and hope-renewing global systems dedicated to promoting and protecting justice. In the very tension of sin and grace, grace is primal and enduring; only in grace and with grace can one come to a deep realization of sin. In the end, when all things come to their final validation, the primacy of grace in the eschatological hope is the ultimate word of soteriology.

Under the primacy of community I treat the doctrines on the nature of the church and of the final communal destiny. To be essentially human is to be in community. For the Christian, the locus of this community is the church. And yet if the church is to be a prophetic sign of liberation in the world, it is in need of transformation, so that its structures may be made consistent with its vision as the church on the side of the poor and a church at the center of the world where massive cultural and political changes are taking place, especially in the roles of women in all realms of society. The discourse on the final things presents a final grand narrative of the whole of humankind, the earth, and the entire cosmos, all sharing a common destiny.

The approach I take is limited. It specifically reconnects doctrinal theology and moral theology only in terms of moral vision and not in terms of moral content or theory. It simply asks how theological anthropology, based on the doctrines of the faith, grounds the moral vision of who we ought to be and what we ought to do. With regard to treating the doctrines of faith, one can choose to take one doctrine and engage in a focused and in-depth discussion, or one can take a more holistic approach based on the primary doctrines of the faith. I chose the latter, and while the breadth and expansiveness of this approach is its merit, it is also its limitation. It is not possible, using this holistic approach, to go into a focused and in-depth discussion of each one of the doctrines.

This holistic approach is deliberately more positive than polemical. I do not enter into the debates of different positions in systematic theology, not only because it is not possible, given the limited space for engagement, but also because it is not the purpose of the chapter.

I present contrary views only when they are necessary to illuminate the meaning of the doctrine. I limit my work with reference to its main thrust, which is to use the doctrines of the faith as the basis of the Christian moral vision. Thus, I select my sources in terms of how they contribute positively to developing a theological anthropology within the hermeneutical framework of the three primacies of love, grace, and community.

Primacy of Love

Underlying the doctrines of creation, Trinity, and Jesus Christ is the primacy of love, of divine love. This reflects a God who seeks to be in communion with all of humanity and of creation. Love means the desire for communion with the beloved. Love is the primal movement from God, as God, for God is love. Thus, the most profound New Testament metaphor is found in 1 John: "God is love" (4:16). God, the origin, sustainer, and end of all reality, is characterized by the radical relationality of that most relational of categories, love.[7]

Creation: Women, Poor, and Earth

Interpreting the Genesis Account

The Bible's accounts of creation were not intended to answer the scientific question of how the world came to be. The thrust of its texts was not scientific but relational—the relationship of God to reality, a relation of the Creator with all of creation.[8] A careful reading of the Yahwist creation narrative clearly indicates that it is not concerned with providing answers about cosmology. Rather, it is an etiology, a story rich in symbolism, which presents the experience of the goodness and intimate relatedness with God, who self-reveals as love, and the contrasting experience of sin, estrangement, and alienation from God.[9] The creation stories in Genesis are concerned on a fundamental level with the establishment of relationship. They are not reports of what actually happened at the beginning. Rather, they are stories of faith; they took shape in Israel's experience of God and in the face of its threatened and contingent existence.

---

[7] David Tracy, "Approaching the Christian Understanding of God," in Schüssler and Galvin, *Systematic Theology*, 1:138.

[8] Anne M. Clifford, "Creation," in Schüssler and Galvin, *Systematic Theology*, 1:198.

[9] Ibid., 201.

The love of God, who is the origin of life, its sustainer, and its ultimate meaning, is abiding. God's power is Israel's sole protection, and God's fidelity is its invincible hope. The creation stories, thus, must be seen through the prism of the faith of Israel, who had encountered God and been delivered from watery chaos, deserts, and slavery to the freedom that comes with a name, a destiny, and a future. If God protects, saves, and brings a people to freedom, all that comes from the hands of this God must be good. A hopeful confidence in the goodness of creation is rooted in Israel's faith experience of God's saving and abiding love.[10] The Priestly account of creation speaks of the good of all that has come to be: "God saw everything he had made, and indeed, it was very good" (Gn 1:31).

The writers reshaped the traditions behind these accounts into a new form reflecting a period in Israelite history that witnesses to a belief in God arising from the very needs and concerns of that time. The Priestly tradition behind Genesis 1 is historically situated in the period of the Babylonian exile in the sixth century BC, a dark period of national devastation and collective loss, both theologically and politically. Those who survived this period reasserted their belief in God's power over chaos and destruction, a belief that found expression in the creation narrative, influenced by the Babylonian epic poem *Enuma Elish*. These influences were reshaped by the authors of the Priestly account to portray a God who brought forth an orderly cosmos out of chaos for the elect people of Israel. Rather than a historical reporting of the beginnings of all things, the Priestly account was intended to renew and rekindle confidence in the providence of God.[11]

The difference between the *Enuma Elish* creation story and the Priestly account of creation in Genesis is the motif of conflict. In *Enuma Elish*, creation came to be from the conflict of Marduk and Tiamat, and the world was believed to have been formed from the dead carcass of Tiamat. In contrast, in the Priestly account all things came to be simply by God's command. God's word created a good and orderly world. Everything has its origin in God's word of command. In the face of the multiplicity of deities that inhabit the Babylonian cosmologies, Genesis sees all of creation by the command of the only sovereign God, before whom all bow down in exaltation and worship.[12] All of creation bears the mark of God and is good,

---

[10] Ibid., 200.

[11] Ibid., 199.

[12] Ibid., 199–200.

for the God of creation is the same God of Exodus who saves, whose love is abiding, and whose fidelity is unbroken. The fundamental truth is that God's saving love and abiding fidelity constitute the ground and foundation of God's relationship with creation and all of humankind.

Feminist Critique of Hierarchical Dualism

The thrust of relationality, characterized by love and fidelity, in the Genesis accounts is contrary to a hierarchical dualism with man as superior over women and nature. This construct was based on the dualism of spirit over matter, equating spirit with the masculine principle and matter with the feminine. This construct has political consequences as it translates into social structures of domination/subordination with man as the ruler, sovereign over woman.[13]

This social dualism in the relationship of man and woman has ecological consequences, as well, for earth is matter, which is seen as antithetical to spirit. The sovereignty of man over woman extends to nature, most often symbolized as female. Just as women give life to every human child, so also the earth brings forth fruits. Within this system of dualism, women and the natural world have no intrinsic worth and value; they have only instrumental value with reference to man whose needs and desires they fulfill. The earth, which is not regarded with reverence as the mysterious source and matrix of life but as dead and lifeless, is instrumentalized in a similar way.[14]

> In our day the mentality that sees nature as something to be dominated more often than not continues to draw on the imagery and attitudes of men's domination of women. For example, the much used phrase "the rape of the earth" reveals the extent to which the exploitation of nature is identified with violent sexual conquest of women. Our language speaks of "virgin forest," as yet untouched by man but awaiting his exploration and conquest. Symbolized as female, earth can be made to yield up her secrets; she can be penetrated, conquered, possessed. She is given to man for mastering and as a resource for his pleasure and need. At the same time, to be truly himself man must transcend

---

[13] Elizabeth A. Johnson, *Women, Earth, and Creator Spirit* (New York: Paulist Press, 1983), 12.

[14] Ibid., 13–14.

nature in the pursuit of culture, inevitably described as a masculine endeavor.[15]

Furthermore, Johnson asserts that the social domination of women and the ecological domination of the earth are inextricably fused in theory and practice. Contrary to the view that ecological crisis lies in an overly anthropomorphic view, she holds that it lies in the dominion of the androcentric view.[16]

Rosemary Radford Ruether, a leading voice in feminist theology, writes: "It is perhaps not too much to say, that the Achilles heel of human civilization, which today has reached global genocidal and ecocidal proportions, resides in the false development of maleness through repression of the female."[17]

We search for a way to undercut the dualism by going back to the heart of the creation accounts. If relationality and love are at the heart of the universe, then we must have a new view of wholeness that unifies rather than stratifies, that reconciles rather than divides—a view where our eyes see the sacredness of all of humankind and all of creation loved unto fullness. Where there is an interconnectedness in reciprocity and mutuality—in love—there the Creator God is most present and active in the world.

This view of wholeness, founded on interconnectedness, is at the core of the kinship model, by which we must conceive our relationship with the earth. This model is different from the kingship model, based on the hierarchical dualism that drives a wedge between humanity and earth and places human beings in a position of absolute dominion over all creatures. Creatures are ranked according to their participation in the fullness of spirit, with the inorganic matter at the lowest of the chain of being, then vegetative matter, followed by animals, human beings, and the nonphysical spirits or angels. Those at the higher levels have the right to use and control those at the lower levels. The stewardship model is similar to the kingship model in the sense that it preserves the hierarchical dualism. But it is different in that the position of human

---

[15] Ibid., 16. Johnson makes reference to Sherry Ortner as the source of her statement. "Is Female to Male as Nature is to Culture?" in *Women, Culture, and Society,* ed. Michelle Zimbalist Rosaldo and Louise Lamphere (Stanford, CA: Stanford University Press, 1974), 67–87.

[16] Johnson, *Women, Earth, and Creator Spirit,* 16.

[17] Rosemary Radford Ruether, *New Woman, New Earth* (San Francisco: Harper and Row, 1975), 11; see also, idem, *Gaia and God: An Ecofeminist Theology of Earth Healing* (San Francisco: Harper San Francisco, 1992).

beings over other creatures is not one of dominion but of stewardship. As stewards, human beings have the duty to protect and care for the weak and vulnerable in creation. In their care for the earth, even for their own self-interest and self-survival, they have a more respectful use of its resources compared to the abuse and misuse that the stance of dominion over the earth promotes.[18]

Beyond the kingship and stewardship models is the kinship model. "If separation is not the ideal but connection is; if dualism is not the ideal but the relational embrace of diversity is; if hierarchy is not the ideal but mutuality is; then the kinship model more closely approximates reality."[19] This model views life as interconnected; the flourishing and damaging of one affects all. It does not categorize beings in terms of a hierarchy of dignity but views each as an inherent part of one whole. The kingship and the stewardship models assign the dominant position to human beings, either as sovereign to other creatures or stewards in relation to them. These two views have placed human beings at the center, and yet in the realm of reality, they are dependent on the rest of creation for their sheer survival. No human life, for instance, is possible without the oxygen that trees create through the process of photosynthesis. But trees could exist for millennia without human care and stewardship. Who needs whom?[20]

Ruether, in imaging this kinship model, uses the metaphor of dance. "We must start thinking of reality as the connecting links of a dance in which each part is equally vital to the whole, rather than the linear competitive model in which the above prospers by defeating and suppressing what is below."[21] From a religious perspective we view the world as sustained and nurtured by the life-giving action of Creator Spirit. The earth, thus, is a sacred space where the Creator Spirit is present, and every created being and every form of life in that space must be treated with reverence, because each and every one is a manifestation of the creative power and energy of the Creator Spirit.

---

[18] Johnson, *Women, Earth, and Creator Spirit*, 29–30. See also Denis Edwards, *Ecology at the Heart of Faith* (Maryknoll, NY: Orbis Books, 2006); Sallie McFague, *Super, Natural Christians: How We Should Love Nature* (Minneapolis, MN: Fortress Press, 1997); Dieter T. Hessel and Rosemary Radford Ruether, eds., *Christianity and Ecology: Seeking the Well-Being of Earth and Humans* (Cambridge, MA: Harvard University Press, 2000); Mary Evelyn Tucker and John Grim, eds., *Worldviews and Ecology: Religion, Philosophy, and the Environment* (Maryknoll, NY: Orbis Books, 1994).

[19] Johnson, *Women, Earth, and Creator Spirit*, 30.

[20] Ibid., 31.

[21] Rosemary Radford Ruether, *To Change the World: Christology and Cultural Criticism* (New York: Crossroad, 1981), 67.

Triple Cries: Interlocking Oppressions

The connection between the social domination of women and the ecological domination of the earth is as deep as the connection between the cry of the poor and the cry of the earth. Leonardo Boff writes: "The logic that exploits classes and subjects peoples to the interests of the few rich and powerful countries is the same as the logic that devastates the Earth and plunders its wealth, showing no solidarity with the rest of humankind and future generations."[22] It is the logic based on "being over" rather than "being with."[23] The ultimate root of this logic is the destruction of the universal relatedness and connectedness at the heart of all of creation.

Feminist theology and ecological theology converge with liberation theology, whose epistemological focus is the preferential option for the poor and their liberation from the degradation and dehumanization of poverty. "The same logic of the prevailing system of accumulation and social organization that leads to the exploitation of workers also leads to the pillaging of whole nations and ultimately to the plundering of nature."[24] In the diminishment of women, the oppression of the poor, and the plundering of the earth, we hear triple cries. All cannot be silenced. Until these cries of oppression are heeded, creation will continue to groan from its depths. Only when relationships are rightly ordered, in a world where all that exists is connected and interconnected, truly life-giving, not death-dealing, is creation one with the Creator Spirit, the origin and source of all love, life, and goodness.

Trinity: Beyond Rahner and Feminist View

Renewing Trinitarian Theology

The doctrine of the Trinity is the specifically Christian way of speaking about God. Catherine Mowry LaCugna, however, holds that there is a gap between the trinitarian doctrine and life, and that there is a need to restore this doctrine to its rightful place at the

---

[22] Leonardo Boff, *Cry of the Earth, Cry of the Poor*, trans. Phillip Berryman (Maryknoll, NY: Orbis Books, 1997), xi. Poor women in developing world are given voice in the following book, among others: Ivone Gebara, *Longing for Running Water: Ecofeminism and Liberation* (Minneapolis, MN: Fortress Press, 1999).

[23] Boff, *Cry of the Earth, Cry of the Poor*, xii.

[24] Ibid., 110–11.

center of Christian faith and practice.[25] She views in the revitalization of the Cappadocian (not the Augustine nor Thomistic) doctrine of the Trinity a great potential for filling this gap and restoring the central place of the Trinity. The Cappadocians—Basil, Gregory of Nyssa, and Gregory of Nazanzius—made person rather than substance the decisive and primary ontological category. This was to assert that the divinity of Godhead originates with personhood (someone in relation with; someone toward another) rather than substance (something in and of itself). As the Greek theologian John Zizioulas states it, "God exists on account of a person, the Father, and not on account of a substance."[26] If God were not personal, God would not exist at all. Against *eunomianism,* which states that what makes God to be God—being unbegotten, unrelated to another—the Cappadocian Trinity shows that "love for and relationship with another is primary over autonomy, ecstasis over stasis, fecundity over self-sufficiency."[27] God by nature is outgoing love and self-donation.

Unlike the Cappadocians, who emphasized the equal but distinct roles of the Father, Son, and the Spirit—the divine unity and divine life located in the communion among equal though unique persons—Augustine held that the personhood of God is derived from essence; the unity of the Father, Son, and Spirit who are coequal is the divine substance, the common essence they share. Augustine's theology, as received by his interpreters and passed on in tradition, led to the image of a self-enclosed Trinity of Persons who in one undifferentiated act reach out to creatures. Although Augustine endeavored to make the Trinity more intelligible, there is a certain abstractness to his formulation. Augustine's theology contributed to the idea of the self as an individual rather than, as with the Cappadocians, someone who comes to self through another.

Thomas's treatment of the Trinity in the *Summa Theologiae* presents God's essence and existence as indistinguishable. God is the pure act of being, with no "real" relation to creation, insofar as God's act of being is not contingent upon the creature's act of being. His point was metaphysical: God alone is the self-sufficient act of being.

---

[25] See Elizabeth T. Groppe, "Catherine Mowry LaCugna's Contribution to Trinitarian Theology," *Theological Studies* 63/4 (2002): 730.

[26] John Zizioulas, *Being as Communion* (Crestwood, NY: St. Vladimir's Seminary, 1985), 41–42.

[27] Catherine Mowry LaCugna, "God in Communion with Us," in *Freeing Theology: The Essentials of Theology in Feminist Perspective,* ed. Catherine Mowry LaCugna, 83–114 (San Francisco: Harper Collins, 1993), 86.

This is the very nature of God, and it is the nature of creature to be totally dependent on God. This metaphysical perspective shows God as the perfect being, one who is not determined by any other being. LaCugna viewed these metaphysical claims as the possible reasons why Thomas's theological system has been perceived as an unsatisfactory theism. Thomas, in his treatment of the Trinity, explores the notions of relations and person: The Son comes from and is begotten by the Father; the Father and the Son together spirate the Spirit. In this sophisticated metaphysics Thomas focuses on the intra-divine relations (God's inner life) rather than on God's relationship with the creature. This approach fits the Scholastic paradigm and Aristotelian metaphysics, but the overall effect is the creation of an ontological chasm between God and the creature that cannot be overcome. The Augustine-Thomist theologies of the Trinity had the overall effect of depicting the Trinity as an intradivine reality, a self-sufficient and contained community.[28]

Beyond Rahner: Theologia *and* Oikonomia

In trinitarian theology the paradigm of the economic and immanent Trinity has been a key in conceiving the trinitarian mystery since the publication of Karl Rahner's work on the Trinity. Rahner affirmed and renewed the appreciation of the trinitarian God as self-communicating and self-expressive, and of the soteriology at the heart of the Trinity. He wrote in 1970, "The economic Trinity is the immanent Trinity and the immanent Trinity is the economic Trinity."[29] Rahner offered a paradigm to relate the inner life of the Trinity and soteriology. All theological paradigms, however, have their limitations. For one, even the term *immanent Trinity* is imprecise and could be open to confusion. In today's theology the word *immanence* used with reference to God refers to God coming close in communion with creatures, whereas the term *immanence* in the expression *immanent Trinity* means the opposite.

LaCugna suggests a moratorium on the terms *economic* and *immanent* as a step to greater precision, and she proposes that theologians develop alternative approaches. In consonance with Rahner's clarion call for a renewed trinitarian theology, she holds that the construction

---

[28] For the development of LaCugna's position regarding the priority of the Cappadocian Trinity over the Augustine-Thomistic Trinity, see ibid., 85–91.

[29] Karl Rahner, *The Trinity*, rev. ed., trans. Joseph Donceel, intro. Catherine Mowry LaCugna (New York: Crossroad, 1997; originally published 1970), 22.

of a trinitarian paradigm must prescind from the very language of the economic and immanent Trinity that Rahner used.[30] She proposes the following alternative paradigm for present-day trinitarian theology: the inseparability of *theologia* (the mystery of God) and *oikonomia* (the mystery of salvation). The term *theologia* does not simply replace the term *immanent,* nor is the meaning of *oikonomia* reduced to *economy.*[31] In LaCugna's work *theologia* refers to the mystery and being of God, and *oikonomia* is the "comprehensive plan of God reaching from creation to consummation, in which God and all creatures are destined to exist together in the mystery of love and communion." *Theologia* and *oikonomia* are distinct but inseparable dimensions of trinitarian theology. "*Theologia* is fully revealed and bestowed in *oikonomia* and *oikonomia* truly expresses the ineffable mystery of *theologia.*"[32]

The doctrine of the Trinity, which is the Christian way of speaking about God, summarizes what it means to participate in the life of God through Jesus Christ in the Spirit. The mystery of God is revealed in Christ and the Spirit as the mystery of love, the mystery of persons in communion who embrace death, sin, and all forms of alienation for the sake of life.[33] Trinitarian theology shows the inseparability of *theologia* and *oikonomia.* In this inseparability LaCugna gives primacy to relational ontology over the metaphysics of substance. At the heart and core of this relational ontology is the principle that "not only does soteriology require an ontological foundation, but soteriology must be decisive in our formulation of ontological statements about the being of God."[34]

> The doctrine of the Trinity is meant to express that who and what God is *with us* (as redemptive love) is exactly who God is *as God.* God can draw completely near to us, share history with us, and never be diminished either as mystery or as God. Indeed, one might add that God is Absolute Mystery not because God

[30] Catherine Mowry LaCugna, "Discussion of God for Us," lecture, Duke University, November 11, 1993. Cited in Groppe, "Catherine LaCugna's Contribution to Trnitarian Theology," 732n8.

[31] Groppe, "Catherine Mowry LaCugna's Contribution to Trinitarian Theology," 743.

[32] Catherine Mowry LaCugna, *God for Us: The Trinity and Christian Life* (San Francisco: Harper Collins, 1991), 223, 221. Elsewhere she described *theologia* as a reference to God's external being.

[33] Ibid., 1.

[34] As cited in Groppe, "Catherine Mowry LaCugna's Contribution for Trinitarian Theology," 747.

remains locked in otherworldly transcendence, but because the transcendent God becomes also absolutely immanent.[35]

The economy of creation and redemption unfolds the mystery of God who "is not self-contained, egotistical, and self-absorbed, but overflowing love, outreaching desire for union with all that God has made."[36] Further,

> if the very nature of God is to be related as love—and this, after all, is the fundamental claim of a trinitarian theology—then one can prescind from this relatedness and still hope to be making statements about the relational God. Far from devolving into a theological agnosticism, a trinitarian theology of God can affirm with confidence that God is who God reveals Godself to be.[37]

LaCugna's Trinity invites us to stand in loving awe at God's inscrutable and unfathomable love, and within this love, to renew our own vocation as persons in communion with God, and with one another, and with creation.

Naming God Rightly: A Feminist Critique of Trinitarian Theology

But even a trinitarian model that gives primacy to the relationality at the heart of the divine being cannot completely be free of a hierarchy of persons, contrary to the concept and experience of a truly mutual love of equals. This hierarchy is present even where the process is characterized as the movement of love, as exemplified in Walter Kasper's retrieval of the trinitarian tradition through the love categories of Richard of St. Victor:

> In the Father, love exists as pure source that pours itself out; in the Son it exists as a pure passing on, as pure mediation; in the Spirit, it exists as the joy of pure receiving. These three modes in which the one being of God, the one love, subsists, are in some sense necessary because love cannot be otherwise conceived.[38]

---

[35] LaCugna, "Problems with a Trinitarian Reformulation," *Louvain Studies* (1985): 330.

[36] LaCugna, *God for Us,* 15.

[37] LaCugna, "Problems with a Trinitarian Reformulation," 340.

[38] Walter Kasper, *The God of Jesus Christ,* trans. Matthew O'Connell (New York: Crossroad, 1984), 308–9.

When the procession of love goes from the First to the Second and to the Third, the First, the Father, assumes an ontological priority, and the Spirit appears to be the least and last of the three.[39] The word *persons* can also lend to a misunderstanding of the trinitarian doctrine, as it drifts from the arcane Greek philosophical concept of hypostasis, which approximately connotes the fundamental subsistence of a thing, to the contemporary understanding of *person* as an individual center of consciousness and freedom. Now to say that God is three Persons inevitably gives rise to tritheism, a belief in three gods. God is personal, interpersonal, and transpersonal in an unimaginably rich way, but the understanding of *person* in the trinitarian symbol escapes our grasp.[40]

Besides the hierarchy of relations within the Trinity, naming God in exclusively masculine terms posed another critical problem. Feminist theologians question whether the far-reaching negative consequences of an exclusively masculine imagery for God provides a religious legitimation of patriarchy. Mary Daly expressed the terms of this legitimation in her classic feminist critique of patriarchy and patriarchal language: "If God is male, the male is God."[41] The controversy on how to name God rightly is a problem in trinitarian theology, not only in feminist theology. Among ways of addressing the problem, what appeals most is to view the naming of God as Father from the perspective of Jesus as the iconoclast, protofeminist, and prophet who, though male, challenged the cultural stereotypes of his time and transformed them. Sandra Schneiders presents her insight into this Jesus perspective:

> In Jesus's culture the father-son metaphor was the only one capable of carrying the meaning of his integral involvement in the work of salvation originated by God. Second, by his use of "Abba" for God and his presentation of God as the father of the prodigal, Jesus was able to transform totally the patriarchal God-image. He healed the father metaphor which had been patriarchalized in the image of human power structures and restored to it the original meaning of divine origination in and through love. Third, he delegitimized human patriarchy by invalidating its appeal to divine institution.[42]

---

[39] Elizabeth A. Johnson, *She Who Is: The Mystery of God in Feminist Discourse* (New York: Crossroad, 1994), 196.

[40] Ibid., 203.

[41] Mary Daly, *Beyond God the Father* (Boston: Beacon Press, 1973), 18.

[42] Sandra M. Schneiders, *Women and Word: 1986 Madaleva Lecture in Spirituality* (New York: Paulist Press, 1986), 48.

This approach, while it remains faithful to the biblical facts, reckons with the historical and cultural conditioning of Jesus' teaching and mission. It is also grounded in the eschatological hope for the healing and transformation of fatherhood and masculinity of the sin of patriarchy. As Schneiders writes: "Jesus' teaching about God as father and his calling together of a new, non-patriarchal faith community of equal disciples constitute a liberating subversion of patriarchy which can no longer claim divine sanction but stands revealed as a sinful human structure."[43]

The fatherhood of God has been used to support the sexist language of complementarity, or gender dualism, and patriarchal language. The work of revision has begun, however, and three models have been presented to work to transform speech about God. The first model introduces feminine traits to the predominantly male image of God in order to transform and revise its overly masculine qualities. The revision, while it is a laudable attempt at including the female in conceiving God, has not redressed the inequality, but in fact has maintained it. The central figure remains male, now made even more appealing because of his integrated feminine qualities. The second model goes beyond integrating feminine qualities into a dominant and central image of God. It illuminates the feminine dimension in the Godself—the Holy Spirit as the feminine dimension in God, the maternal aspect of God. The model is criticized, however, because the trinitarian God is presented as two male images and an amorphous third, conceived as "the feminine" in God. The third model avoids the pitfalls of the first two. It envisions God equivalently as male and female, using parallel biblical images of the shepherd looking for the lost sheep and the woman looking for the lost coin. There is no danger of stereotyping because God's redeeming work is told in images that are equivalently male and female.[44]

The issue, however, goes much deeper than a revision of language about God. While language shapes our world of meaning and creates social systems, and requires ongoing revision so we can always speak rightly, merely changing language does not change reality.[45] "For example, changing from *Negro* to *black* hardly alleviated racism. On the other hand, by being forced to change language, whites were

---

[43] Ibid., 49.

[44] Elizabeth A. Johnson, "Incomprehensibility of God Male and Female," *Theological Studies* 45/3 (1984): 454–65.

[45] LaCugna, "God in Communion with Us," 107.

reminded of deep-seated racism and the ways that language bears and perpetuates racism."[46]

God is ultimately incomprehensible and unnamable. But we strive to come to an understanding of God that makes sense to us. An attempt to overcome the error of tritheism is by using *person* to speak of God's threefold relationship, as we encounter the one and the same God, in a way that is beyond us, with us, or within us.[47] Another suggestion is to speak of God as subsisting in three manners of self-subsistence, which is much closer to the meaning of the Greek word *hypostasis*. One objection to this use, however, is that if this were preached from the pulpit, people would not understand it.[48] What leads to the error of tritheism is a literal understanding of trinitarian language. To assume to know the inner life of God is a bold overreach of the human mind. We can only see darkly, and we can only speak analogically, for God is and yet is not what we say about God. Yet, we cannot stop speaking about God, for how can we be silent about the ultimate reality in our life?[49]

We need to deconstruct our imagination, set it free from our narrow and naive literalism, and then go right to the heart of the trinitarian theology characterized by self-giving and self-receiving. For God "to be" is "to be in relation." In the end, more important than the transformation of God language is the transformation of our hearts into who God is. "Commitment to inclusive language must be matched by commitment to inclusive commitment." This is where the trinitarian and Christian feminist agendas intersect. The doctrine of the Trinity affirms that the God into whose name we are baptized is neither the patriarchal Father-God nor a God who created women "less" than men. The God we know, love, and worship is the God we have come to know through Jesus, in and through the power of the Holy Spirit—Jesus in whom "there is no longer Jew or Greek, there is no longer slave or free, there is no longer male and female" (Gal 3:28). "The self-revelation of God in Christ remains the only sure source for overcoming distortions in theology and church practice, because it is only by living *in Christ* that we meet the living God whom Jesus proclaimed and through Christ are faithful to the true, living God."[50]

---

[46] Ibid.

[47] Elizabeth A. Johnson, *Quest for the Living God: Mapping Frontiers in the Theology of God* (New York: Continuum, 2007), 204.

[48] Ibid., 212–13.

[49] Johnson, *She Who Is*, 200.

[50] LaCugna, "God in Communion with Us," 105–7.

Jesus Christ: Kenosis, Reign of God, Atonement, Reusrrection, Global Christ

Jesus, Kenosis of God: A Feminist and Liberationist Perspective

The Trinity should not be thought of literally as three different people, but as the triune Mystery of self-donating, self-giving love. When the Trinity is understood this way, it becomes possible to see Jesus "existing as the Word of God in time, who, in his humanness, embodies the self-emptying of the God of love."[51] "The Word became flesh and lived among us" (Jn 1:14). This is beyond our nameable experience, but it is made expressible with the help of the biblical concept of *kenosis*, or self-emptying. God, who is eternally self-giving and self-donating within the divine Mystery, empties Godself in the human/historical realm in the person of Jesus of Nazareth. God's self-emptying of the glory of divinity to be human in Jesus is contemplated in Philippians 2:6–7:

> who, though he was in the form of God,
>   did not regard equality with God
>   as something to be exploited,
> but emptied himself,
>   taking the form of a slave.

Elizabeth Johnson writes:

> As this human being, Jesus is the Son of God. Precisely as this human being he is God in time. He is fully human, fully free, fully personal, and as such he is God who has self-emptied into our history. At the end of this progression of thought, what is restored to our consciousness is a way of envisioning Jesus to be genuinely human at the same time that the confession of his genuine divinity does not slip from view.[52]

---

[51] Elizabeth A. Johnson, *Consider Jesus: Waves of Renewal in Christology* (New York: Crossroad, 1990), 30.

[52] Ibid., 31. Also see Karl Rahner, "On the Theology of the Incarnation," *Theological Investigations,* vol. 4, *More Recent Writings* (New York: Seabury Press, 1974), 105–20; and idem, "Christology Within an Evolutionary View of the World," *Theological Investigations,* vol. 5, *Later Writings* (Baltimore: Helicon, 1966), 157–92. See also Leo O'Donovan, ed., *A World of Grace* (New York: Seabury Press, 1980), which helps facilitate the reading of Rahner by presenting both the context and thrusts of his theology; and Piet Schoonenberg, *The Christ: A Study of the God-Man Relationship in the Whole of Creation and in Jesus Christ* (New York: Herder and Herder, 1971).

While it is true that God has no sex, Jesus does, and the sex is male. The maleness of Jesus has been used to support the claim that the God revealed in Jesus is male and to legitimize male dominance and superiority in relation to women. It is also viewed as the justification of maleness as the norm of humanity. Schneiders writes: "If any of these ideas are true, the incarnation can only be seen as an unmitigated disaster for women."[53] She argues that Jesus as referred to in creed and cult as the Son of God incarnate does not reveal the maleness of the Second Person. For if the Second Person is male, so are the other two; they differ only in relationship not in nature. But to speak of God as male is to attribute to the divine nature a human limitation, sex.[54] This means that the Second Person of the Trinity came to be called son because Jesus is male, and not the other way around.[55]

But if Jesus is a genuine human being, why is he male rather than female? This question is critical because it is premised on a widely held assumption that Jesus was male because of the privileged place of maleness as the superior form of humanity, making it the appropriate locus for divine self-revelation. The revelation of God, however, has always defied the worldly standards of power and superiority, as shown in the pattern of divine action in both Hebrew and Christian scriptures. God declared to the Jews, "It was not because you were more numerous than any other people that the Lord set his heart on you and chose you—for you were the fewest of all peoples" (Dt 7:7). And this same divine logic is applied by Paul for the early Christians:

> Consider your own call, brothers and sisters: not many of you were wise by human standards, not many were powerful, not many were of noble birth. But God chose what is foolish in the world to shame the wise; God chose what is weak in the world to shame the strong; God chose what is low and despised in the world, things that are not, to reduce to nothing things that are, so that no one might boast in the presence of God. (1 Cor 1:26–29)[56]

One can argue that Jesus had to be male, for if the patriarchal culture of his time was to be redeemed, he had to liberate it from within. He had to be a countersign of the sins and abuses of this culture.

---

[53] Schneiders, *Women and the Word*, 50.
[54] Ibid., 50–51.
[55] Ibid., 51.
[56] Ibid., 57–58.

Jesus repudiated competition, the exercise of coercive power, all forms of domination and control of others, aggression and violence. He espoused meekness and humility of heart, peace-making, non-violence, silent patience in the face of injustice and suffering, recourse to personal prayer in times of difficulty, purity of heart, and a nurturing concern for all, especially the sick, the oppressed, sinners, women, and children.[57]

He invalidated the stereotypically male "virtues" and the masculine approach to reality, and honored the traits of women that both men and women had been taught to despise. Had Jesus been a woman, his espoused way of life, patterned after virtues that are stereotypically identified with women, would not have been revelatory.[58] It would not have challenged the patriarchal society and, thus, would not have been able to transform it.

Jesus' attitude toward women was also revelatory because he was a man in a culture where women were subjugated to the power and dominion of men. Believing in the full personhood of women and in the equality of women and men, he rejected any kind of participation in patriarchal privilege. He called men and women to a new relationship, in which one is not dominated by the other but both are fully flourishing in their humanity. He chose women as disciples and apostles (see Jn 4:4–42; 20:11–18); he praised their faith (Mt 9:22); and he accepted their love and friendship (Lk 7:37–38). He acknowledged them as equal partners in dialogue, unlike the men who rendered them silent or diminished their value (Jn 4:27–30). He defended them against arbitrary divorce and called both men and women to live by the demands of marital fidelity (Mt 19:3–9). He rejected the sexual double standard by defending the woman taken in adultery, who was to be stoned to death while the man, her partner in sin, was set free. And finally, he crowned the work and ministry of women by appearing first to his women disciples after the resurrection and entrusting to them the resurrection kerygma upon which the church was founded (Jn 20:11–18; see also Mk 16:9; Mt 28:9–10).[59] The maleness of Jesus was not an exaltation of maleness but the revelation of the soteriology of his incarnation. He became man, entered deeply into the male culture, but only to liberate it; he called women and men to a new and transformed relationship of equality and mutuality. Today, we call

---

[57] Ibid., 58–59.
[58] Ibid., 59.
[59] Ibid., 60.

Jesus a feminist in his belief in the full personhood of women and their equality with men in a new and transformed relationship.[60]

The kenosis of God, which is beyond all human construct, was made even more radical by Jesus's total solidarity with the poor. "Birds of the air have nests, but the Son of Man has nowhere to lay his head" (Lk 9:58). He was born into a poor family, was laid in an animal's feeding trough, and fled as a refugee from the murderous wrath of a king. Gustavo Gutiérrez captures the meaning of God's radical option for the poor by being poor in Jesus when he speaks of the advent of God in Jesus Christ as "an irruption smelling of the stable."[61] At the outset of his ministry, Jesus, reading from the scroll of Isaiah, set his heart on a ministry for the poor and the downtrodden:

> The Spirit of the Lord is upon me
> because he has anointed me
> to bring good news to the poor.
> He has sent me to proclaim release to the captives
> And recovery of sight to the blind,
> to let the oppressed go free
> to proclaim a year of the Lord's favor. (Lk 4:18–19)

Out of the reading of Jesus from the perspective of the poor and oppressed has come a potent christological title: Jesus Liberator. By imaging Jesus as Liberator, liberation theology (or specifically liberation Christology) takes a definite stance. This is not a neutral and objective portrayal of Jesus; this is Jesus in the prophetic-liberating tradition of the biblical faith of both the Jewish scriptures and in the Christian testament.[62] Highlighted in Jesus' ministry is its political dimension, which is the central hermeneutical key in Juan Luis Segundo's Christology.[63] Segundo's Christology is premised on the

---

[60] Ibid., 62. There has been much research done on the biblical testimony regarding Jesus and women. See, for example, works by Elisabeth Schüssler Fiorenza, Raymond Brown, Meir Tetlow, and Elizabeth Moltmann-Wendel. For popular treatments of the same theme, see Rachel Conrad Walberg, *Jesus According to a Woman* (New York: Paulist Press, 1975); and idem, *Jesus and the Freed Woman* (New York: Paulist Press, 1978). See also Leonard Swidler, "Jesus Was a Feminist," *New Catholic World* 214 (1971): 771–73.

[61] Gustavo Gutiérrez, *The God of Life* (Maryknoll, NY: Orbis Books, 1991), 84.

[62] Roger Haight, *Jesus: Symbol of God* (Maryknoll, NY: Orbis Books, 1999), 377–78.

[63] See Juan Luis Segundo, *The Historical Jesus of the Synoptics* (Maryknoll, NY: Orbis Books, 1985), 71–85. The following books address the theme of social

fact that Jesus' teaching posed a challenge and threat to the imperial colonial system of his day and subverted its entire way of life. Elisabeth Schüssler-Fiorenza writes, "Jesus was not crucified because of his theological teachings but because of their potentially subversive character and the political threat to the imperial colonial system."[64] It is the very religiosity of Jesus, the very faith at the foundation of his life, that profoundly engaged him with the political and public issues of his day.[65] There was no separation. The religiosity and faith that drew him intimately in prayer with God is the very same religiosity and faith that put him in the arena of the public and political issues of his day. This is liberation Christology at its edge, in Jesus as the Liberator against all forms of injustice and exploitation. Jesus, thus, as the kenosis of God, is the self-disclosure of God, who fully entered into the human condition, became one among us, and, embracing the poverty of the poor as his own, acts as a saving and liberating God.

Reign of God: Parables as Subversive

With Jesus at the center, the reign of God entails a reversal of worldly values, turning upside down the common standards of worthiness and acceptability. In the parables of the kingdom Jesus shows a love that exceeds all expectations and conditions, a prodigal love that reaches all, especially those who are in need, whether they are deserving or not. Such a love, which discipleship must imitate, reaches the edge in its forgiveness of enemies and its utter self-abandonment in the story of the good Samaritan and as instituted in the Sermon on the Mount in Matthew 5–7.

Jesus shared meals with the social underclass, like tax collectors, who were reviled because they were perceived as opportunists and grafters. Defying norms and laws of social relationships, Jesus' table fellowship was iconoclastic. It destroyed the boundaries that separated the pure and the impure, and it instituted a whole new and inclusive communal ethos rather than one that was exclusive, discriminatory, and hierarchical. The spirit of Jesus' table fellowship permeated his

justice in Christology: Thomas E. Clarke, ed., *Above Every Name: The Lordship of Christ and Social Systems* (Ramsey, NJ: Paulist Press, 1980); Sharon H. Ringe, *Jesus, Liberation, and the Biblical Jubilee: Images for Ethics and Christology* (Philadelphia: Fortress Press, 1985); and Carol Frances Jegen, *Jesus the Peacemaker* (Kansas City, MO: Sheed and Ward, 1986).

[64] Elisabeth Schüssler Fiorenza, *Jesus: Miriam's Child, Sophia's Prophet: Critical Issues in Feminist Christology* (New York: Continuum, 1994), 93.

[65] Haight, *Jesus*, 379. The deep connection of Jesus' ministry with the public and political issues of his time is the primary thrust of liberation Christology.

whole stance to the world of relations: he approached women directly without the usual practice of male intermediary in a patriarchal culture; he touched the sick, the lepers, those considered untouchables; he protected women from the practice of divorce as governed by patriarchal domination and caprice by forbidding divorce. Elisabeth Schüssler Fiorenza writes:

> the Jesus movement had experienced in the praxis of Jesus a God who called not Israel's righteous, but its religiously deficient and its social underdogs. In the ministry of Jesus, God is experienced as all inclusive love . . . a God who specially accepts the impoverished, the crippled, the outcast, the sinners, and prostitutes, as long as they are prepared to engage in the perspective and power of the *basileia*.[66]

Biblical portrayals of Jesus show that Jesus' ministry subverted institutionalized power relationships. However, although he represented a radical alternative social vision, he did not create a new social entity. The reign of God was immediate in the very presence, teaching, and miracles of Jesus, but it too had an eschatological nostalgia. The nostalgia for the final consummation of the reign of God sustains one's faith in its irrepressible power in the face of suffering, conflict, and failure. In the traditional societies of ancient Palestine, where the resources were limited and their distribution was determined by the patron-client relationship, the few who belonged to the elite class lived in excess, while the poor and the marginalized had, at best, only their basic subsistence needs met. The reign of God preached by Jesus posed a reversed worldview to that of the patron-client structural relationship and moved the early Christians to gather in communities, where they gave what they had without conditions and received according to need. This sharing and distribution of goods, inspired by the spirit of fellowship, solidarity, compassion, equality, and dignity, subverted the expectations and relationships of the social reality at that time.[67]

"Purity" societies in first-century Palestine define the social boundaries by their contrasting views of pure and impure, clean and unclean,

---

[66] Elisabeth Schüssler Fiorenza, *In Memory of Her: A Feminist Theological Reconstruction of Christian Origins*, tenth anniv. ed. (New York: Crossroad, 1994; originally published in 1983), 130.

[67] See, among others, Halvar Moxnes, *The Economy of the Kingdom: Social Conflict and Economic Relations in Luke's Gospel* (Philadelphia: Fortress Press, 1988); and John Dominic Crossan, *Jesus: A Revolutionary Biography* (San Francisco: Harper San Francisco, 1994).

qualities that apply to both individuals and groups. Purity is concerned in particular with what passes in and out of bodily orifices, representing the entrances and exits of society. Purity laws are connected with economics because they impose markers between the elite and the marginalized.[68] As such, these laws were wielded by the elite as their ideological tool in determining who is of lesser status and thus should have no access to material and political goods. In purity societies women are classified as impure because menstruation and childbirth are considered impure; so is any sexual contact with women.[69]

The ethos of Christianity, as opposed to the ethos of the Jewish purity laws, upsets the whole worldview where control, domination, and bias determine social relations. This Christian ethos draws its intrinsic spirit from Jesus, whose iconoclastic table fellowships with social outcasts—including tax collectors, sinners, and prostitutes—and whose healing of those afflicted believed to be ritually impure and socially ostracized, undermined the social markers and distinctions and opened a new way of social relations that were open and inclusive.[70] Embodying in his very being a whole new way of personal and social relations, Jesus undercut the bias and exclusion of the purity system and replaced it with a radical eclecticism that abandoned rigid social distinctions. More than instituting an abandonment of controls, he instituted a way of being characterized by invitation and inclusion. This love of God in Jesus Christ is manifested in his inclusive hospitality for all, bursting all social expectations and conditions, and breaking all barriers determined by class, gender, status, and religion. Such a love was as dangerous as it was iconoclastic, subverting all systems or institutions that were discriminatory and oppressive of the poor, women, and all who were marginalized.

Many of Jesus' parables proclaim the coming of the reign of God. These parables have been a subject of numerous studies, and the past decades have seen a flourishing of approaches. The historical analysis in the seminal work of Jeremias and Dodd has been supplemented and challenged by other methods premised on various disciplines. In particular, the book by William R. Herzog, *Parables as Subversive Speech,*

---

[68] Marcus J. Borg, *Meeting Jesus Again for the First Time: The Historical Jesus and the Heart of Contemporary Faith* (San Francisco: Harper San Francisco, 1994), 108; and idem, *Conflict, Holiness, and Politics in the Teachings of Jesus* (New York: Edwin Mellen, 1984).

[69] See Lisa Sowle Cahill, *Sex, Gender, and Christian Ethics* (Cambridge: Cambridge University Press, 1996), 129–30.

[70] Crossan, *Jesus,* 68–69, 82.

has revolutionized the study of Jesus' parables.[71] A groundbreaking book, it uses the methodologies of social scientists and applies them to a sampling of two groups of biblical parables. To the first group Herzog gives the title "Unmasking the World of Oppression," and to the second group, "Opening Up New Possibilities: Challenging the Limits." In the first group are the following parables: the laborers in the vineyard (Mt 20:1–16); the wicked tenants (Mk 12:1–12); the rich man and the Lazarus (Lk 16:19–31); the unmerciful servant (Mt 18:23–35); and the talents (Mt 25:14–30; Lk 19:11–27). In the second group are the following parables: the Pharisee and the tax collector (Lk 18:9–14); the friend at midnight (Lk 11:5–8); the unjust judge (Lk 18:1–8); and the dishonest steward (Lk 16:1–9).

Herzog premises his approach to the parables on his vision of who Jesus is and what his mission entails: "The comparison of the quest for the parables of Jesus with the quest for the historical Jesus raises a fundamental question. Any study of Jesus' parables will be predicated on some larger understanding of what Jesus' public life was all about."[72] He argues that if Jesus was a teacher of heavenly truths dispensed through literary gems called parables, it would be difficult to understand why he was crucified between two social bandits. It appears that the Jewish leaders conspiring with their Roman overlords executed Jesus because they saw him as a threat to their interests. His teaching challenged the social systems and structures that maintained their positions of political and economic power and privilege. If they did not perceive him to be a threat, they would have not subjected him to such degradation and humiliation before executing him in as ignominious a way as possible. The main thrust of Herzog's book is to bring together the teacher who spoke in parables and the subversive who threatened the powers of his day. He does this by interpreting the parables of Jesus as subversive speech and by showing him as a pedagogue of the oppressed.

Herzog uses the work of Paulo Freire, especially *Pedagogy of the Oppressed*, as a guide for understanding some of the parables.[73] Freire used his pedagogy as a tool of analysis, so as the poor were learning how to read, they were also learning how to read their culture, including the systems of domination, exploitation, and marginalization. The key that unlocked this process was *codification*. Herzog viewed Jesus

---

[71] William R. Herzog II, *Parables as Subversive Speech: Jesus as Pedagogue of the Oppressed* (Louisville, KY: John Knox, 1994).

[72] Ibid., 14.

[73] See Paulo Freire, *Pedagogy of the Oppressed*, 30th anniv. ed. (New York: Bloomsbury Academic, 2000; originally published in 1970).

using storytelling as codifications designed to stimulate social analysis of the power structures and systems of his day in order to expose the contradictions between their present situation and the reign of God's justice. Freire's pedagogy of the oppressed is not neutral; it is political to the core. The parables of Jesus also were not neutral; they provoked the hearers to decode the oppressive reality or limit situations or boundaries of their closed world. Like Freire's codifications, the parables begin with everyday events in the lives of the listeners—hiring and paying of day laborers; contracting with tenants to tend a vineyard; providing hospitality for a visitor to a small village; settling an estate claimed by a widow; and the conflicts among steward, merchants, and absentee landlord. In the long history of interpretation of parables, it has been held that the parables presented scenes from everyday life to show that the reign of God is so intimately woven into everyday life.[74]

But, as Freire knew, the danger of beginning with daily life was that the poor had internalized the world of their oppressors and had been reduced to interpreting their reality through the lens of their oppressors. Therefore, the codification had to shock the hearers out of their instinctive acquiescence to the interpretation of reality imposed on them. A critical dissonance is created between the reality in the parable and the reality of their everyday lives. Herzog writes:

> Thus, for example, a lofty elite goes to the marketplace to hire day laborers; a lowly day laborer challenges a member of the ruling class; Lazarus ends up in Abraham's bosom while the rich man burns in Hades; violence breaks out unaccountably and unexpectedly in the vineyard; a royal act of forgiveness of debt leads to the torturer's dungeon, not to the reign of God; a highly placed retainer buries a talent rather than invests it; a widow beats the system and gets justice; and a steward, with the deck stacked against him, wins the hand, even though the master held all the cards.[75]

This critical dissonance is interpreted by most as the incongruity between life on earth and life in the reign of God. Herzog takes this dissonance to hold the parable up as an object for contemplation and analysis by the hearers. It lured them into the process of decoding and problematizing their world. And then they are led to move from the

---

[74] See Herzog, *Parables as Subversive Speech*, 16–29.
[75] Ibid., 261.

parable to the larger systemic realities, from the surface to the depths of the structures and systems of oppression. The parables in the first group explore the world of oppression and the way it works:

> The parable of the laborers in the vineyard problematizes the relationship between wages and work; the parable of the wicked tenants problematizes the issues of land tenure, ownership, and inheritance in the context of the spiral of violence and aggression; the parable of the rich man and Lazarus problematizes the relationship between earthly status and kinship with Abraham; the parable of the unmerciful servant problematizes the hidden contradictions in popular messianic hopes; and the parable of the talents problematizes the dilemma of whistle-blowing retainers. At a deeper level, a number of the parables problematize the relationship between the debt code and the purity codes of the Torah as they were worked out in daily life.[76]

The parables in the second group probe limit situations and pursue limit actions that can bring about a twist or turn of events. To analyze the systems of oppression is one thing, but it is quite another to envision how to change them. The parables in group two present characters who rebel against the situations they are in, refusing to be victims of their circumstances; for example, a tax collector "claims the value of the rituals of the redemptive media for the outcast and receives justification; and a villager refuses to hoard and extends hospitality; a widow breaks the culture of silence and demands justice at the gate; a steward refuses to become a statistic and outsmarts his master."[77] Jesus' concerns were rooted in the Torah as it was used as a tool by the ruling elites of Jerusalem and the Herodian client-rulers to control the lives of the people of the land. His was a prophetic reading of the Torah that condemned injustice and oppression and invited his hearers to a new order, the reign of God. The parables were part of this larger vision at the center of which is Jesus' compassion and justice for the poor.[78]

One clear implication of this approach to parables as subversive speech is that Jesus' ministry was not removed from the economic and political realities of his day. Matters of justice were at the core of his ministry; there was no separation between the things of the

---

[76] Ibid., 262.
[77] Ibid.
[78] Ibid., 264.

spirit and matters of justice. In fact, we can say that justice was at the center of Jesus' spirituality. It is possible to interpret the parables without regard for its social realities, as it is also possible to engage in ministry without regard for social context. But when theology is not premised on social, political, and economic analysis, it becomes a theology in a vacuum. The parables grew out of the world of the hearers, and it lured them to codify and problematize their situations and to enter into analysis and dialogue within a larger context. Today, we must learn to tell new parables that codify and problematize our world as well as Jesus told parables for his world. That the parables were anchored in daily life points to a theology that does not begin with "mysteries of God but with the perplexities of daily life." When this happens, we discover a different kind of "spirituality not confined to an ethereal realm beyond time and space but rooted in and growing out of their historical and social context. Justice and justification, righteousness, and right relations, gospel and social analysis and spiritual reflection are dimensions of a single whole, not antithetical opposites."[79]

Death and Atonement: Feminist Critical Voices

Did Jesus die because of the way he lived? Or was it a design of God? Sharp debates about the death of Jesus sparked by feminist and womanist theologians are at the cutting edge of discussions about Christology and atonement. The critical feminist voices are directed against Anselm's satisfaction atonement theory, which assumes that the sin of humankind offended God and that the penalty exacted by this sin has been paid by Jesus' death on the cross. Sin was atoned for because it was punished, but this full atonement could only be made possible by the death of the incarnate God, for no less than God's ultimate justice and honor had been offended by humankind. Satisfaction-atonement is founded on the assumption that doing justice means to punish, and that a wrong deed is balanced by violence.

There are variants of the feminist and womanist critical discourse on Christology and atonement, but one of the sharpest criticisms is articulated by Joanne Carlson Brown and Rebecca Parker. According to them, women have been conditioned to accept suffering. The authors point to Christianity as a central force in shaping women's acculturation to abuse. The image of Christ on the cross teaches that suffering is redemptive, and only if women pattern their lives after

---

[79] Ibid., 264–66.

the suffering Christ can they find their own identity and value. The pernicious impact of such a christological symbol leads women to keep silent for years about experiences of sexual abuse, not to report rape, and to stay in marriages in which they are both physically and mentally abused.[80]

What complicates the image of the suffering Christ on the cross is his silent submission and obedience to his father's will. Brown and Parker use the image of the divine child to depict this suffering at the behest of his father. "Divine child abuse is paraded as salvific and the child who suffers 'without even raising a voice' is extolled as the hope of the world."[81] Rita Nakashima Brock, arguing along the same lines, writes that satisfaction-atonement reflects views of divine power that sanction child abuse on a cosmic scale.[82]

Brown and Parker state that many are persuaded to live a life of "self-sacrifice and obedience" with the resurrection as the promise of the reward for enduring pain, humiliation, and lack of freedom, even at the cost of their sacred right to self-determination, wholeness, and freedom. Since women have been acculturated to accept the role of the suffering servant, this belief in divinely sanctioned, innocent suffering contributes to the victimization of women in both church and society.[83] It is the patriarchalization of Christology, as analyzed by Rosemary Radford Ruether, that provides the theological grounding of women as suffering servants and subservient victims.[84]

Christine Gudorf asserts that the sacrifice of a surrogate does not interrupt the cycle of violence. It serves to protect those in power from violent protest by those whom they oppress. By ritualizing the suffering and death of Jesus and by lifting it up as an exemplar of perfect obedience and self-sacrifice for the powerless in society and church, Christian ministry and theology continue to foster the cycle of evil.[85] Elisabeth Schüssler Fiorenza states: "A theology that is silent about the sociopolitical causes of Jesus' execution and stylizes him as the

---

[80] Joanne Carlson Brown and Rebecca Parker, "For God So Loved the World?" in *Christianity, Patriarchy, and Abuse: A Feminist Critique,* ed. Joanne Carlson Brown and Carole R. Bohn, 1–30 (Cleveland: Pilgrim Press, 1989), 2.

[81] Ibid.

[82] Rita Nakashima Brock, *Journeys by Heart: A Christology of Erotic Power* (New York: Crossroad, 1998), 56.

[83] Brown and Parker, "For God So Loved the World?" 2–3.

[84] See Rosemary Radford Ruether, *Sexism and God-Talk: Toward a Feminist Theology* (Boston: Beacon Press, 1983), 122–26.

[85] Christine E. Gudorf, *Victimization: Examining Christian Complicity* (Philadelphia: Trinity Press International, 1992), 14–15.

paradigmatic sacrificial victim whose death was either willed by God or was necessary to propitiate God continues the kyriarchical cycle of violence and victimization instead of empowering believers to resist and transform it."[86]

J. Denny Weaver proposes an alternative to the abusive atonement images rejected by Brown and Parker, although he takes seriously their critique of the traditional christological atonement. Weaver restores to the equation the devil that Anselm removed in his satisfaction-atonement. By removing the devil from the equation and making humankind responsible directly to God, Anselm made God the only agent behind the death of Jesus. Weaver writes:

> Since the death is aimed at God as part of the equation but sinners cannot pay the debt to God's honor for themselves; and *since the devil is not paying anything to God nor obeying the will of God nor even any longer in the equation,* God is the possible one remaining who can oversee the death of Jesus so that it pays the divine debt to justice. The logic behind Anselm's atonement image points to God as the agent behind the death of Jesus.[87]

Weaver's devil is not a personified being who may or may not have rights in the divine order of things. Following Walter Wink, he regards the devil or Satan as the accumulation of evil, with a rule so comprehensive that it exists at all levels, from the individual to the cosmic. Its reality is found through systems and institutions and the people who compose them. None of these systems and institutions is good or evil in itself, but the moral character of its agency depends on its alignment or lack of alignment with the reign of God.[88]

It was this accumulation of evil, the reign of Satan, that put Jesus to death. Jesus did not seek his own death; neither did God will it. It was his prophetic work for the reign of God that brought him into a deadly conflict with systems and institutions of his time that were

---

[86] Schüssler Fiorenza, *Jesus,* 106. For a feminist discussion of sacrifice and ritual by a sociologist of religion, see Nancy Jay, *Throughout Your Generations Forever: Sacrifice, Religion, and Paternity* (Chicago: University of Chicago, 1992).

[87] J. Denny Weaver, *The Nonviolent Atonement* (Grand Rapids, MI: Eerdmans, 2001), 200.

[88] Ibid., 210–11. See Walter Wink's power trilogy: *Naming the Powers: The Language of Power in the New Testament; Unmasking the Powers: The Invisible Forces That Determine Human Existence;* and *Engaging the Powers: Discernment and Resistance in a World of Domination* (Minneapolis, MN: Fortress Press, 1982, 1984, 1992).

opposed to the reign of God. To pose a threat to the established power could be fatal. Those who dared challenge such enormity of power put themselves at the edge. This is what Jesus did in his proclamation of the reign of God in his person and in his mission.[89]

This is not a passive sufferer of satisfaction-atonement made to pay the debt of sin that has offended God. This is an active resister who turned upside down ways of being and doing that betray the values of the reign of God. He opposed sin, injustice, and oppression. Consider the many stories of Jesus confronting evil people and institutions—defying prejudice against Samaritans, confronting greed, defending women against their accusers, healing on the Sabbath, cleansing the Temple, and much more. This is not a model of passive submission to abuse; this is not an imagery of suffering that is salvific in and of itself, to be desired and wanted. On the contrary, it opposes all forms of suffering that oppression and injustice weigh down on people; it sets free both oppressed and oppressors from the systemic evils that bind them. And it calls victims out of their victimization to become active resisters.[90]

Finally, salvation and justice are no longer based on the violence of justice equated with punishment. Salvation does not depend on balancing sin by retributive violence, with God as the ultimate punisher. Justice is accomplished by doing the work of justice. Salvation is fulfilled by the very fruit of one's work of justice.[91] Jesus came "that they may have life, and have it abundantly" (Jn 10:10). He did not come to die, believing that this was his fate. No, he lived to the fullest, excluded no one from his radical embrace of love, but was willing to face death as the final act of a life so fully lived. Death, then, was the consequence of a life of love; it was not the ultimate end of a divinely sanctioned fate or design.

Liberation theology takes the same stance. In *Jesus Christ Liberator,* Leonardo Boff writes:

Death was not a catastrophe that came abruptly into the life of Christ. His message, life, and death form a radical unity. Violent death is in one way or another implied in the demands of his preaching. . . . He knows that whoever tries to change the human situation for the better and free people for God, for others, and for themselves must pay with death. He knows that all the

---

[89] Weaver, *The Nonviolent Atonement,* 211.
[90] Ibid., 221–22.
[91] Ibid., 212.

prophets died a violent death (Luke 11:47–51; 13:34; Mark 12:22). He also knows of the tragic end of the last and greatest of all the prophets, John the Baptist (Mark 9:13).[92]

The Mystery of Resurrection

The resurrection of Jesus is the foundation of the Christian faith. But how to move from the historical witness to a theological hermeneutics of the resurrection that is intelligible is a critical question. While the resurrection accounts are told as straightforward stories, to understand them exactly as they are told is to misread them, because at the bottom this is not what they are. One has to negotiate the tension between history and theology, because resurrection faith demands both fidelity to the gospel testimony and a critical reflection on this testimony. This task of correlating history and theology, however, is made complicated by the pluralism of interpretations both on the level of gospel data and theological construction. There is no consensus on the historical character of the empty tomb tradition and the appearance narratives, just as there is a whole spectrum of theological glosses of the meaning and significance of the resurrection for Christian faith.[93]

In the face of the aforementioned pluralism, and given the limited purpose of this chapter, I pursue one way of understanding the meaning of the resurrection, as proposed by Roger Haight. Haight holds that the resurrection of Jesus was a passage into another world, into the sphere of the ultimate and absolute reality who is God, which is totally beyond any human construct of imagination. In this sense he does not speak of the resurrection as a historical event, because if it is spoken of this way, an event of transcendence is turned into a worldly event that can be subjected to empirical investigation.[94]

Haight's position stands in contrast to those who take an empirical-historicist interpretation. For example, Wolfhart Pannenberg asserts that the resurrection was a public historical event that historians can study and probe. Fueled by his apologetic concern, he understands revelation as mediated through history. The resurrection of Jesus

---

[92] Leonardo Boff, *Jesus Christ Liberator: A Critical Christology for Our Time,* trans. Patrick Hughes (Maryknoll, NY: Orbis Books, 1978), 111. Boff presents a meditation on the cross from a liberationist perspective in *Passion of Christ, Passion of the World* (Maryknoll, NY: Orbis Books, 1987).

[93] Haight, *Jesus,* 119–20.

[94] Ibid., 124.

must be a historically demonstrable event. This historical necessity is needed as a divine confirmation of the personal claims raised by Jesus' public life and as the foundation of the meaning of history as a whole.[95] He, however, fails to reckon with critical epistemological questions of how the historical event of the resurrection might be imagined by historians.[96] "Is the resurrection of Jesus historically demonstrable to an open-minded but neutral observer?" is one of the questions which remains.[97] Nicholas Lash also insists that the resurrection of Jesus is a historical fact. He states: "If the doctrine of the resurrection is true, it is factually true, and the fact to which it refers is a fact about Jesus."[98] Haight writes that Lash rejects the position that reduces the resurrection to an entirely subjective perception, devoid of an objective historical testimony based on public testable data.[99]

Haight holds that what motivates the insistence on the historicity of the resurrection is legitimate; it does not, however, warrant the unqualified assertion that it is a historical fact, in a way that it strongly associates it with the empirical, making it a this-worldly event. Haight asserts that such historicizing undermines the fundamental nature of the resurrection as a transcendent object of faith.[100] He writes:

> What happened to Jesus in and through his death is transcendent; it is an eschatological reality that transpired in a region that is not circumscribed by the physicality of the finite world. . . . Because being exalted is transcendent, the term "resurrection" is symbolic in pointing attention to another order of reality, that of existing within the creator God's own life, which cannot be grasped directly or immediately. Being resurrected is an object of faith-hope: faith, as an engaged commitment to the reality

---

[95] See Wolfhart Pannenberg, *Jesus—God and Man* (Philadelphia: Westminster, 1968), 88–106. His position is dramatically opposed to that of Rudolf Bultmann. See Rudolf Bultmann, "New Testament and Mythology: The Problem of Demythologizing the New Testament Proclamation," in *New Testament and Mythology and Other Basic Writing*, ed. Schubert M. Ogden, 1–41 (Philadelphia: Fortress Press, 1984).

[96] Haight, *Jesus*, 124.

[97] John Galvin, "Jesus Christ," in Schüssler and Galvin, *Systematic Theology*, 1:251–324, esp. 306.

[98] Nicholas Lash, "Easter Meaning," *Heythrop Journal* 25 (1984): 12.

[99] Haight, *Jesus*, 124.

[100] Ibid.

symbolized in the story of Jesus; hope, as openness to the future, and as involving concern about one's own destiny.[101]

In summing up the nature of the resurrection, he states:

> It is the assumption of Jesus of Nazareth into the life of God. It is Jesus being exalted and glorified within God's reality. This occurred through and at the moment of Jesus' death, so that there was no time between his death and his resurrection and his exaltation. This is a transcendent reality which can only be appreciated by faith-hope. I take this to be a middle and mediating position between an existential and an empirical-historicist interpretation of the New Testament witness.[102]

In taking this position Haight does not deny the fact of the resurrection but insists on its transcendence beyond an empirical-historicist worldview. All transcendent reality, however, is historically mediated. And the historical mediation of the resurrection is Jesus of Nazareth; he is the necessary ground of the resurrection. "Jesus of Nazareth remains the concrete focal point of primitive Christian faith in the resurrection itself. In other words, the external, objective, and historical referent of Christian faith in the resurrection of Jesus is the Jesus of history, the person Jesus in his pre-Easter life."[103] The one who was resurrected is Jesus, so there is a radical continuity between the personal identity of Jesus during his lifetime and his being with God. "One cannot affirm a resurrection of Jesus without reference to Jesus of Nazareth."[104]

Haight proceeds by explaining the historical grounds for belief in Jesus' resurrection. By grounds, he means "factors that focus attention on Jesus as the object of God's action,"[105] which have taken hold of the minds and hearts of the disciples and everyone who encountered him. First is the impelling moral coherence of Jesus' teaching, which manifests the love, goodness, and justice of God. And his teaching

---

[101] Ibid., 125.

[102] Ibid., 126.

[103] Ibid., 148. Rudolf Pesch takes the same position. For a summary of Pesch's position and the debate it evoked, see John P. Galvin, "Resurrection as *Theologia Crucis Jesu*: The Foundational Christology of Rudolf Pesch," *Theological Studies* 38/3 (1977): 513–25. Pesch's current view has shifted to a more traditional position.

[104] Haight, *Jesus*, 142.

[105] Ibid.

comes with an awe-inspiring authority that makes him stand above the content of his message; people experience God in his sheer word and presence. Finally, the moral coherence of his teaching and the authority with which he taught are validated by the way he lived and died. In the end it is this life so fully lived in utter goodness and compassion for others that reveals who God is.[106]

The resurrection faith—faith in Jesus as alive in the life of God—can only be the initiative of God as Spirit. But the action of the Spirit is not unmediated; rather, it operates within a religious human experience that is accessible to faith as a reasonable act. It is mediated through the lingering memory of the disciples' encounter with the humanity of Jesus, and their lingering commitment to his person as the one in whom they encountered God.[107] It is this graced memory and commitment that enabled them to see beyond the empty tomb and recognize Jesus in the resurrection appearances. And they were never the same again. They who cowered in fear behind doors now fearlessly preached their faith in the risen Christ in Jerusalem, where they too could easily meet the same fate as their master. But the chains of death had been broken, and the new life in the resurrection engulfed them with a new power and hope.

The resurrection is the ultimate shaper of reality. Sin is not the last word. Love is. Death is not the final power. Life is. Haight writes

> What God begins in love, because of the complete boundlessness of that love, continues to exist in that love, thus overcoming the power and finality of death. . . . What God did in Jesus, God always does and has always done. For the salvation accomplished in Jesus Christ consists in revealing the true nature and action of God.[108]

The life, death, and resurrection of Jesus are indivisible; they constitute the whole meaning of the Incarnation of God—the full kenosis of the love of God in Jesus Christ.[109]

---

[106] Ibid., 142–43.

[107] Ibid., 145–46.

[108] Ibid., 147.

[109] For Karl Rahner, the resurrection is inseparable from the crucifixion. The resurrection of Christ is not *another* event *after* his suffering and after his death. See "Dogmatic Questions on Easter," in *Theological Investigations,* vol. 4, *More Recent Writings,* trans. Kevin Smyth (Baltimore: Helicon, 1966), 128. For Edward Schillebeeckx's position, which diverges sharply from Karl Rahner's position, see Galvin, "Jesus Christ," 310.

Search for the Global Christ

Miguel A. De La Torre recounts the following:

During Holy Week of 2001, the Discovery Channel and British Broadcasting Corporation coproduced a television documentary titled *Jesus: The Complete Story*. While some interpretations based on so-called recent scientific discoveries were questionable, of interest was the attempt to re-create Jesus' physical appearance. Using a two-thousand-year-old Jewish skull, a forensic artist created a computer-generated image of what Jesus might have looked like. Skin pigmentation and hair color were based on third-century frescoes of Jewish faces found in the ruins at Dura-Europos in Syria. The final image revealed an olive-skinned man with short dark curly hair. This image of Jesus challenged the traditional one that dates from the fifth century, as well as the more modern white-skinned, blue-eyed, blond-haired Jesus popularized on stained-glass windows and portraits.

For purposes of our inquiry, it really is unimportant if this reconstructed image represents how Jesus might have looked. Of greater interest is the reaction of some members of the dominant culture to this non-Eurocentric-looking Jesus, a reaction best illustrated by newspaper columnist Kathleen Parker of the Tribune Media Services in an article titled "Jesus Falls Victim to Makeover Madness." She bemoaned the fact that "this new Jesus looks like no one familiar. The willowy, long-haired figure who in picture books attracted children . . . now looks like the kind of guy who wouldn't make it through airport security." She was specifically disgusted with the new Jesus' jaw, which "looks likely to chomp down on a brontosaurus thigh," and his wide nose, which she calls a "snout that snorts." In short, she voices her anger that the white Jesus she grew up with is being replaced by an ethnic-looking Jesus, a Jesus who looks more like someone from the margins of society. She concludes by blasting the tendency of academic researchers to "debunk" the Aryan Jesus, insisting that Jesus was *really* a bisexual, cross-dressing, whale-saving, tobacco-hating, vegetarian African Queen who actually went to temple to lobby for women's rights.[110]

---

[110] Miguel A. De La Torre, *Reading the Bible from the Margins* (Maryknoll, NY: Orbis Books, 2001), 104–5. Parker's article, to which he refers, appeared in *The Grand Rapids Press* (April 14, 2001).

Whatever Jesus might look like, what is important is *who* he is and what he means in our life. The question that Jesus posed—"Who do you say that I am?" (Mt 16:15)—can be expressed in other ways: What do I mean to you? How does belief in me make a difference in your life? How do you reckon with the imperatives of my word and witness in the way you love and hope? The answers arise from the situations in which people live, spiritualities shaped by their cultures, their communities of faith, and by the circumstances of their lives.

Michael Amaladoss argues that images can be as important as doctrines in grasping who Jesus is.

> All images of Jesus arise in the context of the dialectic between his person and life and the life of the disciples. They answer the question: what does he mean to us today? They have double roots, one in his life as reported to us in the gospels, and the other in the culture and history of the disciples, though one of these roots may be stronger in a particular image. For example, while the crucified Jesus is more rooted in his life, the Sacred Heart is more cultural.[111]

Amaladoss explores images of Jesus in the Asian context of cultural and religious pluralism. Jesus was born, lived, preached, and died in Asia, yet he is often seen as one from the West. Jesus as sage, guru, way, *satyagrahi,* avatar, servant, pilgrim, and even as dancer "jolt our imagination from its dogmatic slumber and awaken it to the richness and diversity of our Christological heritage."[112]

A lay theologian of the Presbyterian Church of Korea, Chung Hyun Kyung, reflects on this question: Who is Jesus for Asian Women? She writes that Asian women draw from those traditional images of Jesus to which they can deeply relate from the depths of their life experiences. The most prevailing is the image of the suffering servant.[113] According to a 1987 statement developed by the Asian Women's Theological Conference, Asian Christian women from many different countries define Jesus as "the prophetic messiah whose role is that of the suffering servant," "the one who offers himself as ransom for many," and "through his suffering messiahship he creates a new

---

[111] Michael Amaladoss, *The Asian Jesus* (Maryknoll, NY: Orbis Books, 2006), 2.

[112] Ibid., Peter Phan's endorsement, back cover.

[113] Chung Hyun Kyung, *Struggle to Be the Sun Again: Introducing Asian Women's Theology* (Maryknoll, NY: Orbis Books, 1990), 53.

humanity."[114] They reject images of Jesus as "triumphal king" and "authoritative high priest" because these images have "served to support a patriarchal religious consciousness in the Church and in society."[115] The image of Jesus' suffering gives Asian women the wisdom to distinguish suffering imposed by an oppressor and suffering that is the consequence of one's stand for justice and human dignity.

Smokey Mountain was a huge garbage dump in the heart of the city of Manila, Philippines. Several thousand tons of garbage collected daily from all over the city were dumped on Smokey Mountain. More than twenty-five thousand people lived on the dump site and scavenged in the sea of trash in order to survive. Benigno P. Beltran, a Filipino priest, lived with the people for thirty years as their chaplain. In his book *Faith and Struggle on Smokey Mountain* he reflects on who Christ is for the scavengers. Written with powerful eloquence, this book is about the faith and song of a people, the jewels of the pauper, amid unspeakable squalor, stench, and degradation. Beltran writes that there are no atheists on Smokey Mountain.

> Faith is as natural to the scavengers as breathing. They have an intuitive understanding of the human need to believe in the transcendent. . . . Their brains are hard wired for faith, partly because of their culture, partly because of their poverty. The poor know they are in urgent need of redemption. The omnipresent symbols of Catholicism in make-shift altars inside their hovels depict their deep feeling of intimacy and their belief in the easy accessibility of the divine.[116]

The birth, life, death, and resurrection of Christ constitute the faith narrative that is deeply woven into the fabric of their lives. In the traditional *panunuluyan* (the search of Mary and Joseph for a place to lodge for the night) the scavengers depict it with a Smokey Mountain touch. After having been rejected by the rich, powerful, and famous in society, Mary faints from hunger and weariness, and it is the scavengers who rush to help. They let her ride on their pushcart among the tin cans and pieces of plastic they gathered and bring her to their humble shanty in the garbage dump where she gives birth

---

[114] "Summary Statement from the Theological Study Group," presented at the Consultation on Asian Women's Theology Singapore, November 20–29, 1987.

[115] Chung, *Struggle to Be the Sun Again*, 53.

[116] Benigno P. Beltran, *Faith and Struggle on Smokey Mountain: Hope for a Planet in Peril* (Maryknoll, NY: Orbis Books, 2012), 64.

to Jesus. The entire scene brings tears to their eyes.[117] Believing that Christ is truly in their midst, and having been taught that Calvary was a garbage dump outside the gates of Jerusalem, they regard the dump site as a sacred place where they follow the steps of Jesus in the Way of the Cross on Good Friday. They carry the dead Christ *(Santo Intierro)* in procession as some men whip themselves with lashes that have broken pieces of glass tied at the ends. On Easter, the images of the victorious Christ and blessed Mother are marched in procession as the people celebrate with dance and song. Ritual and symbol are as necessary to the scavengers as food and water.[118]

In *Galilean Journey* Virgilio Elizondo relates the story of the Galilean Jesus to the story of a new mestizo people. He states the Galilee principle: "What human beings reject, God chooses as his very own." He contends that the Galilean identity is the essential starting point of Christian identity and mission today. He writes:

> We have to be aware of what Galilee was and what it meant to be a Galilean so as to discover the places and peoples with a similar identity and role in today's world. It was said that nothing good come out of Galilee. God ignored them and chose it as his starting point. He revealed himself in what the world ignored. It is there that the unsuspected event took place. It is in the unsuspected places and situations of the world and through the "unlikely" persons that God continues to work today.[119]

The Galilean principle strikes a deep resonance in the hearts of Mexican Americans. In their mingling of ethnicity, race, and culture, as *mestizaje,* they find their profound connection with Jesus, whose marginalized Galilean identity marked him as a mestizo too. In their struggle for their own identity in a world that marginalizes them, they find new life and hope in the Galilean Jesus.

African American theologians James Cone and J. Deotis Roberts understand Christ's blackness as symbolic. When the finite mind is unable to fathom an infinite Being, it takes recourse in the use of symbols which, however, cannot fully capture the essence of the Divine. But in identifying with the black Christ, African Americans are enabled to define who they truly are in a racist society. Jesus' blackness is his

---

[117] Ibid., 62-63.

[118] Ibid., 88–93.

[119] Virgilio Elizondo, *Galilean Journey: The Mexican Promise,* rev. and exp. ed. (Maryknoll, NY: Orbis Books, 2000), 91–92.

solidarity with the oppressed and despised people of the world, "the least of my people." While Cone points to Jesus' blackness to Christ's particular identification with African Americans, Roberts extends its meaning to the universal, to Christ's relationship with all of humanity. The claim of African Americans to a black Christ is the same claim that white, red, yellow, and brown people have to Jesus in their own likeness.[120]

Symbols, though finite, create a relationship with the subject of the symbol. For black people, Jesus' blackness transforms blackness from a quality that is abhorred to one that is raised to dignity, one that is honored and loved. Because the Divine is black, Christ's identification with the struggle of African Americans is affirmed, and Christ's commitment to black liberation is sealed.[121]

The search for Christ by people of different cultures and races makes this search global. But the question "Who do you say I am?" cannot ever be silenced, and its hidden depths cannot be fully exhausted. This is a question of ultimacy and mystery, and the human heart continues to search for answers.

Primacy of Love and Christian Moral Vision

The primacy of love is the one thread that is woven into and through the God narrative of the Christian faith—the mysteries of the God of creation, the trinitarian God, and Jesus Christ. The breadth and richness of these doctrines unravel the mystery of God as profoundly relational and communal. The creation narratives in Genesis are not about cosmology but about relationship. They are about God, the origin of life, revealed as love, abiding and saving love. The God of creation is also the God of the Exodus, who saves and brings people to freedom. The Trinity is not rooted in the mystery of substance and essence, but in the mystery of persons in communion—the mystery of love, outgoing and outpouring love, not self-enclosed or self-sufficient, but flowing with desire for union with all of creation. The trinitarian God is God for us. The mystery of the fully divine and fully human Jesus Christ is God's disclosure in time and history. It is a disclosure of love that is inclusive and all-embracing, with a preferential option for the poor and the marginalized

---

[120] The position of Roberts is cited and developed in De La Torre, *Reading the Bible from the Margins*, 122.

[121] See Kelly Brown Douglas, *The Black Christ* (Maryknoll, NY: Orbis Books, 1994), 55–64.

in society; a love that subverts systems and structures of bias and discrimination based on class, gender, status, and religion; a love willing to face death as the final act of a life fully lived for others; a love so boundless and invincible that it overcomes the power and finality of death.

So, what is the Christian moral vision that is shaped on the basis of this theological anthropology? Who is the human person and the connection with who God is? By *moral vision* we mean the way we see who we are and how we ought to live—our way of being and way of doing. The revelation of God in creation, in the Trinity, and in Jesus Christ brings to light the mystery of the human person created by God who is love, through love, and for love. Moral life is founded on love, and the Christian moral life is patterned after Jesus' love.

If to be moral is to love, then all moral strivings must be strivings of love. Love requires the constant shifting of center from the "me" to the "other," seeking the good of the other as if it were our own. Love means that our hearts must expand to include those whom we may not even know by name, but with whom we share a common humanity. The striving of the heart to love may not always result in right decisions and actions, for finite as we all are, our discernment and our efforts may fall short of what we ought to be and to do. But it is in the very striving to love that we become moral, and in becoming moral, we become more human.

Love, based on what is at the heart of creation, on what is truly trinitarian, and what is profoundly christic, grounds the ethical call to solidarity. Solidarity means to live by the spirit of inclusive hospitality to all. No one is excluded; everyone is invited to the table of fellowship, especially the poor and the many who live at the margins of society. Solidarity is women and men in equal dignity, truly partners in relationships of mutual respect, for when women are demeaned, men are diminished, but when women are empowered, men are transformed, both flourishing in their common humanity. Solidarity takes a global meaning as rich nations make the plight and struggle of poor nations their own, sharing from their wealth, creating just structures for global trade and economy, and helping find solutions to massive problems of poverty, hunger, corruption, violence, disease, and illiteracy. And solidarity means to be deeply connected with the earth and the cosmos, to be a bearer of life where there is death, and to be the sanctuary of hope where there is destruction. Solidarity is to heed the cries of the poor, of women, of the earth, and of the entire cosmos and to allow their cries to be heard, never silenced.

To be men and women of solidarity constitutes the Christian moral vision founded on the primacy of love as drawn from the doctrinal theology of creation, Trinity, and Jesus Christ.

Primacy of Grace

The primacy of grace asserts one of the most fundamental beliefs of the Christian faith. Even where sin abounds, grace abounds even more. There is no sin so deep that God's grace is not deeper still. It is this fundamental belief from which we draw hope—a hope that is invincible because it is grounded and rooted in God.

Doctrine of Grace: Personal, Communal, and Global

One can understand the experience of grace in its three dimensions: (1) as the personal presence of God in love; (2) as ecclesial and communitarian; and (3) as transforming and liberating.

Grace as Personal Self-Presence of God in Love

First, grace is the personal presence of God in love—the deep communion of love of God and human beings. Even before the exercise of human freedom, before the yes or no of the human person, God has made a bestowal of Godself in love. This creates a radical openness to God in the person, evoking an unconditional desire for God. This desire is unconditional because God has constituted Godself as the very end of every human being. "There are no conditions remaining to be met—by God—before human beings actually have God in self as their ultimate end. Hence, this desire for God is 'unconditional.'"[122] This very desire for God is a gift, for a person cannot desire an unknown God. The very offer of Godself to the person is gratuitous, a grace in a mode in what Rahner calls the supernatural existential, which is directed toward the possession of grace, sanctifying grace, the state of being in communion with God, founded on one's personal acceptance of the offer. But the very acceptance of grace is borne by grace, insofar as the supernatural existential is the very ontological possibility for the acceptance of sanctifying grace.[123]

---

[122] David Coffey, "The Whole Rahner on the Supernatural Existential," *Theological Studies* 65/1 (2004): 102.

[123] Conversely, without prejudice to its gratuity, God's self-communication must be present in every person as the condition which makes its personal acceptance possible. "But in the truth of God's absolute God-communication, in which he is

Because of God's universal love we are dynamically structured toward the infinite. Though finite, we have a supernatural destiny. And living within this supernatural existential bids us to approach, enfolding us in an ultimate and radical love. This love, experienced at the ground of our being, is God's gift of self, which allures us beyond ourselves to others, and through others to God, in whom alone we find the ultimate meaning of our being. We can say no to the divine allure of love, but our supernatural existential is what we are, rooted in our nature as human beings, created in the divine image of God. And so even in our no, the supernatural existential asserts its ontological claim, and in our rejection, we experience an existential emptiness of what truly is and what we truly are.

Grace is the personal presence of God in love—the deep communion of love of God and human beings. Neo-Scholastic theology understood grace primarily as *created* grace, a finite gift that removes sin and restores our relationship with God. This understanding of grace led to the unfortunate misreading of grace as a "third thing" between God and human beings, something lost by sin and regained by penance. Thus, it could be under the determination of willful actions of persons. Drawing from biblical, patristic, and medieval theology, Rahner shifted to the primordial understanding of grace as *uncreated* grace. Grace is God's self-communication, not a special gift that shows up now and again. Uncreated grace is the Holy Spirit dwelling at the heart of our existence, permeating the world at its inmost roots—the Spirit of love, for love is what God is. When the Spirit comes to us, we are brought into the actual presence of love, the love in the Trinity, the love that is the very essence of God. Grace is not some*thing*; it is some*one*. As Rahner states, in the most tremendous statement that can be made about God, "the Giver Himself is the Gift."[124] Insofar as we are receptive to the Giver, we become the reality that we are being touched by. Being loved, we become lovers. In and through grace, we come to see who we are, for the truth of being loved and of loving is the truest thing about who we are.

Grace as Ecclesial and Communitarian

Love as the primary action of the Holy Spirit was manifested at Pentecost:

---

at once giver and gift and the ground of the acceptance of the gift, it is also said to us that whoever loses himself completely finds himself in the presence of infinite love." Karl Rahner, *Foundations of Christian Faith: An Introduction to the Idea of Christianity*, trans. William V. Dych (New York: Crossroad, 1978), 125.
    [124] Ibid., 120.

> All of them were filled with the Holy Spirit and began to speak in
> other languages, as the Spirit gave them ability. Now there were
> devout Jews from every nation under heaven living in Jerusalem.
> And at this sound the crowd gathered and was bewildered, be-
> cause each one heard them speaking in the native language of
> each. (Acts 2:4–6)

Total strangers now can hear and speak to one another. This is the
work of the Spirit, who draws people together in community, where
there were only "I's" before.

The babel of language symbolizes separation and alienation,
rooted in our incapacity to be present to another and to have the
other present to us. When mutual presence is absent, we hear and
speak "foreign languages" to one another. If mutual love is to be
possible at all, it must begin with the capacity to hear the other and
to be heard. This is an imperative in every level of human encounter
and interchange, from the interpersonal, to the international, interreligious, interracial, and interethnic. The Spirit's coming creates us as
lovers as we experience God as love and ourselves as being loved.[125]

This communitarian dimension of grace manifested by the Holy
Spirit is the main thrust of Yves Congar's theology of the Holy Spirit,
which unifies pneumatological anthropology and pneumatological
ecclesiology. From the Reformation through the twentieth century,
much of Catholic theology divorced these two domains of the theology. Theologians reflected on the indwelling of the Holy Spirit in
the human soul and the consequent bestowal of spiritual gifts and
fruits, but they did so apart from the ecclesial life and mission of
the church. Congar saw that the Spirit of God is given to us not as
individuals but as persons in communion with one another. "His
pneumatological anthropology presents a vision of human persons
transformed by grace like iron glowing in fire,"[126] and having been
transformed this way, called to live in communion and holiness with
others.

---

[125] John C. Haughey, *The Conspiracy of God* (Garden City, NY: Doubleday,
1973): 77, 85–86. For a discussion of natural metaphors used by early Christian
theology to elucidate the presence of the Spirit in the world, see Johnson, *Women,
Earth, and Creator Spirit*, 41.

[126] Elizabeth Teresa Groppe, *Yves Congar's Theology of the Holy Spirit* (New
York: Oxford University Press, 2004), 170.

Beyond the Church: Grace in the World

This communitarian dimension of grace is extended beyond the church, as the "indwelling Spirit leads, pulls, and attracts human communities toward a better world."[127] The Spirit as the builder of inclusive communities; the Spirit as an ecological Spirit; and the Spirit as an eschatological presence constitute the images and functions of the Holy Spirit as transforming and liberating grace in the world. Only in and with the power of the Spirit can inclusive communities be built that are founded on full participation and genuine solidarity in the face of divisions and alienations, and against exclusions and discriminations.[128]

The Holy Spirit is the ecological Spirit because it is the role of the Spirit to "enable each creature to be and to become, bringing each into relationships with other creatures in both local and global systems, and in this process of ongoing creation, relating each creature in communion within the life of the divine Persons-in-communion."[129] The cosmic mutuality of all creation, which is the deep relatedness of both human and nonhuman, is the work of the Holy Spirit, in creation, in the world, and in the entire cosmos.[130] As eschatological Spirit, the Holy Spirit breaks into the present from the future, and in the tension of the already and the not yet is transforming all social, political, economic, and religious systems into the eschatological city of God.[131]

Sin: Feminist and Liberationist Perspectives

Sin is the very rejection of grace, for in self-aggrandizement, we take a direction against the movement of grace to the path of perdition of ourselves and others. God engages a human freedom that is so

---

[127] Mary Elsbernd, "Toward a Theology of Spirit That Builds Up the Just Community," in *The Spirit in the Church and the World*, ed. Bradford E. Hinze, College Theology Society 49, 152–66 (Maryknoll, NY: Orbis Books, 2004), 159.

[128] Ibid., 161–62.

[129] Denis Edwards, "For Your Immortal Spirit Is in All Things: The Role of the Spirit in Creation," in *Earth Revealing, Earth Healing: Ecology and Christian Theology*, ed. Denis Edwards, 45–66 (Collegeville, MN: Liturgical Press, 2001), 64.

[130] Dawn M. Nothwehr, "The Ecological Spirit and Cosmic Mutuality: Engaging the Work of Denis Edwards," in Hinze, *The Spirit in the Church and the World*, 177.

[131] Elsbernd, "Toward a Theology of Spirit That Builds Up the Just Community," 160–61.

other than God and so free that through sin it can refuse God's offer of grace. The profound duality and contrast arise out of the context of the relation of human freedom to God. Human freedom, which constitutes the human person, stands before God in its dual propensity for creativity and destruction.

Original sin, the sinful condition into which all human beings are born, experienced personally and interiorly as concupiscence, entraps an individual in a profound tendency to sin, beyond the person's power to overcome apart from grace.[132] Piet Smulders expresses this reality of concupiscence: "In the heart of human beings lies a kind of will not to love God; anterior to personal choice, it encompasses and fetters that choice."[133] Original sin explained not only the universality of human alienation from God and the origin of evil but also the reason for Christ's incarnation and the grace of forgiveness, the necessity of infant baptism for salvation, and the role of the church as mediator of Christ's redemption.[134]

When this pivotal doctrine is under siege, the whole of the Christian creed is threatened. There has been a diminishment of focus on original sin, but the doctrine has not been ignored by theologians. The classical doctrine of original sin accounted for the universality of sin by way of physical transmission. All human beings, thus, inherit the actual sin of Adam. Taking seriously modernity's challenges, and placing original sin against a new intellectual and cultural horizon, theologians like Piet Schoonenberg seek to reinterpret this traditional doctrine, which is hinged on the historicity of Adam, and the critical difficulties that accompany it. Schoonenberg uses the primary category of original sin as *being situated,* which is "an existential determination and a permanent feature of human existence."[135] This category corresponds with original sin as a condition of sin into which all are born, and the Fall in this view remains historical but not in the sense

---

[132] Roger Haight, "Sin and Grace," in Schüssler and Galvin, *Systematic Theology,* 2:88; see also Stephen J. Duffy, "The Heart of Darkness: Original Sin Revisited," *Theological Studies* 49/4 (1988): 616.

[133] Piet Smulders, *The Design of Teilhard de Chardin: An Essay in Theological Reflection,* trans. Arthur Gibson (Westminster, MD: Newman, 1967), 176. For Karl Rahner's views on concupiscence, see Rahner, "The Theological Concept of Concupiscentia," in *Theological Investigations,* vol. 1, *God, Christ, Mary, and Grace,* trans. Cornelius Ernst (Baltimore: Helicon, 1961), 347–82.

[134] Tatha Wiley, *Original Sin: Origins, Developments, Contemporary Meanings* (New York: Paulist Press, 2002), 127.

[135] As cited in ibid., 135.

proposed by early church writers. It is existential, as it occurs in each person's refusal to seek and to love God.[136]

Feminist Perspectives on Sin

The critique of the classical doctrine of original sin is at the heart of feminist theology. The myth of Eve is rejected as a victim-blaming ideology that mislabels evil. "Real evil exists precisely in this false naming, projection, and exploitation."[137] This evil emerges out of patriarchy, which used the doctrine of original sin to denigrate women, to blame them for evil, and to subjugate them to male rule. Tertullian's invective against women exposes this patriarchal view of original sin.

> You are the devil's gateway: you are the unsealer of that (forbidden) tree: *you* the first deserter of the divine law: *you* are she who persuaded him whom the devil was not valiant enough to attack. *You* destroyed so easily God's image, man. On account of *your* desert—that is, death—even the Son of Man had to die.[138]

In the same treatise, drawing on man's fear of being tempted by woman, Tertullian interprets Genesis 3 as a story of sexual temptation and cast all women in the role of Eve:

> Do you not realize that you are each an Eve? The curse of God on this sex of yours lives on even in our times. Guilty, you must bear its hardships. You are the gateway of the devil; you desecrated the fatal tree; you first betrayed the law of God; you softened up with your cajoling words the one against whom the devil could not prevail by force. All too easily you destroyed the great image of God, Adam. You are the one who deserved death, and because of you the Son of God had to die.[139]

This explanation of original sin depicts the root sin that destroys the created order—the claim of superiority of some over others that legitimizes their denigration of them as well as their domination over

---

[136] See ibid., 132–37. For an understanding of original sin in contemporary theology, see, among others, Gabriel Daly, "Original Sin," in *The New Dictionary of Theology*, ed. Joseph Komonchak, Mary Collins, and Dermot A. Lane (Wilmington, DE: Glazier, 1987), 726–31.

[137] Ruether, *Sexism and God-Talk*, 163.

[138] Tertullian, "On the Apparel of Women" 1.1.

[139] Ibid.

them. From the vantage point of gender, this theology of original sin is founded on a gender dualism of male superiority and female inferiority, on an exclusive male claim to being the image of God, and an assumption that male privilege and rule are the divinely guaranteed order of creation.[140] Female subordination is portrayed as God's punishment for Eve's sin. In interpreting Genesis 3 as the divine revelation of woman's inferior nature and her responsibility for the Fall, male theologians rendered sacrosanct a social order distorted by patriarchy as the order of creation. "Male theologians have used the doctrine of original sin to denigrate women, blame them for evil, and prohibit them from full participation in the life of the church. By deeming female subordination a divine punishment, instead of exposing it as human bias, the doctrine reinforced a cultural ideology of male superiority."[141]

From the feminist point of view, the woman was not the cause of evil but the victim of it. The Fall is not due to a woman but to patriarchy:

> Feminist theology has shown that our societal oppression and ecclesial exclusion is not women's "fault," it is not the result of Eve's sin nor is it the will of God or the intention of Jesus Christ. Rather it is engendered by societal and ecclesiastical patriarchy and legitimized by androcentric world-construction in language and symbol systems.[142]

Patriarchal societies uphold and reinforce what should not be—hierarchy, domination, privilege—and obstruct and eliminate what should be—relations of mutuality. This patriarchal view of original sin must be reconstructed based on an anthropology "expunged of gender hierarchy and privilege, a critical theory of history, and a social analysis of the dynamics of power and ideology,"[143] for a true revelatory word for women and men.

Liberationist Perspectives on Sin

Liberation theologians criticize the privatization of sin. Even the universality of sin as understood in classical theology is in the terms

---

[140] Wiley, *Original Sin*, 156.

[141] Ibid., 178.

[142] Elisabeth Schüssler Fiorenza, "Breaking the Silence—Becoming Visible," Concilium 182, *Women: Invisible in Church and Theology*, ed. Mary Collins and Elisabeth Schüssler Fiorenza, 3–16 (Edinburgh: T. and T. Clark, 1984), 14.

[143] Wiley, *Original Sin*, 178.

of the individual inheritance of original sin. An individualistic theology of sin does not have the standpoint from which to expose the systems and structures that perpetuate evil. This evil is embedded in social, political, economic, and cultural structures and systems that institutionalize oppression, domination, and privilege. New Testament scholar Walter Wink describes these as domination systems and structures. They are characterized by "unjust economic relations, oppressive political relations, biased race relations, patriarchal gender relations, hierarchical power relations, and the use of violence to maintain them all."[144] While sin is rooted in personal acts, it is facilitated and perpetuated by these systems and structures. Liberation theologians, however, have also articulated the unconscious dimension of social sin, the more involuntary ideological influences and subconscious dynamics that have an impact on personal agency. Gregory Baum speaks of "guilt by personal implication" and "guilt by common heritage" to distinguish what is rooted in personal sin and what is referred to as involuntary social conditioning.[145]

The perspective of sin in liberation theology is grounded in scripture. Both the Johannine "sin of the world" (Jn 1:29) and the Pauline "evil age" (Gal 1:4) speak of evil that permeates every dimension of human life. The prophets denounce evil that is not only personal but social. The prophet Amos speaks words of warning:

> Hear this, you that trample on the needy,
>   and bring to ruin the poor of the land . . . (Am 8:4)

Isaiah urges all to cease evil by doing justice:

> cease to do evil,
>   learn to do good;
> seek justice,
>   rescue the oppressed,
> defend the orphan,
>   plead for the widow. (Is 1:16–17)

The nature of social sin is rooted in social solidarity; each individual sin in some ways affects others and threatens the common

---

[144] Walter Wink, *The Powers That Be: Theology for a New Millennium* (New York: Doubleday, 1998), 39.

[145] See Gregory Baum, *Essays in Critical Theology* (Kansas City, MO: Sheed and Ward, 1994), 198–201.

good. Social sin involves sinful relationships among and within human communities, class struggles, and confrontations among blocs of nations. There is an intrinsic connection between personal sin and social sin, because structural sins are always linked to concrete acts of individuals who introduce these structures, consolidate them, and make them difficult to remove. They spread, grow stronger, and become the source of other sins. The evil found deep in social structures is an inducement to sin; it can be overcome only with strenuous effort and the assistance of grace. Sin in its social dimension is what Piet Schoonenberg speaks of when he calls original sin the sin of the world. Sin has come about from the accumulation of sin in history. This sin has an infectious power of entrapping all in a profound tendency to sin.[146] These evils are the sinful structures of injustice, oppression, exploitation that threaten or even destroy fundamental human rights and values that are at the foundation of society.

Our lives are so deeply intertwined that the burden of one becomes the suffering of another, the death of one becomes the grief of another; indeed, there is no one's joy or pain that is not our own too. Thus, when we speak of sin, we have to speak of it in its broad social, public, and global spheres—sin that is found deep in the web of relationships institutionalized in structures and systems that cause widespread poverty, corruption, violence, disease, and death. People are oppressed, their human dignity is violated, and death-dealing relationships are fostered, like the sins of sexism and racism. The consequences of social sin are witnessed in the massive misery and suffering wrought by poverty, widespread violation of basic human rights, racial violence and slaughter, abuse of women's human rights, child molestation, human and drug trafficking, corporate greed and corruption, and environmental catastrophes.

Grace as Primal: Final Word of Soteriology

Sin, as a personal or social reality, is the rejection of grace; sin is a movement away from love. But even in the gutters of sin, grace can abound. Before love, all sin, personal and social, stands in its puniness. If sin takes on a structural and social dimension, so does grace.

---

[146] See Piet Schoonenberg, *Man and Sin: A Theological View*, trans. Joseph Donceel (Notre Dame, IN: University of Notre Dame Press, 1965), 104–5. Also, Roger Haight points out that "the term *original* sin has had simultaneously two interrelated referents: the originating sin at the dawn of human existence called the fall and the damaging effects of sin resulting in a sinful condition of the whole race" (Haight, "Sin and Grace," 85).

Where sin abounds, grace abounds. Social grace is found in structures, institutions, and systems that are dedicated to the nurture and care of human life; the protection of peoples, cultures, and human dignity; and promotion of the common good. These structures and systems are life giving and hope renewing in their corporate efforts to address and respond to the massive problems of suffering, sickness, poverty, and injustice in the global context.[147]

In the end, when all things come to their final validation, grace is and remains primal. Christian faith teaches that heaven and hell are not to be viewed logically as two equal alternatives, for heaven is a reality and hell is only a possibility. The possibility of hell is the most radical theological statement about the nature of human freedom. What is so terrible about human freedom is that it has the power to destroy itself in its refusal of God. And yet, hell is not a creation of a God who punishes out of vengeance. God does not take vengeance but leaves evil to its own limited logic. Salvation and loss are not on the same plane. Heaven is God's embrace of love for all, intended for all from eternity. The very movement of divine Love is communion that seeks to embrace all. Thus, though hell is a possibility, there is no claim or certitude from scripture or church tradition that anyone has been or will be damned.[148]

Some theologians, like Hans Urs von Balthasar, push the Christian eschatological vision of hope to its most radical limits by holding that there is no point beyond which God in Christ will not go to save sinners, as suggested by the mystery of Holy Saturday. Christ descended to the depths of hell, where the all-holy God is absolutely excluded.[149] Von Balthasar's position is echoed by Edith Stein, who considers improbable that the free human will of the damned will remain perpetually closed to the love of God, in all its splendor, magnanimity, and kenosis. "Human freedom can be neither broken nor neutralized by divine freedom, but it may well be, so to speak, outwitted. . . . The descent of grace to the human soul is a free act of divine love. And there are *no limits* to how far it may extend."[150]

---

[147] Haight, "Sin and Grace," 130.

[148] Peter C. Phan, "Contemporary Context and Issues in Eschatology," *Theological Studies* 55/3 (1994): 531. See also Joseph Ratzinger, *Dogmatic Theology: Eschatology: Death and Eternal Life*, trans. Michael Waldstein and Aidan Nichols (Washington, DC: Catholic University of America Press, 1988), 205.

[149] See John R. Sachs, "Current Eschatology: Universal Salvation and the Problem of Evil," *Theological Studies* 52/2 (1991): 244.

[150] As cited in Hans Urs von Balthasar, *Dare We Hope "That All Men Be Saved"?* trans. David Kipp and Lothar Krauth (San Francisco: Ignatius Press,

This belief in the power of grace that surpasses human sin grounds the radical hope that all men and women will in fact be saved. In the face of the irresistibility and persistence of divine love, the person whose freedom is neither neutralized nor supplanted will be drawn to this love and only to this love. Such a hope, radical as it may be, is not merely possible but is well founded, even while one remains convinced that God's offer of grace must be accepted in freedom. For if grace is truly efficacious and if freedom possesses an innate capacity for God, then one does not hope in vain in the possibility, if not the reality, of all being saved. This hope for the salvation of all demands that we must truly live what we hope for, and "such hope is not an idle posture but constitutes a moral imperative to act in a way that all will be saved."[151] We are called to labor for the universal communion of all people in love and justice in the here and now. This is not to deny the real possibility of hell. But just as real is the possibility of universal restoration, which has not been given as much emphasis as it should. Thus, when the eschatological hope is driven to its edge, one dares believe that, in the end, all will be saved, that the primacy of grace is and will be the final word of soteriology.

Primacy of Grace and Christian Moral Vision

The mystery of grace is the personal presence of God in women and men through the indwelling and interdwelling Spirit, in whose initiative and power individuals are transformed and communities are built—inclusive, global, ecological, and eschatological. But there too is the tragedy of sin, the awful destruction of persons, communities, nations, the earth, and the cosmos—a tragedy and destruction that threaten to annihilate every throb of hope in human hearts and in the cosmic spirit. Yet grace is primal, overcoming sin to become the final word of soteriology. "The light shines in the darkness and the darkness did not overcome" (Jn 1:5).

There is this eschatological hope, this profound expectation and insistence that things as they are, are not what they were meant to be, that all that was lost may be found, and that all that was bound in death may find new life. This belief in eschatology pushes hope to the edge, there where it is most powerful because it knows no limits. This is a hope so profound as it is radical, for it is rooted in God,

---

1988), 219–21.

[151] Phan, "Contemporary Context and Issues in Eschatology," 532.

whose very offer of Godself is absolutely gratuitous as the origin and finality of all that is and all that could ever be. In the invincibility of that hope is the primacy of grace.

What is our moral vision of who we are and what we ought to do if we live based on the primacy of grace? We must envision ourselves in a prophetic mission in a world plagued by evil and sin. Subversion is a prophetic mission. It is a call to break down all systems of oppression, inequality, and violence—patriarchy, sexism, racism, classicism, colonialism, religious fundamentalism, terrorism—and the unspeakable human suffering they cause.

Subversion is active resistance to evil, so comprehensive that it exists at all levels, from the personal, to the global, to the ecological, to the cosmic. It is iconoclasm—the destruction of all that stands in conflict with the reign of God. This prophetic work brings us into conflict, and sometimes into deadly conflict, with deeply entrenched powers. But to struggle against these powers we must find a center, live by that center, and be sustained by that center. At the center of Jesus' life is the reign of God—the disposability of his life, the radicality of his death, and the hope of the resurrection all are centered on the reign of God.

Subversion is a breaking down, but it is also a building up. It is the building up of structures, systems, and institutions that promote the common good, particularly the protection of the most vulnerable in society. At its heart is a radical reversal of attitudes, values, and dispositions. For subversion means to see the world through a different lens, from a different perspective. We see the world from the underside, from the margins, from the edges. A whole new narrative shapes our vision. And that narrative influences our moral decisions and actions. When our vision is changed, our doing is transformed. The old way of seeing is displaced by a whole new way of being. Subversion becomes a faith calling, grounded in and sustained by our belief in the primacy of grace.

Primacy of Community

The deepest truth about God is that God is relational. As deeply as this truth relates to God, so does it relate to the human being. Relationality is the foundation of community. The mystery of the Trinity is the mystery of communion within God and with us. We do not, however, look at the Trinity as a model, external to us, on which to pattern our lives. Rather, the Trinity is within us, through grace, through the indwelling and inter-dwelling Spirit, enabling and empowering us to build communities. This topic on the primacy of community is developed in two general sections: church as community, and the common eschatological destiny.

Church as Community: Equal, Democratic, and Global

Here we view the church as community in three ways: the call to the discipleship of equals; the church as democracy; and the church as a global/world church. A feminist perspective is taken on the first two topics to address the call and challenge of the church to be truly a sign of what it claims to be as church in the world today.

The Call to the Discipleship of Equals

To be essentially human is to be in community. For the Christian, the locus of this community is the church. What does it mean to be church? How is being church essential to being human? To be church is basically to be human together in Christ through the Spirit. It is a particular way of being community as people who have been called by the Spirit of Jesus to keep his memory alive as they live by his teaching, hope in the power of his cross and resurrection, and stand as prophetic witnesses to his justice and love in the world. And yet, if the church is to be truly a prophetic sign of liberation in the world, it requires transformation, a systemic change. This change starts with its internal structures, that they may be consistent with its vision as a church in the world—a church for the poor and for the oppressed,[152] and a church in dialogue with massive cultural and political changes in the world. If the church is in the midst of the world that is constantly changing, it must reexamine and rethink its structures in the light of the signs of the times.

While the church sees its role as a key player in the theater of contemporary life, its structures have been trapped in the past. For instance, in the face of the global emergence of women in positions of leadership in different realms of social life, the church continues to deprive women of full participation in its ecclesial life. Its vision of ecclesial life is still patriarchal and hierarchal, contrary to the vision

---

[152] See *Justice in the World* (Washington, DC: United States Catholic Conference, 1972), 34; James B. Nickoloff, "Church of the Poor: The Ecclesiology of Gustavo Gutiérrez," *Theological Studies* 54/3 (1993): 512–35; and Joyce Murray, "Liberation for Communion in the Soteriology of Gustavo Gutiérrez," *Theological Studies* 59/1 (1998): 51–59.

of an egalitarian community. It is this vision of egalitarian community
that inspires the inclusive feminist reading of Christology, which holds
that it is the humanity of Jesus and not his maleness that is normative for a full human existence and that to be *imago Christi* lies not
in sexual similarity with the male Jesus but in becoming a man or
woman after Jesus' heart.

Mary Hines notes, however, that while it cannot be denied that the
continued exclusion of women from ordination remains a potent symbol of women's wider exclusion in the Roman Catholic Church, it is
not at the center of the struggle for church reform. Beyond the question
of women's exclusion from ordained ministry is a need for a systemic
change in the church. The ordination of women is not the sufficient or
adequate answer to a problem that is far deeper and more complex.[153]

Such systemic change in the church must be directed toward more
inclusive leadership and decision-making structures inspired by the
spirit of the "discipleship of equals" and the principles of justice and
democracy. Such change must be visionary, that the church may truly
be a church of many peoples and cultures, a church that empowers
other voices rather than silences them, a church that is truly a communion, *koinonia,* in diversity and plurality. The church as a discipleship of equals undermines the hierarchical ordering of powers and
functions in the church where a dominant male elite governs. In the
discipleship of equals, there is no place for structures of dominance
and subordination, since all are called to be sharers of Jesus' liberating
mission and ministry on the basis of their different gifts rather than
on the basis of any ontological sacramental status.[154]

The Church and Democracy: Fuller Participation of Women

Related to the image of the church as a community of disciples
is the church as democracy. This questions the presumption that the
church's present hierarchical structures are divinely ordained and
therefore cannot be changed. Biblical and hermeneutical studies have
challenged this position, showing that the structures of the church have
been adapted to the social and cultural circumstances of the times.
Schillebeeckx writes: "The community which calls itself the church
of Christ never lives in a social, cultural, or political vacuum."[155] The

---

[153] Mary Hines, "Community for Liberation," in LaCugna, *Freeing Theology,*
170.

[154] Schüssler Fiorenza, *In Memory of Her,* 105–33.

[155] Edward Schillebeeckx, *Church: The Human Story of God* (New York: Crossroad, 1993), 187.

church, however, is not to pattern itself after any existing democratic system or to duplicate any particular democratic social order; it is summoned to go to the very core vision of the democratic principle which is the creation of a just society based on the consent of the governed.[156] If the church is to reform its structures according to this core democratic principle, then it has to allow broad-based participative processes in all aspects of its life, its governing, and its teaching functions. The decision-making powers in the church should be made radically inclusive, with women's voices heard in church assemblies on an equal basis with those of men. Participation, conciliarity, pluralism, accountability, and dialogue are the five principles that must govern the democratic restructuring of the church.[157]

The truth that the human person is the image of God constitutes the foundation of a communal life lived in equality and justice. Church teaching declares explicitly that all human beings are created in the image and likeness of God, together and equally. There has been, however, an ongoing discourse on the meaning and implications of this teaching. Two anthropological theories have emerged in the process: an egalitarian anthropology of partnership and an anthropology of complementarity. The first emphasizes equality; the second accentuates difference. Representing two ways of understanding the nature and relation of man and woman, these two theories are not confined to the locus of ideas and concepts, for they hold real consequences for the social, cultural, and political world.

The discourse has divided feminists. Some feminist theologians are convinced that complementarity is irreconcilable with genuine equality, while others take the view that there is no need to choose

---

[156] See Eugene C. Bianchi and Rosemary Radford Ruether, eds., *A Democratic Catholic Church: The Reconstruction of Roman Catholicism* (New York: Crossroad, 1992), 12. See also, among others, Leonardo Boff, *Church, Charism, and Power: Liberation Theology and the Institutional Church*, trans. John W. Dierchsmeier (New York: Crossroad, 1985); and Letty M. Russell, *Church in the Round: Feminist Interpretation of the Church* (Louisville, KY: Westminster/John Knox, 1993).

[157] See Bianchi and Ruether, *A Democratic Catholic Church*, 253–60. The sexual abuse scandals that have plagued the Catholic Church have led many Catholics to ask how to expand the role of the laity within the governance of the church. This is the thrust of Stephen J. Pope, ed., *Common Calling: The Laity and Governance of the Catholic Church* (Washington, DC: Georgetown University Press, 2004). For a comprehensive analysis of numerous issues, controversies, and developments in the US Catholic Church in changing and evolving times, see Charles E. Curran, *The Social Mission of the US Catholic Church: A Theological Perspective* (Washington, DC: Georgetown University Press, 2011).

between complementarity and equality, for both are true. Sara Butler writes:

> Man and woman are equal in humanity, but not identical. On the one hand, they are of equal dignity or worth and possess equal rights as persons. On the other hand, male and female are two different bodily ways of being human, ordered to one another, that is ordered to communion. In my opinion, the "either/or" formulation must give way to the typically Catholic "both/and"; we are both equal and complementary.[158]

Feminist theologians criticize the anthropology of complementarity as promoting relations of power or value. They hold that the anthropology of complementarity gives advantage to men because it defines men as normative and women as auxiliary. Elizabeth Johnson rejects the unrelieved binary thinking that accompanies the anthropology of complementarity, which "casts men and women as polar opposites, each bearing unique characteristics from which the other is excluded."[159] This presents a view of humanity that sees man and woman as two halves of a whole, with human qualities and social roles divided down to the middle. This clean and sharp divide of human qualities is not only invalidated in real life, as "women can be rational and great at leadership; men can be loving and nurturing."[160]

Johnson suggests replacing the theory of complementarity with an anthropological model (one nature celebrated in an interdependence of multiple differences) that eliminates an exaggerated focus on sexual difference. Along with sex, race, social condition, nationality, age, state of health, sexual preference, and cultural location are anthropological constants that contribute to shaping one's humanity. Unlike the proponents of anthropology of complementarity, Johnson argues against the primacy of sexual difference in defining a person's identity, but without denying its importance. She states that the present teaching on the equality of men and women is a radical departure from tradition, where women were demonized as temptresses and were considered "misbegotten males" or defective males and were denied of the dignity

---

[158] Sara Butler, "Embodiment: Women and Men, Equal and Complementary," in *The Church Women Want*, ed. Elizabeth A. Johnson, 35–44 (New York: Crossroad, 2002), 35.

[159] Johnson, *She Who Is*, 154.

[160] Elizabeth A. Johnson, "Imaging God, Embodying Christ: Women as a Sign of the Times," in Johnson, *The Church Women Want*, 55.

of being fully created in the image of God.[161] However, she notes that despite John Paul II's endorsement of women's equality with men as the image of God, women are not given equal access with men to all ministries of church life and governance. The pope's use of anthropology, based on a dualistic view that men and women embody human nature in two contrasting ways, leads to the conclusion that women possess characteristics that define the distinct social roles they play.[162]

Without denying the givenness of sexual difference of men and women that constitutes the foundation of the most splendid and profound relationship, Johnson holds that the dualistic anthropology based on innate difference between men and women is deficient in a complex world where relations are played out under the force of social and historical realities. She proposes a holistic, egalitarian anthropology of partnership in which a person's characteristics and roles are not determined by sex, essential as this is to his or her identity. Characteristics and roles are spread out over a wider spectrum for both women and men, with a whole range of similarities or dissimilarities, between and among them, and the calling of each is shaped by his or her gifts, strengths, education, contexts, and circumstances.[163] This holistic, egalitarian anthropology of partnership is the bedrock of a truly just society, in which both women and men are called to full actualization of their persons, in wide and broad contexts. A community where women recover their full humanity is envisioned as the same community where men arrive at their full humanity. The primacy of community calls for both to come to their full human flourishing.

Global Church

The image of the world church Rahner envisioned evokes new and powerful changes that must take place in the shaping of the church today and in the future.[164] The church must emerge from within the diversity of people, cultures, and religions and assume a plurality of faces—an African face, a Latin American face, an Asian face. *World church* is a church that emerges from the ground up, in which

---

[161] Ibid.

[162] Ibid., 52–53.

[163] Ibid., 54–55.

[164] Rahner speaks of three epochs in church history: the first was the very short period of Judeo-Christianity; the second was the long period of Christendom; and the third, ushered in by Vatican II, moved the church to the world stage. See Karl Rahner, "The Abiding Significance of Vatican II," *Theological Investigations*, vol. 20, *Concern for the Church* (New York: Crossroad, 1981), 90–102.

the universal church comes to shape in the gathering of local and indigenous churches, each a whole church, in a unity that is not uniformity.[165] This church, situated in the midst of enormous social and cultural plurality, in a constantly changing world, continues to commit itself as a visible sign of God's gracious will to save and liberate all people, but it no longer is the only locus of that salvation. Rather than a triumphalistic church, as it was in the past, it has to be a humble church, amid many and diverse voices, in a world of plurality of cultures, peoples, and religions. A church in the world, embracing its joys, anxieties, and griefs, must be in dialogue with this plurality. To view the church in this way fills one with hope and faith in the Spirit who is within the church. Only when the church can truly be church of equal discipleship, a just and democratic church, and a world church, will it be the presence of the Christ in the world—a liberating presence for all men and women, for all peoples and cultures. It also will be the icon of the Trinity, the communion of diversity, the unity in love—the church as *koinonia*.[166]

At the heart of a world church is dialogue, particularly interreligious dialogue. The church that has become global must enter into profound dialogue with all other faiths and cultures. There are four fronts of interreligious dialogue—dialogue of life, dialogue of action, dialogue of theological exchange, and dialogue of religious experience. The dialogue of life takes place in homes, workplaces, social gatherings, the marketplace—anywhere people encounter one another in many ways, and yet come to know that though different, they share a common humanity. They recognize in one another fellow human beings, companions on life's road, even treasured friends, through shared joys or griefs, common hopes or dreams.

In the dialogue of action the arena is the world. People of different faiths unite in the common struggle for justice, in solidarity with the poor, for the transformation of social structures and systems. They strive to build a new world where all may live in peace.

In the dialogue of theological exchange, we sit at the feet of others and learn from the richness of their faith. We do not enter into this dialogue with a mind to convert others, or even to arrive at religious consensus. We encourage others to speak from their own traditions, so that we may know, understand, and appreciate. And in knowing, understanding, and appreciating, we are transformed. Although there

---

[165] Hines, "Community for Liberation," 177.
[166] Carl F. Starkloff, "The Church as Covenant, Culture, and Communion," *Theological Studies* 61/3 (2000): 409–31.

may be differences and even conflicts of beliefs and visions, even then, dialogue is possible. While we remain true to our own tradition, respect for the others' traditions is essential (*Dialogue and Proclamation*, no. 42).

In the dialogue of religious experience, people do not pray together, for that would be syncretism, but rather are together to pray. In addressing the religious representatives to the World Day of Prayer for Peace held in Assisi, on October 27, 1986, John Paul II said: "Our meeting attests only—and this is its real significance for the people of our time—that in the great battle for peace, humanity, in its very diversity, must draw from its deepest and most vivifying sources where its conscience is formed and upon which is founded the moral action of all people."[167]

Dialogues are engaged at different levels, but the questions that would continue to challenge interreligious dialogue are regarding the status of Jesus Christ in relation to other religious mediations and the question of his divinity. These two questions are intertwined, and they are sensitive issues, evoking intense inquiry and discussion. There is no promise of easy answers. But as the church becomes more and more global, the increasing fact of pluralism, particularly religious pluralism, opens a new spatial framework, creates a new temporal frame of reference, and expands the horizon of experience for these questions.[168]

When the story of Jesus is put within this new framework, seen from the lens of religious pluralism, there are possible shifts in understanding his status in relation to other religious mediations and the question of his divinity. While the truth of Jesus as the mediator of God's salvation to Christian believers remains constant, how would this truth be negotiated with others who have no conscious relation with him and who have their own understanding of the Absolute or Ultimate that grounds their lives? In a church that is truly global, reaching out to people of all faiths, how would the doctrine on the divinity of Jesus, while it remains central to the Christian faith, be understood? Would a theology that affirms Jesus' divinity in a distinctive and historically unique way, but that does not deny possible

---

[167] For a development of the four dialogues, see Johnson, *Quest for the Living God*, 163–74.

[168] See Roger Haight, "The Future of Christology: Expanding Horizons, Religious Pluralism, and the Divinity of Jesus," in *Christology: Memory, Inquiry, Practice*, the annual publication of the College Theology Society, 2002, vol. 48, ed. Anne M. Clifford and Anthony J. Godzieba, 47–61 (Maryknoll, NY: Orbis Books, 2003).

"incarnations" of God in other religions, be accepted?[169] Whatever the answers to these challenging questions, in a changing world of religious pluralism, the fact remains that, as Schillebeeckx stated, there can be no return to the former age when the church could claim that Christianity is the one true religion, for that would be "a virtual declaration of war on all other religions."[170]

A Common Eschatological Destiny: Continuity of Present and Future

The Christian belief in eschatology is not a belief in a future that is discontinuous with systems of justice and communities of compassion that have been built. All that is good, true, and noble will come to final meaning and consummation with the restructuring and transformation of the political, economic, and social structures in which communal relationships are determined. It is inconceivable to accept the present order with the cumulative consequences of the deeds of human violence, greed, and domination as inevitable and enduring, and then hope that one day the reign of God would suddenly break in.

There is an essential interrelatedness and communality of our destiny, and we are called to the formidable task of building a just society, for our eschatological hope in the future is and should be inseparably bound with historical contemporaneity and urgency. It is this hope that must permeate, sustain, and energize our work for liberation and justice in the here and now. Monika Hellwig writes that eschatology is a "matter of salvation of the world rather than salvation of souls out of the world."[171] Echoing the same eschatological stance, Gustavo Gutiérrez asserts:

> The claim that the victory which has conquered death is our faith will be lived, inescapably, at the very heart of history, in the midst of a single process of liberation which leads that history to its fulfillment in the definitive encounter with God. To hope in Christ is at the same time to believe in the adventure of

---

[169] Ibid.

[170] Edward Schillebeeckx, "The Uniqueness of Christ and the Interreligious Dialogue," paper delivered to the Catholic Academy, Munich, Bavaria, April 22, 1997, manuscript, 5.

[171] Monika Hellwig, "Eschatology," in Schüssler and Galvin, *Systematic Theology* 2:362.

history which opens infinite vistas to the love and action of the Christian.[172]

In view of eschatology, in the belief in the final things, the discourse on embodiedness brings to light our common humanity, for our body is our way of relating with others and with the world. Starting with our experience of our body as a common ground, we recognize that we are all heirs of the same finite human condition, and death is the great leveler. We are not a duality of body and soul but a body-soul unity—the body is the visibility of the soul, and the soul is the actuality of the body. The feminist critique of embodiedness rejects the notions of the body that view female flesh as inimical to eternal life. This opposition between female flesh and eternal life led to the belief that if women's bodies were to be redeemed at all, they had to be transformed into male bodies.[173]

Rahner states: "All eschatological assertions have the *one* totality of man in mind, which cannot be neatly *divided* into two parts, body and soul."[174] This view of the person as total and integral unity changes the whole notion of death. Sallie McFague underscores embodiment as the basis of our common life, connecting us in a deep, intricate, and permanent ways not only with other human beings but with all forms of life. These connections link us with God, who is the source of all embodiment. She envisions eschatology as a decentering of human beings in the whole scheme of creation and their recentering as they "side with the oppressed, create communities embodying concern for the basic needs of the life-forms on earth, aware of their profound interdependence as well as individuality."[175] Human beings are called to remove themselves from the center, where all of creation is laid at their feet, that they may take on the humble task of stewardship—a solidarity in vulnerability with all of life forms that have been abused and misused, that all may ultimately be brought to redemption in the

---

[172] Gustavo Gutiérrez, *A Theology of Liberation: History, Politics, and Salvation*, rev. ed., trans. and ed. Sister Caridad and John Eagleson (Maryknoll, NY: Orbis Books, 1988), 140.

[173] Ruether, *Sexism and God-Talk*, 248.

[174] Karl Rahner, "The Hermeneutics of Eschatological Assertions," in *Theological Investigations*, vol. 4, *More Recent Writings*, trans. Kevin Smyth (Baltimore: Helicon, 1966), 340.

[175] Sallie McFague, *The Body of God: An Ecological Theology* (Minneapolis, MN: Fortress Press, 1993), 206.

resurrection of the one collective body in which all becomes one in Christ.

Eschatology should be seen not as a linear historical progression but rather as a centering movement in the heart's conversion to other human beings, to the earth, and to the cosmos. Bringing the earth and the cosmos into the whole eschatological vision is a necessary qualification to the anthropocentric focus of the traditional eschatology. This approach to eschatology implies ethical imperatives relative to earth and all its resources. Christian eschatology envisions a particular resurrection in death, the raising up of the whole, embodied spiritual subject, who retains a relationship to the world and a continuing individual impact on the transformation of world history, the earth, and the cosmos, until the universal resurrection, when all will reach the fullness of finality.

The grand narrative of our common and collective lives is that our individual stories are all woven into the whole story of human history and the world, with all of us sharing a common destiny. The good that we do is redemptive of others, and the evil that we commit becomes their burden. In the end, all that is and that was, will become one in God in Christ, through the Spirit, there where all things change but are not ended.

Primacy of Community and Christian Moral Vision

For the Christian, to be community is to be church, which is to be human together in Christ through the Spirit. But for the church to be true to its prophetic mission in the world, it must become a church of equals, where women participate as fully as men in the ecclesial life, and a church that is democratic at its core, where no voice is marginalized or silenced, where without respect to social roles shaped by sexual hierarchy and dualism, people come together in true dialogue and conciliarity. The primacy of community calls the church to look into its internal structures that they may be reconciled with its avowed mission of justice in the world.

There is also the call to be a world church, a church of today and tomorrow, situated in the midst of enormous social and cultural plurality in a constantly changing world. This is a call to be a humble and listening church in the spirit of fellowship where no voice claims superiority or dominance over others, but each, true to its own tradition, participates in the common search for truth.

Finally, there is the promise based on a grand narrative of eschatology. Whatever good we do is not lost or diminished in time, but with all other acts of love and goodness has a place in the universe of meaning. There is a promise of eternity in God of all that is true, good, and honorable. And for all that is not, there is hope of transformation, of being brought into new life. This grand narrative of eschatology declares that the whole of humankind, the earth, and the entire cosmos share a common destiny in Christ, through the Spirit, in whom all things become one.

What is the Christian moral vision that must govern our lives if we believe in the primacy of community and in this grand narrative of eschatology? We have to live the ordinariness of our lives with a profound sense of transcendence. The moral choices we make are not discrete acts; rather, they enter into the shaping of the fundamental orientation of our entire lives. And with our lives so deeply intertwined with other lives, our choices have far-reaching consequences. The abiding call is to build human communities, that all may find in their common and shared humanity the basis for reconciliation and hope. The worth of all—man, woman, and child—must be upheld and their inalienable human dignity and freedom protected.

The call of transcendence is a call to go beyond ourselves, to reach out to others, to embrace the world, to have a kinship with earth and with the cosmos—to live with a deep sense of the future and of eternity already present in the now, being shaped in the arena of life, in its joys and griefs, in its lights and shadows. Christian moral life, thus, is a life of faith. Persons of faith do not perceive morality as simply morality but as morality situated decisively in their relation to God. Religious faith is not regarded as only one option among other options in life. Of its nature, religious faith is a fundamental choice that engages, shapes, and evaluates the whole of life.[176]

Conclusion

For moral theology to be a genuine theological discipline, it must be infused with the truths of the faith. Making moral theology, in terms of its vision, truly theological necessitates its connection with systematic theology. This connection is located in the area of theological anthropology based on the doctrines of the faith that systematic theology is primarily concerned with. Drawing from the richness and depth of the theological discourse on the doctrines of the faith in

---

[176] Rene Latourelle, "Revelation and Faith: Personal Encounter with God," *Theology Digest* 10 (Autumn 1962): 237.

systematic theology, a theological anthropology is developed around the three primacies—love, grace, and community. These three primacies are used to provide a hermeneutical framework in understanding who God is and who the human person is. Our understanding of ourselves is very much connected with how we view God, and our understanding of God brings to light the mystery of who we are in relation to all of creation.

The theological anthropology developed in the light of faith, as reflected and interpreted in systematic theology, is shown as grounding the Christian moral vision, which essentially is the way we view the world and reality, with reference to two interrelated questions—Who are we? and How ought we to live? They are interrelated because the way we envision who we are makes claim on how we ought to live. The three primacies of love, grace, and community that constitute a coherent theological anthropology are seen as answering the aforementioned questions. If love, grace, and community are the three thrusts in our faith understanding of who God is and who the human person is, what is their bearing on the kind of people are we? The answer is that we are relational and communal with an eschatological destiny. How ought we to live? We must be driven by the call to solidarity, by the prophetic witness of subversion, and by a deep sense of transcendence inspired by faith.

The truths of the faith are not abstract truths; they are saving truths. In their depth, expanse, beauty, and sublimity, they reveal the grand narrative of creation being loved unto fullness by God, in one divine embrace.

PART II

NORM

The necessary function of moral norms is mediating the moral vision in the peculiarities and complexities of human choices and acts. Their binding force lies in the moral vision that they explicate and mediate. Moral norms are the repository of the accumulated communal and ecclesial experience of values. As such, they are necessary points of reference and criteria for determining what is right regarding complex human problems and social issues. Catholic social teaching constitutes a substantial body of norms on social questions and issues. I propose in this section an ethical framework for the study and analysis of Catholic social teaching for an ordered, substantive, and effective reading of its voluminous documents. The proposed framework consists of historical context; principles and norms of judgment, directives for action, and critical excursus.

The historical context *shows how a social encyclical was shaped by the social, economic, political realities of its own time.* Principles and norms of judgment *refer to the moral criteria that govern ethical judgment on specific issues that are addressed.* Directives for action *refer to the call to moral praxis.* Critical excursus *refers to an assessment of the relevance of a social teaching, of its prophetic message or narrow view, and of its radical vision or limited horizons as it engages with the social issues of our times.*

This framework is proposed for reconfiguring the matter of the encyclicals without losing its substance. It rearranges the content in an order that makes reading more accessible, and it reappropriates the language to evoke interest that leads to critical thought and inquiry while remaining faithful to the meaning. The goal is to give serious readers of Catholic social teaching greater access to the texts of Catholic social teaching than summaries or excerpts, which cannot replace the academic experience of coming into contact with the full texts.

The proposed framework is applied in the study and analysis of selected encyclicals, showing both change and continuity in the social tradition: Rerum Novarum *ushered in a new era in Catholic social thought;* Mater et Magistra *gives us a glimpse of Catholic social teaching in transition;* Octogesima Adveniens, *on the eightieth anniversary of* Rerum Novarum, *represents developments in Catholic social teaching after Vatican II; and* Centesimus Annus, *recognizing the centenary of* Rerum Novarum, *demonstrates the ongoing development of the tradition while still looking back at its predecessors.*

4

Rerum Novarum

Rerum Novarum (1891) crystallized critical international discussions of social issues, especially those concerned with the status of workers. The church, deeply engaged in these issues of the day, brought the institutional weight of its tradition to bear on them. The significance of *Rerum Novarum* is that not only did it represent a church which spoke to the issues of its own time, but it also began a whole tradition of the church as a prophetic voice of justice for every era and age. No previous pope had addressed matters of ethics as applied to the social order, with a focus on economic realities in general and the question of justice for workers specifically.

Readers should note that with the exception of directly quoted material, I have paraphrased the source material in O'Brien and Shannon's *Catholic Social Thought* and also provided a paragraph number for the original text.[1] In the directly quoted sections, I do not identify with the gender exclusion of women in the language used. I quoted as is, however, to preserve the historicity of the original text.

Historical Context

The world of *Rerum Novarum* was one of incredible economic and political complexity. It was a time of tumultuous changes resulting from the shift from feudalism to capitalism, which reached its zenith in the Industrial Revolution. While the effects of this shift were first felt in England, they soon spread across Western Europe.

---

[1] David J. O'Brien and Thomas A. Shannon, *Catholic Social Thought: The Documentary Heritage* (Maryknoll, NY: Orbis Books, 1992). The official texts of these encyclicals are also available on the vatican.va website. Please note that paragraph numbers may vary, depending on the translation used.

Economic Context

Feudalism, with its complex political, social, and economic system, largely based on the reciprocal obligations among the various members of the social order, was followed by the early modern monarchical or princely forms of a more or less centralized authority. Between 1750 and 1850, Europe also experienced a doubling of population, partly because of the absence of plagues.[2] This new surge of population, composed largely of single males in search for a new life, was met by widespread moves from a rural setting where living was eked almost entirely from the tilling of the land to a town-centered society which engaged progressively in factory manufacture.

With the move from the rural setting to the town, a market economy began to emerge. Cottage industries operated on a system of contractors, wage arrangements, and some centralization of production. After contractors estimated the demand for particular products in various markets, they contacted at-home workers, who produced these products with advance payments. There was a central place for preparatory work for products like wool, but the weaving was done in homes. All this changed once the hand looms were replaced by mechanized power looms in factories, which were run by the steam engine and fueled by coal. "All that was required for the transition to industrialization after a while was to stop supplying the weavers with hand looms and start installing mechanized power looms in a large central workshop, namely the factory."[3]

The change from hand tools and handmade items to mass-produced products also caused massive social dislocations. Factory jobs in the cities, with year-round wages as opposed to seasonal wages, lured the people from the countryside. But because of the surge of population moving to the cities seeking jobs, factory owners were able to hire at low wages and require twelve- to fifteen-hour days. Working long hours away from their families under deplorable conditions in factories put great strain on individuals and families. Many were also left unemployed, for the available jobs could not meet the ever-growing population moving to the cities. This created social problems in the cities, which became fertile ground for widespread social discontent,[4] due to "the suffering of impoverished industrial workers, great

---

[2] Paul Misner, *Social Catholicism in Europe: From the Onset of Industrialization to the First World War* (New York: Crossroad, 1991), 8, 11.

[3] Ibid., 13, 14.

[4] Thomas A. Shannon, "Commentary on *Rerum Novarum*: The Condition of Labor," in *Modern Catholic Social Teaching: Commentaries and Interpretations*,

concentrations of wealth and associated abuses within the capitalist system, the dangers of untrammeled markets, and the need to establish a more equitable social equilibrium."[5]

While the feudal world of the past was radically changed by the Industrial Revolution, its social hierarchy remained; that is, a few enjoyed most of the benefits, while the majority lived with scarcity. The existence of a social hierarchy, however, was not always the cause of social discontent or dissent; there was an interesting social interdependency, with the poor serving the needs of the rich and the rich caring for the poor through alms distribution. "The hope was that this social complementary and paternalistic interdependence would result in a spirit of *noblesse oblige* that would help smooth some of the rough edges of the beginnings of industrialization."[6]

While the social hierarchy remained, the historical prohibition on the practice of usury—interest on loans—changed. The rapid growth of business fueled by the new industrial economy necessitated the availability of credit. Usury went from simply charging interest to adding a finance charge for the inconvenience suffered by the lender. Eventually a credit system with established practices for loans became an integral part of capitalism and industrialism, which led to the rise of the bourgeoisie.[7] These entrepreneurs "could appreciate that the inequalities marking the old world would remain, but not necessarily at *their expense*."[8]

Political Context

Rerum Novarum was not only written during rapid economic changes, with accompanying social dislocations, but it also emerged during an era when the Catholic Church was challenged by political developments hostile to its authority. The French Revolution of 1789 was at the forefront of these developments. In France the properties of the church were nationalized, its institutions were assaulted, and individuals affiliated with it were persecuted. In Germany, the authority of

---

ed. Kenneth R. Himes, 127–50 (Washington, DC: Georgetown University Press, 2004), 129.

[5] See Gerard P. Fogarty, "Leo XIII and the Church in the United States," in *Le pontificat de Léon XIII: renaissances du Saint-Siège?* ed. Philippe Levillain and Jean-Marc Ticchi (Rome: École Française de Rome, 2006), 356–57.

[6] Shannon, "Commentary on *Rerum Novarum*," 129.

[7] See James F. Keenan, "The Casuisty of John Mair, Nominalist Professor of Paris," in *The Context of Casuistry*, ed. James F. Keenan and Thomas A. Shannon, 85–103 (Washington, DC: Georgetown University Press, 1995).

[8] Misner, *Social Catholicism in Europe*, 21.

abbots and bishops was taken away, as was the ecclesiastical control of many universities. All this existed as part of a larger movement to denounce tradition, and the Catholic Church symbolized tradition.[9]

In Germany, Bismarck initiated the *Kulturkampf* (1870–82), the primary goal of which was to redefine German politics and culture.[10] However, it also aimed to diminish the role and status of the Catholic Church. It enacted laws that removed all guarantees in the Prussian constitution to safeguard the Catholic Church, according to the principle of "a free Church in a free State."[11] In 1872, the Jesuits were suppressed; in 1873, other religious orders were silenced.

In Italy, the Papal States, consisting essentially of areas of central Italy that had been given to the papacy by the Carolingian kings in the eighth century, brought the church into the center of the political entanglements. During the Franco-Prussian War, Napoleon withdrew the French troops defending the papacy, rendering Pius IX "a prisoner of the Vatican" as Italian troops took Rome and unified Italy. After the death of Pius IX few held high hopes for the bold initiatives of his successor, Leo XIII. In the world of *Rerum Novarum* in 1891, the institutional status of the church, to say nothing of its role in society, was challenged and greatly diminished, if not entirely put in jeopardy.[12]

Thomas Massaro points out that it is crucial to recall that the papacy of Leo XIII began at the precise midpoint between the French Revolution and the Second Vatican Council. The church took a posture of extreme defensiveness regarding the modern liberal order, which it viewed from under the lingering dark shadows of the French Revolution. On the specific topic of politics, Leo's approach to government was viewed as a bridge to twentieth-century Catholic political thought. His teaching on the Christian position regarding core principles of political justice laid the groundwork for change and positioned the church to face the challenges of a new century.[13]

---

[9] Shannon, "Commentary on *Rerum Novarum*," 129.

[10] See Ronald J. Ross, *The Failure of Bismarck's Kulturkampf: Catholicism and State Power in Imperial Germany, 1871–1877* (Washington, DC: Catholic University of America Press, 1998).

[11] Joseph N. Moody, ed., *Church and Society: Catholic Social and Political Thought and Movements, 1789–1950* (New York: Arts, 1953), 456.

[12] Shannon, "Commentary on *Rerum Novarum*," 130. The historical context was developed based on ibid., 128–30.

[13] Thomas Massaro, "The Social Question in the Papacy of Leo XIII," in *The Papacy Since 1500: From Italian Prince to Universal Pastor,* ed. James Corkery and Thomas Worcester, 143–61 (New York: Cambridge University Press, 2010), 147.

To consider Leo XIII as a bridge figure in this way highlights two aspects of his contribution. First, Leo's political writings analyzed with keen insight the conditions of his day and unraveled the possibilities these conditions contained for religious communities and their members in Europe and North America. Second, Leo's influence was fundamentally transitional. He stood alongside eighteenth- and nineteenth-century popes who lived through the nightmare of the fallout of the French Revolution as they came to grips, often in wrenching ways, with the church being stripped of much of its power in Western Europe. Some of this power was temporal, involving large landholdings and financial interests. Leo XIII was the first pope to reign after the church had lost control of the Papal States during the Italian national unification.[14]

The wounds inflicted on the prestige and power of the Catholic Church were still raw, and the effects of the resultant backlash had to be reckoned with. Nineteenth-century church leaders were faced with redefining the public role of the church in a secular world. Leo's political writings denounced the trends toward secularism, and successive popes throughout this era sought to reassert their authority. But they finally realized that the world in which they could exercise direct control over worldly events had passed. The church gradually had to embrace the mantle of "moral advocacy" in the new world, which denied direct political power to religious authority. Leo and the popes who came after him took new directions, adopted new approaches, and in the process found new allies in their efforts to protect and promote key values in the context of a new world order.[15]

Norms and Principles

At the heart of the encyclical was a cry of protest against the treatment of workers. It was significant that Leo XIII chose to speak out at that time and intervened in a most solemn and official way in the burning issues of the day. Putting the institutional weight of the church on the side of the poor, he proposed his teaching as a remedy for the social problems of the time, at the heart of which was the "misery and wretchedness which press so heavily at this moment on the large majority of the very poor. . . . A small number of very rich men have been able to lay upon the masses of the poor a yoke little better than slavery itself" (no. 2).

---

[14] Ibid.

[15] Ibid., 147–48.

The first of the social encyclicals, *Rerum Novarum* demonstrated that social issues are not marginal to the mission of the church and not to be treated as an optional extra but are at the core of its mission. Its call to people to heed the cries of the poor is central to the mission of the church.

In the following pages I draw upon the principles of judgment enshrined in the encyclical. The purpose of highlighting these norms is to cut to the kernel of its teachings, which are germane for future analysis and commentary. In a broad stroke, as an introduction, the focus of the encyclical is the relation between capital and labor, employee and employer, wealthy and poor. Leo framed this focus in terms of three core issues: the meaning of labor and the rights of workers, private property as a natural right, and the role of the intervention of the state. There are subsidiary issues, like Leo's moral stance regarding the economic systems of capitalism and socialism, that relate to these core issues.

The Meaning of Labor and the Rights of Workers

Rerum Novarum posits that human labor has an intrinsic dignity because it enables people to live their lives in an upright and creditable way. Labor cannot be treated as a commodity, because to do so is to degrade persons to the status of things. Leo gives this a human face by relating it to the brutal reality of the underpaid workers. In the words of the encyclical:

> Religion teaches the rich man and the employer that their workpeople are not their slaves; that they must respect in every man his dignity as a man and as a Christian; that labor is nothing to be ashamed of, if we listen to right reason and to Christian philosophy, but is an honorable employment, enabling a man to sustain his life in an upright and creditable way; and that it is shameful and inhuman to treat men like chattels to make money by, or to look upon them merely as so much muscle or physical power. (no. 16)

The encyclical states that we can contemplate the dignity of labor by reflecting on the life of Christ, "'who whereas he was rich, for our sakes became poor'; and who, being the son of God, and God himself, chose to seem and to be considered the son of a carpenter—nay, did not disdain to spend a great part of his life as a carpenter himself" (no. 20). The church teaches that "in God's sight, poverty is no disgrace, and that there is nothing to be ashamed of in seeking one's bread by labor" (no. 20).

Among the rights of workers to be protected, Leo ranks the spiritual life of the workers as first: "Life on earth, however good and desirable in itself, is not the final purpose for which man is created; it is only the way and the means to that attainment of truth, and the practice of goodness in which the full life of the soul consists" (no. 32). The spiritual needs of the workers are most sacred, for not only are basic human rights in question, but also the inviolable rights of God. God has a sovereign claim on the human heart in worship and adoration, and thus the obligation holds for the cessation of work on Sundays and certain festivals. Leo argues, however, that "this rest from labor is not to be understood as mere idleness; much less must it be an occasion of spending money and a vicious excess, as many would desire it to be; but it should be rest from labor consecrated by religion" (no. 32). Sunday's rest and religious observance make God the focus of our mind and heart in a sacred space where the business of daily life is put aside.

Then the encyclical addresses the question of hours of work. The core principle is that human beings should not be used as mere instruments for making money—"To grind men down with excessive labor as to stupefy their minds and wear out their bodies" (no. 33). Daily labor must be regulated so that it is not protracted, because there are limits to human strength. Rather than specifying a definite number of hours for work, Leo sets certain conditions for determining these limits. The time of work should depend "upon the nature of the work, on circumstances of time and place, and on the health and strength of the workman" (no. 33). He states, for instance, that those who labor in mines and quarries within the bowels of the earth should have proportionately shorter hours, as their labor severely challenges their bodies and health. He notes too that the season of the year must be taken into account, for a kind of labor might be easy during a particular time of the year and be intolerable at another time (no. 33). He further stresses that "work which is suitable for a strong man cannot reasonably be required from a woman or a child" (no. 33). The basic principle that Leo identifies is that "a workman ought to have leisure and rest in proportion to the wear and tear of his strength; for the waste of strength must be repaired by the cessation of work" (no. 33).

Leo's focus is to ease the burdens of workers, with particular care for children and women. Children must not be made to bear the burdens of labor until their bodies and minds are sufficiently mature. Too early an experience of hard work blights the promise of a young mind and makes education impossible. Leo compares what happens to a child in the workforce to what happens to the buds of spring destroyed by rough weather. He also addresses the condition of women, who he believes are not suited to certain trades by their nature, which is centered on taking care of children and the well-being of the family (no. 33). Clearly, the pope's view of women's nature was conditioned by the worldview of his time, that is, that a woman's work is limited by biology. While this frame of analysis is criticized today, it does not deny that women have been subjected to the same abuses as men in the workplace, and additionally, have often been victims of sexual harassment and discrimination.

The discussion of a just wage in *Rerum Novarum* has yielded enduring principles. "Extreme inequality is not desirable. Workers have certain rights and must be treated with respect. The economy is chock-full of moral significance and ethical obligations."[16] Leo attacks using consent to set wages, the prevailing practice, in which the employer and the worker are bound to a wage based on a mutual agreement that is broken only if the worker does not complete the work or the employer does not pay the full remuneration for the work. For Leo, this practice was open to abuses because it left out important considerations. The proper norm or principle to follow regarding wages is based on the meaning of work. First, work is personal; we leave on our work a stamp of our person and powers, which are employed for the personal profit for which it was given. Second, labor is necessary, for without the fruit of our labor, we cannot live, and self-conservation is a law of nature that must be obeyed (no. 34). Leo concludes that if a person's work were only personal, for one's pleasure or profit, then the contract model would be acceptable. But since work is necessary for one's self-preservation and that of one's family, "each one has a right to procure what is required in order to live; and the poor can procure it in no other way than by work and by wages" (no. 34).

To use the consent model for work renders the poor vulnerable to the employer. The poor are forced by their desperate circumstances to accept any wage contract, even under very harsh work conditions. But often they practically end up living on what seems not even enough for survival, which violates the law of nature. They become victims of force and injustice. As Leo notes, "There is a dictate of nature more imperious and more ancient than any bargain between man and man that the remuneration must be enough to support the wage earner in reasonable and frugal comfort" (no. 34).

---

[16] Massaro, "The Social Question in the Papacy of Leo XIII," 156.

Private Property as a Natural Right

Leo's core assertion is that "the right to possess private property is from nature, not from man; and the State has only the right to regulate its use in the interests of the public good, but by no means to abolish it altogether" (no. 35). It must be assumed as a principle that private ownership is sacred and inviolable. The law, therefore, should favor ownership and should encourage as many people as possible to become owners (no. 35). This teaching regarding private property is viewed as Leo's reaction to the socialist threat of undercutting rights to property and redistributing it. He also upholds ownership of property as the way for the poor to get out of the trap of poverty. And he sees the necessity of a just wage not only to give security to workers, but also to enable them to save money to buy property. Given the critical importance of property ownership for social justice and social mobility, he asserts that everyone has the right by nature to possess private property.

> And to say that God has given the earth to the use and enjoyment of the universal human race is not to deny that there can be private property. For God has granted the earth to mankind in general; not in the sense that all without distinction can deal with it as they please, but rather that no part of it has been assigned to any one in particular, and that the limits of private possession have been left to be fixed by man's own industry and the laws of individual peoples. . . . Now, when man thus spends the industry of his mind and the strength of his body in procuring the fruits of nature by that act he makes his own that portion of nature's field which he cultivates—that portion on which he leaves, as it were, the impress of his own personality, and it cannot but be just that he should possess that portion as his own, and should have a right to keep it without molestation. (no. 7)

This paragraph is key, because it shows that while Leo roots the right of private property in nature, there is also a relationship between property and labor. "For every man has by nature the right to possess property as his own" (no. 5). Shannon points out that "this statement of theory of private property qualifies, if not rejects the theory of property identified by Thomas Aquinas."[17] Aquinas's position is that "a private property system of control is a social convention that *does*

---

[17] Shannon, "Commentary on *Rerum Novarum*," 142.

not violate the natural law but can be justified on grounds of practical expediency."[18] Aquinas further states:

> Now, according to the natural order instituted by divine providence, material goods are provided for the satisfaction of human needs. Therefore the division of and appropriation of property, that proceeds from human law, must not hinder the satisfaction of man's necessity for such goods. Equally whatever a man has in superabundance is owed, of natural right to the poor for their sustenance.[19]

What can be gleaned from this statement is that possession of property may not be a natural right for Aquinas in the way Leo expresses it. Aquinas holds that no one should hinder another's claim to property, but he sees that its possession can be qualified by the needs of others. In other words, while Aquinas emphasizes the social issue surrounding property, Leo holds the natural right to property.[20]

Leo further states his argument for private property: "Now when man thus spends the industry of his mind and the strength of his body in procuring the fruits of nature by that act he makes his own that portion of nature's field which he cultivates" (no. 7). Shannon points out that Leo's claim in this statement is quite interesting when it is read in the light of John Locke's theory of property in *Two Treatises of Government*.[21] Locke argues for the rights of individuals to life, liberty, and property. If individuals place themselves under government, it is only for the protection and preservation of property. Government is not the origin of the right of property. Rather, according to Locke,

> though the earth and all inferior creatures be common to all men, yet every man has a "property" in his own "person." This nobody has any right to but himself. The "labor" of his body and the "work" of his hands, we may say, are properly his. Whatsoever, then he removes out of the state that Nature

---

[18] Manuel Velasquez, "*Gaudium et Spes* and the Development of Catholic Social-Economic Teaching," in *Questions of Special Urgency: The Church in the Modern World, Two Decades After Vatican II*, ed. Judith A. Dwyer (Washington, DC: Georgetown University Press, 1986), 197.

[19] Thomas Aquinas, II-II, Q.66, A.7.

[20] Shannon, "Commentary on *Rerum Novarum*," 142.

[21] Ibid.

hath provided and left in it, he hath mixed his labor with it, and joined to it something that is his own, and thereby makes it his property.[22]

Leo's view seems in some ways to coalesce with the beliefs of Locke. This interesting blend of their teachings entered Catholic thought through the influence of the Jesuit Luigi Taparelli D'Azeglio in his 1840 book *Saggio teoretico di dirritto natural appogiato sulfatoo*.[23] Leo used his ideas to argue that property is a natural right, putting weight more on this notion of property rather than on the priority of the communality of all property. When Leo's view of property is read together with his other statement that it is "a duty, not of justice (except in extreme cases), but of Christian Charity to share with the poor out of one's superfluity" (no. 19), not only is a strong case made for the inviolability of the natural right to private property but also for individualism.[24]

Referring to the work of Patricia Werhane, who makes the point that the key to reconciling the right to ownership and social obligation is stewardship,[25] Shannon writes, "This concept of stewardship, later taken up in Vatican II, provides an interesting and important resolution to the tension on the right of property set up by the juxtaposition of Thomistic and Lockean thinking in the encyclical."[26] Arguing for how Leo links rights and obligations with stewardship as the mediator between the two, Werhane writes:

> Thus *Rerum Novarum* challenges both Marxism and economic egoism. It links alienation to poor working conditions and the inability to own property rather than to the nature of work itself. The economic leveler of greed is not socialism nor the market but the obligation to expand and extend property ownership. Stewardship thus conceived linking property with concomitant obligations implies a sense of social justice parallel to the demands

---

[22] John Locke, *The Second Treatise on Civil Government*, par. 26.

[23] See Velasquez, "*Gaudium et Spes* and the Development of Catholic Social-Economic Teaching," 197.

[24] Shannon, "Commentary on *Rerum Novarum*," 142–43.

[25] See Patricia Werhane, "The Obligatory Nature of Stewardship in *Rerum Novarum* and Its Relevance to the American Economy," in *Rerum Novarum: Celebrating 100 Years of Catholic Social Thought*, ed. Ronald F. Duska, 184–97 (Lewiston, NY: Edwin Mellen, 1991).

[26] Shannon, "Commentary on *Rerum Novarum*," 143.

of the nineteenth century populists that safeguard individualism without sacrificing the goal of economic redistribution.[27]

From the text of *Rerum Novarum* and what commentators have written, we can see Leo's arguments for the right to private property. First, he states that it is undeniable that the very reason and motive for remunerative labor is to acquire property. The full right to the dignity of labor is not just to remuneration but also to the disposal of that remuneration as one pleases. It is precisely in this power of disposal that ownership is important, whether the property is land or movable goods. Leo criticizes socialists for their view of society, in which private property is transferred to the community. This, Leo states, deals a blow to the right of wage earners to dispose of their earnings to acquire what would increase their stock and better their lives (no. 4).

Second, Leo suggests that the natural right to possess property is what distinguishes human beings from animals. Beyond the sheer instincts of self-preservation and the propagation of the species, which humans share with animal creation, the functions of reason and choice contribute to what makes a human fully human (no. 5). In this account of reason setting human beings apart from other animals, it must be within the right of every person to "have not only things which perish in the using, but also those which, though used, remain for use in the future" (no. 5). The capacity to conceive enduring goals for the future is a distinct capacity of human reason, as contrasted to the mere animal instinct for survival.

Third, what is necessary for the preservation of life and for life's well-being has been provided in great abundance by the good Creator. But only when we spend the industry of our mind and the strength of our body in procuring what is available in nature do we make that portion of nature's bounty our own. Not only should we possess that portion as our own, since it bears our imprint, but we should have the right to keep it without molestation (no. 7). Leo asserts that the claim to property comes from the creative toil of those who take as their own what they have made.

Fourth, seen in the situation of Leo's world, there is a great divide between those who hold power because they hold wealth and who have within their grasp all labor and trade, and those who are needy and powerless. When more people are owners of property, "the gulf between vast wealth and deep poverty will be bridged over, and the

---

[27] Werhane, "The Obligatory Nature of Stewardship in *Rerum Novarum* and Its Relevance to the American Economy," 190.

two orders will be brought nearer together" (no. 35). Leo sees that excessive inequality creates social unrest and class conflict, and he asserts that only through ownership of property by those at the lower ranks of the social hierarchy can there be some relative leveling of economic relationships.

Fifth, ownership of property (such as the land one tills) would result in an increase of the abundance of the fruits of the earth:

> Men always work harder and more readily when they work on that which is their own; nay, they learn to love the very soil which yields in response to the labor of their hands, not only food to eat, but an abundance of the good things for themselves and those that are dear to them. It is evident how such a spirit of willing labor would add to the produce of the earth and to the wealth of the community. (no. 35)

Leo argues here that it is the fruit of the labor of the workers that enriches the community, and the more the workers are enabled to produce more fruit, the better for them and for all. Ownership of property thus contributes not only to the flourishing of individuals and families, but also to the common good.

Finally, since the family is the first natural society, the father, in his capacity as head of the family, has the duty to provide for his family now and in the future, keeping them from want and misery in the uncertainties of this mortal life. In no other way can a father fulfill his obligation except by ownership of profitable property that he can pass on to his children as inheritance (no. 10). Leo's assessment of the value of property ownership includes its importance as protection against the onslaught of life's challenges both for oneself and as a security for one's progeny—ensuring the well-being of generations to come.

The Role of the State

Another enduring legacy of *Rerum Novarum* is its affirmation of the role of the state, though limited, in resolving social issues. To understand the position that Leo took in relation to the role of the state, we must first discuss the two contrasting views of the role of the state in society. First, there is the classical theory of liberal capitalism. It holds that the state should be confined to political matters such as ensuring internal order and stability and protecting the country from external aggression. The economic sphere is generally left without interference; the state allows private enterprise, open competition, and the forces of the market to operate freely. This is based on the assumption that the state and all its agencies should be neutral and independent. They should not be engaged in any economic conflicts or rivalries that take place in society. The state only provides the framework within which economic activity can take place effectively within its own mores. Marxist theory holds a radically different view, holding that the state is not neutral. Political power is not separate from economic power, as those with economic power gain political power, and likewise those with political power use it to gain economic power. As one might expect, the lower classes are exploited by those with political power who control the apparatus of the state for their economic benefit.[28]

What is the view of Leo? He basically disagrees with both of these views, but in speaking about the role of the state in *Rerum Novarum*, he comes fairly close to each at different times. Though agreeing with the neutrality of the state in matters of economics, his account of what happens in practice comes quite close to the Marxist view. According to the principles laid out in *Rerum Novarum*, economic power should not overlap with political power. The wealthy should not use their power to manipulate the apparatus of the state to protect their interest. The state should be neutral, above the interests of all classes, and should keep balance and harmony among them. To the state, the interests of all are equal, whether high or low. Poor and rich are equal members of the national community; they are component parts, living parts, that make up the living body. The poor are by far the majority. "It would be irrational to neglect one portion of the citizens and to favor another; therefore, public administration must duly and solicitously provide for the welfare and the comfort of the working people, or else that law of justice will be violated which ordains that each shall have his due" (nos. 26–27). Leo cites the wise words of Thomas Aquinas: "As the part and the whole are in a certain sense identical, the part may in some sense claim what belongs to the whole" (no. 27).

What is assumed here is that cooperation and not conflict is to be the basis of the social order, for each person is part of the whole. That the contrary has been held, Leo believes, is an error: "The great mistake that is made in the matter now under consideration is to possess oneself of the idea that class is naturally hostile to class; that rich and poor are intended by nature to live at war with one another" (no. 15).

---

[28] Donal Dorr, *Option for the Poor: A Hundred Years of Catholic Social Teaching* (Maryknoll, NY: Orbis Books, 1983), 20.

This mistaken view is due to the lack of appreciation of the design of nature for the body politic:

> Just as the symmetry of the human body is the result of the disposition of the members of the body, so in a State it is ordained by nature that these two classes should exist in harmony and agreement, and should, as it were, fit into one another, so as to maintain the equilibrium of the body politic. Each requires the other; capital cannot do without labor nor labor without capital. (no. 15)

What Leo describes is an ideal, but in the actual situation what he saw was much closer to what the Marxists described in their view of society—the rich held the state hostage in their power and used its apparatus to protect and promote their economic interest:

> On the one side there is the party which holds power because it holds the wealth; which has in its grasp all labor and all trade; which manipulates for its own benefit and its own purposes all the sources of supply; and which is powerfully represented in the councils of the State itself. On the other side there is the needy and powerless multitude, sore and suffering, always ready for disturbance. (no. 35)

Faced with this reality, Leo sees that the recourse to remedy the situation is for as many workers as possible to become owners of property (no. 35). As long as wealth is concentrated in the hands of the few, these few use the power to control the economy to benefit themselves. This means that for as long as the wealth of the nation is in the hands of one sector of society, the state is hindered in playing its role in protecting the rights of the poor and thus in promoting the common good.

What can be gleaned from this argument is a shift from seeing poverty as a sign of moral failure or laziness to understanding it as a consequence of a systemic failure—the byproduct of unjust economic and political systems.[29] The condition of poverty is not a given to be lived and endured in spirit of resignation but "a state of things that ought not to be and can be changed for the better."[30] Poverty is not exclusively a moral problem but is also a function of a faulty economic

---

[29] Shannon, "Commentary on *Rerum Novarum*," 140.
[30] Misner, *Social Catholicism in Europe*, 40.

system.[31] Since the problem is in the system, the solution must be a change in the system. Misner writes:

> Without laws, without the state setting basic standards, that is, without a political consensus on a certain level of regulation, the social question could not be solved—just as it could not be solved without individual responsibility, without the beneficent influence of religion, or without an effective organization of labor to confront the power of concentrated capital.[32]

This shift in the analysis of the social problem of poverty is considered a critical shift in Catholic thinking, one that first appeared in *Rerum Novarum*. While affirming the limited role of government, Leo upholds that "rulers should anxiously safeguard the community and all its parts" (no. 28). He particularly asserts that the state must intervene whenever the general interest of any particular class suffers or is threatened by evils that cannot be countered except by public authority and force (no. 28). The intervention of the state is legitimate in specific situations:

> If religion were found to suffer through the workmen not having time and opportunity to practice it; if in workshops and factories there were danger to morals through the mixing of sexes or from any occasion of evil; or if employers laid burdens upon the workmen which were unjust, or degraded them with conditions that were repugnant to their dignity as human beings; finally if health were endangered by excessive labor, or by work unsuited to sex or age—in these cases there can be no question that, within certain limits, it would be right to call in the help and authority of the law. (no. 29)

In other words, the state must intervene for those who have no other recourse to negotiate for their rights with those who have the means and power to protect their own interests. Leo insists that the state has a special obligation to care for and protect the poor, who are without power and have nothing to fall back on:

> The richer population have many ways of protecting themselves, and stand less in need of help from the State; those who are

---

[31] Shannon, "Commentary on *Rerum Novarum*," 140.
[32] Misner, *Social Catholicism in Europe*, 143.

badly off have no resources of their own to fall back upon, and must chiefly rely upon the assistance of the State. And it is for this reason that wage earners, who are, undoubtedly, among the weak and the necessitous, should be specially cared for and protected by the commonwealth. (no. 29)

In anticipation of the later development of the principle of subsidiarity, Leo writes: "The law must not undertake more, nor go further, than is required for the remedy of the evil or the removal of danger" (no. 29). What is critical here, because of its enduring impact, is the notion that the church and its work of charity are not enough to respond to or solve social problems. As the discussion shifts from the poor to poverty, the encyclical argues for the legitimacy of state intervention in addressing these problems. With the concentration of economic and political power in the hands of a few, the encyclical upholds the moral imperative of distributive justice:

> Justice, therefore, demands that the interests of the poorer population be carefully watched over by the administration, so that they who contribute so largely to the advantage of the community may themselves share in the benefits they create—that being housed, clothed, and enabled to support life, that they may find existence less hard and more endurable. (no. 27)

In this statement Leo articulates the role of the state in changing the social order to one where equity and justice define social relations. As Thomas Massaro writes, "The moral imperative of protecting workers from degradation and even extinction justifies significant government activism and regulation in the interest of achieving labor justice."[33]

Was there an evolution in the thinking of Leo regarding charity and justice? In exhorting the rich to care for the poor, he taught that

> no one is commanded to give out to others that which is required for his own necessities and those of his household; nor even to give away what is reasonably required to keep up becomingly his condition in life; for no one ought to live unbecomingly. But when necessity has been supplied, and one's position fairly considered, it is a duty to give to the indigent out of that which is left over. (no. 19)

---

[33] Massaro, "The Social Question in the Papacy of Leo XIII," 157.

Leo praises giving out of one's excess in the form of almsgiving and in a spirit of charity. He criticizes those who propose another way: "At the present day, there are many who, like the heathen of old, blame and condemn the church for this beautiful charity. They would substitute in its place a system of State-organized relief. But no human methods will ever supply for the devotion and self-sacrifice of Christian charity" (no. 24).

Then Leo turns to the state and explicates its most critical obligation to the poor. "Among the many and grave duties of rulers who would do their best for their people, the first and chief is to act with strict justice—with that justice which is called in the schools *distributive*—toward each and every class" (no. 27). This is a demand of justice and not of charity. This is giving the workers what is due to them on the basis of their labor, not giving them from the excess of one's goods. In the first, the workers' dignity and power are upheld; in the second, their need and dependency is stressed. Leo seems to assign the work of charity to individuals, while the work of justice is properly assigned to the state. This affirms a shift in the analysis of the problem as structural, not only personal or individual. For the state to meet this critical obligation, it must use its apparatus to "secure from misery those on whom it so largely depends" (no. 27). Leo does not make one the alternative to the other. There is a role for charitable works in society, but only when workers are paid justly, given opportunities to build their assets, acquire property, and when they are fully afforded the dignity of their person and their labor.

Directives for Action

This section focuses on the encyclical's directives for action. It brings the discussions to the level of behavior and praxis, in terms of the reciprocal duties of employers and workers, of the relationships among classes, and of the nature of workers' associations. Leo lays out those actions consonant with the spirit and tradition of the church and those hostile to it.

Reciprocal Duties of Employers and Workers

A key paragraph in the encyclical lists the reciprocal duties of employers and workers, duties that are morally obligatory if harmony and justice are to bind both. The following duties bind the owner and the employer:

Religion teaches the rich man and employer that their work-people are not their slaves; that they must respect in every man his dignity as a man and as a Christian . . . that it is shameful and inhuman to treat men like chattels to make money by, or to look upon them merely as so much muscle or physical power. Thus, again, religion teaches that, as among the workmen's concerns are religion herself, and things spiritual and mental, the employer is bound to see that he has time for the duties of piety; that he be not exposed to corrupting influences and dangerous occasions; and that he be not led away to neglect his home and family or to squander his wages. Then, again, the employer must never tax his work-people beyond their strength, nor employ them in work unsuited to their sex or age. His great and principal obligation is to give to every one that which is just. Doubtless before we can decide whether wages are adequate many things have to be considered; but rich men and masters should remember this—that to exercise pressure for the sake of gain, upon the indigent and destitute, and to make one's profit out of the need of another, is condemned by all laws, human and divine. To defraud any one of wages that are his due is a crime which cries to the avenging anger of heaven. . . . Finally the rich must religiously refrain from cutting down the workman's earnings, either by force, fraud, or by usurious dealing: and with the more reason because the poor man is weak and unprotected, and because his slender means should be sacred in proportion to their scantiness. (nos. 16–17)

The whole passage constitutes a moving and eloquent call to conversion, not only a change of heart but a change of behavior and practice in the sphere of economics. But could this eloquent call be only rhetorical, as shown in the gap between the words of the encyclical and the actual facts? Leo was well aware of the injustices so prevalent in his time. Workers were treated like chattel, denied of all dignity, and valued only for the money gained through their labor; children were made to work beyond their capacity; women were subject to sexual harassment in the workplace; human laws governing business in an unbridled liberal capitalist society legitimized the rich making profit out of the needs of the poor; employers paid unjust wages; and workers were taxed beyond their strength. And above all, the state failed to protect the workers against these injustices.

What action does Leo recommend to workers in the face of these abuses? The following is a list of the duties which *Rerum Novarum* lay down for workers:

Religion teaches the laboring man and the workman to carry out honestly and well all equitable agreements freely made, never to injure capital, nor to outrage the person of an employer; never to employ violence in representing his own cause, nor to engage in riot and disorder; and to have nothing to do with men of evil principles, who work upon the people with artful promises, and raise foolish hopes which usually end in disaster and in repentance when too late. (no. 16)

A close examination of the list shows that Leo is against any kind of confrontation that would cause damage to the property of an employer or would cause disorder. There is no encouragement of any form of activism in the struggle of the workers to protect their rights. If taken strictly, Leo seems to imply that a strike is wrong whenever it poses a threat to peace and order, but he does not provide guidelines on when a strike is legitimate. He acknowledges that strikes do occur, and with causes and consequences, but he does not address their moral legitimacy:

When work-people have recourse to a strike, it is frequently because the hours of labor are too long, or the work too hard, or because they consider their wages insufficient. The grave inconvenience of this not uncommon occurrence should be obviated by public remedial measure; for such paralysis of labor not only affects the masters and their work-people, but is extremely injurious to trade, and to the general interests of the public; moreover, on such occasions, violence and disorder are generally not far off, and thus it frequently happens that the public peace is threatened. The laws should be made beforehand, and prevent these troubles from arising; they should lend their influence and authority to the removal in good time of the causes which lead to conflicts between masters and those whom they employ. (no. 31)

While Leo sees the strike as a recourse of the workers to fight for their cause in the economic sphere, the consequences could quickly spill over into the political sphere, which would pose a threat to a public order. He puts a strict boundary between the economic and the political, so that using a strike to challenge the status quo in the economic sphere would not turn into a political incitement. Is this realistic? And could this result in the church undermining the rights of the workers by creating a political cover for those in power?

Class Relationships

What seems to be keeping Leo from confronting the reality of conflict in unjust situations is his ideal of harmony between and among classes, so exalted and perfect that it becomes almost abstract. His teaching on the relation of classes is a core theme in the encyclical. Leo envisions a hierarchical society as part of the very fabric of nature, which he believes the socialists are intent on tearing apart by stirring up class warfare by making the poor dissatisfied with their lot. Though social classes exist in hierarchical relationships, the church "lays down precepts yet more perfect, and tries to bind class to class in friendliness and good understanding" (no. 18). This is pursued within the transcendental horizons of our mortal life, for

> the things of this earth cannot be understood rightly without taking into consideration the life to come, the life that will last forever. . . . Money and the other things which men call good and desirable, we may have them in abundance or we may want them altogether; as far as eternal happiness is concerned, it is no matter; the only thing that is important is to use them aright. (no. 18)

Thus, while there may be differences and divisions between and among classes, they do not ultimately matter because, in the end, all stand fully equal before God.

Leo's view of the relationship of classes is articulated in two key assertions. First, he holds that the differences and inequalities between classes are natural. "There naturally exist among mankind innumerable differences of the most important kind; people differ in capability, in diligence, in health, and in strength; and unequal fortune is a necessary result of inequality in condition" (no. 14). He argues, however, that the differences and inequality are "far from being disadvantageous either to individuals or to the community; social and public life can only go on by the help of various kinds of capacity and the playing of many parts, and each man, as a rule, chooses the part which peculiarly suits his case" (no. 14). What Leo is arguing here is that differences and inequality, which are part of nature, all come together in the common life people live, with each contributing according to who he or she is.

Second, rejecting the Marxist notion of class warfare, he argues that classes are not naturally hostile to one another, with the poor intended by nature to live at war with the rich. On the contrary, using the symmetry of the different parts of the body, the rich and poor live in harmony; they need each other to keep the equilibrium of the body politic (no. 15). The differences do not destroy the dignity of any person, regardless of class position. Each has duties to the other—this is particularly true of property owners—and carrying these out in fidelity to the duties of one's state guarantees social harmony and well-being. Leo very carefully spells out the rights and duties of each class to the other, and then notes: "Were these precepts carefully obeyed and followed, would not strife die out and cease?" (no. 17).

Workmen's Associations

One force that might bring about a transformation required for a structurally just society is the trade union. History has shown that major changes can be brought about by a strong trade union movement. Through unions, workers could have a say in the shaping of government policies, and they could negotiate from a position of collective strength for their causes. The trade unions could also take on quasi-political roles in addressing issues that affect employer-worker relationships. What was the teaching of *Rerum Novarum* on associations or organizations of workers?

Leo does not call such associations labor unions; he calls them workmen's associations, a precursor of our current understanding of labor unions. In speaking of such associations he alludes to the positive benefits of the older guild system and calls for the adaptation of such associations to the needs of the current age.

> History attests what excellent results were effected by the artificer's guilds of a former day. They were the means not only of many advantages to the workmen, but in no small degree of the advancement of art, as numerous monuments remain to prove. Such associations should be adapted to the requirements of the age in which we live—an age of greater instruction, of different customs, and of more numerous requirements in daily life. (no. 36)

He defends the basic right of workers to form associations, calling the most important of these workmen's associations (no. 36). It is not clear exactly what he means by these associations, but it seems that they are organized to meet a plurality of needs and consist of either workmen alone or of workmen and employers together. Leo argues that it is the natural right of individuals to form societies for their mutual help and benefit (no. 38). While the state cannot prohibit the creation of societies, it can interfere when such societies pose harm or danger to the state. But caution must be taken that individual rights are not violated and that unreasonable regulations are not imposed under the pretense of public benefit (no. 38).

The main danger that Leo sees in such associations is that they would be under the sway of leaders whose beliefs are not compatible with Christianity and the public well-being. He writes: "But there is a good deal of evidence which goes to prove that many of these societies are in the hands of invisible leaders, and are managed on principles far from compatible with Christianity and the public well being; and that they do their best to get into their hands the whole field of labor and to force workmen either to join them or to starve" (no. 40). Leo makes reference here to the practice called the closed shop, where only members of a particular association would be able to get a job. He also notes here how workers could be won over by atheistic and/ or socialist labor movements that take up their cause against abusive employers. For this reason he lavishes praise on Catholics who work for the cause of the workers without compromising their principles. "Those Catholics are worthy of all praise—and there not a few—who, understanding what the times require, have, by various enterprises and experiments, endeavored to better the conditions of the working people without any sacrifice of principle" (no. 41). He encourages Christian workmen to form their own associations as an alternative to joining those that expose their religion to peril.

Leo teaches that the spiritual is not dissociated from the temporal. Religion must be the foundation of the workmen's associations. Special and principal attention must be given to piety and morality, which gives these associations their special character compared to those that take no account of religion at all. To ensure that members are well grounded, the associations must provide for religious instruction and for the proper celebration of religious feasts and reception of the sacraments (no. 42). Leo lays out specific instructions on how the associations are to operate so that members "may live together in concord":

Office-bearers should be appointed with prudence and discretion. . . . Let the common funds be administered with strictest honesty, in such a way that a member receives assistance in proportion to his necessities. The rights and duties of employers should be the subject of careful consideration as compared with the rights and duties of the employed. If it should happen that either a master

or a workman deemed himself injured . . . there should be a committee composed of honest and capable men . . . whose duty it
should be, by the laws of the association, to decide the dispute.
Among the purposes of society should be an effort to arrange
for a continuous supply of work at all times and seasons; and
to create a fund from which the members may be helped in their
necessities, not only in the case of accident, but also in sickness,
old age, and misfortune. (no. 43)

The aforementioned instructions are founded on the following
principles:

to infuse the spirit of justice into the mutual relations of employers and employed; to keep before the eyes of both classes the
precepts of duty and the laws of the Gospel—that Gospel which,
by inculcating self-restraint, keeps men within the bounds of
moderation, and tends to establish harmony among the divergent
interests and various classes which compose the State. (no. 41)

Leo's vision is different from the idea of the trade union as presently
understood. The workmen's association's membership is not confined
to workers alone, and the main emphasis is self-restraint and harmony.
Leo carefully avoids words that imply conflict and struggle. As a
whole, the workmen's associations are to serve both the spiritual and
temporal needs of the workers and their families. And through its support of these associations, the church is able to address the problems
of the workers and contribute to the common good.

Though Leo's writings show his reluctance to encourage workers to
take organized political and militant action to secure their rights, he
was attentive to their cries against the hardheartedness and greed of
employers. He saw how they were held hostage by the unchecked and
cutthroat competition in which they had no chance for survival. At the
beginning of *Rerum Novarum* there is a perceptive passage in which
the pope reflects on the reason workers were exploited and abused:

But all agree, and there can be no question whatever, that some
remedy must be found, and quickly found, for the misery and
wretchedness which press so heavily at this moment on the
large majority of the very poor. The ancient workmen's guilds
were destroyed in the last century, and no other organization
took their place. . . . Hence by degrees it has come to pass that
workingmen have been given over, isolated and defenseless,

to the callousness of employers and the greed of unrestrained competition. (no. 2)

Donal Dorr remarks that while this has sometimes been dismissed as a pointless pining for an outdated social order, it contains one of the most important insights in the entire encyclical. Certainly there was nostalgia for things past, but what is critical is the assertion that it was the loss of organizational support for the workers, with the abolition of the guilds, that caused them to be left isolated, abandoned, and helpless against the hardheartedness of employers and the greed of unchecked competition. The workers had no protection against abuse and exploitation precisely because they had no organization to defend themselves.[34]

Again we see a shift from seeing the social problem as purely a moral matter, such as how virtuous the employers are, to seeing it as a structural issue. The greed and hardheartedness of employers may still be present, but if the workers have protection in an organization, they are able to fight for their cause. The passage indicates how Leo had gone a fair way toward an analysis of structures of society of his time and saw the profound connection between poverty and powerlessness.[35] Much was left to be desired, however, in how he pursued this insight to its practical conclusions. In the words of Dorr, his "prophetic voice seemed to falter when it came to drawing practical conclusions from his insight about the importance of trade unions."[36]

One might expect that after seeing the disastrous aftermath of the demise of the guilds, Leo would recommend the establishment of a strong movement of workers that would work for structural change. But perhaps partly because of uncertainty about how this movement would develop, the practical proposals he put forward fell short of his insight.

Critical Excursus

After reading the encyclical one is left with the question of whether *Rerum Novarum* measured up to the prophetic call of the church to be on the side of the poor. It seems that Leo was pulled in different directions and that the positions he took were sometimes ambivalent. To understand his positions, one has to go beyond *Rerum Novarum*

---

[34] Dorr, *Option for the Poor,* 28.
[35] Ibid., 29.
[36] Ibid.

and see the background for his teachings in his past writings. His theology of civil authority, his political philosophy, and his spirituality influenced the shape of his position on the relation of the church to the state and had implications for his view of private property, his reservation on political action for structural change, and his stance regarding poverty and injustice. While in *Rerum Novarum* he articulates his positions in an authoritative teaching, these must be put in the context of his worldview, which was influenced by the historical times in which he lived.

Theology of Civil Power

According to Leo's theology of civil power, authority of rulers comes from God: "From the heads of States, to whom as the Apostle admonishes, all owe submission, and on whom the rights of authority are bestowed by God Himself, these sectaries withhold obedience."[37] So he maintains that it is "impious" to rise up against one's rulers. Later in the same encyclical he says that the church constantly urges on everybody the apostolic precept that one should obey rulers as a matter of conscience. Two and a half years later, in 1881, Leo issued an encyclical, *Diuturnum,* in which he once again addressed the origin of civil power. Rejecting the modern view that power and authority come from the mandate and will of the people, Leo asserts that civil power has its source in God. He draws from the authority of scripture, the teachings of the fathers of the church, and the arguments of reason to ground his teaching. He teaches in his 1882 encyclical *Auspicato Concessum* that "those who are imbued with the Christian religion know with certainty that they are bound in conscience to submit to those who lawfully rule them" (no. 23). He points out that in early Christian times, even in the face of persecution, the great martyrs continued to believe that the powers of the rulers were founded on the authority of God.[38]

The conclusion that Leo draws from his theology of civil power is that the church must strengthen and help the state. In his encyclical *Inscrutabili,* issued in 1878, he also made a strong appeal to civil authorities to cooperate with the support that the church offered them:

> We address ourselves to princes and chief rulers of the nations and earnestly beseech them . . . not to refuse the Church's aid

---

[37] Cited in ibid., 36–37. See also *The Great Encyclical Letters of Pope Leo XIII,* pref. John J. Wynne (New York: Benziger Brothers, 1903).

[38] Cited in Dorr, *Option for the Poor,* 37.

. . . but with united and friendly aims to join themselves to her as the source of authority and salvation . . . considering that their own peace and safety, as well as that of their people, is bound up with the safety of the Church and the reverence due to her.[39]

Does this mean that the church gives unqualified and unconditional obedience to civil authority? Leo makes qualifications to his teaching regarding allegiance or obedience to the state where its command is opposed to the law of God or the will of God. One is only bound to obey the state when its law is within the boundaries of its divine sanction. As he explains in *Diuturnum*, those rulers whose will is in opposition to the will of God have lost their claim on the obedience of those under their sovereignty. In another encyclical, *Au milieu des sollicitudes*, written in 1892, his response to a delicate political situation demonstrates a rather circumspect nuance in his distinction between the constituted powers of the state, on the one hand, and legislation, on the other. The fact that odious legislation is passed by a regime does not prove that it is not a duly constituted political authority. On the other hand, one is not bound to obey any law that is hostile to religion, even those enacted by those who hold lawful political authority. Any resistance to a law must be within the limits imposed by the civil authority that remains legally constituted. From Leo's religious worldview, the divine sanction of civil authority is founded on that which is much deeper and beyond human legitimation, and which remains even with a flawed human institution.[40]

Political Philosophy

Leo's political philosophy articulates further his stance regarding socialism and liberal capitalism. For Leo, socialism was the epitome of all social evils. In the document *Auspicato Concessum* he pictured socialism at its worst: "The beginning and the instruments of 'Socialism' are violence, violations of injustice, the craze for a new order and envy between the different classes of society."[41] He linked socialism with political extremism which results in anarchy and nihilism. Excluding God from public life and denying the notion of reward and punishment in the future, socialism leaves the poor discontented with their lot, coveting the wealth of the rich.[42]

---

[39] Cited in ibid., 36.
[40] Cited in ibid., 42.
[41] Cited in ibid., 54.
[42] Cited in ibid.

The pope's fear and rejection of socialism led him to revise an earlier draft of *Rerum Novarum* in which the right to private property was founded on the universal principle that the goods of the earth are for the common good.[43] He thought that this statement might be interpreted as aligning the church with the socialist view, and so in *Rerum Novarum* he gave a restrictive interpretation to the universal teaching by saying that God has granted the earth to humankind in general, which means that no part of it was assigned to anyone in particular, and that the limits of private possession have been left to be fixed by people's own industry and by the laws of the individual races (no. 7).

Leo's teaching on political issues was not worked out in an academic environment in which he dealt with issues in the abstract. His teaching was immediately related to actual situations. The context of the historical times and the challenge that the church faced amid social realities shaped his views. He saw the abuse and exploitation of industrial workers and was shocked at their poverty and defenselessness. He was cautious, however, in encouraging any radical upheaval of the established system, because of his fear of revolution. The word *revolution* conjured memories of historical upheavals that brought into question the self-understanding of the Catholic Church and endangered its very existence. The first upheaval was the French Revolution, which overthrew the old order in France and was followed by major social and political changes in other countries in Europe, which affected the Catholic Church in a very serious way. The second was the loss of papal temporal power during the time of Pope Pius IX, who died as a "prisoner of the Vatican," demonstrating in a way nothing else could how the existence of the church was not guaranteed.[44]

Leo endeavored to negotiate a balanced position between liberal capitalism and socialism, rejecting the extremes of both. His formal rejection of socialism served his purpose of condemning the unchecked abuses of the capitalist system without leaving himself vulnerable to the accusation that he was aligning with socialism. He took extreme caution at any hint of a militant political action against the established capitalist system. Nevertheless, his teaching on the intervention of the state seemed to be influenced by socialist principles. Leo navigated his way between the extremes of the economic systems from his position on the side of the poor and the working class. It may be argued that

---

[43] See Marie-Dominique Chenu, *La 'doctrine sociale' de L'Église comme idéologie* (Paris: Cerf, 1979), 22; and John Molony, *The Worker Question: A New Historical Perspective on Rerum Novarum* (Dublin: Gill and MacMillan, 1991), 69.

[44] Dorr, *Option for the Poor*, 51–52.

he could have pushed for a stronger political action against the capitalist system and its abuses if he was on the side of the workers, but Leo was limited by other considerations of profound import for him.

Escapist Spirituality

The way Leo links economics and politics with life after death is linked to his teachings on spirituality. He saw one answer to the inequality between the rich and poor on earth in the promise of rewards in heaven that are proportionate to the miseries one endures on earth. This spirituality was applied by Leo even in situations where rulers abuse their God-given authority. In his 1878 encyclical *Quod Apostolici Muneris*, directed against socialism, communism, and nihilism, he nullified the right of subjects to rebel against abusive rulers:

> Should it, however, happen at any time, that in the public exercise of authority rulers act rashly and arbitrarily, the teaching of the Catholic Church does not allow subjects to rise against them without further warranty, lest peace and order become more and more disturbed, and society run the risk of greater detriment. And when things have come to such a pass as to hold out no further hope, she teaches that a remedy is to be sought in the virtue of Christian patience and in urgent prayer to God.[45]

In one passage in another encyclical from 1886, *Quod Multum*, addressed to the bishops of Hungary, this form of escapist spirituality is even more clearly articulated:

> The best and most effective way of avoiding the horrors of socialism . . . is for the citizens to be completely imbued with religion. . . . For just as religion requires the worship and fear of God so also it demands submission and obedience to lawful authority; it forbids any kind of seditious activity and wills that the property and rights of everybody be safeguarded; and those who are more wealthy should magnanimously help the poor masses. Religion cares for the poor with every form of charity; it fills the stricken with the sweetest comfort by offering them the hope of very great and immortal good things which are all the more plentiful in the future in proportion to the extent to which one has been weighed down more heavily or for a longer time.[46]

---

[45] Cited in ibid., 39.
[46] Cited in ibid., 38.

Leo comforted the poor by setting before them the example of Jesus, reminding them that Jesus called them blessed and that he said their hope is in their reward in eternal life.[47] This comfort comes with an exhortation to prayer as the final recourse of the poor in the face of injustice. If they cannot obtain justice within the existing system, they cannot resort to illegal means to topple the system. At that point the limit has been reached, and injustice must be endured. Even the most political of Leo's encyclicals remain at their core religious documents, concerned with how to live out a life of faith in a complex world. John Courtney Murray discerns in Leo's writings many of the core principles found in traditional Christian teachings regarding life in human society.[48]

At the time of the release of *Rerum Novarum*, some speculated that Leo was prompted to issue it because the church was rapidly losing the working classes to socialism. The fear of an ascendant socialist or communist menace in a rapidly industrializing Europe would have shaken the ground on which Catholic officials stood. While it might be possible to impute some cynical motives to the pope for issuing *Rerum Novarum* as a strategic attempt to address this fear or to bolster the power and influence of the universal church, it is crucial to assert that the first of the great social encyclicals is at its heart a pastoral intervention aimed at the horrifying conditions of workers living under grinding poverty and exploitation. It is, above all, a religious document concerned with the faithful, their earthly welfare and supernatural well-being. Leo often makes reference to the will and plan of God to justify and ground his recommendations.[49] "These are not the admonitions of a political economist or even of a diplomat. They are the earnest entreaties of a universal pastor."[50]

Implications of Rerum Novarum

A study of *Rerum Novarum* reveals how Leo's theology of civil power, his political philosophy, and his escapist spirituality all influenced his view of social realities and what the stance of the church

---

[47] Cited in ibid., 39.

[48] See John Courtney Murray, "Leo XIII: Two Concepts of Government," *Theological Studies* 14/4 (1953): 551–67; and idem, "Leo XIII: Two Concepts of Government, II: Government and the Order of Culture," *Theological Studies* 15/1 (1954): 1–33.

[49] Massaro, "The Social Question in the Papacy of Leo XIII," 153, 158.

[50] Ibid., 158.

should be. As a whole, his past teachings were centered around harmony and stability as primary values. His theology of civil power protects stability in society, even in the face of injustice; his political philosophy nullifies any ideological extreme and is envisioned to protect the poor and powerless, whose discontent could cause social upheaval; his spirituality employs religion and prayer to placate the poor with the promise of reward in the afterlife. These views and values are reflected in the principles and norms of judgment and directives of action in *Rerum Novarum*. In addressing the meaning of labor and the rights of workers, the basic principles of *Rerum Novarum* are that human labor has an intrinsic dignity and that workers should not be treated as commodities. They are persons with dignity with a spiritual life, whose minds and bodies must not be worn out by excessive labor. Leo speaks against the contract model for wages, believing it renders the poor vulnerable to the mercy of the employer. A just wage must meet the requirements of a life lived in reasonable and frugal comfort for the worker and his family. These norms are necessary to order the relationship between the employers and employee, which alone can ensure harmony and stability in society.

Leo's assertion of private property as a natural right cuts into what he believes is the evil of socialism, which turns property into a collective ownership by the state. Leo's position has been criticized as a misreading of socialism, because, as some scholars hold, socialists did not reject private ownership of personal property but only criticized the private ownership of the means of production. Other scholars also criticized his view as a misstatement of the Thomistic doctrine of private property as a natural right. Aquinas's position, while it respects an individual's claim to property, does not hold this claim to be absolute, as it might be interpreted from the language of a natural right. He sees that property is subjected to social organization and social expediency, and as such becomes more a social issue than a right. The possession of property is qualified by the needs of others, stressing the social character of property beyond the individual's natural right.

Be that as it may, Leo's arguments for private property in defense of human dignity, human flourishing, and human progeny in an equitable sharing of the goods of the earth are classical and enduring. Again, he sees the acquisition of property by the poor as the way to prevent social unrest and conflict caused by excessive inequalities. James Bailey draws from the teaching of *Rerum Novarum* and the encyclicals that followed in its tradition to make a compelling case for property ownership and asset building as integral to the mission of the church to reduce poverty, which is foundational for building a just society.[51] Throughout his entire encyclical Leo envisions a society that exists in harmony, becoming a reality only when the wide chasm between the rich and poor is bridged and they meet in a common place of dignity and peace.

Another enduring legacy of *Rerum Novarum* is its argument for the legitimate intervention of the state in social issues and problems. Discernible in this intervention is the critical shift in the analysis of social problems from individual causes to systemic causes. The state has to intervene to protect the poor. At issue is a society in which the rich, who hold the country's wealth and are sovereign over its labor and trade, can manipulate the whole system to enrich and empower themselves even more, while millions are left to live in grinding poverty. Where there is wealth, there is power; where there is poverty, there is defenselessness. The state is obliged to act on behalf of those who are poor and vulnerable, if for no other reason than because its failure as their last recourse would lead them to take desperate means to take what they need to survive. For Leo, the ultimate goal of state intervention is the harmony and stability of society, which can be ensured when the poor can rely on the assistance of the state to pursue and protect what is justly theirs.

This same notion of the promotion and protection of the primary values of harmony and stability runs through the directives for action in *Rerum Novarum*. In a key passage Leo lists the duties of employers to workers and calls them to a conversion of heart that translates into a change of behavior and practice in the sphere of economics. They must do this for the poor workers who are weak and unprotected. The pope urges the workers, however, if the employers fail to do their duty or abuse and exploit them, not to seek redress that would cause damage to property or lead to rioting and disorder. While Leo sees a strike as a recourse of the workers to fight for their rights, more important for him is the preservation of public peace.

A man of his time whose view of the world was also largely ahistorical, Leo taught that the hierarchical relationships in society—there are rich and there are poor; there are differences and inequalities—are part of the very fabric of nature. He accuses socialists of tearing this natural order apart by their philosophy of class warfare. Leo asserts that, contrary to the belief that classes are naturally hostile to each other, they need one another for mutual benefit, as the different parts

---

[51] James P. Bailey, *Rethinking Poverty: Income, Assets, and the Catholic Social Justice Tradition* (Notre Dame, IN: University of Notre Dame Press, 2010).

of the body function in symmetry. In the context of transcendental values that defy differences and divisions, because all stand equal before God in the end, Leo calls the rich and poor to do their duty to each other in "friendliness and good understanding" (no. 18).

Leo, while correctly addressing social problems as structural issues more than purely moral matters, did not champion the establishment of a strong movement of workers that would work for structural change. He was reluctant to encourage workers to take organized political and militant action to secure their rights. He did defend the basic rights of workers to form associations, but associations that had as their main emphasis self-restraint and harmony. With religion as their foundation, and with special and principal attention given to piety and morality, the workmen's associations Leo envisioned were far different from trade unions as presently understood.

To ensure that Catholic workers would not be led astray by associations that deny God and religion, and also to protect them from the practice of the closed shop, which limited job opportunities to members of a union, Leo encouraged Catholic workers to form their own associations. There were two unfortunate results of this directive. First, it contributed to the fragmentation of the trade union movement. Instead of uniting with other workers in one united and strong workers' movement, many Catholic workers formed their own unions. This weakened the solidarity of workers, for inevitably different unions began to compete with one another and to differ in the positions they took on policies and strategies. Second, it diminished the influence that Catholic worker activists could have had on the trade union movement, as Catholic associations were isolated from similar worker movements outside of the church and "secular" trade unions turned anti-Catholic at times.

Conclusion

We end by asking once again, did *Rerum Novarum* measure up to the prophetic call for the church to be on the side of the poor? Or did the theology, political philosophy, and spirituality of Leo XIII put severe limits on his response to this prophetic call?

There is no doubt that *Rerum Novarum* put the institutional weight of the church on the side of the poor. It was a major intervention of the church in their defense. Not only was there clarity in its articulation of the defense of the poor, but also there was a heartfelt compassion for their cry. The official voice of the church was heard in the world of the industrial proletariat as a voice of care for their lot and of protection for their rights. The social problems of the times became a concern of the church; no longer was the church hidden behind its walls, isolated from the world. *Rerum Novarum* laid the foundations of church teaching on social questions with regard to the dignity of labor, a just wage, property ownership as a means to reduce poverty, the legitimate intervention of the state for the protection of the weak, and the right of workers to organize. The encyclicals that followed continued its enduring legacy for changing times and contexts.

However, *Rerum Novarum* was also written in its own historical context. Leo's ahistorical and hierarchical view of society, founded on neo-Scholasticism, affected his view of everything from the role of women to the consequences of revolutionary political movements. This explains why his theology, political philosophy, and spirituality were all based on the values of harmony and stability. He rejected any cause or force that could ignite the fire of revolution, largely by a discontented proletariat, whom he urged to remember the promise of reward in the afterlife.

Leo's analysis of social problems was astute; he saw them as more structural than individual, and he envisioned the most critical changes to be possible only when the state acts on behalf of the workers as demanded by structural (distributive) justice. He was, however, not prepared to follow his analysis to its practical consequences. He endeavored to negotiate the middle way and took the path of non-confrontation in a situation that seemed too volatile. He may have made the ethical calculation that the anarchy and destruction that might result from militant political action would cast the poor into a much worse situation than the injustices they currently bore. He held that the protection of public order and peace is not contrary to the cause of justice; it is a precondition for justice, and might even be an integral part of the just society. But above all else he believed that destroying the order and stability of society violated the very authority of God as embodied in civil authority.

According to the pope's argument, subversive action was illegitimate not solely because of the violence that those involved in it might engage in. Working so that the order of society might be overturned and its stability disrupted was in his mind a flouting of God's authority, since the existing authorities are God's agents. It follows that to seek to overthrow a regime even by *nonviolent* means would also be fundamentally wrong. Questions about just means do not arise, since there can be no just means by which one could reject God's authority as embodied in the regime.[52]

But both in theory and praxis there can be no change of structures without organized political action and its attendant social consequences. When the rich have taken control of the political structures of society to defend and protect their economic interest, there can be no change unless action is taken on both fronts, because economics and politics are so intricately intertwined. Only in theory can one be distinguished from the other; in the arena of life and praxis, they coalesce and conspire to place a heavy burden on the poor and weak. When Leo argues that the will and authority of God are embodied in an existing regime, and thus no force should threaten its authority, could it be that he consequently legitimized the regime with religious validation? And by legitimizing a regime that commits unjust acts against the poor, had he compromised his position on the side of the poor? In the end, where is the true authority and will of God? In the regime that acts against the poor? Or in the legitimate struggle of the poor for their God-given right to dignity, equality, and justice?

This gap between the theology, political philosophy, and spirituality of Leo and his social analysis caused his response to the prophetic call of the church to falter; ultimately, beyond his profound compassion and urgent exhortations, in the real world of conflict and change the encyclical did not fully support the poor. The limitations of the encyclical, however, do not overshadow its enduring legacy. Thomas Massaro brings this legacy into sharp light:

All the backward-looking aspects of *Rerum Novarum*—its tendency to lapse into an other-worldly spirituality of resignation, its rigid defense of nearly absolute rights to private property, a nostalgia for medieval institutions, a restorationist brand of ecclesiology that grates on contemporary ears—are eclipsed by this one remarkable development. A nineteenth-century pope had adopted a surprisingly sophisticated structural view of economic forces responsible for the exploitation of millions, and urged both church and state to act as agents of social justice and economic reform on behalf of the poor. While the encyclical remains cautious in tone and exhibits a fair dose of clericalism and paternalism in denying a thorough program of empowerment to the poor, it is nevertheless a stunning breakthrough.[53]

---

[52] Dorr, *Option for the Poor*, 48.
[53] Massaro, "The Social Question in the Papacy of Leo XIII," 158.

Leo's teaching threw long-lasting ripples into the institutions of church and society. One effect with momentous significance was support for the practice of collective bargaining by labor unions, which now defines the core practice of industrial relations in much of the world.[54] By legitimizing Catholic participation in organized labor, *Rerum Novarum* "opened the door to the union movement, particularly in the United States."[55] Leo's teachings on the ethical obligation of employers to pay a "family wage" or "living wage" took longer to win enactment, but minimum-wage legislation was eventually upheld in all major industrialized economies to protect the well-being of the worker.[56]

Michael Schuck and Joe Holland, two distinguished commentators on Catholic social teaching, consider Leo's work a landmark that divides all church social teaching into pre-Leonine, Leonine, and post-Leonine eras.[57] As Massaro notes, "It remains important, however, to think of *Rerum Novarum* not as an isolated and discrete contribution of a single pope, however important in itself, but rather to situate it in a tradition of social teachings with certain predecessor and successor documents, understandings, and practices."[58] Schuck, upholding this stance, asserts that *Rerum Novarum* cannot be understood without reference to what came before it.[59] Massaro says that Holland negates the portrayal of *Rerum Novarum* as a "big bang" that eclipses the importance of all social teachings that came before or after. "Even the brightest stars in the galaxy must remain in proper context."[60]

In assessing the legacy of *Rerum Novarum,* it remains true that no pope before Leo produced as momentous a message as that contained in his encyclical. His work became the leading light to all the popes who served after him when they sought to address the social questions of their own day, shaped by the circumstances of the times in which they lived.

---

[54] Ibid., 159.

[55] Shannon, "Commentary on *Rerum Novarum,*" 147.

[56] Massaro, "The Social Question in the Papacy of Leo XIII," 159. The first minimum-wage laws in the United States were enacted by Massachusetts in 1912 (ibid., n23).

[57] See Michael J. Schuck, *That They Be One: The Social Teaching of the Papal Encyclicals, 1740–1989* (Washington, DC: Georgetown University Press, 1991); and Joe Holland, *Modern Catholic Social Teaching: The Popes Confront the Industrial Age, 1740–1958* (New York: Paulist Press, 2003).

[58] Massaro, "The Social Question in the Papacy of Leo XIII," 160.

[59] Michael J. Schuck, "Early Modern Roman Catholic Social Thought, 1740–1890," in Himes, *Modern Catholic Social Teaching,* 100.

[60] Massaro, "The Social Question in the Papacy of Leo XIII," 160.

5

Mater et Magistra

Mater et Magistra, Pope John XXIII's first social encyclical, was written in 1961, on the threshold of a whole new era in Catholic social thought. Along with *Pacem in Terris* and the convening of Vatican II, *Mater et Magistra* brought a new spirit to the church's engagement in social issues. This spirit was largely because of the person of Pope John himself—his spirit of joyful openness and his genuine pursuit of dialogue—a person walking with humanity in a time of new changes and challenges in the world.

Readers should note that with the exception of directly quoted material, I have paraphrased the source material in O'Brien and Shannon's *Catholic Social Thought* and also provided a paragraph number for the original text.[1] In the directly quoted sections, I do not identify with the gender exclusion of women in the language used. I quoted as is, however, to preserve the historicity of the original text.

Historical Context

Turn of World Events

During the four-and-a-half years of John's pontificate critical world events shaped the economic and political landscape of the time and brought a context to his papacy, defining his threefold agenda. These events included the following:

- Fidel Castro's guerilla warfare took a successful turn in Havana (1959);

---

[1] David J. O'Brien and Thomas A. Shannon, *Catholic Social Thought: The Documentary Heritage* (Maryknoll, NY: Orbis Books, 1992). The official texts of these encyclicals are also available on the vatican.va website. Please note that paragraph numbers may vary, depending on the translation used.

- John Kennedy was elected as the first Catholic US president (1960);
- the Organization of Petroleum Exporting Countries (OPEC) was established (1960);
- the United States entered the Vietnam War (1965);
- the Berlin Wall was erected (1961);
- the first human orbited the earth (1961);
- the Cuban missile crisis brought the United States and the Soviet Union close to a nuclear catastrophe (1962); and
- Algeria declared its independence from France, and Uganda declared its independence from Great Britain (1962).[2]

Prior to Pope John's election some other important historical events dramatically altered the global landscape. In 1952 the United States detonated the first hydrogen bomb and also launched the first atomic submarine. Five years later the Soviet Union launched Sputnik 1 and Sputnik 2. The Cold War between the Soviet Union and its allies and the United States and the North Atlantic Treaty Organization (NATO) chilled the world. All the nonaligned nations in the Third World were caught in the ideological battle of the two big powers. Other non-aligned nations—twenty-nine African and Asian nations—condemned colonialism at the Bandung conference.[3]

John was elected pope on October 28, 1958, a month before his seventy-seventh birthday. He served the church as John XXIII for only four years and seven months. He died on June 3, 1963. But in that short period of time he forged a new relationship between the church and the world. The self-understanding of the church was changed forever in its interactions with a complex and ever-changing world. John envisioned a renewed Catholic Church, a leaven of transforming unity for other Christian denominations and faiths. His was a clear and strong voice on the issues of economic justice, the threat of nuclear war, and conflict between nations. The threefold agenda of Pope John can be envisioned in three concentric circles: the core circle is the renewal of the Catholic Church; the middle

---

[2] Marvin L. Mich, "Commentary on *Mater et Magistra*: Christianity and Social Progress," in *Modern Catholic Social Teaching: Commentaries and Interpretations*, ed. Kenneth R. Himes, 191–216 (Washington, DC: Georgetown University Press, 2004), 193.

[3] Ibid., 193.

circle is the peace of the Christian churches; and the outer circle is the unity and peace of humanity.[4]

In 1959, in the chill of the Cold War, John announced his vision of an ecumenical council to bring about *aggiornamento* (modernization), pointing the church toward the future as an agent of change and justice. This council aimed to renew the Catholic Church in terms of its liturgy, the role of bishops, the nature of the church, and other issues that concern the inner life of the church. It also reached out to other Christian churches in the pursuit of ecumenical dialogue and cooperation. Finally, it turned to the world and brought its institutional presence to the issues of justice and peace with a new attitude that was dynamic and engaging yet open and humble.[5] E.E.Y. Hales writes:

> This third circle, the circle of world co-operation, of world peace, was growing steadily clearer and more compelling to the Pope. Somehow the light from the first circle—the circle of Catholic unity, as represented by the Council—had to spread out to clarify not only the second circle, Christian Unity, but the third circle, the Unity of Mankind.[6]

The Making of a Pope

The death of Pius XII and the election of John XXIII marked the end of an era. A rotund and smiling John was a contrast to the ascetic and gaunt Pius. The difference, however, went beyond the impact of their presence. John brought a vision to the church and the world that was shaped by his personal history, particularly his early days in northern Italy and his ministry as priest and bishop.

Angelo Roncalli was born to a poor peasant family on November 25, 1881, the fourth of thirteen children. His father was a peasant farmer in Sotto il Monte, near Bergamo, central Lombardy, in northern Italy. His great-uncle Zaverio had a significant role in forming his later theology and pastoral ministry. Zaverio was active in the Catholic social action movement in the diocese of Bergamo. Inspired

---

[4] E.E.Y. Hales, *Pope John and His Revolution* (Garden City, NY: Doubleday, 1965), 132; and Paul Johnson, *Pope John XXIII* (Boston: Little Brown, 1974), 141.

[5] Mich, "Commentary on *Mater et Magistra*," 194.

[6] Hales, *Pope John and His Revolution*, 125.

by *Rerum Novarum* the bishop of Bergamo had encouraged involvement in Catholic social action. The diocese had over two hundred associations, with forty thousand members. These associations included

> study circles, mutual assistance projects, cooperatives, and credits banks. John's early thinking was shaped by the witness of his uncle and by the communal influence of the diocese. Roncalli saw in action a theology which formed the social conscience of the community. If he wanted to be a priest in the diocese, his theology would have to have a social dimension. 'Uncle' Zaverio had disposed him to understand that.[7]

After his ordination Roncalli returned to Bergamo and served as secretary to the new bishop of Bergamo, Radini Tedeschi. Like his predecessor, Tedeschi was a progressive bishop who committed himself to social action. His teaching that Christ's preference goes to the disinherited, the weak, and the oppressed matched his actions. He supported a strike in 1909, and he defended the church's involvement and intervention in social action. The influence of Bishop Tedeschi further deepened Roncalli's formation. Work as a hospital orderly in 1915 and as a chaplain during World War I convinced him that war is evil.[8]

Later, Roncalli's assignments took him as apostolic delegate beyond Catholic Italy—to Bulgaria from 1925 to 1934, and to Turkey and Greece from 1934 to 1944. These positions opened him to a world-view influenced by ecumenical and interfaith perspectives. He saw things more through a pastoral prism than a creed or ethnic tradition. His following assignments expanded his world experience. In 1944, he was sent as nuncio to France, where he had contact with the worker-priest movement and the cardinal of Paris Maurice Feltin, who was the president of Pax Christi. In Paris, he briefly served as the Vatican observer to UNESCO before he became archbishop and patriarch of Venice in 1953.

It was in France and in UNESCO that Roncalli saw there is more value to a united world than a divided one. "It was possible to set aside ideological barriers and address 'all men of good will.'"[9] With characteristic optimism he stressed what unites rather than what

---

[7] Peter Hebblethwaite, *Pope John XXIII: Shepherd of the Modern World* (Garden City, NY: Doubleday, 1985), 19.

[8] Seán Mac Réamoinn, "John XXIII, Pope," in *The Modern Catholic Encyclopedia*, ed. Michael Glazier and Monika Hellwig (Collegeville, MN: Michael Glazier/Liturgical Press, 1994), 434–35.

[9] Hebblethwaite, *Pope John XXIII*, 231.

divides. He was open to all positions, including that of the left, as demonstrated in his welcome to the Italian Socialist Party when it held its congress in Venice in 1957.

The papacy of John was brief, but it left the church forever changed. His impact surprised many who had low expectations of this rotund peasant priest from northern Italy. They thought that he would be a provisional and transitional pope, one who would leave no enduring legacy to the church and the world. He confounded those who thought he would be a "do nothing" pontiff. John wrote: "Yet here I am, already on the eve of the fourth year of my pontificate, with an immense programme of work in front of me to be carried out before the eyes of the whole world, which is watching and waiting."[10] Just a year before, in 1961, *Mater et Magistra,* John's social encyclical, had been promulgated. *Pacem in Terris,* his international encyclical, was published in 1963.[11]

Norms and Principles

The principles and norms of judgment necessary to grasp the significance of *Mater et Magistra* can be grouped in the following three major sections: continuity and discontinuity with past encyclicals; developing and expanding tradition; and new aspects of the social questions.

Continuity and Discontinuity with Past Encyclicals

There are differences in opinion regarding the continuity of John's teachings with *Rerum Novarum* and *Quadragesimo Anno.* British historian and political commentator Paul Johnson, who emphasizes *Mater et Magistra*'s discontinuity, states:

> John did his best to emphasize its continuity with previous teaching. He was not anxious to repudiate earlier popes more than was absolutely necessary. This led him into some well-meaning exaggerations, what might almost be termed a falsification of the record. . . . What John taught had very little in common with any previous papal announcement.[12]

---

[10] Pope John XXIII, *Journal of a Soul,* trans. Dorothy White (New York: McGraw-Hill, 1964), 303.

[11] This development of the historical context is essentially based on Mich, "Commentary on *Mater et Magistra,*" 192–94.

[12] Johnson, *Pope John XXIII,* 145–46.

Others, such as Paul-Emilie Bolte and Richard Camp, argue from the opposite side. They see considerable continuity between John's encyclical and the teachings of his predecessors. Camp cites *Mater et Magistra* as "filled with the Pius XII's spirit of humanitarian idealism coupled with the desire to be as realistic as possible; there was little in its spirit or in its letter which Pius could not have approved."[13]

Donal Dorr takes a middle position. He sees *Mater et Magistra* as continuing the direction of his predecessors while breaking new ground: "In one sense his position was by no means a radical one, nor did it represent any major departure from the direction set by earlier popes, especially Pius XII. . . . Pope John had, in another sense, a major role to play in turning the Catholic Church in quite a different direction on social issues."[14] *Mater et Magistra* itself states that the reason for this new encyclical is to keep alive the torch lighted by its great predecessors, but, more than confirming and explaining more fully what its predecessors taught, it is to set forth the church's teaching regarding new and serious problems of its day. Continuity, expansion, and change are the goals of *Mater et Magistra* as it contemplates church social teaching in its own time.

Focusing on the political realm, Michael Schuck identifies four "reversals" in papal political teaching since 1959: first, an acceptance of participatory democracy; second, an acceptance of separation of church and state; third, a guarded acceptance of violent citizen resistance to unjust governments; and fourth, the right of non–Roman Catholics to profess their religion publicly.[15] John contributed to these reversals, particularly to the acceptance of the separation of church and state and the profession of faith in the public arena by non–Roman Catholics. John's vision and leadership created a new situation in which these reversals became part of the mainstream of social mores. Not only were there reversals of the teachings of the church, however; there was also a change in tone and methodology. The tone was appreciated by many as more modern.[16] "Many passages are engaging,

---

[13] Richard L. Camp, *The Papal Ideology of Social Reform: A Study on Historical Development, 1878–1967* (Leiden: E. J. Brill, 1969), 107. See also Donal Dorr, "Pope John XXIII—New Direction?" in *Readings in Moral Theology, no. 5, Official Catholic Social Teaching*, ed. Charles E. Curran and Richard A. McCormick (New York: Paulist Press, 1986), 103.

[14] Dorr, "Pope John XXIII—New Direction?" 77.

[15] Michael Schuck, *That They Be One: The Social Teaching of the Papal Encyclicals 1740–1989* (Washington, DC: Georgetown University Press, 1991), 177.

[16] Donald R. Campion, "The World Wide Response," in *The Challenge of Mater et Magistra*, ed. Joseph Moody and Justus George Lawler (New York: Herder and Herder, 1963), 156.

encouraging, cordial, and affectionate (85 ff., 156, 148 ff., 160, 182, 284, 236)."[17] The openness and optimism of John were reflected in his direct and familiar style, which addressed problems realistically yet positively, and was less preoccupied with doctrinal and theoretical discourse and more with practical directives.[18] John broke from the Leonine style, which used a "double-pulsed" method of social instruction, paralleling negative judgments with positive recommendations.[19] While John did not turn a blind eye to what was wrong in the world and did not lack the courage to address the dangers, threats, and evils plaguing society, he did not focus on them. He turned toward what was good in the world—to the progress and improvements being made, and what could be done to further them. There was a lack of nostalgia for things past while there was an exuberance for things new.[20]

This new tone was paralleled by a turn to a different methodology. Instead of using the old theoretical approach, employing the device of hypotheses and theses, John engaged with different philosophies of life or ideologies and negotiated the common ground where all could meet. His methodology focused on dialogue and collaboration rather than on condemnation; it begins not with what is wrong with the other side but with what is right. John believed that while there were universality and constancy in the teachings of the church, they had to be read and reinterpreted in the light of changing times and contexts, in tune with the spirit of Vatican II that would follow.[21] This methodology generally employed three steps, first expressed by Cardinal Cardijn in the 1920s and used by Catholic action groups thereafter: observe, judge, and act. In other words, first, analyze the situation; second, discern the principles; and third, take action that is appropriate.

Developing and Expanding Tradition

Increased State Intervention

The question of increased state intervention became necessary because of the situation in Europe, where many countries had moved

---

[17] Vivian Boland, "*Mater et Magistra*," in *The New Dictionary of Catholic Social Thought*, ed. Judith A. Dwyer (Collegeville, MN: Liturgical Press, 1994), 581.

[18] Campion, "The World Wide Response," 157.

[19] Schuck, *That They Be One*, 91.

[20] Mich, "Commentary on *Mater et Magistra*," 197.

[21] Ibid., 198.

toward a welfare state after the chaos and devastation of World War II. In some countries welfare took the form of socialism or quasi-socialist systems that employed high levels of taxation on income and profits to redistribute ownership of property and wealth. During the papacy of Pius XII there had been "increasingly bitter and ideological" discussions on the emerging welfare states, which were viewed by some as creating opportunities for abuse and dependency, undermining personal responsibility.[22] In *Mater et Magistra* John promoted a balance between state intervention and personal responsibility, with an expanded role of the state in a wide variety of economic affairs, such as protecting the common good and providing effective measures against mass unemployment (no. 54). Such measures have the good of individuals as their end, for they allow them the opportunity to engage in productive activity and to provide necessities of life for themselves and their dependents (no. 55). The whole purpose of political authority and state intervention is the promotion of the common good. John thought the state must, for instance, exercise stricter control over managers and directors of large businesses, lest they depart from the requirements of the common good (no. 104). In great detail John also stipulates what state intervention must address regarding the special difficulties of those working in agriculture (nos. 128–41).

John further argues for balance between the actions of the state and the initiative of individuals. He states that there cannot be a prosperous and well-ordered society unless both private citizens and the public authorities work together for the common good (no. 56). "Where private initiative of individuals is lacking, political tyranny prevails" (no. 57), and where "appropriate activity of the state is lacking or defective, commonwealths are apt to experience incurable disorders, and there occurs exploitation of the weak by the unscrupulous strong, who flourish" (no. 58). John sees the good in the roles of both the state and individuals for the protection and promotion of the common good.

John defines the common good as the "sum total of those conditions of social living, whereby men are enabled more fully and more readily to achieve their own perfection" (no. 65). The notion of common good is dynamic, for its meaning depends on one's view of society. Does the common good refer to a collection of "goods," or does

---

[22] Rodger Charles, *Christian Social Witness and Teaching: The Catholic Tradition from Genesis to* Centesimus Annus, vol. 2, *The Modern Social Teaching: Contexts, Summaries, Analysis* (Herefordshire, England: Gracewing/Fowler Wright, 1998), 146.

it mean the conditions necessary for human flourishing? One view emphasizes the common good as social reality in which all persons should share through their participation; the second view emphasizes the human rights dimension of the common good: "It is agreed that in our time the common good is chiefly guaranteed when personal rights and duties are maintained" (*Pacem in Terris*, no. 60). In John's writings these are not two different views, but rather two complementary ways of viewing a dynamic reality in different contexts.

The common good for John is not limited to the boundaries of nation-states but constitutes the conditions in the global community where men and women are enabled to live and flourish as persons of dignity. In *Pacem in Terris*, John observes that the present international system of organization and the way its principle of authority operates on a world basis no longer correspond to the objective requirements of universal common good (*PT*, nos. 134–35).

Complexity of Social Structure

Socialization, one of the central themes of the encyclical, is considered the most controversial section of *Mater et Magistra*. John's discussion of socialization without any condemnatory statements about socialist and communist philosophies brings Catholic social teaching to a place where new thinking on matters regarding the state and the common good in a more complex society can emerge.

Mater et Magistra describes socialization as "one of the principal characteristics of our time . . . multiplication of social relationships, that is, a daily more complex interdependence of citizens, introducing into their lives and activities many and varied forms of association, recognized for the most part in private and even in public law" (no. 59). John points out that this "complex interdependence of citizens" arises "from the human and natural inclination . . . whereby men are impelled to enter voluntarily into association" to achieve goals beyond their individual capacities (no. 60).

John highlights the numerous services and advances in this move toward broader social relationships, noting that it makes possible the satisfaction of many personal needs such as healthcare, education, skills training, housing, labor, communication, information, and entertainment (no. 61). But as various forms of associations are multiplied, laws that control and determine relationships of citizens are multiplied as well. This can create a need for a growing intervention by public authorities in the more intimate aspects of personal life. As a consequence, boundaries must be set around the exercise of free action, which could mean that personal rights are hindered (no. 62). John points out that the increased complexity of human life is "the creation of free men," who must "be responsible for what they do. . . . Furthermore, men are not altogether free of their milieu" (no. 63).

As intervention by public authorities increases due to the complexity of society, two important principles must govern the governmental actions: (1) public authorities must have a correct grasp of the common good; and (2) intermediary bodies must be allowed to govern themselves according to their own laws, which bind them in a spirit of sincere concord among themselves (no. 65). Without using the term *subsidiarity*, John alludes to it as the corrective to any tyranny of excess state intervention as a result of socialization.

John sets two conditions for socialization to benefit the individual as well as protect the common good: "(1) the freedom of individuals citizens to act and groups of citizens to act autonomously, while cooperating with one another; (2) the activity of the state whereby the undertakings of private individuals and groups are suitably regulated and fostered" (no. 66). If social systems are organized and governed according to these two norms, individuals will not be "gravely discriminated against or excessively burdened" and human community will be structured for "the adequate fulfillment of rights and duties of social life" (no. 67).

John's support of socialization yields the most important theme of the encyclical, because it begins the process of breaking the long alliance between Roman Catholicism and socially conservative forces. This alliance allowed the church to be used ideologically against structural changes designed to protect the poor.

The Just Wage and Workers' Participation

There is a basic optimism in John's view of the modern world; especially toward scientific and technological advances—the discovery of atomic energy, the growth of automation, the far reach of radio and TV, the progress in transportation, and the initial conquests of outer space (no. 47). Turning to developments in the social field, he highlights the development of systems for social insurance and social security systems, heightened consciousness among workers as members of unions, improvement of basic education, wider diffusion of the conveniences of life, increased social mobility, and a resulting decline in class divisions (no. 48). Besides the developments in science and technology and in socioeconomic life, there were also significant advances in political life: greater participation in public life of citizens from almost all social strata; broader intervention of public authorities in economic and social affairs; freedom for peoples of Asia and Africa from colonial powers; and the establishment of suprational assemblies and councils that take into account the interests of all people (no. 49).

But even in his optimism about the positive developments in the modern world, John is filled with profound sadness over what he calls a "wretched spectacle"—great masses of workers who are not paid according to their labor, leaving their families in stark poverty, in violation of the basic requirements of human dignity (no. 68). This is the old injustice of a few amassing so much wealth amid the extreme need of so many. He adds that one of the reasons for poverty is the fact that these areas are still underdeveloped in terms of modern industrial techniques (no. 68). Later he says that usually an underdeveloped or primitive state of economic development is the fundamental or enduring cause of poverty and hunger (no. 163), such as primitive and obsolete methods of agriculture (no. 154). Clearly he has no serious doubts about the need for modernization and development as the way in which the world must make progress,[23] but he is aware that this kind of development can create social problems (nos. 124–25) and even economic difficulties (no. 154).

John also deplores the condition of nations where large sums of money are devoted to armaments and little is invested in the social needs of the poor (no. 69). While many are perishing from misery and hunger, the technical advances in the pursuit of the arms race are bringing the human race to ruin and horrible death (no. 198). Money is also squandered by governments on prestige projects (no. 69). It frequently happens that tasks of lesser importance are paid much more than those accomplished by whole classes of decent and hardworking citizens who contribute to the life of the community and of the nation (no. 70).

When workers live under conditions where the welfare of the poor is the lowest social priority, John reaffirms the necessity and importance of a just wage that is not left completely to the unregulated market forces. Norms of justice and equity must be strictly followed. He states what should be taken into account in determining what constitutes an appropriate wage to lead a life of individual worth and to fulfill one's family responsibilities:

---

[23] Donal Dorr, *Option for the Poor: A Hundred Years of Catholic Social Teaching* (Maryknoll, NY: Orbis Books, 1983), 117.

(1) the contribution of individuals to the economic effort; (2) the economic state of the enterprises within which they work; (3) the requirements of each community, especially as regards overall employment; (4) finally, what concerns the common good of all peoples, namely, of the various states associated among themselves, but differing in character and extent. (no. 71)

The fourth criterion is new in *Mater et Magistra* and demonstrates John's global perspective. He speaks of the common good of all people. What might serve as a background here is the reality of how the global economy operates, where investments are moved to regions where wages are negotiated at the lowest cost, pitting one group of workers against another.[24] This violates the moral demand of a just wage, which protects the good of all workers across nations in the entire global context. John speaks, instead, for effective aid that should be given to assist economically underdeveloped nations (no. 80).

John also states the strict demand of social justice—that no citizen is excluded from the benefits of the national wealth. Vigilance, thus, must be exercised that wealth is justly distributed and disparity of wealth is progressively eliminated (no. 73). He asserts that "the economic prosperity of any people is to be assessed not so much from the sum total of goods and wealth possessed as from the distribution of goods according to norms of justice, so that everyone in the community can develop and perfect himself. For this, after all, is the end toward which all economic activity of a community is by nature ordered" (no. 74). It is clear here that the ultimate goal of economic prosperity is the more equitable distribution of wealth according to justice.

John, following Pius XI, teaches that because the fruits of production are due to a corporate effort, these should be shared by all and not be accumulated in the hands of few, who in this case are the executives and stockholders. Workers who contribute to the wealth of the corporation have a right to its profits, besides being paid just wages. The demands of the common good, on both the national and world levels, should determine not only a just wage but also profit sharing (no. 81).

Demands of Justice Regarding Workers

John asserts that it is not enough that an economic order produces vast amounts of goods and allows the equitable distribution of these

---

[24] Mich, "Commentary on *Mater et Magistra*," 199.

goods; it must also meet the demands of justice in the participation of workers in productive activity, where they "have the opportunity to assume responsibility and perfect themselves by their efforts" (no. 82). If the human dignity of workers is compromised, their sense of responsibility weakened, or their freedom of action denied, an economic order is unjust (no. 83). In this statement John weighs in on the controversy that involved his predecessor, Pius XII, from 1949 to 1952, around the question of what level of participation or codetermination workers can exercise in the policies, procedures, and direction of their industries. According to Jean-Yves Calvez, Pius XII conflicted with the position of the German Katholikentag (Catholic Day) of Bochum, which held that codetermination is a natural right.[25] This resulted in an exchange of clarifications and warnings that caused "a feeling of uneasiness and hesitation" among Catholics regarding the notions of participation and codetermination.[26]

John concludes that "we do not doubt that employees should have an active part in the affairs of the enterprise wherein they work, whether these be public or private" (no. 91). They must have a say in the efficient running of the enterprise (nos. 92–93), and they must be able to exert their influence, beyond the limits of their places of work, on the national level where policies are being determined (no. 97). In some circumstances employees may be entitled to profit sharing in corporations where they work to overcome inequity in the share of fruits of production, with disproportionate amounts going into the hands of the wealthy and powerful (nos. 75–77). John's position lays the foundations for the development of this principle in Catholic social teaching in the years to follow, as shown in the writings of Pope Paul VI and in the US Bishops' 1986 pastoral letter on the economy, *Economic Justice for All*. The relationship between employers and employees "should be marked by mutual respect, esteem, and good will," with the benefit of everyone as the ultimate goal (no. 92).

The rights of the workers to participate should be protected at all levels in national and international institutions. Their representation in these institutions must be ensured so that their rights, needs, and aspirations are safeguarded (no. 99). John particularly expresses his esteem and praise for the work of the International Labor Organization, through whose effective and valuable work the legitimate rights of workers were recognized and protected (no. 103).

---

[25] See Jean-Yves Calvez, *The Social Thought of John XXIII*, trans. George J.M. McKenzie (Chicago: Henry Regnery, 1964), 38.

[26] Ibid., 37.

Private Property

John reaffirms the right to private property as rooted in the nature of things and recognizes this right as both an economic safeguard and an economic stimulus (no. 109). He does not hold it as a primary right as Leo did, who, faced with what he perceived as the socialist threat, overstated the importance of private property. A primary right refers to that which is necessary for survival, such as the right to food, shelter, and clothing. The Thomistic tradition considers private property a right to the extent that it serves a social function by contributing to the right order in society, a position John upholds (no. 111). In serving this social function the right to private property is connected with a just wage. Justice and equity must be met in the remuneration of labor, because the right to private property is dependent on the fruitfulness of labor. By securing private property, the security and stability of the family are protected, which lay at the foundation of a strong and prosperous nation (no. 112).

While stressing the individual right to private property, John asserts its rootedness in social responsibility and draws inspiration from the Gospels, which reveal Jesus Christ ordering the rich to share their goods with the poor so as to turn them into spiritual possessions. "Do not store up for yourselves treasures on earth, where moth and rust consume and where thieves break in and steal; but store up for yourselves treasures in heaven, where neither moth nor rust consumes and where thieves do not break in and steal" (Mt 6:19–20), and "Truly I tell you, just as you did it to one of the least of these who are members of my family, you did it to me" (Mt 25:40).

John also addresses the necessity of expanding state ownership of goods if the common good requires it, for example, when such ownership carries "power too great to be left in private hands, without injury to the community at large" (no. 116). However, the state must not take over to such an extent that private initiative, right of liberty, and responsibility of action are diminished. State intervention must be balanced with subsidiarity (no. 117).

John notes that economic systems grow as property ownership expands, and as economic systems expand, property ownership then also increases. "It is especially appropriate that today, more than heretofore, widespread private property should prevail, since, as noted above, the number of nations increases wherein the economic systems experience daily growth" (no. 115). John accepts the common assumption that rapid economic growth opens the conditions necessary to overcome the problem of unequal distribution of wealth. But is this an optimism supported by reality? Or is it a blind spot that fails to see the forces that intervene between economic growth and equitable distribution of wealth?

New Aspects of the Social Question

In this section of the encyclical John speaks of the progress of events and of time that has made it increasingly evident that the relationship of workers and management in productive enterprises must be readjusted to norms of justice and equity. He addresses four areas of particular concern.

Agriculture: A Depressed Sector

John first focuses on the struggles of farmers in modern economies. The plight of farmers takes a personal turn for John, who grew up on his family's farm in northern Italy. This section of the encyclical is so down to earth in its specification and vivid in its details that it may well be considered John's rural charter. John notes that as economic life progresses and expands, an imbalance between agriculture and industry is created. Rural workers leave the fields for the larger towns and cities in hope of more prosperous lives. This diminishes the number of workers in the rural areas, while the numbers of industrial and service workers increase (no. 124).

John's fundamental concerns are threefold: first, how to bridge the wide gap between agriculture and industry in terms of production efficiency; second, how to minimize the differences between the rural standard of living and that of city dwellers; and finally, how to empower rural dwellers so they may have a greater appreciation of who they are and the work they do (no. 125).

To prevent the imbalances among agriculture, industry, and the services for productive efficiency, public authorities must endeavor to bring principal services to the rural areas: "highway construction; transport services; marketing facilities; pure drinking water; housing; medical services; elementary, trade, and professional schools; things requisite for religion and recreation; finally, furnishings and equipment needed in the modern farm home" (no. 127). Without the social and economic progress necessary for a dignified farm life, there is nothing to stop farmers from deserting the fields.

To minimize differences between the rural standard of living and that of city dwellers, authorities should attend to following matters: taxation, capital, price protection, and strengthening of farm income, and appropriate organization of farming enterprises. As regards taxation, justice and equity must be observed in assessing ability to pay (nos. 131–32). In the case of the rural enterprise, authorities must consider that rural economy is both delayed and subject to greater risk and that capital to increase return is not easily found (no. 133). Special provision must be made for agricultural financing, considering that investors are more inclined to invest in enterprises rather than in rural economy. Banks must also be established that provide capital to farmers at reasonable rates of interest (no. 134). The prices of agricultural products necessary for the basic needs of people must be protected so that all can afford to buy them, but not, however, at the cost of unjust compensation for the labor of farmers (no. 140). Suitable opportunities must also be given to farm families to supplement their incomes (no. 141). It is also necessary that farmers form among themselves mutual-aid societies and professional associations to receive instruction, be kept informed of new developments, and be given technical assistance to ensure that their labor will yield for themselves and their families decent and humane family living (no. 143).

To ensure that those engaged in agricultural pursuits not regard themselves as inferior to others, they should be helped to recognize that their labor is endowed with a dignity of its own, in the "majestic temple of creation"; their work yields the fruit of the earth that nourishes humankind and also provides raw materials for industry (nos. 144–45). As members of their own professional associations, they stand on the same footing with other classes of workers, and they bring their rights and interests into line with the rights and needs of other classes. They should make their importance and influence felt, demanding that their efforts be aided to enable them to contribute to the common good (no. 147).

Aid to Less Developed Areas

Though *Mater et Magistra* is built upon the tradition of its predecessors, it is the first encyclical that addresses issues of international relations and economic development. Seeing the excessive imbalance among the economically advanced nations, those who are in the process of development, and those that are underdeveloped, John calls for equitable distribution and social solidarity. "On a worldwide scale, governments should seek the economic good of all peoples" (no. 37).

The excessive imbalance is shown in the way some people enjoy life's leisure and conveniences in some countries, while others exist in grinding poverty; food is wasted in countries where there is surplus of it, while elsewhere large masses of people experience want and hunger (no. 161). Underdevelopment is evident in their primitive states of economy; the solution is rapid economic growth, which is to be achieved by acquiring foreign capital and skills and developing new technology (nos. 163–64).

Despite the disparity of resources, countries each day seem to become more interdependent. "Yet today, men are so intimately associated in all parts of the world that they feel, as it were, as if they are members of one and the same household" (no. 157). John believes that it is opportune to stress that "we all share responsibility for the fact that populations are undernourished. It is necessary to arouse a sense of responsibility in individuals and generally, especially among those who are more blessed with this world's goods" (no. 158).

John urges richer nations to make greater efforts to provide developing countries with aid designed to promote science, technology, and economic life. He also calls for help for as many youths as possible to study in the great universities of more developed countries (no. 165). Although seemingly unquestioning about the model of development exported from the West, he also warns the economically developed countries of the errors in the past. While prosperous countries provide development aid to developing nations, they must respect the integrity of the indigenous cultures of these nations. He stresses wealthy countries should "take special care lest, in aiding these nations, they seek to impose their own way of life upon them" (no. 170). They should not use the volatile political situations in many of these nations to their advantage (no. 171).

It is a mistaken view that economic progress can be equated with superior human development. In fact, developed nations tend to neglect spiritual goods, as they give prior value to progress in science, technology, and economy. For all their lack of wealth, people of poor nations have a general awareness and sensitivity to higher values on which moral teachings rest—"an awareness derived from ancient traditional custom which provides them with motivation" (no. 176). These nations must be aware of the dangers in the help provided by more affluent nations that might undermine these higher values, on which true civilization depends—values that should be held in honor, be perfected and refined (no. 177). "John warned that help from the affluent nations could be a Trojan Horse."[27] His warnings to the affluent nations are apt, but he fails to mention that Western prosperity is

---

[27] Mich, "Commentary on *Mater et Magistra*," 201.

itself dependent on cheap labor and raw materials for its development, a process that continues to impoverish the Third World.

John opens a whole new chapter in Catholic social teaching by the global shift in his encyclical.

Population Growth and Economic Development

The question addressed in this section is the need to balance economic goods and population increase in the context of poor countries and in the context of the whole world (no. 185). John argues against the notion that the growing global imbalance between the escalating number of births and the dwindling economic resources is an impending crisis. His position is based on three arguments. First, he considers the arguments of those who see this so-called crisis as "so inconclusive and controversial that nothing certain can be drawn from them" (no. 188); second, he believes that the resources of creation are abundant, with "an almost inexhaustible productive capacity" to feed, clothe, and house humanity (no. 189); and third, he points out that God "has endowed man with such ingenuity that, by using suitable means, he can apply nature's resources to the needs and requirements of existence" (no. 189).

John, however, sees how science and technical advances, rather than being employed to address the problem of scarcity of goods, are being transformed into means to lead the human race to ruin and horrible death (no. 198). He is referring to breakthroughs in science and technology being used primarily for destructive purposes and a senseless arms race. John "links decisively the questions of population, economic development, and the arms race."[28] If there is any solution, it will be found not in the enterprise of destruction and death but in creative and life-giving use of the bounty of nature and creation.

Consistent with Catholic tradition, John rejects any strategy that sees a solution in limiting population by violating the procreative purpose of sexuality. He links human dignity with the transmission of life in marriage. Life is sacred from its inception, since the very action of God is required in the creation of life. John solemnly warns that those who violate the action of God not only offend God's majesty, they also dishonor themselves and the human race, and they weaken the moral fiber of society (no. 194). John, however, does speak of the human misery and suffering in many countries where scarcity of food and resources in the face of an exploding population produces

---

[28] Boland, "Mater et Magistra," 587.

a wretched condition that offends this same divine majesty. He insists that this condition is the consequence when people depart from the providence and directives of God, who has "bestowed upon humanity sufficient goods wherewith to bear with dignity the burdens associated with procreation of children. But this task will be difficult or even impossible if men, straying from the right road and with a perverse outlook, use the means mentioned above in a manner contrary to human reason or to their social nature, and hence, contrary to the directives of God" (no. 199).

International Order and Cooperation

John views a world that has grown more and more interdependent by reason of science and technology. Because of this interdependence, the problems in any country have global consequences (no. 202). But interdependent as countries are, they relate in mutual distrust, rooted in fear of one another—fear that drives them to build and amass armaments to deter and defend against aggression (no. 203). Energy is directed more toward human destruction than to human development, and resources of nature are depleted for this lethal goal (no. 204).

The cause of this state of affairs is to be found in differing philosophies of life (no. 205). Some believe that there is no law of justice that pertains to everyone and binds all. Justice is invoked, but it does not hold the same meaning for everyone. The attempt to articulate its meaning itself becomes a source of contention. But if there is no law of justice that binds all, people have no way of achieving their rights unless they resort to force, the root of serious evils (no. 206).

John, in the tradition of his predecessors, upholds the longstanding belief that the solution to the human problems in the world is the return to religion and to the moral laws that are founded on it. Apart from God, morality collapses. People believe otherwise because of the power of science and technology. It is, however, the very progress of science and technology that has caused global problems that can only be overcome if the authority of God, author of all human life and rule of all nature, is recognized. The power of science and technology is precarious, teetering between good and evil. Scientific advances open up a seemingly limitless horizon, but its vast forces can also be used for destruction. People who have experienced this diabolic use of its power rightly conclude that only when such power is put under the direction of moral laws can it be used for the good of the human race and not for its destruction (no. 210).

In the section entitled "Incomplete and Erroneous Philosophies of Life" this same theme of the primary role of religion is further developed: "This inward proclivity of man to religion confirms the fact that man himself was created by God, and irrevocably tends to him. Thus we read in Augustine: 'Thou has made us for Thyself, O Lord, and our hearts are restless until they rest in Thee'" (no. 214). Religion is implanted in the human person by nature, and no force can destroy it or shrewdness suppress it. "Separated from God, man becomes monstrous to himself and others. Consequently, mutual relationships between men absolutely require a right ordering of the human conscience in relation to God, the source of all truth, justice, and love" (no. 215).

John asserts the fragility of human achievements. In the face of scientific progress and advances, he writes: "People fail to take into account the weaknesses of nature, such as sickness and suffering—weaknesses that no economic or social system, no matter how advanced, can completely eliminate" (no. 213). He includes a profound quotation from Pius XII, stating, "It is a 'monstrous masterpiece' of this age 'to have transformed man, as it were, into a giant as regards the order of nature, yet in the order of the supernatural and the eternal, to have changed him into a pygmy'" (no. 243).[29]

With a spirit of hope and optimism, he sees that many have turned away from the deceptive promise of a happy life to be lived here forever; they have sought spiritual things more intensively (no. 211). When John speaks of religion, he does not refer specifically to the Catholic faith. His basic assumption, however, is that religion, which is above ideological and philosophical divide, could unite people across their differences. Couldn't this assumption be argued against given the fact that religion has, in fact, divided people and nations? What about the fact that religion cannot be totally insulated from social, cultural, economic, and political realities? Might viewing religion as the solution to world problems without looking into how it is intertwined with other realities be too narrow an approach?

Directives for Action

The encyclical's vision of society and of its norms and principles for transforming change "are not only to be explained but also applied. This is especially true of the Church's teaching on social matters, which has truth as its guide, justice as its end, and love as its driving

---

[29] Pius XII, radio broadcast, Christmas Eve, 1953.

force" (no. 226). John recognizes that this is a lofty but difficult task (no. 221). The challenge arises from the following problems: "There is deeply rooted in each man an instinctive and immoderate love of his own interests; today there is widely diffused in society a materialistic philosophy of life; it is difficult at times to discern the demands of justice in a given situation" (no. 229).

New Pedagogical Principle for the Church

It is not enough for people to be instructed; they must experience social teaching in action and be formed by its vision. "We do not regard such instructions as sufficient, unless there be added to the work of instruction that of the formation of man, and unless some action follow upon the teachings, by way of experience" (no. 231). This statement articulates a new pedagogical principle for the church: actions on behalf of social justice are formative of a just person. John stresses that the Christian is not only formed *for* action but *by* action. "This is the first time that any pontifical document has ever brought out this interaction and dependency so clearly. This fusion of education and action fits in with Pope John's desire to give his flock a pastoral letter, a letter directed to concrete action, not to academic disputes."[30] This is no knowledge without love, without compassion. Only in loving and only in being compassionate does one come to know what love means and what compassion means. It is a knowing that comes from doing.

"Observe, Judge, Act"

Action inspired by Christian principles can have a transforming power to be a light for the world. This is what sums up the spirit and intent of *Mater et Magistra*. The "call to action" in Catholic social teaching, first articulated in *Mater et Magistra*, will be followed through in subsequent documents, especially the 1971 apostolic exhortation *Octogesima Adveniens*. With regard to this call to action, *Mater et Magistra* recommends the widely used Catholic Action process—observe, judge, act—as a way to implement the church's social teaching. Described in greater detail, the three steps consist of the following: "first, the actual situation is examined; then, the situation is evaluated carefully in relation to these teachings; then only is it decided what can and should be done in order that the traditional norms may be adapted to circumstances of time and place" (no. 236).

---

[30] Peter J. Riga, *John XXIII and the City of Man* (Westminster, MD: Newman, 1966), 5.

These three steps realize John's exhortation—"We have drawn norms and teachings, upon which we especially exhort not merely to meditate deeply, but also to do what you can to put them into effect" (no. 261). The pope addresses in particular the young who in the school context might end up studying Catholic social teaching but not becoming engaged by it in practice and action.

Spirituality of Engagement

John also calls the laity to the noble task of living the teachings of the church in the conduct of their lives at the heart of the temporal affairs of the world. While this call, like his other exhortations, may seem less striking now, decades after Vatican II, during his era his comments on the role of the laity were significant. From the spirituality of detachment of the late 1950s, John calls the laity to a spirituality of engagement. This shift is shaped by the change of the church's attitude toward society and the problems of "this world." Christians are not only to fix their gaze on the heavenly but must also "dirty their hands" in transforming the temporal world.

This shift in spirituality also reflects a change in the understanding of salvation. In the past, salvation was conceived as otherworldly; the new spirituality calls for men and women to be profoundly engaged in the affairs of the world, and in their very engagement they are redeemed as they become agents of change and witnesses of conversion. There is an integration of spirituality and temporality, of the heavenly and the worldly, of the now and the hereafter, in the new teaching on salvation. From the shift from a spirituality of detachment to a spirituality of engagement emerged a new theology of salvation, which John may not have explicitly taught in his encyclical, but which is infused in his social vision.

Critical Discursus

We assess *Mater et Magistra* in terms of its continuity with the tradition and of the new trails it has blazed, but we also note a certain shortsightedness in its social vision. The norms and principles it promoted have their basis in the core social teachings of the church but are expanded in a new global context. But *Mater et Magistra* is also criticized for what commentators call blind spots in its social vision, resulting from a refreshing and yet uncritical optimism in John's view of the world.

Continuity with Tradition

In the tradition of his predecessors John took his position on the side of the poor and weak in society, and for their protection he upheld the intervention of the state in the affairs of life in the social, economic, and political realms. In line with Leo and Pius XI, John employed the old principles of subsidiarity and common good to prevent the state from overreaching its power, resulting in totalitarian state control. The principle of subsidiarity prohibits the state from taking over that which could be accomplished through the initiative of individuals and communities. The principle of common good, which pertains to the sum total of conditions in society that enable persons to flourish as individuals and members of communities, defines the norm that determines whether state intervention is legitimate or not. If state intervention denies individuals their freedom of thought and action and causes harm to the life of the community or of the nation, such an intervention should be denounced as illegal and immoral. John built on the principle of state intervention as balanced and governed by the principles of subsidiarity and common good at the core of Catholic social teaching.

John also spoke to the old injustice of a few amassing wealth amid the extreme need of so many. Like Leo, he grieved over the wretched spectacle of great masses of workers who were not paid according to their labor, leaving them without the means to provide their families with basic necessities. He reaffirmed the moral requirement of a just wage for workers; this should not be determined by unregulated market forces but by norms that define what is fair and just in proportion to the nature of the work and according to the requirements of overall employment in a given context. Like Leo and Pius he saw the link between a just wage and social mobility through property ownership. Only through ownership can there be a greater distribution of wealth in society, as well as greater security for workers and their families, which redounds to the peace and prosperity of a nation. Also, by protecting the right of private property, human liberty is safeguarded and strengthened. But beyond the concern for individual rights, the social character of private property is stressed, for the Christian spirit is always inclined to the greater needs of others. Clearly, John continued the teachings of his predecessors on a just wage, private property, human rights, and social responsibility.

Consistent with Catholic tradition John also rejected development strategies that seek solutions in limiting population through violating the procreative purpose of sexuality. The solution is in a greater distribution of wealth in a world that is abundantly endowed by divine providence. He also upheld the longstanding belief that the solution to human problems in the world is the return to religion, on which moral laws are founded. When the beguiling dominance of science and technology, of the consuming greed of economic superfluity, and of unmitigated control of political power seize the minds and hearts of men and women, they separate themselves from the true and eternal source of truth, justice, and love. The problems in the world are caused by the loss of its center, and thus the solution to these problems is the return to the center.

Breaking New Ground

Beyond the moral imperative of a just wage, John breaks new ground in laying the foundation of the participation of employees in the affairs of the enterprise in which they are employed. They have a say in the management of the firms where they work and exercise an influence in the determination of policies on the national scale. They are also entitled to profit sharing, as the fruits of production must be shared with those who labored to bring them about and not be accumulated in the hands of a few. These principles of shared management and profit sharing as first enunciated in *Mater et Magistra* were followed and developed in the encyclicals that followed in the next decades.

Mater et Magistra was the first encyclical to address issues of international relations and economic development. It represented a new era of the church turning toward the world and its global social issues. John helped the Catholic Church speak its voice among a plurality of voices, endeavoring to be heard in its call for equality and justice amid vast inequities and deprivations. His was a new theology and spirituality, one infused with a refreshing optimism about the modern world, specifically the kind of society that emerged in the Western world as a result of rapid economic growth. He spoke later, in *Pacem in Terris,* with ringing hope and challenge of the age of the atom and of the conquest of space as an "era in which the human family has already entered, wherein it has commenced its new advance toward limitless horizons" (*PT,* no. 156).

John saw that because the world had become interdependent, that social issues must be seen from a global perspective. When *Mater et Magistra* spoke of the common good, it was not limited within the boundaries of nation-states. It spoke of the common good in the global community. When it stated the norms for determining an appropriate wage to lead a life worthy of a human and one that enables each person to fulfill family responsibilities, the requirement of a just wage was expanded to protect the good of all workers, across nations, in the entire global context. This means workers in regions to which more developed countries go for cheaper labor, pursuing more profit at a lesser cost. Requiring a just wage across nations and countries to satisfy common good on a global scale demonstrated John's broad vision of social problems. He thought of problems not in a linear way but in circles of interdependence, where social burdens borne by one are borne by all.

John did not intend his encyclical to be an abstract and academic discourse on ideas and theories; he meant it to be a pastoral encyclical that formed people through principled action. The inductive methodology of "observe, judge, act" continued to guide Catholic social thought and social ministry through the decades that followed. Various episcopal conferences, like the Conference of Latin American Bishops (CELAM) and the National Conference of Catholic Bishops in the United States, used the methodology to articulate national and regional Catholic social teaching. Another long-term impact of *Mater et Magistra* was the creation of the Pontifical Commission for Justice and Peace. It came to be when a few bishops, including Dom Hélder Câmara, the auxiliary bishop of Rio de Janeiro, suggested that a special commission be established to study the principles and directives of *Mater et Magistra*, drawn from its vision of the world in the modern world and the global problems it addressed, particularly the relationship between the industrialized and underdeveloped countries.[31]

Socialization is considered a central theme of the encyclical and its distinctive contribution to the development of Catholic social teaching. But it is also viewed as its most complicated and controversial theme in the very use of the word *socialization,* given its connotations and the complex history of the concept. Leo condemned the socialization of private property, which Marxist socialism espouses. Marxism, pursuing a classless society in which the productive system is completely socialized, envisions a progressive socialization, or social ownership of the processes of industry. This was the initial meaning of socialization. What the popes since the time of Leo rejected is the extreme form of socialism that abolishes private property, because they believed that the solution to the inequitable distribution in the world was to enable all people to own property for their needs and dignity.

---

[31] Peter Hebblethwaite, *Pope John XXIII: Shepherd of the Modern World* (Garden City, NY: Doubleday, 1985), 462.

A more moderate form of socialism emerged over time. It was this moderate form that Pius had in mind when he wrote in *Quadragesimo Anno* that "it may well come about that gradually these tenets of mitigated socialism will no longer be different from the program of those who seek to reform human society according to Christian principles." There was an opening to state ownership of certain forms of property that are far beyond the capacity of individuals to govern or manage. "It is rightly contended that certain forms of property must be reserved to the state, since they carry with them a power too great to be left to private individuals without injury to the community at large" (*QA*, no. 114).

John took the same stance as Pius, but he described socialization in the terms used by the Forty-Seventh Congress of the *Semaines Sociales de France* held in Grenoble, July 1960, at the same time that the encyclical was being drafted. As stated in *Mater et Magistra*, "One of the principal characteristics of our time is the multiplication of social relationships, that is, a daily more complex interdependence of citizens, introducing into their lives and activities many and varied forms of association, recognized for the most part in private and public law" (no. 59). With the increasing complexity of society, state intervention increases, even in the more intimate aspects of personal life such as healthcare, education of the young, and choosing a career.

But John set the principles of common good and subsidiarity to protect state intervention from turning into a tyranny of excessive control. Intervention of the state must be exercised only to protect the common good; it must not take over where private initiative and enterprise are sufficient in securing benefits for individuals and community. The importance of socialization is articulated in *Mater et Magistra* through a listing of its seven implications:

- Employees are entitled to share in the ownership of the company where they work (no. 75).
- Employees should have a say in the management at the level of the individual firm and in determining policy at various levels, including the national level (no. 92–93, 97).
- The state is to exercise strict control over manager and directors of large businesses (no. 104).
- More state ownership is justified to promote the common good (no. 116–17).
- The state and public authorities should take on a greater role in addressing social problems (no. 120).

- Public authorities must address the special difficulties of the farmers (no. 128–41).
- Specific recommendations are made in regard to tax assessment (no. 133), credit facilities (no. 134), insurance (no. 135), social security (no. 136), price supports (no. 137), price regulation (no. 140), and moving industry into rural areas (no. 141).[32]

All of these state interventions are found to be necessary and legitimate because of the demand of the common good in a more complex society, in which economics is experienced on such large scales that the state is needed to govern such transactions so that the collective good of each one can be protected and promoted.

What broke new ground in John's socialization is his moving the Catholic Church away from the old fears and suspicions of socialistic notions. He began, as Donal Dorr points out, the "process of breaking the long alliance between Roman Catholicism and socially conservative forces."[33] Unlike the previous popes, John did not make any condemnatory statements about socialist and communist philosophies. Certainly this came from his refreshing openness to wherever truth could be found, transcending ideological differences. But of more critical significance was his position of publicly and officially putting the weight of the church on the side of structural changes for the benefit of the poor. For too long the church's anti-socialist and anti-communist stance, and its promotion of private initiative and private property, had been used as an ideological defense of the status quo, where unregulated market forces of free capitalistic enterprise render the poor, those without any negotiating social power, trapped in poverty. By its openness to necessary and legitimate state intervention on much larger scales, to effect structural policies to protect the weakest and most vulnerable in society, *Mater et Magistra* forged a direction other encyclicals would follow. Pope Paul VI, for instance, in *Populorum Progressio* in 1967 asserted the priority of common good over the right to property (*PP*, no. 23), and he criticized unrestrained capitalism and profit (*PP*, no. 26).

In the contemporary debate over the size of government, *Mater et Magistra* provided clear and enduring norms and principles. In multiple and pluralistic societies, where there is increasing interdependence on a

---

[32] Cited in Mich, "Commentary on *Mater et Magistra*," 208.

[33] Donal Dorr, *Option for the Poor and for the Earth: Catholic Social Teaching* (Maryknoll, NY: Orbis Books, 2012), 112.

large scale, and within countries where there are huge gaps between the haves and the have-nots, state intervention for the sake of the common good and for the protection of the poor is an imperative, legally and morally.

Blind Spots and Shortsightedness

Not only did John view the modern world and its developments with optimism, but he also viewed capitalism with the same optimism. It is not that he ignored its deficiencies and abuses, nor did he defend its unrestrained free enterprise. He was not so beholden to it that he could not shift away from it to protect the poor and defend the common good. But some of his views revealed assumptions that are founded on a capitalist free enterprise mode—assumptions that were not critically examined. In his 1959 encyclical *Ad Petri Cathedram* John remarked that class distinctions were less pronounced than before. "Anyone who is diligent and capable has the opportunity to rise to higher levels of society" (*PC*, no. 33; cf. *MM*, no. 48). This implies that within capitalist free enterprise, there is greater possibility for social mobility for people who are diligent and capable. Further, he seems to suggest that the rich in society have earned their privileged place while the poor are poor due to their own failure. John would certainly not adhere to this implication about the poor, since he himself saw the need for structural solutions to social problems; his optimism, however, about the capitalist system, which he saw bring growth and development to society in his time, beguiled him into believing that it could be transformed over time to bring about change.[34]

Other evidence of this blind spot in his view of capitalism is found in his teaching in *Mater et Magistra* regarding the need for wider distribution of property of various kinds (no. 115). He considered it time for societies to adjust their social and economic structures to facilitate a wider distribution of ownership because of the increasing number of countries experiencing rapid economic development. His assumption was based on equating economic growth with wider distribution of ownership, and the notion that if the "economic cake" is enlarged, more can have a piece of it. While this may seem to make sense, in practice those who invest to enlarge the economy want a major share of the new wealth, even at the cost of some delay in a just redistribution of shares.[35]

---

[34] Dorr, *Option for the Poor* (1983), 118–19.
[35] Ibid., 119–20.

This belief that the best way to solve social problems is to speed up economic growth was not confined to Western countries. Almost all third-world countries accepted this view, economic growth was pursued while intolerable sacrifices were asked of the people. The capitalist system is an ideology of growth, promoted by massive advertisements, for without growth, the system would collapse. It is its lifeline. This growth, however, benefits a few—those who have the economic power to create it and the corresponding political power to hold it. The truth is that the capitalist system creates an illusion of free enterprise that offers access to success and wealth to everyone, but in reality the poor often have no competitive chance.[36]

John certainly rejected these illusions, but he seemed to have been affected by them in his belief in the correlation between hard work and initiative and success and prosperity relative to social mobility. Perhaps this equation seemed validated by facts in the years between 1945 and 1961, which saw a considerable increase in prosperity for workers in Western countries. But this new wealth must be viewed in a wider reality, for it came from the use by Western countries of raw materials and energy from the third-world countries, purchased at very low prices. So the progress in the West was due to the imbalance of economic relations of the developed countries and the poor countries. Based on this critical model of development, John appears to be inconsistent with his global vision of interconnectedness of peoples and nations.[37]

While it may be true that under certain circumstances rapid economic growth under a free-enterprise system results in an increase in property ownership, this does not necessarily mean that a more equitable distribution of wealth has been achieved. "The economic prosperity of any people is to be assessed not so much from the sum total of goods and wealth possessed as from the distribution of goods according to norms of justice" (no. 74). The question is—is it possible to reverse the inherent nature of the capitalist system toward inequitable distribution of wealth and power?[38]

Another theme in the encyclical pertains to finding solutions to the social problems in the world in the return to religion and the moral laws founded on it. While this comes from a strong sense of the integrity of Catholic teaching, there is a need to have a more nuanced and critical assessment of the role of religion in the public arena.

---

[36] Ibid., 120–21.
[37] Ibid., 121–22.
[38] Ibid., 123.

Social problems are complex, and solutions to them are complex too. While religion is founded on a transcendental source, it is also a human phenomenon that is affected by social realities. The roots of social problems are multiple, and while they are fueled by political and economic conflicts, religious vindications are almost never absent. Religion can be a source of unity and peace when it is above divisions and conflicts, but religion can be ideologized and can be itself a source of division. What John explicated in *Mater et Magistra* is the transcendental and transformative role of religion, as a vigorous advocate of human rights and social justice. But critical readers of religion must also acknowledge its deadly dark side, if they are to understand the complex and ambiguous reality of religion.

Conclusion

John XXIII did not propose a radical reconstruction of society. He was looking for a moderate and gradual reform of the capitalist order through state intervention to protect the poor. He continued to draw from the old principles of subsidiarity and common good to prevent any state intervention from going to the extreme of totalitarian control. While he was optimistic that the capitalist system could be humanized by social compassion and justice through reforms, there were blind spots in his outlook, because he failed to assess critically the assumptions of free enterprise. He was clear about the end goal of the model of development, which is the equitable distribution of wealth, but there was a kind of naive optimism that the capitalist system through its ideology of growth can realize this end goal. The same lack of critical assessment of the assumptions of the capitalist system is reflected in his treatment of the role of religion in the public arena. His high idealism and optimism tend to focus on what is good and positive, which results in a lack of grasp of the complexity and ambiguity of realities.

John broke new ground as he brought a global perspective to Catholic social teaching and aimed in the encyclical to promote formation by action; this has had a long-term impact on the articulations and application of Catholic social teaching. Moving the church away from its suspicion and fear of socialistic notions, he broke the long alliance between Roman Catholicism and socially conservative forces that employed an anti-socialist stance to prevent structural changes in the status quo maintained by the free enterprise of capitalism. This new direction also appeared in the encyclicals that followed.

John attempted to work with the status quo without being be-holden to it. He worked through it, but he took the necessary shifts to disallow the use of Catholic social teaching as an ideological weapon of the rich and powerful to resist social change. The fundamental op-tion—the protection of the poor and the defense of the most vulner-able in society—gave him a hermeneutic with which to view economic and political systems.

6

Octogesima Adveniens

Issued on May 14, 1971, *Octogesima Adveniens* is the apostolic letter of Paul VI to Cardinal Maurice Roy, president of the Pontifical Commission for Justice and Peace, marking the eightieth anniversary of *Rerum Novarum* and the tenth anniversary of *Mater et Magistra*. It emphasizes that action for justice is a personal responsibility of all Christians, in their personal contexts as well as in their witness in solidarity with others in the public arena. All analysts and commentators of *Octogesima Adveniens* agree that the distinctive contribution of this encyclical is found in its shift from economics to politics as the realm of the work of justice, as well as its shift from the universal church to the local churches as the locus of solutions to social problems.

Readers should note that with the exception of directly quoted material, I have paraphrased the source material in O'Brien and Shannon's *Catholic Social Thought* and also provided a paragraph number for the original text.[1] In the directly quoted sections, I do not identify with the gender exclusion of women in the language used. I quoted as is, however, to preserve the historicity of the original text.

Historical Context

New Global Issues and Challenges

By 1971, it was clear that the globalization of capital had created enormous economic inequity, since the political mechanisms provided by national labor unions and laws were not sufficient to meet the

---

[1] David J. O'Brien and Thomas A. Shannon, *Catholic Social Thought: The Documentary Heritage* (Maryknoll, NY: Orbis Books, 1992). The official texts of these encyclicals are also available on the vatican.va website. Please note that paragraph numbers may vary, depending on the translation used.

requirements of economic justice. Many emerging nations, multiethnic and multicultural, posed challenges to the previous state models. In other parts of the world crisis after crisis seemed to arise: the Paris student uprisings (1968), the political assassinations in the United States (1963, 1968), the Six Day War (1967), the Vietnam War (1955–75), the invasion of Czechoslovakia (1968), and the genocide in Biafra (1967).[2]

As people in many parts of the world became increasingly educated and rose in the social hierarchy, they demanded greater participation in decision making. The traditional structures could not meet this new demand and its accompanying challenge, showing a need to reexamine the traditional views of decision making, power, and authority in all sectors of society, including the church. When Paul presided over the concluding session of Vatican II, he was overseeing the most massive changes in Catholic theology since the Council of Trent four hundred years earlier.

> At the time of Trent, the vast majority of human persons did not face personal decisions about where they would live and die, which religion to follow, which gender or sexual orientation to claim, which nationality or occupation to adopt, which social class to strive for. All of these aspects of personal identity were given at birth; later most persons were assigned by parents either a spouse or a religious habit. For the married, there was little or no choice of whether to have children, or how many to have. All of these assignments were for life, and individual choice played little or no role in them. By the pontificate of Paul VI, individuals in much of the world made personal choices of locality, education, occupation, class, sexual identity, marital status, spouse, family size, and often even nationality. Faced with such a burden of responsibility for self-creation, modern individuals demanded greater and greater degrees of freedom and participation in decision making.[3]

The Impact and Influence of Medellín

The shift of *Octogesima Adveniens* from economics to politics reflected the issues and challenges of the times. Paul VI saw that

[2] Mary Elsbernd, "Whatever Happened to *Octogesima Adveniens*?" *Theological Studies* 56/1 (1995): 41–42.

[3] Christine E. Gudorf, "Commentary on *Octogesima Adveniens*," in *Modern Catholic Social Teaching: Commentaries and Interpretations*, ed. Kenneth B. Himes, 315–32 (Washington, DC: Georgetown University Press, 2004), 318.

ultimate decisions rest with political power (no. 46). Political power, its proper use, and its potential for abuse constitute the encyclical's major themes. *Octogesima Adveniens* was issued less than three years after the Conference of Latin American Bishops in Medellín, Colombia, and its stress on liberation for the poor (nos. 28, 45). The use of *development* is not a focus, or a binding theme, as it was in *Populorum Progressio*. Many analysts attribute this change to Paul's trip to Medellín in 1968 and to his relationship with liberationist Latin American prelates, such as the Franciscan archbishop of São Paulo, Evaristo Arns. The Latin American Episcopal Conference (CELAM), inspired by the empowered role of the local church envisioned by Vatican II, addressed the challenges to the gospel within its situation. The Medellín conference was led by the Brazilian bishops, many of whom had been victims of the massive human rights violations that followed the 1964 military coup. Radicalized by their experience, the bishops broke with hundreds of years of ecclesial history in Latin America. In their statements in the Medellín documents they called for the church to become the church of the poor, particularly in Latin America, where the majority are weighed down by crushing poverty caused by structural and systemic injustice.[4]

In Latin America many worker and student movements had long been Marxist in orientation or were connected to its different strains. By 1971, liberation theologians called upon the church in Latin America to go beyond its magisterial role of denouncing the unjust reality of poverty, and actually take the side of the poor. This position would pit the church against the rich, entrenched in their positions of power and privilege, with whom the church had been allied for centuries. Breaking from this historic alliance, it would create a new solidarity with the poor. The primary attraction of socialism for the Latin American advocates for the poor was the social ownership of the means of production in a continent where the resources have been controlled by the richest ten percent.[5]

Liberation theologians argue that while one might reject the ideology of Marxism, its tools for social analysis can still be valuable in recognizing injustice and how to address it.[6] Socialism, which had been treated in *Rerum Novarum* and the encyclicals that followed,

---

[4] Ibid., 317.

[5] Ibid., 325.

[6] Gonzalo Arroyo et al., "Declaration of The 80," in *Christians and Socialism: Documentation of the Christians for Socialism Movement in Latin America,* ed. John Eagleson, trans. John Drury (Maryknoll, NY: Orbis Books, 1975), 4.

was also treated by Paul VI.[7] He showed a greater openness to Marxist socialisms, speaking of socialisms, in the plural, and recognizing the many divisions and permutations of socialism in the world (no. 31). None of the predecessors of Paul had come to grips with the complexity of socialism.

Though John had opened the door for Christian collaboration with socialists, and Paul had upheld such a collaboration in *Populorum Progressio*, none of the popes before Paul had approved of the use of the tools of Marxist thought.[8] *Octogesima Adveniens* broke even further by proposing the possibility that, if accompanied by careful discernment, Marxist tools such as social analysis could be useful in the work of social justice.[9]

Norms and Principles

New Social Problems

Universal Call of Justice

Paul speaks of having gone into the crowds and having heard the appeals, cries of distress, and also cries of hope. From the human faces of suffering he saw the grave problems of the times, problems that may seem particular to each part of the world but are common to all of humankind, posing a threat to its future. He speaks of flagrant economic, cultural, and political inequalities: while some regions are heavily industrialized, others are still at the agricultural stage; while some are enjoying excess prosperity, others are crushed by starvation; while some people have reached the highest lights of culture, others

---

[7] Socialism and communism were condemned in several papal documents of the nineteenth century. See Pius IX, *Qui Pluribus* (1846) and *Syllabus of Errors* (December 8, 1864). Socialism was among the evils of the day in Leo's first encyclical, *Inscrutabili* (1878). And in 1878, in an entire encyclical, *Quod Apostolici Muneris,* Leo condemned socialism. See Christine E. Gudorf, *Catholic Social Teaching and Liberation Themes* (Washington, DC: University Press of America, 1980), 109–65.

[8] Some commentators leave out of their consideration the development and shifts in the doctrine between Paul VI and John XXIII. They read Paul's cautions about the dangers of Marxist ideology and praxis as general condemnations of Marxism. See, for example, James Finn, "Beyond Economics, Beyond Revolution: *Octogesima Adveniens,*" in *Building the Free Society: Democracy, Capitalism, and Catholic Social Thought,* ed. George Weigel and Robert Royal, 149–62 (Grand Rapids, MI: Eerdmans; Washington, DC: Ethics and Public Policy Center, 1993).

[9] Gudorf, "Commentary on *Octogesima Adveniens,*" 325.

are trapped in the darkness of illiteracy. Paul makes a universal appeal for more justice, peace, and mutual respect among individuals and peoples (no. 2).

Paul points to the urgent questions that must be addressed today—questions caused by the modern economy in the wider context of a new civilization (no. 7). He reflects on changes that are rapid and profound, so that persons are challenged by the meaning of their own being and by the urgency of their collective survival. While persons think of the past as over and done with, they face a future whose meaning must be shed upon with the light of permanent and eternal truths (no. 7).

Urbanization

Paul speaks of the flight to the cities as the agrarian civilization continues to weaken. This results in populations swelling up in the cities where neither employment nor housing is sufficient. The extent of this flight is almost unimaginable; people in the tens of millions are grouped in cities better called by the term "megapolis" (no. 8).

As the inordinate growth of cities is not accompanied by proportionate growth in the social and economic structures to tend to the incessantly growing needs, social problems are exacerbated: "professional or regional unemployment, redeployment and mobility of persons, permanent adaptation of workers, and disparity of conditions in the different branches of industry" (no. 9). Unlimited competition for the purchase of new products results in consumerism, as superfluous needs are ingeniously created while many people cannot even satisfy their primary needs. This leads Paul to ask if, after endeavoring to control nature, persons have now become slaves of the objects that they made (no. 9).

The rise of the urban civilization has upset both the ways of life and habitual structures of existence: the family, the neighborhood, and the very framework of the Christian community. Persons experience a new loneliness, not in the face of a hostile nature, but amid a vast and faceless society. In a disordered existence new proletariats are born. They find themselves in the heart of the cities. Instead of meaningful human encounters and mutual gifts of assistance, life in the city fosters discrimination and indifference. People's needs are taken advantage of for profit, and they become victims of new forms of exploitation and domination. There is so much misery hidden behind the facades of city life—misery brought about by the degradation of human dignity with the rise of delinquency, criminality, abuse of drugs, and eroticism (no. 10).

"It is, in fact, the weakest who are the victims of dehumanizing living conditions, degrading for conscience and harmful for the family institution." These conditions do not allow even the minimum of intimacy; and "youth escape from a home which is too confined and seek in the street compensations and companionships which cannot be supervised" (no. 11). Paul speaks of the

> urgent need to remake at the level of the street, of the neighborhood, or of the great agglomerative dwellings the social fabric whereby man may be able to develop the needs of his personality. Centers of special interest and of culture must be created at the community and parish levels with different forms of associations, recreational centers, and spiritual and community gatherings where the individual can escape from isolation and form new fraternal relationships. (no. 11)

This is a task that Christians must undertake—to build up the city, to renew human bonds, and to foster new hope in the face of the collective future that all share (no. 12). Paul calls all Christians to live by the norms and principles of concern and solidarity in recreating the city and making it a space where people are profoundly connected as human beings amid loneliness, alienation, discrimination, and exploitation.

Youth

Urban life and industrialization have changed the society in which the young live. Paul speaks of the generational divide between young and adult generations. This divide is "a source of serious conflicts, divisions, and opting out, even within the family, and a questioning of modes of authority, education for freedom, and the handing on of values and beliefs, which strikes at the deep roots of society" (no. 13).

The Role of Women

Paul's position on women reveals ambiguity. He refers to the charter for women that declares an end to their discrimination, establishes relationships of equality in rights, and demands respect for their dignity. He specifically says that he does not have in mind false equality, which denies the distinctions of a woman from a man designed by the Creator, and which contradicts the woman's proper role at the heart of the family (no. 13). This proper role in all other papal teachings is a role dedicated to motherhood and domesticity. At the same time, however, he advocates for women to participate equally in cultural, economic, social, and political life. "Developments in legislation should on the contrary be directed to protecting her proper vocation and at the same time recognizing her independence as a person, and her equal rights to participate in cultural, economic, social, and political life" (no. 13). The ambiguity of Paul's position casts a double burden on women, who are called to do their proper role in the home and at same time contribute to the life of the community and the nation. Paul does not address the need for men to share in domestic work and in family care to relieve women of this double burden and enable them to exercise their equal right to participate in the public realm.[10]

Workers

Paul declares upholding of the human person as "the beginning, the subject, and the goal of all institutions." He further declares that "every man has the right to work, a chance to develop his qualities and his personality in the exercise of his profession, to equitable re-muneration which will enable him and family to lead a worthy life on the material, social, cultural, and spiritual level, and to assistance in case of need arising from sickness or age" (no. 14). Although in demo-cratic societies the principle of labor union rights is accepted, workers are often stopped from exercising these rights. Unions make possible the lawful and collective participation of workers in the economic life of a nation in the pursuit of the common good (no. 14). Actions taken by union organizations are not without difficulties. They can take advantage through their collective power (including the right to strike) to impose conditions that might harm the financial solvency of a company or are too burdensome for the overall economy of a nation. It is necessary to determine the limit beyond which the harm caused by strikes becomes inadmissible (no. 14).

Victims of Change

Paul turns his attention to those he calls the new poor—"the handi-capped and the maladjusted, the old, different groups of those on the fringe of society, and so on—in order to recognize them, help them, defend their place and dignity in a society hardened by competition and the attraction of success" (no. 15). He turns his attention to them because in the speedy and rapid changes in an industrialized society,

---

[10] Ibid., 328.

these are the ones who are left at the margins of society, without voice and identity.

Discrimination

Paul considers among the victims of injustice those who are discriminated against "on account of their race, origin, color, culture, sex, or religion." Racial discrimination stirs up tension within countries and on the global level. Racial prejudice in laws and systems is to be totally rejected and condemned. The basic principle is that all humankind shares the same basic rights and duties, as well as the same supernatural destiny; all should be equal before the law; all must be integrated into the economic, cultural, civic, and social life, and all should benefit from the wealth of a nation (no. 16).

Right to Emigrate

Paul also turns to the precarious situation of a great number of emigrant workers whose condition as foreigners deprives them of their social vindication, in spite of the contribution of their labor to the economic life of the country that receives them. Paul calls people to go beyond their narrow nationalist attitude in this regard and to grant emigrants a charter that assures them "a right to emigrate, favor their integration, facilitate their professional advancement, and give them access to decent housing, where if such is the case, their families can join them" (no. 17). He also speaks of the situation of people who, to find work, to escape a disaster, or survive a hostile climate, leave their countries, only to find themselves without any home among other peoples. Paul exhorts everyone, but especially Christians, to recognize their duty to work for authentic justice and enduring peace based on the established universal human bonds. He writes: "We cannot in truthfulness call upon that God who is the Father of all if we refuse to act in a brotherly way toward certain men, created to God's image. A man's relationship with God the Father and his relationship with his brother men are so linked together that scripture says: 'He who does not love does not know God' (1 John 4:8)" (no. 17).

Employment and Overpopulation

With the growth of population, especially in young nations, the number of those failing to find work and driven to misery and parasitism will increase, unless systemic and structural changes are effected that would bring an increase of investment, trade, and production, which would benefit not only a few but the majority. There must also be an increase in opportunities for education, for skills are necessary to gain access to these benefits. Such changes must be founded on the spirit of genuine solidarity. Paul expresses his disquiet over the sense of fatalism that is gaining hold on people in positions of responsibility. It is this sense of fatalism, he says, which drives them to Malthusian solutions and promotes propaganda for contraception and abortion. He does not deny the state responsible intervention, within the limit of its competence, through providing appropriate information and adopting suitable measures, on the provision that these be in conformity with the moral law and that they respect the rightful freedom of married couples. He states the principle: "Where the inalienable right to marriage and procreation is lacking, human dignity has ceased to exist" (no. 18).

Social Communication

Mass media, says Paul, is the new power in the world. Its reach is wide, as is its influence. It can bring about shifts in mentalities and knowledge, as well as transformation of organizations and of society itself. It wields positive effects, it cuts the distances between nations and peoples by bringing the news in an instant, establishing contacts across the globe, and creating bonds of unity among people. Through the media, greater spread of education and culture is made possible. But the power of mass media is so immense that those who hold it must exercise it with social responsibility in terms of their aims, the means they use, and the effect of their pursuits on the political and ideological spheres and in social, economic, and cultural life. They have a grave responsibility to the truth and the values they put forward. They must be governed by the demands of the common good, as enshrined in the common heritage of values on which orderly civil progress in based (no. 20).

The Environment

Paul speaks of the dark consequences of human exploitation of the environment. By exploiting nature, people risk destroying it and becoming, in turn, victims of its degradation. There is the constant threat of pollution and refuse, new illnesses, and other forms of destruction, and there are wide-ranging social problems that arise from the degradation of the environment. Paul exhorts Christians to take responsibility, together with the rest of humanity, for a destiny that from now on is shared by all (no. 21).

Fundamental Aspirations and Current Ideas

Equality and Participation

In the face of scientific and technological progress, there are two aspirations that will never lose their hold, and they grow stronger as people become better informed and better educated: the aspiration to equality, and the aspiration to participation. These are intrinsic to human dignity and freedom (no. 22). Paul points out how these two aspirations are threatened by the various forms of discrimination that continually appear—ethnic, cultural, religious, and political. Human rights are often disregarded, if not scoffed at. While laws are necessary to protect justice and equality, often they are not sufficient. Paul holds that preferential care is to be given to the poor and the special situation they have in society; "the more fortunate should renounce some of their rights so as to place their goods more generously at the service of others" (no. 23). Without compassion for and solidarity with others, even equality before the law can become a subterfuge for flagrant discrimination, continued exploitation, and actual contempt. Many people taken over by individualism will be only after what is due them, without care for others or for the common good (no. 23).

Political Society

Paul states that the aspirations to equality and to participation seek to promote a democratic society. But people continue to search through various models that could more perfectly satisfy these two basic human aspirations. Christians are exhorted to take part in this search as a matter of duty. As social beings, persons build their destinies in relation to others, in their own groupings. These seek to extend to a vaster society, the political society, where the common good must be upheld (no. 24). In light of the common good, people must not be concerned only about their individual rights but also recognize their duties toward one another (no. 24).

Paul holds that the worst kind of dictatorship is the dictatorship over minds. He exhorts cultural and religion groups in their exercise of freedom to pursue ultimate values and convictions that are founded on the true nature, origin, and end of person and society (no. 25). It is good to keep in mind the principle proclaimed in the Second Vatican Council's *Dignitatis Humanae*: "The truth cannot impose itself except by virtue of its own truth, and it makes its entrance into the mind at once quietly and with power" (*DH*, no. 1).

Ideologies and Human Liberty

Paul warns that Christians who are involved in political activity must discern how ideologies contradict the Christian faith. He cites in particular the atheistic materialism of Marxist ideology, its dialectic of violence, its violation of freedom in collectivity, and its denial of all transcendence. Just as Christians cannot adhere to the Marxist ideology, neither can they accept a liberal ideology that, because it believes only in individual initiatives, exalts individual freedom without limits and, being exclusively oriented to interest and power, does not view the necessity of social organization in the pursuit of the common good (no. 26).

Many ideologies are rooted in a worldview that denies transcendent faith in God either in their belief system or their praxis system (no. 27). When an ideology, even if it does not theoretically deny God, promotes a way of life where ultimacy lies in the goods of the earth, it is atheistic at the heart of its praxis. Those who adhere to such an ideology "imagine they find in it a justification for their activity, even violent activity, and an adequate response to a generous desire to serve." Those who allow themselves to be consumed by an ideology become its slaves (no. 28).

Paul speaks of a retreat of ideologies worldwide, which could point to an openness to the transcendence of faith. However, "it may also be a more accentuated sliding toward a new positivism: universalized technology as the dominant form of activity, as the overwhelming pattern of existence, even as a language, without the question of its meaning being really asked" (no. 29).

Historical Movements

The teaching of John XXIII in *Pacem in Terris* states that historical movements that originated from ideologies are in part distinct from them. The possibility of making a distinction is based on the fact that historical movements are products of their times and have their own economic, social, cultural, or political ends. Those ends are pursued in view of changing needs and challenges and thus are in constant evolution, even though they may continue to draw inspiration from the ideology from which they originated. These historical movements, Paul notes, insofar as they are guided by right reason and inspired by the lawful aspirations of people, may even yield elements that are positive and deserving of approval (no. 30).

Attraction of Socialist Currents

Paul appeals for some caution in the attraction of some Christians to socialist currents and their various developments. Recognizing therein a certain number of aspirations that they believe are compatible with their faith, they seek to be a part of these currents and developments. Paul warns that oftentimes this attraction is directed to very general ideals—a will for justice, solidarity, and equality—so that one is blinded to the fact that socialist movements, in whatever new forms they have emerged, remain conditioned by the ideologies from which they originated. Paul calls for careful judgment. "Distinctions must be made to guide concrete choices between the various levels of expression of socialism: a generous aspiration and a seeking for a more just society; historical movements with a political organization and aim, and an ideology which claims to give a complete and self-sufficient picture of man" (no. 31). He says that these distinctions should not lead one to consider such levels as completely separate and independent. The link that connects them together must be carefully discerned in order to enable Christians to determine the degree of commitment they could give, "while safeguarding the values, expecially those of liberty, responsibility, and openness to the spiritual, which guarantee the integral development of man" (no. 31).

Historical Evolution of Marxism

Some question whether a historical development of Marxism might not authorize certain concrete rapprochements. "Those who pose this question cite a certain splintering of Marxism, which until now showed itself to be a unitary ideology which explained in atheistic terms the whole of man and the world." Given the conflicting interpretation of Marxism-Leninism, and the opposition between the political systems that are aligned with it, there is an emerging view of establishing distinctions between Marxism's various levels of expression (no. 32). At the first level Marxism remains no more than the practice of class struggle—the relationship of domination and struggle among peoples. At the second level it is the collective exercise of political and economic power by a single party, depriving individuals and other groups of initiative and choice. At the third level it is a socialist ideology based on an atheistic totalizing ideology that explains the origin and meaning of the person and society apart from God (no. 33).

At other times Marxism presents itself as a rigorous scientific method of examining political and social reality, employing the dynamics of theory and praxis. Although the type of analysis it offers is partial to certain aspects of reality to the detriment of the rest, through the prism of its ideology, it furnishes some people not only with a working tool but also a "certitude preliminary to action: the claim to decipher in a scientific manner the mainsprings of the evolution of society" (no. 33).

Paul warns that while these different levels of Marxism can be distinguished, it would be illusory and dangerous not to view all of them as intimately linked by their origin. To those who say they are only using the Marxist tools of analysis but not its atheistic ideology, Paul warns against forgetting the intimate link that radically binds all the levels together. It is deceptive to hold that Marxist analysis is not infused by its ideology of class struggle and the kind of totalitarian and violent society to which its process leads (no. 34).

Liberal Ideology

Paul notes the renewal of a liberal ideology that asserts itself in the name of economic efficiency and as a defense of the individual against the overreach of large organizations and the totalitarian tendencies of political powers. He upholds the protection of personal initiative and freedom. He warns, however, against idealizing liberalism, which leads to forgetting that at its very root it is an erroneous affirmation of the autonomy of the individual that diminishes the importance of community and solidarity. He calls for careful discernment of liberalism and its attractions (no. 35).

Christian Discernment and Utopias

Christians must draw from the sources of the faith and the church's teaching the necessary principles and criteria to guide their encounters with ideologies, lest they be beguiled by their attractions. Paul appeals for greater knowledge of the specific character of the Christian contribution for a positive transformation of society (no. 36).

The weaknesses of ideologies, according to Paul, take concrete form through the systems that incarnate them—bureaucratic socialism, technocratic capitalism, and authoritarian democracy. These systems show how difficult it is to solve the great human problem of living together in justice and equality. All these systems carry within themselves the materialism, egoism, and lack of constraint that afflict all things human. Paul speaks of a rebirth of utopias, which offer alluring solutions to the problems of the times. The appeal of utopias is that they offer an escape from the concrete tasks in the present. But Paul rejects their appeal because they allow people to live in an imaginary future and thus find facile alibis to reject immediate responsibility. However, from a different perspective, the present can contain hidden possibilities that direct one toward a fresh future. This evokes the Christian notion of the Spirit of the Lord, who animates persons to break down every limit and urges them to go beyond every horizon. Paul teaches that at the heart of the world dwells the mystery of persons discovering themselves in the struggle of constraint and freedom, as they are weighed down by sin or lifted up by the Spirit. He envisions a new earth, which he says must not weaken but strengthen our concern for cultivating our present life as one that foreshadows all that was promised to come (no. 37).

The Questioning of the Human Sciences

Addressing technological and scientific advances in the world, Paul notes that those human persons who have subdued nature by use of their reason are now trapped within their own rationality, becoming the object of science. He notes that human sciences explain reality from a purely quantitative or phenomenological point of view and claim for such an explanation an all-embracing interpretation. Paul rejects this as a dangerous presumption: "To give a privileged position in this way to such an aspect of analysis is to mutilate man and under the pretext of a scientific procedure, to make it impossible to understand man in his totality" (no. 38). This scientific reductionism can also result in a model of society in which science can manipulate the desires and needs of persons, modifying their behavior and even their system of values (no. 39).

As he did in *Populorum Progressio*, Paul upholds the special contribution of the church to civilizations: "Sharing the noblest aspirations of men and suffering when she sees them not satisfied, she wishes to help them attain their full flowering, and that is why she offers men what she possesses as her characteristic attribute: a global vision of man and of the human race" (no. 40). Should the church in its turn contest the conclusions of human sciences? Paul writes that the church has confidence in scientific research and urges Christians to contribute to this endeavor. Seeking to know the human person better through scientific study and research, those who are enlightened by faith could themselves begin a dialogue between the church and the various fields of discovery (no. 40).

Scientific research will yield its understanding of the human person from its particular sphere, but a complete and full picture of the person escapes scientific methodology. Still, the contributions of sciences are welcomed by the church. They could assist Christian social morality in making a critical judgment and taking an overall view of societies. "These sciences are a condition at once indispensable and inadequate for a better discovery of what is human. They are a language which becomes more and more complex, yet one that deepens rather than solves the mystery of the heart of man; nor does it provide the complete and definitive answer to the desire which springs from his innermost being" (no. 40).

Progress

Progress is the motive, measure, and goal of modern sciences. Since the nineteenth century Western societies (and as a result, many others) have put their hopes in ceaselessly renewed and indefinite progress. Progress is viewed as that which frees the human person from the demands of nature and social constraint, and, as imaged and communicated by the modern media, has become an omnipresent ideology. Yet one is confronted by the ambiguity of its values and results. Paul articulates this ambiguity and also the elusiveness of progress: "What is the meaning of this never-ending, breathless pursuit of a progress that always eludes one when one believes one has conquered it sufficiently in order to enjoy it in peace? If it is not attained, it leaves one dissatisfied" (no. 41). When economic growth becomes the sole measure of progress, it exalts the quantitative order of existence. But there is more to life than economic goods. There is the quality of human relationship and participation which is as essential to the good and future of society as the quantity of goods produced and consumed (no. 41).

There is a certain tendency to measure everything in terms of efficiency and trade, in terms of the interplay of forces and interests— quantitative criteria of progress. Such a tendency must be overcome, Paul teaches, and in place of quantitative criteria there must be qualitative criteria that attend to "the intensity of communication, the spread of knowledge and culture, mutual service, and combining of efforts for a common task" (no. 41). Genuine progress is found in the development of moral consciousness, which bears fruit in greater openness to God and greater solidarity with others. Christians are called to understand this in the context of the death and resurrection of Christ and the outpouring of the Spirit, where they find "the only hope which does not deceive" (no. 41).

Christian Engagement with Social Questions

Dynamism of the Church's Social Teaching

In the face of so many questions, the church seeks to give an answer from the sphere of truth. The questions have grown in their depth, and the search for answers has become even more urgent. Paul offers the social teaching of the church to accompany the human search for answers. The church reflects on the application of principles in the light of the changing situations of the world, under the inspiration of the gospel, as a source of renewal when its message is accepted in its totality and with all its demands, especially justice for the poor (no. 42).

There is a need to establish greater justice in the distribution of goods on both national and international levels. In the case of the latter, there is a need to go beyond the use of force, for force only creates situations where opposing groups struggle, opening the way to the use of extreme violence and abuse. Dialogue must be pursued because there is no true and lasting peace forged in situations of struggle and violence (no. 43). But, as often stated, Paul teaches that the most important duty in the realm of justice is to allow each country to promote its own development, free from any economic or political domination. This does not deny the need of mutual assistance and the imperative of solidarity. The model of growth of rich nations, however, is to be questioned, as well as its impact on production, the structure of exchanges, the control of profits, and the monetary system. There remains the abiding and urgent call for justice, which must inspire international organizations to renew their effectiveness in heeding this call (no. 43).

Paul speaks of the new economic powers emerging in the multinational enterprises that are breaking down national frontiers. They conduct autonomous economic deals and exchanges largely independent of the national political powers, and they seek their own interests whether or not doing so could threaten or even destroy the common good. In these private organizations new and abusive forms of economic domination and abuse are committed on the social, cultural, and even political level. Paul warns against the excessive concentration of means and powers, which Pius XI also condemned in *Quadragesimo Anno*, written in 1931 on the fortieth anniversary of *Rerum Novarum* (no. 44).

True liberation, Paul teaches, starts with the interior freedom that persons must find again in relation to goods and powers—an interior freedom that can be reached only through the power of a transcendent love for others, expressed in a genuine readiness to serve. Ideologies lead only to a change of masters, who, when they are in positions of power, pursue privileges only for themselves and their cohorts, and cause widespread violations of justice. Similarly, nations are in competition to attain technological, economic, and military power. Caught in this pursuit of power, they live in a climate of distrust and struggle that compromises peace (no. 45).

Shift from Economics to Politics

"Is it not here that there appears a radical limitation to economics?" Paul asks. He continues, "economic activity is necessary and, if it is at the service of man, it can be a source of brotherhood and a sign of Providence. It is the occasion of concrete exchanges between men, of rights recognized, of services rendered, and of dignity affirmed in work" (no. 46). While the economic enterprise can engage people in confrontation and domination, it can also foster dialogue and cooperation. "This is why the need is felt to pass from economics to politics," because "the ultimate decision rests with political power" (no. 46).

Political power is exercised to ensure the cohesion of the social body. While protecting legitimate liberties of individuals, families, and subsidiary groups is important, the realization of the common good is the final responsibility of those in positions of political power. Paul teaches that such power must always intervene with care for justice and devotion for the common good. Achieving the common good requires the participation of individuals and intermediary bodies that are proper to them. Political activity helps individuals become engaged members of the social body, but it never absorbs them. In pursuit of the common good political power must be free from the interests of particular groups, and even go beyond national limits for the good of all in the global realm. Politics calls one to a vocation, a demanding one, of living the Christian commitment to the service of others. "The domain of politics is wide and comprehensive, but it is not exclusive." While it acts within its competence from people to people, from country to country, its true pursuit is to find solutions to problems within structures and systems of relationships. Christians who are called to a vocation in politics are exhorted to make choices that are consistent with the gospel and that give witness to a life singularly spent in service to others (no. 46).

Sharing in Responsibility

The passing from economics to politics is made imperative by people's insistence on a greater sharing in responsibility and decision making. This legitimate demand broadens as educational and cultural levels rise. People have also become more aware of the world that they live in, the uncertain future that it faces, and that choices being made on both the personal and communal levels determine the life of tomorrow. Paul refers to the teaching of John XXIII in *Mater et Magistra* that stresses that responsibility is a basic demand of human nature, a concrete exercise of freedom, and a path to human development. John showed how this sharing in responsibilities must be ensured in economic life. Paul, going beyond the teaching of his predecessor, speaks of a wider view of sharing in responsibility that extends to the social and political sphere. He sees that choices to be made are more complex, the considerations that are to be discerned are more numerous, and the consequences involve more risk. There are limits that are sometimes called for, but no obstacle should be placed to a wider participation in decision making. Paul counsels that to counterbalance increasing technocracy, modern forms of democracy must devise far-reaching ways to inform people and to involve them in shared responsibility (no. 47).

To share responsibility is to learn to live more and more as a member of community. Freedom, often understood as an assertion of one's autonomy at the cost of the freedom of others, is now to be realized in its most authentic and deepest reality, which is living in solidarity with others. For Christians, it is by losing themselves in God, who sets them free so that they find true freedom, renewed in the death and resurrection of the Lord (no. 47).

Diversity of Situations

"In some places they [Christians] are reduced to silence, regarded with suspicion, and as it were kept on the fringe of society, enclosed without freedom in a totalitarian system." In other places Christians are a weak minority without a voice. Even in some nations where the church is officially recognized, it is caught in the crises that unsettle society. Some of its members are tempted by radical and violent solutions to problems of society, beguiled as they are by the revolutionary ideologies and their promise of a better world. Others are happy living in the status quo, unaware of the injustices inflicted on others by the system that sustains their way of life (no. 3).

In the light of the diversity and even complexity of the situations that Christians are in, Paul enunciated the most striking norm or principle of the encyclical in the following:

In the face of such widely varying situations it is difficult for us to utter a unified message and to put forward a solution which has a universal validity. Such is not our own ambition, nor is it our mission. It is up to the Christian communities to analyze with objectivity the situation which is proper to their own country, to shed on it the light of the Gospel's unalterable words and to draw principles of reflection, norms of judgment, and directives of action from the social teaching of the church. (no. 4)

Paul recognizes that the social teachings are worked out in the course of history as they are shaped by the conditions of the times. Since *Rerum Novarum* put the institutional weight of the church on the side of the workers, the social teachings of the church since then did likewise for other victims of injustice (no. 5).

Paul speaks of the evolution of social teaching as the demand of social justice is applied in different contexts. Today, Paul says, the social question has become a worldwide issue: "A renewed consciousness of the demands of the Gospel makes it the Church's duty to put herself at the service of all, to help them grasp their serious problem in all dimensions, and to convince them that solidarity in action at this turning point in human history is a matter of urgency" (no. 5).

Directives for Action

Call to Action

Paul begins by stating what the church has always envisioned in the social sphere. He speaks of the double function the church assumes—"first to enlighten minds in order to assist them to discover the truth and to find the right path to follow amid the different teachings that call for their attention; and secondly to take part in action and to spread, with a real care for service and effectiveness, the energies of the Gospel." He makes a fresh and insistent call to action. Laypeople, he says, should take up as their proper task to renew the temporal order. If the role of the hierarchy is to teach and to interpret the norms of morality authentically, it belongs to the laity to "infuse Christian spirit" into the human contexts and cultures in which they live—a task they must do on their own initiative and competence. Paul exhorts people to examine their lives and evaluate what they have done and what they ought to do. "It is not enough to recall principles, state intentions, cry against injustice, and utter prophetic denunciations," if these are not accompanied by effective action (no. 48).

Paul also points out that it is easy to blame others for injustices without seeing one's share in the responsibility that may have brought them about. One must also recognize first of all the need for personal conversion. Basic humility rids actions of "all inflexibility and sectarianism; it will also avoid discouragement in the face of a task that seems to be limitless in size" (no. 48). The hope of the Christian lies in the belief that Christ continues to work in his body, which is the church, and through the church, in the whole of humankind, by the redemption of the cross and the victory of the resurrection. People of other faiths, and also men and women of good will, are undertaking actions of justice and peace, working for the same common end. For beneath the exterior of indifference, Paul believes that there is in the heart of every person a thirst for justice and peace and a desire to live within the bonds of a common humanity (no. 48).

Amid diversity of many kinds, Paul calls all people to determine in their conscience what actions they are called to do. He particularly calls Christians to make wise and vigilant choices and avoid aligning themselves with those who violate the principles of true humanism under the guise of solidarity. Christians who engage in actions in accordance with their faith, as unbelievers would expect them to do, must clarify their motives and must take an all-embracing stand against "selfish particularism and oppressive totalitarianism" (no. 49).

Plurality of Options

Because there is a legitimate variety of possible options, Christians, inspired by the same faith, can take different directions of action and engagement. The church invites all Christians to help adapt all structures to the real needs of today. Paul calls for Christians who may appear to be in opposition, because of different starting points, to make real efforts to understand each other's positions and motives, and in the spirit of profound charity, to work toward common ground. "The bonds which unite the faithful are mightier than anything which divides them" (no. 50). Rising above their own particular conditions, they must be open to the common call to transform society (no. 50).

Paul also calls Christian organizations to work toward collective action. They embody in their vision and action the concrete demands of the Christian faith for a just and transformed society. Today, more than ever, the word of God is proclaimed by the witness of service and action for others under the inspiration of the Holy Spirit, where existence and the future meet (no. 51).

Critical Excursus

From the themes explicated and developed in the encyclical, we can identify three themes that are strikingly innovative: a new norm or principle on power and authority; a shift from economics to politics; and a stress on human aspirations to equality and decision making. Then we can ask whatever happened to *Octogesima Adveniens*? This question addresses the failure to implement *Octogesima Adveniens* in the decades since its promulgation.

Innovative Norms and Principles

New Norm or Principle on Power and Authority

Regarded as the single most striking theme in *Octogesima Adveniens* when it was issued was its new principle of power and authority. *Octogesima Adveniens* holds that the church does not seek to exercise authority over decisions that could be made alone by those in the context in which Christians find themselves. The abdication of power and authority by the church in such contexts, Charles Curran notes, "reflects a heightened awareness of historical consciousness and the need for a more inductive approach."[11] Before *Octogesima Adveniens* Catholic social doctrine had been taught as holding the definitive answers to social questions and the final solutions to social problems. This was particularly asserted in *Rerum Novarum* by Leo, who spoke of the church's role regarding the social problem of labor: "No practical solution of this question will ever be found without the assistance of religion and the church. It is we who are the chief guardian of religion, and the chief dispenser of what belongs to the Church, and we must not by silence neglect the duty that lies upon us" (*RN*, no. 13). He does not deny the roles of other sectors of society, but he concludes, "All the striving of men will be in vain if they leave out the Church" (*RN*, no. 13).

Pius XI also claimed the authority to deal with social and economic problems insofar as they raise moral questions. In *Quadragesimo Anno* he set the clear parameters of the authority of the church. "For

---

[11] Charles E. Curran, *The Catholic Moral Tradition Today: A Synthesis* (Washington, DC: Georgetown University Press, 1999), 149.

the deposit of truth entrusted to us by God, and our weighty office of propagating, interpreting and urging in season and out of season the entire moral law, demand that both social and economic questions be brought within our supreme jurisdiction, insofar as they refer to moral questions" (QA, no. 41).

Paul, expressing a new view, speaks of the work of the Spirit all over the world, in all Christian communities: "On all the continents, among all races, nations and cultures, and under all conditions, the Lord continues to raise up authentic apostles of the gospel" (no. 2). Because of the unbounded and ubiquitous presence of the Spirit in every place and time, the church, he believes, cannot claim to be the only source of answers and solutions. He enunciates a striking norm/principle regarding the limits of the power and authority of the church relative to social problems, in oft-quoted lines of *Octogesima Adveniens*:

> In the face of such widely varying situations it is difficult for us to utter a unified message and to put forward a solution which has universal validity. Such is not our ambition, nor is it our mission. It is up to the Christian communities to analyze with objectivity the situation which is proper to their own country, to shed on it the light of the Gospel's unalterable words and to draw principles of reflection, norms of judgment, and directives for action from the social teaching of the church. . . . It is up to these Christian communities, with the help of the Holy Spirit, in communion with the bishops who hold responsibility and in dialogue with other Christian brethren and all men of good will, to discern the options and commitments which are called for in order to bring about the social, political, and economic changes seen in many cases to be urgently needed. (no. 4)

The entire passage contains a number of new principles: First, it says that answers must come from the local church communities, from the laity, working with their bishops, and in "dialogue with other Christian brethren and all men of good will." They must analyze with objectivity the situation proper to their country, in the light of the gospel, from which they draw "principles of reflection, norms of judgment, and directives for action." Second, using a less authoritative "social teaching" rather than *social doctrine*,[12] and taking a historical rather

_____

[12] The terms *social doctrine* and *social teaching* are used interchangeably by many commentators. Theological approaches, however, have distinguished the terms, with *social doctrine* having a more authoritative meaning. The debate around these terms shows that their difference is not just a matter of words and

than an ahistorical perspective, it recognizes that the church's teachings are worked out in the course of history, shaped by the conditions of the times. And third, it disclaims the exclusive papal responsibility to declare a unified and universal solution to social problems. This is neither its ambition nor its mission.

Octogesima Adveniens refers to the forthcoming synod of bishops, representing all the local churches of the world, whose mandate is to examine in greater detail how the church should respond to global injustice (no. 6). All in all, what is discerned in *Octogesima Adveniens* regarding the theme of power and authority is the spirit of conciliar collegiality rather than exclusive papal authority, a decentralizing of power and sharing of responsibility between the pope and bishops, and also between Christian communities and clerical hierarchies.

Theologians of stature have praised *Octogesima Adveniens*'s rejection of power and authority exclusively from the top down. Philip Land describes this position as a dramatic departure from the approach of previous papal documents. He views this as Rome reversing its old practice of exercising power by handing down from the top solutions to specific questions.[13] M.-D. Chenu also praises this inductive method, in which different situations are viewed as the loci from which theology springs through discernment of signs.[14] This change of approach reflects a revision in the role of the pope as a moral teacher, who, recognizing the limit of his reach, leaves the discernment of problems at the local or regional level, and also a change in theological method whose starting point is shifted from abstract ahistorical truths applied to situations to experiential truths discerned from a variety of cultural and geographical situations from which transcultural and universal truths are drawn.

Related to this shift in understanding power and authority in the church is the pluralism of Christian options. If decision making is now put in the hands of those in the situation or context, then one is not surprised that *Octogesima Adveniens* treats at the end of its en-

---

meanings. The term *social teaching* is preferred by theologians and commentators who uphold the more inclusive and broad approach to participation and decision making of *Octogesima Adveniens*, while the term *social doctrine* is preferred by those who emphasize papal authority. See Todd David Whitmore, "The Loyal Dissent of Neo-Conservative Economics, Part 2," *The Observer* [University of Notre Dame], October 16, 1998.

[13] Philip S. Land, "The Social Theology of Pope Paul VI," *America* 12 (May 1979): 394.

[14] Marie-Dominique Chenu, *La 'doctrine sociale' de l'Eglise comme idéologie* (Paris: Cerf, 1979), 80.

tire statement the legitimate pluralism of Christian options. For if all Christians, and if indeed all humans, are to make decisions and accept responsibility for them, it would not be possible to expect that they would all see a situation in a similar way. They will view it through the prism of their own background and experience. The likelihood that they will arrive at the same decision or action is minimal or nil. Paul says that the same Christian faith can lead to different commitments. He calls for mutual openness to one another's positions and a willingness to work toward convergence and collaboration. A profound charity must infuse this openness and willingness, but one that is not blind to the complexity and diversity that need to be negotiated. What is refreshing in this new approach is that unity among members of the church is no longer to be sought in the directives of the local bishop or in the universal norms taught by papal authority. In *Octogesima Adveniens* the Catholic layperson is exhorted to work for justice in the world through collaborative action amid complexity and diversity.[15] "The suspicion of democratic politics as a field of activity for Christians, which had bedeviled the Church since the French Revolution seemed to have been dissolved."[16]

A Shift from Economics to Politics

In the few years after *Populorum Progressio* was issued, it began to dawn on more and more people that economic problems and political problems are so linked that underlying most economic difficulties are political problems. Thus, those in the Latin American context cry for liberation rather than for development. If *development* is used to approach social issues, problems such as poverty, apathy, and poor distribution of resources would be viewed as not yet solved because they are still in the process of development. Also, when one speaks of *development*, the emphasis tends to be only on economic issues; when *liberation* is used, it implies a perspective in which political action is central. From the perspective of development, the poor are viewed at the bottom of a ladder that all can climb. The truth is, however, that peoples and nations are poor not because they are at the bottom of this ladder of development, but because they have been prevented from climbing this ladder or even pushed down the ladder. When

---

[15] Gudorf, "Commentary on *Octogesima Adveniens*," 322.
[16] Ibid., 323.

poverty is seen from this view, the solution is more in the realm of liberation than of development.[17]

The more radical committed Christians in Latin America, as represented by their bishops at Medellín, rejected the very notion of development. The Medellín documents are notably political in their perspectives. The influence of Medellín on *Octogesima Adveniens* shows in its shift from economics to politics; the encyclical states that "in the social and economic field, both national and international, the ultimate decision rests on political power" (no. 46). Paul offers a nuanced response to Medellín, or at least some aspects of it. He, however, is reluctant to use the word *liberation* in place of *development*, presumably because it might be taken to mean revolution. The fact is, however, the major issues that he deals with in *Octogesima Adveniens* are not purely economic ones. The focus has shifted from economics to politics.[18]

Paul is "in notable contrast to papal tradition when he recognizes that most social problems are at bottom political problems."[19] Donal Dorr agrees with this statement in one sense, but he says that it needs some qualification. He points out that the encyclicals that preceded *Octogesima Adveniens* had proposed political remedies to socioeconomic problems—ranging from a corporative type of system within the state as explicated in *Quadragesimo Anno* and the need for new international institutions leading toward a world government in *Populorum Progressio*. Dorr argues that

> it is one thing to propose political solutions to economic and social problems, but quite a different thing to recognize clearly that designing and bringing into effect such solutions brings one into the sphere of political activity. The novelty of *Octogesima Adveniens* lies largely in the extent to which it consciously addresses itself to the some of the political problems involved in choosing and implementing an equitable order in society.[20]

As he calls for a shift from economics to politics, Paul sees the need to revise the relationships between nations in the economic

[17] Donal Dorr, *Option for the Poor: A Hundred Years of Catholic Social Teaching* (Maryknoll, NY: Orbis Books, 1983), 212.

[18] Ibid., 213.

[19] Land, "The Social Theology of Pope Paul VI," 394.

[20] Dorr, *Option for the Poor*, 214.

sphere and criticizes the models of growth of the rich nations (no. 42). He particularly expresses his concern over the uncontrolled power of multinational corporations (no. 44), which could be kept within limits by political action. He also addresses the power that the media hold and the need for political control to prevent abuses of this power (no. 20). This political power can be exercised over economic activity in new forms of democracy, where people are well informed and able to participate more in decision making on the local and national levels. Paul goes beyond John XXIII in this regard. John called for sharing of responsibility in economic life, in the policies of companies and businesses. Paul extends this participation to the social and political sphere (no. 47). He does not delineate in great detail how this participation is be exercised, but he cites the role played by trade unions in the pursuit of the common good (no. 14).[21]

Clearly, it is Paul's view that trade unions confine their role in "lawful collaboration in the economic advance of society" (no. 14). He speaks, however, of the times they use force, which is directly political in nature, as fundamental means to defend their collective position. He states that this could create conditions too burdensome for the overall economy, and thus the limit beyond which the harm caused society becomes inadmissible must be assessed (no. 14). An ambivalence is discerned in Paul's shift from economics to politics, however, when applied to the case of trade unions. He finds himself forced at this point to make distinctions between economics and politics. It is not difficult to see why, if one is to view it from the consensus model of political action that has long been upheld by papal teaching. There is a caution about moving toward any kind of confrontation that would exacerbate class divisions in society. Strikes, which are employed to rectify specific economic abuses, should not be turned into political weapons to destabilize the government. This, in the mind of Paul, is directly political.[22]

Paul's distinction between economic and political, in relation to the role of trade unions, is primarily to protect the stability of society. But the same question that confronted Leo confronts Paul too. Should one protect the stability of society at the cost of injustice? Is it possible to keep a demarcation line between economics and politics, when underlying the economic problems are political problems, relative to the wide gaps of power between the rich and poor at the

---

[21] Ibid., 215.
[22] Ibid., 220–21.

root of economic inequity and injustice? Those with political power maintain their economic positions to the detriment of the poor, who are marginalized and without power. When workers are confined to the economic sphere and closed out from direct political power, they are condemned to impotence and futility. Paul recognizes the need to shift from economics to politics, and that greater participation should be extended to the political sphere. This is because it is in politics that the ultimate solution lies, should be pursued to its fullest meaning and implication relative to trade unions, and not remain on the level of an abstract principle.

This shift from economics to politics yields a broad discussion on ideologies. For Paul, political activity is not an autonomous activity. It is based on a vision or model of society, and in deep and broad ways, on an understanding of the nature and the end of the human person as well as the purpose and goal of society. Paul holds that neither Marxist ideology nor liberal ideology is compatible with the Christian understanding of the human person (no. 26). Both ideologies absolutize what is finite to offer a total and comprehensive view of the human and of the world. Marxism exalts the ultimacy of the collective society to the detriment of the dignity of the individual; liberal ideology exalts the autonomy of the individual to the detriment of the common good. Both deny transcendence. Marxism, in its atheistic vision, holds that everything comes to be through conflict and struggle of classes till the classless society is achieved. Liberal ideology promotes a way of life in which the ultimacy lies in the consumption of goods—a practical atheism that denies the transcendent meaning of human fellowship, as rooted in God.

Paul holds that there is an intimate link between and among the various levels of Marxism, and it is an illusion to think that employing it at one level—the Marxist tools of analysis—is confined to that level alone and is not infused with the ideology of class struggle and the kind of totalitarian and violent society that Marxism envisions. Paul appeals for Christian discernment based on faith-inspired principles and criteria, that those who are attracted to certain aspects or principles of ideologies may see them as they are.

Human Aspirations to Equality and Decision Making

The third substantive innovation in *Octogesima Adveniens* is found in Paul's treatment of the fundamental human aspirations to equality and decision making.

> While scientific and technological progress continues to overturn man's surroundings, his patterns of knowledge, work, consumption, and relationships, two aspirations persistently make themselves felt in these two contexts, and they grow stronger to the extent that he becomes better informed and better educated: the aspiration to equality and the aspiration to participation, two forms of man's dignity and freedom. (no. 22)

In the earlier encyclicals this aspiration to equality was not viewed as innate to human nature or to human dignity. In fact, what is innate to nature is inequality. Leo writes in *Rerum Novarum* that "humanity must remain as it is. . . . There naturally exist among mankind innumerable differences of the most important kind; people differ in capability, in diligence, in health, and in strength; and unequal fortune is a necessary result of inequality in condition. Such inequality is far from being disadvantageous either to individuals or to the community" (*RN*, no. 14). Hierarchy and inequality are natural, and "all striving against nature is in vain" (*RN*, no. 14). Far from being disadvantageous, Leo viewed hierarchy and inequality as necessary for the good of all. There are roles and functions for each one to fulfill, some high and some low, but all are essential for society to be sustained. "There is nothing," he writes, "more useful than to look at the world as it really is" (*RN*, no. 14). And that for him means to see the consequences that sin has on human work. To endure the punitive burden of work is bitter and hard, but it is expiation of sin, the reality of which shall remain with humankind as long as life lasts. "To suffer and endure, therefore, is the lot of humanity. . . . No strength and no artifice will ever succeed in banishing from human life the ills and troubles which beset it" (*RN*, no. 14).

This view of the world, in which hierarchy and inequality are the lot of humanity, because it was the way the world was ordained, is reiterated in other papal teachings after Leo. In 1937, Pius XI, in *Divini Redemptoris*, writes: "It is not true that all have equal rights in civil society. It is not true that there exists no lawful social hierarchy" (*DR*, no. 33). In his Christmas address of 1945 Pius XII clarifies the view that inequality belongs to the nature of things:

> In a nation worthy of the name, inequalities among the social classes present few or no obstacles to their brotherly union. We refer, of course, to those inequalities which result not from human caprice, but from the nature of things—inequalities in intellectual and spiritual growth, with economics, with differences in

individual circumstances, within, of course, the limits prescribed by justice and mutual charity.[23]

Papal teachings since Paul VI and John XXIII have broken radically from this view that inequalities are due to nature. For if the gross inequalities in the human lot are all due to nature, then there is no place for human effort and creativity. All are trapped in their given conditions; no one can go beyond the limits to which he or she has been assigned. This view of the human person is bereft of the eschatological hope that gives impetus to the development of persons and societies. And it is also blind to what sin has done to creation and humanity, in the structures and systems of the world, beyond the punitive burden it has imposed on individuals. This view is as old as it is static and myopic.

Paul built on and extended the view of John, who forged the transition from the old to the new in papal teachings. Although John still quoted both Leo and Pius XII regarding the inevitability of classes as founded in nature, in *Mater et Magistra* he pointed out that "the greater amount of responsibility desired today by workers in productive enterprises, not merely accords with the nature of man, but also is in conformity with historical developments in the economic, social, and political fields" (*MM*, no. 93). With his insistence on some degree of participation in decision making even by the workers, given historical developments, like more universal access to education, he completely broke from the traditional understanding of hierarchized inequality, where some, by virtue of nature, rule, and others follow.[24]

Paul teaches that participation in decision making is essential to human nature and the development of its potential. People are not unequal at fixed levels, because as persons share more and more responsibility in decision making, human potential that is open ended is developed at higher levels. Equality is founded in human dignity. In correlation with greater equality is Paul's emphasis on participation.[25]

---

[23] *Acta apostolic sedis* (AAS) 37 (1945), 14.

[24] See Gudorf, "Commentary on *Octogesima adveniens*," 321.

[25] Paul VI's interpretation of John XXIII's *Mater et Magistra*, nos. 91–97, noted in *Octogesima Adveniens*, no. 47, assumes that natural human equality requires participation, but *Mater et Magistra* explains the reason for participation in decision making: "It should be emphasized how necessary, or at least very appropriate, it is to give workers an opportunity to exert influence outside the limits of the individual productive unit, and indeed within the ranks of the commonwealth. The reason is that individual productive units, whatever their size, efficiency, or importance within the commonwealth, are closely connected with the overall economic and social situation in each country, wherein their own prosperity ultimately depends" (nos. 97–98).

In *Octogesima Adveniens* he upholds the critical value of participation in ensuring quality rather than just quantity in economic growth:

> Without doubt, there has been just condemnation of the limits and even the misdeeds of a merely quantitative economic growth; there is a desire to attain objectives of a qualitative order also. The quality and the truth of human relations, the degree of participation and responsibility, are no less significant and important for the future of society than the quantity and variety of the goods produced and consumed. (no. 41)

John spoke of participation in the realm of economics; Paul goes beyond and shifts it to the realm of politics:

> The passing to the political dimension also expressed a demand made by the man of today: a greater sharing in responsibility and in decision making. The legitimate aspiration becomes more evident as the cultural level rises, as the sense of freedom develops and as man becomes more aware of how, in a world facing an uncertain future, the choices of today already condition the choices of tomorrow. (no. 47)

Paul is aware of the increasing complexity and the heightening risks of decision making, but rather than limiting participation, modern forms of democracy must be devised within which people are more informed and are able to express themselves and be engaged in shared responsibility.

Thus Paul, building on John's earlier call for worker participation in decision making in economic enterprises and broadening the extent of his teaching on equality and participation in political decision making, renders the traditional view of hierarchical inequality based on nature a foregone reality. A new view of the human and of human interactions and relationships in the various spheres of life has been established, and the church, rather than being a steward of the old, becomes a prophet of the new. How the church would itself live out its own vision is, however, another story.

Whatever Happened to Octogesima Adveniens?

Mary Elsbernd addresses the failure to implement *Octogesima Adveniens*'s innovative vision and principles. *Octogesima Adveniens*, says Elsbernd, "held that Catholic social teaching had been worked out in history, i.e., that Catholic social teachings are historically constituted, that the local Christian community contributed to the development of Catholic social teachings, and that a single universal message is not the papal mission."[26] From the time of John Paul II, the church reversed these new directions set by *Octogesima Adveniens*. John Paul referred to Catholic social *doctrine,* not to Catholic social *teaching,* to stress the authoritative language of the term, as if it goes back to the gospel in an unbroken chain.[27] The *Catechism of the Catholic Church,* issued under John Paul II, upholds the message that the social teaching of the church is a single universal message (no. 2032), which reverses the teaching of Paul on the diverse expressions and thrusts of the social teaching arising from different contexts.

Furthermore, John Paul never cited *Octogesima Adveniens,* no. 4, which stated that it is neither the ambition nor the desire of papal teaching to put forth a unified message or put forward a solution that claims a universal validity. His reversal of this principle is attested in *Laborem Exercens,* where he upholds the role of the magisterium in bringing up to date "ageless Christian truth"; only the application of this truth is the role of the laity in their historical contexts. It is not within their competence to give shape to the development of the Christian truth.[28]

It seems the failure of *Octogesima Adveniens* is largely because of John Paul II. But commentators on *Octogesima Adveniens* point also to Paul VI himself. The factors that brought about the failure of its implementation were present in Paul, and in the council, and throughout the self-understanding of Christian communities as well. Contrary to its apparent impact on many appreciative Latin American liberationists and European and North American progressives, there are clues in *Octogesima Adveniens* that explain its subsequent lack of influence.[29] Before looking into these clues, however, it is important to look first into the change in historical context that emerged after its issuance—the collapse of the communist bloc.

The demise of Soviet communism, the progressively economic downtrend of communist Cuba, and the poverty and underdevelopment of North Korea (while capitalism rose in China and in Vietnam) brought new currents into the world. Marxism was discredited throughout most of the globe in the face of the triumph of Western

[26] Elsbernd, "Whatever Happened to *Octogesima Adveniens?*" 40.
[27] Ibid.
[28] Ibid., 50.
[29] Gudorf, "Commentary on *Octogesima Adveniens,*" 326.

capitalism, despite the cry for economic justice on a world scale. *Octo-gesima Adveniens*'s discourse on Marxism and its openness to Marxist tools turned into a historical footnote in this turn of world events.[30]

But beyond this development outside of the church, the failure to implement the innovative principles of *Octogesima Adveniens* was due to the context in which these principles were conceived. Paul's insistence on participation in decision making was only so for the socioeconomic and sociopolitical world. There was no reference to the internal life of the church. His was only a call to Christians to be engaged and to participate in the world. Nowhere in *Octogesima Adveniens* does he indicate how Christians can participate in the church's decision making regarding the social issues and problems in the world. The new vision of participation of more and more people in the shaping of the world to come does not replace the old vision of non-participation of the laity in the shaping of the church to come. The internal life of the church remained as it was, while Paul taught and preached how life in the world should change.[31]

While *Octogesima Adveniens* is replete with the language of historicity, development, newness, complexity, risks, as in all papal teaching, it continues to refer to the light of the gospel. This is the language of timeless, permanent, and unchanging teaching. While the words of the gospel do not change, biblical scholarship has shown how the meanings of these words are interpreted in new social contexts and from different historical perspectives. Christians are to adhere to the meaning of the gospels, not to the words. The implication of this apparent split between church teachings that are affected by historical consciousness and development and the gospel, which is beyond and outside of any historical change, is that while the church attempts to forge ahead, it is pulled back by old structures of thinking. There is a deep ambivalence that comes from long entrenched ways of thinking, even as the church negotiates new avenues and approaches to evolving reality.[32]

This same split is shown in the ethical method that deals with medical/sexual issues, on one hand, and social teaching, on the other hand. Social teaching was open to the historical hermeneutic, while teaching on medical/sexual issues continues to draw its principles from the classical approach. This classical approach affects the way the other aspects of the life of the church are treated; the church as an institution; the

---

[30] Ibid.
[31] Ibid.
[32] Ibid., 326–27.

roles of laity, clergy, and religious; and issues of due process are all put under juridical norms defined as unchangeable, rooted in revelation, as mediated in nature, scripture, or tradition. Thus, the norms that govern the fixed structures of our sexual nature as well as equally fixed structures of the inner life of the church are different from those which govern all our other aspects and capacities as human beings. Why this is so baffles the mind. There is nothing that is not created or human, even the mediations of revelation. And all creation is subject to change and development, or at least possesses the potential for change and development.[33]

The gaps and ambivalence in papal teaching result in contradiction—contradiction between its assertions on participation of Christians and all people of good will in decision making in social, economic, and political affairs in accord with human nature and dignity and the exclusion of laity from decision making on the inner life of the church; contradiction between assertions of episcopal collegiality based on the collaborative search for the truth, and assertions of papal authority that claim it as the exclusive locus of power and authority. These contradictions are manifested in Paul himself. His rejection of exclusive power and authority in *Octogesima Adveniens* is contradicted by his refusal to admit collegial power sharing in his executive decision to eliminate discussion of birth control from the Second Vatican Council's sessions on the pastoral constitution. This was followed by *Humanae Vitae,* which defied the results of the broader consultation of theologians, experts, and married people. When the pope who authored *Octogesima Adveniens*, which declared universal participation in decision making as integral and essential to human nature and human dignity, refuses to share power and authority with his fellow bishops, then how can his encyclical be validated, promoted, and widely accepted?[34]

This same contradiction is present in his teaching on women's roles. While he advocates that women participate equally in cultural, economic, and social life, he also teaches that women's primary role is in the home as mothers, for the care and welfare of children. Without stressing as well the responsibility of men to share in domestic duties, he made it seem as if women are made to carry a double burden if they are to fulfill papal teaching. And while he advocates women's rights to participation in world affairs, he excludes them from participation in the affairs of the church. He excludes women first from

---

[33] Ibid., 327.
[34] Ibid., 327–28.

being acolytes and lectors, and then from being ordained as priests. In *Ministeria Quaedam* the exclusion was especially a cause for consternation, because in the document Paul claimed that in continuity with the opening of the church to the world at Vatican II, and its increased emphasis on the church as community, these roles are opened to the unordained by virtue of their baptism.[35]

> Mother Church earnestly desires that all the faithful should be led to that full, conscious and active participation in liturgical celebrations which is demanded by the very nature of the liturgy. Such participation by the Christian people as "a chosen race, a royal priesthood, a holy nation, a purchased people" (1 Pt 2, 9) is their right and duty by reason of their baptism. In the restoration and promotion of the sacred liturgy, this full and active participation by all the people is the aim to be considered before all else.[36]

The document, however, summarily excluded women from becoming lectors and acolytes despite their baptism.[37] His exclusion of women from ordination cannot be reconciled with his assertions and declarations in *Octogesima Adveniens*, because unordained women have no right or authority to participate in sacramental administration and in the governance of the church.[38] If excluded from participation in the very life of the church, women are, thus, not worthy of the human dignity that is at stake in participation in decision making.

Whatever happened to *Octogesima Adveniens*? I believe that Christine Gudorf has best responded to this question:

> If in Vatican II the church opened its door to historicity, Paul nevertheless attempted to preserve some small space for stasis. OA thus contains at least some hints prefiguring the later gulf that developed between the methods and assumptions governing papal thought on the Church itself, its internal governance, its teaching on sexuality, and, to far lesser extent, its interpretation of scripture and tradition, as opposed to its teaching on the

---

[35] Ibid., 328.

[36] Paul VI, *Ministeria Quaedam*, August 15, 1972, *AAS* 64 (1972): 530; trans. *The Pope Speaks* 17/1 (1972): 256.

[37] "In accordance with the venerable tradition of the church, installation in the ministries of lector and acolyte is reserved to men" (*Ministeria Quaedam*, 553; *The Pope Speaks*, 261).

[38] *Code of Canon Law*, trans. Canon Law Society of America (Washington, DC: Canon Law Society of America, 1983), c.129.1.

world, its politics, culture, economics, and interrelationships as revealed by the sciences. This gulf widened under John Paul II, but it began with Vatican II and Paul VI himself.[39]

Conclusion

Was *Octogesima Adveniens* a visionary document written ahead of its time? Or was it written in one moment of enlightenment when the church saw things as they ought to be? If it was written ahead of its time, we hope that Catholic social teaching will again revisit the teachings of *Octogesima Adveniens* and will pursue the precedents it set within the cycle of change, decline, and renewal. If it was written at a moment of enlightenment when the church saw things as they ought to be, then we hope that the church will define itself more and more clearly by the light of this moment and become the church that moves and is directed by the ever renewing and life-giving Spirit.

[39] Gudorf, "Commentary on *Octogesima Adveniens*," 328.

7

Centesimus Annus

Pope John Paul II issued *Centesimus Annus* on the one hundredth anniversary of *Rerum Novarum*, the 1891 encyclical of Pope Leo XIII and the first of the social encyclicals of the Catholic Church in the modern era. Amid the historical changes of the time, John Paul II declares how the Catholic Church should respond in light of the primary values that define its vision. He is, however, no mere observer of events. He writes from his experience as a catalyst of the dramatic changes that took place in Poland, his homeland, and their ripples in Eastern Europe. Contextualizing the encyclical in these changes allows us to view the forces that shaped its vision and thrust.

Readers should note that with the exception of directly quoted material, I have paraphrased the source material in O'Brien and Shannon's *Catholic Social Thought* and also provided a paragraph number for the original text. In the directly quoted sections, I do not identify with the gender exclusion of women in the language used. I quoted as is, however, to preserve the historicity of the original text.[1]

Historical Context

The writing of the encyclical was influenced by the political movements of the day and by the ecclesial stance of the church in regard to the current matters of politics and economics. The church was at the threshold of a new era, and it responded with the weight of its tradition as challenged by the contemporary world.

---

[1] David J. O'Brien and Thomas A. Shannon, *Catholic Social Thought: The Documentary Heritage* (Maryknoll, NY: Orbis Books, 1992). The official texts of these encyclicals are also available on the vatican.va website. Please note that paragraph numbers may vary, depending on the translation used.

Political Movement for Change

The radical turn of events that resulted in the dramatic trans-formation of communism in the Soviet Union and Eastern Europe became the context of *Centesimus Annus*. The document is infused with the spirit of its writer, who lived under the harsh rule of com-munism in Poland. As a manual laborer, a teacher, and later a bishop in Krakow, Karol Wojtyla heard the cries of his people in their fight for freedom from the shackles of authoritarian rule. These cries were never silenced in his memory, and as he wrote this centenary encyclical, they came back to him, more real than they ever were, as he saw the events unfolding in his homeland and elsewhere in Eastern Europe.

Poland was the leader of the nations of Eastern Europe that were extricating themselves from the rule of the Soviet Union. At the helm of this movement was a labor union, Solidarity, based at a shipyard. While practically all the sectors of society—intellectuals, students, business people—were involved in the movement propelled by Soli-darity, it was the working people, through their organization, and with their grit and determination, who were its heart and soul. A revolution that was nonviolent in its spirit and struggle, in the face of the overwhelming state police power, it was upheld by John Paul as a model of an effective political movement. It was clearly given his support as the Roman pontiff, without accusation of preference or bias, because of its momentous significance not only for Poland but for the world.

While the historical drama was still unfolding at the time of the publication of *Centesimus Annus*, its timeliness was far more novel than prophetic. When Leo wrote his encyclical, he spoke of "new things" *(Rerum Novarum)* that were revolutionizing the world. But while these "new things" that he spoke of actually had been simmer-ing for the past 150 years, those that John Paul wrote about emerged over only two or three years and rapidly turned the world upside down. Given the fact that he was not a mere observer of these events but personally supported them, particularly in Poland, he had an un-precedented opportunity to speak as a teacher and pastor to the social questions faced by the world at the threshold of a new era.[2]

---

[2] This historical development is adapted from Daniel Finn, "Commentary on *Centesimus Annus (On the Hundredth Anniversary of* Rerum Novarum)," in *Modern Catholic Social Teaching: Commentaries and Interpretations,* ed. Kenneth Himes, 436–66 (Washington, DC: Georgetown University Press, 2004), 437–41.

Church Engagement with Systems of Thought and Ideologies

The ecclesial context of the encyclical was marked by a shift in the church's engagement of its institutional wisdom on secular matters of politics and economics. This was a shift from the position of triumphalism that the church took during the age of Leo and Pius XI—a position taken even on matters that were not directly within the competence of the church. This resulted in certain errors in assessment of systems and ideologies.

Early papal teachings pointed to the medieval approach to the organization of economic life, primarily based on the guild system. Leo writes: "If society is be cured now, in no other way can it be cured but by a return to the Christian life and Christian institutions" (*RN*, no. 22). In the guild system the custodians of the morality of economics were the producers in each line of artisanship. Pius promulgated corporatism: workers, managers, and owners in each line of industry are organized to deal with problems specific to them. Meanwhile, however, the rights and demands of workers were being fought for and negotiated in contexts beyond these medieval structures promulgated by the church, with the involvement of national governments.[3] With the emergence of trade unions, beyond the concept of Leo's workmen's associations, the struggles of the workers were waged in the public arena, between trade unions and companies.

When John Paul set out to write his encyclical, he did not propose new institutions, as Leo and Pius did, but became a critical voice of values relative to the structures of economic and political life.[4] Here, he demonstrated the competence of the church relative to matters of economics and politics, as negotiating between two extremes: one, the claim that the church has no competence in economic and political issues; and the other, the answers to complex and complicated economic and political questions can be directly and neatly provided in an unmediated way by scriptures and the Christian faith.[5] The competence of the church lies in the realm of morality, and all human realities, including economics and politics, have a moral dimension. To this dimension the church addresses its teaching. A critical moral

---

[3] One of the factors that caused the demise of corporatism was a distorted version of its original idea. For further discussion, see Marie J. Giblin, "Corporatism," in *The New Dictionary of Catholic Social Thought*, ed. Judith A. Dwyer (Collegeville, MN: Liturgical Press, 1994), 246.

[4] Finn, "Commentary on *Centesimus Annus*," 439.

[5] Ibid.

view of economics and politics, however, is based on a technical understanding of the workings of their systems and structures. The church thus relies on experts for this understanding, as it discerns its moral position relative to human values that these systems and structures promote or violate.

Another aspect of the ecclesial context of the encyclical was the quarter-century of theological developments concerning the relation of faith and economics since Vatican II. Daniel Finn cites liberation theology, the neoconservative defense of capitalism, and the publication of detailed responses to economic issues by various national episcopal conferences as deserving mention in considering these developments.[6] The first development was the emergence of a new theology following the shift from the first-world theology that Gustavo Gutiérrez and other Latin American theologians criticized as not addressing the realities of their people, many crushed by the weight of extreme poverty, while a few live wasteful and opulent lives.[7] These theologians developed what is called liberation theology, based on three central insights.

First, theology is a second moment, not a first moment, in any given situation. The first and prior moment is an already existing life of faith. This means that theology is engaged as a second moment of reflection on the praxis of faith. Second, liberation theology is built on the witness of Christ in the gospel in a life totally committed to the poor and the marginalized in society. And third, it teaches that the work of God in the world is a work of liberation, which reached its fullness in the ministry of Christ, and which continues today in our times. "This commitment embodies the 'preferential option for the poor,' a phrase that within a decade began appearing in episcopal and papal documents."[8]

Liberation theology has also taken root in other parts of the world; it has taken various articulations among women and racial and ethnic minorities. It counts as its adherents theologians and other academics in North America and Europe. Liberation theology has been viewed with suspicion by church authorities. They hold that this theology criticizes the abuses of capitalism, but it also endorses socialism, a point that can conflict with Catholic social teaching. In particular, its uncritical use of the Marxist tools of analysis deviates from the

---

[6] Ibid.

[7] See Gustavo Gutiérrez, *A Theology of Liberation: History, Politics, and Salvation*, trans. and ed. Caridad Inda and John Eagleson (Maryknoll, NY: Orbis Books, 1973).

[8] Finn, " Commentary on *Centesimus Annus*," 440.

caution the church counsels in their use because of their intrinsic connection with the ideological vision of Marxism. It also opposes the concept of development espoused by the United Nations and even in church teaching, which views poverty as a state at the lower level of development and as a process, rather than as a consequence of structural and systemic injustice that the poor must be liberated from.[9]

A second important development prior to *Centesimus Annus* was the moral defense of capitalism by conservative Catholics. Many have criticized the capitalist system; a few have defended it. One of these few is Michael Novak, who views the economic system as only one element of a three-part social system referred to as "democratic capitalism." Together with the economic system are the political system and the institutions of the "moral-cultural system," which act as checks and balance for each other. Thus, while free economy leaves people to make their choices, good and bad, the moral-cultural systems (especially churches) can avert the bad by exhorting people to choose good.[10] John Langan, however, chides the neoconservatives for naiveté in thinking that the moral-cultural systems are independent of the economic order and act as a sort of check on it. He points out that some of the largest institutions with a hold on the cultural shape of American society (television networks, large entertainment conglomerates, and so on) are profitable and powerful economic corporations. Many of these institutions can be blamed for what is empty and superficial in American culture.[11]

Neoconservatives also hold that it is not the maldistribution of goods that is the cause of poverty. They view the prosperity of the industrialized countries as the result of the productivity of their citizens. They reject the equation of prosperity of industrialized nations with the exploitation of the poor nations, even if abuses are not always avoided. They hold that the market is still the best economic arrangement for human flourishing if it is backed up by strong cultural institutions and an appropriately restrained political system. Although still an opinion of a few, it has appealed to the secular conservative circles and has gathered a growing support from church people.[12]

The third development in the ecclesial context was the drafting of pastoral letters and other documents on economic life by numerous

---

[9] See Congregation for the Doctrine of the Faith, "Instruction on Certain Aspects of the Theology of Liberation," *Origins* 14/13 (September 13, 1984): 193–204.

[10] Finn, "Commentary on *Centesimus Annus*," 440.

[11] John Langan, "Ethics, Business, and the Economy," *Theological Studies* 55/1 (1994): 112–14.

[12] Finn, "Commentary of *Centesimus Annus*," 440.

national conferences of Catholic bishops around the world.[13] These global initiatives created a context of welcome and expectation for the centenary encyclical of John Paul. Although *Rerum Novarum* and *Centesimus Annus* were one hundred years apart, the cries of the poor are heard in both, the struggle for justice is their common theme, and the hope for social transformation remains their ultimate goal.

In this historical and ecclesial context, we study the encyclical by drawing out its norms and principles for judgment for politics and economics and its directives for action, and in our critical excursus we offer our positive and negative assessments.

Norms and Principles

We draw the norms and principles for judgment from the encyclical based on structured study of it; first, from its rereading of *Rerum Novarum*; second, from its presentation of the Christian anthropology that grounds its ethics of politics and economics; and third, from its focus on norms that govern politics and economics respectively.

Rereading Rerum Novarum

Fragmented Society

Centesimus Annus begins with a rereading of *Rerum Novarum* that describes the fragmented society of its time and then reiterates the human rights of the workers declared by Leo as basic and fundamental, and it upholds the abiding and constant preferential option of the church for the poor. In chapter 1, John Paul reflects on the encyclical of Leo and reiterates his key teachings. First, he situates the encyclical at a time when "a traditional society was passing away and another was beginning to be formed—one which brought the hope of new freedom but also the threat of new forms of injustice and servitude" (no. 4). In this society a new form of property had appeared—capital—and a new form of labor—labor for wages. This new situation divided society into "two classes separated by a deep chasm" (no. 4). There was the enormous wealth of a few as opposed to the poverty of many. Society was torn apart by the conflict between capital and labor, a "conflict between the extremes of mere physical survival on one hand and opulence on the other" (no. 5). John Paul writes that Leo

[13] See Charles E. Curran, "The Reception of Catholic and Social and Economic Teaching in the United States," in Himes, *Modern Catholic Social Teaching*, 469–92.

exercised his papal position and mission as the head of the church—he who was called to feed the lamb and tend the sheep—when he intervened for justice for workers. He envisioned peace as founded on justice in the social and economic context of his time (no. 5).

Rights of Workers

At the core of Leo's encyclical is the dignity of the worker and the dignity of work. "Work belongs to the vocation of every person; indeed, man expresses and fulfills himself by working." There is a social dimension to work because of its intrinsic relationship not only to the family, but also to the common good (no. 6). The largest section of this chapter is devoted to the fundamental rights of the worker, the fulfillment of which is the condition for peace.

The right to property is a basic value, not an absolute value, for it must be complemented by the other principle of the universal destination of the earth's goods. John Paul affirms once again the basis of this right—to possess the things necessary for one's personal development and the development of one's family. He also affirms the relation of the deprivation of private property and poverty, which means that unless the poor are enabled to build their assets, they remain mired in poverty for the rest of their lives (no. 6). In close connection with the right to private property, which is inalienable and proper to the person, is the natural human right to form private associations. In Leo's view this was the right to establish professional associations of employers and workers, or workers alone. The church defends such associations, which have evolved into trade unions, not for ideological prejudices or in order to perpetuate a class mentality, but because this right is a natural right of the human being (no. 7).

Together with this right is the right to the limitation of working hours, the right to legitimate rest, and the restriction against children and women working under conditions not suited to their constitution (no. 7). John Paul quotes the severe statement of Leo: "It is neither justice nor humanity so to grind men down with excessive labor as to stupefy their minds and wear out their bodies" (*RN*, no. 33). The right to a just wage cannot be left to the free consent of the parties, because the employers are only bound to pay according to what is agreed upon. The inequality of the power relationship between the workers and corporations is too large, and the right to subsistence and the obligation to support self and family is too strong, for the work contract to be left to their mutual consent. The "poor who can procure in no other way than by what they can earn through their work" are left at the mercy of the employers who could impose the conditions of the agreement (no. 8). To be just and humane, workmen's wages should be sufficient to support their families (no. 8).

John Paul regrets that, even today, because of what he calls unbridled capitalism, there are still instances of contracts between employers and employees that violate the most elementary justice regarding "employment of women and children, working hours, hygienic condition of the workplace, and fair pay, and this is the case despite the international declarations and conventions on the subject and the internal laws of states." He asserts, as Leo did, that the public authority has the strict duty of protecting the welfare of the workers, because a failure to do so is a severe violation of justice (no. 8).

To all these rights Leo added another right, which John Paul gives as much importance—the right to discharge freely one's religious duties. And in relation to this right is the need for Sunday rest, so that people could have a sacred space where they are freed from the demands of daily living, to turn their thoughts to heavenly things and to the worship they owe to God. No one can take away this human right, which is based on a commandment. In the words of Leo, "No man may with impunity violate the human dignity which God himself treats with great reverence" (no. 9).

State Intervention

John Paul takes note of passages in *Rerum Novarum* that are relevant today, especially in the face of the new forms of property in the world. He first reiterates that Leo criticized the two social and economic systems of socialism and liberalism—socialism for its violation of the right to private property, and liberalism for its neglect of the poor and defenseless. In the criticism of both systems Leo attempted a balance between an overly collective system and an overly individualistic system. The decisive moral criterion is the protection of the poor. Quoting Leo, John Paul writes:

When there is question of defending the rights of individuals, the poor and helpless have a claim to special consideration. The richer population have many ways of protecting themselves, and stand less in need of help from the state; those who are badly off have no recourse of their own to fall back upon, and must chiefly rely upon the assistance of the state. And it is for this reason that wage earners, who are, undoubtedly, among the weak and necessitous, should be specially cared for and protected by the commonwealth. (*RN*, no. 29)

In his reflection on this passage John Paul writes that "this is an elementary principle of sound political organization, namely the more individuals are defenseless within a given society, the more they require the care and concern of others, and in particular the intervention of governmental authority" (no. 10).

John Paul calls this stance for the poor and defenseless "solidarity," which he views as one of the fundamental principles of the Christian view of social and political organization.[14] Leo did not use the same word, but he referred to the same reality in what he called "friendship," a concept already found in Greek philosophy. Paul VI expands the meaning of the term to refer to a "civilization of love" (no. 10).

Rereading the encyclical in the light of contemporary realities enables one to appreciate the church's abiding concern for the poor. "The preferential option for the poor," defined as a special form of primacy in the exercise of Christian charity, is a constant and continuing call in the church teaching. Leo's encyclical on the condition of the workers is an encyclical on the poor and the terrible conditions that industrialization has cast on them, a situation in which multitudes of people find themselves today (no. 11).

John Paul recalls Leo's principle of state intervention to protect the common good, which includes all sectors of life and presupposes the rightful autonomy of each sector. While intervention of the state is necessary, Leo required limits to its instrumental character, inasmuch as in the hierarchy of values, the individual, family, and society are prior to the state and the state exists to protect their rights and not stifle them (no. 11). John Paul asserts that Christian anthropology—a view of the human person as one on whom is imprinted God's image and likeness, and who possesses an incomparable dignity—is the foundational principle of the church's social doctrine (no. 11).

Christian Anthropology: The Foundation of the Ethics of Politics and Economics

From his perspective the person is the entry point of Catholic social thought into the ongoing discussion on the questions in the sphere of politics and economics. Without models to present about economic and political institutions, the church offers its teaching on the fundamental dignity of the human person as the foundation of these institutions.

---

[14] For a further description, see Franz H. Mueller, "Solidarism," in Dwyer, *New Dictionary of Catholic Social Thought*, 906–8.

The Person as the Way of the Church

John Paul speaks of the church over one hundred years as continuously addressing the social question Leo confronted in his time. The sole purpose of the church is care and responsibility for the human person, who has been entrusted to the church by Christ, for the person is the only creature on earth that God willed for its own sake, and for which God has his plan that is a share in eternal salvation. This is not the person in the abstract, but the real, concrete, historical person—each individual. Each is included in the mystery of redemption through which Christ has united himself with each one forever. The church upholds the person as the way of the church and the way of its mission in the church. This and this alone is the principle that inspires the church's social doctrine, for the church's whole wealth of doctrine is the person in his or her concrete reality as sinful and righteous. Only through faith is the person's true identity fully revealed, and it is precisely on faith that the church's social teaching is founded (no. 53).

Christian Anthropology as Theological

John Paul teaches that the meaning of the person is received by the church from divine revelation. He quotes Paul VI: "In order to know man, authentic man, man in his fullness, one must know God." He also quotes Saint Catherine of Siena, who in prayer expressed the same idea: "In your nature, O eternal Godhead, I shall know my own nature."[15] He concludes that Christian anthropology is a chapter of theology, and the church's social doctrine, by its fundamental concern for the human person, "belongs to the field of theology and particularly of moral theology" (no. 55). Founding his teaching on politics and economics on this anthropology, he argues not from technical politics or economics, but from the faith vision of the human person and of society and its bearing on the norms and principles that must govern structures and systems in economics and politics. The way the human person and society are viewed from a faith perspective poses a critique to socialism and capitalism.

Anthropological Errors

John Paul views the fundamental error of socialism as anthropological. When persons are reduced to elements or molecules within a

---

[15] Paul VI, Homily at the final public session of the Second Vatican Council (December 7, 1965), in *Acta apostolic sedis* (AAS) 58 (1966): 58.

social organism, they are devalued and their good is equated to socio-economic data. Denied the exercise of freedom, their moral autonomy as persons is violated; deprived of something they could call their own through their initiative, they are made to depend on the social machine and those who control it. This takes away from them their dignity as persons and destroys the possibility of building an authentic human community (no. 13).

He further says that when the moral autonomy of persons is violated, their "subjectivity" is violated, and so also is the subjectivity of society. This subjectivity of society is "realized in the various intermediary groups, beginning with the family, and including economic, social, and political, and cultural groups, which stem from human nature itself and have their autonomy, always with view of the common good" (no. 13).

The Christian vision upholds the value and grandeur of persons, who enter into relationships of solidarity and communion with others, the reason for which they were created by God. Indeed, it is through the free gift of self that persons truly find themselves. This gift has its origin in the person's essential capacity for transcendence. And by virtue of this capacity, persons cannot only give themselves to a "purely human plan, to an abstract ideal, or to a false utopia." As persons, we give ourselves to another person, to other persons, and to God, who alone can fully accept the gift of ourselves. A person is alienated when this capacity for transcendence is denied, and a society is alienated if it threatens, prevents, or even destroys solidarity and communion (no. 41).

The theological dimension of the Christian anthropology that John Paul stresses contradicts the "atheistic" solution, which deprives the person a most essential dimension of human life, namely, the spiritual. It also contradicts the permissive and consumerist solutions of unbridled capitalism, which views life as lived as if there is no God, as people absolutize the value of material things enjoyed in selfishness, without any regard for the needs of others—a self-absorption that ultimately harms them and others. The church continues to preach its religious and transcendent mission on behalf of humankind (no. 55).

John Paul's view of the person makes him understand the preferential option for the poor as not limited to material poverty, for he holds that there are many other forms of poverty, especially in modern society. There is economic, cultural, as well as spiritual poverty. He says that this preeminent option of the church, which is founded in the gospel, is never exclusive or discriminatory toward other groups. The church's love for the poor is essential for what the church is and what constitutes its constant and abiding tradition (no. 57).

John Paul speaks of solidarity as the way to overcome the widespread individualistic mentality. This solidarity begins in the family with the mutual support of husband and wife and the care different generations give to one another. The family must be a community of work and solidarity. He calls for social policies by the state that provide families with support for bringing up children and for looking after the elderly. In addition to the family are intermediate communities, which are networks of solidarity that strengthen the social fabric, preventing society from becoming an anonymous and impersonal mass. People are neither only producers and consumers of goods nor simply objects of state administration, for the meaning or purpose of life is not circumscribed by the state and the market. Human persons remain above all beings who seek the truth and strive to live in the truth (no. 49).

John Paul holds that *Rerum Novarum*, more than its valid contribution to socioeconomic analysis of the end of the nineteenth century, derives its special value as part of the evangelizing mission of the church. The encyclical proclaims the mystery of God and the mystery of the human person in the light of the mystery of salvation in Christ. Only in this light does the church concern itself with everything else—"the human rights of the individual, and in particular of the 'working class,' the family and education, the duties of the state, the ordering of national and international society, economic life, culture, war, and peace, and respect for life from the moment of conception and death" (no. 54).

Political Ethics

The heart of *Centesimus Annus* is found in the echoes of personal reflections of a man who was part of the transformation of Europe in the extraordinary events of the years 1989 and 1990, when the world saw the collapse of communism. John Paul was not a detached observer of the extraordinary turn of events. The former Soviet president, Mikhail Gorbachev, testifies to the major political role played by the pope in the collapse of communism: "Everything that happened in eastern Europe during these last few years would not have been possible without the presence of this pope, without the leading role—the political role—that he was able to play on the world scene."[16] When reading the encyclical, readers get a feel of John Paul's beliefs and

---

[16] Quoted in Donal Dorr, *Option for the Poor: A Hundred Years of Catholic Social Teaching* (Maryknoll, NY: Orbis Books, 1983), 342.

principles, which are carved from out of his own experience and out of the struggle of his own people in Poland, and he shares these beliefs and principles with his worldwide audience, making a significant contribution to the corpus of norms and principles that grounds ethics in the political sphere.

The Fall of an Oppressive Regime: Factors and Reasons

John Paul presents what he calls the new things of today. He recalls Leo stating (*RN*, no. 3) that by doing away with private property, and turning individual possessions into common property of all, the socialists "rob the lawful possessor, distort the functions of the state, and create confusion in the community" (no. 12).

Speaking in the same vein as Leo, John Paul believes that the violation of the rights of the workers was the decisive factor in the fall of an oppressive regime. It was the throng of working people in Poland in the name of solidarity who toppled the system that presumed to champion their cause—the dictatorship of the working class. It was this people, he says, who out of their lived experience of work and oppression, recovered the content and principles of the church's social doctrine (no. 23). Of great significance is that the collapse was brought about by peaceful protest using only the weapons of truth and justice. Against the teaching of Marxism, which held that only by intensifying social conflicts could they be resolved by violent confrontations, John Paul upholds the power of negotiation, dialogue, witness to the truth, appeal to the conscience of the adversary, and reawakening in the enemy a sense of shared human dignity. "Violence, he teaches, always needs to justify itself through deceit." He calls people to fight for justice without violence, renouncing class struggle in their internal disputes as well as in international conflicts (no. 23).

Without denying the necessity of social conflict, and in fact affirming its positive role when it takes the form of a struggle for social justice, John Paul asserts that what is condemnable in class struggle is the idea that conflict is not restrained by ethical or juridical considerations, or by respect for the dignity of others and consequently of oneself. No reasonable compromise could ever be reached because what is pursued is not the general good of society but a partisan interest, and anything that stands in its way is destroyed. John Paul compares this to the doctrine of total war, at the base of militarism and imperialism, which takes the reins of international relations. Every force is used, including lies, terror tactics against citizens, and weapons of destruction, to impose the absolute domination of one side through the decimation of the other side. John Paul concludes that class struggle and militarism have the same roots, namely, "atheism and contempt for the human, and the use of force above reason and law" (no. 14).

The second factor in the collapse of Marxism was the inefficiency of the economic system, which for John Paul was not simply a technical problem but rather a consequence of the violation of the human rights to private initiative, ownership of property, and freedom in the economic sector. For him, the core problem is the human anthropology at the base of Marxism, which understands the human person only on the basis of economics or class membership. He teaches that the human person is understood more fully in the realm of culture (language, history, and the key human events of birth, love, work, and death). At the heart of every culture is the human person in relation to the deepest of all mysteries—the mystery of God. Different cultures are essentially different expressions of people facing the meaning of personal existence in the face of this mystery. When this mystery is eliminated, John Paul teaches, the cultural and moral life of nations are corrupted (no. 24).

Thus, the true cause of the collapse of Marxism was the spiritual void that resulted in the loss of a sense of direction for the young, but which also led them to an "irrepressible search for personal identity and for the meaning of life." This brought them to a rediscovery of the roots of their national culture and led them to the person of Christ, who alone could satisfy the desire in every human heart for goodness, truth, and life. The witness of those who remained faithful to God under the most difficult human circumstances and in the face of persecution gave courage to those who were searching for meaning. Marxism could not uproot from the human heart the need for God (no. 24).

The events of 1989 showed that law and morality could not be banished from the public arena. But only when sacrifice, suffering, and struggle were united with Christ on the cross could a miracle of peace be possible. And only in this union with Christ could one discern the cowardice that gives in to evil and the violence that gives an illusion of fighting evil (no. 25). In the light of Christ one comes to see the true reality of sin that touches all things that are human. John Paul warns that when people think they possess the secret of a perfect social organization that makes evil impossible, they also think that they can use any means in order to bring that organization into being. Politics then becomes a "secular religion," which draws people to believe in a paradise in this world. No political society can claim to be the kingdom of God, which is ultimately and fully realized at the end of time. Only through Christ's sacrifice on the cross has the victory of the kingdom of God been achieved once and for all. But here and now the Christian life is lived in the struggle between good and evil, in the arena of the human heart itself (no. 25).

After the Collapse of Communism

John Paul writes that it is on the basis of the world situation as he earlier described it, and which he elaborated in the encyclical *Sollicitudo Rei Socialis*, that the unexpected and promising significance of the events of the recent years can be understood. Although these events reached their climax in 1989 in the countries of Central and Eastern Europe, they had roots over a longer period of time and over a wider geographical area. In some countries of Latin American and also of Africa and Asia, dictatorial and oppressive regimes fell one by one in the decade of the 1980s. A difficult transition toward more participatory and just political structures began. The church was a decisive voice for the protection of human rights, especially in situations where polarization, influenced by ideology, threatened human dignity. The church declares that every person, whatever his or her personal convictions, bears the image of God and therefore deserves respect. John Paul observes that the vast majority of people who identify with this faith conviction sought forms of protest and political solutions that are respectful of the dignity of the person (no. 22).

The events of 1989 took place principally in the countries of Eastern and Central Europe, but they had consequences on the entire human family—consequences that were not mechanistic or fatalistic but that were played out in the human arena, where freedom cooperates with grace, within the merciful plan of God, who acts within history. The first consequence was an encounter in some countries between the church and the workers' movement, which had fallen under the influence of Marxism and appropriated Marxist economic and materialistic theories. But the crisis of Marxism reawakened the demand for justice and dignity of work according to the doctrine of the church. The workers' movement was part of a more general movement of people of good will for the liberation of the human person and for the protection of human rights. This movement, far from opposing the church, looked to it for wisdom (no. 26).

But even with the collapse of Marxism, the injustice and oppression that it exploited and on which it fed still plagued the world. John Paul, addressing those searching for new and authentic theory and praxis of liberation, offers the social doctrine of the church, the teaching about the human person, and the church's commitment to fight marginalization and oppression. He calls to memory what in the past led many believers to attempt various ways to find a compromise between Marxism and Christianity. Now, he says, there is a reaffirmation of the theology of integral human liberation. He reflects on the events of 1989 as important not only for the countries of Central and Eastern Europe but also for the countries of the Third World (no. 26).

There were also other social forces and ideological movements that opposed Marxism by setting up systems of national security aimed at controlling the whole society in a systematic way. John Paul warns that increasing the power and control of the state to stop the invasion of communism could run the risk of threatening or even destroying the very freedom and protection of human rights that are necessary to oppose communism. Another way that people sought to defeat Marxism was on the level of pure materialism, by showing how a free-market society could achieve the material human needs not attainable by communism. John Paul argues that while this social model may show the failure of communism, it ends like it, in the sense that it reduces the human person to the sphere of economics and the satisfaction of material needs (no. 19).

During the same period a widespread process of "decolonization" occurred as countries gained or regained their independence and their right to national self-determination. But this put many countries at the beginning of their social reconstruction toward a genuine independence. Their economies were not yet freed from the hold of large foreign companies, which were not committed to the long-term development of host countries. These companies leave after they ravage the resources of host countries. Just as the economic life of these countries was troubled, so also was their political life by the vestiges of foreign control. And because of the problems of education in these countries, they had not developed a class of competent professional people capable of running the state apparatus efficiently and justly, nor were there qualified experts to manage the economy to meet the challenges of development. Given this situation, some people turned to Marxism for a possible shortcut for building the nation and state, and thus, variants of socialism emerged. What mingled in the many ideologies that took shape were legitimate demands for "national recovery, forms of nationalism, and also of militarism, principles drawn from ancient popular traditions that are sometimes in harmony with Christian social doctrine" (no. 20).

Turning once again to the concerns of the peoples of Europe, John Paul expresses his concern that the hatred and ill will due to the widespread injustices committed during and prior to the years in which communism dominated would reemerge unless people grew in the spirit of peace and forgiveness. What is needed, he believes, are concrete steps to consolidate international structures to arbitrate conflicts and build peace. A great effort must be directed to the moral and economic rebuilding of countries that have abandoned communism. The fall of Marxism has highlighted the reality of interdependence among peoples, for peace and prosperity are goods that belong to the whole human race. John Paul teaches that peace and prosperity cannot be enjoyed at the cost of other people's rights and well-being (no. 27). He particularly speaks of the need for aid from other nations for former communist countries that are rebuilding their social order and economic systems. These are countries that have suffered the consequences of historical events that were violently imposed on them and that prevented them from pursuing their own path of economic and social development (no. 28).

The assistance he asks for former communist countries, particularly from the countries of Europe, is also good for the interest and welfare of Europe as a whole, because there can be no peace if people live in situations of "economic disorder, spiritual dissatisfaction, and desperation." John Paul, however, asks that the help that is given to rebuilding the former communist countries not lessen the assistance for the third-world countries, whose people live under worse conditions of poverty. What he envisions is the mobilization of resources, which he says are not lacking in the world, for economic growth and common development. Enormous resources could be diverted from disarming huge military machines, which were constructed for the conflict between East and West. He says that there could even be more abundant resources if in place of war, reliable procedures for conflict resolutions could be set up that would result in greater arms control and arms reduction. There should also be measures against the arms trade, especially in third-world countries. When he speaks of the need for assistance for people in great want and need, he warns against the mentality that considers the poor as burdens. The poor have a right to the goods of the earth, through the dignity of their work, in a world that is just and prosperous for all. John Paul teaches that the advancement of the poor is the advancement of the whole human race (no. 28).

Ideologies, War, Peace

When hatred and injustice are systematized by ideologies, violating the most fundamental truth about the person, these ideologies take over entire nations and drive them to act (no. 17). *Rerum Novarum*, writes John Paul, opposed ideologies of hatred and taught that violence and resentment could be overcome by justice. He warns that true peace is never just the silencing of guns, as a result of military victory. Peace is the removal of the causes of war and the establishment of genuine reconciliation among peoples. It is for this reason that for many years there has been in Europe and in the world "a situation of non-war rather than genuine peace." Half of the continent lived under the communist dictatorship while the other half lived under its threat. The ideological domination of communism destroyed the historical memories of peoples and the roots of their culture; many were compelled to leave their homeland or were forcibly deported (no. 18).

John Paul speaks of the unbridled self-interest that brings so much darkness into the world against the light that comes from the good in people's hearts. He speaks of the error of freedom that violates the truth and the duty to respect the rights of others. The extreme consequences can be seen in the tragic wars that ravaged Europe and the world in the twentieth century. Some of these resulted from militarism and exaggerated nationalism and from related forms of totalitarianism; some were civil wars of an ideological nature. These wars, as John Paul reflects, have built up hatred and resentment caused by so many injustices on the national and international levels, violating the most basic of human rights as entire peoples were exterminated. The Holocaust remains a diabolical symbol of the aberration of the heart when it turns against God (no. 17).

Extremist groups that took the path of violence found ready military and political support, while those that took the path of peaceful and humane solutions were left unaided. John Paul points to the precariousness of peace following the Second World War, which led to the militarization of many third-world countries and to the fratricidal conflicts that tore apart their societies, as well as to the spread of terrorism. He also speaks of the threat of atomic war that could exterminate the world. Such destruction is in the hands of science, which created a lethal weapon and put it at the disposal of ideologies of hatred and destruction (no. 18). On the occasion of the tragic war in the Persian Gulf, John Paul wrote his impassioned cry against war:

"Never again war!" No, never again war, which destroys the lives of innocent people, teaches how to kill, throws into upheaval even the lives of those who do the killing and leaves behind a trail of resentment and hatred, thus making it all the more difficult to find a just solution of the very problem which provoked the war. . . . It must not be forgotten that at the root of war there are usually real and serious grievances: injustice suffered, legitimate aspirations frustrated, poverty, and the exploitation of multitudes of desperate people who see no real possibility of improving their lot by peaceful means. (no. 52)

John Paul describes a world besieged by an insane arms race that takes away massive resources which could have built and developed poverty-stricken countries and used them instead for war and destruction. Science and technology are made to conspire with the lethal goals of war. Wars fought with enormous bloodshed in various parts of the world are fueled by ideologies that provide them with doctrinal justification (no. 18).

The culture of a nation derives its character from the open search for truth, which is renewed in every generation (no. 50). This truth continually speaks to us of our active commitment to our neighbor and demands of us a shared responsibility for building peace. This commitment is not limited to one's own family, nation, or state, but embraces all of humankind, for no one should be excluded from concern, especially in times of great need (no. 51). John Paul particularly calls for ways other than war to resolve conflict; because of the ever-closer links among people, it would be very difficult to limit its human cost.

Human Rights and Democracy

The reality that took center stage was the spread of communist totalitarianism over more than half of Europe and over other parts of the world. John Paul saw some hope in the positive efforts in some countries to rebuild a democratic society inspired by social justice to break the hold of communism on masses of exploited and oppressed people. These were efforts to preserve the free-market mechanisms and to strengthen the stability of currency and to foster harmony of social relations—"the conditions for steady and healthy economic growth in which people through their own work can build a future for themselves and their families." He also notes the efforts to avoid making market mechanism the only point of reference for social life, and to subject these mechanisms to public control to protect the principle of the common destination of material goods. "Abundance of work opportunities, and a solid system of social security, professional training, the freedom to join trade unions and the effective action of these unions, the assistance provided in cases of unemployment, the opportunities for democratic participation in the life of society—all these are meant to deliver work, from the mere condition of a 'commodity' and to guaranteeing its dignity" (no. 19).

John Paul notes that after the Second World War, in reaction to its horrors, there arose a more lively sense of human rights, attested in a number of international documents and recognized by the new "rights of nations" to which the Holy See has always contributed. At the center of this new turn is the United Nations. Not only was there a development in awareness of the rights of individuals, but also in awareness of the rights of nations and the realization of the need to overcome the wide chasms and gross imbalances between and among the geographical areas of the world. This shifted the social question from the national to the global (no. 21).

While John Paul notes these developments with satisfaction, he says that there is so much work left to be done for many nations and peoples. Moreover, the United Nations has not yet been able to build true and effective resolutions of international conflicts that could stop war. He sees this as the most urgent challenge of the times (no. 21).

The church warns against the danger of fanaticism or fundamentalism in the name of ideology, religious or scientific. The danger lies in the imposition of concepts of true and good as defined by these ideologies on people. "Since it is not an ideology, the Christian faith does not presume to imprison changing sociopolitical realities in a rigid schema, and it recognizes that human life is realized in history in conditions that are diverse and imperfect" (no. 46). The Christian faith constantly affirms the dignity of the person and upholds the value of respect for freedom. But only when freedom is rooted in truth does it reach its full development. In a world without truth, freedom loses it foundation, and persons are exposed to the manipulations of ideologies (no. 46).

John Paul upholds the rule of law, but its power must be balanced by other powers and by other spheres of responsibility that keep it within bounds, as *Rerum Novarum* presented the organization of society according to the three powers of legislative, executive, and juridical. The rule of law is violated by totalitarianism, which in its Marxist-Leninist form maintains that some people, because of their knowledge or their class membership, can arrogate to themselves the exercise of absolute power. Totalitarianism arises out of the denial of a transcendental truth, through obedience to which persons achieve their full identity and dignity. Without this truth there is no ultimate arbiter of the law. People's self-interest as a class, group, or nation would pit them against one another. If transcendent truth is not acknowledged, then the force of power pushes people to a struggle, with the one who wields the most power dominating the others, mindless of their rights. John Paul states that the root of modern totalitarianism is found in the denial of the transcendent dignity of persons rooted in their being the visible image of the invisible God, whose rights may not be violated by any individual, group, class, nation, or state (no. 44).

Like his more recent predecessors, John Paul endorses democracy. The church, he writes, upholds the values of the democratic system, which promotes the participation of citizens in making political choices and in which power rests in the governed to elect those who govern them and to replace them through peaceful means. The church, thus, rejects the formation of narrow ruling groups that violate the power of the state for ideological ends. Authentic democracy is exercised by a state ruled by law and on the basis of a correct concept of the human person. It creates the conditions for the development of persons through education in true ideals and of the "subjectivity" of society through participation and shared responsibility. In a democratic society, agnosticism and skeptical relativism may seem to be upheld because any claim to certitude of truth and principles to govern human life goes against the democratic point of view that truth is determined by the majority or is subjected to plurality of ideas. John Paul asserts that "if there is ultimate truth to guide and direct political activity, then ideas and convictions can easily be manipulated for reasons of power. As history demonstrates, a democracy without values easily turns into open or thinly disguised totalitarianism" (no. 46).

Following the collapse of communist totalitarianism and of many other totalitarian and national security regimes, there was a resurgence of democratic ideals and human rights. For democracy to be solidly founded, human rights must be promoted and protected. John Paul points out, however, that even in countries with democratic forms of government, human rights are not always respected. Here he is referring not only to the scandal of abortion, but to all violations of justice and morality. He means also the failure to protect the common good, as groups with electoral and financial power pursue their narrow interest, denying the participation of the general population in the civic and political life of the nation. The church respects the legitimate autonomy of the democratic order and does not engage in the technical aspects of politics by promoting this or that institutional or constitutional solution. The contribution of the church is its vision of the dignity of the human person revealed in all its fullness in the mystery of the Incarnate Word as the transcendent value that must ground politics as a human activity (no. 47).

Ethics of Economics

John addresses a number of issues that concern ethics and economics within the horizon of his theological anthropology—the human dignity of the person as the image and likeness of God. As he deals with issues of economics—private property, work and wages, the role of trade unions, the promise or peril of capitalism, and the call to social transformation—it is his theological anthropology that infuses his appeals for the protection of the poor and the weakest in society.

Private Property and New Wealth

John Paul states: "In *Rerum Novarum*, Leo XIII strongly affirmed the natural character of the right to private property, using various arguments against the socialism of his time." This right, John Paul stresses, which is fundamental for the autonomy and development of the person, has always been defended by the church up to the present day. He points out that the church teaches the right to private property is not absolute, because by its very nature as a human right, it has limits (no. 30). Daniel Finn points out "the subtler shift of the argument from the right *of* private property toward the right *to* property as John Paul phrases it in the opening sentence of chapter 4, the most important section of his encyclical. Not only do those who own property have a right to it but all persons have a claim on property, a right to have sufficient amount of it to maintain themselves and those for whom they have responsibility."[17] John Paul says that while Leo proclaimed the right to private property he also upheld with equal clarity the common destination of created goods. And quoting Saint Thomas Aquinas, he adds: "But if the question be asked, how must one's possessions be used? The church replies without hesitation that man should not consider his material possessions not as his own, but as common to all," because "above the laws and judgments of men stands the law of the judgment of Christ" (no. 30).

---

[17] Finn, "Commentary on *Centesimus Annus*," 446.

He quotes *Gaudium et Spes* (nos. 69, 71), which contains Vatican II's teaching on the social dimension of private property:

> In making use of the exterior things we lawfully possess, we ought to regard them not just as our own but also as common, in the sense that they can profit not only the owners but others too. . . . Private property or some ownership of external goods affords each person the scope needed for personal and family autonomy, and should be regarded as an extension of human freedom. . . . Of its nature private property also has a social function which is based on the law of the common purpose of goods. (no. 30)

The question raised is the origin of material goods that sustain human life, satisfy people's needs, and are object of their rights. As we know from Genesis, the original source of all that is good is the creative act of God. God gave the earth to the whole human race for the sustenance of all, without exception. The fruitfulness of the earth, which satisfies human needs, is God's gift for life. But the earth yields its fruit only through human work. Persons, using their intelligence and exercising their freedom, make part of the earth their own, the part they acquire through work. This, John Paul teaches, is the origin of individual property. No one should stop anyone from having a share of the earth, but all should cooperate so that together they can dominate the earth (no. 31). Finn points out that John Paul's "reliance on the notion of the universal destination of goods stresses the idea underlying the right of individuals to the goods they need, but puts the stress where Aquinas puts it: on God's creative intention for the goods needed, with somewhat reduced emphasis on the claims of individuals."[18]

John Paul speaks of another form of ownership that is becoming no less important than land: possession of "know how," technology, and skill. He stresses that for this new wealth, people need to collaborate in a community of work, which extends to widening circles. People who produce other than for their own use do so in order that others may use it after a just price is established. This kind of interaction, which necessitates a skill to foresee the needs of others and to

---

[18] Ibid., 447. For an extended discussion of rights in Catholic social thought, see Julie Clague, "'A Dubious Idiom and Rhetoric': How Problematic Is the Language of Human Rights in Catholic Social Thought?" in *Catholic Social Thought: Twilight or Renaissance?* ed. Jonathan S. Boswell, Frank P. McHugh, and Johan Verstraeten (Leuven: Leuven University Press, 2000), 125–40.

be able to acquire the necessary combinations of productive factors to meet these needs, is another important source of wealth today. Many goods cannot be produced in isolation but only in cooperation with others, in the pursuit of the common good. "Organizing such a productive effort, planning its duration in time, making sure that it corresponds in a positive way to the demands which it must satisfy, and taking all the risks—all this too is a source of wealth in today's society." In this new kind of wealth the role of creative imagination and discipline is an essential part, as well as initiative and entrepreneurial ability (no. 32). David Hollenbach states that John Paul's inclusion of skills and technology within the property doctrine means that the universal destination of goods requires "the participation of others in this network of solidarity." Without this inclusion, the ownership even of this intellectual property "has no justification."[19] With this new understanding of property, not only does the universal destination of goods refer to those found in nature but also to those that are the result of human work and ingenuity. This makes it even more morally urgent that education, skill formation, and access to technology be made available to all and not simply to the privileged.[20]

John Paul carves out his own position regarding ownership of the means of production, whether in industry or in agriculture. He is against the socialists as far as the right of persons to own the means of production, but he criticizes the capitalists for their disregard for the common good. Setting the moral norm, he teaches that ownership of the means of production is just and legitimate if it is for the service of productive work. It becomes illegitimate when it is used to impede the work of others, in pursuit of profit at the cost of the overall expansion of work and of the good of society, resulting in illicit exploitation, speculation, and the breaking of solidarity among workers (no. 43).

"The obligation to earn one's bread by the sweat of one's brow also presumes the right to do so. A society in which this is systematically denied, in which economic policies do not allow workers to reach satisfactory levels of employment, cannot be justified from an ethical point of view, nor can that society attain social peace" (no. 43).

---

[19] David Hollenbach, "Christian Social Ethics After the Cold War," *Theological Studies* 53/1 (1992): 86.

[20] Jorge Maria Mejía, "*Centesimus Annus*: An Answer to Unknowns and Questions of Our Times," *Ecumenical Review* 43/4 (October 1991): 406.

Work, Wages, and Trade Unions

Wage levels should be adequate for the maintenance of workers and their families, including some savings. This means a continuing provision for skill training for workers and also adequate legislative interventions to stop shameful forms of exploitation, like paying inhumane wages to the most vulnerable workers, such as immigrants and those on the margins of society. John Paul refers to the decisive role of trade unions in negotiating just wages and humane working conditions. They also provide places where workers can express themselves, and thus build a culture where workers share in a fully human way in the life of their places of employment (no. 15).

John Paul writes that besides the earth, persons' principal resource is themselves. It is their intelligence that enables them to discover the potential of the earth's productivity and the many ways it can satisfy human needs. It is their disciplined work with others that makes possible new ways of transforming the natural and human environments. He says that in this process of creation and transformation, important virtues are developed, such as diligence, industriousness, courage in making difficult decisions, and prudence in calculating reasonable risk. Because work is now in the context of a community, rather than in isolation, there is need also to develop reliability and fidelity in interpersonal relationships (no. 32). Citing in particular the business economy, he says that many risks and decisions taken in this field are part of the exercise of responsible freedom. Whereas land and capital were formerly the decisive factors of production, today the most decisive factors are human persons themselves—their knowledge, particularly their scientific knowledge, their capacity for interrelated and compact organization, as well as their ability to perceive the needs of others (no. 32).

John Paul, however, raises the question of how people can truly participate in the new process of creating wealth. The fact is that many people, perhaps the majority today, do not have the means to acquire the basic knowledge to enable them to express their creativity and develop their potential. They have no access to the network of knowledge and intercommunication, and thus, to a large extent they are marginalized. While economic development takes place at increasing levels, they are trapped in the narrow scope of their old subsistence economies (no. 33).

Beguiled by the dazzle of opulence that is beyond their reach, and driven by the need for survival, people in many countries crowd the cities, where they lose their cultural roots, are rendered vulnerable to danger and uncertainty, and are left at the margins of society, disintegrated and unwanted. There are even threats through coercive forms of demographic control that violate human dignity (no. 33). Here we see the role of trade unions and other organizations of workers in defending the rights of workers and protecting their interests as persons, "while fulfilling a vital cultural role, so as to enable the workers to participate more fully and honorably in the life of their nation and to assist them along the path of development" (no. 35).

Speaking again of the right to private initiative and ownership, John Paul teaches that the foundation of this right is the exercise of intelligence and freedom in utilizing the goods of the earth for human development and fulfillment. The social dimension of work is found in the collaboration of people in work for the service of one another and of the community. Here the social character of work becomes critically important, as very little of the world's industry and technology would have been possible were it not for this inherent social character of labor. Various sorts of intellectual property are impossible without social collaboration. When people collaborate in their work for a common goal, they progressively expand the chain of solidarity. The fruit of work contributes to the needs of the family, to the growth of community, of the nation, and ultimately of humanity (no. 32).

If the work of persons is not to be reduced to the level of commodity, the following must be satisfied: "sufficient wage for the support of the family; social insurance for old age and unemployment; and adequate protection for the conditions of employment" (no. 34). John Paul upholds the right to struggle against an economic system which protects the "absolute predominance of capital and promotes the possession of the means of production and of the land, in contrast to the free and personal nature of human work." He, however, does not propose the socialist system as an alternative. What he proposes is a society of free work, of enterprise, and of participation, one not directed against the market; the market, however, must be appropriately controlled by the forces of society and by the state, so as to ensure that the basic needs of the whole society are satisfied (no. 35).

State Intervention: Subsidiarity and Solidarity

John Paul sees the two principles of subsidiarity and solidarity as guiding the extent and limits of state intervention. The principle of subsidiarity was first articulated by Pius XI in *Quadragesimo Anno*. Pius states that it is "gravely wrong to take from individuals what they can accomplish by their own initiative and industry and give it to the community" (*QA*, no. 79). It is similarly unjust "to transfer to the larger and higher collectivity functions which can be performed and provided for by the lesser and subordinate bodies. Inasmuch as every social activity should, by its very nature, prove a help to members of the body social, it should never destroy or absorb them" (*QA*, 79). *Centesimus Annus* states: "A community of a higher order should not interfere in the internal life of a community of a lower order, depriving the latter of its functions, but rather support it in case of need and help to coordinate its activity with the activities of the rest of society, always with view to the common good" (no. 48).

Subsidiarity is used to protect the economic freedom of individuals in the market. Governments should not take over the functions that individuals can properly do themselves. Correspondingly, John Paul upholds the principle of solidarity. A term that appears fifteen times in the document, it is considered "one of the fundamental principles of the Christian view of social and political organization" (no. 10). He does not define solidarity, but drawing from the content and spirit of his writings, one can define it as helping to bear the burden of others as if it is one's own burden, especially that of the poor and weakest in society, and a committed action on the level of individuals, communities, nation, and the entire world to lift them out of their situations of human deprivation on all levels.

These two principles of solidarity and subsidiarity are seen in the subsequent statements John Paul makes in the encyclical. First, he establishes the principle that economic activity, especially the activity of a market economy, cannot be conducted in an "institutional, juridical, or political vacuum." In other words, it is not an autonomous human activity that is not bound to laws that protect individual rights and the common good. Any economic activity presupposes "guarantees of individual freedom and private property, as well as stable currency and efficient services." The principal role of the state is to protect these guarantees—to ensure that those who work can enjoy the fruit of their labor and are paid according to the rules of equity. The violation of these rules by corrupt public officials and illegal economic practices for easy profits weaken the economic order (no. 48). Thus, John Paul supports the mechanisms of the market but insists "that the market be appropriately controlled by the forces of society and by the State, so as to guarantee that the basic needs of the whole society are satisfied" (no. 35).

Rerum Novarum rejected state control of the means of production, which would dehumanize persons as cogs in the state machine. The state, however, has the task of imposing a juridical framework on the economic affairs to ensure that in what is called a free economy, there is a relatively equal playing field, so that one party is not so powerful as to crush the other into subservience. Just reforms should also be enacted to ensure that both the state and society protect the workers from the terror of unemployment. Historically, this protection has been instituted through balanced growth and full employment or through unemployment insurance and retraining programs (no. 15).

The state contributes to the goals trade unions pursue both directly and indirectly: indirectly, according to the principle of subsidiarity, by creating favorable conditions for the free exercise of economic activity that bears fruit in employment and in sources of wealth; directly, and according to the principle of solidarity, by defending the weakest, by setting juridical limits on the autonomy of parties who determine working conditions, and by ensuring the necessary support for unemployed workers. The role of the state in protecting the rights of workers has yielded various support systems through social security, pensions, health insurance, and compensation in case of accidents. These reforms were brought about not only through the instrumental role of the state but also through the workers' movement (no. 15).

Another task of the state is that of overseeing and directing the exercise of human rights in the economic sector. The primary responsibility in this area, however, belongs to individuals and various groups or associations that make up society. This is so because the state could not control every aspect of economic life without restricting the free initiative of individuals. What is within the power of the state is to sustain the conditions for job creation and to stimulate business and economic activities, and to transform practices and policies that are detrimental to growth and progress (no. 48).

The state also has the right to intervene when monopolies cause obstacles to development. In exceptional cases the state can exercise a substitute function to strengthen weak social sectors or business systems to protect the common good. But such functions should be temporary, lest a too-large state take over what properly belongs to these systems and sectors to the detriment of both economic and civil freedom. In recent years the range of the state has vastly expanded, to the point of creating the so-called welfare state. Some countries have taken this direction to respond to widespread poverty and deprivation. However, excesses and abuses in the system have provoked very harsh criticisms of the welfare state. John Paul points out that malfunctions and defects in the social assistance state are caused when the principle of subsidiarity is not respected: "A community of a higher order should not interfere in the internal life of a community of a lower order, depriving the latter of its functions, but rather should support it in case of need and help to coordinate its activity with the activities of the rest of society, always with a view to the common good" (no. 48).

When the state intervenes directly, society is deprived of its responsibility. The social-assistance state leads people to a condition of dependency that diminishes their human initiative and effort. Such a condition is encouraged by an inordinate increase in public agencies, resulting in wasteful spending, and through an excessive bureaucratic system, which reduces people to mere objects of assistance. John Paul says that many needs are not material; there are human needs that can be responded to only by genuine fraternal support and kindness. The human touch of care and compassion can be lost when needs are left to the bureaucratic system of state agencies. The church, faithful to the mission of Christ, has been present and active among the needy, offering them assistance, in ways that do not humiliate them but rather uphold their dignity (no. 48).

Avoiding an excessive impersonal role of the state, John Paul upholds the importance of intermediate communities, starting from the family, that vary in size from local social and cultural groups to much larger economic and political organizations, that "develop as real communities of persons and strengthen the social fabric, preventing society from becoming an anonymous and impersonal mass" (no. 49). These intermediary groups, which he calls "networks of solidarity," when well structured and well led, can truly serve the common good, which is serving the needs of individuals and of the specific groups, with an impact on the entire society, since into the fabric of society is woven all these intermediary groups. He endorses the reliance on society, rather than on the state, in meeting human needs, especially those unmet ones, because they are "best understood and satisfied by people who are closest to them and who act as neighbors to those in need" (no. 48).

With reference to the rightful intervention of the state, it is the task of the state to provide for the defense and preservation of common goods such as the natural and human environments, which should not be left simply to market forces. The collective goods that everyone has a right to in the legitimate pursuit of personal goals must be protected by the state and all of society (no. 40). The common good includes the well-being of every person and the provision of the common goods necessary for the thriving of both individuals and society.

Capitalism: Promise or Peril?

Though not directly stated by John Paul, one of the central questions of the encyclical, and surely the most widely reported theme, is whether capitalism offers promise or is itself a peril. John Paul writes:

> Can it perhaps be said that, after the failure of communism, capitalism is the victorious social system, and that capitalism should be the goal of the countries now making efforts to rebuild their economy and society? Is this the model which ought to be proposed to the countries of the Third World which are searching for the path to true economic and civil progress? (no. 42)

First, John Paul sets the limits within which the church answers the question. He states that the church does not have models to present, because models that are real and truly effective are those that evolve from situations through the efforts of people of good will, who responsibly confront concrete problems in their social, economic, political, and cultural aspects. To solve human and social problems the church offers its social teaching as an indispensable and ideal orientation, a teaching that recognizes the positive value of the market and of enterprise but at the same time calls for the common good as the direction and orientation of the market economy. Church teaching has also consistently protected the rights of the workers, the dignity of their work, and their participation in the broader fields of the industrial enterprise through the exercise of their intelligence and freedom in solidarity with others (no. 43). In other words, it is in the realm of ethics, not in the sphere of technical economics, that the voice of the church is heard.

John Paul states that the evil of capitalism in its earliest period still exists in the condition of "ruthlessness in no way inferior to the darkest moments of the first phase of industrialization" (no. 33). This is true even in the face of great changes that have taken place in highly advanced countries, for capitalism is most inadequate in its placing the dominion of things over people. The poor, besides their extreme deprivation of material goods, lack knowledge and training, which imprisons them in their humiliating subjection (no. 33).

From addressing the problems of the weaker countries, John Paul moves to address those of the more developed countries. He says that "a given culture reveals its overall understanding of life through the choices it makes in production and consumption" (no. 36). It is here that he brings up the phenomenon of consumerism. He criticizes capitalism for the consumerist lifestyle it promotes. He says that consumerism turns upside down the value system which puts interior and spiritual values over material and instinctive wants, while guided by a comprehensive picture that respects all the dimensions of a person. He warns against direct appeals to a person's instincts, while ignoring in many ways the person's intelligence and freedom. The creation of consumer attitudes and lifestyle is objectively improper and is often inimical to physical and spiritual health. The economic system does not have of itself the criteria to distinguish higher forms of human needs from artificial needs which compromise genuine development. What is needed is a great deal of educational and cultural formation, which includes consumer education regarding the responsible use of the power of choice, which also includes formation in social responsibility of producers and people in the mass media. In these matters, which have consequences on society at large, John Paul calls for necessary intervention by public authorities (no. 36).

A striking example of artificial consumption cited as contrary to the health and dignity of the human person, which is beyond control when it becomes an addiction, is the use of drugs. Widespread drug use is a "sign of a serious malfunction in the social system; it also implies a materialistic and, in a certain sense, destructive 'reading' of human needs." Drugs, as well as pornography and other forms of consumerism, exploit human frailty and are taken to fill a void (no. 36).

Equally of concern is the ecological degradation that comes with consumerism. Because of people's unmitigated desire to satisfy their needs, they consume the resources of the earth in an excessive and disordered way. "At the root of the senseless destruction of the natural environment lies an anthropological error" (no. 37). Because human beings have discovered their power to change and transform the world through their work, they have forgotten that everything, even that which they hold in their power, has its origin in God's prior and original gift. They start playing God, setting themselves in the place of God, as they arbitrarily exploit the earth, subjecting it to their unrestrained will, mindless of the God-given purpose of all creation. They end up provoking a rebellion on the part of nature, as it lashes back with its fury, tyrannized as it is by people rather than governed by them (no. 37).

But there is a destruction that is more serious than the irrational destruction of the environment: the destruction of the human environment. This destruction is given even less attention than the preservation of various animal species threatened with extinction, though that is important to preserve the balance of nature in general. There is too little effort, John Paul says, to safeguard the moral conditions for an authentic "human ecology" (no. 38). Not only has God given the earth to humankind, who must use it with respect for the original good purpose for which it was given, but the person too is God's gift. The first and fundamental structure of human ecology is the family, which is formative of persons because it is the place where they receive their education about truth and goodness, about love and being loved, about what it means to be a person. Upholding the family as the sanctuary of life, and at the heart of the culture of life, John Paul condemns all threats to and destruction of life, which includes abortion (no. 39). *Sollicitudo Rei Socialis* denounces the "systematic campaigns against birth. . . . In any event, there is an absolute lack of respect for the freedom of choice of the parties involved." People are "often subjected to intolerable pressures . . . in order to force them to submit to this new form of oppression" (*SRS*, no. 25).

His denunciations are directed not so much against an economic system as against an ethical and cultural system. The economy is only an aspect of the whole of human activity. If consumerism plagues a society as the consumption of goods becomes the center of life and is society's only value, mindless of any other value, the reason is to be found not in the economic system itself, but in the entire sociocultural system, which is bereft of ethical and religious values. Economic freedom is only one dimension of human freedom. When this freedom becomes autonomous of all other values, the human person is seen only as a consumer of goods; economic freedom then loses its essential connection to the essence of human persons and ends up alienating and oppressing them (no. 39).

It appears on the level of individual nations and international relations that the free market holds the most promise of utilizing resources and effectively responding to needs. But he immediately notes this is true only for the needs that are "solvent" in terms of purchasing power and for those resources that are "marketable" insofar as they are capable of obtaining a satisfactory price. But there are many human needs that find no place on the market. And these needs should not be abandoned, allowing those who are burdened by these needs to perish. He also notes that the very poor do not have the purchasing power to buy all the marketable goods. It is urgent that the poor should be helped to "acquire expertise, so they can be included in the circle of exchange, and that they be able to develop skills that make best use of their capacities and resources." But even prior to what John Paul calls the "logic of a fair exchange of goods and the forms of justice appropriate to it," there exists something that is due to human persons, by virtue of their humanity and by virtue of their lofty dignity. He writes: "Inseparable from that required 'something' is the possibility to survive and at the same time, to make an active contribution to the common good of humanity" (no. 34).

Marxism blames capitalist bourgeois societies for the commercialization and alienation of human existence. This critique, however, is based on a materialistic foundation, which is solely in the sphere of relationships of production and ownership. It is for this reason that Marxism, with its myopic view, affirms that only in collective society can alienation be eliminated. John Paul points out that the historical experience of socialist countries has sadly demonstrated that collectivism does not eliminate alienation; in fact, it exacerbates it, on top of its failure to provide basic necessities and economic sufficiency (no. 41).

The historical experience of alienation takes different expressions and contexts. In the West consumerism traps people in the cycle of alienation, as they are completely taken over by false and superficial gratifications rather than experiencing their personhood in authentic ways. Alienation is also found in work, when it is only instrumentalized for maximum returns and profit with no concern whether workers, through their labor, grow as human beings in relationships within a genuinely supportive community, or are diminished in increasing isolation through a maze of relationships of competition and estrangement, in which people are only considered as means and not ends (no. 41).

> Returning now to the initial question: "can it perhaps be said that, after the failure of communism, capitalism is the victorious social system and that capitalism should be the goal of the countries now making efforts to rebuild their economy and society? . . . The answer is obviously complex. If by *capitalism* is meant an economic system which recognizes the fundamental and positive role of business, the market, private property and the resulting responsibility for the means of production, as well as free human creativity in the economic sector, then the answer is certainly in the affirmative, even though it would perhaps be more appropriate to speak of a *business economy, market economy,* or simply *free economy.* But if by capitalism is meant a system in which freedom in the economic sector is not circumscribed within a strong juridical framework which places it at the service of human freedom in its totality, and which sees it as a particular aspect of that freedom, the core of which is ethical and religious, then the reply is certainly negative. (no. 42)

In contrast to some who claim that he gives an unqualified endorsement of capitalism, John Paul criticizes a radical capitalistic ideology that sees all attempts to solve problems are doomed to failure and blindly entrusts solutions to the free play of market forces (no. 42).

Call to Social Transformation

John Paul calls for transformation, not only the transformation of individual lives but also transformation of systems and structures on the national and international levels. It is a comprehensive call for transformation if massive social problems are to be addressed. He teaches that another name for peace is development. "Just as there is a collective responsibility for avoiding war, so too is there a collective responsibility for promoting development." Just as within societies a solid economy must be built and directed toward the common good, so also there must be interventions on the international level to protect the broader common good. But for this to happen, "great effort must be made to enhance mutual understanding and knowledge, and to increase the sensitivity of consciences." The culture that must be built must be one that "fosters trust in the human potential of the poor, and consequently in their ability to improve their condition through work or to make a positive contribution to economic prosperity." But to make this come to fruition, the poor—whether individuals or nations—need to be given realistic opportunities and be provided access to both material and human resources. This demands a concerted worldwide effort to promote development, an effort that will require the more developed to pay some cost that involves sacrificing their positions of power and income, so the needs of those who have so little can be provided for (no. 52).

John Paul takes note of how these reforms are to be established through effective instruments of solidarity that are capable of sustaining an economic growth more respectful of the values of the person. Here he honors the numerous contributions of Christians in establishing "consumers and credit cooperatives, in promoting general education and professional training, and in experimenting with various forms of participation in the life of the workplace and in the life of society in general" (no. 16).

John Paul calls for a change of life in order to limit waste of environmental and human resources, to enable all to have a sufficient share of these resources. Much of the wealth enjoyed by the few is the result of the work and culture of peoples who live on the margins of the international community (no. 52). Unfortunately, the great majority in the Third World still live in this marginalized condition. John Paul, however, said that it would be a mistake to understand this "world" in purely geographic terms. In some regions and in some sectors of that world, development programs have been developed that depend not so much on the use of material resources but on human resources. He mentions that in recent years poor countries were thought to develop if they were isolated from the world market and able to depend on their resources. The result of this was dismal, as these countries suffered stagnation and recession, while those that took part in the economic activity at the global level experienced development. John Paul concludes that the chief problem is fair access to the international market, where poor countries are not exploited for their natural resources and their human resources are properly used (no. 33).

The methods of production, which are constantly changing, require constant retraining and updating to meet the demands of new skills and professional expertise. Those who fail to keep up with the times can become marginalized, as in the case of the elderly, the young people who cannot find their place in society, and in general, those who are the weakest, those who reside in the so-called Fourth World. John Paul particularly cites the situation of women who are in this condition (no. 33).

John Paul rejects the view that the defeat of so-called real socialism leaves capitalism as the only model of economic organization. He admonishes that all barriers and monopolies should be broken down, those which leave so many countries on the margins of development. In their place should be systems and structures that provide individuals and nations with the basic conditions for development. This calls for the entire international community to address such needs and problems. He calls stronger nations to assist the weaker ones so they can find their place in the global economy; the weaker nations must also make the necessary efforts and sacrifices to ensure political and economic stability, to improve the skills of their workers, and to train competent business leaders to manage their economies (no. 35).

The positive efforts being made in the poorer and weaker countries toward development are being derailed by their foreign debt. While the principle that debts must be paid must be upheld, it is not right to demand or expect payment that would bring about consequences as detrimental as pushing an entire people to hunger and despair. The debt should not be paid at the price of sacrifices that are beyond bearing.

It is morally imperative to find ways to lighten, defer, or cancel the debt and to protect the fundamental right of peoples to subsistence and progress (no. 35).

Although the Marxist solution has failed, John Paul says the realities of marginalization and exploitation remain in the world, especially in the Third World, as does the reality of alienation in the more advanced countries. The church raises its voice amid these phenomena that diminish the human person in different ways. The church carries in its heart the burden of vast multitudes, "a yoke little better than that of slavery" (no. 61), as they live in conditions of extreme material poverty.

John Paul again asserts his vision of development, understood not solely in economic terms but in a way that is fully human. It is more than raising peoples to economic levels enjoyed by those in the richest countries; it is rather building a more decent human life by enhancing all individuals' dignity and creativity in their response to their personal vocation in the face of God's call. The apex of development is the exercise of the right and duty to seek God, to know God, and to live with that knowledge (no. 29). This vision becomes a reality if there is a change of lifestyle inspired and sustained by a greater concern for the marginalized. "Justice will never be fully attained unless people see in the poor person who is asking for help in order to survive, not an annoyance or a burden but an opportunity for showing kindness and a chance for greater enrichment" (no. 58).

It is to this individual transformation, as well as systemic and structural transformation, that can be inspired only by the radical spirit of solidarity for the poor, that John Paul calls his readers.

Directives for Action

The encyclical ends with directives for action that implement the principles and norms in the ethical sphere of politics and economics. When convictions and commitments are incarnated in action, they hold the power to change and transform society.

Social Message: Basis for Action

John Paul expresses his desire that his teaching be made known to the Western countries, which, thinking the collapse of "real socialism" is a one-sided victory of their own economic system, fail to see the need to transform it. He also hopes that his message will reach the Third World, where massive populations live in extreme poverty and underdevelopment. He calls and inspires people to urgent action: "Everyone should put his hand to the work which falls to his share, and that at once and straightway, lest the evil which is already so great become through delay absolutely beyond remedy" (no. 56).

The social message of the gospel, John Paul teaches, must not be considered a theory but above all else a basis and a motivation for action. He brings to mind the first Christians, who distributed their goods so no one in the community would be left without food and other necessities. They bore witness to the truth that despite different social origins, it is possible for people to live in peace and harmony. And down the centuries, "the monks tilled the land, the men and women religious founded hospitals and shelters for the poor, the confraternities as well as individual men and women of all states of life devoted themselves to the needy and to those on the margins of society." They were all inspired to live by Christ's words, "just as you did it to one of the least of these who are members of my family, you did it to me (Mt 25:40). These words did not remain a pious exhortation but were made the foundation of concrete Christian life commitment (no. 57).

Witness of Action: Structural and Systemic Change

The social message of the church gains power from its incarnation in the witness of action, rather than from the presentation of its internal logic and consistency. Such witness is particularly empowered by the church's preferential option for the poor—an option that is not limited to material poverty but to all other forms of poverty as well. The church's love for the poor, which is constant in its teaching, impels it more than ever to give attention to a world in which poverty threatens on a large scale in spite of technological and economic progress. There are many faces of the poor who live at the margins of society—the elderly and sick, the victims of consumerism, and refugees and migrants (no. 57).

Love for the poor is made concrete in the promotion of justice. John Paul states:

Justice will never be fully attained unless people see in the poor person, who is asking for help in order to survive, not an annoyance or a burden, but an opportunity for showing kindness and a chance for greater enrichment. . . . It is not merely a matter of "giving from one's surplus," but of helping entire peoples which are presently excluded or marginalized to enter into the sphere of economic and human development. For this to happen, it is not enough to draw on the surplus goods which in fact our world abundantly produces; it requires above all a change of lifestyles, of models of production and consumption, and of the established structures of power which today govern societies. (no. 58)

In other words, because the problem is systemic and structural, the solution should also be systemic and structural.

Action on the Global Level

Because of the globalization of the economy, there is a need for international agencies to institute safeguards for the common good. This is something no individual country, even given its position of global power and leadership, can do. John Paul lists his directives for action regarding this matter. There should be greater coordination and collaboration among the powerful countries; the international agencies must be representative of the collective interests of the family of nations; the situation of peoples and countries that yield the least power in the global arena but are the most burdened with acute and desperate needs must be the primary consideration in the weighing of decisions and consequences (no. 58).

John Paul also stresses the interdisciplinary dimension of the church's social teaching, as it is incarnated in different and constantly changing social, economic, and political contexts. In its dialogue with different disciplines the church opens them up to broader horizons, infused by faith, which upholds the person who is acknowledged and loved in the fullness of his or her dignity. Besides the interdisciplinary aspect is the experiential dimension of the church's social teaching. At the crossroads where Christian life and conscience come into contact with the real world, the church's prophetic voice is heard. There at the crossroads are individuals, families, politicians and statesmen, and other good persons of good will who live by the church's social teaching (no. 59).

Appeal to All Peoples

John Paul makes an appeal to the Christian churches and to all the great world religions, inviting them to offer the "unanimous witness of our common convictions regarding the dignity of man, created by God." He upholds the preeminent role of religions in preserving peace and in building a society worthy of the human person. He calls for openness to dialogue and cooperation among all people of good will, and he addresses particularly individuals and groups with specific responsibilities in the areas of politics, economics, and social life, at both the national and international levels (no. 60).

Critical Excursus

As the centenary encyclical, *Centesimus Annus* is a critically important document in the history of Catholic social thought. It bears witness to the continuity of tradition, but at the same time it breaks open this tradition to an ever-changing world. This critical excursus begins by establishing the genre of *Centesimus Annus*.

Context of Critique: Genre of Centesimus Annus

To offer a critique of *Centesimus Annus* is to first contextualize it in its genre. As John Paul states, the encyclical, just like *Rerum Novarum*, derives its special value as part of the evangelizing mission of the church. As the church engages its institutional wisdom on secular matters, it does not claim an expertise in technical politics and economics. Its competence lies in the realm of morality, and it relies on experts for the understanding of the technical aspects and presents its moral position relative to human values that the political and economic systems and structures promote or violate. John Paul is praised for having demonstrated the competence of the church relative to matters of politics and economics as negotiating between two extremes: one, the claim that the church has no competence in economic and political issues and must be relegated to those that are explicitly spiritual and religious of nature, and the other extreme which is that the answers to complex and complicated political and economic questions can be drawn from scriptures and the Christian faith in a clear, neat, and unmediated fashion.

Given its aforementioned competence, I hold that the most significant contribution of *Centesimus Annus* to the discourse on politics and ethics is its theological anthropology, which grounds the moral criteria against which political and economic structures and systems are judged. The church upholds the value and grandeur of the human person, as the visible image of the invisible God, and only in this light does the church concern itself with everything else. The person is the way of the church, the route the church travels in fulfilling its mission. Only for the protection of the dignity and rights of individuals does the church exist. And it is from this principle that it speaks in its prophetic voice as it puts all of its institutional power on the side of the poorest and weakest in society.

Positive Assessment of the Encyclical

I develop my positive assessment of the encyclical by navigating the moral ecology of politics and economics based on the writing of John Paul. By *moral ecology* I mean the patterns and interrelationships of persons and systems and structures that promote moral values as founded on the theological anthropology of the encyclical. These are the values that must be upheld and promoted if politics or economics meet the requirements of ethics. I consider the moral ecology of politics and economics as the distinctive contribution of the encyclical as it seeks to be a prophetic voice in the arenas of politics and economics.

Moral Ecology of Politics

Hardly any commentator on *Centesimus Annus* has given attention to the corpus of ethical norms and principles on politics in the encyclical. The focus of discourse and debate has been on economics and largely on John Paul's views on capitalism. To miss the teachings of John Paul on politics is to miss the soul of his experience, which he expresses in this centenary encyclical—the events of 1989 and 1990. Although the primary context of his teaching was Central and Eastern Europe, with particular focus on Poland, the relevance of the norms and principles drawn from that context can be wide ranging, as the consequences of the dramatic turn of events in Europe spread to countries in Latin America, Africa, and Asia.

There are primary ethical criteria that constitute the moral ecology of politics in *Centesimus Annus*. First, the ethical determination of any political system is its concept of the human person; second, law and morality should govern in the public arena of politics; third, true peace is not merely the silencing of the guns but the removal of the causes of war and the establishment of genuine reconciliation. In relation to the first ethical criterion, John Paul views the fundamental error of Marxism as anthropological—its concept of the person at its base. It understands the human person only on the basis of economics or on the basis of class membership, and thus it denies the deepest mystery of who the human being is as a person with a supernatural orientation. When this mystery is eliminated, the moral life of any political system is corrupted. The person can be reduced to a cog in a machine and be instrumentalized for ideological ends. But the truth of the matter is, Marxism or any other political system cannot uproot from the human heart the irrepressible need for transcendence, which many give the name God.

The second ethical criterion that requires the necessity of law and morality in the public arena of politics is violated by totalitarianism, which in its Marxist-Leninist form maintains that some people, because of their knowledge or their class membership, can arrogate to themselves the exercise of absolute power. When the transcendent value of the dignity of the human person and the all-embracing value of the common good are denied, then people's self-interests as a class, group, or nation are pitted against one another. John Paul does not deny the necessity of social conflict, and in fact affirms its necessary role in the pursuit for social justice. But what he condemns in what he calls class struggle is the use of force above reason and law, and of all tactics that violate every criteria of truth and justice to decimate the other side for one's partisan interests to dominate, even at the cost of the general good of society. When politics is not restrained by ethical and juridical considerations, it becomes an arena of destruction of the dignity of persons and of the common good. The church upholds the values of authentic democracy, where power rests in the governed and those in power are accountable to those they lead. It rejects any use of power of the state for ideological ends of narrow ruling groups. A democracy that is not founded on true participation and sharing of power, and which violates human rights, descends into totalitarianism.

The third ethical criterion relates to principles that govern war and peace. True peace is never just the silencing of guns. Peace that is founded on justice requires the removal of the causes of war: wide-scale poverty, massive social inequity, violation of basic human rights, oppression of peoples, systemic discrimination, and so forth. Conflicts between and among nations in war take a high human toll. John Paul speaks of the insane arms race, which uses science and technology for destruction and usurps resources for the alleviation of global poverty and social programs for underdeveloped nations. Although the use of violence may sometimes be allowed to stop genocide, John Paul calls for ways to resolve conflict other than war, because the links of lives in a global interdependence are ever so close that the human cost of war cannot be limited. In place of violence and war should be conflict resolution founded on the power of negotiation, dialogue, witness to the truth, appeal to the conscience of the adversary, and reawakening in the enemy a sense of shared dignity—all upholding the theological anthropology at the base of the encyclical.

These three criteria, which shape the moral ecology of politics, are transcultural and universal, for they present values that cut across cultures as they represent what is genuinely and authentically human.

Moral Ecology of Economics

There are those who hold the view that within the mainstream of economics, moral questions have no place, on the grounds that economics can and should limit its efforts to empirical science. There is no dimension of human life, however, that does not have a moral dimension. Moral questions touch everything that is human, and those involved in the discourse on economics have to accept this fact at the start.

Centesimus Annus received a lively reaction in the popular press and among scholarly critics. But many commentators saw the encyclical through the prism of their prior commitments and, thus, careful readers must assess commentaries judiciously. Jorge Mejía warns against any "partial or selective reading of the text" or "one aimed at serving particular purposes."[21] A number of neoconservative scholars praised the encyclical for its promotion of capitalism. Michael Novak, known as one of the strongest Catholic defenders of capitalism, praised the encyclical as "the great Magna Carta for the twenty-first century" and as the "fullest and best [encyclical] in the whole tradition."[22] He particularly cited the encyclical's support of a type of reformed capitalism, a model, he claims, the pope "now proposes" for the nations of formerly communist Eastern Europe and the Third World.

In the same vein of thought, Richard John Neuhaus claims that the encyclical has provided the moral-theological grounding for "the new capitalism." In his words, "the market economy comes with a price, and the Pope is deeply concerned about unemployment, social dislocation, and 'the whole ultra-liberal, consumerist system which is devoid of values, and introducing it with the power of propaganda."[23] He further states that the pope teaches that "the poor of the world are not oppressed because of capitalism . . . but because of the absence of capitalism." He claims that the pope is for more freedom in the economy and not less and is in fact convinced that "state interventions . . . no

---

[21] Ibid., 403.

[22] Michael Novak, "The Hundredth Year," *Crisis* 10 (May 1992): 2–3.

[23] Richard John Neuhaus, quoting John Paul II, as reported in a published interview by Polish journalist Jas Gawronski in R. J. Neuhaus, "John Paul's 'Second Thoughts' on Capitalism," *First* no. 41 (March 1994): 66.

matter how well intended, almost always turn out to be oppressive and stifling."[24] Pursuing the same perspective as Novak and Neuhaus, Robert A. Sirico asserts that John Paul II and *Centesimus Annus* "endorse capitalism as essentially in accord with Christianity."[25] Contrary, however, to the triumphant praise of the encyclical by neoconservatives, in line with what they claim is the patronage of John Paul of their project, John Pawlikowski notes that John Paul reiterated his refusal to endorse capitalism.[26] He condemned "the selfish demands inherent in current economic models."[27]

Todd Whitmore, arguing against Michael Novak's claim that we, including the pope, are now all capitalists,[28] points out that Novak, in fact, rejects the fundamental teachings of John Paul regarding economic rights, the gap between the poor and the rich, and various limits on private property, and that John Paul himself explicitly states that he rejects capitalism's ideology.[29] Charles Wilber charges Novak, as well as William Simon and Robert Sirico, with misinterpreting the pope as advocating a free-market capitalism that the entire tradition of Catholic social thought has condemned, along with socialism, for over a century. He states that the "socially regulated capitalism" endorsed by John Paul calls for a strong role of government in economic life contrary to what Novak would allow.[30]

John Paul's refusal to be a proponent of capitalism is based on three reasons: (1) The abuses of capitalism resulting in situations of injustice and exploitation are too widespread. "There are situations in which the rules of the earliest period of capitalism still flourish in conditions of ruthlessness in no way inferior to the darkest moments of the first phase of industrialization" (no. 33); (2) Property is not

---

[24] R. J. Neuhaus, in "The Pope, Liberty, and Capitalism: Essays on *Centesimus Annus*," *National Review* 43/11 (June 24, 1991): 9.

[25] Robert A. Sirico, in "The Pope, Liberty, and Capitalism: Essays on *Centesimus Annus*," *National Review* 43/11 (June 24, 1991): 13.

[26] See John T. Pawlikowski, "Government and Economic Solidarity: The View from the Catholic Social Encyclicals," *Bridges: An Interdisciplinary Journal of Theology, Philosophy, History, and Science* 7/3–4 (2000): 281–95.

[27] John Paul II, "The World's Hunger and Humanity's Conscience," address to the UN International Conference on Nutrition," *Origins* 22/28 (December 1992), 475.

[28] Michael Novak, *The Catholic Ethic and the Spirit of Capitalism* (New York: The Free Press, 1993), 101.

[29] Todd David Whitmore, "John Paul II, Michael Novak, and the Differences Between Them," *Annual of the Society of Christian Ethics* 21 (2001), 215–32.

[30] Charles K. Wilber, "Argument that the Pope Baptized Capitalism Holds No Water," *National Catholic Reporter* (June 7, 1991), 10.

only private but common. This necessitates limits on the legitimacy of private property at the core of capitalism. "The church teaches that the possession of material goods is not an absolute right, and that its limits are inscribed in its very nature as a human right" (no. 30); and (3) The church, in its eschatological witness, should maintain its independence as a critic of temporal matters. "The Church offers her social teaching as an indispensable and ideal orientation, a teaching which recognizes the positive value of the market and of enterprise, but which at the same time points out that these need to be oriented toward the common good" (no. 43).

In this light I hold that the distinctive contribution of *Centesimus Annus* is its economic vision as articulated in its moral ecology of economics, which is shaped by the norms and principles that must govern the enterprise of economics. These are the norms and principles that must guide the correction of capitalism as a system. I take up four primary ethical criteria in the sphere of economics, as founded on the theological anthropology of *Centesimus Annus*, against which it holds up any economic system. Any system that falls short of these criteria is outside of the encyclical's moral ecology. These four ethical criteria constitute what Daniel Finn calls "the moral ecology of markets."[31]

First, economic activity is a human activity that must be bound by laws. It cannot be conducted in a political vacuum. It must function within a juridical framework. Within this framework the following must be promoted: initiative and industry, private property, continuing education for increased productivity, development of science and technology, full employment for workers, and just wages. What must be prohibited are unsafe working conditions, subjecting women and children to detrimental work, profit-driven pursuits by owners of capital or means of production by reducing the opportunities for work, degradation of environment, and violation of the rights of workers to organize. The state must respect the principle of subsidiarity but at the same time it must intervene if the common good of the workplace and of the community is endangered. Included here is the role of government in granting a stronger legal power to labor unions and strengthening of the legal status of laborers in the face of corporate power.

Second, the possession of "know how" and technology, a new kind of wealth, stresses the social dimension of property and of work. It also upholds the universal destination of good, found not only in nature but in the result of human work and ingenuity. Social inequity,

---

[31] See Daniel Finn, "John Paul II and the Moral Ecology of Markets," *Theological Studies* 59/4 (1998): 662–79.

thus, is found not only in the possession of goods as found in nature but also in the access to science and technology. The poor are trapped in a subsistence level of existence and are cut off from the world of technological communications and productivity because of their lack of access to technological knowledge and skills. This is the new form of social injustice. Given the new wealth acquired by knowledge and skills in science and technology, in the context of collaboration with others, the social nature of work requires more than ever the "subjectivity" of persons in interpersonal and transpersonal relationships. The Catholic doctrine of wealth and property has evolved from the "natural fruitfulness of the earth" to the fruit of human work and ingenuity, particularly in the context of technological developments. The church needs the work of moral theologians to do further theoretical work to develop the ethics of property in the light of the contemporary shifts of its nature and meaning.

Third, networks of solidarity must be built for those who have the least access to the common goods. The rights of the poorest and weakest in society must be defended and protected. They must be provided the most essential goods and services, which they, through no fault of their own, are unable to provide for themselves. They must, however, not be reduced to mere recipients of impersonal and bureaucratic assistance. It is important to note here, as Kenneth Himes has pointed out, that this critique of excessive government bureaucracy is taken from a communitarian and not from a libertarian perspective. That is, John Paul is not proposing the end of government responsibility, but a more humane approach and the employment of alternative delivery systems, considering that the persons in need are persons, with profound human needs, which are not only material in nature.[32] With reference to the critique of the welfare state, Donal Dorr holds that this should not be seen as "approval by the pope of the liberal capitalist approach. It can rather be understood as a challenge to people to develop caring societies where the State protects the weaker sectors but does not cripple their initiative or make them dependent on the State."[33]

John Paul upholds the importance of intermediate communities from the family to civil society groups wherein the "subjectivity" of society is fostered. He endorses reliance on society rather than on the state, without denying the intervention of the latter in meeting human

---

[32] Kenneth R. Himes, "The New Social Encyclical's Communitarian Vision," *Origins* 21/10 (August 1, 1991): 167.

[33] Dorr, *Option for the Poor*, 350.

needs in the spirit of solidarity. Central to John Paul's analysis is the distinction between state and society. The state is the apparatus of the government that is distinct from and yet emerges from society—that which constitutes the nation. The relation of society and government in *Centesimus Annus* is thoroughly grounded in Catholic social thought.[34] "For John Paul, the State, when things are working as they should, expresses the society's values and aspirations."[35] But the distinction, however, holds. As Russell Hittinger states: "The state is an instrument of, rather than the substance of, of human solidarity."[36] John Paul upholds the subjectivity of society through the vibrancy of social organizations, where people are bound in solidarity. This is contrary to libertarians' "methodological individualism," which is based on the conviction that individuals gather in various groups only to pursue their own goals. And it is also contrary to communism, which destroys the subjectivity of individuals and the subjectivity of society by its prohibition of the establishment of groups that represent vibrant democratic life.[37]

Fourth, beyond the juridical framework that governs the economic behavior to protect the common good, particularly the protection of the most vulnerable, the law can do only so much unless men and women are virtuous in their practice of economy.[38] If they do not behave according to fundamental moral virtues, economic life will be left to the rule of the survival of the fittest, and the economic system will collapse under the force of vicious and mindless competition.[39] John Paul appeals to business leaders in his homilies, as he did in Poland in 1997: "Do not let yourselves be deceived by visions of immediate profit, at the expense of others. Beware of any semblance of exploitation."[40] He summons men and women to practice virtues within the market system, including "diligence, industriousness, prudence in undertaking reasonable risks, reliability and fidelity in interpersonal

---

[34] Finn, "Commentary on *Centesimus Annus*," 449–50.

[35] Ibid., 451.

[36] Russell Hittinger, "Making Sense of the Civilization of Love: John Paul II's Contribution to Catholic Social Thought," in *The Legacy of Pope John Paul II*, ed. Geoffrey Gneuhs (New York: Crossroad, 2000), 83.

[37] Finn, "Commentary on *Centesimus Annus*," 450–51.

[38] The juridical framework can govern behavior, but John Paul recognizes what Thomas Aquinas argued centuries earlier: the law cannot prohibit all evil actions for fear that many good things will be eliminated in the process (*Summa Theologiae* 1–11, q. 91, a.4.).

[39] Finn, "Commentary on *Centesimus Annus*," 457.

[40] John Paul II, "The Necessity of Jobs, the Meaning of Work," homily at Legnica, Poland, *Origins* 27/6 (June 26, 1997): 89.

relationships, as well as courage in carrying out decisions which are difficult and painful but necessary, both for the overall working of a business and in meeting possible setbacks" (no. 32). What John Paul exhorts is that the behavior of men and women who hold the reins of the economic system must be founded on a moral core.

The moral ecology of the economy as envisioned by John Paul in *Centesimus Annus* is a prophetic call in an economic society ruled by self-interest and profit. The world of economics must not be isolated from the broader moral values of a people. It cannot operate within its own rules without having to be made accountable to the rules of common decency, to the imperative of social justice, and to the call of solidarity for the vulnerable. When such values do not enter into the fabric of its interactions and relationships, then, as with any human institution existing on excessive self-aggrandizement, it will cause its own destruction.

Negative Assessment of the Encyclical

Centesimus Annus is a critically important document in the history of Catholic social thought because of its fidelity to tradition and also its contemporary thrust. At the same time, however, it has been found wanting in some areas. There are four areas to address in our negative assessment of the encyclical: its uncritical reading of *Rerum Novarum*, its Eurocentric view of socialism and Marxism, its augmented meaning of the preferential option for the poor, and its failure to address justice within the church.

Uncritical Reading of Rerum Novarum

Centesimus Annus devotes a whole chapter to reaffirming the teaching of *Rerum Novarum*. However, John Paul does not bring the critical eye of an academic historian to the one-hundred-year-old document. Rather, his reading is "unashamedly selective," as directed by his pastoral intent. He particularly focuses on how to present the enduring relevance of *Rerum Novarum* today, and to assert once again the continuity of the teaching of the church, relative to private property, work, the economic process, the role of the state, and the nature of the human person.

Without a critical eye, and with a pastoral agenda, John Paul does not refer to the inadequacies of *Rerum Novarum*. For instance, Leo overemphasized the right to private property in his effort to oppose socialism in the nineteenth century. John Paul does not highlight this point, but the fact is that Leo XIII and Pius X "represent the high water mark of individualism in the trajectory of Catholic views on private property."[41] Leo made reference to Thomas's notion of the common use of material goods, but it was clear that it was not his intention to highlight this notion. Thomas teaches that people should possess things not as their own but in common, which means that although the owner of an object has the authority to decide its use, he or she cannot use it in just any way he or she needs, in the face of needs of others. Material things are intended to meet human needs; it is their purpose according to God's intention. So with bread; if one has too much and another has none at all, we are under an obligation to share the bread with the other.[42] Thomas goes even further when he argues that when the need is so urgent that it places a person in imminent danger, and there is no other recourse, that person may take the property of those with excessive abundance without being morally accountable.[43] Leo does not take this radical turn of Thomas in limiting the right to private property; in fact, he tends to go to the other side. The right to private property was enshrined in his writings in the face of what he viewed as the socialist threat.[44]

Rerum Novarum also proposed a very limited concept of work-men's associations, which did not have the same political status as our trade unions today, but were reminiscent of the artificer's guilds of the medieval ages. Leo was wary of trade unions with political status, which might exercise their collective power to cause instability in society. The economic dislocations that would be caused by strikes and that destabilize society were viewed by Leo as far worse than existing injustices. Leo promotes groups that serve to help workers among themselves, and between employers and workers, in times of need, sickness, calamity, and in the event of death. They are meant to build harmony and interdependence, founded largely on religious bonds, rather than to cause conflict and polarization in the struggle for justice. During the time of Leo, many workers left these associations and joined the more secular trade unions. In the rereading of *Rerum Novarum* John Paul avoided any critical assessment of the workmen's

---

[41] Finn, "Commentary on *Centesimus Annus*," 444. For a treatment of Leo XIII and Thomas Aquinas on private property, see Charles E. Curran, *Catholic Social Teaching, 1891–Present: A Historical, Theological, and Ethical Analysis* (Washington, DC: Georgetown University Press, 2002), 175–79. See also Ernest L. Fortin, "'Sacred and Inviolable': *Rerum Novarum* and Natural Rights," *Theological Studies* 53/2 (1992): 216.

[42] Finn, "Commentary on *Centesimus Annus*," 445.

[43] Thomas Aquinas, *Summa Theologiae*, II-II, q.66, a. 7.

[44] Finn, "Commentary on *Centesimus Annus*," 445.

associations in view of protecting the needs and rights of workers in the face of the unbridled abuse of corporate power.

Eurocentric View of Socialism and Marxism

British economist Ronald Preston gave the encyclical his general approval but found its view of socialism and Marxism too simplistic and drawn only from the view of Eastern European communism.[45] Paul VI had a grasp of the complexity of socialism and Marxism compared to the limited view of John Paul. In *Octogesima Adveniens* Paul VI speaks of the various expressions of socialism, the socialist currents, and their various developments (*OA*, no. 31), speaks of the historical evolution of Marxism, and makes distinctions between the atheistic ideology and philosophy of Marxism and its rigorous scientific method of social analysis, without denying their intimate link.

Most people who look back on the extraordinary months of late 1989 and early 1990 are left with two powerful images. The first is the fall of the Berlin Wall, and the second is Nelson Mandela walking into the light out of the dungeon where he was confined in darkness for twenty-seven years. If John Paul were an African, he might have hailed this second event as more glorious than the first. And he might have it as the key event out of which he would have carved his encyclical. And if it were so, he might have the world divided not between East and West but North and South, with the East and West division a variant of the North. The collapse of communist economies and ideology in Eastern Europe might have been viewed as the early stage of the malaise of the whole "Northern" approach to the world. So while the Eurocentric Polish experience of the pope at the core of the encyclical was its strength, it was also its limitation.[46]

John Paul did not criticize the simplistic view of socialism in *Rerum Novarum*. In his fear of the threat of atheistic socialism, Leo condemned what he believed was the socialist rejection of all private property.

> To remedy these evils the *socialists*, working on the poor man's envy of the rich, endeavor to destroy private property, and maintain that individual possessions should become the common property of all, to be administered by the state or by municipal bodies. They hold that, by thus transferring property

---

[45] Ronald H. Preston, "*Centesimus Annus*: An Appraisal," *Theology* 95 (1992): 405–16.

[46] Dorr, *Option for the Poor*, 342–43.

from private persons to the community, the present evil state of things will be set to rights, because each citizen will then have his equal share of whatever there is to enjoy. But their proposals are so clearly futile for all practical purposes, that if they were carried out the workingman himself would be among the first to suffer. Moreover they are emphatically unjust, because they would rob the lawful possessor, bring the State into a sphere that is not its own, and cause complete confusion in the community. (RN, no. 3)

The truth of the matter, however, is that very few socialists ever called for the common holding of all goods. Marxists only condemned private ownership of the means of production like tools, machines, and factories that produced other goods.[47] John Paul articulates his precise position regarding ownership of the means of production:

Ownership of the means of production whether in industry or agriculture, is just and legitimate if it serves useful work. It becomes illegitimate, however, when it is not utilized or when it serves to impede the work of others, in an effort to gain a profit which is not the result of the overall expansion of work and wealth of society, but rather is the result of curbing them or of illicit exploitation, speculation or the breaking of solidarity among working people. Ownership of this kind has no justification, and represents an abuse in the sight of God and man. (no. 43)

Augmented Meaning of the Preferential Option for the Poor

An editorial in *America* criticized the encyclical's broadening of the preferential option for the poor to include all forms of poverty, including spiritual poverty. But in doing so, has the pope emptied the concept of its specific and historical intent? This term was not just academic, for it carried the story of masses of people in the Latin American continent without food, water, and shelter, the most basic of human needs, amid the opulence of the rich. When the Latin American bishops coined this term in their 1968 and 1979 meetings at Medellín, they were thinking of their people, weighed down by material poverty, not of "spiritual paupers who sniff cocaine in Swiss villas or

---

[47] Finn, "Commentary on *Centesimus Annus*," 445.

Park Avenue penthouses."[48] As Patrick McCormick puts it in another context, "Shall we be for both Lazarus and Dives?"[49]

Not only has the encyclical emptied the term of its specific and historical intent, but it has also compromised its radicality. To give preference to the materially poor is the most radical of love, for it means to defy all the common standards of preference. It is the option of looking at a person with the heart, beyond all differences in status or position, and in its depths to reach the common humanity that binds one to another. It is the option of seeing another in the way Jesus sees him or her, as the poor with whom he became one. In Jesus, God not only became poor, but God *is* poor.

Failure to Address Justice Within the Church

The encyclical's broadening the meaning of the preferential option for the poor is in contrast to its narrowing of the focus of the meaning of justice to political and economic justice. It gives no evidence of addressing ecclesial justice or justice within the church. The criteria the church uses to judge other systems should be the same criteria used to judge the church. As stated in *America,* John Paul's critiques "will be read in a knowing way by those who feel the church's own structures and disciplines need reform."[50] John Paul articulates this challenge himself: "Today more than ever, the Church is aware that her social message will gain credibility more immediately from the witness of actions than as a result of its internal logic and consistency" (no. 57).

Conclusion

As a centenary encyclical, *Centesimus Annus* presents a continuity of tradition as it grounds its norms and principles and its directives for action on those that have been fundamentally upheld by Catholic social thought over the century, and particularly as enshrined in *Rerum Novarum,* which it commemorates. But it also broke new grounds by contextualizing its teaching in a technological world. This is exemplified, for instance, in its new understanding of wealth and property in terms of possession of "know how," technology, and skill; the social

---

[48] Editorial, "*Centesimus Annus,*" *America* 164/20 (May 25, 1991): 555–56.

[49] Patrick McCormick, "That They May Converse: Voices of Catholic Social Thought," *Cross Currents* 42/4 (1992): 527.

[50] Editorial, "*Centesimus Annus,*" 556.

nature of this type of wealth and property; and the new social inequities in relation to it.

Centesimus Annus must be read based on its genre, deriving its special value as part of the evangelizing mission of the church. Its distinctive contribution to the discourse on politics and economics is its theological anthropology, on which is based its moral criteria in judging the structures and systems of politics and economics. Apart from its theological anthropology, its teaching on politics and economics loses its religio-moral core.

The prophetic voice of the church on politics and economics must be heard, for there is something essential to the human that is lost when its voice is silenced or ignored. Its teaching, which comes from its religio-moral core, provides a wealth of tradition and wisdom to draw from for critical discernment of theories, principles, and practices in politics and economics. The church, admittedly, is flawed as a human institution, and its witness to its religio-moral core has been imperfect. But this core, the foundation of its teaching on the dignity of the human person, the protection of the most vulnerable in society, the communal nature of work and wealth, the imperative of subsidiarity and solidarity, and the building of a just and caring society, is what the church is all about, what it exists for, what it strives to be—the core that cannot be eradicated even in failure and sin.

PART III

CHOICE

Moral vision and norm are incarnated in specific choice, influenced by values and virtues, directed by reason and principles, and inspired by spirituality. In developing an ethical methodology for decision making in conflict situations, I have integrated virtue ethics and the ethics of holistic reasoning into the process. By integrating a virtue-centered approach and a principle-centered approach, we can reach a comprehensive account of what it means to be moral.

At the heart of an integrated ethical methodology for conflict situations is systematic analysis and discernment, which involves the consideration of a reflective equilibrium, the weighing and balancing of virtues and principles in the process of moral reasoning in conflict situations. Both virtue ethics and ethics of holistic reasoning are necessary in the reflective equilibrium to arrive at a decision that is truly human and Christian. Virtue ethics and ethics of holistic reasoning profoundly intersect in the person of virtue or in the community of virtuous persons who seek to do because of who they are. What precedes the systematic analysis and discernment is the primacy of context—thinking with stories—and this context put in a larger framework of reference beyond the stories.

Moral decision making is not a matter of technique or skill; it is not merely a rationalistic and analytical approach. At the center of decision making are the moral agents in community. It is their formation in vision and norm that directs, influences, and shapes their choice. Moral agents formed in moral vision and moral norm do not enter in the process of decision making in a moral vacuum. They bring a specific Christian ethos as they understand virtues and principles as shaped by culture and religion, scriptures, and systematic theology (moral vision) and as grounded in Catholic social teaching (moral norm).

While the integral ethical methodology proposed is virtue oriented and principle directed, it remains on the level of discursive reasoning. In Ignatian discernment the power of affectivity and spirituality come into full force as one brings into shape a choice or decision in a conflict situation. It is when reason is bathed in the waters of affectivity and spirituality that it reaches a depth of illumination. The proposed ethical methodology is integrated into the third mode of Ignatian discernment where one weighs his or her options, then into the second mode, where one seeks affective confirmation through the judgment of the heart, and finally into the first mode, where one is disposed, in complete abandon of self, to the pure gift of love and peace God alone can give.

8

An Ethical Methodology
for Conflict Situations

Over the past three decades the theological and philosophical debate on proportionalism has generated voluminous amounts of literature. The rhetoric of the debate has sometimes been inflammatory, yielding more heat than light, but nonetheless the issues and questions it posed were of significant importance. Since the term *proportionalism* suggests to some a "dissenting view" relative to the instructions of *Veritatis Splendor,* I propose that it be changed to "ethics of holistic reasoning." Proportionalism has represented the general move in moral theology to see norms in a more holistic and contextual way. As stated in the Preface, scholars of repute who use the ethical methodology of proportionalism have expressed their objection to *Veritatis Splendor*'s blanket critique of proportionalism without making the necessary distinctions across the entire range, resulting in what they call strawman caricatures of the method as they actually use it.

After the dust of the debate settled, and we have moved on to the post-debate era, with the emergence of new ethical approaches, in particular virtue ethics, we can step back and ask what insights and perspectives have evolved about ethical thought as a whole and about moral reasoning in general. In relation to this overall question, we ask more specifically: What is the positive contribution of the ethics of holistic reasoning? What is virtue ethics? What new direction has virtue ethics brought to moral reasoning? How does the ethics of holistic reasoning relate to virtue ethics?

There is no perfect ethical methodology. All have epistemological limits or constraints. The entire effort of this chapter, however, is to present the ethical approaches in their truest light, as they provide a moral compass amid the complexities of being moral. I first demonstrate why I am using the term *ethics of holistic reasoning* for proportionalism, to highlight what the method is at its core. An accurate assessment of its contextual and holistic approach shows its distinctive contribution to moral thought. While this type of moral reasoning has no causal relationship with virtue ethics, it precedes it with its turn to the subject in relation to the act. I present virtue ethics in Thomistic thought and in its contemporary retrieval and then discuss the relation of the ethics of virtue and the ethics of principles. The end goal is to develop an ethical methodology for moral reasoning in conflict situations, integrating the ethics of holistic reasoning and virtue ethics. This is to respond to the need of an ethical methodology that fills in the lacunae of a purely virtue-centered approach and also that of a purely principle-centered approach. Integrating the ethics of holistic reasoning and virtue ethics to achieve a comprehensive account of being moral in conflict situations is an effort to move forward the ongoing discourse in the field.

Ethics of Holistic Reasoning

Contrary to the criticism that it is only an act-oriented method, proportionalism is in fact holistic and integral, as it sees the act in relation to the agent and the agent in relation to the act, and all that specifies the circumstances that surround them.[1] I draw from specific elements of proportionalism as evidence for my thesis that the primary positive contribution of proportionalism to moral reasoning is that it insisted and pursued a holistic ethical method. Elements that show this drive for holism are the primacy of context for moral objectivity, the concept of premoral *vs.* the privileging of the *finis operis*, the new hermeneutics of direct and indirect, and proportionalism as a Christian non-utilitarian teleology.[2] While referring back to these elements of proportionalism may appear to be rehashing old arguments, the consolidation of these arguments to present proportionalism in a positive light and to demonstrate its primary contribution to moral

---

[1] Edward Vacek seems to suggest that placing proportionalism within the traditional deontology versus teleology framework might be the reason why its interest in moral agency has been overlooked. See his "Proportionalism: One View of the Debate," *Theological Studies* 46/2 (1985): 289. See also Aline Kalbian, "Where Have All the Proportionalists Gone?" *Journal of Religious Ethics* 30/1 (2002): 7.

[2] John Mahoney speaks of the drive for totality in contemporary moral theology that rejects the Scholastic method that led to the fragmentation of the whole into atomic elements. See *The Making of Moral Theology* (Oxford: Clarendon Press, 1987), 310. This drive for totality and integration is identified as a central feature of the post–Vatican II renewal in moral theology.

theology as an ethics of holistic reasoning is new. In the heat of the debate in the past decades the individual trees were mistaken for the forest, so to speak. We have missed the much broader perspective in appreciating the enduring value of the methodology proportionalism has offered for moral reasoning in conflict situations. In looking back and seeing with new eyes, we are able to see the old in a new way. In the subsequent sections of this chapter, the term *ethics of holistic reasoning* is used in place of *proportionalism*.

The Primacy of Context for Moral Objectivity

The insistence on the primacy of context by scholars of ethics of holistic reasoning shows the direction of this approach to moral reasoning, which takes into account all of reality in any given situation to determine moral objectivity.

I begin with Josef Fuchs's key argument that all morality must be rooted in its concrete context and that moral absolutes are to be understood in terms of moral objectivity but not moral universality. Fuchs cites the directives of Paul concerning women in his letters. Fuchs says that while these directives are binding for the women of Paul's cultural milieu, and thus are morally absolute in the objective sense, they are not so in the universal sense. As the social positions of women have changed and evolved, what was normative during the Pauline age is not normative in another age and era.[3]

The church arrives at moral pronouncements in the sphere of natural law morality, based on the nature of the human person. The person, however, is not a static being, incapable of change and development. Our anthropological understanding changes and evolves because of new experiences, insights, and evaluations. The church is also not a "spiritualized" reality, engaging with the world in a vacuum, totally untouched by time and culture.[4] Edward Vacek notes that all or almost all of what were considered in the tradition as intrinsically binding prohibitions have over time been modified. At one time, lying, birth control, taking money as interest, and divorce and remarriage were forbidden. Now, under special conditions, all are tolerated. He cites the example of the Pauline privilege, which considered a peace-filled faith life to be a higher value than the permanence of a marriage

---

[3] Josef Fuchs, "The Absoluteness of Moral Norms," in *Proportionalism: For and Against,* ed. Christopher Kaczor, 60–99 (Milwaukee: Marquette University Press, 2000), 64–65.

[4] Ibid., 70–71.

between a Christian believer and a pagan. Vacek concludes that Paul legitimated divorce and remarriage under these circumstances.[5]

Social, cultural, technological, and economic facts change. Not only facts but also the mind's grasp of facts and realities changes, as the locus and perspectives of meaning change. One thinks, for example, of the changing and expanding concept of sex and marriage in the milieu of the Catholic Church in the recent past.[6] One must see reality, thus, through changing prisms to determine the truth of the total action, which is not divorced from the actual reality. What we strive for is moral objectivity as rooted in the context, which takes into account all of a given situation as it is discerned, evaluated, and judged. Moral objectivity is neither relativism nor subjectivism. It is not arbitrary, but rather it is *recta ratio,* which requires that one think and judge which decision or action is oriented to what is right, reasonable, and human in a given context.

Fuchs does not deny moral absolutes, but he distinguishes *absolute* in the sense of objectively valid affirmation from *absolute* in the sense of a universal norm. For clarity and accuracy of moral thinking, however, one distinguishes formal norms from material norms, and value terms and an "act in itself."[7] No one denies the universality of formal norms that commend general values and attitudes (be just, be fair, be chaste, be honest, or "do good and avoid evil"), although their substantive meaning remains to be filled out, since they do not precisely delineate which actions embody these attitudes and values. Material behavioral norms relate to concrete sorts of action we ought to do, which are still to be specified by actual circumstances (entrusted secrets ought to be kept; do not use artificial contraceptives). To speak of murder is no longer just the naming of an "act in itself." It is called a value term because implicit in its description is a value relation and therefore a moral judgment. Value terms need no further specification and discussion (murder is morally evil). In contrast, killing without the extenuating circumstances is only a naming of an "act in itself" and is either right or wrong, depending on the context.

---

[5] Vacek, "Proportionalism," 306.

[6] Fuchs, "The Absoluteness of Moral Norms," 78.

[7] See the discussion of different types of norms in Lisa Sowle Cahill, "Contemporary Challenges to Exceptionless Moral Norms," in *Moral Theology Today: Certitudes and Doubts* (St. Louis: The Pope John Center, 1984), 121–35. See also idem, "Teleology, Utilitarianism, and Christian Ethics," *Theological Studies* 42/4 (December 1981): 601–29, esp. 614–16; and Richard Gula, *Reason Informed by Faith: Foundations of Catholic Morality* (New York: Paulist Press, 1989), 283–99.

Fuchs's understanding of absolute in terms of moral objectivity and not moral universality does not refer to formal norms or to value terms but to material behavioral norms. It is clear from the definition of formal norms that he does not deny their moral imperative in a universal sense. Neither does he question the universality of value terms, which suggests circumstances in which the act in question has no moral justification and thus needs no further specification. He limits his assertion of moral objectivity as absolute but not universal to concrete material behavioral norms. For this type of norms, "conscience ought to assist action toward objectivity, toward truth, in conformity with concrete human reality."[8] It seems to me that the impasse in the ethical debate was often caused by the confusion in the use of the different types of moral norms and under which type or category of moral norms certain acts fall.

While material behavioral norms are tied to particular and concrete situations and, thus, do not apply for all and every other situation in a universal sense, Fuchs sees an exception in that there can be "norms stated as universals, including, that is, a precise delineation of the action, to which we cannot conceive of any kind of exception" (such as cruel treatment of a child that is of no benefit to the child).[9] Richard McCormick uses *virtually exceptionless* to refer to situations in which the degree of evil in certain acts is such that it is virtually impossible to conceive circumstances that would justify them morally. Richard Gula explains the position of Richard McCormick in the following:

> For McCormick, "virtually" indicates we cannot prove without the sharpness of deductive syllogistic logic that no exception could ever occur. Yet these norms light up values which human experience tells us in the general course of events and all practical purposes, ought to take precedence even though their preference in every instance cannot be demonstrated absolutely.[10]

Albert Di Ianni considers some norms as virtually exceptionless because their absoluteness cannot be demonstrated theoretically but we must act on them as if they were absolute.[11] The notion of virtually

---

[8] Fuchs, "The Absoluteness of Moral Norms," 74.

[9] Ibid., 89.

[10] Richard M. Gula, *Reason Informed by Faith: Foundations of Catholic Morality* (New York: Paulist Press, 1989), 295.

[11] Albert Di Ianni, "The Direct/Indirect Distinction in Morals," *Readings in Moral Theology*, no. 1: *Moral Norms and Catholic Tradition*, ed. Charles Curran and Richard McCormick, 215–43 (New York: Paulist Press, 1979), 236–38.

exceptionless is different from the traditional notion of intrinsic evil, which categorizes an act as morally evil in its very nature or object, apart from intention and circumstance. Acts are considered virtually exceptionless after the full assessment of the object of the act, all possible intention, and every circumstance conceivable.

McCormick speaks of "direct killing of non-combatants in warfare" as virtually exceptionless.[12] Louis Janssens identifies the norm "you shall render help to a person in extreme distress" as an example of a virtually exceptionless norm.[13] For Paul Ramsey, virtually exceptionless norms are prohibitions of premarital sex, rape, and medical experimentation on persons without their informed consent.[14]

For Grisez, the critical question is whether Fuchs's view is vulnerable to cultural reductionism: "This reduction of morality to social convention leaves no room for moral criticism which transcends cultures and epochs."[15] He further writes: "The ultimate horizon of the good need not be settled by what contributes to human progress in one's actual earthly society. For while natural virtues promote the good life of earthly society, Christian virtues equip one for life in the kingdom. The kingdom is no mere abstraction but a reality which relativizes the particularities of historical epochs and cultures."[16] It is for this reason, he asserts, that Vatican II affirms in *Gaudium et Spes*: "The Church also maintains that beneath all changes there are many realities which do not change and which have their ultimate foundation in Christ, who is the same yesterday and today, yes, and forever" (*GS*, no. 10).

Grisez also points out that while the whole concrete reality of persons and their societies must be taken into account, not everything of this reality should be accepted uncritically as determinative of what is morally right or wrong.[17] And from his deontological view, he argues by quoting David Bidney's words: "In the last analysis, *culture is not the measure of things, but nature is,* and there are more things in

---

[12] Richard A. McCormick, "Ambiguity in Moral Choice," in *Doing Evil to Achieve Good,* ed. Richard A. McCormick and Paul Ramsey, 7–53 (Chicago: Loyola University Press, 1978), 42.

[13] Louis Janssens, "Norms and Priorities in a Love Ethics," *Louvain Studies* 6 (Spring 1977): 217.

[14] See Paul Ramsey, "The Case of the Curious Exception," *Norm and Context in Christian Ethics,* ed. by Gene Outka and Paul Ramsey (New York: Charles Scribner, 1968), 116–17; 127–30.

[15] Germain Grisez, "Moral Absolutes: A Critique of the View of Josef Fuchs," in Kaczor, *Proportionalism,* 333.

[16] Ibid., 339–40.

[17] Ibid., 336.

nature than are ever grasped through our human cultural symbols."[18] I cannot see, however, why a sharp demarcation line is drawn by Grisez between nature and culture, unless nature is considered a static concept. Nature, if understood as a dynamic reality, interacts with culture. And it is in this interaction that the texture and substance of nature are enriched and developed.

For Fuchs, the "nature" upon which the moral law is inscribed is preeminently and formally nature as *ratio*, but only, of course, as *recta ratio*. He states: "Whatever is not *recta ratio* is necessarily non-human, not worthy of man, antithetic to a steadily advancing 'humanization.'"[19] There is a shift here from nature to person. He writes: "It would be possible and perhaps more meaningful to speak of 'person' as moral norm instead of 'nature.'"[20] Fuchs apparently avoids the immutability that has traditionally characterized nature by shifting to the historicity of person. Self-realization, he says, requires that persons discover the available possibilities for their development and determine on the basis of their present understanding of themselves which of these possibilities are right, reasonable, and human in the full positive sense of these words.[21]

The context grounds the holistic approach to moral reasoning. It is the starting point of ethical reflection, and it provides the data for moral choosing. Divorced from context, and when based on a priori norms and principles, the entire ethical process is bereft of its human texture and substance. Holistic reasoning is engaged in the fullness and richness of the human context to determine moral objectivity.

The Use of Premoral/Nonmoral Concept vs. the Privileging of Finis Operis

A more integral relation of the act, agent, and circumstances is shown in the use of the premoral/nonmoral concept of the ethics of holistic reasoning.[22] It rejects the privileging of the *finis operis* over *finis operantis* and circumstances and consequences in determining what is moral. According to moral theology, human action has three aspects: the act-in-itself or the object of the act *(finis operis)*, the intention of the act *(finis operantis)*, and the circumstances *(circumstantiae)*.

---

[18] Cited in ibid., 333.

[19] Fuchs, "The Absoluteness of Moral Norms," 76.

[20] Ibid., 73.

[21] Ibid.

[22] Ethics of holistic reasoning scholars use premoral and nonmoral interchangeably. They refer to acts or realities that are not yet moral or immoral.

Peter Knauer discusses this three-font principle in his influential article in 1967 that started the proportionalist debate. He supported this principle because he held that only by taking into account the intention of the person acting and the circumstances surrounding his or her action can one determine the true nature of the object of the act. One can cite here the classic example of almsgiving. The *finis operis* (object of the act) of almsgiving is the relief of the needs of a poor person. The *finis operantis* qualifies the object of the act by the intention of the agent, whether the act is a true act of compassion or a way to make a good impression or done only to obtain a tax advantage. The circumstance surrounding the act may show whether the giving of the alms has held up the dignity of the recipient or has shamed him or her. Only by integrating all three aspects can the morality of almsgiving be fully determined.[23]

The privileging of the *finis operis* appears in the *Catechism of the Catholic Church*. It is interesting to note that while the catechism speaks of the three fonts of a moral act, it refers to the *finis operis* by itself as morally determinative: "A morally good act requires the goodness of the object, of the end, and of the circumstances together. . . . The object of the choice can by itself vitiate an act in its entirety" (no. 1755). It further states, "it is therefore an error to judge the morality of human acts by considering only the intention that inspires them or the circumstances (environment, social pressure, duress, or emergency, etc.) which supply their context" (no. 1756). There is no doubt, then, that while intention and circumstances (including consequences) can alter or corrupt an action, from the perspective of the catechism, it is the object by itself that is morally determinative.

The privileging of *finis operis* is most strongly established in the traditional concept of intrinsic evil. In a statement from *Veritatis Splendor*, teleological and what was called proportionalist theories are rejected on the ground that they do not hold that certain acts are morally good or evil according to their object, apart from intention, circumstances, and consequences. The object of the act is the primary criterion in determining whether the act is bad or good.

> One must therefore reject the thesis, characteristic of teleological and proportionalist theories, which holds that it is impossible to qualify as morally evil according to its species—its "object"—the deliberate choice of certain kinds of behavior or specific acts,

---

[23] Peter Knauer, "The Hermeneutical Function of the Principle of Double Effect," in Kaczor, *Proportionalism*, 28.

apart from a consideration of the intention for which the choice is made or the totality of the foreseeable consequences of that act for all persons concerned. (*VS*, no. 79)

The moral logic of what *Veritatis Splendor* condemned as proportionate reasoning is, however, used in *Evangelium Vitae* to justify capital-punishment cases. The encyclical recognizes that the question of capital punishment is one in which a conflict situation is involved. Executing the offender is an extreme measure to be taken only when it would not be possible otherwise to defend society and to protect the safety of persons:

This should not cause surprise: to kill a human being, in whom the image of God is present, is a particularly serious sin. *Only God is the master of life!* Yet from the beginning, faced with the many and often tragic cases which occur in the life of individuals and society, Christian reflection has sought a fuller and deeper understanding of what God's commandment prohibits and prescribes. There are in fact situations in which values proposed by God's law seem to involve a genuine paradox. This happens for example in the case of *legitimate defense,* in which the right to protect one's own life and the duty not to harm someone else's life are difficult to reconcile in practice. (*EV,* no. 55)

Public authority must redress the violation of personal and social rights by imposing on the offender an adequate punishment for the crime, as a condition for the offender to regain the exercise of his or her freedom. In this way authority also fulfills the purpose of defending public order and ensuring people's safety, while at the same time offering the offender an incentive and help to change his or her behavior and be rehabilitated. (*EV,* no. 56)

Evangelium Vitae is guided by the principle that punishment is for the purpose not only of defending the public order but also rehabilitating the offender. If the logic of proportionate reasoning is used—the logic implied in the encyclical—while life is a fundamental value, in cases of extreme conflict situations, where the defense of society is on the line, the taking of the life of the offender is evil but not moral evil. It is a premoral or nonmoral evil, and the whole action is morally justified.

Traditional moral theology classifies certain acts as intrinsically evil in the sense that they are morally evil by their very nature, acts that are so gravely evil that no actual set of circumstances can qualify them. Acts of masturbation, contraception, sterilization, and homosexuality are intrinsically evil, and hence always immoral, whatever the circumstances, motives, or consequences. The moral quality of these acts is already determined before the person engages in them, in any or all possible situations, and for whatever reason or intention. Lisa Cahill writes that several authors have raised the question:

> How can a physical act like masturbation or contraception be prohibited absolutely, even granting that it is a disvalue, i.e., something to be avoided all other things being equal, that is, in the absence of proportionate reason? Would circumstances, e.g., masturbation for a semen test, contraception to safeguard a woman's health make no difference? Is masturbation "intrinsically" more evil than other acts, such as killing a human being, which can be justified in extreme circumstances?[24]

By introducing the concept of premoral/nonmoral good and evil, the notion of intrinsic evil was revised in view of a more holistic moral reasoning where the agent and circumstances have a determinative function in defining the moral meaning of an act. Holistic ethical reasoning is built on a clear and sharp distinction between moral good and evil, on the one hand, and premoral/nonmoral good and evil, on the other hand. This distinction is pivotal to holistic ethical reasoning. It holds that the moral goodness or evilness of an act cannot in itself be defined in a definitive way apart from its uniquely human features and circumstantial qualifiers. This does not mean that premoral/nonmoral judgment has no moral weight, but that, on the first level, judgment it is not yet morally decisive. For example, on a premoral/nonmoral level, giving gifts is a good act. But until further evaluation in relation to intention and circumstances, it cannot be judged as morally good or bad. This means that whether the gift is given out of love and not as a bribe, or grudgingly, or under duress, determines its moral meaning.

Premoral/nonmoral realities, however, are not neutral. To the contrary, premoral/nonmoral evil is regarded as something generally not fulfilling for human nature, and indeed harmful to it, and must be avoided if possible. It counts as a negative factor in a total moral evaluation. But taken by itself, it not yet morally decisive.[25] Arguing

[24] Cahill, "Teleology, Utilitarianism, and Christian Ethics," 611.
[25] Cahill, "Contemporary Challenges to Exceptionless Moral Norms," 124.

from this position, Fuchs holds that an action cannot be judged morally in its materiality (killing, wounding, going to the moon) without reference to the intention of the agent. For only when the intention of the agent enters into consideration is one dealing with a human action. And only with respect to human action may one be able to make a true judgment of moral goodness or evil. The evil in a premoral/nonmoral sense must be judged in terms of the totality of the action with the intention of the agent and circumstances as integral to the final moral assessment.[26] It is at least confusing to speak of death, suffering, and poverty as moral evil, regardless of how they are caused, because the word *moral,* while analogous, has always referred to the sphere of human freedom and responsibility. Premoral/nonmoral realities, both good and evil, exist independent of choosing, but they attract choice and influence choice. In that sense they already belong to the moral realm, even in a minimal sense. In identifying premoral/nonmoral realities, however, one must take note of realities into which are already built the final moral evaluation of an act. Terms such as lying (withholding the truth unjustly) or stealing (taking property unjustly) describe actions that are always immoral. These actions are described in conditions that already contain their final moral condemnation or disproportion and therefore need no further moral evaluation.[27]

Needless to say, the distinction between premoral/nonmoral and moral good/evil is rejected by some scholars. Paul Ramsey, for instance, concludes that there is really not much sense in the "bifurcation of the moral universe into moral and nonmoral values or into physical and human actions or values."[28] And he is resistant to the inclusion of killing among premoral evils, maintaining instead that it is something never to be done directly. He asks: "What argument can there be for classifying the slaying of one person by another as a nonmoral evil? Doubtless, it is sensible to call *death* a nonmoral evil. But at issue here is the moral evil of killing a human being; he is the image of God and is holy ground."[29] What the ethics of holistic reasoning holds is not different from the traditional teaching that killing is not to be avoided at all costs. There are killings that are allowed and thus are justifiable under some extreme circumstances. They remain evil, but they are not moral evil; they are premoral/nonmoral evil.

---

[26] Fuchs, "The Absoluteness of Moral Norms," 84.

[27] Philip Keane, *Sexual Morality: A Catholic Perspective* (New York: Paulist Press, 1997), 51.

[28] Paul Ramsey, "Incommensurability and Indeterminacy in Moral Choices," in McCormick and Ramsey, *Doing Evil to Achieve Good,* 92.

[29] Ibid., 82.

All in all, the introduction of the premoral/nonmoral concept demonstrates the drive toward holism—the object, agent, and circumstances as mutually determinative of the final moral judgment of an act. The premoral/nonmoral concept protects moral judgment from the privileging of the *finis operis* that abstracts moral realities from persons and human situations and leads to a narrow and constricted moral view and judgment.

The New Hermeneutics of Direct and Indirect

This same drive toward holism is also demonstrated in a new hermeneutics of the direct and the indirect principle, a concept embedded in the traditional theory of double effect. Over the past decades, however, the absoluteness of this principle has been questioned, especially in complicated cases. The theory provided a useful tool of moral evaluation for a time, but the increasing objections to its use and application weakened its influence. Its most controversial application is in the case of ectopic pregnancy.

Using the principle of double effect, in the event of an ectopic pregnancy, the removal of the fallopian tube with the fetus inside is morally permissible, but to remove the fetus directly in order to save the damaged uterus is abortion and murder. The reasonableness of this position has been seriously questioned. Vincent MacNamara states the basis of the objection:

> The position just did not make sense to reasonable people. The fact that it held that to do greater rather than lesser physical harm to the mother was what was morally right and the difference between the procedure of removal and that of repair—the foetus dies in both—was that between moral legitimacy and murder, shattered the confidence of many authors in the principle.[30]

Even moralists who defend the direct/indirect principle find it difficult to sustain their arguments. They find it necessary to explain the presence of direct/indirect with more ramifications. They contend that an evil is indirectly intended if it is the unintended byproduct of an act. The agent here is aiming at the good effect, though evil effects are foreseen. Relative to this view a distinction is made between "morally intended" and "psychologically intended." Something could be psychologically intended—in the sense of foreseen—but morally unintended.

---

[30] Vincent MacNamara, *Love, Law, and Christian Life: Basic Attitudes of Christian Morality* (Wilmington, DE: Michael Glazier, 1988), 142.

Clearly, the theory got caught up in hairsplitting complications.[31] The ethics of holistic reasoning maintains the use of direct and indirect but steers clear of the complications and proposes a more straightforward approach to moral evaluation.

While affirming the moral relevance of the difference between an intending will and a permitting will, McCormick goes on to say that it is not this difference that constitutes the decisive criterion of the moral judgment of an act. If there is truly a holistic ethical reason for acting, the person is properly disposed to what constitutes the order of good, whether the premoral evil occurs as an indivisible effect or as a means within the action.[32]

> Concretely, it can be argued that where the higher good is at stake and the only *means* to protect it is to choose to do a non-moral evil, then the will remains properly disposed to the values constitutive of human good. (Grisez's basic goods, Schüller's *ordo bonorum*), and the person's attitude or intentionality is good because he is making the best of a destructive and tragic situation. That is to say that the intentionality is good even when the person reluctantly and regretfully to be sure, intends the nonmoral evil if a truly proportionate reason for such a choice is present.[33]

McCormick, while pointing to the presence or absence of a holistic ethical reason for an action as the decisive criterion, takes a more nuanced position than Schüller relative to the function of the principle of direct and indirect.[34] He holds that an action involving an intending will is a different human moral action from that involving a permitting will. Therefore, it is not only the existence or nonexistence of evil effects that determines the meaning of an action, but also the relation of the will to the occurrence. If the premoral evil is directly intended rather than merely permitted, there would have to be a greater proportionate reason established for the act to be moral and there would be a greater likelihood of the premoral evil in the act becoming moral evil.

---

[31] Ibid., 143–44.

[32] McCormick, "Ambiguity in Moral Choice," 40.

[33] Ibid., 39.

[34] Schüller takes the position that direct and indirect have no moral significance where nonmoral evil is associated with human conduct. See Bruno Schüller, "The Double Effect in Catholic Thought: A Reevaluation," in McCormick and Ramsey, *Doing Evil to Achieve Good,* 165–92. In contrast, see McCormick, "Ambiguity in More Choice," 34–35.

The nuanced position of McCormick is illustrated in his judgment of killing noncombatants as a means to bringing enemies to their knees and weakening their will to fight. The difference, he holds, is not the number of deaths, which could numerically be the same whether they are killed incidentally or killed directly. But how they occur has a good deal to say about the present meaning of the action and the effect on the agent and on others. Here we see evil as a means and evil as an effect change the meaning of the action. McCormick states precisely his position:

> In other words, the teleological character of all our norms does not eliminate the relevance of the distinction between direct/indirect where nonmoral values and disvalues are involved. Rather precisely because these norms are teleological is the indirect/direct distinction relevant. For the relation of the evil as-it-happens to the will may say a great deal about the meaning of my action, its repercussions, and implications, and therefore what will happen to the good in question over the long haul. If one asks why, I believe the answer is to be found in the fact that an intending will represents a closer relation of the agent to the disvalue and therefore indicates a greater willingness that the disvalue occurs.[35]

McCormick, while seeing the moral relevance of the notion of direct or indirect, but without assigning it the final and decisive criterion, holds that it is too readily concluded that if evil in an action is directly intended as a means, the whole action is immoral. He uses the following example:

> If a woman has cancer of the ovaries, a bilateral oophorectomy is performed. The result: sterility. If a family has seven children, the wife is weak, the husband is out of a job, the woman may have a tubal ligation on the occasion of the last delivery. The result: sterility. The immediate effect (nonmoral evil) is the same in both cases: sterility. Obviously these actions are different human actions in terms of their overall intentionality—the good sought. One is a lifesaving intervention, the other is a family-saving or family-stabilizing act, so to speak. But even within the larger difference, the bearing of the will toward the sterility is,

---

[35] McCormick, "Ambiguity in Moral Choice," 33.

I believe, distinguishable in two instances. For the moment no moral relevance will be assigned to this difference. But it seems that there is a difference and the difference originates in the relation of the nonmoral evil to the good sought. In the one instance the non-moral evil is chosen as a means; in the other it is not.[36]

The first case shows the equal immediacy of the good and evil effects, which is grounded on the unity of human action. This unity or indivisibility accounts for the direct intent of the good and the indirect intent of evil. McCormick accepts Grisez's criterion for this case: "If the evil occurs within an indivisible process, then in the moral sense, it is equally immediate with the good effect, and hence not a means. If, however, the process is divisible so that the good effect occurs as the result of a subsequent act, we are dealing with a means and an intending will."[37]

McCormick holds that the traditional understanding of evil as an indivisible aspect of an action is only one form of evil that is morally allowed relative to a good end. He maintains, however, that in the case of evil as a means in a divisible act, what is decisive is to establish the necessary causal relation between the means and the end to establish a holistic ethical reason. With the establishment of holistic ethical reason, the evil remains premoral evil and the whole action is morally justified. In instances when the only way to save the life of a pregnant woman is by surgery that kills the fetus, the evil is necessary and the surgery is permissible.[38] When the use of force is judged the only way to achieve self-defense against an unjust aggressor, it is also necessary and permissible.[39] In these cases, if the action of the agents were not taken, a far greater evil would have been caused. And if this is so, the good of the act would have been contradicted—a moral disproportion was caused.

But there is a difference between evil as aspect/effect and evil as a means. It comes down to the posture of the will in relation to premoral evil. The will is closer to the premoral evil when it is used as

---

[36] Ibid., 37.

[37] Ibid.

[38] McCormick, "A Commentary on the Commentaries," in McCormick and Ramsey, *Doing Evil to Achieve Good*, 193–265, see esp. 238.

[39] See John Langan, "Direct and Indirect—Some Recent Exchange Between Paul Ramsey and Richard McCormick," *Religious Studies Review* 5/2 (April 1979): 100; and Louis Janssens, "Ontic Evil and Moral Evil," in Kaczor, *Proportionalism*, 118.

a means. "An intending will is more willing that the evil be than is a permitting will. . . . This can have morally significant repercussions."[40] The holistic ethical reason sufficient for allowing evil as an effect may not be sufficient for choosing it as a means. When premoral evil is used as a means, a much greater holistic ethical reason is required, and most likely might not be established. McCormick cautions, thus, that since premoral evil as means and premoral evil as effect are different realities, they demand different holistic ethical reasons. What is sufficient for allowing a premoral evil as an effect may not in all cases be sufficient for choosing it as a premoral means. This view maintains the moral relevance of direct and indirect, but it is the presence or absence of holistic ethical reason for the act that is morally decisive.[41]

Scholars of holistic ethical reasoning, however, stress that the distinction of premoral evil and moral evil is pivotal in reference to the use of evil as means. Only premoral evil is allowed to be used as a means, not moral evil. The traditional moral principle holds that the end does not justify a morally evil means. Ethicists hold that if a holistic ethical reason is established, the means used, though involving some form of premoral evil, is allowable, and the whole action is morally justified. Thus, contrary to what its critics hold, the ethics of holistic reasoning does not deny the traditional moral principle, for only in the absence of a truly holistic ethical reasoning does premoral evil become moral evil.

Holistic ethicists criticize arguments that appear to be trapped in physical categories. For instance, Gerald Glesson applies the criterion of closeness to determine what effects are or are not included in the object of the human act. He writes: "That an agent knowingly and voluntarily does what is certain to be lethal is surely strong evidence that the agent is intending to kill. Some effects of what one does are simply 'too close' to the realization of one's formal intention to be merely incidental effects."[42] Arguing in the same vein, Eugene Diamond concludes: "It is difficult to see how the direct removal of

---

[40] McCormick, "Ambiguity in Moral Choice," 36. Vacek speaks of a different consciousness and hence a different personal posture (see "Proportionalism," 311–12). See also Knauer, "The Hermeneutic Function of the Principle of Double Effect," 42; and McCormick, "Ambiguity in Moral Choice," 41.

[41] McCormick, "Ambiguity in Moral Choice," 40–41.

[42] Gerald Glesson, "Is the 'Medical Management' of Ectopic Pregnancy by the Administration of Methotrexate Acceptable?" in Issues for a Catholic Bioethic, ed. L. Gormally, 359–70 (London: Linacre Center, 1999), 364. Using this criterion of closeness, salpingostomy (removal of embryo alone) is direct or intentional abortion.

both the embryo and the trophoblast with a forceps could constitute indirect abortion."[43] What is gleaned from these two positions is that touching the fetus to extricate it from the diseased uterus is considered a lethal touch, an act of murder, while removing the uterus with the fetus inside is allowed. What is decisive is whether the fetus is physically touched or not, which determines whether it is direct or indirect, the basis of its moral goodness or evilness. In a recent article Martin Rhonheimer argues against this physicalist understanding of *direct* and *indirect*, which he holds is in defense of the core teaching of *Veritatis Splendor.* He states:

> Physical action is an object for the will not as far as it is good or evil as *a physical action* (including its natural per se effects), but as it is good in the judgment of the reason. To use Aquinas's terminology, the physical act—the exterior act—is a good insofar as it is a *bonum rationis*: a good for the reason and in the perspective of reason.[44]

He proposes an understanding of *direct* and *indirect* that nullifies the argument against procedures of salpingostomy (removal of the embryo alone) and craniotomy. He understands *direct* and *indirect* in an intentional and not a physical way. An act is not direct when it is outside of the intention of the agent, as in Aquinas's *praeter intentionem*, and thus does not specify the act morally.[45] With reference to craniotomy Rhonheimer states:

> In a constellation of vital conflict, instead, the immediately lethal intervention on the baby can be judged by the reason as "good" in terms of the simple *removal of the baby* to save the mother's life, without considering the lethal effect of its death as belonging to the *reason* why this act is chosen (because, as I have already shown, this death *can no longer be* an object of choice and therefore actually is not the reason for acting: the craniotomy is not informed by a choice to let the mother survive *instead of the child*, but only and alone to save the mother). Hence, the non-intentionality of the baby's death is not due to the actor's simply

---

[43] Eugene Diamond, "Moral and Medical Considerations in the Management of Extrauterine Pregnancy," *Linacre Quarterly* 66/3 (1999): 11.

[44] Martin Rhonheimer, "Vital Conflicts, Direct Killing, and Justice: A Response to Rev. Benedict Guevin and Other Critics," *The National Catholic Bioethics Quarterly* 11/3 (Autumn 2011): 533.

[45] Ibid., 522.

subjective "shifting" of the intention away from considering that he is killing the baby, but to the *objective constellation* which makes it impossible that one reasonably choose the baby's death (either as an end in itself or as a means to save the mother's life, that is, preferring the mother's survival to the baby's survival so that for this reason the baby is killed). The fact that the killing is *praeter intentionem*, that is, that it falls outside the intention, is nothing other than a consequence of this objective constellation, and not simply of (subjectively) not wanting the baby's death.[46]

Rhonheimer further argues that saving the mother (a life-saving intentionality) is that which morally shapes the action on the level of its very moral object, as the baby's death is not the consequence of not intending it subjectively, but is an intrinsic characteristic of the objective (and tragic) constellation of the case, which is not the consequence of subjective preferences.[47] However, how can the lethal crushing of the skull that is deliberately and intentionally done, in the full knowledge that the act will immediately cause the baby's death, be considered *praeter intentionem*? Is this turning reality on its head when we argue that what we are choosing to do is not what it really is but something else?[48] Rhonheimer holds as critical the distinction between "what is intentionally done" and "what is intended in what is intentionally done." He further points out that the critical question is *what it really is* that we do in each case. And arguing against physicalism, he holds that this cannot be made out by simply looking only at what is physically observable in terms of the effects caused by one's doing.[49] "If this were a criterion for what one *intends* in doing what one does, and thus chooses to do, neither killing in self-defense nor hysterectomy would be licit, because what someone who defends himself intentionally and knowingly does is an action which by its nature and immediate causal effect foreseeingly results in the aggressor's death; despite this, we consider the causing of death to be *praeter intentionem*."[50] If the distinction is not made between what one does

---

[46] Ibid., 534. A different viewpoint is presented in Thomas A. Cavanaugh, "Double-Effect Reasoning, Craniotomy, and Vital Conflicts: A Case of Contemporary Catholic Casuistry," *National Catholic Bioethics Quarterly* 11/3 (September 2011): 453–64.

[47] Rhonheimer, "Vital Conflicts, Direct Killing, and Justice," 537.

[48] This question is posed by Benedict Guevin in "Vital Conflicts and Virtue Ethics," *National Catholic Bioethics Quarterly* 10/3 (Autumn 2010): 480.

[49] Rhonheimer, "Vital Conflicts, Direct Killing, and Justice," 536.

[50] Ibid.

on purpose (intentionally) and *knowingly* and what one necessarily *intends* in doing something and thus chooses as a means, it would, Rhonheimer warns, destroy all traditional notions of morality. It would also render the principle of double effect inapplicable.[51]

Ethicists like McCormick would not disagree with Rhonheimer on his understanding of *direct* and *indirect* beyond the physicalist terms. But they hold that what decisively determines moral judgment is the absence or presence of a holistic ethical reason, without denying the direct/indirect distinction. Nancy Rourke compares the two most cited histories of the principle of double effect, which reflect the polarization of a tradition focusing on the direct and indirect criterion and the other focusing on proportionate reason criterion. She concludes that if the principle of double effect is to be effectively used, its irreducible four-part principle must be maintained and moralists should resist simplifying it.[52] I hold that the direct/indirect distinction has been given disproportionate focus, and it has not been contextualized in the total human situation. And while the criterion of proportionate reason is only one of the criteria of the principle of double effect, in the principle of proportionate reason, it is the very structure and substance of its moral reasoning.

In the case of ectopic pregnancy, from the ethics of holistic reasoning view, the final decisive criterion in the removal or repair of the uterus—in both the fetus dies—is what is truly right, human, and compassionate for the mother, who loses not only her child but also her capacity for childbearing. This ethical understanding is contextualized in a broad and holistic human context, that is, the person as integrally and adequately considered. The ongoing discussion of ectopic pregnancy, which began in the 1880s, has not abated. There has been a flurry of articles that have addressed the issue offering several positions: non-intervention, salpingectomy (removal of tube with embryo), salpingostomy (removal of embryo alone), and the use of methotrexate (MXT).[53] Although not an ectopic pregnancy case, the excommunication *latae sententiae* (automatically) of Sister Margaret

[51] Ibid., 537.

[52] Nancy Rourke, "Where Is the Wrong: A Comparison of Two Accounts of the Principle of Double Effect," *Irish Theological Quarterly* 76/2 (2011): 150–63.

[53] These positions are reviewed in Christopher Kaczor, "Moral Absolutism and Ectopic Pregnancy," *Journal of Medicine and Philosophy* 26/1 (2001): 61–74. See also James Keenan, "The Function of the Principle of Double Effect," *Theological Studies* 54/2 (1993): 309; and William E. May, "Martin Rhonheimer and Some Disputed Issues in Medical Ethics: Masturbation, Condoms, Craniotomies, and Tubal Pregnancies," *The Linacre Quarterly* 77/3 (August 2010): 329–52.

McBride, the chair of the ethics committee of St. Joseph's Hospital in Phoenix, Arizona, by Bishop Thomas J. Olmstead for permitting the abortion of an eleven-week-old fetus in order to save the life of its mother brings into question the traditional hermeneutics of direct and indirect abortion. The patient, who was also the mother of four children, was suffering from acute pulmonary hypertension, which her doctors judged would prove fatal for both her and her pre-viable child. The ethics committee believed abortion was permissible in this case under the principle of double effect. Bernard G. Prusak, in his article pertaining to this case, subjects the principle of double effect to another round of philosophical scrutiny, examining particularly the third condition of the principle in its textbook formulation, namely, that the evil effect in question may not be the means to the good effect, with reference to the traditional hermeneutics of direct and indirect abortion.[54] I hold that the new hermeneutic of direct and indirect contextualized in a more holistic grasp of the human situation is necessary and crucial, because decisions are not made in the world of abstract concepts or ideas but where the life and death of persons hang in the balance.

Ethics of Holistic Reasoning as a Non-Utilitarian Christian Teleology

Is the ethics of holistic reasoning utilitarian? Utilitarianism holds that acts are obligatory if they pass the test of utility, that is, if they maximize the happiness of a larger number of people than would alternative courses of action. The *telos* of utilitarianism is most adequately defined as net social good, which precludes, if necessary, the participation of the minority for the sake of the welfare of the majority. In utilitarianism the principle of justice has no meaning if considered independently of the principle of utility. Justice means social expediency. All persons are deemed to have a right to equality of treatment except when some recognized social expediency requires the reverse. At the bottom line of a utilitarian theory of morality is the sum total welfare conceived in a relatively immediate, empirical, and quantifiable sense.[55]

Frederick Carney maintains that a utilitarian calculus is at the heart of McCormick's teleological method; the theory is unquestionably a

---

[54] See Bernard G. Prusak, "Double Effect, All Over Again: The Case of Sister Margaret McBride," *Theoretical Medicine and Bioethics* 32 (2011): 271–83.

[55] See Cahill, "Teleology, Utilitarianism, and Christian Ethics," 601–29.

form of utilitarianism.[56] William Frankena, based on his thoughtful study of methods and models of ethics, writes, "I see no alternative but to interpret McCormick as a utilitarian of some sort."[57] There may be reasons for these scholars to judge the works of ethicists like McCormick to be utilitarian. McCormick's overriding reason, for instance, in judicial murder or the bombing of noncombatants seems to take a utilitarian approach. He argues that killing noncombatants and judicial murder are wrong because of the likelihood that they will result in the value of life being eroded in the "long run."[58] This seems to be consequentialism, a form of utilitarianism thinly disguised.[59]

In his rejoinders McCormick retracts his quasi-utilitarian arguments. He says that while long-term consequences of acts bring about deleterious social effects, these do not constitute their immorality. They only point to the lack of proportion in the act itself, which makes it wrong. Thus, consequences in the long term are not the final and decisive moral determination of an act. When consequences bring about a disproportion in the sense that the very good end of an act is contradicted, the act is immoral. One sees here that while he maintains the teleological thrust of his moral reasoning, he abandons the quasi-utilitarian appearance of his argument. He writes: "I would abandon the *long-term effects* explanation of teleology; but I see no reason for abandoning the teleology itself."[60]

Thus, consequences constitute only one of the indicators of the disproportion in the act. The means used to realize the good in the act if it does not meet the last resort also brings about disproportion. To meet the requirement of last resort, there must be a simultaneity of the good and evil effects of an indivisible act, or the premoral evil means used by an agent must stand in necessary causal relationship to the premoral good sought, and not only in factually efficacious relation to the end.

In assessing the means used, the theory of moderation of traditional moral teaching is also taken up by the ethics of holistic reasoning, which prohibits the causing of more evil than necessary. The moral

---

[56] Frederick Carney, "On McCormick and Teleological Morality," *The Journal of Religious Ethics* 6 (1978): 81–107.

[57] William Frankena, "McCormick and the Traditional Distinction," in McCormick and Ramsey, *Doing Evil to Achieve Good*, 159.

[58] McCormick, "Ambiguity in Moral Choice," 44.

[59] Lisa Cahill writes that this accusation comes from Christian ethicists who share McCormick's theological tradition as well as those who oppose it ("Teleology, Utilitarianism, and Christian Ethics," 612–13).

[60] McCormick, "A Commentary on the Commentaries," 265.

consideration of the means distinguishes ethics of holistic reasoning from utilitarianism, which ultimately operates according to utility: what can bring about the desired end, regardless of the morality of the means used. In summary, the simultaneity of good and evil effects, the causal necessity of the evil to achieve the good, and the curtailing of superfluous evil determine the ethics of the means that, besides the consequences, indicate the presence or absence of holistic ethical reasoning.[61] The drive toward holism is demonstrated in the plurality of moral factors that are brought into the moral calculus.

The consequences and the means used must be related to the value or good that the act seeks to realize. If, however, the value or good sought is lesser than the value or good sacrificed in a conflict situation, there is no holistic proportionate reason for the entire act. And if this is so, from the very start, it is futile to proceed with the process of ethical reasoning. One must first establish that the good or value that is the end of the act must be greater or at least equal to the good or value sacrificed. This weighing of values is held as one of the epistemological challenges of the ethics of holistic reasoning.

The criterion of weighing values can be put negatively: an action is disproportionate if a lesser value is preferred to a higher value. Thus, a moral agent is causing more evil than is necessary if he or she chooses a lesser value over a higher value, other things being equal. The evil aspect of an act should never outweigh the good aspect. McCormick offers a specifying explanation of this criterion, bringing its overall positive thrust: "To see whether an action involving evil is proportionate in the circumstances, we must judge whether this choice is the best possible service of all the values in the tragic and difficult conflict."[62] Our communal experience and wisdom tell us that all the ends of values will be best served by certain actions and the reverse happens by other actions. Charles Curran puts it succinctly: "All of the moral values must be considered and a final decision be made after all the moral values have been compared."[63]

Paul Quay says that ethical reasoning in the school to which McCormick belongs "is less a calculus than a mercantilism of values. . . . Values are balanced, exchanged, and traded off for one another, the moral judgment becomes a commerce and merchandizing in human

---

[61] See Christopher Kaczor, "Proportionalism and the Pill: How Consistent Application of Theory Leads to Contradiction to Practice," in Kaczor, *Proportionalism*, 466–76, esp. 468, 475.

[62] McCormick, "Ambiguity in Moral Choice," 46.

[63] Charles Curran, *A New Look at Christian Morality* (Notre Dame, IN: Fides, 1970), 239.

conduct and Christian behavior."[64] But aren't we always weighing values when we make decisions? In traditional morality a weighing of values is engaged when one is faced with keeping a secret or disclosing it in a situation where someone's well-being is at stake. Weighing values is at the heart of many of our ordinary decisions: we forgo career advancement in order to have more time with family; we choose to work with less pay rather than take a high-powered and lucrative position for the sake of a more tension-free life; one decides to be a labor-union lawyer rather than be a corporate lawyer in order to engage in structural and systemic change for social justice. I hold, as McCormick states, that in our weighing of values, we do all we can to guarantee that our calculus be truly adequate and fully Christian.

Grisez holds that basic goods such as life, knowledge, and integrity are incommensurable; they cannot be weighed against one another, for they have no common denominator or reference. Christopher Kaczor states the view of Grisez in the following: "In so far as proportionalism presupposes that one can find a proportion between various different basic goods, proportionalism is no more than a rationalization of any choice the agent wishes."[65] As such, Grisez considers proportionalism not only nonsense but "dangerous nonsense."[66] He and Boyle, among others, oppose proportionalism because it is altogether unworkable. It is, they charge, a calculative method, and this calculation cannot be done unless the values of various outcomes can be measured against one another; but such outcomes are simply incommensurable.[67] A number of proportionalists and non-proportionalists have criticized Grisez's theory of incommensurability of basic human goods.[68]

We can, in fact, make value comparisons and assessments. Edward Vacek offers an insightful comment: "We are sure that loving a friend

---

[64] Paul Quay, "Morality by Calculation of Values," *Theology Digest* 23 (1975): 352.

[65] Christopher Kaczor, "Introduction," in Kaczor, *Proportionalism,* 15. See Germain Grisez, *The Way of the Lord Jesus,* vol. 1, *Christian Moral Principles* (Chicago: Franciscan Herald Press, 1983), 156.

[66] Germain Grisez, "Against Consequentialism," in Kaczor, *Proportionalism,* 246.

[67] Germain Grisez and John Boyle, *Life and Death with Liberty and Justice* (Notre Dame, IN: University of Notre Dame Press, 1979), 349–51. See also William Cosgrave, "The Principle of Double Effect—An Unresolved Debate," *The Furrow* 40/12 (December 1989): 713.

[68] Among proportionalists, see Garth Hallett, *Greater Good: The Case for Proportionalism* (Washington, DC: Georgetown University Press, 1995). From a non-proportionalist perspective, see Russell Rittenger, *A Critique of the New Natural Law Theory* (Notre Dame, IN: University of Notre Dame Press, 1987).

is in itself more valuable than tasting peaches, even if the former is fraught with pain and the latter consistently gives pleasure. Anyone who could not make such a comparison of these 'incomparables' would have to be value-blind, bereft of value judgment."[69] In conflict situations, where evil is inevitable, the rule of Christian reason, as it is governed by the *ordo bonorum*, is to choose the lesser evil. This, it seems, is beyond debate, for the only alternative is to choose the greater evil, which is patently absurd. Likewise, if one has to choose the good, one must choose the greater good, or that which is at the best service of the good.

Grisez, however, insists that basic goods are "equally ultimate."[70] The word *equal* presumably does not suggest a term of comparison, but rather is meant negatively, that is, a matter of incommensurability. He further claims that we can never act directly against a basic good.[71] Respect for all basic goods means "one should never act directly against any of the fundamental goods."[72] However, some kind of commensurability of good is implied in another statement he makes: "Not even the parent and physician need always act to preserve and promote life, for sometimes other goods also are very pressing."[73] This led Vacek to inquire: "On what rational basis might one choose to realize one incommensurable good, omit another, and not preserve still another, if in fact they are incommensurable?"[74] Grisez and other critics of the ethics of holistic reasoning can be taken to task for their inconsistency in applying their critique on commensurability of goods.[75] McCormick takes up Grisez's issue of basic goods and gives quite a thoughtful, balanced, and nuanced position:

> Further reflection by practical reason tells us what it means to remain open and to pursue these basic human values. First we must take them into account in our conduct. Simple disregard of one or other shows we have set our mind against this good.

[69] Vacek, "Proportionalism," 304.

[70] Germain Grisez, *Abortion: The Myths, the Realities, and the Arguments* (Washington, DC: Corpus Books, 1970), 315.

[71] Grisez and Boyle, *Life and Death with Liberty and Justice*, 368.

[72] Germain Grisez and Russell Shaw, *Beyond the New Morality: The Responsibilities of Freedom* (Notre Dame, IN: University of Notre Dame Press, 1974), 130.

[73] Grisez, *Abortion*, 319.

[74] Vacek, "Proportionalism," 310.

[75] Among proportionalists, see Hallett, *Greater Good*. From a non-proportionalist perspective, see Rittenger, *A Critique of the New Natural Law Theory* (Notre Dame, IN: University of Notre Dame Press, 1987).

Second, when we can do so as easily as not, we should avoid acting in ways that inhibit these values, and prefer ways that we realize them. Third, we must make an effort on their behalf when their realization in another is in extreme peril. If we fail to do so, we show that the value in question is not the object of our efficacious love and concern. Finally, we must never choose against a basic good in the sense of spurning it. What is to count as "turning against a basic good" is, of course, the crucial moral question. Certainly it does not mean that there are never situations of conflicted values where it is necessary to cause harm as we go about doing good.[76]

Ethics of holistic reasoning scholars admit, however, that what needs to be further developed in holistic reasoning is its "value theory." There should be an in-depth analysis of value assessment that would result in consensus on objective hierarchical relations of potentially conflicting values. Probing the hierarchy of complex relations of goods is the substantive task of moral philosophers and theologians. Lisa Cahill holds that formulating a theory of value assessment is vital for the ethics of holistic reasoning epistemology.[77] Paulinus Odozor, however, does not share Cahill's view.[78]

I hold that any assessment of value or determination of hierarchy of goods should not be abstracted from the context of lived experience. For example, in the case of the lived experience of the poor, the basic human needs of food, shelter, education, and medical care surpass all other basic goods. Until these basic human needs are satisfied, other goods are subordinate. Likewise, the lived experience underlying the feminist agenda can challenge perceptions of basic good and what constitutes authentic personhood. The lived contexts, thus, of socioeconomic oppression and gender oppression

---

[76] Richard McCormick, "Does Religious Faith Add to Ethical Perception," in *Introduction to Christian Ethics: A Reader*, ed. Ronald P. Hamel and Kenneth R. Himes, 140–45 (New York: Paulist Press, 1979), 142.

[77] Cahill, "Teleology, Utilitarianism, and Christian Ethics," 617.

[78] Odozor does not agree with Cahill's view that the lack of a hierarchy of values constitutes a shortcoming in McCormick's teleology. In fact, he says, this indicates that if one has to take a route to ethics, it has to be through responsible teleology. He holds that the difficulty Cahill points out stems from the finite condition, the fact that we have individual, social, and cultural differences. He further argues that determining a hierarchy of values is not foreign to any normal adult; it is not something that theoreticians instead of adult decision makers do. See Paulinus Odozor, *Richard A. McCormick and the Renewal of Moral Theology* (Notre Dame, IN: Notre Dame Press, 1995), 108–9.

can bring to question a hierarchy of goods that is universalized in the abstract.[79]

Todd Salzman writes: "While basic goods are incommensurable, each equal in relation to other, this is only so in the abstract realm. Actual moral judgment takes place not in the abstract, within the world of ideas, but in the lived contexts which provide the common denominator by which basic goods can be compared, prioritized, and chosen in relation to one another."[80] When goods conflict in human situations, commensuration becomes necessary. Holistic ethical reasoning is the norm or principle for commensuration. "While commensuration of goods is not a precise science, and indeed is very difficult at times, this difficulty does not render proportionate reason meaningless, irrational, or a principle of justification and rationalization."[81] What commensuration and proportionate reason recognize is that the way of arriving at a judgment of proportionality is not monolithic, and the prudent person is best to make this judgment.[82]

McCormick refers repeatedly to the "prediscursive" elements of moral judgment, coming primarily from good moral common sense. He speaks of a moral instinct of faith, which "cannot be adequately subjected to analytic reflection but is also chiefly responsible for one's ultimate judgment, in concrete moral questions."[83] This demands a qualitative sensitivity to the depth and breadth of value. It is the well-ordered heart that is both the origin and result of ethical decision. "Compassion and depth of feeling are more important than calculation."[84] Even if this is profoundly true, the ethicist is not dispensed of the task to probe unceasingly the conceptual and normative warrants for moral judgment. "The judgment of proportionality in conflict situations is not only a very decisive judgment; it

---

[79] See Todd A. Salzman, *What Are They Saying About Catholic Ethical Method?* (New York: Paulist Press, 2003), 75. See also Lisa Sowle Cahill, "Feminist, Ethics, Differences, and Common Ground: A Catholic Perspective," in Readings in Moral Theology, no. 9, *Feminist Ethics and the Catholic Moral Tradition*, ed. Charles E. Curran, Margaret A. Farley, and Richard A. McCormick, 184–204 (New York: Paulist Press, 1996), 185; and Grisez, *The Way of the Lord Jesus*, 298.

[80] Salzman, *What Are They Saying About Catholic Ethical Method*, 40.

[81] Ibid.

[82] McCormick, "Notes on Moral Theology: 1985," *Theological Studies* 47/1 (1986): 87–88.

[83] Richard A. McCormick, "Reproductive Technologies: Ethical Issues," *Encyclopedia of Bioethics*, ed. Warren T. Reich, 1454–64 (New York: Free Press, 1978), 1459.

[84] Vacek, "Proportionalism," 303.

is also a difficult one."[85] We have discussed the three conditions that are required for holistic ethical reasoning to be established, which McCormick has systematically formulated in the following:

1. The value sought is greater or at least equal to the value sacrificed.
2. There is no less harmful way of protecting this value here and now.
3. The manner of its protection here and now will not undermine it in the long run.[86]

Only by meeting these three conditions is a holistic ethical reason established. The foregoing could be put negatively. An action is disproportionate: (1) If a lesser value is preferred to a greater value; (2) If evil is unnecessarily caused in the protection of the greater good; and (3) If the circumstances, the manner of protecting the good will undermine it in the long run.

Ethics of holistic moral reasoning not only asks *What?* and *Why?* to determine the values that the moral agent seeks; it also asks *How?* and *What else?* to inquire into all possible courses of action to establish that the means taken is the last resort in protecting this value in the least harmful way; and finally it asks *What if?* to inquire into all possible consequences of the means used that might undermine the value sought in the long run. The three conditions are so integrated that if one condition is not realized, there is moral disproportion. When stated simply, and to show how the three conditions constitute one holistic ethical movement, we can say that the very means used to protect the greater value must not bring about consequences that will undermine it in the long run.

All three conditions, as a whole, show if there is a moral proportion between the act and its end (reason). The very structure of holistic ethical reasoning protects moral choice from mere subjective arbitrariness. If, in the final analysis, there is a contradiction between the act and its end, then the act undermines its very rationale. Or, in other words, the act becomes counterproductive because there is a moral disproportion between it and its end. Knauer writes: "An act becomes immoral when it is contradictory to the fullest achievement of its own end in relation to the whole of reality."[87]

---

[85] McCormick, "Ambiguity in Moral Choice," 46.
[86] Ibid., 45.
[87] Knauer, "The Hermeneutic Function of the Principle of Double Effect," 37.

Holistic ethical reasoning in the school of McCormick and others draws primarily upon the Aristotelian-Thomistic interpretative tradition of a teleological ethics. The primary difference between the utilitarianism of Bentham and Mill and the teleology of Aristotle and Aquinas is that the good *(telos)* sought is perceived differently. Utilitarianism pursues the greatest good for the greatest number and the greatest sum total of social welfare. In contrast, Aristotle and Aquinas envision the *telos* of human life as the realization of virtue, a life oriented to the *summum bonum*, God, from the Christian faith view. Beyond the utilitarian *telos* that is finite and material and limited, the *telos* from the faith view is all-encompassing and transcendent, for God is the ultimate end of all that is.[88]

The moral theory of Richard McCormick exemplifies Christian teleology. The full Christian experience, he writes, provides the refinement of sensitivity to human values. The Christian perspective provides the broader and deeper horizon of meaning to moral reasoning. A value judgment distanced from this horizon of meaning might otherwise be determined solely by empiricism.

> The Christian story tells us the ultimate meaning of ourselves and the world. In doing so, it tells us the kind of people we ought to be, the goods we ought to pursue, the dangers we ought to avoid, the kind of world we ought to seek. It provides the backdrop or framework that ought to shape our individual decisions. When decision making is separated from this framework, it loses its perspective. It becomes a merely rationalistic and sterile ethics subject to distortions of self-interested perspectives and cultural fads, a kind of contracted etiquette with no relation to the ultimate meaning of person.[89]

It is within this framework of the Christian story that the conditions of holistic ethical reasoning are realized in terms of the choice of higher over lower values in a hierarchy *(ordo bonorum)* that is properly ordered; this constitutes human flourishing precisely because the finite order of values originates in and is oriented to the *summum bonum*, God. As a whole, a holistic ethical method refers not only to results. "It also pertains to the agent, to expressive and evolving

---

[88] See Cahill, "Teleology, Utilitarianism, and Christian Ethics," 627–29.

[89] Richard A. McCormick, *Health and Medicine in the Catholic Tradition* (New York: Crossroad, 1984), 50. For a critique of McCormick's views, see Peter Clark, "Richard McCormick, SJ, and Dual Epistemology," *Christian Bioethics* 14/3 (2008): 236–71.

natural tendencies, to intentions, acts, and manners of acting, to the circumstances as well as social situations . . . and to the religious context."[90]

All in all, the important aspects of the ethics of holistic reasoning include the primacy of context for moral objectivity, the use of pre-moral concepts *vs.* the privileging of *finis opera,* the employment of a new hermeneutics of direct and indirect principles, and holistic ethical reasoning as a non-utilitarian Christian teleology. These demonstrate the drive for holism in the pursuit of moral objectivity.

Virtue Ethics

Since Vatican II the human person as integrally and adequately considered is the fundamental criterion of Christian morality, since morality has turned to the moral subject and away from the finality of bodily structures and functions. Catholic moral theology, in particular, has become more open to the language of character and virtue, beyond the questions on rightness or wrongness of acts, which many hold largely characterized the dilemma ethics that has dominated Christian ethics and moral theology for three decades. I argue, however, that the ethics of holistic reasoning does not separate the act from the agent and thus is not focused alone on the rightness or wrongness of the act apart from the agent as moral subject. Virtue ethics pushes further the focus on the moral agent, as it completely addresses the person as a moral character.

The proponents of virtue ethics state that as an ethical method it attends to the development of virtues that perfect the agent as a moral person while acting morally well. It is not interested in particular actions but in the formation of person and character. It shifts the stress of the question from *What should I do?* to *Who am I? Who should I become?* It holds that, opposed to the focus of dilemma ethics on major and controversial ethical questions of abortion, gay marriage, contraception, gene therapy, and war, virtue ethics attends to what people face morally in their everyday lives.[91]

In treating here the issues of virtue ethics in Thomistic thought, a contemporary retrieval of virtue ethics, and the ethics of character and ethics of principles, my end goal is to locate the meeting grounds of virtue ethics and the ethics of holistic reasoning, though of different

---

[90] Vacek, "Proportionalism," 290.

[91] See James F. Keenan, "Virtue Ethics," in *Christian Ethics: An Introduction,* ed. Bernard Hoose (Collegeville, MN: Liturgical Press, 1998), 84–94.

ethical modes, in view of proposing an ethical methodology for moral reasoning in conflict situations.

Virtue Ethics in Thomistic Thought

Aquinas makes a general distinction between infused virtues and acquired virtues. The infused virtues (faith, hope, and charity) are directed to our supernatural end. They cannot be acquired by human power; they must be infused in us directly by God. Through grace, faith, hope, and charity are bestowed upon us, making us partakers of the divine life. Through charity, we come to a friendship with God, a knowing and intimate relationship, in which all our impulses and desires are oriented to God, transforming our entire being.

Acquired virtues can be obtained through our habitual behavior oriented toward our full human flourishing. Aquinas names four acquired virtues, called cardinal virtues because they are the principal virtues for a well-ordered life: prudence, justice, fortitude, and temperance. Aquinas's four cardinal virtues are hierarchical, with justice as the chief moral virtue and temperance subordinate to fortitude, but both auxiliary to justice, while prudence functions to determine the mean of all three and also to unite them in the same way that charity unites the infused virtues. Justice is superior to all the other virtues because it is closest to reason and also is the only relational virtue, governing our exterior actions. With justice on the top of the hierarchy of the Thomistic virtue ethics, it presents a virtuous person as primarily a just person. Justice governs all actions; temperance and fortitude serve justice, in the sense that we are called to be temperate and brave, so we can be just.

In their hierarchical relationships the virtues have no competitive claims, but only distinctive roles or functions. Prudence orders our practical reason; justice perfects our will; courage and temperance perfect our emotions and passions. Prudence sets the agenda of the virtues, aligning it to the overall end of life and discerning the standards of action for attaining the end. But the ultimate goal of prudence, as it is for temperance and fortitude, is for the person to become what he or she is called to be—a virtuous person, who is to be a just person.[92]

Thomistic virtue ethics is criticized for privileging justice, and thus diminishing or neglecting the place of other virtues like care and love. Simply to be just is insufficient, for there are other relational claims on us. Whereas one must be just—that is, one must treat everyone

---

[92] James F. Keenan, "Proposing Cardinal Virtues," *Theological Studies* 56/4 (1995): 709–29, esp. 717–19.

equally—one needs to attend to the immediate needs of friends, family, and community. Thomistic virtue ethics is also criticized for being abstracted from real lives and real conflicts. Its unity is found in some theoretical/hierarchical apportioning of cardinal virtues to specific powers or functions rather than in the actual living out of the virtues. But when virtues make claim on us in a variety of ways, they can conflict. Stanley Hauerwas states that we face the task of sorting out "conflicting loyalties" throughout our lives.[93] The insufficiency of the classical list of virtues and its hierarchical uniformity reveals an anthropology that understands moral agents as objects rather than subjects, as it is focused on the perfection of what they have rather than who they are, on the things inside them rather than on their ways of being.[94]

A Contemporary Retrieval of Virtue Ethics

James Keenan proposes a new vision of virtue ethics that speaks of persons as relational in three ways: generally, specifically, and uniquely. Each way demands a cardinal virtue. "As a relational being in general, we are called to justice. As a relational being specifically, we are called to fidelity. As a relational being uniquely, we are called to self-care."[95] Moving away from the hierarchical anthropology of Aquinas and the privileging of justice, Keenan holds that justice, fidelity, and self-care are ends in themselves, with none as ethically prior or auxiliary to the other. Each one is cardinal. The fourth virtue is prudence, which determines which way of life is just, faithful, and self-caring.

Keenan describes justice as directed to the common good, which treats people as equal and basic rights as universal. The goal of moral life is to become impartial, and thus to break all forms of bias and prejudice. As impartiality and universality are to justice, partiality and particularity are to fidelity. Fidelity protects our special and particular bonds, as we are called to be faithful to those who are closest in the hierarchy of relationships. Justice and fidelity, pursuing their own ends, can come into conflict. Keenan, drawing from classic plays and movies, describes this conflict: Antigone is caught as she stands between

---

[93] Stanley Hauerwas, *A Community of Character* (Notre Dame, IN: University of Notre Dame Press, 1981), 144.

[94] Keenan, "Proposing Cardinal Virtues," 723. See also Stephen Pope, "The Order of Love and Recent Catholic Ethics: A Constructive Proposal," *Theological Studies* 52/2 (1991): 255—88.

[95] Keenan, "Proposing Cardinal Virtues," 723.

the demand of peace for her city and obedience to law and her filial love for her brother, who remains unburied outside the city walls; in the film *The Music Box* a lawyer turns her back on her fidelity to her father, as she becomes his accuser of the crimes he committed against humanity; in *The Long Walk Home*, a wife rejects her husband's claim on her in her pursuit of civil and human rights.[96]

These examples show people choosing justice over fidelity. The following examples show the reverse: In the movie *Scent of a Woman*, a prep-school student decides not to report on his classmates in the face of the harm they have caused to the whole school; in *Terminator* a boy called to save the world endangers humanity's entire existence when he saves his mother first. The characters in these dramas were torn between two distinct and opposed claims.[97]

The third cardinal virtue is self-care, with self-esteem as its subcategory. It is a mistaken view to diminish or neglect this virtue. It is as important as the other two; in fact, self-care is the foundation of love for others. It is from the wellspring of self-care and self-worth that one draws one's resources for attending to the needs of others. And the fourth virtue is prudence, which is necessary to discern and determine how to live a life of justice, fidelity, and self-care in the complexity of being human and in the face of conflicts.[98]

Other scholars introduce ways of integrating seemingly conflicting virtues, such as the following formulation by Walter Burghardt: "not faith nor justice; one word, a newly coined word . . . faithjustice. This is the faith that does justice. Each word is significant in itself, but it is the two in combination that shapes a spirituality of justice."[99] Margaret Farley speaks of sexual love as just love, that is, founded on love and a justice that is loving.[100] Other scholars, however, see that there are virtues that cannot be integrated. For instance, A.D.M. Walder argues that justice and kindness cannot cohere in a single person. "One's

---

[96] Ibid., 726.

[97] Ibid.

[98] Keenan makes his own proposal of the cardinal virtues in view of the inadequacy of the classical list of cardinal virtues in the face of contemporary challenges. See ibid., 723–28.

[99] Walter Burghardt, "Characteristics of Social Justice Spirituality," *Origins* 24/9 (July 1994): 159. See also Fred Kammer, SJ, *Doing Faithjustice: An Introduction to Catholic Social Thought* (New York: Paulist Press, 2004).

[100] Margaret A. Farley, "An Ethic for Same Sex Relations," in *A Challenge to Love: Gay and Lesbian Catholics in the Church*, ed. Robert Nugent (New York: Crossroad, 1983), 93–106; see also idem, *Personal Commitments: Beginning, Keeping, Changing* (San Francisco: Harper and Row, 1990).

impartial commitment to principles may be inimical to attachments to certain persons because of their particular individuality."[101]

This debate between caring and justice echoes a longstanding discussion in moral psychology. Carol Gilligan claims that there are gender differences when it comes to virtue orientations. She holds that women tend toward the ethics of care, while men tend toward the ethics of justice. These gender differences go back to the two distinct paths of childhood of boys and girls, as the former tend toward separation from mother to assert independence and the latter tend toward attachment to mother to possess intimacy.[102]

The debate evokes strong reactions. Sidney Callahan asserts that the "two voice" hypothesis of Gilligan is flawed. Moral reasoning transcends sex differences. Women are as principled and justice oriented as men. Rather than sex and gender, class, age, and power influence moral reasoning.[103] Claudia Caird, in the same vein, holds that Gilligan's reliance on psychological explanations ignores political forces in explaining sex differences in relation to the practice of virtues.[104] Mary Ellen Ross charges that Gilligan's theory reinforces sexist and gender stereotypes; that is, women are relegated to the nurturing domestic sphere while men are assigned to the impersonal public realm of power and institutions.[105] Owen Flanagan sets out the most devastating critique of Gilligan's theory, judging it empirically false and philosophically inadequate, because it is based on a dubious neo-Freudian framework. He holds, however, that the failure of the two-voice hypothesis does not deny significant gender differences in moral experiences; like many other scholars, he looks to other avenues as more promising than the neo-Freudian analysis of childhood for reasons for these differences, like self-concept, personal ideals, cultural formation, and others.[106]

---

[101] A.D.M. Walder, "Virtue and Character," *Philosophy* 64 (1989): 356.

[102] Carol Gilligan, *In a Different Voice: Psychological Theory and Women's Development* (Cambridge, MA: Harvard University Press, 1993).

[103] Sidney Callahan, *In Good Conscience: Reason and Education in Moral Decision Making* (San Francisco: Harper and Collins, 1991), 196.

[104] Claudia Caird, "Gender and Moral Luck," in *Identity, Character, and Morality: Essays in Moral Psychology,* ed. Owen Flanagan and Amélie Oksenberg Rorty (Cambridge, MA: MIT, 1990), 199–218; see also idem, "Women and Moral Theory," *Ethics* 91 (1998): 125–35.

[105] Mary Ellen Ross, "Feminism and the Problem of Moral Character," *Journal of Feminist Studies in Religion* 5/2 (Fall 1989): 57.

[106] Owen Flanagan, *Varieties of Moral Personality: Ethics and Psychological Realism* (Cambridge, MA: Harvard University Press, 1991), 240.

What one can glean from this discussion is that moral experience is too complex to be reduced to any one virtue. Moral reasoning must be likened to a Swiss army knife, with its multiple gadgets, rather than just one or two. Human life is rich, complex, and multileveled. A narrow and monolithic approach to it does not correspond to reality. And when culture is thrown into the entire mix, there is an explosion of differences. MacIntyre holds that the practices that shape the excellent person are determined by local communities. He notes that Homeric culture held the warrior as the prototypically excellent person and therefore emphasized the virtue of bravery, while Aristotle presumed the Athenian gentleman as the excellent person and promoted the virtue of prudence.[107]

Flanagan argues that to create a single anthropological portrait normative for moral conduct is pointless, because individuals are complex and human experience is original.[108] This is exemplified in the moral excellence of saints who are originals, not imitations: Thérèse of Lisieux is not John the Baptizer.[109] What is proposed instead is a modest and minimal portrait of a virtuous person that would be given specific content in diverse cultures. Nussbaum advocates an understanding of the human that can create a common ground for intercultural discourse. There are virtues so basic that any person can recognize them in himself or herself, that can be articulated in different and diverse ways across cultures and peoples.[110] What is needed is an exchange across time and place of what it means to be and to act in minimally integrated virtuous ways, using basic virtues as referential points.[111]

Ethics of Virtue and Ethics of Principles

Aline Kalbian concludes that there are no clear causal relationships between proportionalism and other approaches. She, however, asserts

[107] Alasdair C. MacIntyre, *After Virtue: A Study in Moral Theory* (Notre Dame, IN: University of Notre Dame Press, 1981); also see idem, *Whose Justice? Which Rationality?* (Notre Dame, IN: University of Notre Dame Press, 1988).

[108] Flanagan, *Varieties of Moral Personality.*

[109] Caroline Walker Bynum warns us against considering a saint as a model of virtue. See *Holy Feast and Holy Fast* (Berkeley and Los Angeles: University of California Press, 1987), 7.

[110] Martha C. Nussbaum, "Non-Relative Values: An Aristotelian Approach," in *Moral Disagreements: Classic and Contemporary Readings,* ed. Christopher W. Gowans (New York: Routledge, 2000), 168–79.

[111] See cross-cultural studies on courage and honor in Lee H. Yearley, *Mencius and Aquinas: Theories of Virtue and Conceptions of Courage* (Albany: State University of New York Press, 1990); and Frank Henderson Stewart, *Honor* (Chicago: University of Chicago Press, 1994).

that proportionalism has created a conceptual space that has encouraged a hospitable atmosphere for more particularistic approaches.[112] In the same light I argue that the ethics of holistic reasoning has preceded and facilitated agent-centered and context-driven ethical approaches.

There has been much discussion on how virtue ethics, as an ethics of character, relates to the ethics of principles, which we call here the ethics of holistic reasoning. How exactly does virtue relate to rules and principles? There are three schools of thought: one, virtue ethics is auxiliary to ethics of principles; two, virtue ethics is more primal than the ethics of principles; and three, the ethics of character and ethics of principles are mutually necessary.

The first school of thought holds that virtue ethics cannot be an independent method of moral reasoning. Virtues are auxiliary to rules and principles. They enable us to accomplish what the principles and rules direct. Strict deontologists hold that virtues are dispositions to act upon moral imperatives; they merely restate rules and duty in motivational terms.[113] Furthermore, virtues rely upon feelings, which cannot be relevant to morality, since morality is directed by clear moral action guides. If feelings alone were to govern our moral action, morality would be justified by personal intuitions that elude public scrutiny and accountability.[114]

The second school of thought, which Martha Nussbaum represents, argues for the primacy of virtues to judge moral conduct. They can adequately provide the standards of morally right conduct. Virtues, not principles, constitute the basis of normative conduct; rules and principles are derived from virtues and obtain their content from them.[115] Following rules and principles without the requisite virtue is only going through the motions. It is impossible, for instance, to be grateful without having the virtue of gratitude. Gratitude is more than a disposition to obey a moral rule. It also consists in "having certain beliefs, feelings, and attitudes toward, and about one's benefactors."[116]

---

[112] Kalbian, "Where Have All the Proportionalists Gone?" 19.

[113] See John Rawls, *A Theory of Justice* (Oxford: Oxford University Press, 1971), 192, 437. See also Alan Gewirth, "Rights and Virtues," *The Review of Metaphysics* 38 (1985): 757.

[114] William Spohn cites other philosophical problems with virtue ethics. See "The Return of Virtue Ethics," *Theological Studies* 53/1 (1992): 60–75, esp. 63–64.

[115] Martha C. Nussbaum, *The Fragility of Goodness: Luck and Ethics in Greek Tragedy and Philosophy* (New York: Cambridge University Press, 1986), 299; see also John Kekes, *The Examined Life* (Lewisburg, PA: Bucknell University Press, 1988).

[116] Walter E. Schaller, "Are Virtues No More Than Dispositions to Obey Moral Rules?" *Philosophia* 20 (July 1990): 201.

Virtue is needed to apply standards, because much of right conduct cannot be codified in rules or principles. Life is so complex and moral principles are so general that the virtues of justice, empathy, compassion, and sensitivity can alert us to the moral demands and needs of situations.[117] The judgments of virtue by persons of wisdom and prudence would be the most right, the most practical, and the most human in such situations.[118]

The third school of thought is located at the midpoint of the two other schools. Jean Porter shows that Thomas intimately relates virtue ethics and ethics of principles. She states: "The current distinction between virtue-based ethical systems and rule-based ethical systems cannot be applied to Thomas. For him true moral rectitude is necessarily grounded in the orientation of the whole personality that charity creates; and yet, charity cannot be exercised or even exist, unless the moral rules generated by right reason are observed."[119] Gregory Trianosky takes the same position, arguing that virtues are not complete alternatives to moral principles; both are needed for ethics to be practical. He agrees that virtues are indispensable for applying rules and determining what to do when no rules apply. But in the first case, rules must be applied and conflicts between rules must be resolved. The rules, however, do not tell us how to apply them in specific situations, let alone apply them well, or indeed when to excuse people for failing to comply with them.[120]

I take the position of the third school of thought, which I consider to be inclusive of the second school of thought. I take a different direction, however, from the sharp distinction of virtue ethics as an ethics of character and the ethics of holistic reasoning as an ethics of principles; that is, that virtue ethics only asks *Who ought we to be?* and not *What ought we do?* and, on the reverse, that the ethics of holistic reasoning only asks *What ought we do?* and not *Who are we?* I argue that these questions are so integral to moral reasoning that

---

[117] For discussions on the role of virtues in practical matters, see Rosalind Hursthouse, "Virtue Theory and Abortion," *Philosophy and Public Affairs* 20 (1991): 223–46; David Fisher, "Crisis in Moral Communities: An Essay in Moral Philosophy," *Journal of Value Inquiry* 24 (1990): 17–30.

[118] Sidney Callahan relates psychological research to moral experience in *In Good Conscience: Reason and Emotion in Moral Decision Making* (San Francisco: Harper Collins, 1991).

[119] Jean Porter, "*De Ordine Caritatis*: Charity, Friendship, and Justice in Thomas Aquinas' *Summa Theologiae*," *Thomist* 53 (1989): 213.

[120] Gregory Trianosky, "What Is Virtue Ethics All About?" *American Philosophical Quarterly* 27/4 (October 1990): 342.

they are never separated. The question of being/identity enters deeply into the question of actions, and likewise the question of actions is founded on the question of being/identity. I grant that these questions are not articulated with the same clarity, depth, and intensity at all times, but this does not mean that they are not always making claims on our moral reasoning and decision making. In the words of Thomas Aquinas, "Virtue is that which makes its possessor good, and his work good likewise."[121]

The common critique of virtue ethics is that while it has so much to offer to moral life in general, it does not provide the methodology to resolve difficult moral dilemmas. It fails to be action guiding, and it does not offer any means of act appraisal.[122] Christine Swanton asks: "The rightness of an act is critically determined by a qualified agent, but how qualified is a virtuous agent?"[123] On the other hand, answers to real moral issues are premised ultimately on what is truly good and worthwhile in life. And only virtuous persons with fine sensibilities and discriminatory powers can judge right and desire to act accordingly because it is their disposition to act well. Tom Beauchamp offers his observation in the healthcare context of the importance of persons motivated by virtue:

> Virtue theory is of the highest importance in a health-care context because a morally good person with the right motives is more likely to discern what should be done, to be motivated to do it, and to do it. The person who simply follows rules and possesses no special moral character may not be morally reliable. The person who simply follows rules and possesses no special moral character may not be morally reliable. Often the reactions people have to those in the past who wronged patients—in research for example is that they lacked discernment, compassion, and trustworthiness, not that they failed to act in accordance with a rule or principle.[124]

---

[121] Thomas Aquinas, *Summa Theologiae* 1a2ae q.56. a.3.

[122] See Ann Marie Begley, "Practising Virtue: A Challenge to the View That a Virtue Centred Approach to Ethics Lacks Practical Content," *Nursing Ethics* [Belfast, Northern Ireland] 12/6 (2005): 622–37. See also Donald N. Bersoff, "The Virtue of Principle Ethics," *The Counseling Psychologist* 24/1 (January 1, 1996): 86–91.

[123] Christine Swanton, "A Virtue Ethical Account of Right Action," *Ethics* 112 (October 2001): 34.

[124] Tom L. Beauchamp, "Principlism and Its Alleged Competitors," *Kennedy Institute of Ethics Journal* 5/3 (September 1995): 194–95.

The point here is not "to demonstrate the superiority of one normative theory over the other, but rather how to relate one to the other in a matrix that does justice to each and assigns to each its normative force."[125] The virtuous person uses rationality (practical wisdom) in order to make good choices in acting well. And by acting well, he or she flourishes as a person of virtue.[126] In virtue ethics, persons must exercise prudential reasoning to negotiate all the competing allegiances in order to know what justice, fidelity, and self-care require of them in the concrete human context. In the ethics of holistic reasoning, prudential reasoning is exercised as guided by principles. At the center of the proposed ethical methodology for moral reasoning in conflict situations is a person of virtue engaged in a profound moral inquiry.

A Proposed Methodology for Conflict Situations

The methodology I propose takes an approach that integrates the ethics of virtue and the ethics of holistic reasoning. It also proposes the use of narrative as a method that privileges life stories as a source of personal and moral intelligibility, in light of the primacy of the human context of moral reasoning.

Primacy of Context: Thinking with Stories

No moral theory can be adequate if it does not take into account the narrative of our experience. Thinking with stories is a concept borrowed by David Morris from sociologist Arthur W. Frank.[127] I interpret this concept as that way of allowing our stories to shape our thinking and reasoning. It is a thinking which collaborates reasoning with feeling and imagining, because stories engage our minds as well as our hearts. The purpose of taking into account the narrative of our moral experience is critical for moral reasoning, because it is necessary to establish the context, the human locus, of moral objectivity. All moral reasoning begins with, is shaped by, and is determined by the context. The context provides the resource for moral reasoning;

---

[125] Edmund Pellegrino, "Toward a Virtue-Based Normative Ethics for the Health Professions," *Kennedy Institute of Ethics Journal* 5/3 (September 1995): 273.

[126] P. Gardiner, "A Virtue Ethics Approach to Moral Dilemmas in Medicine," *Journal of Medical Ethics* 29 (2003): 298.

[127] Arthur W. Frank, *The Wounded Storyteller: Body, Illness, and Ethics* (Chicago: University of Chicago Press, 1995), 23–25. Also see Osborne P. Wiggins and Annette C. Allen, eds., *Clinical Ethics and the Necessity of Stories: Essays in Honor of Richard M. Zaner* (New York: Springer, 2011).

apart from it, moral reasoning exists in a vacuum, abstracted from the actual human situations where people are struggling with their human choices.

The first-person narrative, or personal story, or story of a people is a rich source for qualitative data about the unique lives of individuals. They are also a means for making moral life intelligible—why individuals and societies do what they do. While narratives privilege personal stories, plurality of stories is encouraged so that multiple voices are heard from all those whose lives are involved in and affected by the moral conflict. The richer the texture of the narrative, the better; one sees reality as it is, with its shared meanings and competing perspectives in people's lives.

Alasdair MacIntyre claims that what is significant about human beings is their social embeddedness. He considers that an individual's very capacity for choice is shaped, enabled, and made meaningful by the traditions of the person's community.[128] Narratives navigate the coherence of people's lives with the deep values that have shaped them—values rooted in their cultures and religions or in their particular way of life. Engaged with the subjective, intersubjective, and intrasubjective, narratives witness to the particular, provisional, partial, subjective, fragmented dimensions of life, seeking to find intelligibility and coherence.

A good narrativist must have the critical and empathetic skills to observe and identify patterns of meaning; to follow complex plots; to understand different cultural, social, and religious perspectives; to consider and test multiple narratives; and to fit fragments and parts within a larger frame of meaning. A good ethicist is a good narrativist, because thinking with stories is itself theoretically robust, as one cuts through the rich fabric of narratives to see the ethical justifications of decisions intricately woven into the relational, interrelational, and communal dimensions of moral situations.[129]

One must gather necessary information from all available sources to bring to light what is required in determining the moral objectivity on which judgment and decision are based. McCormick stresses that the "strength of our moral norms touching concrete conduct is an elaboration of what we judge within our culture, with our history and experience to be proportionate or disproportionate."[130] Thus, to

---

[128] See MacIntyre, *After Virtue*, 181–225.

[129] J. McCarthy, "Principlism or Narrative Ethics: Must We Choose Between Them?" *Medical Humanities* 29/2 (2003), 5.

[130] McCormick, "Ambiguity in Moral Choices," 44.

bring a careful, subtle, and balanced moral discernment to a particular human situation is a total human enterprise involving the relationship of faith, religion, culture, and experience in dialogue with theology and other human sciences.

A Larger Framework for Thinking with Stories

There is a need to put thinking with stories within a larger frame of reference beyond the experiential. All pertinent data and information regarding the issue or problem relative to the story or stories must be gathered to provide a larger frame for study and analysis of the context. One draws this data and information from social science, behavioral science, empirical science, and any other fields of study or research that are relevant to the said issue or problem. While putting the thinking with stories within a larger frame of reference is necessary for a broader and more enlightened understanding, James Gustafson also recommends a critical engagement with the sources that one uses. He sees the value of social and other sciences for more precise insight into the circumstances in which a moral problem occurs, for uncovering its possible causes, and for considering possible options for action.[131] But one must be critically aware of the value biases of the studies that one uses and be able to make a judgment whether the data provided are adequate and reliable.[132] The more problematic use of empirical sciences, he writes, is in "the development of moral norms. It is problematic because it raises the philosophical questions of the relations of the fact to value, of the *is* to the *ought*."[133]

In the same vein of thought, Charles Curran holds that theological ethics must be open to the data of science and technology. This openness stems from an acceptance of human reason and its ability to arrive at true wisdom and knowledge, and also from a basic recognition of the goodness of the natural and of the human.[134] He recognizes the limitations of science and technology, as there is no perfect identity between what is empirical and what is human. "The human realities of freedom, wonder, awe, and suffering all transcend

---

[131] James Gustafson, *Theology and Christian Ethics* (Philadelphia: Pilgrim Press, 1974), 219–20.

[132] Ibid., 228.

[133] Ibid., 222.

[134] Charles Curran, *Critical Concerns in Moral Theology* (Notre Dame, IN: University of Notre Dame Press, 1984), 105–6.

the empirical and the technological. Empirical science and technology can contribute much to the meaning and enhancing of the human, but there are important aspects of the human that transcend the empirical and the technological."[135]

The complexity of what is human renders the view of any one particular science narrow. There are many different sciences that contribute to our understanding of the human—the psychological, sociological, the hygienic, the eugenic, the medical—but the perspective of any one empirical science can never be equated with the total human perspective. And there is no one view within any particular empirical science. Within most disciplines there exists a great diversity of opinions that exacerbates the complexity of issues and problems.[136] An ethicist must be able to negotiate the diversity of opinions and to make a judgment on which view or opinion is more adequate, accurate, or at least plausible with reference to the understanding of what is human. Being his or her own thinker, an ethicist takes full responsibility in using empirical data, which must be subjected to critical judgment and to revision.[137] I propose the use of mutual critical correlation to characterize the relation between what is ethical and what is empirical. In this mutual critical correlation there may be identity, similarity-in-difference, and confrontation. The end goal is the conversion or transformation of both poles through open dialogue. To bring a careful, subtle, and balanced moral discernment to a particular human situation is a total human enterprise.

Reflective Equilibrium: Systematic Moral Analysis and Discernment

I refer to this element of systematic moral analysis as reflective equilibrium, because it involves weighing and balancing of virtues, values, rules, and principles in the process of moral reasoning.[138] Reflective equilibrium asks two key questions in moral reasoning: *What ought we be?* and *What ought we do?* We all find ourselves in moral dilemmas in our personal and social lives. Both virtue ethics and the ethics of holistic reasoning are necessary in our reflective equilibrium to arrive at a decision that is truly human and Christian.

---

[135] Ibid., 108.
[136] Ibid., 108–10.
[137] Gustafson, *Theology and Christian Ethics*, 227–28.
[138] See McCarthy, "Principlism or Narrative Ethics?" 2.

Virtue Ethics

One must ask what virtue is demanded of the moral agent in the concrete human situation that he or she is in. Contrary to the Thomistic theory of virtue ethics, contemporary virtue ethics shows that virtues can conflict in concrete human situations: the claims of justice over claims of fidelity; the claims of self-care over fidelity and also over justice. The virtue of prudence is necessary to discern and determine what it means to be just, faithful, or self-caring in the face of competing allegiances. I suggest that related values of common good, solidarity, compassion, respect, acceptance, forgiveness, and others fall under the general virtues of justice, fidelity, and self-care. Justice protects the common good; fidelity protects our special and particular bonds; and self-care protects our self-esteem and respect. Virtues are not abstract; they take different personal, cultural, and religious expressions and configurations. There is not one dominant paradigm for interpreting and applying virtues, given the demands of particular relationships and situations.

Thus, asking *What ought I be?* or *What kind of person should I seek to be?* or *What ought I do?* or, in a communal context, *What kind of people are we?* or *What kind of community or nation are we?* relative to virtues, requires moral analysis and discernment. How one responds to these questions is critical, because the kind of person one seeks to be enters into what one seeks to do. It creates the horizon of meaning against which one actualizes one's being into one's doing. Without this horizon of meaning, living an ethical life by only following principles can be empty and sterile. It can also be futile. Those, for instance, who have gotten into the habit of cheating can never get out of that habit unless they confront themselves at the core of their person: *What kind of person am I becoming? What kind of person do I seek to be?* Unless the problem is resolved at this level, it can be futile to attempt to break any habit of sin.

In a real sense one does not go from rule or principle to choice; one decides from a horizon of meaning. Following a rule or principle makes sense only when it is coherent to this horizon of meaning. There is, thus, an intrinsic connection between the ethics of character and the ethics of principles, and both are engaged with the concrete narrative/context of the moral situation.

Integrating Virtue Ethics and Ethics of Holistic Reasoning

Basic principles and specific actions guiding rules govern the decision-making process. In a given situation any decision or course of action is morally justified if it is consistent with ethical principles and rules. The strength of the ethics of principles is that it provides a common ground for moral reasoning beyond the vagaries of culture or creed in the public forum. People may arrive at different decisions in the end, but the ethics of principles provides objective referential points for public discourse. The ethics of holistic reasoning provides an ethical framework for moral decision in conflict situations. I attempt to translate this framework in a way that can facilitate moral reasoning by using reality-seeking questions for all three criteria of moral reasoning and integrating virtue ethics into the process:

First, What? and Why? *The value sought should be greater than or at least equal to the value sacrificed (the principle of greater good over lesser goods; the principle of best service of the good).* This criterion raises the questions of *What?* and *Why?* and requires, first of all, a thorough and accurate appraisal of the moral situation. One has to see the concrete situation in all its details and entirety. Thus, one has to investigate the "whatness" of the situation and explore all the values that are at stake in any and every possible course of action that one can opt to take. This draws information from the work done on thinking with stories and its larger framework based on data from social and empirical sciences. One determines the value or good that one seeks to protect and weighs whether that value or good is higher or at least equal to the value sacrificed. The weighing of values or goods is not done in a vacuum but in the actual context of the given moral situation, with the person integrally and adequately considered.

Asking *What?* and *Why?* is a critical moment in the ethics of holistic reasoning, for it pivots on the value or good that moral agents seek, the end of their total moral action. The means used and the consequences are directed toward this value or good. Asking *What?* is as important as *Why?* because it summons the moral agents to see reality as it is, as they investigate the objective moral reality that confronts them and all the possible courses of action they can take. Asking *Why?* places moral agents in a true discernment of not only what they are seeking to do but more primarily on who they are, for the weighing and balancing of values is grounded in the integrity of their person and character. And this is where virtue ethics and the ethics of holistic reasoning profoundly connect.

It is the virtuous person or community of virtuous persons whose calculus of values is human and Christian. The weighing of values should be governed by the virtues in asking these questions: *Who am I? What kind of person do I seek to be? What ought I do? What kind of people are we? What kind of nation do we seek to become?*

It is here that the previous critical reflection on virtue ethics in terms of the consonance or conflict of the virtues can be brought to bear on determining through prudential judgment which values should be pursued as higher values over lesser values in a given human context.

In seeking the greater good and what is in the best service of this good, McCormick offers a way of being and doing. He says that we must seek the guidance of others whose maturity, experience, reflection, and detachment from the situation could offer a counterbalance to our involved and self-interested tendencies. Furthermore, he says, we must bring our religious faith and its intentionalities to bear on our decisions. So informed, we are asked only to do the best that we possibly can. But we must depend on communal discernment, or we would only be considering from our individualistic perspectives.[139] Persons of virtue, thus, must continue to wrestle with the reality questions of *How? What else? What if?* with their sensitivity to values and their capacity for discernment in the context of community.

A second principle for moral reasoning, How? What else? *There should be no other way to realize this value in the here and now with the least possible harm (principle of last resort).* The second criterion raises the question *How?*, that is, in what manner and by what means the value is sought and realized. *What else?* is asked to ensure that one has explored all possible means and is taking the last resort to protect the value or good, with the least possible harm. What distinguishes the ethics of holistic reasoning from utilitarianism is that not just any means is taken to pursue a good or value. The morality of the means is discerned to realize the end good or value.

To avoid mere intuitionism or subjectivism in determining whether what one does to pursue the end value is the last resort and that it causes the least possible harm, one must be guided by the following subset of subsidiary principles:

---

[139] McCormick remarks that the determination of proportionality is relatively easy in cases where instrumental goods and basic goods conflict. Based on the hierarchy of goods, the instrumental goods are sacrificed for the basic goods. Thus life is chosen over property. Here a strict weighing and measuring of values is easy and possible. Other cases where proportionality is also relatively easy to determine are cases involving commensurability along quantitative lines. For instance, if one were to steer a runaway train, and there are two directions in which it can turn, but in either, people are bound to be killed, one ought to steer the train in the direction where fewer people will be killed, other things being equal. See Philippa Foot, "The Problem of Abortion and the Doctrine of Double Effect," in *Moral Problems,* ed. James Rachel (New York: Harper and Row, 1971), 41. In cases, however, where basic goods are in conflict, a more complex and subtle moral reasoning is required. See McCormick, *Ambiguity in Moral Choice,* 35.

- *The principle of indivisibility:* When the means used involves two effects, there must be an intrinsic link between the good effect and the evil effect in one indivisible act. Ethics of holistic reasoning scholars like McCormick align with this traditional principle, which is grounded on the immediacy of good and evil effects in a unity of action. For instance, in the case of surgery the very same physical act that amputates also removes a threat to life.

- *The principle of necessity of cause:* The traditional understanding of evil as an indivisible aspect of an action is only one form of evil that is morally allowed relative to a good end. The ethics of holistic reasoning maintains that when the premoral evil is a means rather than an effect, there must be a necessary causal relation between this premoral evil means and the premoral good pursued, and not only a factually efficacious relation. For example, the killing of innocent civilians is factually efficacious in the sense that it ends the war, but it does not mean that there was a necessary causal relation between killing innocent civilians and ending the war. If efficacy is made the criterion of moral rightness, then we judge actions by a crude form of consequentialism. A sheriff may not frame an innocent person for a murder he did not commit, even to prevent a riot that will kill many others. There is no necessary connection between framing an innocent person and preventing a riot, even if it factually stopped the riot. Factually efficacious is different from necessary cause.

- *The principle of lesser evil:* If evil is inevitable to protect the higher good, evil that is more than necessary is not allowed. For instance, if one can defend oneself by injuring rather than killing, then one should only injure. If one can defend oneself without even injuring, one must be bound by this limit. Superfluity of evil is forbidden.[140] For example, if the abortion of the fetus is the only way thinkable, given our medical tools, of saving the mother, otherwise both mother and fetus die, there is a necessary causal relationship between the evil done and the good achieved. And all things considered, abortion is the lesser evil in this tragic

---

[140] What is argued here is that when evil is inevitable, one must be guided by the principle of lesser evil. Georg Spielthenner examines the principle of lesser evil and holds that this principle is not well understood by most of its advocates. In his article, he first analyzes the principle of lesser evil; second, offers a critical assessment of lesser evil reasoning; and third, discusses the most common pitfalls writers tend to fall into; and finally, explores the application of lesser evil reasoning to choices under uncertainty. "Lesser Evil Reasoning and Its Pitfalls," *Argumentation* 24 (2010): 139–52.

instance. To determine what is the lesser evil in complex situations requires rigorous moral discernment. The main pitfall to be avoided in lesser evil reasoning is narrowly reducing the options. Practical problems include multiple conflicting values.[141]

Finally, a third principle for proper moral reasoning: What if? *The means used to protect this value will not undermine it in the long run.* This criterion asks *What if?* regarding the foreseeable effects and consequences of the means used to protect the good or value. In the protection of higher values, risks are taken that may involve inevitable harm. But the risks must be so calculated that the consequences will not in the long run undermine the very value that one seeks to protect. Serious attention must be given to foreseeable consequences, both short term and long term. Hence, the factual and ethical necessity to ask the question *What if?*

One must investigate all possible and foreseeable consequences not only for oneself but for others and for the larger community, both in the short run and the long run. For example, the suffering made inevitable by violent revolution must be more tolerable than the suffering perpetuated by a tyrannical regime, and there must be solid hope that the just goals of the revolution will be attained. One cannot consider only short-term gains, because the long-term consequences can in the end bring about more harm than good.

These three conditions or criteria are intrinsically related. If one criterion is not realized, this affects the other two, resulting in a moral disproportion and thus rendering the whole action immoral. The value sought must always be higher or at least equal to the value sacrificed; if this criterion is not met, to continue the process is morally futile. If the means used to protect the value brings about consequences that undermine this very value, then there is moral disproportion, and the whole action is not morally justifiable. Holistic ethical reasoning involves a multileveled analysis and discernment in determining the moral rightness of an act.

Judgment and Decision

The final moment of the moral reasoning process is judgment and decision. One makes a judgment based on the results of moral analysis, as shaped by the concrete narrative of the ethical situation. And founded on this judgment, one makes a moral decision. In the end all

---

[141] See ibid.

that is asked is that we do everything possible to make an informed decision, based on accurate facts, a well thought-out decision based on principled discernment, and an ethical decision, governed by the good that we seek to become and do within the context of the actual moral situation. The ultimate goal is to arrive at moral objectivity and its claim on our personal and collective conscience in the light of the Christian system of values.

Conclusion

No one ethical theory can fully and perfectly grasp the dynamics of thinking and knowing in the realm of morality. Such is the nature of theories. Debate on theories will go on endlessly, and transcending some impasses might never happen. The theory expressed here puts the ethics of holistic reasoning and virtue ethics in their truest light and integrates them for the purpose of proposing an ethical methodology for moral reasoning in conflict situations. I sought a methodology that overcomes the defects of certain approaches that tend to be one-dimensional, either solely virtue based or principle based, and that corrects the extremes of other approaches that focus exclusively on the object or the intention or the consequences of moral actions. Whatever limitations this proposed framework may have, it was conceived to create richer possibilities in responding to moral dilemmas in our lives, in a holistic and integral way, taking moral persons in relation to their acts, at every level of interaction, in view of an adequate account of moral objectivity or truth. In the final analysis the person of virtue is where virtue ethics and the ethics of holistic reasoning meet, for one who lives a life of virtue can engage in moral reasoning in a way that is truly human and Christian.

9

Ignatian Discernment—
A Critical Contemporary Reading

The capacity to make decisions is at the heart of the human project. All the powers of the intellect, affectivity, and imagination are summoned when one brings into shape a choice or decision that could define one's life, affect for weal or woe the lives of others, or even determine the destiny of a people or of the world. Some decisions may be of such great import—some are of ordinary circumstances—but nonetheless, in all decisions of small or great magnitude, the place of affectivity and spirituality is critical. Contrary to the thinking of rigorous rationalists, it is in the affective and spiritual region that persons are profoundly engaged in their fundamental moral experience. The rational, however, is a constant, for persons are creatures of reason, and what is moral must be reasonable, but when reason is bathed by the waters of affectivity and spirituality, it reaches a depth of illumination.

Making moral decisions is a lifelong challenge. Throughout our lives we are confronted by moral dilemmas, and we ask again and again what is the right thing to do. The situations range from the intimate issues of personal morality to the larger contexts of social issues, involving global questions of war, politics, and economics. Collective decisions are made on issues of broad import, where we, at various levels, participate as members of society in the shaping of such decisions as individual moral agents based on our conscientious discernment.

This chapter, in a slightly different form, integrates two previously published articles: "Ignatian Discernment: A Critical Contemporary Reading for Christian Decision Making," *Horizons* 32 (Spring 2005): 72-99, and "A Reading of Ignatian Discernment from a Theological Epistemology," *Loyola Schools Review* 5 (2006): 24-36.

The modes of Ignatian discernment for Christian decision making must be contextualized in the three dimensions of human life, as the personal and interpersonal cannot be separated from the social structures within which people live. The societal dimension of discernment is real, as it impinges on the personal and interpersonal decisions made. A heightened awareness of the depth and complexity of human decisions makes one see how persons can directly or indirectly contribute to social sin or social grace. Various authors have addressed the social or public dimension of Ignatian discernment.[1] Making a choice can prove to be most demanding. The complexity of human problems, the pluralism of values, and the shifting sense of what is right and wrong make moral decisions difficult. Very often there are no easy answers; sometimes there are no clear answers or even no answers at all.

In relation to this fundamental engagement of persons in decision making, Ignatian discernment is the distinctive contribution of Ignatius's *Spiritual Exercises* to humanity and to Christian spirituality. But any treatment of the writings of Ignatius must be cognizant of the cultural context in which they were shaped and of the worldview that underlies them. How can one be faithful to the Ignatian vision while negating Ignatian fundamentalism? This is a challenge one faces in any serious study of Ignatian writings. Furthermore, how can one read the Ignatian writings in a contemporary world without diminishing in any way their core meaning or inner logic? The answers to these questions are not as easily stated or formulated as the questions themselves. Commentaries on Ignatian discernment are sharply divided on fundamentals, especially on the interpretation of the three Ignatian "times" or modes of discernment.[2] There have been debates on what

---

[1] See Margaret Ellen Burke, "Social Sin and Social Grace," *The Way Supplement* 85 (Spring 1996): 40–54; Alexander Lefrank, "The Spiritual Exercises as a Way of Liberation: Social Dimension," *The Way Supplement* 46 (Spring 1983): 56–66; Charles Wookey, "Making Christian Choices in the Political World," *The Way Supplement* 64 (Spring 1989): 103–14; John J. English, "Discerning Identity: Toward a Spirituality of Community," *The Way Supplement* 64 (Spring 1989): 115–28; Paul Boateng, "Faith and Politics," *The Way Supplement* 60 (Autumn 1987): 40–50; Thomas E. Clarke, "Ignatian Prayer and Individualism," *The Way Supplement* 82 (Spring 1995): 7–14. See also the whole issue of *The Way Supplement* (Autumn 1988), entitled *Spirituality and Social Issues*.

[2] For a discussion of terms, see Jules J. Toner, *Discerning God's Will: Ignatius of Loyola's Teaching on Christian Decision Making* (St. Louis: Institute of Jesuit Sources, 1991), 103–4; and Thomas Greene, *Weeds Among the Wheat* (Notre Dame, IN: Ave Maria Press, 1984), 83–84, 91, 98, 100.

Ignatius means by each of these three times or occasions for reaching a good decision, their interrelationships, and their comparative value.

Any reading of Ignatian discernment with theological seriousness is confronted by substantive theological questions that need to be addressed. They are substantive because they address the theological epistemology and worldview with which we read and understand Ignatian discernment. Unless these questions are first addressed, the horizons of interpreting discernment from the Ignatian perspective is constricted and the understanding of its rules can be misconstrued. I formulate these questions as follows: How is the incomprehensible God experienced? What is the relation between divine providence and human freedom in seeking God's will? Is belief in Satan, in good and evil spirits, a matter of Christian faith? This chapter addresses these three questions in view of a consideration of Ignatian discernment. The first part of the chapter, a critical reading of Ignatian spirituality, provides a stance for any serious theological reading of Ignatian discernment. The second part of the chapter presents and expands on Ignatian modes of discernment.

I present my concluding statement under the title "Reappropriating Ignatian Discernment"—my attempt at a contemporary reappropriation of Ignatian discernment for our time. If theology is to illumine reality, it must flow back to life. The study of Ignatian discernment shapes one's way of seeing the world and of one's own reality in manifold ways. Appropriation is a way of disclosing what these manifold ways mean in one distinct way, as theology is made to flow back to life. In a real sense, appropriation is the final act of interpretation.[3]

Ignatian Spirituality from a Theological Perspective

Discernment goes beyond the question of whether an action is morally right, though it presupposes it. It is more focused on these questions: Who am I? What do I desire to become? Is this action most resonant with who I seek to be, in the face of the God who beckons me to fullness of life? Drawing less from abstractions than from resources of memory and imagination, discernment is directed by a judgment of affectivity, without denying the place of reason, for reason is always necessary to make any kind of judgment. But the scrutiny engaged by reason here is different from formal logic

---

[3] See Paul Ricouer, *Hermeneutics and the Human Sciences: Essays on Language, Action and Interpretation* (Cambridge, England: Cambridge University Press, 1981), 190–93.

that puts to test the moral principle as it is applied to a relevant case to yield a moral conclusion. Beyond the reasoning mind, but not in opposition to it, the reasoning heart stirs and moves one to take the path of authenticity as one comes to terms with whom one is before the loving and liberating God. The word *heart* here is understood in the biblical sense as the deepest level of ourselves, where God's Spirit joins our spirit (Rom 8:16). It is at this level that God addresses us as a Thou, in the fullness of our integrity and freedom.[4]

How Is the Incomprehensible God Experienced?

What is presupposed here is a God who is known and experienced by human persons as being deeply and personally accessible. This is a God who crosses the infinite expanse of God's incomprehensibility to make Godself and God's will known to human beings. Anyone who is engaged in Ignatian discernment finds himself or herself pondering on how God, who is beyond all that can be seen and known, can be experienced. It is a question that provokes one's mind and unless one finds some intelligible answers, it can block any process of discernment. Here I use Rahner's approach to the experience of God and the method of his approach to answer this concern.

Rahner's Approach to the Experience of God

The experience of God is not the privilege of mystics alone; it is accessible to all, and is in fact inescapable in the sense that it is present in every person, whether consciously or unconsciously, whether suppressed or accepted, whether rightly or wrongly interpreted. It is not an experience conceived as one particular experience among others at the same level, but rather is the ultimate depth and radical essence of every spiritual experience.[5] What is a spiritual experience? Rather than defining it, Rahner describes it by contemplating the depth of significant human experiences: our holding our silence even when we have been unfairly treated; forgiving someone who takes our forgiveness for granted; deciding a course of action against all odds purely upon the dictate of conscience; fulfilling a duty at the radical cost of self; continuing to love for no reason other than simply that it is good to love; persevering in faith in the abyss of pain and suffering;

---

[4] See William C. Spohn, "The Reasoning Heart: An American Approach to Christian Discernment," *Theological Studies* 44/1 (1983): 30–44.

[5] Karl Rahner, "The Experience of God Today," *Theological Investigations*, vol. 11, *Confrontations*, trans. David Bourke, 149–65 (New York: Seabury Press, 1974), 150, 154.

doing what is good because it is good without any thought of praise or reward.[6]

Rahner holds that such experiences are truly spiritual in the sense that in them we live in the Spirit and discover that our meaning is not exhausted by the fortunes of the world. Living at the border between God and the world, we experience the taste of the pure spirit, the secret passion of great saints and martyrs. When we live in the spirit this way, we have already in fact experienced the supernatural.[7] We have done so perhaps in an anonymous and inexpressible way, but then in actual fact, Rahner says, it is God who is at work in us. At the bottomless depth of our existence, there where we lose our claim on ourselves, we encounter God. He writes:

> The seemingly uncanny, bottomless depth of our existence as experienced by us is the bottomless depth of God communicating himself to us, the dawning of his approaching infinity which no longer has any set paths, which is tasted like a nothing because it is infinity. When we have let ourselves go and no longer belong to ourselves, when we have denied ourselves and no longer have the disposing of ourselves, when everything (including ourselves) has moved away from us as if unto an infinite distance, then we begin to live in the world of God himself, the world of the God of grace and of eternal life.[8]

In looking for this experience of grace in the contemplation of our lives, we can only recognize it in our giving of ourselves to God and to others in a love that utterly forgets self. It is an experience that has the special quality of the ineffable, namely, mystery. It is mystery not so much because it is still unexplored or it defies all knowing, but because it is the substrate that sustains the very reality that we know. It is at the same time inconceivable and self-evident, as it is mediated

---

[6] Karl Rahner, "Reflections on the Experience of Grace," *Theological Investigations*, vol. 3, *The Theology of the Spiritual Life,* trans. Karl-H. and Boniface Kruger, 86–90 (London: Darton, Longman, and Todd, 1967), 87. Rahner defines mysticism as "an ultimate and absolutely radical experience of transcendence in the mystery of God. . . . It is a condition where the 'mystical' subject undergoes an 'immediate' experience, transcending mediation by categorical objects of the everyday." See Karl Rahner, *The Practice of Faith: A Handbook of Contemporary Spirituality* (New York: Crossroad, 1983), 70, 72. Also see Michael Stoeber, "Mysticism and the Spiritual Life: Reflections on Karl Rahner's View of Mysticism," *Toronto Journal of Theology* 17/2 (2001): 263.

[7] Rahner, "Reflections on the Experience of Grace," 88.

[8] Ibid.

through what is familiar and yet it extends to that which is limitless, inexhaustible, summoning us to constantly reach out beyond ourselves to an ever greater reality. In the face of mystery we come to experience that which is not ours to shape or control, and yet it is most interior to us but not subject to us. It permeates everything, giving it a unifying center and yet remaining in itself incomprehensible.[9]

At the heart of this mystery is a personal encounter in which one experiences a love that is absolute and unconditional, and finds no adequate reason whatsoever why one is loved so in this way; yet it is abiding, forever summoning one to seek to love in the same way, and there is no rest until all has come to all in this love. Rahner states that this experience of mystery, at the heart of which is unconditional love, is centrally connected to one's experience of God.[10] He writes that "the ultimate depths of this experience of God to which we have sought to appeal are precisely the experience of an ineffable nearness of God to us such that for all the adorable inconceivability which abides throughout, God bestows on us an immediacy that brings forgiveness and a share in divine life."[11] It is possible to suppress this experience, yet it remains, and at the crucial turns of our lives, it breaks in upon our awareness once more with irresistible force.

It is possible, thus, to experience God. In the human search for meaning, however, one is confronted by the question: How can the eternally incomprehensible God be the meaning of our life? Incomprehensibility does not belong only to God as God is in Godself, but it defines who God is relative to us. How can the incomprehensibility of God be understood in a way that it does not annihilate God's accessibility, making it beatifying rather than alienating? Rahner says that if incomprehensibility implies that the human being has no reasoning capacity to know God, then God as the meaning of human life has to be rejected from the very outset. Reason, thus, must be understood as the capacity for the incomprehensible, the capacity of the *excessus,* as going out into the inaccessible. This capacity does not mean the power of comprehending, of gaining mastery or subjugating; rather, it is the capacity of being seized by what is ineffable, the power of coming face to face with incomprehensibility itself.[12]

---

[9] Rahner, "The Experience of God Today," 156–57.

[10] Ibid., 164.

[11] Karl Rahner, "The Human Question of Meaning in the Face of the Absolute Mystery of God," in *Theological Investigations,* vol. 18, *God and Revelation,* trans. Edward Quinn (New York: Crossroad, 1983), 96–99.

[12] Ibid., 100–104.

In what kind of an act can the person as a reasoning being face the incomprehensibility of God and not be radically diminished by his or her puny finitude, alienated and separated from God? Rahner says that if we look for a name for such an act derived from our basic experiences, we can only speak of love. Interpersonal love gives us a hint of our own relationship with God as its creaturely reflection. In loving another, we give ourselves in trusting surrender, without reassurance, to that which we cannot completely comprehend, to that which we cannot master in the other, for loving means leaving the other free and incalculable at every given point. A knowing that bears the marks of domination and appropriation is not a knowing in true loving. Thus only in the act of resigned and self-forsaking surrender to the incomprehensibility of God as God, in God's nature and freedom, can one truly love God. And in loving God as God, in all that God is, divine incomprehensibility ceases to be a limit to such a love but becomes its very content.

Corollary to the question that we have raised regarding the possibility of finding our meaning in an incomprehensible God is the question of how prayer can be a dialogue with God, which presupposes that in prayer not only does the human person speak, but also Godself speaks and addresses the person. In what sense is prayer a dialogue, and how does God speak in prayer? To speak of prayer as a dialogue between God and the person must not be so stretched that it loses the analogical character of such speaking. From the outset, when we refer to the partnership of the divine and human in prayer, we recognize what is radically unique and unparalleled and, thus, cannot be understood univocally according to the pattern of a relationship between human beings in a partnership.

The difficulty in seeing and acknowledging that in prayer we experience God, who speaks a personal word to us, is not without basis. Prayer can seem to be a monologue, or at best a conversation with oneself. God's most fundamental word to us is not an external word, something added on as one object among other objects of experience. Rather, the word of God spoken to us is interior and integral to us, a word that we ourselves recognize as such, in all our uniqueness and freedom and in our total dependence on God. In prayer, God's universal salvific love is radicalized in immediacy by what is called grace—God's self-disclosure in loving communion with us spoken to and addressed in our actual nature, in the very concreteness and particularity of our personal context. We hear ourselves as God's addressee, filled with God's gracious disposal of Godself, and received in faith, hope, and love. We do not hear "something" added to ourselves, but ourselves spoken to us as we are, constituted as the hearers of the word of God as the abiding answer to the infinite question that we are.[13]

Theological Anthropology: The Method of Rahner's Approach

What is the theological method or framework operative in Rahner's approach to the experience of God? Rahner explains it as theological anthropology.[14] According to this theological approach or method, anything that one says about God has a deep connection with who the human person is, and anything that profoundly relates to the human person opens one to the mystery of God. All theology, thus, must have the human person as a referent in its speech about God and salvation, for without this referent, it loses its intelligibility and its agency for empowerment and transformation in the human context. This method is grounded in a definite view of God, the person, and human existence. The loving, incomprehensible God relates as a gracious and gracing God to the human person. And this divine disposal orders the human person with a radical openness *(potentia obedientialis)* toward God as his or her final end and ultimate meaning.[15] The human person is a hearer of the word, having some kind of "ear" within for a revelation, a built-in natural capacity for hearing a possible revelation from God, of which God's bestowal of Godself in grace is the source and origin.[16] This constant and fundamental experience of God drawing close, enabling the addressee to be open to the infinite and being embraced by it, is called "supernatural existential."[17] It is a fundamental condition, a basic pattern not only in individual experience but also in history. For Rahner, human beings can truly experience God in "mediated immediacy" at the heart of the world, where grace is abidingly

---

[13] Karl Rahner, "Dialogue with God," in *Theological Investigations*, 18:122–31.

[14] Karl Rahner, "Theology and Anthropology," *Theological Investigations*, vol. 9, *Shape of Contemporary and Future Theology*, trans. Graham Harrison (London: Darton, Longman, and Todd, 1972), 28–45. Paul Molinar, in "Can We Know God Directly? Rahner's Solution from Experience," *Theological Studies* 46/2 (1985): 228–61, accuses Rahner of philosophical reductionism. See also Leo J. O'Donovan's response to Molinar in "A Journey into Time: The Legacy of Karl Rahner's Last Years," *Theological Studies* 46/4 (1985): 625.

[15] Karl Rahner, *Foundations of Christian Faith: An Introduction to the Idea of Christianity*, trans. William V. Dych (New York: Crossroad, 1995), 126–33.

[16] Albert M. Libatore, "Karl Rahner: Hearer of the Word: Laying the Foundation for a Philosophy of Religion," *Louvain Studies* 21 (Spring 1996): 93–95. See Karl Rahner, *Hearer of the Word*, trans. Joseph Donceel, ed. Andrew Tallon (New York: Continuum, 1994).

[17] Rahner, *Foundations of Christian Faith*, 127.

present. The belief that in grace the transcendent God is immanent and the creaturely finite being becomes transcendent is at the core of Rahner's theology.

The very concept of theological anthropology shows that the human experience is the locus of divine activity, without itself being identified with the divine. God draws near in profound human experiences. Because grace is omnipresent, reality is not radically divided into sacred and profane. Rather, all reality is potentially sacred, for when experienced in its depth, any reality is brought to the realm where the divine and human meet. All revelation is mediated. There is no direct revelation in the sense that God is known in Godself without mediation. Revelation is rooted in time and place and in the vicissitudes of historicity, because of the fact that the addressee of God's revelation is an embodied being. The word *direct* is used to differentiate transcendental from categorical revelation. *Direct* does not mean here that one comes face to face with God in the beatific vision.[18] It means a revelation beneath the support of particular categorical explications and prior to the exercise of human will. The inner word of graced transcendental revelation draws a person affectively toward God without any prior influence of thought or image. Very simply, it is an experience of being taken over completely in love by God without any effort of one's own. This means that the experience of "being loved by God" is due solely to God's free action on the soul of the human being, without previous human seeking or willing. In that sense, it is God's direct act, without any proportionate human imaginative or rational intentionality.[19] What is being asserted here is the initiative of God and the absolute gratuity of God's love. In the originating moment of the divine-human encounter, it is God's initiative and not the human person's.

Rahner explains this transcendental revelation with reference to *quasi-formal* causality. Because God offers Godself to the human spirit in a way that is analogous to form being present to matter, we are ontologically modified by the presence of God. Thus, though human and finite, we have a divine and infinite end that defines us ontologically, disposed as we are to an immediate communication of the divine Being. But there is no real union as between form and matter. The word *quasi* is used to remind us that this *forma* remains absolutely transcendent and free and that the ontological divinization of our

---

[18] Karl Rahner, "The Logic of Concrete Individual Knowledge in Ignatius Loyola," in *The Dynamic Element in the Church* (Quaestiones Disputatae 12), trans. W. J. O'Hara (New York: Herder and Herder, 1964), 106.

[19] Ibid., 129–42.

being is analogical. This means that although we are divinized by the offer of God as our final end, we do not ourselves become God. What is given to us in the transcendental revelation seeks categories of the outer word as explications of the inner transcendent reality. Whether transcendental or categorical, however, revelation comes to us through mediated immediacy.[20] It is God we encounter, not an image of God, not a replica of God. The personal transcendent God is known and loved in immanence, in mediated immediacy, through grace. In the direct transcendent revelation, however, God is experienced without the person's active free agency, only through his or her sheer radical receptivity and openness to God. The divine disclosure is direct only in this sense.

What Is the Relationship Between Human Freedom and Divine Providence?

Ignatian discernment suggests an image of God in which God has a particular will for each individual person, within a specific divine plan that is communicated through special divine disclosure; when received, this leaves one with no power to resist or disobey. If such an image is pushed to the extreme, God would be seen as the Great Manipulator of the universe, who determines every action. It is in the light of this image of God that the second theological question relative to Ignatian discernment arises regarding the relationship of freedom and divine providence. The question asked is whether there is an unchanging blueprint of God's will for our life that we must discover through discernment. And if there is, how does it reckon with the reality of human freedom? Does divine providence obliterate human freedom, with all claims to creativity and responsibility negated? How can divine providence and freedom be understood in a way that freedom is not denied and belief in providence is not compromised?

A new paradigm for understanding providence attempts to keep the tension between freedom and providence, showing God and the human person in collaboration, and this collaboration is illustrated in the Thomistic dual agency of the divine and human. Beyond this dual agency, basically understood in terms of the Thomistic relation of cause and effect, is the "logic of intersubjectivity," which shows God and the human person in a relation of intersubjective "thous," with God truly taking divine risks in the face of the creativity and

---

[20] Karl Rahner and Joseph Ratzinger, *Revelation and Tradition* (New York: Herder and Herder, 1966), 13–21.

spontaneity of human freedom. In view of the discussion of the relationship of freedom to God's will, I propose a revised understanding of God's will.

New Paradigm for Understanding Providence

In the classical model of providence God's power is imagined as control over our lives and all of creation; prayer is conceived as discerning one's place in the divine scheme of things. The appropriate religious response is obedient surrender or abandonment to the divine will. And if the divine will is to be known through the structures of our individual and collective life, then as Anne Carr points out, the benevolent God could thus be perceived to give divine legitimation to the hierarchical order of paternalism that once reigned throughout the created order: master ruled over slave, king over subject, man over woman, children, and the earth. The more contemporary view of providence, influenced by the emergence of historical consciousness in the nineteenth century, images God not as controlling the human will but luring it toward the goal and responsibilities that are the person's, enabling and liberating human freedom in its very power to determine and create itself as one chooses from the manifold ways God opens for human flourishing. Prayer, from this new perspective of providence, is understood as discernment of God's lure and direction from within us, amid the complex ambiguities of our personal and communal lives.

This change in the understanding of the relation of divine providence and human freedom has resulted in some reversals in our image of God. Such reversals bring to focus, to use one example, the feminist critique of the masculinized divine image that has long been entrenched in tradition. Perception of the divine power not as a dominating power but as a relational empowerment changes the image of God from a sovereign king and master (ruling, controlling, determining) to mother, lover, friend (caring, persuading, and enabling).

Human agency is endowed with a self-determining power and a relative autonomy in the search for creative ends within the scheme of things. Such autonomy is relative and not absolute, for human agency remains within the orbit of divine providence which enables, directs, and sustains it.[21]

---

[21] Anne E. Carr, "Providence, Power, and the Holy Spirit," *Horizons* 29/1 (2002): 80–93.

Does God Play Dice? Providence and Change

Elizabeth Johnson engages the particular question of how God's providential activity can be affirmed in a world where chance plays an essential role. The conclusion that the fact of genuine randomness in the world does not conflict with divine providence can be seen as shedding light on the mystery of divine providence and human freedom in a dynamic relation. She draws upon the scientific data that attest to the interplay of providence and chance in the universe and interfaces this with the Thomistic notion of dual agency in her pursuit of the question of how to reconcile divine providence, freedom, and chance in a way that is theologically intelligible.[22]

The mechanistic view of the world associated with Newtonian physics has been replaced by a dynamic, open-ended view of the world that perceives a built-in "indeterminacy in the physical systems at the quantum level, unpredictability of chaotic systems at the macro level, and the random emergence of new forms through the evolutionary process."[23] This built-in indeterminacy and unpredictability, which is called the play of chance, undermines the belief that the world operates according to a fixed blueprint or plan.[24] This reversal impinges on the classical idea of the laws of nature. These laws are to be taken only as descriptive and not prescriptive. They are descriptive of what is observable, approximating how the forces in nature relate from what can be seen, but their illustrations do not show what is at the depths of nature which remains veiled, for nature itself is a mystery.[25] Contemporary science, however, sees the essential role of chance in enabling matter to explore all its potentialities. In the rapid randomization that chance brings to play, matter is brought to its full actualization. Chance, thus, is not seen as diametrically opposed to law; it is, rather, the very means by which law becomes creative. Contemporary science calls for a modified notion of an overall design or pattern in the world, one that includes as essential the play of chance, indeterminacy, and

---

[22] Elizabeth A. Johnson, CSJ, "Does God Play Dice? Providence and Change," *Theological Studies* 57/1 (1966): 3–18. Johnson's article is used extensively in this section.

[23] Ibid., 7.

[24] Paul Davies, *The Cosmic Blueprint* (New York: Simon and Schuster, 1988), 202.

[25] William A. Stoeger, "Contemporary Physics and the Ontological Status of the Laws of Nature," in *Quantum Cosmology and the Laws of Nature: Scientific Perspectives on Divine Action*, ed. Robert Russell, Nancy Murphy, and C. J. Isham, 209–34 (Vatican City: Vatican Observatory; Berkeley, CA: Center for Theology and the Natural Sciences, 1993).

unpredictability in the shaping of the universe, within a manifold of open possibilities.[26]

This contemporary view of the world provides an evocative context in which to understand God's creative and providential action and human agency and freedom. "There is a deep compatibility between the autonomous ways physical, chemical, and biological systems operate through the interplay of law and chance on the one hand, and human consciousness and freedom on the other."[27] This participatory relationship is made possible by the dual agency of God and the human person, with God as the primary cause working through secondary created causes. Aquinas's theology of dual agency provides insights into divine agency that allow the potential for chance in the world. All that exists participates in its own way in divine being through the very gift of creaturely existence. This notion of participation explains how the creating and sustaining God is present in all things, as the very inner source of their being, power, and action, and yet is distinct from all things, for Godself alone simply exists while every creature exists only insofar as it participates in being.[28] Though bringing about one effect, each cause stands in a fundamentally different relationship to the effect, as God works through secondary causes with genuine causal efficacy in their right. In other words, God grants the secondary cause its own integrity and autonomy, even while it is not itself its own cause—God is.[29] It is, thus, inconceivable to think of God working in this world apart from secondary causes, but only "in and through them, not beside, in addition, or in competition with them."[30]

This notion of double agency with respect to efficient causality is correlated with final causality to illumine that, as the finite secondary causes work according to their intrinsic natures, their very self-direction toward the good is itself an imprint *(impressio)* from God. God, in giving creatures their own being, built into them the inclination by which, through their own natural actions, they tend toward the good. This direction toward the good, while it is their natural orientation,

---

[26] Johnson, "Does God Play Dice?" 8.

[27] Ibid.

[28] See Thomas Aquinas, *Summa Theologiae* 1, q.104, a.1; *ST* 1, q.103, a.2; *ST* 1, q.19, a.2.

[29] Johnson, "Does God Play Dice?" 12. See also Etienne Gilson, "The Corporeal World and the Efficacy of Second Causes," in *God's Activity in the World: The Contemporary Problem,* ed. Owen C. Thomas, 213–30 (Chico, CA: Scholars Press, 1983); see also David B. Burrell, *Aquinas: God and Action* (Notre Dame, IN: University of Notre Dame Press, 1979).

[30] Johnson, "Does God Play Dice?" 12.

pursued freely by the force of their own desires and strivings toward
the good, is ultimately a participation in the ultimate good, which is
God. God is immanent in the universe as the final cause.[31] As a whole,
we see that "God as the primary cause endows all created beings
with their own participation in divine being (enabling them to exist),
in divine agency (empowering them to act) and in divine goodness
(drawing them toward their goal)."[32]

Combining the interplay of chance and randomness with structures
of regularity with Aquinas's understanding of the dual agency of God
and the human person, in the dialogue of science with Christian faith,
yields interesting results. For one, it shows how chance, randomness,
and self-direction, present in both the universe of physical causes and
in the universe of freedom, can be held without surrendering belief
in divine providence. It also brings in a new hermeneutics of the perfection and power of God. Divine perfection is a perfection of love
and relationality rather than that of self-sufficiency and control, and
divine power is not a "power over" but a power that empowers and
enables as seen in the divine work within the processes in the universe
and within free human acts. The relationship of responsible human
action with God's providential action is illumined through the prism
of new images and symbols. One outstanding image is that of God as
lover waiting upon the beloved, with urges and lures of love toward
fullness of life, but only waiting, with ever-gracious patience in the
face of the whole free play of acceptance or rejection, vulnerability or
intransigence, always within the orbit of divine love and providence,
and all out of respect for the integrity and autonomy of the beloved in
casting his or her lot in the field of many dreams. Johnson concludes
that "not the monarch but the lover becomes the paradigm."[33]

Beyond Dual Agency: "Logic of Intersubjectivity"

In a response to Elizabeth Johnson's article, Joseph A. Bracken
completely agrees with her that creaturely spontaneity ought to be
compatible with a proper understanding of divine providence. However, he does not concur with her use and defense of Aquinas in this
regard. For one, he points out that there is ambiguity in the way God
as the Subsistent Being and the person as the creaturely being can
concur to bring about the same effect in the way Johnson describes
it. What is missing in the argument is the recognition of a distinction

[31] *ST* 1, q. 103, a.8.
[32] Johnson, "Does God Play Dice?" 13–14.
[33] Ibid., 15–17.

between person and nature within God. God is the transcendent First Cause because God exists by nature without any antecedent cause. The nature of God is simply to be; the personal reality of God is the subject of the unlimited act of being. If nature is not distinguished from person, and God is simply the act of being, pantheism or pancosmism results, because all finite beings exist by the sheer participation in the act of being and "God is simply the name for the collection of finite entities that here and now exists."[34] This distinction between nature and person relative to God is required to justify God's transcendence vis-à-vis creation, even as God is immanent in creation as its ground of being or existence. The divine nature is immanent within creation as its intrinsic principle of existence and activity; God as a personal being transcends all of God's creatures, but creatures in their ontological freedom also "transcend" God as individual entities distinct from God and from one another. Bracken elucidates this point:

> When humans and other created beings are said to share in the divine being, this means that they too participate in the ground of being, that is, in the underlying nature of God or the activity of existing. But they do not share in the initiative reality of God. For they are not God, but remain themselves as independent finite realities, even though they draw their existence from the ground of being, the divine nature of the divine act of being.[35]

Bracken perceives an implicit reference to the distinction between nature and person in Johnson's statement: "The mystery of God is the livingness of Being who freely shares being which creatures participate."[36] He says that Aquinas, by referring to God as Subsistent Being, *subsistent* referring to God as the subject of the act of being, also makes an implicit reference to the same distinction. He wonders why the distinction between person and nature, which Aquinas himself uses later in the *Summa Theologiae* in his exposition of the Trinity, is not clearly explicitated or operative in the discussion of the God-creature relationship, as it is in Johnson's discussion. In his judgment it is because the Thomistic understanding of the God-world relationship is governed by the logic of objective cause-and-effect relationships and

---

[34] Joseph A. Bracken, "Response to Elizabeth Johnson's 'Does God Play Dice?'" *Theological Studies* 57/4 (1996): 721.

[35] Joseph A. Bracken, *Divine Matrix: Creativity as Link Between East and West* (Maryknoll, NY: Orbis Books, 1995), 29.

[36] Johnson, "Does God Play Dice?" 11.

not the logic of intersubjectivity, with God and creation as objects of thought rather than genuine subjects of experience.[37]

If the logic of subjectivity had been used more forcefully, Bracken points out, it would have made Johnson's claim of a risk-taking God more persuasive. He has no problem with the notion that divine nature empowers the creature to act according to its creaturely nature and produce an effect consonant with that creaturely nature. He is in full accord with whatever Johnson says in this regard, provided that what is being referred to is clearly divine nature rather than specifically God as being or entity. But he has difficulty when this notion is used to explain how God, as the primary cause, and the creaturely being, as the secondary cause, bring about the same effect, with each cause standing in a fundamentally different relation to the effect. That they bring about the same effect is possible only if one of them is instrumental to the purpose of the other. But if God and the creature are two ontologically independent subjects of the act of being, God may resist what the creature intends to do, and the creature as an ontologically independent subject of the act of being can choose to do what he or she wills. Within this scheme God and the creature, related to each other as Thou, can mutually condition and affect one another.[38]

My difficulty with Bracken's line of thought is that if pushed to its logical conclusion, it would imply that there is temporality and change in God. If, however, he suggests that God as God is not temporal and subject to change, but that only God's relations with creatures in the temporal order changes, he offers a qualification that makes the dynamics in the relationship of God and creature as he conceives it more acceptable. William J. Hill pursues the same line of qualification:

> What is achieved in history is not a new acquisition *in God*, but does become a new acquisition *for God* in the finite realm. God becomes what God was not—not in Godself but in the world and in history. It is not simply the case that what is other than God changes, but rather that God changes—not in Godself but in the other and by way of the other. God changes not absolutely but relationally, i.e., in terms of those dispositions of knowing and loving that God chooses to adopt towards a

[37] Bracken, "Response to Elizabeth Johnson's 'Does God Play Dice?'" 722. See also Kitty Ferguson, *The Fire in the Equations: Science, Religion, and the Search for God* (Grand Rapids, MI: Eerdmans, 1995), 149–63.

[38] Ibid., 723–24, 728. See also Catherine Mowry Lacugna, "The Relational God: Aquinas and Beyond," *Theological Studies* 46/4 (1985): 663.

universe of creatures that in finite and temporal ways determine themselves.[39]

In the same vein Langdon Gilkey speaks of God's self-limitation insofar as "he will have to act in the future as he has in the past, namely *through* our freedom and limited by our freedom. History in the future, therefore, will remain open to the wayward as well as the creative possibilities of freedom."[40] If these statements about God's relationality toward the world are disturbing, then perhaps it is the price to pay for a profound belief in God as a genuine subject of the act of being in relation to creatures, a relation of an intersubjective Thou, beyond a relation of cause and effect. In that sense God truly takes risks in relation to creaturely beings. Bracken says that Johnson seems to move in that direction in the latter part of her article. He writes: "As I see it, this is where the logic of Elizabeth Johnson's argument seems implicitly to lead her. My quarrel is not with her conclusions but with the metaphysical conceptuality she uses to get there."[41] No one scheme or conception of the God-world relationship, however, can claim to have a final say, for each scheme is radically limited in the face of God, who is ineffable and incomprehensible. In understanding any scheme we may go to the edge of the waters but refuse (theologically and existentially) to dive into the deep end, because, like human freedom, the mystery of God can be a burden we must bear.

A Revised Understanding of God's Will

God's will seems unyielding; it connotes predetermination and absoluteness. I propose that in place of God's *will*, we speak of God's *desire*. "Desire is an inclination toward some object accompanied by a positive effect. The quality of desire is determined by the object whereas its intensity comes from affect."[42] Desire is the inner force of the heart that creates and drives our striving. Our deepest desires move and direct all else in our life.[43] There is a deep connection be-

---

[39] William J. Hill, "Does God Know the Future? Aquinas and Some Moderns," *Theological Studies* 36/1 (1975): 15.

[40] Langdon Gilkey, *Reaping the Whirlwind: A Christian Interpretation of History* (New York: Seabury Press, 1976), 279.

[41] Bracken, "Response to Elizabeth Johnson's 'Does God Play Dice?'" 730.

[42] E. Edward Kinerk, "Eliciting Great Desires: Their Place in the Spirituality of the Society of Jesus," *Studies in the Spirituality of Jesus* 19/4 (September 1987): 3.

[43] Thomas McGrath, "The Place of Desires in the Ignatian Exercises," *The Way Supplement* 76 (Spring 1993): 27.

tween our human desires and our knowledge. As Mark Doty writes, "I am certain that the part of us that desires, that loves, and longs for encounter and connection—physical and psychic and every other way—is also that part of us that knows something about God."[44] Also, the more authentic our desires are, as we go more deeply into ourselves, the more they become communal. What is most uniquely personal in ourselves points to our most profound connection with others in community and in larger society.[45] To know the desire of God is consistent with the spirit of Ignatius, a man of great desires whose longing to know God's desires characterized all of his life. "The one who is desired longs to be possessed by the one who desires and understands their lives as being fully for the other and understandable only in relation to the desire of the other."[46] Ignatius vividly expresses throughout the Exercises his desire to do what his Divine Majesty desires of him.

Discernment may then be expressed in the language of desire: God having a desire for each one of us, as God loves us in a singular way, radically unique and unrepeatable. Like any desire, it seeks expression in a special disclosure that only the beloved understands. And the beloved, resonating with God's desire as his or her own desire, is so moved that he or she cannot but utter yes. This reality is present in a way that divine providence and human freedom are fathomed in deeply relational and affective terms.

Is Belief in Satan and in Good and Evil Spirits a Matter of Christian Faith?

The third question we raise in this chapter concerns belief in Satan, in good and evil spirits as a matter of Christian faith. Ignatian discernment is engaged in a world where there are preternatural forces that come to influence the thoughts and emotions of men and women. Any serious study of Ignatian discernment is confronted with the question of whether created spirits, angels or devils, exist. This is an issue that is unsettling to many who make or direct the *Ignatian Exercises* and who use the discernment of the spirits for Christian decision making. The issue is sometimes dismissed or trivialized, or if judgments are made on it, they are made without sufficient nuance based on a critical study.

[44] Mark Doty, "Sweet Chariot," in *Wrestling with the Angel: Faith and Religion in the Lives of Gay Men*, ed. Brian Bouldrey (New York: Riverhead, 1995), 6.
[45] Kinerk, "Eliciting Great Desires," 4. See also Michael Panicola, "Discernment in the Neonatal Context," *Theological Studies* 60/4 (December 1999): 729.
[46] McGrath, "The Place of Desires in the Ignatian Exercises," 29.

Jules J. Toner cites two reasons why contemporary Christians feel a certain unease with belief in created personal spirits, both good and evil ones. First, belief in these spirits appears to belong to a primitive era and culture that lie outside of the epistemology and worldview of the scientific age. Second, belief in Satan and demons looks back to a dreadful history of superstitions, punishment, and cruelty. Toner holds that however true these reasons are, they do not justify the renunciation of such a belief. He asks, "Could not much the same reasons be alleged for renouncing belief in God?"[47]

The question is not simply whether created personal spirits exist and influence human life, but whether Christians should believe in their existence and influence as a matter of faith, based on scripture and church teaching. While there has been no sustained in-depth theological writing that bears on this question, a study of those writings available does reveal a spectrum of positions.

Spectrum of Positions

Rahner holds that unbelief in good and evil spirits cannot hold in an age when the existence of intelligent beings other than persons is readily supposed. These spirits are "principalities and powers," who belong to our world by the very ground of their being and who exert their superhuman influence on human history, for its perdition or salvation. The great danger at the present time, Rahner points out, is that good and evil spirits are rejected as mythological, beyond what is acceptable as credible and intelligible. He takes a clear position that the existence of angels and devils cannot be disputed in view of the conciliar declarations, and their scriptural attestation cannot be merely assumed as a hypothesis that could be dropped today.[48]

Based on the teaching of the Fourth Lateran Council in 1215, Rahner concludes that the personal principles of goodness and wickedness cannot be trivialized into abstract ideas. Particularly in reference to the devil, he holds that he "is not to be regarded as a mere mythological personification of evil in the world; the existence of the devil cannot be denied."[49] Such a belief in the devil and angels, however, must not be exaggerated in a Gnostic or Manichean way,

---

[47] Jules J. Toner, *A Commentary on Saint Ignatius's Rules for the Discernment of Spirits* (St. Louis: The Institute of Jesuit Sources, 1982), 260.

[48] See Karl Rahner, "Angels," in *Sacramentum Mundi: An Encyclopedia of Theology*, ed. Karl Rahner et al. (New York: Herder and Herder, 1968), 1:27–35.

[49] Karl Rahner, "The Devil," in Rahner et al., *Sacramentum Mundi*, 2:73–74. See also Adolf Darlap, "Demons," in Rahner et al., *Sacramentum Mundi*, 2:70–73.

elevating them as God's equals or rivals.⁵⁰ It will be well to have
the teaching of the Fourth Lateran Council before us, because the
debate relative to this belief revolves around the interpretation of
this Church teaching.

> We firmly believe and profess without qualification that there is
> only one true God, eternal . . . omnipotent and indescribable:
> three persons but one essence. . . . They are the one and only
> principle of all things—creator of all things visible and invisible,
> spiritual and corporeal, who, by his almighty power, from the
> very beginning of time has created both orders of creatures in
> the same way out of nothing, the spiritual or angelic world and
> the corporeal or visible universe. And afterwards, he formed
> the creature man, who in a way belongs to both orders, as he is
> composed of spirit and body. For the devil and the other demons
> were created by God good according to their nature, but they
> made themselves evil by their own doing. As for man, his sin was
> at the prompting of the devil.⁵¹

Studying more closely the teaching, which was a declaration against
the Albigensians, Schoonenberg points out that the issue was not the
existence and the creation of angels and devils. The crucial point
of the teaching affirmed by the council against the Albigensians, he
says, was that everything has been created by one God. Even this
doctrinal statement that most explicitly speaks of angels and devils
assumed or presupposed rather than explicitly declared their existence.
Thus, he believes, theologians could not claim without qualification
that the existence of angels and devils is "*de fide*." They should ask
if this teaching on angels and devils is a presupposition required by
the content of other revealed truths, and by this necessity is a matter
of Christian faith, or if it is merely part of a historically conditioned
worldview in which these truths were revealed. In other words, the
existence of devils and angels is not essential to the teaching of the
faith but is only accidental to its teaching in a particular historical
context. Schoonenberg relativizes the importance of the question in
relation to the core meaning and value of the Christian faith grounded
in God's disclosure of Godself as love and salvation in the face of sin

---

⁵⁰ Rahner, "Angels," 35.
⁵¹ J. F. Clarkson, SJ, et al., trans., *The Church Teaches: Documents of the Church* (St. Louis: Herder, 1955), 146.

and evil. The focus is on God's saving action, not on the nature and kinds of beings existing in the whole of creation.[52]

Henry Ansgar Kelly concludes that theologians cannot justly give or call for an unqualified assent of faith to the existence of evil spirits.[53] Most of his 1968 book is a critical account of demons in the Old and New Testaments and in the history of Western thought, illuminating the harmful effects of such a belief. Demythologizing many beliefs about the nature, origin, and activity of the devil and demons, he explicitly interprets the declaration of the Lateran Council in direct contrast with Karl Rahner. His is a firmly held opinion that we have no grounds for a theological certainty about the existence of the devil and demons.[54] Since the existence of the evil spirits is more improbable than probable, and since belief in evil spirits is not necessary to enable us to cope with life's problems and, in fact, has been shown to bring about greater problems, Kelly concludes that "it would seem best to act as though evil spirits did not exist, until such time as their existence is forced upon us."[55] Only when such a belief is necessary for some perceived advantage that cannot be achieved otherwise should it be brought into the scheme of reality.

Ernest Lucier holds that the question regarding the existence of evil and good spirits, demons and angels cannot be attested with any kind of certainty through the methods of profane sciences, for by definition demons and angels can only be known by revelation, the basic source of which is scripture. The faith tradition, patristic and conciliar, he says, must not be too easily rejected as obscurantist. Answering the core question of his essay, "Is belief in a personal Satan and devils part of the divine revelation?" he asserts that it is, but it is not an essential part of revelation, only secondary. But while it is so, he holds a theologian is misinformed and misguided in abandoning the ordinary teaching of the church. Belief in a personal Satan, though, is not beyond the possibility of a practical doubt, in the face of the mystery that shrouds demonic existence. In the end, however, evil is conquered not by any kind of speculation on the existence of Satan, but by deciding for goodness in every given situation, through the act of personal

---

[52] Peter J. Schoonenberg, *God's World in the Making* (Pittsburgh: Duquesne University Press, 1964), 8–9.

[53] Henry Ansgar Kelly, *The Devil, Demonology, and Witchcraft: The Development of Christian Belief in Evil Spirits* (Garden City, NY: Doubleday, 1968).

[54] Ibid., 131.

[55] Ibid.

liberty for which a person is accountable and responsible and which no evil, moral, physical, or personal, can ever put under constraint.[56]

Louis Monden, writing in 1966, took a firm stand for the personal existence of Satan.[57] He writes that contemporary thought is prone to regard all mention of the diabolical in a figurative sense. All personifications of evil and whatever symbolizes it found in the Old and New Testament are seen as part of the mythological garb of God's entire message. In this matter, as in all others, contemporary theology seeks to extract from Christian teaching every mythical element, remove it from outmoded worldviews, and translate it into a religious language and expression that is intelligible and acceptable. He says, however, that if the scripture is read with an open mind, free from preconceived notions, one can see that if the existence of Satan as a personal entity is denied or eliminated, this changes the Christian message in its very essence. In New Testament thought, at the heart of which is Christ's preaching, evil is first of all not some *thing* but some *one*. Monden elaborates as follows:

> The struggle against the "Evil One" is of a strikingly personal character; and exactly for this reason the battle on behalf of the Kingdom of God, like the battle which marks our work-a-day lives, takes on an earnestness, an inexorable dramatic tension, which is the very touchstone of a true Christian life. The custom adopted by Christians, since the last century, of "demythologizing" Satan often, therefore, takes on the nature of a flight from the serious exactions of the Christian situation.[58]

Paul M. Quay submits a careful study of the teaching of the council.[59] Engaging in a critical analysis of arguments against the teaching, in view of what the council actually said and so far as can be ascertained what it intended, he seeks to discover whether, on this one basis at least, we are held as Catholics to believe that angels and demons exist. This is to presume, however, that whatever the council intended to define as faith is indeed accepted as an essential element or part of the content of Catholic faith.

---

[56] Ernest Lucier, "Satan," *The Catholic Mind* (September 1974), 24–25.

[57] Louis Monden, *Signs and Wonders: A Study of the Miraculous Element in Religion* (New York: Desclee, 1966), 140.

[58] Ibid. Reviews heaped praise on Monden's book.

[59] Paul M. Quay, "Angels and Demons: The Teaching of IV Lateran," *Theological Studies* 42/1 (March 1981): 20–45.

The position under debate is that the Lateran Council did not formally propose as revealed truth the existence of angels and demons. Again, the main argument in support of this position holds that the council presumed or presupposed the existence of devils and angels but did not directly address it; thus, it did not formally define it. This argument appeals to the hermeneutical principle that "any dogmatic definition ought not to be extended beyond the scope of the error it intends to condemn."[60] It held that the council's intent was only to defend the universality and unicity of God's creative activity and the creaturely origins of sin and evil against the heresy that held otherwise. It did not teach formally on the existence of demons and angels, because that was not the subject of the error it sought to condemn. The proposition about angels and demons is only part of the psycho-cultural framework of the council, within which truth or falsehood about the world is asserted, which in our own psycho-cultural framework of today we can just as persuasively and effectively explain without any mention of angels or demons. Thus, demons and angels are elements of a long-gone worldview that once served as a vehicle for revealed truth.

Quay submits his own arguments on the basis of the text of the Lateran teaching. He holds that it is the worst sort of legalism or quibbling to say that the teaching on the existence of angels and demons has not been defined and hence is not a matter of Christian faith on the basis of the Lateran teaching, because formal statements of existence have not been made. He points out that we are not concerned with stretching what the council said but understanding it. He cites the example of the teaching of Nicaea that declares, "We believe in God the Father Almighty." The Nicene Creed does not define the existence of God, just as no council states that Jesus Christ exists. Quay writes: "It will not do to say that, even if God did not exist, it would still be true that the Christian concept of God implies his unicity, hence that declaration of his unicity gives no grounds of itself for asserting his existence; for, did He not exist, faith in His unicity would be erroneous. Professions of faith are solely factual and existential; conceptual elaboration is not of direct concern to them."[61] He concludes that the *de fide* declaration of the existence of angels and demons is in accord with both the text and the context of the Lateran teaching, and thus doubts or denials that the existence of angels and demons is an article of Catholic faith are without serious grounding.

---

[60] Charles R. Mayer, "Speak of the Devil," *Chicago Studies* 14 (1975): 10.
[61] Quay, "Angels and Demons," 38n26.

Theological and Pastoral Position

Given this wide spectrum of theological positions on whether the existence of demons and angels is a matter of faith, what are we to make of it for our prayer and discernment? I take the fundamental stance that the existence of Satan and good and evil spirits does not constitute a core belief of the Christian faith. This means that one can live a meaningful Christian life apart from belief in their existence. Even as there is no one definitive answer to the question regarding their existence, it is wise from the outset to put the question within the wider faith context and to avoid any form of exaggeration that may rise from such a belief resulting in groundless fears and vicious super-stitions, which would annihilate the very life of faith. What matters is that one is committed to the love of God, for which one responds with greater generosity to the good and opposes with courage all and every form of evil.

Evil ultimately assumes a human face in the reality of sin. The final power lies in the exercise of human freedom. Beyond locating evil in individual persons, it is important to see it in its structural and systemic manifestations—social situations that cause or support evil and institutionalize it in cultural, political, and economic systems. Social or structural sins, however, are rooted in personal sin and thus are always linked to the concrete acts of individuals who create these structures and consolidate them with others through their complicity, indifference, and neglect. Drawing the more social dimension of evil puts it in a much wider social arena, beyond individualistic notions and concepts of temptation and sin. Peter McVerry describes sinful structures in the following terms: "the formal set of relationships which result in the oppression of groups of people, while enabling other groups of people to benefit from the oppression, even without those benefiting fully knowing or fully consenting to the oppression."[62] In the same vein, Peter Henriot defines social sin as follows:

(1) structures that oppress human beings, violate human dig-nity, stifle freedom, impose gross inequality; (2) situations that promote and facilitate individual acts of selfishness; (3) the complicity of silent acquiescence of persons who do not take responsibility for the evil being done.[63]

---

[62] Peter McVerry, "Sin: The Social, National, and International Aspects," *Way Supplement* 48 (Fall 1983): 39.

[63] Peter Henriot, "The Concept of Social Sin," *The Catholic Mind* (October 1973), 40.

In engaging in Ignatian discernment where human decisions are shown to be influenced by evil or good spirits, a pastoral stance must be taken in relation to individuals. Prudential judgments must be made as to when a person's belief in Satan, demons, and angels is to be taken into account in the process of prayer and discernment or excluded from it. One may decide to omit such a belief because of uncertainty, or one may do so because one cannot get a handle on exactly when and how Satan, demons, or angels are involved. It is particularly necessary to downplay or to omit totally concerns about evil and good spirits if one does not have the psychological capacity to deal with them profitably. The ultimate purpose is to open oneself to be led and guided by the Holy Spirit and to struggle against any force or influence that works against the divine promptings, from whatever source it may come, with or without the mediation of an evil spirit. One may be directed by the natural promptings of one's heart, which like all else in the universe, are under God's providence.[64]

Reading Ignatian discernment with theological seriousness by addressing the three questions—How is the incomprehensible God experienced? What is the relationship between human freedom and divine providence? and Is belief in Satan, in good and evil spirits a matter of Christian faith?—lays the groundwork and provides the horizon for a critical and contemporary reading of the modes of Ignatian discernment.

A Contemporary Reading of the Modes of Discernment

On the modes of Ignatian discernment I take a critical approach, considering that there is not one single interpretation of these modes; this can be seen as the reason for debates and discussions among reputable theologians on this key issue. I also bring to bear on my reading of Ignatius's classical writing, a product of his sixteenth-century religious worldview, the new hermeneutical lens of contemporary theology and philosophy. While this does not negate the value of accurate exegesis of the Ignatian texts, it is important to be mindful that fidelity to the past does not mean rigid fundamentalism. In fact, this provides a liberating and evocative context for linking the past to new worldviews and horizons of human meaning, thus assuring the fresh continuity of its spirit and vision in the present. I make an explicit effort to translate in a more general language the terms used

[64] Toner, *A Commentary on Saint Ignatius's Rules for the Discernment of Spirits*, 34–37, 270.

by Ignatius. This is to make accessible the inner logic of the Ignatian discernment in a language that is understood by all.

The Three Modes of Discernment: A Continuing Discourse

The most diverse and sharply debated of the interpretations of Ignatian discernment are those that pertain to its three modes. There are conflicting views of what these modes mean, how they are inter-related, and what their comparative value is in reference to a life lived according to God's reality and truth. Before issues and problems are addressed, what needs to be first clarified is when Ignatian discernment is properly used as a mode for Christian decision making. Is it only used in situations when a person is faced with a moral decision of primary significance, when he or she stands before the choice of a state of life or a radical reform thereof? The common but not universal opinion is that occasions for the use of Ignatian discernment are frequent, even daily. Ignatius made no direct and explicit reference on the matter, but what can be gleaned from his writings strongly supports the common opinion. That only a few important life choices are worthy of God's personal concern is not Ignatian in spirit and principle. There is no choice that is so unimportant as to lie outside God's divine love.[65] Edward Pousset asserts that Ignatius's ways of making an election relate to all of life:

> They are valid not merely for the macro-decision that involves an entire life, nor even merely for the decision of a moderate mag-nitude that plans a reform. They are also suited for directing the multitude of choices implied in the running of a household, the carrying out of a profession, and all our relationships with oth-ers, even if it is only a question of saying or not saying a word. In short, there is micro-decision in our daily life, however tiny it may be, that does not fall within their competence.[66]

We need, however, to enlarge the space of our tents, as Isaiah puts it, beyond the micro-decisions or macro-decisions of our personal and interpersonal lives. When we truly give our lives to others beyond our inner circle of relations, we get involved in the struggle of those who lack the resources to live humanly. We work to change structures that

---

[65] Toner, *Discerning God's Will*, 30–32.

[66] Edward Pousset, *Life in Faith and Freedom: An Essay Presenting Gaston Fessard's Analysis of the Dialectic of the Spiritual Exercises*, trans. and ed. Eugené L. Donahue (St. Louis: Institute of Jesuit Sources, 1980), 130. See also Sandra M. Schneiders, "Spiritual Discernment in the Dialogue of Saint Catherine of Siena," *Horizons* 9/1 (1982): 49.

violate their dignity and their basic right to decent human life. Christian discipleship involves the three dimensions of human experience, all of which must be taken into account—personal, interpersonal, and public. The public dimension is as intrinsic to our discernment and to our spiritual life as a whole as the personal to interpersonal dimensions are.

Anne Patrick defines spirituality as constituting the whole of Christian religious life, beyond prayer and spiritual exercises, and she points out that commitment to social justice involves the continual effort to right unjust relationships at levels ranging from the interpersonal and the transnational.[67] If spirituality is the whole of Christian religious life, there are no impenetrable boundaries between ethics and spirituality. The work for social justice is central to ethics as it is to spirituality, in the intra-, inter-, and social dimensions of human existence.

The First Mode of Discernment

The first mode of discernment, says Ignatius, is "a time when God our Lord so moves and draws the will that, without doubting, the faithful person follows what is shown, as St. Paul and St. Matthew did in following Christ our Lord."[68] There are three essential factors in this first mode. First, something is said to be shown to the person. What is shown is God's direction of that which the person must follow. Second, the will of the person is moved and drawn to the divine direction precisely as God acts in the person; and third, the person is so moved without doubt that the movement is from God and what is shown is truly God's will.[69]

---

[67] Anne E. Patrick, "Ethics and Spirituality: The Social Justice Connection," *The Way Supplement* 63 (Autumn 1988): 105. See also Margaret A. Farley, "New Patterns of Relationship: Beginnings of a Moral Revolution," *Theological Studies* 36/4 (1975): 627–46; David Hollenbach, *Justice, Peace, and Human Rights: American Catholic Social Ethics in a Pluralistic World* (New York: Crossroad, 1988); Karen Lebacqz, *Six Theories of Justice: Perspectives from Philosophical and Theological Ethics* (Minneapolis: Augsburg, 1986); and Daniel C. Maguire, *The Moral Revolution: A Christian Humanist Vision* (San Francisco: Harper & Row, 1986).

[68] Ignatius of Loyola, *Exercitia Spiritualia* (Rome: In Collegio Romano eiusdem Societatis, 1915 [1615]), [175]. Hereafter referred to as *SpEx* with the standard numbering in the text. (The text number referred to in brackets is translated into English in Toner, *Discerning God's Will*, 108).

[69] Toner, *Discerning God's Will*, 109. Some refer to Ignatius's visions at Cardoner River and at La Storta (*Autobiography*, [30] and [96]) as experiences of the first mode of discernment. See Harvey D. Egan, *The Spiritual Exercises and the Ignatian Mystical Horizon*, foreword by Karl Rahner (St. Louis: The Institute of Jesuit Sources, 1976), 135.

Rahner refers to this first mode as God's free and special disclosure of divine will, beyond the ordinary ways and sources of knowing, for an individual recognizing it as such follows it with absolute certitude. He writes: "It must be a kind of knowledge of this will that is distinct from usual kinds. . . . God himself 'speaks' here in a way that goes beyond those sources of knowledge. Consequently the object about which God 'speaks' must itself be different from what other means of knowing give access to."[70] Avery Dulles, explaining Rahner's thought on the matter, states that this special disclosure comes down to a private revelation like that given to certain saints who were divinely called to various tasks and missions, disclosures they could not have known apart from revelation.[71]

Ignatius and Rahner seem to put forward an image of God having a particular will for each person, within a specific divine plan that is communicated through special divine disclosure, which, when received, leaves one with no power to resist or disobey. Roger Haight proposes a new way of looking at this question that deals with divine omnipotence, providence, and governance, on the one hand, and human freedom, on the other. He distinguishes between a general will and a specific will of God. The general will of God is found in the scriptures, especially in the New Testament as mediated by the person of Jesus. In the message of the kingdom, for instance, is God's general will for social history, as justice characterizes our public and personal relations, and love as the fundamental motive and character of all our human actions. God, he holds, has no specific will for concrete and individual decisions in people's lives. Thus, what is at stake is not God's will but the individual's will. And one's personal decision cannot be equated with God's specific will, but only as conforming to God's general will, in greater or lesser degree, in one's concrete context. This releases people from the anxious quest for certainty about God's specific will, because in this view, it does not exist. While this view limits God's general will to the vision and norm for life, it bestows on human decisions a responsibility and seriousness that can energize them.[72]

---

[70] Karl Rahner, "The Logic of Concrete Individual Knowledge in Ignatius Loyola," in *The Dynamic Element in the Church* (London: Burns and Oates, 1964), 106.

[71] Avery Dulles, "Finding God's Will: Raher's Interpretation of Ignatian Election," *Woodstock Letters* 94 (1965): 142.

[72] Roger Haight, "Foundational Issues in Jesuit Spirituality," *Studies in the Spirituality of Jesuits* 19/4 (September 1987): 32–35.

This provocative view puts strength on the side of human freedom, but it lacks the richness and dynamism of the more recent contemporary views that keep divine providence and human freedom in creative tension, as in the model of intersubjectivity of two "thous" in the process theology model. Seeing God as one who does not remain only on the general level but is as much engaged on the level of the personal, where providence and human freedom are most deeply and intimately involved, I propose a revision to the phrase *God's will*. It seems unyielding; it connotes predetermination and absoluteness. As aforementioned, I propose that in place of God's will we speak of *God's desire*. Desire is an inclination of the heart toward some object accompanied by a positive affect. The quality of desire is determined by the object, whereas its intensity comes from affect. It is the inner force of the heart that impels all striving. That which one desires most is that which moves and directs all else in one's life.[73] There is a deep connection between our human desires and our knowledge of God. The more authentic our desires are, as we go more deeply into ourselves, the more they become communal. What is most uniquely personal in ourselves points to our most profound connection with others in community and in the larger society.[74]

The reference to the desire of God is consistent with the spirit of Ignatius, who longed to be the object of God's desire all of his life. "The one who is desired longs to be possessed by the one who desires and understands their lives as being fully for the other and understandable only in relation to that desire of the other."[75] Throughout the Exercises Ignatius vividly expresses his desire to do what his Divine Majesty desires of him.

The interpretation of the first mode of discernment, then, may be expressed in the language of desire: God has a desire for each one of us, because God loves us in a singular way. Like any desire, it seeks expression in a special disclosure that only the beloved can understand. And the beloved, resonating with God's desire as the beloved's own desire, is so moved that he or she can only utter his or her yes.

Inevitably, one must ask how frequently any person enters this first mode. What Ignatius thought about this question cannot be established,

---

[73] McGrath, "The Place of Desires in the Ignatian Exercises," 29. See also Kinerk, "Eliciting Great Desires," 1–29.

[74] Kinerk, "Eliciting Great Desires," 4. See also Panicola, "Discernment in the Neonatal Context," 729.

[75] McGrath, "The Place of Desires in the Ignatian Exercises," 29. See also Lachlan M. Hughes, "Affectivity, Conscience, and Christian Choice," *The Way Supplement* 24 (Spring 1975) 36–45.

although some point out that Ignatius himself frequently experienced it. Some take the extreme view that this is as rare as a private revelation;[76] others say that it is exceptional, but not as rare as it is commonly made out to be.[77] The other extreme opinion is that it is of frequent ordinary occurrence.[78] Ignatius, a master of brevity but not of clarity, said nothing to enlighten us on the matter.[79]

The other question raised is whether the "consolation without previous cause" is intrinsic to the first mode of discernment. The nature of this consolation is such not because of its suddenness or by its mystical quality, but rather by the absence of any antecedent intentionality towards its expression and manifestation. One is deeply drawn toward God without any conscious intervention that may have moved one's affectivity. One simply finds himself or herself deeply in love with God, without having sought it, either by prayer or contemplation, or by any other way. There could be a note of suddenness or surprise, but neither is necessary or intrinsic to the experience. "It is rather the total movement of affectivity and sensibility towards God without any proportional influence of imaginative or rational intentionality prior to the experience—whether this priority is conceived temporally or naturally."[80]

Again, there is a whole range of positions relative to the question. Some say that the first mode of discernment involves a time of great consolation, a rare moment of felt union.[81] Others specify it as consolation without previous cause but keep it distinct from the first mode of discernment. The consolation without previous cause is seen by others as essential in understanding the first mode of discernment. Some simply see the identification of the two, being that the consolation without previous cause is the first principle of all Ignatian discernment, and without it the first mode of discernment loses its basis or validity.[82] Some merely hold that the first mode must

---

[76] James Walsh, "Discernment of Spirits," *The Way Supplement* 16 (Summer 1972): 64.

[77] Hugo Rahner, *Ignatius the Theologian*, trans. Michael Barry (New York: Herder and Herder, 1968), 145.

[78] Bertrand de Margerie holds that the first mode is normal in the sense of usual. *Theological Retreat* (Chicago: Franciscan Herald Press, 1976), 155.

[79] Toner, *Discovering God's Will*, 129.

[80] Ibid.

[81] Michale J. Buckley, "The Structure of the Rules for Discernment of Spirits," *The Way Supplement* 20 (Autumm 1973): 33.

[82] Hervé Coathalem, *Ignatian Insights: A Guide to the Complete Spiritual Exercises,* 2nd edition, trans. Charles McCarthy (Taiching, Taiwan: Kuanchi, 1971), 187-88.

be seen in relationship with consolation without previous cause, the latter as necessary in understanding the former.[83] And others assert that consolation without previous cause belongs to the first mode, meaning that the first mode always includes the consolation without previous cause but not vice versa.[84] Ignatius is silent on the matter. He makes no mention of the consolation without previous cause in what he means by the first mode of discernment. This is in contrast with his clear reference to the presence of consolation and desolation present in the second mode of discernment that distinguishes the second from the first as well as the third. It is argued that Ignatius would have been expected to make mention or at least imply it, if consolation without previous cause is essential or intrinsic to the first mode of discernment. But his silence on the relationship of the first mode of discernment and consolation without previous cause in key texts is significant. Thus one many have the experience of the first mode of discernment but only with the quiet certitude of God's truth, without the notable sweetness and joy of the consolation without previous cause. On the other hand, one may have the fill of consolation without previous cause, but none may truly bring clarity to the choice one is making. Thus, the first mode of discernment and consolation without previous cause are not intrinsically or essentially related.[85]

The Second Mode of Discernment

Ignatius's statement in the *Spiritual Exercises* describing this mode of discernment is marked by brevity far more than his description of the first mode of discernment: "The second is a time when sufficient light and understanding are gathered, through experiences of consolations and desolations and through experience of discerning diverse spirits."[86] I do not intend to discuss in great detail all the rules or guidelines under this second mode of discernment. Instead, I wish to draw insights from the Ignatian rules or guidelines in how one can discern the connaturality of one's desires with God's desires as mediated through the interplay of consolation and desolation, and

---

[83] De Margerie, *Theological Retreat*, 155-56.

[84] Egan, *The Spiritual Exercises and the Ignatian Mystical Horizon*, 140-41.

[85] Toner, *Discerning God's Will*, 115-118.

[86] *SpEx*, [176] (Toner, *Discerning God's Will*, 131). For the study and understanding of the rules for discernment of spirits for this second mode, see Michael Buckley, "The Structure of the Rules for Discernment of Spirits," *The Way Supplement* 20 (Autumn 1973): 19–37.

how one can understand the ways of evil and good in the process of discernment.

God's desires are stirred in our hearts by way of consolation or desolation, that we may come to resonate with these desires as our own desires for our meaning and authenticity. Consolation is any interior movement of feeling or emotionality that draws us to God. The primary matrix of consolation is that of the love of God. And within that matrix, we experience tears of remorse or joy, increase of faith, hope, and charity, and a deep quiet and peace.[87] The feeling of love for God, to qualify as consolation, must be experienced by the person as "aflame." "Love has to be love for God if the lover's experience is to count as spiritual, but love for God has to be love with delightfully inflamed sensibility if the lover's experience is to count as consolation."[88] This is spiritual consolation in the proper sense. Desolation brings a reverse affective disposition. While consolation has its origin in the love of God, desolation comes from feeling separated from that love, which brings about a state of confusion, tepidity, cynicism, and distrust.[89] "Consolation and desolation do not identify necessarily with pleasure and pain."[90] They are denoted not by their sensibilities but by their direction or orientation.

No equivalence, thus, is posited between consolation and pleasure, desolation and pain. Consolation is any movement of human sensibility, irrespective of the cause, which directs one to God, whether a consolation of quiet peace or of exuberant joy, and whether it is accompanied by pain or pleasure. In consolation the soul is on fire with love of God, as no created love can ever fill the soul. Consolation is rooted in faith; it is joy despite tragic pain. There is a peace that is deeper than the pain. It is having a deep sense that "where there is great suffering, there's also that great sense of hope and joy and knowledge that God is there."[91]

To act directly against desolation, one must resist any impulse or suggestion to change one's previous decision or commitment made during the time of consolation. One must remain firm, for in desolation the

---

[87] *SpEx*, [316], Rule 1:3. (The English translation used is "The Text of St. Ignatius Rules for the Discernment of Spirits," in Toner, *A Commentary on Saint Ignatius's Rules for the Discernment of Spirits,* 24–25. Hereafter referred to as *Text* in relation to the English translation used.)

[88] Toner, *A Commentary on Saint Ignatius's Rules for the Discernment of Spirits*, 98.

[89] *SpEx*, [317], Rule 1:4 (*Text*, 25).

[90] Buckley, "The Structure of the Rules for Discernment of Spirits," 29.

[91] "An Interview with Dorothy Day," *National Jesuit News* (May 1972), 10.

evil spirit becomes our counsel, as when in consolation, the good spirit becomes our lead. One must also go the way contrary to the way of desolation and abide in the Spirit's protection against the destructive effects of desolation through prayer, meditation, and penance. To overcome spiritual desolation, one must make oneself reflectively aware of it. By doing so, one detaches oneself from the concrete experience of desolation as an object distinct from one's person.[92]

To act directly against the thoughts that may arise from desolation, we must consider the ways of the Lord, whose graced presence may not be sensibly felt but who remains faithful. Directed toward the future, where consolation is awaiting, we must endure some desolation. Understanding why God sometimes allows desolation helps one face it with faith and courage. God allows desolation as the consequence of our personal sins and failures, that we may be purified. Desolation also makes us experience the cost of loving God without the rewards of consolation, and in the process learn in humility that consolation is due to grace alone.[93]

The other kind of consolation, differentiated from consolation without previous cause, is brought about by the intervention of imaginative or rational intentionality. This is called consolation with previous cause. Because both good and evil can cause consolation, the origin of the consolation must be discerned with astuteness. To see signs or glimpses into the true source of consolation, one must be attentive to the process of consolation itself, which will end either in destruction or in further development. As it unfolds little by little, this process helps reveal prior good or evil influences in their true light.[94]

As one gains in spiritual sensitivity to the ways of the divine, one discerns the subtlety of consolation from its moment of initiation. The coming of true consolation to a person given over to the Lord is likened to a drop of water entering a sponge—gentle, quiet, imperceptible. On the contrary, that which is not of God will enter with noise and disturbance, as when a drop of water hits a rock. The condition of affectivity or disposition of the receiver of the consolation indicates the quality of consolation.[95] In Ignatian discernment consolation and desolation are recognized by the obvious moral

---

[92] Toner, *A Commentary on Saint Ignatius's Rules for the Discernment of Spirits*, 150.

[93] *SpEx*, [322], Rule 1:9; [323], Rule 1:10; [324], Rule 1:11 (*Text*, 26–27).

[94] *SpEx*, [331], Rule 2:3; [332], Rule 2:4; [333], Rule 2:5; [334], Rule 2:6 (*Text*, 28–29). See also William K. Delany, "Discernment of Spirits in Ignatius of Loyola and Teresa of Avila," *Review for Religious* (July-August 1987): 606–7.

[95] *SpEx*, [335], Rule 2:7.

direction and orientation of what has caused them. This is, however, not always the case. The apparent moral worth of what is proposed may be beyond doubt at the beginning, but its real worth is judged ultimately by feelings of peace and joy. Affectivity is the criterion by which consolation can be judged as coming from God.[96] This brings us to the ways of evil and good in the process of discernment.

Though belief in the personal existence of Satan, angels, and demons is not essential to the Christian faith, it is not entirely removed from the Christian faith experience. So much the better for us, even those for whom belief in preternatural beings is not congenial to their spirituality, to draw wisdom from Ignatius's profound understanding of how the ways of good and evil have a bearing on the process of discernment. These ways stand in relation to the two kinds of persons, who represent two different dispositions. For those whose lives are dominated by sin, their mode of temptation is pleasure, which maintains them in their state of sin. For those who represent a contrary disposition, whose conscience is progressing through a period of purification and who are no longer simply taken over by imagination and pleasure, their mode of temptation is now focused on thought, and the evil spirit through false reasoning causes them to be sad, to be focused on their pain, and to give up on themselves. The frontal attacks of the evil spirit, without subtlety, without deception, are focused on wearing down the victim. The good spirit, acting in a reverse manner, moves one's thoughts to effect feelings of courage, consolation, inspiration, and calm.[97]

Three similes are used to dramatize the power and strategy of the evil spirit and show how to wage a counterattack. First, Ignatius uses the simile of a shrewish woman (the word *shrewish* as a qualifying term is a slight liberty taken by Toner with the text, in deference, he explains, to Ignatius's respect for and friendship with women, and also to the fact, I assert, that being shrewish is not intrinsic to women).[98] As seen from tradition, religion has often connected the feminine to the diabolical, to the extent that late Jewish and early Christian thought virtually demonized women.[99] Such a view must be completely corrected. The feminist approach to Ignatian spirituality brings the values

---

[96] Buckley, "The Structure of the Rules for Discernment of Spirits," 35–36.

[97] *SpEx*, [314], Rule 1:1; [315], Rule 1:2 (*Text*, 23).

[98] Toner, *A Commentary on Saint Ignatius's Rules for the Discernment of Spirits*, 26.

[99] Walter H. Wagner, "The Demonization of Women," *Religion in Life* 42 (Spring 1973): 56. See also Mary Aquin O'Neill, "The Nature of Women and the Method of Theology," *Theological Studies* 56/4 (1995): 730.

of solidarity, equality, and inclusiveness into the personal and public realms of human engagement and involvement.[100] A greater gender sensitivity in the approach to Ignatian spirituality brings a new depth and richness from the woman perspective.[101] Kathleen Fischer articulates this perspective as

> a vision of life emphasizing inclusion rather than exclusion, connectedness rather than separateness, and mutuality in relationships rather than dominance and submission. Feminism also entails the conviction that full individual development can take place only within a human community that is structured in justice. And so, feminism works for social change.[102]

To continue with the point of the first simile, one must face without hesitation the enemy's threats and pressures, likened to the shrewish woman out to get her way through her nagging, screaming, and sobbing. Before a show of strength, the shrewish woman turns to flight. In the face of the enemy's warfare of wits, one must go contrary to where one is being led. "Resist the devil, and he will flee from you" (Jas 4:7).

The second simile is that of a false lover. This enemy can be dealt with by exposing his counterfeit to the light. In the concrete, this means that one must be open about his or her spiritual life to a spiritual master or director who is familiar with the ways of the good and evil spirits.

The third simile is that of a military commander-in-chief who attacks when the defense of the other side is weakest. The strategy of the evil spirit is to take us where we are most vulnerable. The obvious practical conclusion is that true self-knowledge is our best preparation and defense against the ways of the Evil One.[103]

The insidiousness and disguise of evil, appearing as an angel of light, is seen in its intrusion into the good in a slow and subtle manner, carried over in a gradual unfolding and devolution, and tempting the

---

[100] Loretta Piper, "A Feminist Reflection on Ignatian Mission," *The Way Supplement* 79 (Spring 1994): 34.

[101] See Pamela Hayes, "Women and the Passion," *The Way Supplement* 58 (Spring 1987): 56–73; Ursula King, "Women's Contribution to Contemporary Spirituality," *The Way Supplement* 84 (Autumn 1995): 26–37. See also the whole issue of *The Way Supplement* 93 (1998) entitled "Where Now? Women's Spirituality After the Ecumenical Decade."

[102] Kathleen R. Fischer, *Women at the Well: Feminist Perspectives on Spiritual Direction* (Mahwah, NJ: Paulist Press, 1988), 2.

[103] *SpEx,* [325], Rule 1:12; [326], Rule 1:13; [327], Rule 1:14 (*Text,* 26–27). See Toner, *A Commentary on Saint Ignatius's Rules for Discernment,* 198–210.

person to hidden falsehoods and perverse designs.[104] Because of the deceptive nature of evil, one must be attentive to the process as well as the first moment of consolation. The call here is to confront not only the obvious ways of evil, but more so its deceptive ingress into what is good. Thus, one must attend to one's attractions toward any good by analysis of its entire beginning, middle, and end, and discern at what precise moment evil has sneaked in. One can determine the deceptive nature of false consolation by the reality to which it has led, obliterating the peace and quiet that was initially present.[105] The Evil One could be the very origin and source of what appeared to be good. The masquerade of evil must be disentangled and exposed in the light.

As one's life of faith grows and matures, one is tempted less by the appearance of obvious evil and more by that of deceitful good. In this lies the most significant insight of Ignatian discernment. For the good person who is searching out the authenticity and meaning of his or her life, the true danger is not obvious moral compromise but deceitful good.[106] Noteworthy in Ignatian discernment is that there is less discussion of desolation in relation to those who have matured in their faith, as they have disposed their entire lives toward God. This is so because desolation is a movement of affectivity away from God in some sort of evident and obvious manner. It is pseudo-consolation, deceptive or deceitful, that more often confronts the mature person of faith.

Thus, even in the case of consolation without previous cause, Ignatius warns that the actual consolation without previous cause and the time of the afterglow be distinguished. The afterglow is the lingering memory and feelings that remain after the source of the consolation has ceased. Consolation without previous cause is without deception, but in the time that immediately follows it, thoughts and feelings may come to us that may not have God as their origin but the Evil One, and thus we can be deceived. To guard ourselves against deception, we must subject our whole experience to scrutiny, reflection, and prayer, so we can see the serpent's tail lurking in the afterglow.[107]

The Third Mode of Discernment

What Ignatius does for the third "time" or moment of discernment, which he does not do for the first or second mode, is to follow it up

---

[104] *SpEx*, [332], Rule 2:4 (*Text*, 28).

[105] *SpEx*, [333], Rule 2:5; [335], Rule 2:6 (*Text*, 28–29).

[106] Buckley, "The Structure of the Rules for Discernment of Spirits," 32–33.

[107] *SpEx*, [336], Rule 2:8 (*Text*, 29).

with many paragraphs of detailed instructions on how to carry it out. The opening statement is stated as follows:

> The third is a tranquil time when one considers first for what a person is born, that is to praise God, our Lord, and to save his soul; and, when desiring to do this, the person elects as a means to help serve God and save his soul a way of life or state in life within the boundaries of the Church. I said a tranquil time, a time when a person is not stirred up by diverse spirits and has free and tranquil use of his natural powers.[108]

In this mode one makes a comparative evaluation of alternatives for choice, during a tranquil time, in view of one's ultimate end. Ignatius's explanatory statement yields two factors: the third time is a time when there are no diverse spirits stirring up the discerner, and it is also a time when he or she has a free use of his or her natural powers. Tranquil time may be interpreted differently from different perspectives. Some interpret the tranquility of the third time as spiritual consolation. Others, like Karl Rahner, designate the third time as the absence of consolation; therefore, the discerner is left to fend for himself or herself without divine aid.[109] Rahner, however, seems then to contradict the aforementioned explanation by saying that the third time may be regarded as a sign of motion by the good spirit, a motion so delicate that the discerner "does not notice it at all and so he thinks that he has found the right solution by pondering and calculating acutely and lucidly, pencil in hand, without being moved by any spirit at all."[110]

Harvey Egan interprets the time of tranquility as a time of being moved by diverse spirits either to consolation without high crests or to desolation without deep troughs. It is a time of some kind of plateau for consolation and desolation.[111] In Ignatius's thought, however, the data of consolation and desolation are not relied on as heavily as a source of evidence in the third mode; otherwise, the election would still be of the second mode, not the third.[112] The "natural powers" of the person are used in decision making; these include insight, reason,

---

[108] *SpEx,* [177] (English translation in Toner, *Discerning God's Will,* 161–62).

[109] Rahner, "The Logic of Concrete Individual Knowledge in Ignatius Loyola," 168.

[110] Ibid.

[111] Egan, *The Spiritual Exercise and the Ignatian Mystical Horizon,* 147.

[112] Toner, *Discerning God's Will,* 166.

imagination, memory, and will, which are not under the influence, whether impeding or liberating, of diverse spirits.[113]

After stating what he means by a third time for a sound and trustworthy election, Ignatius points out the next step to take:

> After going back and forth [over the advantages and disadvantages] in this way and having reasoned on the matter proposed [for election] from all sides, to observe toward which alternative reason leans. Thus, in accord with the prevailing movement of reason, and not in accord with any sensual movement, a decision on the matter proposed ought to be made.[114]

One brings to mind all the options in the situation for one's choice, opens to the Spirit, and prays that one's will may be moved toward what is truly for the greater glory of God. After these initial preparations, one looks over the options well and faithfully, sees each and every aspect, draws out evidences, weighs the advantages or disadvantages, sees certain or foreseen consequences of each alternative—all these considerations within the vision of which option is truly for the greater glory of God. The main norm or principle that guides discernment in the third mode is this greater service to and glory of God—the *magis* principle, or the greater-glory principle.[115]

When Ignatius uses "the glory of God," he means our participation in God, the transformation of created life by its union with God in Jesus, in which God is present and revealed. God's glory is God's glory *in* us, and *for* us and others. It is achieved through the free decisions and actions of human persons, for we are not only recipients and vessels of divine glory, but we are God's collaborators in bringing it about in ourselves, in others, and in the whole world.

This might be compared to the rule of God that Jesus preached. Much of the second week of the *Spiritual Exercises* is focused on meditations on Jesus's preaching and actions that manifest the glory of God. For Ignatius, to advance the rule of God is to give God more glory. In the concrete personal choice, what does the glory of God mean? It means the expression of divine love that seeks for us to come to know the joy and fullness of a life in God and will not settle for a lesser good for us. The glory-of-God principle does not always require choosing hard things; it sometimes requires hard decisions,

---

[113] Ibid., 167.
[114] Ibid., 180.
[115] Ibid., 173.

yes, but sometimes thoroughly delightful and easy ones too, much more delightful than we often allow ourselves to have. What counts is not whether the alternative is hard or easy, pleasant or unpleasant, but whether it is truly for the glory of God in us, and for others. In every case, accepting and living by the greater-glory principle is truly accepting and living by love, love for God and others. And in the full measure we give ourselves in love and for love, in every shifting of our centers from ourselves to others, we give praise and glory to God.[116]

There are special situations, however, when the giving of ourselves is asked to a much greater degree, when a special *magis* norm governs our choice—a greater likeness to Christ in his poverty and humiliation as a norm for deciding and choosing, not in every situation for choice, but in one special kind of situation. This is a special choice and must be discerned with much prudence and wisdom. The *magis* principle is the primary norm; the greater-likeness norm is secondary, in the sense that it is not what is expected of every choice.[117] "It can never justify a choice of actual poverty and humiliation over riches and honors if the latter are seen to be more for the service of God in a particular situation for choice, with all its concrete circumstances, including the agent's responsibilities to others and his or her own psychological and spiritual development."[118]

The Relationship of the Three Modes

How do the three modes interrelate, if they can be brought into such a relationship at all? The answers to this question by interpreters of Saint Ignatius vary, depending on how they view the modes in themselves. In the spectrum of interpretations I take up three major positions, those of Rahner, Egan, and Toner; two positions are located at each end of the spectrum, and one position is somewhere in the middle, although much closer to one end than to the other. At one end is the interpretation proposed by Karl Rahner. The three modes, in his view, constitute one identical kind of choice or election; they have one and the same nature and are distinguished only by the different degrees to which they realize that nature.[119] All Ignatian discernment of God's will, in Rahner's view, is ultimately a second mode discernment, with the first mode as an extraordinary phenomenon,

---

[116] Ibid., 174–75.

[117] Ibid., 177–78.

[118] Ibid., 178.

[119] Rahner, "The Logic of Concrete Individual Knowledge in Ignatius Loyola," 105.

the practical importance of which is secondary.[120] The third mode is
a deficient modality, which appears in its more fully developed form
in the first and second mode. The third mode, thus, could be seen as
the less perfect mode of the second, but whose rationality must be an
intrinsic part of the second.[121] His elaboration on the place of reason
in discerning the spirits in the second mode probes deep into the very
nature of such a discernment. Rahner's position on this matter is critically important:

> Even with this second mode of making the Election and within
> the stirrings of the spirits, rational reflection can and must de-
> velop as an indispensable element in the motion of the spirits.
> After all, these stirrings do not consist of merely indifferent, blind
> drives like hunger, thirst and so on. They consist of thoughts, acts
> of knowing, perception of values, etc. They themselves contain
> an objective conceptual element, they can be expressed and
> verified. The experience of consolations and desolations is not
> the experience of merely physiological states but of impulsions
> having a rational structure. They are always also the product
> of one's own activity of an intellectual kind. They cannot not
> be so. But that immediately implies that what has to be done in
> the third mode of making the Election must also take place in
> the second. The second mode of Election differs from the third
> not by total disparity but as the larger whole differs from a part
> which is necessarily contained in the whole even though by itself
> it does not constitute the whole. And the third mode in its turn is
> rather to be conceived as the deficient form of the second, a way
> of making the Election which, as we have already said, aspires
> to be integrated into the greater, more comprehensive whole.[122]

For Rahner, therefore, the positive value of the third mode is seen
in its intrinsic relationship with the second mode. Apart from this
relationship, discerners are left only with the modest help of rational
reflection and must fend for themselves. Rahner holds that the consolation without previous cause is the *sine qua non* of all discernment.
During such consolation, however, there can be no thought about a
finite object of choice, no counsel regarding any act to be done, because one's soul is on fire with the love of God, and no created reality

[120] Ibid., 127–28n25.
[121] Ibid., 103–6.
[122] Ibid., 102–3.

could stand in the way of such love. The time for discernment happens during the "time immediately following," with the consolation still lingering, still actual but no longer pure. It is now a consolation of the second degree with the admixture of thoughts and impulses with finite objects. Only in this time is it possible to carry on discernment of God's will.[123]

What is the discernment process that is carried out during this time? Rahner states that one discerns whether there is a congruence between the will to the object of choice or election with the pure receptivity to the love of God, the transcendent orientation of the consolation without previous cause, which while it is no longer in its pure form, is still actual. When there is a congruence between the object of choice or election and this fundamental transcendence, there is peace, quiet and tranquility, true gladness and joy. The heart of full discernment then, in Rahner's view, is not so much the experience of consolation without previous cause, or the consolation of second degree or the action or choice that proceeds from consolation, but rather the coherence and congruence of the proposed choice with the fundamental orientation of consolation. This coherence must be tested, and whenever there is dissonance, there is no true peace or joy.[124]

Egan tends toward Rahner's position but differs from him on some points. He holds that the three modes are not three distinct ways of finding God's will but actually aspects of one core experience and one election in which all three are present in varying degrees of intensity. There are three aspects of the experience of the divine-human encounter at different levels. Where the experience is at the very core of one's being, where one is most deeply taken over by the God who is love, this is the first mode. If the purity of this experience dissipates into consolation and desolation with finite objects, then this is the second mode. And finally when this core experience is manifested in tranquility, leaving the exercitant to his or her own abilities, this is the third mode.

Egan points out, in agreement with other commentators, that without the direct immediacy of the experience of God in some way, election is not possible. This means that what is constituted in the first mode is also found in the second and in the third. And the consolation without previous cause present in the first mode, accompanying a God-guaranteed communication, is also present as the touchstone experience in the second mode, on whose basis motions are judged. It

---

[123] Ibid., 160–62.
[124] Ibid., 158.

is also present in the third mode as the tranquility in God for whose glory and praise alone one is moved to make a choice. The second and third modes contain the God-initiated experience of the first mode.[125]

Egan basically follows the interpretation of Rahner in his consideration of the three modes as constituting aspects of one core experience, present in varying degrees, but he differs from Rahner's interpretation in the sense that, for him, the three are interpenetrating, with elements of each way in the other two.[126] If all three interpenetrate or fuse, then no one mode is deficient in relation to the others in terms of content. This view is in contrast to Rahner's interpretation, which considers the third mode as substantially different in content from the other two modes. In both Rahner's and Egan's interpretations there is no claim of autonomy for any one of the modes.[127]

Toner takes a position that sharply contrasts with that of Rahner and Egan, bringing a parallel richness to the discourse. He holds that any position that claims that consolation without previous cause is the first principle of all discernment of the spirits and of the divine will of God conflicts with the teaching of Ignatius. In contrast to Rahner's position that all Ignatian discernment is ultimately that of the second mode, and that each mode of discernment interpenetrates each other as Egan holds, Toner asserts that Ignatius presented each mode as fully distinct from the others and that each is able to function autonomously, itself, although when reason may warrant and as the situation demands, he seems to call upon both the second and third modes of discernment together.

Toner refers to Ignatius's use of the third mode as an autonomous way of discernment for major decisions of his own life and for decisions of others, even for vocation decisions. He questions the grounding of Rahner's interpretation of the consolation of the second degree or the afterglow of consolation without previous cause as a time of discernment in the second mode. It does not fit into what Ignatius taught about the nature of the second mode. That there is no communication from God regarding the object for choice during consolation without previous cause, as Rahner holds, is opposite to the Ignatian teaching that one may have a joyful certitude of the divine impulses and intentionalities precisely during this time. Ignatius teaches that one must be sensitive to the divine impulses toward an object of choice during times of consolation. For Rahner, the locus of the discernment

---

[125] Egan, *The Spiritual Exercises and the Ignatian Mystical Horizon*, 152–54.
[126] Ibid.
[127] Toner, *Discerning God's Will*, 237.

is not in the choice itself but in the harmony of the choice with the fundamental orientation of consolation.[128]

Limitations in Discernment

It is important to talk about the limitations of discernment, lest people become cynical about its truth and integrity. When we discern a decision we have to make regarding a particular issue or problem, we are discerning within the limits of our freedom. We can only discern God's desire for us in conjunction with our own desire for our life. We cannot discern what other people would desire for themselves in relation to what we desire. It could be that what they discern would conflict with our choice.[129] This does not mean that our discernment is wrong. It only means that our discernment, though true and authentic, is limited. Relational as freedom is, the fruit of our discernment is limited.

For example, future events can be beyond the limits of discernment. Discernment is not prophetic knowledge. The actual consequences of the choice one makes in discernment are not completely within one's horizon at the time of choosing. One can only weigh in the choice what *could* be possible consequences, and discernment is limited to what the person contemplates as the desire of God resonating with his or her own desires, with projected consequences only insofar as the mind and heart can envisage, within the vision of what is truly for the glory of God.[130]

Another limit of discernment is the nature of its certitude. We cannot speak of a scientific certitude, given the phenomenon of chance on both the micro and macro levels. Those things in life of which we are certain, on which we base the meaning of our lives, are not things about which we can be absolutely sure, in the sense that we can prove them.[131] Discernment brings us to a different realm, that of intersubjectivity, where there is a connaturality of hearts in a relationship characterized by knowledge, commitment, and self-surrender.

---

[128] Ibid., 152–55.

[129] Ibid., 320–22.

[130] Ibid., 52–53. Michael Kyne points out the need for constant purification of our choices and that we should not invest them with pseudo-infallibility. See "Difficulties in Discernment," *The Way* 14 (1974): 109. See also Lawrence J. Murphy, "Psychological Problems of Christian Choice," *The Way Supplement* 24 (Spring 1975): 26-35.

[131] Richard M. Gula discusses the difference between scientific reasoning and practical moral reasoning of discernment in his *Moral Discernment* (New York: Paulist Press, 1997), 50–52.

And the certitude that is proper to such a relationship is "subjective certitude."[132]

> God can be known only from within a subjective relationship, and this necessarily involves commitment. There is no aspect or element of God which could be known as "object." Any true awareness of God can be disclosed only through an authentic relationship, in which the human self stands before the Infinite who is Love: Love who calls for a totality of commitment and self-surrender. For this reason, the only certitude proper to man's knowledge of God can be a "subjective certitude" which comes through the act of commitment and self-surrender.[133]

The term used in Ignatian discernment is *sentir*, a Spanish term that connotes the same meaning of "subjective certitude." *Sentir* is a felt knowledge that comes from one's emotional resonance or connaturality with the desire of God, born of a personal knowledge and loving commitment. It is an affective and intuitive knowledge in contrast to an intellectual grasping of abstract propositions. It is likened to the knowledge of a mother of her child, or of the lover of the beloved. This is a kind of knowledge that involves one's "bent of being," engaging persons at their depth, where they are authentically self-disposed to God and others. It is through attentiveness to *sentir* that one senses the congruence of one's choice with God's desire for one's authentic living of personal identity in community. *Sentir*, however, does not negate the importance of adequacy of evidence for judgment. Thus, every effort must be made to gather complete data for prayerful reflection and "felt knowledge."

Philip Keane warns against the misunderstanding of discernment as merely deciding on gut level reactions. He says that Ignatius's reference to *sentir* does not mean merely making a decision on the basis of emotion or feeling. While the word includes feeling, it refers to more than that, in the sense that it includes a broad intuitive process in the context of prayer. He also stresses that discernment does not occur in a state of complete obliviousness of objective norms, of the sound traditions and experiences of the Christian community. It is false to dichotomize the objective and subjective, as they are inextricably

---

[132] Ibid., 62–64.

[133] Michael Simpson, "Philosophical Certitude and the Ignatian Election," *The Way Supplement* 24 (Spring 1975): 61.

intertwined in the concrete human person in a concrete context.[134] Discernment engages the whole person, summoning all his or her human capacities:

> Christian discernment is an art form that engages the whole network of human capacities in helping us decide what our relationship with God demands in present circumstances. It is a process that works back and forth to intertwine faith, reason, emotion, intuition, and imagination. . . . The overall process of Christian discernment consists of three structural components: personal reflection, contextual analysis, and critical evaluation.[135]

Affirming the full use of the natural human faculties in discernment, Ladislas Orsy warns against any anti-intellectual trend in spirituality. He says: "Christian wholeness does not consist in by-passing the intelligence in pursuit of holiness, but rather in a healthy integration of our humanity with God's grace. . . . In all cases, critically trained intelligence is a good instrument to buttress spiritual discernment."[136]

Reappropriating Ignatian Discernment

With the voluminous matter that we have gathered from the erudite discourses on Ignatian discernment and on the theological questions that presuppose it, we sift what can flow back to life, into the day-to-day decisions and choices we make for ourselves, for our family, our inner circle of significant others; in our larger interpersonal relationships; and in our public commitments in the world of politics, economics, and ideologies. Theology flows back to life.

I seek to reappropriate the whole theological discourse on the matter of discernment, sifting through the ideas, arguments, and debates in order to clarify for those of us trying to make a sense of our relationships, of our endeavors for others, and of our hopes for a new world, even as we struggle against a lingering sense of futility in what all this is about in the end.

---

[134] Philip S. Keane, "Discernment of Spirits: A Theological Reflection," *American Ecclesiastical Review* 168 (1974): 50–51.

[135] Panicola, "Discernment in the Neonatal Context," 734–35. Panicola bases his description on Gula's *Moral Discernment*, 41–53. Gula builds on the work of Sidney Callahan, *In Good Conscience* (New York: Harper Collins, 1991).

[136] Ladislas Orsy, "Toward a Theological Evaluation of Communal Discernment," *Studies in the Spirituality of Jesuits* 5 (October 1973): 171–72.

At the heart of discernment is God and the human person in an encounter. We relate with God who is love, who has great desires for our human flourishing and that of others, and who lures us into the direction of these desires; finding that our own desires resonate with the divine desires, we make choices that are truly and deeply ours, and yet are enabled and empowered by the very love of God in which we live and have our being. But even to begin to engage in Ignatian discernment, we are confronted with basic questions: How can God, the ineffable and incomprehensible God, be experienced? Does God, in whose hands the world is held up by awesome power, address us and love us as if we were the only ones who exist in this vast universe? And if God speaks and addresses us, how is it so? Rahner's theological anthropology speaks of this divine-human dialogue at the very heart of life itself, of depth experiences that bring us to the edge of our humanity, at boundary situations where our human questions become God questions. It is at the arena of our lives, where we celebrate our joys and bear our sorrows, where we live our longings and hopes for a better world, that we meet God. Nowhere else.

Concomitant to knowing God and the ways of divine love is knowing the ways of the Evil One in the context of Ignatian discernment. The question regarding the reality of Satan, angels, and demons, which draws us into a polemic of various positions, does not involve the Christian faith at its core. With reference to preternatural creatures in the Ignatian discernment process, prudence must be exercised for people who may not have the psychological maturity to deal with this possibility, and to whom more harm than good might be done. The same adjustment must be made for those who simply cannot be comfortable with this belief in their own spirituality, and yet still hold the existence of evil in the human realm. What is stressed is that evil ultimately assumes a human face in the exercise of freedom and is manifested in structures and systems that consolidate and propagate it. The ultimate calling is for one's openness to the leadings of the Holy Spirit for the good and against evil, wherever it may come from.

The encounter between God and the human person brings into question the meaning of divine providence and human freedom. Theology proposes ways of knowing, imaging, and speaking about God; similarly, the academic scholars of the discourse on divine providence and human freedom impinge on our spontaneous and natural ways of speaking to and about God. How can human freedom be upheld without canceling the truth of divine providence? Or how can freedom remain within the orbit of divine providence without losing its autonomy and integrity? Contemporary theology rejects the idea of God having a blueprint of the divine will, which the person merely seeks to find and obey. New paradigms of the divine and human encounter show God in collaboration with persons in the shaping of their free choices. The Thomistic dual agency of the divine and human provides some way of understanding the divine risk that allows the spontaneity and creativity of human freedom. But this risk is more comprehensible, beyond the Thomistic relation of cause and effect, in the paradigm of intersubjectivity, where God and the human person relate to each other as I and Thou. Thus, God truly takes risks in the exercise of human freedom, but if any reference to change is made relative to God, it is not change in the Godself, but change in the relationality of God with the free agency of persons.

God's desires are much bigger than ours, and they pull us out of ourselves, posing exhilarating challenges to our freedom, so that we have fuller lives in the enlarged contexts of community and society, inspired by the demands of Christian discipleship and solidarity. The creative tension of divine providence and our freedom is not in the abstract; it is in the very existentials of our own living, giving, and loving. It is a freedom that can say no, and it is the radical self-limitation of the divine love that allows freedom to be. We must keep the tension of the two truths—God as the ultimate source of our freedom, and human freedom as given a relative autonomy by God. We are not dealing with an either/or truth, but rather, with truths in tension. We are not independent of God insofar as God is our ultimate source but are relatively independent of God because of our freedom. If we do not assert the relative autonomy of human freedom, we cannot explain the reality of sin as a result of a free human act.

Our exercise of freedom in a sense can limit God's freedom, especially when such freedom is exercised in sin, because sin is precisely the arrogant self-assertion of human freedom in the face of God. God does not supplant the human act. Even to stop evil, God does not deny us of our freedom. By creating a being other than Godself who is free, God in a way has limited divine freedom. This way of speaking about God limiting God's freedom certainly suffers from a poverty of language. But poor as it is, it is a way of understanding the divine risk that allows the spontaneity, autonomy, and integrity of human freedom. In the case of authentic freedom, grace makes human freedom more free as freedom finds its ontological possibility in grace and its fulfillment. But the tension remains—the act in authentic freedom, while made possible in grace, remains integrally the act of the person as an agent.

To know God's desires for us, and even to understand our own desires for ourselves as we are in relation with others in community, is an arduous task. And this is where Ignatian discernment proposes a way of knowing what truly matters, not what only seems to matter. In the divine and human encounter God comes as God in "mediated immediacy," sometimes through the "inner word" of our hearts, without any "outer word" or external mediation, a non-conceptual presence, theologians would say, but a presence that can simply take over our hearts, and we know far beyond knowing that it is the Lord God who has come. One example of this is consolation without previous cause, because God has come prior to our desiring God in our thought and affectivity—God loving us before we love, and even before we can desire to love. The absolute gratuitousness of divine love has visited our lives, and no created love could ever fill our hearts in the same way.

Ignatius came to know God and the ways of divine love. Concomitant to this knowing is a knowing of the ways of the Evil One. Contemporary minds resist this belief, which in their worldview should be demythologized. Essential, however, to any process of demythologization is to locate the sources of evil in society and its structures and systems that promote and propagate evil, even without negating the rootedness of social evil in personal sins. The point is to draw individualist interpretations of evil and sin into the social arena, where evil is seen in its interrelatedness and its propagation through complicity and connivance.

The spirituality of Ignatius shows us that our decisions, our most particular and personal decisions, are within the orbit of God's personal love and providence. God is the God of our micro (personal) universe, as God is the God of the macro universe. There is nothing so little and so puny that is beyond the divine providential care. Through the faith language of his worldview, Ignatius gives witness through his writings of how God addresses us and manifests God's divine desires for us, as we make our choices and decisions, in the supreme exercise of our freedom. Through different modes or times of election, God mediates God's divine presence. In the first mode God comes as pure presence and gives us a certitude of the direction that our choice must take, a certitude that may or may not come with the sweet joy of consolation without previous cause, but it is as deep as it is unshakable. In the second mode God lures and directs us to the ways of the divine desires through consolation and desolation. God speaks to our hearts in a true sense. The choice that we make, when our heart resonates with God's desires, is accompanied with great consolation experienced with tears of joy; increase of faith, hope, and charity; and with deep quiet and peace. Desolation accompanies choices we make that are contrary to God's desires for our own human flourishing and in relation to others in community. Any choice rooted in empathy, as we dethrone ourselves from the center of our universe for us to live for others, can be filled with consolation, for this is consonant with God's own desires. But a choice with others as the reference point, which requires self-abandonment, is often accompanied by pain and suffering. There is no equivalence, thus, between consolation and pleasure, or desolation and pain. It could be that consolation comes with deep pain, but the peace is much deeper than the pain, as one is willing to pay the cost of loving. The peace comes with the certitude that God is present even in the depths of pain, in the very choice for love.

Likewise, sometimes a choice may be accompanied with some pleasure, perhaps the pleasure that comes from doing what one wants, freed from the burdens of the cares and concerns of others, and yet one is filled with desolation, a state of confusion, disturbance, restlessness—a deep sense of being separated from God. Desolation does not have God as its origin and source, but God sometimes allows desolation for our own purification and also for our humility. The true challenge, however, for those who have their lives so taken over by God, is no longer in desolation but in a false consolation that accompanies what is deceitfully good. Temptation does not always appear in what is obviously evil; sometimes it is in what is apparently good. Thus, consolation must be discerned with astuteness, from its time of onset, through its duration, and to its end, for what was initially good may slowly disintegrate into its very opposite. The insidiousness of evil lurking in what is apparently good is what confronts a person of faith. In Ignatian discernment, under the disguises of good, evil is recognized ultimately through what comes to one's affectivity, because if one were to depend only on the apparent worth of what is proposed to one's choosing, one can be deceived. This means that one must discern the feelings of peace and joy that accompanies one's choices, feelings that are not produced by some psychological conditionings, for such feelings of peace and joy are given by God. As such, they are gifts of grace.

If affectivity is the criterion, then it must be so ordered by the intimacy and depth of one's love for God in Christ Jesus. Ultimately, only one who has come to know the intimacy and depth of this love and has become familiar with its ways would know this love and recognize its voice and calling. In the end, Ignatian discernment is a discernment of God's love in Christ, in one's connaturality with it, born of the constant and faithful gift of self to this love, in one's tireless labor for the kingdom, in a life so arduously spent for others—such a life and love sustained by prayer, meditation, and the Eucharist, until one can say with Paul, "It is no longer I that live, but this Christ who lives in me" (Gal 2:20). Ignatian discernment cannot be separated from a gospel-inspired and directed life, which is at the heart of the entire *Spiritual Exercises*.

The third mode for discernment is characterized by tranquility; one is not moved by the diverse influences of the spirits or by the crests and troughs of emotions engendered by thoughts. Some commentators say that in the third mode we are left to our natural powers to fend for ourselves. I tend more to think that the time of tranquility is a time of quiet grace, when God is not present in the same ways as in the first and second mode. At this time reason is fully engaged, as we evaluate and weigh our options and their short-term and long-term consequences, all within the vision of what is truly for God's glory in ourselves, in others, and in the world.

The discourse on how the three modes or times of discernment relate illumines the nature of all three. I take the position that no distinctions should be made on the basis of the presence or absence of reason being engaged. Reason is engaged in all three, in various ways. In the first mode contemplative reasoning enables one to see and recognize the presence of God and the certitude of one's choice in the face of the divine presence. There is a different kind of reasoning operative in the second mode, an affective reasoning, or what is called the judgment of the heart. It is reason engaged through feelings of consolation and desolation, joy, peace, pain, and sorrow, judging one's intuitions. The third mode is characterized by a greater degree of discursive reasoning, as one brings the operations of the mind to bear on the options, comparing and evaluating the facts and data, weighing the advantages and disadvantages, and looking into the most likely short-term and long-term consequences. This third mode is guided more by objective norms, norms that go beyond us and exist outside of us, while the second mode is guided by interior subjective norms, our own interior feelings, thoughts, and impulses. The interior or subjective norms are not subjective in the sense of being arbitrary; rather, they are rooted in the action of the Spirit in the interior of the "subject" of the person praying over his or her decisions. Both norms are important.

The second and third modes are made available for human effort and striving in decision making; the first mode is a pure gift from the freedom of God's love. But for as long as people are creatures of thought, feelings, intuitions, and senses, any process of decision making must involve both the judgment of the mind and the judgment of the heart, both discursive and affective reasoning, both objective and subjective norms. There is no point, I believe, in driving a wedge between the different modes, claiming autonomy for one or the other. There can be no autonomy of one mode if persons are addressed by God as persons, embodied beings, immersed in time and history, moved and directed by all that is human, as rational and affective beings. There is a need, thus, for an integral approach to Christian decision making that brings all that is human in us to bear on the choices we make.

I propose that when one makes a choice or decision, one is open to all three modes. I do not think that Ignatius classified the three modes as first, second, and third in terms of their chronological order in making decisions, but in terms of the nature of the mode with reference to the certitude and intensity of the divine presence. What I propose is a chronological order of making decisions. The preliminary stage is what Ignatius calls the third mode, where directed by the *magis* principle for the glory of God, one gathers all the facts and pieces of evidence, thinks through the pros and cons, mulls over the alternative decisions, ponders the various options and their possible consequences in the intra-, inter-, and social dimensions of human existence. In the stage that Ignatius calls the second mode, one brings one's options to prayer, bringing each of them before God and then discerning the feelings of peace and joy, the movements of consolation or desolation, as one prays over the options, ever mindful of the deceptions that one can fall into, especially false consolations and the disguises of evil in what is apparently good. One must be attentive to impulses that come from one's own disordered inclinations, timidity, pride, fear, anxiety, anger, ambition, or resentment—impulses that do not come from the directions and inspirations of the Holy Spirit. The last stage, which Ignatius calls the first mode, is a gift God gives of a certitude that surpasses all human knowledge, beyond one's calculation and expectations, a certitude that comes like a light piercing the darkness of fear, anxiety, and confusion. Since the first mode is a gift, it is not something that one arrives at through one's efforts, but that toward which one makes oneself completely open and disposed.

In the end, the touchstone of Ignatian discernment is what is truly and genuinely human, within the orbit of divine providence enabling and empowering freedom to reach the heights of its potential, there where the human and the divine meet in an intersubjective encounter, in which love is the final criterion, in line with the demands of discipleship and of the kingdom.

PART IV

INTEGRATION

10

Integration of
Vision, Norm, and Choice

Summary and Conclusion

After the preceding presentations of vision, norm, and choice, the goal of this concluding section (indeed, the goal of the entire book) is to show how they are integrated. Vision and norm are integrated into the very act of choice. Also serving as the summary and conclusion of the book, this section makes references to its key points and how they are related to social issues.

Without choice, vision and norm do not have an existential realization. Moral choosing, however, is not just a question of skill or technique; it is not a process in which reason and concepts alone are involved. At the heart of moral choosing are moral agents who are engaged in the social issue they are confronted with in a conflict situation. The premise of the entire book is that moral agents must first be formed in the Christian moral vision and moral norm, for only those whose awareness and consciousness are nourished by the rich sources of the Christian faith can decide from within its horizons and perspectives. Integrating both the ethics of holistic reasoning and virtue ethics, the ethical methodology proposed provides the guiding process in making decisions in moral dilemmas. It is within this process that vision and norm are integrated. To deepen the moral deliberation one has made, one brings it through the process of Ignatian discernment, whereby one confirms one's choice in affective integrity and interior spiritual peace.

The integration of vision, norm, and choice is at the base of this proposed holistic theo-ethical method for social ethics, particularly in dealing with moral dilemmas in conflict situations. In presenting the integration of vision, norm, and choice, I discuss the elements that must be present in a holistic consideration of a proposed method for social ethics as a discipline. As I venture into a whole new way of teaching social ethics, I am reminded of how John Mahoney describes the challenge and demand of developing a moral theology according to the ideal that Vatican II envisioned: "It was not simply a matter of tuning the engine and tightening the steering of moral theology, but of a thorough systematic overhaul of the whole vehicle and sending it off into quite new and uncharted areas of modern living."[1]

The formation of moral agents in vision and norm is central to the method. It is the basis of Christian moral decision making. This metaphysics influenced and inspired by faith grounds the process of formation. It provides a prism through which the moral agent looks at reality. Those who are nourished by moral vision and are rooted in moral norms are those who decide with a specific stance and perspective. They do not decide in a rational vacuum, but with a fullness of a vision of life which inspires commitment and action.

Vision

All ethics is social ethics. All ethical issues have a social dimension, whether in the areas of sex and gender, economics and politics, race and culture, environment, just war, bioethics, or other areas. There are social roots to ethical problems just as there are social consequences. What is recommended is a broad approach to these problems drawing from the rich sources of culture and religion and from the primary sources of the Christian faith.

Culture, Religion, and Moral Vision

Using the perspective of Paul Tillich, culture is a form of expression of religion, and religion is the substance of culture. Culture as a form of expression of religion is a broad understanding of religion, grounded in the principle that reality is not sharply divided into the sacred and profane, but rather that all reality is potentially sacred. If religion provides depth to all things, then culture, which is all pervasive and not only limited to some areas of life, is the realm of religion. In and through the world of the finite, persons encounter the holy in whatever is true, whatever is honorable, whatever is just, whatever is pure, whatever is gracious in their cultures. What must be engaged

---

[1] John Mahoney, *The Making of Moral Theology: A Study of the Roman Catholic Tradition* (Oxford: Clarendon Press, 1987), 307.

here is what is called cultural exegesis, which is an interpretative activity that makes explicit what is implicit in culture, unfolding the transcendent meaning it holds. Cultural exegesis has been neglected because of the focus on the structures of economics and politics seen at the base of social problems. But a social analysis that does not include the cultural dimensions cannot get at the depths of the dynamics shaping social movements. The most important changes are symbolic and cultural. We quote once again Robert Bellah, who writes, "We are used to thinking of change in economic and political terms, but it is the symbolic that goes the deepest and lasts the longest."[2]

Religion as the substance of culture refers to the "spiritual substantiality, which alone gives form its significance."[3] Religion, however, is a complex reality and phenomenon, as it is both incarnated in a culture and also points to some trans-social and transcendent reality. A study of religion as a phenomenon, both from the perspective of theology and cultural anthropology, as well as its relation with morality, is necessary in understanding the force of religion in social transformation. As a whole, what I propose as essential in the formation in moral vision is cultural and religious exegesis, using the methodology of the hermeneutics of appreciation that highlights the positive in the phenomena of culture and religion as forces of social transformation. The dynamics of culture and religion have a bearing on moral vision. The way people image themselves, what they do with their lives, and how they choose and act are influenced by their culture (a particular way of being human) within the horizons of their experience of the divine, in their quest for transcendent and ultimate meaning (religion).

On the second level, culture and religion are treated in a specific way in relation to social issues. The positive forces in culture and religion and their impact on the moral vision of truths and values relative to concrete social issues need emphasis. For instance, in dealing with the problem of immigration, one must look at the elements in the culture and religion of a people that are positive social forces in forming their communal moral vision. In my specific work on the nonviolent Filipino revolution, I probed into our Filipino core-culture values that were at the base of a gracious and graceful nonviolent revolution: *lakas ganda* (gracious power); *lakas awa* (compassionate force); and *lakas-saya* (indomitable joy). In my reflection on the Filipino revolution I saw with immense clarity that there can be no

---

[2] Quoted in John Coleman, "The Renewed Covenant: Robert N. Bellah's Vision of Religion and Society," in *Sociology and Human Destiny: Essays on Sociology, Religion, and Society,* ed. Gregory Baum (New York: Seabury Press, 1980), 89.

[3] Paul Tillich, *What Is Religion* (New York: Harper and Row, 1969), 73.

liberation apart from the beliefs and values of a people, the deepest source of which is their religion. The popular religion of a people in love with Mary *(pueblo amante de Maria)*, regarded as a deadening opiate by a contrary worldview, was precisely that which empowered people to put their lives on the line in their nonviolent struggle for freedom and liberation. The use of cultural and religious exegesis, through what is called the hermeneutics of appreciation, would prove to be a fruitful endeavor in appreciating the breadth and richness of cultures and religions and the moral visions they shape.

Scripture and Moral Vision

Vatican II speaks of scriptures as the soul of moral theology. If moral theology is to be a genuine theological discipline, it must be rooted in scripture as a source. The place of scripture in moral theology is indisputable, but the question of how it is to be used generates no consensus. Both Catholic and Protestant moral theologians continue to grapple with this question. My proposal of how to use scripture in moral theology focuses on its use as illuminative rather than prescriptive. While using scripture as prescriptive provides moral precepts and rules for action, using it as illuminative awakens moral awareness and sensitivity as engendered by a vision of life. This illuminative approach uses scripture as story, bringing the reader into an encounter with the scriptural text and its world of characters, events, and meaning, into the inner reality of scripture that is missed when it is studied only from a historical-scientific perspective. It is reading scripture, not only reading *about* scripture. The method used to study scripture as story is narrative criticism, which approaches scripture as a literary text, with a point of view, characterization, and plot.

While narrative criticism offers the best method for drawing out the power of story in scripture in shaping moral vision and character, like any other method, it is limited, and it leaves lacunae that need to be filled by other methods—like historical criticism and cultural criticism—for a fuller interpretation of scripture. It is apt to refer again to Francis Moloney, who writes that given the fact that scripture is historically and culturally conditioned, there is inevitably something "strange" and "foreign" about the text that demands that we wrestle with it. The world behind the text must be respected and studied in order to understand the strange distance of this world and the world in front of the text. And although from the view of narrative criticism, the real historical author and the reader(s) do not play an active role in the events in the narrative, they leave their traces.[4] Wolfgang Iser refers to the "reader's repertoire" as that which comprises all the data and information necessary for a full interpretation of the scriptural work.[5]

One major lacuna of narrative criticism, which is also true of both historical criticism and cultural criticism, is the lack of engagement with flesh-and-blood readers who significantly contribute to the meaning of the text. This lacuna is filled by contextual biblical pedagogy, which is exemplified by a reading of scripture from the eyes of the disenfranchised, a feminist reading of the scripture, and a reading with a global optic. What I finally propose is an integral biblical pedagogy that makes use of various pedagogies across the entire spectrum of biblical criticism for a full and rich reading and interpretation of scripture with reference to the use of narrative criticism. In a comprehensive theory the sheer volume of content and subject matter, not only at the level of texts but also at the level of readings, and readers of texts, however, could pose a problem and challenge.

Engaging with texts as historical, literary, rhetorical, and ideological, and readers as constructed and as flesh and blood, who are contextualized and perspectival, could result in an explosion of meanings of a text, with each claiming to be as good as the others, ending in what might become a "free for all" approach. I propose three principles to provide a critical framework within which meanings can be negotiated in terms of some hierarchy of preference and priority. First, priority must be given to the voice of contemporary readers over the voice of historical and rhetorical readers of the text. The text is being read now by contemporary readers. The historical and rhetorical readers are employed only insofar as the profound meaning of scripture could come alive to contemporary readers, evoking them to reconfigure their own lives according to this meaning that touches them in their unique circumstances. Second, among the competing perspectives of readers, an interpretational privilege exists with reference to the disenfranchised, which is called the hermeneutical privilege of the oppressed. This principle, founded on the broader theme of the preferential option for the poor, is, however, not accepted without contention; it is a subject of critical discourse. Third, we must remember that scripture is the written testimony of the fullest revelation of

---

[4] Francis J. Moloney, *The Gospel of John*, Sacra Regina Series, no. 4, ed. Daniel J. Harrington (Collegeville, MN: Liturgical Press, 1998), 18, 14.

[5] See Wolfgang Iser, *The Implied Reader: Patterns of Communication in Prose Fiction from Bunyan to Beckett* (Baltimore: Johns Hopkins University Press, 1974).

God in Christ. The entire Bible should be read through the primordial interpretative lens of the call to abundant life in Christ (Jn 10:10). As such, any interpretation that advocates the subjugation of one person to another, or that promotes discrimination against a certain kind of people, or that protects the interest of the dominant culture to the detriment of others, or that renders women and children as victims should be repudiated as anti-gospel or anti-scripture. All deny the full life that Jesus has promised for all.

On the general level one can use narrative criticism for moral vision by mining the wealth of an integral biblical pedagogy, with a focus on contextual biblical pedagogy. On the specific level scriptural stories can be chosen and studied relative to social issues. For instance, the story from the Gospel of Luke—"And at his gate lay a poor man named Lazarus, covered with sores, who longed to satisfy his hunger with what fell from the rich man's table" (Lk 16:20–21)—is an excellent scriptural story to use in the face of our current reality, of poor nations lying at the door of rich nations, unheeded and neglected. Gustavo Gutiérrez, however, observes that the poor today are not only lying at the door; they leave homes and families, sometimes at the risk of their own lives, and put themselves under the constant threat of deportation. Global poverty and unemployment are driving millions of people from their countries to chart their destinies in foreign lands.[6] The parable provides rich material as a story for moral vision, applying the use of an integral biblical pedagogy. It would be a fertile area of study and research to engage in narrative criticism in reading scriptural stories within the breadth of an integral biblical pedagogy and from the various perspectives of contextual interpretation relative to social issues.

Systematic Theology and Moral Vision

The reconnection of systematic theology and moral theology, particularly in terms of Christian moral vision, is at the heart of the renewal of moral theology as a genuinely theological science. Systematic theology helps to develop a coherent theological anthropology and its implications for Christian moral vision. The doctrines of the faith give a particular view of what it means to be human and the basic attitudes and dispositions a Christian ought to have toward the world. What underlies the understanding of the human person from

---

[6] Gustavo Gutiérrez, "Poverty, Migration, and the Option for the Poor," in *A Promised Land, A Perilous Journey: Theological Perspectives on Migration,* ed. Daniel G. Groody and Gioacchino Campese, 76–86 (Notre Dame, IN: University of Notre Dame Press, 2008), 76.

the light of faith is the conviction that who the human person is cannot be separated from the question of who God is. From the breadth and richness of the doctrines of the faith, what must be unraveled are three fundamental realities that enter into the faith narrative of who God is and who the human person is—the primacy of love, the primacy of grace, and the primacy of community. These three primacies constitute the hermeneutical framework within which I bring the doctrines of faith into a coherent and holistic synthesis, taking a feminist, liberationist, and global stance.

Under the primacy of love, the doctrines of creation, Trinity, and Jesus Christ show that the one singular thread that runs through the God-narrative of the Christian faith is that God is love, outgoing and outpouring love, and that this love draws all to a communion of love. Under the primacy of grace we can see the tension of grace and sin, supernatural existential and original sin—the ambiguity that cuts into the very depths of the person, in the face of the eschatological hope that is the ultimate word of soteriology. Under the primacy of community are the doctrines of the church and of the final communal destiny. To be essentially human is to be in community. For the Christian, the locus of this community is the church. The discourse on the final things presents a grand narrative of the whole of humankind, the earth, and the entire cosmos, all sharing a common destiny.

How is Christian moral vision shaped by the primacy of love, the primacy of grace, and the primacy of community? The revelation of Godself in creation, in Trinity, and in Jesus Christ brings to light the mystery of the human person created by God, who is love, through love, and for love. Moral life is founded on love, and Christian moral life is patterned after Jesus' love, his radical hospitality to all, and his solidarity with the poor. What is our moral vision of who we are and what we ought to do if we live based on the primacy of grace? We must envision ourselves as being called to a prophetic mission in a world plagued by evil and sin. Subversion is a prophetic mission; it is a call to break down all systems of oppression, inequality, and violence. Subversion is breaking down, but it is also building up, that the old may be renewed and transformed. What is the Christian moral vision that must govern our lives if we believe in the primacy of community? We live our lives deeply intertwined with other people's lives, with our choices having far-reaching consequences. The moral call is to go beyond ourselves, to reach out to others, to embrace the world, to have a kinship with the earth and with the cosmos, and to live with a deep sense of the future and of eternity already present in the now, being shaped in the arena of life, until all will become all in Christ.

The use of this hermeneutical framework presents a broad synthesis of the doctrines of the faith and the moral vision they shape. But another approach may be taken by choosing a particular doctrine of the faith and drawing out the moral vision of truths and values that relates to social issues. For instance, the moral vision of the doctrine of creation relates to the issue of environmental integrity; the doctrine of the Trinity grounds the call to solidarity and the common good; the doctrine of Jesus and his radical hospitality and preferential option for the poor inspires the moral vision for addressing the issue of immigration; the doctrine of eschatology grounds the moral vision of global peace in the face of war and terror. Whatever approach is taken, the theological anthropology developed based on the truths of faith as interpreted in systematic theology grounds the Christian moral vision of who we are and how we ought to live.

Norm

Moral norms are the criteria used for judging the sort of person we ought to be and the sort of actions we ought to take. They preserve the collective wisdom of the human community regarding the truths and values that must govern its communal life. They mediate in propositional forms the moral vision of truths and values, drawing from this vision their binding force. The value of moral norms is that they bring to our moral judgments a breadth and depth based on their communal grounding that we could not attain if we were to depend only on our limited personal/individual experience. They prevent moral paralysis by providing patterns of behavior and common denominators of value that inform our conscience when confronted with moral dilemmas. Since none of us has a total grasp of the conflicts of values in situations we find ourselves, precedents of right behavior as governed by good norms can help illumine our moral judgments. Moral norms also provide consistency and stability as reliable points of reference and direction for moral living, and at the same time they challenge our moral living by pointing out to us the goal toward which we ought to live, which stretches us beyond our individual experiences to the broader vision that binds us to the community, as well as makes us attentive to the far-reaching consequences of our actions, as beings in relation to others.[7]

---

[7] Richard M. Gula, *Reason Informed by Faith: Foundations of Catholic Morality* (New York: Paulist Press, 1989), 284–85.

Catholic social teaching constitutes a substantial body of norms on social questions and issues. Brian Hehir writes that in the twentieth century the church's social teaching provided a system of norms relating the social vision of the faith to the concrete conditions of the century.[8] Judith Merkle says that "social teaching is a hybrid of moral doctrine, societal criticism, and social vision. It is a complex act of the church in context."[9] Thomas Massaro notes that

> Catholic social teaching has often been called "our best kept secret." In fact, some people are astonished when they first hear of the Church's commitment to justice throughout the world. How did it come to pass that an institution like the Catholic Church, long associated with a conservative approach that resists change and looks to the past, has for so long been delivering a progressive message that challenges the global economic and political order to achieve greater justice?[10]

But Catholic social teaching is not only a "secret" seemingly kept from the world, it is also "kept" from the Catholic faithful in the sense that it has not been accessible to their knowledge, understanding, and much less to their appreciation. I grant that accessibility takes on different levels depending on the audience one addresses. The medium of this accessibility is different in a parish context and an academic context. In an academic course in social ethics, the accessibility must be made in a way that facilitates its reading as a text for a more in-depth understanding and interpretation. Many find the language of the texts dry and dense and lacking an order of ideas that is easily followed, so that reading the texts becomes increasingly burdensome, and as interest diminishes, thoughtful inquiry is not evoked. But serious students of social ethics are shortchanged when they are only given summaries of the encyclicals, which cannot replace the academic richness of coming into contact with the text.

The ethical framework I offer in this book for reading Catholic social teaching is used to reconfigure the content of the encyclicals

---

[8] See Brian Hehir, "Personal Faith, the Public Church, and the Role of Theology," *Harvard Divinity Bulletin* 26/1 (1966).

[9] Judith A. Merkle, "From Catholic Social Teaching to Catholic Social Tradition," in *Theology and the Social Sciences: College Theology Society Annual* 46 (2000), 241–58 (Maryknoll, NY: Orbis Books, 2001), 245.

[10] Thomas Massaro, *Living Justice: Catholic Social Teaching in Action*, 2d classroom ed. (Lanham, MD: Rowman and Littlefield, 2012), 9.

without losing its substance. It gives an order to reading the texts and reappropriates the language in less dense and dry expressions while remaining faithful to its essence. The goal is to facilitate reading to evoke critical thought and inquiry. The proposed framework consists of the following: looking at historical context, principles and norms of judgment, directives for action, and a critical excursus. To illustrate the use of the proposed framework, I apply it in the study and analysis of selected encyclicals, showing both change and continuity of the social tradition. An introduction to Catholic social teaching and an overview of the entire Catholic social tradition precede the study of the selected documents. With the basic content of the selected documents studied, one can engage in a critical discursus relative to current social issues.

Choice

Vision and norm are integrated into choice, because in the very act of choice, the moral agent actualizes his or her view of life, the truths and values that shape this view, and the principles that ground it. Having engaged in the study of Christian moral vision and moral norms, he or she enters into the realm of choice with a particular faith horizon and stance. The study of the ethical methodology for conflict situations and of Ignatian discernment does not exist in a moral vacuum, but within a Christian ethical vision.

Ethical Methodology for Conflict Situations

My ethical methodology for conflict situations is based on the integration of the ethics of holistic reasoning and virtue ethics. This responds to the need for a methodology that goes beyond a purely virtue-centered approach and a purely principle-centered approach, yet draws from the richness of both. The ethics of holistic reasoning has four core principles: the primacy of context for moral objectivity; the use of the premoral/nonmoral concept *vs.* the privileging of *finis operis;* the new hermeneutics of direct and indirect principle; and the understanding of ethics of holistic reasoning as a non-utilitarian Christian teleology. Following the study of the ethics of holistic reasoning is the study of virtue ethics, with an introduction to its thrust in comparison with that of the ethics of holistic reasoning. This study covers three essential topics: virtue ethics in Thomistic thought; a contemporary retrieval of virtue ethics; and the three schools of thought regarding the relation of the ethics of character and the ethics of principles.

There is no perfect ethical approach. All have epistemological limits or constraints. Cognizant of such limits or constraints of the ethics of holistic reasoning and virtue ethics, my point is not to demonstrate which approach is superior, but rather to relate one to the other in a matrix that does justice to each and assigns to each its normative force. This matrix is the use of prudential reason in both virtue ethics and the ethics of holistic reasoning in addressing conflict situations. At the heart of the entire ethical endeavor is the person of virtue engaged in a profound moral inquiry. The ethical methodology I propose for addressing moral dilemmas in conflict situations is divided into three main themes: thinking with stories, reflective equilibrium, and judgment and decision.

Primacy of Context: Thinking with Stories

A good ethicist is a good narrativist, because a good story requires insight into the human condition, where people are struggling with their choices in the face of competing allegiances and perspectives, amid different social forces in culture, politics, and religion that come into play and make claims on the choices to be made. Thinking with stories is reasoning with feeling and imagining, because stories engage our minds as well as our hearts. It is thinking that is shaped by the concrete context, the human locus of moral objectivity. Outside of this context is a moral vacuum.

Whether stories are personal or communal, there are multiple voices that are heard, voices that are often are in conflict. The ethicist who is also a narrativist must draw necessary information from all available sources to bring to full light what is required in determining the moral objectivity-truth on which judgment is to be based. Thus, there is a need to put "thinking with stories" within a larger frame of reference beyond the experiential. To do research into all relevant and pertinent data is necessary for a broad and enlightened understanding of social issues and problems. This is where ethics depends on data from social science, behavioral science, empirical science, and other fields of study.

In the interaction, however, of ethics and other fields of study, ethicists must be critically aware of the value biases of studies they use and be able to make discerned judgment on the adequacy and reliability of their data or information. I propose the use of what I call *mutual critical correlation* to characterize the relation between what is ethical and what is empirical. In this mutual critical correlation, there may be identity, similarity-in-difference, and confrontation. The end goal that must be sought through an open dialogue is the conversion or transformation of both poles. To bring a careful, subtle, and balanced moral discernment to particular human situations is a vital part of being human.

If a particular social issue is taken up, a story, whether real or constructed, must show a conflict situation in which a person, community of persons, or institution faces a moral dilemma. The richer the texture of the stories or narratives, the better they show reality in all its complexity.

Reflective Equilibrium: Systemic Analysis and Discernment

I use the term *reflective equilibrium* to indicate that which lies at the core of an ethical methodology involving systematic moral analysis, because such analysis involves the weighing and balancing of virtues, values, rules, and principles. These are all necessary to determine which is to be given priority in conflict situations where not all the goods can be protected; protecting one may entail the loss of another. Both virtue ethics and the ethics of holistic reasoning are necessary in our reflective equilibrium to arrive at a decision that is truly human and Christian. Holistic moral reasoning in the school of McCormick and other Catholic authors draws upon the Aristotelian-Thomistic interpretative tradition of teleological ethics, which is distinguished from the utilitarianism of Bentham and Mill. Utilitarianism pursues the greatest good for the greatest number and the greatest sum total of social welfare, understood empirically. In contrast, Aristotle and Aquinas envision the *telos* of human life as the realization of virtue, a life oriented to the *summum bonum,* God. The moral theory of Richard McCormick exemplifies Christian teleology. The full Christian experience, he writes, provides the refinement of sensitivity to human values. The Christian perspective provides the broader and deeper horizon of meaning to moral reasoning. A value judgment distanced from this horizon of meaning might otherwise be determined solely by empiricism, but Christian ethics requires a broader vision.

What is required is a qualitative sensitivity to the depth and breadth of value. A well-ordered heart is both the origin and result of ethical decisions. Edward Vacek writes: "Compassion and depth of feeling are more important than calculation."[11] Even if this is true, the ethicist is not dispensed of the task to probe the normative warrants for moral

---

[11] Edward Vacek, "Proportionalism: One View of the Debate," *Theological Studies* 46/2 (1985): 303.

judgment that this proposed ethical methodology provides. In asking *What ought we be?* and *What ought we do?* in the face of conflict situations, we are guided by the moral compass of virtue ethics and the ethics of holistic reasoning.

Virtue Ethics: Integrating Vision and Norm

The stories of which we speak can be analyzed and reflected upon in the light of the claims of justice, fidelity, and self-care relative to the social issues they address. Justice is directed to the common good, which protects the equality of persons and the universality of basic rights against all forms of bias and prejudice. Fidelity protects our special and particular bonds, as we are called to care for those who are closest to us in the hierarchy of relationships. And self-care, with self-esteem as its subcategory, is the foundation of the love for others. These virtues may be translated into values like common good, solidarity, compassion, kindness, forgiveness, and acceptance. The virtues of justice, fidelity, and self-care indicate the realms of relationship—the larger society (nation, community), the inner circle of relationships (family, friendships), and the self.

The meaning of these virtues and values is first understood within the framework of moral vision and moral norm. This is the moment of integration of vision, norm, and choice in relation to virtue ethics. How does the study of religion and culture, of scripture, and of systematic theology deepen one's understanding of the virtues of justice, fidelity, self-care, and related values? How does the study of Catholic social teaching provide the norm for these same virtues and related values? Moral reflection and analysis must take place within the framework of the Christian system of values.

The meaning of these virtues and values in light of moral vision and norm, when translated to the concrete context of the stories in relation to social issues can conflict. The demand of justice can conflict with the demand of fidelity and the demand of fidelity can conflict with the demand of self-care. There are conflicts between and among the claims of virtues and values, and the dissonances can reflect the conflicts between and among claims of religion, culture, and politics, the larger contexts of the issues/problems. The virtue of prudence is necessary to make a Christian moral weighing of conflicting virtues and values by understanding first the nature of the conflicts, their causes, and possible consequences if one virtue or value is chosen over another. Prudence is necessary to determine how to live a life of justice, fidelity, and self-care in the complexity of being human and

in the face of moral dilemmas. At this juncture the integration of virtue ethics and the ethics of holistic reasoning is necessary, and at the
heart of this integration is the person of virtue, who makes the moral
judgment with the help of the ethical methodology provided by the
ethics of holistic reasoning.

Integrating Virtue Ethics and the Ethics of Holistic Reasoning

The ethical methodology provided by the ethics of holistic reasoning consists of basic principles and specific guiding rules that govern
the decision-making process. The strength of these guiding principles
is that they provide a common ground for moral reasoning in the
public forum beyond the vagaries of culture or creed. People arrive
at different decisions in the end, but the ethics of principles provides
referential points for public discourse. To facilitate moral reasoning I
use reality-seeking questions for the criteria of moral deliberation in
conflict situations. The specific questions (What? Why? How? What
else? and What if?) enable the moral agent to probe in a holistic
manner the two key questions—*What ought I be?* and *What ought
I do?*—for being and doing are related and interrelated in the deep
integration of virtue ethics and ethics of holistic reasoning.

Asking the questions, *What?* and *Why?* is a critical moment in the
ethics of holistic reasoning, for it pivots on the value/good that one
seeks, which is the end of one's total moral action. Whatever means
that is used is directed toward the realization of this value/good. Asking "what" is as important as asking "why" because it summons the
moral agents to see reality as it is, as they investigate the objective reality that confronts them and the possible courses they can take. Asking
"why" places moral agents in a true discernment of not only what they
are seeking to do but more primarily on who they are, for the values/
goods they choose over others reflect their person and character. And
this is where virtue ethics and ethics of holistic reasoning profoundly
connect. It is the virtuous person or community of virtuous persons
whose calculus of values is human and Christian. The weighing of
values should be governed by virtues in asking the questions: *Who
am I? What kind of person do I seek to become? What ought I to do?*
And in the larger context, we ask, *What kind of people are we? What
kind of nation do we envision to become?* It is here where the previous
ethical reflection on virtue ethics within the framework of moral vision
and moral norm is brought to bear on determining through prudential
judgment which of the values/goods should be pursued as higher in
a concrete human context, or whether the values in question are at

least equal. The study and reflection of culture and religion, scripture, systematic theology, and Catholic social teaching enter profoundly into the weighing of values/goods in conflict situations.

Asking *How?* and *What else?* refers to the means used to realize the value/good sought. The question "how?" inquires in what manner and by what means the value/good is sought and realized. And the question "what else?" is asked to ensure that one has explored all possible means and that one is taking the last resort to protect the value/good with the least possible harm. What distinguishes the ethics of holistic reasoning from utilitarianism is that not just any means is taken to pursue a good/value. The morality of the means is discerned to realize the end value. Persons of virtue wrestle with the ethics of the means used. To avoid mere intuitionism or subjectivism in determining whether what one does to pursue the end value/good is the last resort and that it causes the least possible harm, one must be guided by the principle of indivisibility; principle of necessary causal relation between means and ends; and the principle of lesser evil. The principle of indivisibility holds that when the means used involves two effects, there must be an intrinsic link between the good effect and evil effect in one indivisible act. The ethics of holistic reasoning aligns with this traditional principle, which is grounded on the immediacy of good and evil effects in a unity of action. It maintains, however, that when a premoral evil (not moral evil) is a means rather than an effect, there must be a necessary causal relation between this premoral evil means and the good/value pursued and not only a factually efficacious relation. The principle of lesser evil prohibits superfluity of evil, even if it is necessary. If evil is inevitable to protect the higher good, evil that is more than necessary is not allowed.

The question *What if?* is asked to discern the consequences of the means used to realize the value/good sought. The "what if" criterion raises the question regarding both the short-term and long-term effects and consequences. In the protection of values/goods, risks are taken that may involve inevitable harm. The risks, however, must be so calculated that the consequences will not in the long run undermine the very values that one seeks to protect.

The three criteria are intrinsically related. This means that even if only one criterion is not realized, the action is not morally justified. The value sought must always be higher or at least equal to or at least equal to the value sacrificed. If this criterion is not met, to continue with the process is morally futile. If the means used to protect the end value/good brings about consequences which undermines it in the long run, then the whole action is not morally justified. The ethics of holistic reasoning involves an integral moral reasoning in determining moral rightness and wrongness.

Judgment and Decision

The final moment of the moral reasoning process is judgment and decision. One makes a judgment based on the results of the moral analysis, as shaped by the concrete narrative of the ethical situation. Founded on this judgment, one makes a decision. In the end, all that is asked is that we do everything possible to make informed and enlightened choices, based on accurate facts that we consider well, grounded on a principled discernment of what best serves the highest good, and consonant with who we are and what we ought to be and do.

Integrating Ethical Methodology and Ignatian Discernment

The ethical methodology I proposed using the ethics of holistic reasoning for conflict situations employs the rigor of reason. But I also hold, contrary to the thinking of rigorous rationalists, that it is in the affective and spiritual regions that persons are most profoundly engaged in their fundamental experience. The rational is constant for creatures of reason, and it must be so because what is moral is reasonable, but it is when reason is bathed by the waters of affectivity and spirituality that it reaches a depth of illumination.

Using the resources of memory and imagination, discernment is directed by a judgment of affectivity, without denying the place of reason, for reason is always necessary to make any kind of judgment. But the scrutiny engaged by reason here is different from formal logic, which puts to the test the moral principle as it is applied to a relevant case to yield a moral conclusion. Beyond the reasoning mind, but not in opposition to it, the reasoning heart stirs and moves one to take the path of authenticity as one comes to terms with who one is before the loving and liberating God.

Ignatian discernment is necessary for the final part of the ethical process because, as Rahner once wrote, theology finds its climax in prayer. Decision making is at the core of being human, and one reaches one's depth in union with God in Christ through the Spirit. The human mind is limited, and the human heart is divided, but when elevated to the realm of the spirit, they reach new depths of clarity and illumination. Spiritual discernment engages one's entire person, for there at the center of prayer and discernment one's mental powers, affective inclinations, and spiritual connaturalities are directed toward the realm of transcendence, where one finds a place of interior peace and wholeness.

To this end this new method benefits from an academic study of Ignatian discernment, the distinctive contribution of Ignatius's *Spiritual Exercises* to humanity and to Christian spirituality. But any treatment of the writings of Ignatius must be cognizant of the cultural context in which they were shaped and of the worldview that underlies them.

A critical reading of Ignatian discernment from a theological perspective is confronted by basic questions that must be addressed to prepare one to enter into the worldview of the Ignatian context: How is the incomprehensible God experienced? What is the relation between divine providence and human freedom in seeking God's will? Is belief in Satan and in good and evil spirits a matter of Christian faith? In the critical and contemporary reading of the three Ignatian modes of discernment, commentaries are sharply divided on fundamentals on the interpretation of the three Ignatian times or modes. There have been many debates on what Ignatius means by each of these three times or occasions for reaching good decisions, their relationship, and their comparative value.

It is essential to employ new hermeneutical lenses of contemporary theology and philosophy to read Ignatius's classical writing, a product of the sixteenth century. With the voluminous matter gathered from the erudite discourse on Ignatian discernment by scholars, we sift what can flow back to life, back into our day-to-day decisions. At the heart of discernment is God and the human person in an encounter. We relate with God, who is love, who has great desires for our human flourishing and that of others, and who lures us in the direction of these desires. Finding that our own desires resonate with God's desires, we make choices that are truly and deeply ours and yet enabled and empowered by the very love of God, in which we live and have our being.

The focus of this study of Ignatian discernment is its three modes. I propose that when one makes a choice or decision, one is open to all the three modes, and Ignatius did not classify the three modes as first, second, and third in terms of their chronological order in making decisions, but in terms of the nature of the mode with reference to the intensity and certitude of the divine presence. Through different modes God mediates God's divine presence. The preliminary stage is the third mode, where one gathers all the facts and pieces of evidence, thinks through the pros and cons, mulls over the alternative decisions, and ponders the various options and their possible consequences. In this third mode where discursive reasoning is engaged, one easily sees how the ethical methodology for conflict situations is integrated into the discernment process. In this mode, one is not moved by the crests and troughs of emotions but is engaged fully in discursive reasoning. One seeks the higher good or value that must be upheld and protected relative to other goods or values, all for the greater glory of God.

In the second mode affective integrity is the criterion. There is a different kind of reasoning operative in the second mode, as one brings one's decision to prayer for an affective reasoning, or what is called the judgment of the heart. In this mode God lures and directs one to the ways of the divine desires through consolation and desolation. God speaks to one's heart in a true sense. The choice that one makes, when it resonates with God's desires, is accompanied by great consolation experienced with tears of joy; increase of faith, hope, and charity; and a deep quiet and peace. Desolation eventually accompanies choices one makes that are contrary to God's desires for one's flourishing and in relation to others in community. But there is no equivalence between consolation and pleasure, or desolation and pain. It could be that consolation comes with deep pain, but the peace is much deeper than the pain, as one is willing to pay the cost of loving. The peace comes with the certitude that God is present even in the depths of pain, in the very choice for love.

In the second mode affectivity is the criterion, but the love of Christ is its focus. As one wrestles with one's feelings regarding the choice one has made using the exercise of reason in the first mode, one keeps one's loving gaze on Christ and asks: "Lord, what are you asking of me?" "What is your loving desire?" "What does it mean to love and to follow you?" Ultimately, only one who has come to know the intimacy and depth of this love and has become familiar with its ways will know this love and recognize its voice and calling. Ignatian discernment is a discernment of God's love in Christ, in one's con-naturality with it, born of the constant and faithful gift of self to this love, in one's tireless labor for the kingdom, in a Gospel-inspired and directed life arduously spent for others.

In what Ignatius calls the first mode, God gives one a certitude that passes all human knowledge, beyond one's calculation and expectations; a certitude that comes like a light piercing through the darkness of fear, anxiety, and confusion. At this moment one might possess absolute clarity about one's choice. Engaged here is contemplative reasoning, which enables one to see and recognize the presence of God and the certitude of one's choice. The second and third modes are made available to human effort and striving in decision making; the first mode is a pure gift from the freedom of God's love. Since it is a gift, one can only make oneself completely open and disposed to its absolute gratuity.

A decision made within the Christian framework of values should be based on moral vision and rooted in moral norms that inform and influence the ethical process, engaging virtue ethics and the ethics of holistic reasoning in determining what is morally right in a conflict situation. Brought to discernment, such a decision finds illumination and confirmation through a recognition of affective integrity and interior peace. This is concisely the integral and holistic method for social ethics I propose regarding decision making in conflict situations.

A Final Word

As I come to the end of the book, I recall once again the words of Richard McCormick, "the problem of elaborating a satisfying value system within the totality of Christian realities remains one of the most important unfinished tasks in the field of Christian morality."[12] It is my hope that the method I have proposed in this book for social ethics is a worthy contribution to the accomplishment of this unfinished task, in the light of Vatican II's grand vision for moral theology as a science of faith, in the global church, in the midst of an ever-shifting world in need of a moral compass.

---

[12] Richard A. McCormick, *Notes on Moral Theology 1965 through 1980* (Washington, DC: University Press of America, 1981), 295.

Selected Bibliography

Adams, Carol, ed. *Ecofeminism and the Sacred*. New York: Continuum, 1993.

Adams, Carol J., and Marie M. Fortune, eds. *Violence Against Women and Children: A Christian Theological Sourcebook*. New York: Continuum, 1995.

Amaladoss, Michael. *The Asian Jesus*. Maryknoll, NY: Orbis Books, 2006.

Arroyo, Gonzalo, et al. "Declaration of the 80." In *Christians and Socialism: Documentation of the Christians for Socialism Movement in Latin America,* edited by John Eagleson, translated by John Drury, 3–6. Maryknoll, NY: Orbis Books, 1975.

Baier Anne, "Claims, Rights, Responsibilities." In *Prospects for a Common Morality,* edited by Gene Outka and John P. Reeder, 149–69. Princeton, NJ: Princeton University Press, 1993.

Bar-Efrat, Simon. *Narrative Art in the Bible*. New York: T. and T. Clark International, 2004.

Baum, Gregory. "Liberation Theology and 'the Supernatural.'" *The Ecumenist* 19/6 (September-October 1981): 81–87.

Bausch, William J. *Storytelling: Imagination and Faith*. Mystic, CT: Twenty-Third Publications, 1984.

Beardslee, William A. *Literary Criticism of the New Testament*. Philadelphia: Fortress Press, 1970.

Beauchamp, Tom L. "Principlism and Its Alleged Competitors." *Kennedy Institute of Ethics Journal* 5/3 (September 1995): 181–98.

Beauchesne, Richard J. "The Spiritual Existential as Desire: Karl Rahner and Emmanuel Levinas." *Église et théologie* 23 (1992): 221–39.

Beltran, Benigno P. *Faith and Struggle on Smokey Mountain: Hope for a Planet in Peril*. Maryknoll, NY: Orbis Books, 2012.

Bianchi, Eugene C., and Rosemary Radford Ruether, eds. *A Democratic Catholic Church: The Reconstruction of Roman Catholicism*. New York: Crossroad, 1992.

Black, Carl Clifton. "Rhetorical Criticism." In *Hearing the New Testament: Strategies for Interpretation,* edited by Joel B. Green, 256–77. Grand Rapids, MI: Eerdmans, 1995.

Black, Peter. "The Broken Wings of Eros: Christian Ethics and the Denial of Desire." *Theological Studies* 64/1 (2003): 106–26.

Boff, Clodovis, and Leonardo Boff. *Introducing Liberation Theology*. Translated by Paul Burns. Maryknoll, NY: Orbis Books, 1987.

Boff, Leonardo. *Cry of the Earth, Cry of the Poor.* Translated by Phillip Berryman. Maryknoll, NY: Orbis Books, 1997.

———. *Jesus Christ Liberator: A Critical Christology for Our Time.* Translated by Patrick Hughes. Maryknoll, NY: Orbis Books, 1978.

———. *Liberating Grace.* Translated by Patrick Hughes. Maryknoll, NY: Orbis Books, 1981.

Boff, Leonardo, and Virgilio Elizondo, eds. *Ecology and Poverty: Cry of the Earth, Cry of the Poor.* Concilium, no. 5. Maryknoll, NY: Orbis Books, 1995.

Boland, Vivian. "Mater et Magistra." In *The New Dictionary of Catholic Social Thought,* edited by Judith A. Dwyer. Collegeville, MN: Liturgical Press, 1994.

Bracken, Joseph. *Divine Matrix: Creativity as Link Between East and West.* Maryknoll, NY: Orbis Books, 1995.

———. "Response to Elizabeth Johnson's 'Does God Play Dice?'" *Theological Studies* 57/4 (1996): 720–30.

Brock, Rita Nakashima. *Journeys by Heart: A Christology of Erotic Power.* New York: Crossroad, 1998.

Brown, Joanne Carlson, and Rebecca Parker. "For God So Loved the World?" In *Christianity, Patriarchy, and Abuse: A Feminist Critique,* edited by Joanne Carlson Brown and Carole R. Bohn, 1–30. Cleveland: Pilgrim Press, 1989.

Brown, Neil. "Teleology or Deontology." *Irish Theological Quarterly* 53/1 (1987): 36–51.

Brown, Raymond. "Roles of Women in the Fourth Gospel." *Theological Studies* 36/4 (1975): 688–99.

Buckley, Michael. "The Structure of the Rules for Discernment of Spirits. " *The Way Supplement* 20 (Autumn 1973): 19–37.

Burghardt, Walter. "Characteristics of Social Justice Spirituality." *Origins* 24/9 (1994): 157–64.

Burke, Margaret Ellen. "Social Sin and Social Grace." *The Way Supplement* 85 (Spring 1996): 40–54.

Burrell, David B. *Aquinas: God and Action.* Notre Dame, IN: University of Notre Dame Press, 1979.

Bussert, Joy M. K. *Battered Women: From a Theology of Suffering to an Ethic of Empowerment.* New York: Division for Mission in North America/Lutheran Church in America, 1986.

Butler, Sara. "Embodiment: Women and Men, Equal and Complementary." In *The Church Women Want,* edited by Elizabeth A. Johnson, 35–44. New York: Crossroad, 2002.

Cahill, Lisa Sowle. "Contemporary Challenges to Exceptionless Moral Norms." In *Moral Theology Today: Certitudes and Doubts,* 121–35. Saint Louis, MO: The Pope John Center, 1984.

———. *Family: A Christian Social Perspective.* Minneapolis: Fortress Press, 2000.

―――. "Feminism and Christian Ethics." In *Freeing Theology: The Essentials of Theology in Feminist Perspective*, edited by Catherine Mowry LaCugna, 211–34. San Francisco: Harper, 1993.

―――. "Feminist Ethics." *Theological Studies* 51/1 (1990): 49–64.

―――. "Feminist Ethics, Differences, and Common Ground: A Catholic Perspective." In *Readings in Moral Theology, no. 9, Feminist Ethics and the Catholic Moral Tradition*, edited by Charles E. Curran, Margaret A. Farley, and Richard A. McCormick, 184–204. New York: Paulist Press, 1996.

―――. "The New Testament and Ethics: Communities of Social Change." *Interpretation* (December 1990): 383–95.

―――. *Sex, Gender, and Christian Ethics*. Cambridge: Cambridge University Press, 1996.

―――. "Teleology, Utilitarianism, and Christian Ethics." *Theological Studies* 42/4 (1981): 601–29.

―――. *Theological Bioethics: Participation, Justice, and Change*. Washington, DC: Georgetown University Press, 2005.

―――. "Toward Global Ethics." *Theological Studies* 63/2 (2002): 324–44.

Callahan, Sidney Cornelia. *In Good Conscience: Reason and Emotion in Moral Decision Making*. San Francisco: Harper San Francisco, 1991.

Calvez, Jean-Yves. *The Social Thought of John XXIII*. Translated by George McKenzie. Chicago: Henry Regnery, 1964.

Camp, Richard L. *The Papal Ideology of Social Reform: A Study on Historical Development: 1878–1967*. Leiden: E. J. Brill, 1969.

Campion, Donald R. "The World-wide Response." In *The Challenge of Mater et Magistra*, edited by Joseph N. Moody and Justus George Lawler, 155–205. New York: Herder and Herder, 1963.

Carney, Frederick. "On McCormick and Teleological Morality." *The Journal of Religious Ethics* 6 (1978): 81–107.

Carr, Anne E. *Transforming Grace: Christian Tradition and Women's Experience*. New York: Continuum, 1988.

Cates, Diana Fritz. *Aquinas on the Emotions: A Religious-Ethical Inquiry*. Washington, DC: Georgetown University Press, 2009.

Cavanaugh, Thomas A. "Double-Effect Reasoning, Craniotomy, and Vital Conflicts: A Case of Contemporary Catholic Casuistry." *National Catholic Bioethics Center* 11/3 (September 2011): 453–64.

Charles, Rodger. *Christian Social Witness and Teaching: The Catholic Tradition from Genesis to Centesimus Annus*. Vol. 2, *The Modern Social Teaching: Contexts, Summaries, Analysis*. Herefordshire: Gracewing/Fowler Wright, 1998.

Chiba, Shin, George R. Hunsberger, and Lester Edwin J. Ruiz. *Christian Ethics in Ecumenical Context: Theology, Culture, and Politics in Dialogue*. Grand Rapids, MI: Eerdmans, 1995.

Childs, Brevard S. *The New Testament as Canon: An Introduction*. Philadelphia: Fortress Press, 1984.

Chopp, Rebecca S. *Power to Speak: Feminism, Language, God.* New York: Crossroad, 1989.

Christ, Carol P. "Embodied Thinking: Reflections on Feminist Theological Method." *Journal of Feminist Studies in Religion* 5/1 (1989): 7–15.

Clague, Julie. "'A Dubious Idiom and Rhetoric': How Problematic Is the Language of Human Rights in Catholic Social Thought?" In *Catholic Social Thought: Twilight or Renaissance?* edited by Jonathan S. Boswell, Frank P. McHugh, and Johan Verstraeten, 125–40. Leuven: Leuven University, 2000.

Clark, Peter. "Richard McCormick, SJ, and Dual Epistemology." *Christian Bioethics* 14/3 (2008): 236–71.

Clarke, Thomas E., ed. *Above Every Name: The Lordship of Christ and Social Systems.* Ramsey, NJ: Paulist Press, 1980.

———. "Discerning the Ignatian Way in Poverty Today." *The Way Supplement* 19 (Summer 1973): 88–95.

———. "Ignatian Prayer and Individualism." *The Way Supplement* 82 (Spring 1995): 7–14.

———. "Ignatian Spirituality and Societal Consciousness." *Studies in the Spirituality of Jesuits* (September 1975): 127–50.

Claver, Francisco. F. "Social Theory and Social Change in the Philippines." *Pulso* 1 (1994): 42–48.

———. "People Power and Value Transformation: A Faith Perspective." In *Toward a Theology of People Power: Reflections on the Philippines February Phenomenon,* edited by Douglas J. Elwood, 54–61. Quezon City: New Day, 1986.

Clifford, Anne, and Anthony J. Godzieba, eds. *Christology: Meaning, Inquiry, Practice.* College Theology Society no. 48. Maryknoll, NY: Orbis Books, 2003.

Clines, David J. "Possibilities and Priorities of Biblical Interpretation in an International Perspective." *Biblical Interpretation: A Journal of Contemporary Approaches* 1/1 (1993): 67–87.

Coffey, David. "The Whole Rahner on the Supernatural Existential." *Theological Studies* 65/1 (2004): 95–118.

Coleman, John A. "The Renewed Covenant: Robert N. Bellah's Vision of Religion and Society." In *Sociology and Human Destiny,* edited by Gregory Baum, 86–109. New York: Seabury Press, 1980.

Conn, Walter E. *Conversion.* New York: Alba House, 1978.

Connery, John R. "Catholic Ethics: Has the Rule for Norm-Making Changed?" *Theological Studies* 42/2 (1981): 232–50.

Cosgrave, William. "Our Emotional Life." *Furrow* 49/5 (May 1998): 270–76.

———. "The Principle of Double Effect—An Unresolved Debate." *The Furrow* 40/12 (December 1989): 703–14.

Coward, Howard G., and Daniel C. Maguire, eds. *Visions of a New Earth: Religious Perspectives on Population, Consumption, and Ecology.* Albany: State University of New York, 2000.

Crosby, Michael A. *House of Disciples: Church, Economics, and Justice in Matthew.* Maryknoll, NY: Orbis Books, 1988.

Crossin, John W. *What Are They Saying About Virtue?* New York: Paulist Press, 1985.

Crysdale, Cynthia S. W. "Revisioning Natural Law: From the Classicist Paradigm to Emergent Probability." *Theological Studies* 56/3 (1995): 464–84.

Culpepper, R. Alan. "Story and History in the Gospels." *Review and Expositor* (1984): 467–78.

Curran, Charles E. "Bernhard Häring: A Moral Theologian Whose Soul Matched His Scholarship." *National Catholic Reporter* 34 (July 17, 1998): 11.

———. *The Catholic Moral Tradition Today: A Synthesis.* Washington, DC: Georgetown University Press, 1999.

———. *Catholic Social Teaching, 1891–Present: A Historical, Theological, and Ethical Analysis.* Washington, DC: Georgetown University Press, 2002.

———. *Faithful Dissent.* Kansas City, MO: Sheed and Ward, 1986.

———. "The Reception of Catholic and Social and Economic Teaching in the United States." In *Modern Catholic Social Teaching: Commentaries and Interpretations,* edited by Kenneth R. Himes, 469–92. Washington, DC: Georgetown University Press, 2004.

———. "Utilitarianism and Contemporary Moral Theology: Situating the Debate." *Louvain Studies* 6 (Spring 1977): 239–72.

Curran, Charles, E., Margaret A. Farley, and Richard A. McCormick, eds. *Readings in Moral Theology, no. 9, Feminist Ethics and the Catholic Tradition.* New York: Paulist Press, 1996.

Curran, Charles E., and Richard A. McCormick, eds. *Readings in Moral Theology, no. 7. Natural Law and Theology.* New York: Paulist Press, 1991.

———. *Readings in Moral Theology, no. 4, The Use of Scripture in Moral Theology.* New York: Paulist Press, 1984.

Daly, Mary. *Beyond God the Father.* Boston: Beacon Press, 1973.

De La Torre, Miguel A. *Reading the Bible from the Margins.* Maryknoll, NY: Orbis Books, 2002.

De Mesa, José M. "Providence as Power and Graciousness." In *Toward a Theology of People Power: Reflections on the Philippines February Phenomenon,* edited by Douglas J. Elwood, 37–61. Quezon City: New Day, 1986.

———. "A Hermeneutics of Appreciation: Approach and Methodology." *MST Review* 4/2 (2000): iv–113.

Di Ianni, Albert. "The Direct/Indirect Distinction in Morals." In *Readings in Moral Theology, no. 1, Moral Norms and Catholic Tradition,* edited by Charles E. Curran and Richard A. McCormick, 215–43. New York: Paulist Press, 1979.

Diamond, Eugene. "Moral and Medical Considerations in the Management of Extrauterine Pregnancy." *Linacre Quarterly* 66/3 (1999): 5–15.

Donaldson, Laura E. *Decolonizing Feminisms: Race, Gender, and Empire-building*. Chapel Hill: University of North Carolina, 1992.

Dorr, Donal. *Option for the Poor: A Hundred Years of Catholic Social Teaching*. Maryknoll, NY: Orbis Books, 1983, 1992.

———. *Option for the Poor and for the Earth: Catholic Social Teaching*. Maryknoll, NY: Orbis Books, 2012.

———. "Pope John XXIII—New Direction?" In *Readings in Moral Theology*, no. 5, *Official Catholic Social Teaching*, edited by Charles E. Curran and Richard A. McCormick, 77–109. New York: Paulist Press, 1986.

Douglas, Kelly Brown. *The Black Christ*. Maryknoll, NY: Orbis Books, 1994.

Duffy, Stephen J. "The Heart of Darkness: Original Sin Revisited." *Theological Studies* 49/4 (1988): 597–622.

Dulles, Avery. "Finding God's Will: Rahner's Interpretation of the Ignatian Election." *Woodstock Letters* 94 (Winter 1965): 139–52.

Duska, Ronald F. "The US Bishops and Capitalism: An Unstable Alliance?" *Peace and Justice Studies* 1 (November 1989): 57–79.

Eagleson, John, and Philip Scharper, eds. *Puebla and Beyond: Documentary and Commentary*. Translated by John Drury. Maryknoll, NY: Orbis Books, 1979.

Ebest, Sally Barr, and Ron Ebest, eds. *Reconciling Catholicism and Feminism?* Notre Dame, IN: University of Notre Dame Press, 2003.

Egan, Harvey D. *The Spiritual Exercises and the Ignatian Mystical Horizon*. St. Louis: The Institute of Jesuit Sources, 1976.

Eilers, Franz-Josef, ed. *For All the Peoples of Asia: Federation of Asian Bishops Conferences Documents from 1992 to 1996*. Vol. 2. Quezon City, Manila: Claretian, 1997.

Elizondo, Virgilio. *The Future Is Mestizo: Life Where Cultures Meet*. Boulder: University Press of Colorado, 2000.

———. *Galilean Journey: The Mexican Promise*. rev. and exp. ed. Maryknoll, NY: Orbis Books, 2000.

Elliott, John H., ed. *Social Scientific Criticism of the New Testament and Its Social World*. Semeia 35. Decatur, Ga: Scholars Press, 1986.

Elsbernd, Mary. "Toward a Theology of Spirit That Builds Up the Just Community." In *The Spirit in the Church and the World* 49 (annual publication of the College Theology Society), edited by Bradford E. Hinze, 152–66. Collegeville, Minnesota: Liturgical Press, 2003.

———. "Whatever Happened to *Octogesima adveniens?*" *Theological Studies* 56/1 (1995): 39–60.

Elwood, Douglas J. "Prologue: Prospect for Indigenous Philippine Theology. In *Toward a Theology of People Power: Reflections on the Philippine February Phenomenon*, edited by Douglas J. Elwood, 1–16. Quezon City: New Day, 1986.

Fabella, Virginia, and R. S. Sugirtharajah, eds. *Dictionary of Third World Theologies.* Maryknoll, NY: Orbis Books, 2000.

Farley, Margaret A. "Feminism and Universal Morality." In Outka and Reeder, *Prospects for a Common Morality,* 170–90.

———. "Feminist Ethics." In *Westminster Dictionary of Christian Ethics,* edited by James F. Childress and John Macquarie, 229–31. Philadelphia: Westminster, 1986.

———. "New Patterns of Relationship: Beginnings of a Moral Revolution." *Theological Studies* 36/4 (1975): 627–46.

———. *Personal Commitments: Beginning, Keeping, Changing.* San Francisco: Harper and Row, 1990.

Ferguson, Kitty. *The Fire in the Equations: Science, Religion, and the Search for God.* Grand Rapids, MI: Eerdmans, 1995.

Finn, Daniel. "Commentary on *Centesimus Annus* (On the Hundredth Anniversary of Rerum novarum)." In *Modern Catholic Social Teaching: Commentaries and Interpretations,* edited by Kenneth R. Himes, 436–66. Washington, DC: Georgetown University Press, 2004.

———. "John Paul II and the Moral Ecology of Markets." *Theological Studies* 59/4 (1998): 662–79.

Finn, James. "Beyond Economics, Beyond Revolution: *Octogesima Adveniens.*" In *Building the Free Society: Democracy, Capitalism, and Catholic Social Thought,* edited by George Weigel and Robert Royal, 149–62. Grand Rapids, MI: Eerdmans, 1993.

Finnis, John. *Moral Absolutes: Tradition, Revision, and Truth.* Washington, DC: The Catholic University of America Press, 1991.

Fischer, Kathleen R. *Women at the Well: Feminist Perspectives on Spiritual Direction.* Mahwah, NJ: Paulist Press, 1988.

Fitzmyer, Joseph A. "Historical Criticism: Its Role in Biblical Interpretation and Church Life." *Theological Studies* 50 (1989): 244–59.

Flanagan, Owen. *Varieties of Moral Personality: Ethics and Psychological Realism.* Cambridge, MA: Harvard University Press, 1991.

Foot, Philippa. "The Problem of Abortion and the Doctrine of Double Effect." In *Moral Problems: A Collection of Philosophical Essays,* edited by James Rachels, 28–41. New York: Harper and Row, 1971.

Fortin, Ernest L. "'Sacred and Inviolable': *Rerum Novarum* and Natural Rights." *Theological Studies* 53/2 (1992): 203–33.

Frankena, William K. "Conversations with Carney and Hauerwas." *Journal of Religious Ethics* 3 (Spring 1975): 45–62.

———. "Ethics of Love Conceived as an Ethics of Virtue." *Journal of Religious Ethics* 1 (Fall 1973): 21–36.

———. "McCormick and Traditional Distinction." In *Doing Evil to Achieve Good,* edited by Richard A. McCormick and Paul Ramsey, 145–64. Chicago: Loyola University Press, 1978.

Fuchs, Josef. "The Absoluteness of Moral Terms." In *Proportionalism: For and Against,* edited by Christopher Kaczor, 60–99. Milwaukee: Marquette University Press, 2000.

———. "Basic Freedom and Morality." In *Introduction to Christian Ethics: A Reader,* edited by Ronald P. Hamel and Kenneth R. Himes, 187–98. New York: Paulist Press, 1989.

———. *Human Values and Christian Morality.* Dublin: Gill and Macmillan, 1970.

———. "Sin and Conversion." In *Introduction to Christian Ethics: A Reader,* edited by Ronald P. Hamel and Kenneth R. Himes, 206–16. New York: Paulist Press, 1989.

Gaillardetz, Richard. "The Ecclesiological Foundations of Modern Catholic Social Teaching." In *Modern Catholic Social Teaching: Commentaries and Interpretations,* edited by Kenneth R. Himes, 72–98. Washington, DC: Georgetown University Press, 2004.

Galilea, Segundo. "The Theology of Liberation and the Place of Folk Religion." Concilium 136, *What Is Religion? Inquiry for Christian Theology,* edited by Mircea Eliade, David Tracy, and Marcus Lefébure, 40–45. New York: Seabury Press, 1980.

Galvin, John P. "Jesus Christ." In *Systematic Theology: Roman Catholic Perspectives,* edited by Francis Schüssler Fiorenza and John P. Galvin, 1:251–324. Minneapolis: Fortress Press, 1991.

Gardiner, P. "A Virtue Ethics Approach to Moral Dilemmas in Medicine." *Journal of Medical Ethics* 29/5 (2003): 297–302.

Gebara, Ivone. *Longing for Running Water: Ecofeminism and Liberation.* Minneapolis: Fortress Press, 1999.

Geertz, Clifford. "The Growth of Culture and the Evolution of the Mind." In *Theories of the Mind,* edited by Jordan M. Scher, 713–40. New York: Free Press, 1962.

———.. "Impact of the Concept of Culture on the Concept of Man." In *The Interpretation of Cultures: Selected Essays,* 33–54. New York: Basic Books, 1973.

———. "Religion as a Cultural System." In *Anthropological Approaches to the Study of Religion,* edited by Michael Banton, 1–46. London: Tavistock, 1966.

Gewirth, Alan. "Common Morality and the Community of Rights." In Outka and Reeder, *Prospects for a Common Morality,* 29–52.

———. "Ethical Universalism and Particularism." *Journal of Philosophy* 85 (1988): 283–302.

Gilkes, Cheryl Townsend. "The 'Loves' and 'Troubles' of African-American Women's Bodies: The Womanist Challenge to Cultural Humiliation and Community Ambivalence." In *A Troubling in My Soul: Womanist Perspectives on Evil and Suffering,* edited by Emilie M. Townes, 232–49. Maryknoll, NY: Orbis Books, 1993.

Gilkey, Langdon. *Reaping the Whirlwind: A Christian Interpretation of History.* New York: Seabury Press, 1976.

Gilleman, Gérard. *The Primacy of Charity in Moral Theology.* Westminster, MD: Newman, 1959.

Gilligan, Carol. *In a Different Voice: Psychological Theory and Women's Development.* Cambridge, MA: Harvard University Press, 1993.

Gilson, Etienne. "The Corporeal World and the Efficacy of Secondary Causes." In *God's Activity in the World: The Contemporary Problem,* edited by Owen C. Thomas, 213–30. Chico, CA: Scholars Press, 1983.

Gioia, Francesco, ed. *Interreligious Dialogue: The Official Teaching of the Catholic Church (1963–1995).* Boston: Pauline and Media, 1997.

Girard, René. *Violence and the Sacred.* Stanford, CA: Stanford University, 1977.

Glesson, Gerald. "Is the 'Medical Management' of Ectopic Pregnancy by the Administration of Methotrexate Acceptable?" In *Issues for a Catholic Bioethic,* edited by L. Gormally, 359–70. London: Linacre Center, 1999.

Grabowski, John S., and Michael J. Naughton. "Catholic Social and Sexual Ethics: Inconsistent or Organic." *Thomist* 57/4 (October 1993): 555–78.

Grant, Jacquelyn. "Feminist and Womanist Criticism." In *The Postmodern Bible,* edited by Elizabeth A. Castello, Stephen D. Moore, Gary A. Philipps, and Regina M. Schwartz, 225–71. New Haven, CT: Yale University Press, 1995.

———. "Womanist Jesus and the Mutual Struggle for Liberation." In *The Recovery of the Black Presence: An Interdisciplinary Exploration,* edited by Randall C. Bailey and Jacquelyn Grant, 125–42. Nashville, TN: Abingdon, 1995.

Green, Garrett. *Imagining God: Theology and the Religious Imagination.* San Francisco: Harper and Row, 1989.

Grisez, Germain. *Abortion: The Myths, the Realities, and the Arguments.* Washington, DC: Corpus Books, 1970.

———. "Against Consequentialism." In *Proportionalism: For and Against,* edited by Christopher Kaczor, 239–94. Milwaukee: Marquette University Press, 2000.

———. *The Way of the Lord 1: Christian Moral Principles; The Way of the Lord 2: Living a Christian Life.* Chicago: Franciscan Herald Press, 1983, 1993.

Grisez, Germain, Joseph Boyle, and John Finnis. "Practical Principles, Moral Truth, and Ultimate Ends." *American Journal of Jurisprudence* 32 (1987): 99–151.

Grisez, Germain, Joseph Boyle, and William May. "Every Marital Act Ought to Be Open to New Life: Towards a Clearer Understanding." *The Thomist* 52/3 (July 1988): 365–426.

Grisez, Germain, and Russell Shaw. *Beyond the New Morality: The Responsibilities of Freedom.* Notre Dame, IN: University of Notre Dame Press, 1974.

Grisez, Germain, and Joseph M. Boyle, Jr. *Life and Death with Liberty and Justice: A Contribution to the Euthanasia Debate.* Notre Dame, IN: University of Notre Dame Press, 1979.

Groody, Daniel G., ed. *The Option for the Poor in Christian Theology.* Notre Dame, IN: University of Notre Dame Press, 2007.

Gudorf, Christine E. *Catholic Social Teaching and Liberation Themes.* Washington, DC: University Press of America, 1981.

———. "Commentary on *Octogesima Adveniens.*" In *Modern Catholic Social Teaching: Commentaries and Interpretations,* edited by Kenneth B. Himes, 315–32. Washington, DC: Georgetown University Press, 2004.

———. *Victimization: Examining Christian Complicity.* Philadelphia: Trinity Press International, 1992.

Guevin, Benedict. "Vital Conflicts and Virtue Ethics." *National Catholic Bioethics Quarterly* 10/3 (Autumn 2010): 471–80.

Gula, Richard M. *Moral Discernment.* New York: Paulist Press, 1997.

———. *Reason Informed by Faith: Foundations of Catholic Morality.* New York: Paulist Press, 1989.

Gustafson, James. "Nature: Its Status in Theological Ethics." *Logos* E (1982): 5–23.

———. *Theology and Christian Ethics.* Philadelphia: Pilgrim Press, 1974.

Gutiérrez, Gustavo. "Poverty, Migration, and the Option for the Poor." In *A Promised Land, a Perilous Journey: Theological Perspectives on Migration,* edited by Daniel G. Groody and Gioacchino Campese, 76–86. Notre Dame, IN: University of Notre Dame Press, 2008.

———. *A Theology of Liberation: History, Politics, and Salvation.* Rev. ed. Translated and edited by Sister Caridad and John Eagleson. Maryknoll, NY: Orbis Books, 1988.

Haight, Roger. "Foundational Issues in Jesuit Spirituality." *Studies in the Spirituality of Jesuits* 19/4 (September 1987): 1–61.

———. "The Future of Christology: Expanding Horizons, Religious Pluralism, and the Divinity of Jesus." In *Christology: Memory, Inquiry, Practice,* edited by Anne Clifford and Anthony J. Godzieba, 47–61. Maryknoll, NY: Orbis Books, 2003.

———. *Jesus Symbol of God.* Maryknoll, NY: Orbis Books, 1999.

———. "Sin and Grace." In *Systematic Theology,* edited by Francis Schüssler Fiorenza and John P. Galvin, 2:77–141. Minneapolis: Fortress Press, 1991.

Hales, E. E. Y. *Pope John and His Revolution.* Garden City, NY: Doubleday, 1965.

Hallett, Garth. *Christian Moral Reasoning: An Analytic Guide.* Notre Dame, IN: University of Notre Dame Press, 1983.

———. *Greater Good: The Case for Proportionalism.* Washington, DC: Georgetown University Press, 1995.

———. "The Incommensurability of Values." *Heythrop Journal* 28 (1987): 373–87.

Harrington, Daniel J., and James F. Keenan. *Jesus and Virtue Ethics: Building Bridges Between New Testament Studies and Moral Theology.* Lanham, MD: Sheed and Ward, 2002.

Hartin, Patrick J. *Third World Challenges in the Teaching of Biblical Studies.* Occasional Papers 25. Claremont, CA: The Institute for Antiquity and Christianity, 1993.

Hauerwas, Stanley. "Casuistry as a Narrative Art." *Interpretation* 37 (1993): 377–88.

———. *Character and Christian Life: A Study in Theological Ethics.* San Antonio, TX: Trinity University, 1975.

———. "Character, Narrative, and Growth in the Christian Life." In *Hauerwas Reader,* edited by John Berkman and Michael Cartwright, 221–54. Durham, NC: Duke University, 2001.

———. *A Community of Character.* Notre Dame, IN: University of Notre Dame Press, 1981.

———. "The Gesture of a Truthful Story." *Theology Today* 42 (July 1985): 181–89.

———. "Love's Not All You Need." *Cross Currents* 22 (Summer-Fall 1972): 225–37.

———. "Obligation and Virtue Once More." *Journal of Religious Ethics* 3 (Spring 1975): 27–44.

———. "Vision, Stories, and Character." In *Hauerwas Reader,* edited by John Berkman and Michael Cartwright, 165–70. Durham, NC: Duke University, 2001.

Hebblethwaite, Peter. *Pope John XXIII: Shepherd of the Modern World.* Garden City, NY: Doubleday, 1985.

Hellwig, Monika. *Jesus, the Compassion of God.* Wilmington, DE: Michael Glazier, 1985.

Hennelly, Alfred T., ed. *Medellín: "On the Poverty of the Church."* In *Liberation Theology: A Documentary History,* edited by Alfred T. Hennelly, 117–18. Maryknoll, NY: Orbis Books, 1990.

Henriot, Peter. "Grassroots Analysis: The Emphasis on Culture." In *Liberation Theologies on Shifting Grounds: A Clash of Socio-Economic And Cultural Paradigms,* edited by G. de Schrijver, 333–50. Leuven: Leuven University, 1998.

Herzog II, William R. *Parables as Subversive Speech: Jesus as Pedagogue of the Oppressed.* Louisville, KY: John Knox, 1994.

Hessel, Dieter T., and Rosemary Radford Ruether, eds. *Christianity and Ecology: Seeking the Well Being of Earth and Humans.* Cambridge, MA: Harvard University Press, 2000.

Hill, William J. "Does God Know the Future? Aquinas and Some Moderns." *Theological Studies* 36/1 (1975): 3–18.

Himes, Kenneth R. "The New Social Encyclical's Communitarian Vision." *Origins* 21 (August 1, 1991): 166–68.

Hines, Mary. "Community for Liberation." In *Freeing Theology: The Essentials of Theology in Feminist Perspective,* edited by Catherine Mowry LaCugna, 161–84. San Francisco: Harper, 1993.

Hittinger, Russell. "Making Sense of the Civilization of Love: John Paul II's Contribution to Catholic Social Thought." In *The Legacy of Pope John Paul II,* edited by Geoffrey Gneuhs, 71–93. New York: Crossroad, 2000.

Holland, Joe. *Modern Catholic Social Teaching: The Popes Confront the Industrial Age, 1740–1958.* New York: Paulist Press, 2003.

Holland, Joe, and Peter Henriot. *Social Analysis: Linking Faith and Justice.* Rev. and enl. ed. Maryknoll, NY: Orbis Books, 1983.

Hollenbach, David. "Christian Social Ethics After the Cold War." *Theological Studies* 53/1 (1992): 75–95.

———. *The Common Good and Christian Ethics.* New York: Cambridge University, 2002.

———. *The Global Faith of Public Faith: Politics, Human Rights, and Christian Faith.* Washington, DC: Georgetown University Press, 2003.

———. *Justice, Peace, and Human Rights: American Catholic Social Ethics in a Pluralistic World.* New York: Crossroad, 1988.

———. "Religion and Political Life." *Theological Studies* 57/1 (1991): 87–106.

Hughes, Lachlan M. "Affectivity, Conscience, and Christian Choice." *The Way Supplement* 24 (Spring 1975): 36–45.

Inch, Morris A. *Scripture as Story.* Lanham, MD: University Press of America, 2000.

Isasi-Diaz, Ada María. "Creating a Liberating Culture." In *Converging on Culture: Theologians in Dialogue with Cultural Analysis and Criticism,* edited by Delvin Brown, Sheila Greeve Davaney, and Kathryn Tanner, 122–39. New York: Oxford University Press, 2001.

———. "Silent Women Will Never Be Heard." *Missiology* 7 (1979): 295–301.

Janssens, Louis. "Norms and Priorities in a Love Ethics." *Louvain Studies* 6 (Spring 1977): 207–38.

Jobling, David. "Globalization in Biblical Studies/Biblical Studies in Globalization." *Biblical Interpretation: A Journal of Contemporary Approaches* 1/1 (1993): 96–110.

Johnson, Elizabeth A. *Consider Jesus: Waves of Renewal in Christology.* New York: Crossroad, 1993.

———. "Does God Play Dice? Providence and Change." *Theological Studies* 57/1 (1996): 3–18.

———. "Imaging God, Embodying Christ: Women as a Sign of the Times." In *The Church Women Want,* edited by Elizabeth A. Johnson, 45–59. New York: Crossroad, 2002.

———. "The Incomprehensibility of God and the Image of God Male and Female." *Theological Studies* 45/3 (1984): 441–65.

———. "Mary and the Female Face of God." *Theological Studies* 50/3 (1989): 500–526.

———. *Quest for the Living God: Mapping Frontiers in the Theology of God.* New York: Continuum, 2007.

———. *She Who Is: The Mystery of God in Feminist Discourse.* New York: Crossroad, 1994.

———. *Women, Earth, and Creator Spirit.* New York: Paulist Press, 1983.

Johnson, Paul. *Pope John XXIII.* Boston: Little, Brown, 1974.

Johnstone, Brian V. "Objectivism, Basic Human Goods, and Proportionalism." *Studia Moralia* 43 (2005): 97–126.

———. "The Subject Object Relation in Contemporary Moral Theology: A Reply to Joseph A. Selling." *Studia Moralia* 44 (2006): 41–62.

Jonson, Albert R., and Stephen Toulmin. *The Abuse of Casuistry.* Berkeley and Los Angeles: University of California Press, 1988.

Kaczor, Christopher. "Double Effect Reasoning from Jean Pierre Gury to Peter Knauer." *Theological Studies* 59/2 (1998): 297–316.

———. "Moral Absolutism and Ectopic Pregnancy." In *Journal of Medicine and Philosophy* 26/1 (2001): 61–74.

———. *Proportionalism and the Natural Law Tradition.* Washington, DC: The Catholic University of America Press, 2002.

———., ed. *Proportionalism, For and Against.* Milwaukee: Marquette University Press, 2000.

Kalbian, Aline. "Where Have All the Proportionalists Gone?" *Journal of Religious Ethics* 30 (2002): 1:3–22.

Keane, Philip S. "Discernment of Spirits: A Theological Reflection." *American Ecclesiastical Review* 168 (1974): 43–61.

Keenan, James F. "The Casuistry of John Mair, Nominalist Professor of Paris." In *The Context of Casuistry*, edited by James F. Keenan and Thomas A. Shannon, 85–103. Washington, DC: Georgetown University Press, 1995.

———. "Christian Perspectives on the Human Body." *Theological Studies* 55/2 (1994): 330–46.

———. "The Function of the Principle of Double Effect." *Theological Studies* 54/2 (1993): 294–315.

———. *A History of Catholic Moral Theology in the Twentieth Century: From Confessing Sins to Liberating Consciences.* New York: Concilium, 2010.

———. "Proposing Cardinal Virtues." *Theological Studies* 56/4 (1995): 709–29.

———. "The Return of Casuistry." *Theological Studies* 57/1 (1996): 123–39.

———. "Virtue Ethics." In *Christian Ethics: An Introduction*, edited by Bernard Hoose, 84–94. Collegeville, MN: Liturgical Press, 1998.

Keenan, James, F., and Thomas A. Shannon. *The Context of Casuistry.* Washington, DC: Georgetown University Press, 1995).

Kinerk, Edward E.. "Eliciting Great Desires: Their Place in the Spirituality of the Society of Jesus." *Studies in the Spirituality of Jesuits* 16/5 (November 1984): 1–29.

King, Ursula, ed. *Feminist Theology from the Third World: A Reader.* Maryknoll, NY: Orbis Books, 1994.

King, Ursula. "Women's Contribution to Contemporary Spirituality." *The Way Supplement* 84 (Autumn 1995): 26–37.

Knauer, Peter. "The Hermeneutical Function of the Principle of Double Effect." In *Readings in Moral Theology*, no. 1, *Moral Norms and Catholic Tradition*, edited by Charles E. Curran and Richard McCormick, 1–39. New York: Paulist Press, 1979.

Korff, Wilhelm. "Nature or Reason as the Criterion for the Universality of Moral Judgments." Concilium 150, *Christian Ethics: Uniformity, Universality, Pluralism*, edited by Jacques Pohier and Dietmar Mieth, 82–88. New York: Seabury Press, 1981.

Kort, Wesley A. *Story, Text, and Scripture: Literary Interests in Biblical Narrative.* University Park: Pennsylvania State University, 1988.

Küng, Hans. *Global Responsibility: In Search of a New Ethics.* New York: Crossroad, 1991.

———. "The History, Significance, and Method of the Declaration Toward a Global Ethic." In *A Global Ethic: The Declaration of the Parliament of the World's Religions*, edited by Hans Küng, 43–76. New York: Continuum, 1998.

———. ed. *Yes to a Global Ethic.* New York: Continuum, 1996.

Küng, Hans, and Helmut Schmidt. *A Global Ethic and Global Responsibilities: Two Declarations.* London: SCM, 1998.

Kyne, Michael. "Difficulties in Discernment." *The Way* 14 (1974): 103–9.

LaCugna, Catherine Mowry. *Being as Communion.* Crestwood, NY: St. Vladimir's Seminary, 1985.

———. *God for Us: The Trinity and Christian Life.* San Francisco: Harper Collins, 1991.

———. "God in Communion with Us." *In Freeing Theology: The Essentials of Theology in Feminist Perspective*, edited by Catherine Mowry La Cugna, 83–114. San Francisco: Harper Collins, 1993.

———. "The Relational God: Aquinas and Beyond." *Theological Studies* 46/4 (1985): 647–63.

Land, Philip S. "The Social Theology of Pope Paul VI." *America* 12 (May 1979).

Langan, John. "Direct and Indirect—Some Recent Exchange Between Paul Ramsey and Richard McCormick." *Religious Studies Review* 5/2 (April 1979): 95–101.

———. "Ethics, Business, and the Economy." *Theological Studies* 55/1 (1994): 105–23.

Leget, Carlo. "Martha Nussbaum and Thomas Aquinas on the Emotions." *Theological Studies* 64/3 (2003): 558–81.

Levison, John R., and Priscilla Pope-Levison. "Global Perspectives on New Testament Interpretation." In *Hearing the New Testament: Strategies for Interpretation*, edited by Joel B. Green, 329–48. Grand Rapids, MI: Eerdmans, 1995.

Lonergan, Bernard. *Method in Theology.* New York: Herder and Herder, 1972.

Longman, Tremper III. "Storytellers and Poets in the Bible: Can Literary Artifice be True?" In *Inerrancy and Hermeneutic: A Tradition, a Challenge, a Debate*, edited by Harvie M. Conn, 137–49. Grand Rapids, MI: Baker Book House, 1988.

Lottin, Odin. *Au Coeur de la Morale Chrétienne.* Tourrnai: Declees, 1957.

———. *Morale Fondamentale.* Belgium: Tournai, 1954.

Lucien, Richard J. *A Kenotic Christology: In the Humanity of Jesus the Christ, the Compassion of our God.* Lanham, MD: Catholic University of America Press, 1982.

MacIntyre, Alasdair. *After Virtue: A Study in Moral Theory.* 2nd ed. Notre Dame, IN: University of Notre Dame Press, 1984.

Mack, Burton L. *Rhetoric and the New Testament, Guides to Biblical Scholarship: New Testament Series.* Minneapolis: Fortress Press, 1990.

MacNamara, Vincent. *Faith and Ethics: Recent Roman Catholicism.* Dublin: Gill and Macmillan, 1985.

———. *Love, Law, and Christian Life: Basic Attitudes of Christian Morality.* Wilmington, DE: Michael Glazier, 1988.

MacReamoinn, Sean. "John XXIII, Pope." In *The Modern Catholic Encyclopedia*, edited by Michael Glazier and Monika Hellwig, 434–38. Collegeville, MN: Michael Glazier/Liturgical Press, 1994.

Maguire, Daniel C. *The Moral Choice.* Garden City, NY: Doubleday, 1978.

———. *The Moral Revolution: A Christian Humanist Vision.* San Francisco: Harper and Row, 1986.

———. "Ratio Practice and Intellectual Fallacy." *Journal of Religious Ethics* 10 (Spring 1982): 22–39.

———. *Sacred Choices: The Right to Contraception and Abortion in Ten World Religions.* Minneapolis: Fortress Press, 2001.

Mahoney, John. *The Making of Moral Theology.* Oxford: Clarendon Press, 1987.

Malina, Bruce J., and Richard L. Rohrbaugh. *Social-Science Commenatary on the Synoptic Gospels.* 2nd edition. Minneapolis: Fortress Press, 2003.

Mamot, Patricio R. *Profile of Filipino Heroism.* Quezon City: New Day, 1986.

Manuel Velasquez, "*Gaudium et Spes* and the Development of Catholic Social-Economic Teaching." In *Questions of Special Urgency*, edited by J. A. Dwyer, 173–99. Washington, DC: Georgetown University Press, 1986.

Massaro, Thomas. *Living Justice: Catholic Social Teaching in Action.* New York: Sheed and Ward, 2000.

———. "The Social Question in the Papacy of Leo XIII." In *The Papacy Since 1500: From Italian Prince to Universal Pastor,* edited by James Corkery and Thomas Worcester, 143–61. New York: Cambridge University Press, 2010.

Massingale, Bryan N. *Racial Justice and the Catholic Church.* Maryknoll, NY: Orbis Books, 2010.

Mattison, William C., ed. *New Wine, New Wineskins: A Next Generation Reflects on Key Issues in Catholic Moral Theology.* Lanham, MD: Rowman and Littlefield, 2005.

May, William E. "Martin Rhonheimer and Some Disputed Issues in Medical Ethics: Masturbation, Condoms, Craniotomies, and Tubal Pregnancies." *The Linacre Quarterly* 77/3 (August 2010): 329–52.

McCormick, Richard A. "Ambiguity in Moral Choice." In *Doing Evil to Achieve Good,* edited by Richard A. McCormick and Paul Ramsey, 7–53. Chicago: Loyola University Press, 1978.

———. *Corrective Vision: Explorations in Moral Theology.* Kansas City, MO: Sheed and Ward, 1994.

———. *The Critical Calling: Reflections on Moral Dilemmas Since Vatican II.* Washington, DC: Georgetown University Press, 1989.

———. "Does Religious Faith Add to Ethical Perception?" In *Introduction to Christian Ethics: A Reader,* edited by Ronald P. Hamel and Kenneth R. Himes, 140–45. New York: Paulist Press, 1989.

———. *Health and Medicine in the Catholic Tradition: Tradition in Transition.* New York: Crossroad, 1984.

———. *How Brave a New World? Dilemmas in Bioethics.* Washington, DC: Georgetown University Press, 1981.

———. "Incommensurability and Indeterminancy in Moral Choices." In *Doing Evil to Achieve Good,* edited by Richard A. McCormick and Paul Ramsey, 69–144. Chicago: Loyola University Press, 1978.

———. "Moral Theology 1940–1989: An Overview." *Theological Studies* 50/1 (1989): 3–24.

———. "Notes on Moral Theology." *Theological Studies* 32/1 (1971): 107–22.

———. *Notes on Moral Theology 1965 through 1980.* Washington, DC: University Press of America, 1981.

———. "Notes on Moral Theology: 1980." *Theological Studies* 42/1 (March 1981): 74–121.

———. "Reproductive Technologies." *Encyclopedia of Bioethics,* edited by Warren T. Reich, 1454–64. New York: Free Press, 1978.

———. "Some Early Reactions to *Veritatis Splendor.*" *Theological Studies* 55/3 (1994): 481–506.

McDermott, Brian O. "The Theology of Original Sin: Recent Developments." *Theological Studies* 38/3 (1977): 478–512.

McFague, Sallie. *Metaphorical Theology: Models of God in Religious Language.* Philadelphia: Fortress Press, 1982.

McGrath, Thomas. "The Place of Desires in the Ignatian Exercises." *The Way Supplement* 76 (Spring 1993): 25–31.

McKnight, Edgar V. *The Bible and the Reader: An Introduction to Literary Criticism.* Philadelphia: Fortress Press, 1985.

McNamara, Vincent. *Love, Law, and Christian Life: Basic Attitudes of Christian Morality.* Wilmington, DE: Michael Glazier, 1988.

Melchin, Kenneth, R. "Revisionists, Deontologists, and the Structure of Moral Understanding." *Theological Studies* 51/3 (1990): 389–416.

Mich, Marvin L. "Commentary on *Mater et Magistra*: Christianity and Social Progress." In *Modern Catholic Social Teaching: Commentaries and Interpretations*, edited by Kenneth R. Himes, 191–216. Washington, DC: Georgetown University Press, 2004.

Miguel-Bonino, José, ed. *Faces of Jesus: Latin American Christologies.* Maryknoll, NY: Orbis Books, 1984.

Misner, Paul. *Social Catholicism in Europe: From the Onset of Industrialization to the First World War.* New York: Crossroad, 1991.

Modras, Ronald. "The Implications of Rahner's Anthropology for Fundamental Moral Theology." *Horizons* 12 (1985): 70–90.

Molinar, Paul. "Can We *Know* God Directly? Rahner's Solution from Experience." *Theological Studies* 46/2 (1985): 228–61.

Moloney, Francis J. *The Gospel of John.* In Sacra Pagina series, vol. 4, edited by Daniel J. Harrington. Collegeville, MN: Liturgical Press, 1998.

Moody, Joseph N., ed. *Church and Society: Catholic Social and Political Thought and Movements, 1789–1950.* New York: Arts, 1953.

Mueller, Franz H. "Solidarism." *The New Dictionary of Catholic Social Thought*, edited by Judith A. Dwyer, 906–8. Collegeville, MN: Liturgical Press, 1994.

Murphy, Lawrence J. "Psychological Problems of Christian Choice." *The Way Supplement* 24 (Spring 1975): 26–35.

Neuhaus, Richard John. "The Pope, Liberty, and Capitalism: Essays on *Centesimus Annus.*" *National Review* 43/11 (June 24, 1991): 8–9.

Nickoloff, James B. "Church of the Poor: The Ecclesiology of Gustavo Gutiérrez." *Theological Studies* 54/3 (1993): 512–35.

Noddings, Nel. *Caring: A Feminine Approach to Ethics and Moral Education.* Los Angeles and Berkeley: University of California Press, 1984.

Northcott, Michael S. *The Environment and Christian Ethics.* Cambridge: Cambridge University Press, 1996).

Novak, Michael. *The Catholic Ethic and the Spirit of Capitalism.* New York: The Free Press, 1993.

———. *Will It Liberate? Questions for Liberation Theology.* New York: Paulist Press, 1986.

Nussbaum, Martha. *The Fragility of Goodness: Luck and Ethics in Greek Tragedy and Philosophy.* New York: Cambridge University Press, 1986.

———. *Upheavals of Thought: The Intelligence of Emotions.* Cambridge: Cambridge University Press, 2001.

O'Brien, David J., and Thomas A. Shannon. *Catholic Social Thought.* Maryknoll, NY: Orbis Books, 2004.

O'Connell, Maureen H. *Compassion: Loving Our Neighbor in an Age of Globalization.* Maryknoll, NY: Orbis Books, 2009.

O'Donovan, Leo J. "A Journey into Time: The Legacy of Karl Rahner's Last Years." *Theological Studies* 46/4 (1985): 621–46.

———. ed. *A World of Grace.* New York: Seabury Press, 1980.

O'Keefe, Mark. *What Are They Saying About Social Sin?* New York: Paulist Press, 1990.

O'Meara, Thomas F. "Virtues in the Theology of Thomas Aquinas." *Theological Studies* 58/2 (1997): 254–85.

O'Neill, Mary Aquin. "The Nature of Women and the Method of Theology." *Theological Studies* 56/4 (1995): 730–42.

Orsy, Ladislas. "Faith and Justice: Some Reflections." *Studies in the Spirituality of Jesuits* (September 1975): 151–69.

Ortner, Sherry. "Is Female to Male as Nature Is to Culture?" In *Women, Culture, and Society,* edited by Michelle Zimbalist Rosaldo and Louise Lamphere, 67–87. Stanford, CA: Stanford University Press, 1974.

Otto, Rudolf. *The Idea of the Holy.* London: Oxford University Press, 1923.

Outka, Gene, and John P. Reeder, eds. *Prospects for a Common Morality.* Princeton, NJ: Princeton University Press, 1993.

Patrick, Anne E. "Authority, Women, and Church: Reconsidering the Relationship." *Empowering Authority: The Charism of Episcopacy and Primacy in the Church Today,* edited by Patrick Howell and Gary Chamberlain, 17–33. Kansas City, MO: Sheed and Ward, 1990.

———. "Ethics and Spirituality: The Social Justice Connection." *The Way Supplement* 63 (Autumn 1988): 103–16.

———. "Narrative and the Social Dynamics of Virtue." Concilium 191, *Changing Values and Virtues,* edited by Dietmar Mieth and Jacques Pohier, 69–80. Edinburgh: T. and T. Clark, 1987.

Phan, Peter C. "Contemporary Context and Issues in Eschatology." *Theological Studies* 55/3 (1994): 507–36.

———. "Method in Liberation Theologies." *Theological Studies* 61/1 (2000): 40–63.

Piper, Loretta. "A Feminist Reflection on Ignatian Mission." *The Way Supplement* 79 (Spring 1994): 30–37.

Pope, Stephen J. "Descriptive and Normative Uses of Evolutionary Theory." In *Christian Ethics,* edited by Lisa Sowle Cahill and James F. Childress, 166–82. Cleveland: Pilgrim Press, 1996.

———. *The Evolution of Altruism and the Ordering of Love.* Washington, DC: Georgetown University Press, 1994.

———. "The Order of Love and Recent Catholic Ethics: A Constructive Proposal." *Theological Studies* 52/2 (1991): 255–88.

———. "Proper and Improper Partiality and the Preferential Option for the Poor." *Theological Studies* 54/2 (1993): 242–71.

Porter, Jean, "*De Ordine Caritatis*: Charity, Friendship, and Justice in Thomas Aquinas' *Summa Theologiae*." *The Thomist* 53/2 (1989): 197–213.

———. "Desire for God: Ground of the Moral Life in Aquinas." *Theological Studies* 47/1 (1986): 48–68.

———. "'Direct' and 'Indirect' in Grisez's Moral Theory." *Theological Studies* 57/4 (1996): 611–32.

———. *Natural and Divine Law: Reclaiming the Tradition for Christian Ethics*. Grand Rapids, MI: Eerdmans, 1999.

———. "The Natural Law and the Specificity of Christian Morality." In *Method and Catholic Moral Theology: The Ongoing Reconstruction*, edited by Todd A. Salzman, 209–29. Omaha, NE: Creighton University Press, 1999.

———. *Nature as Reason: A Thomistic Theory of the Natural Law*. Grand Rapids, MI: Eerdmans, 2005.

———. *The Recovery of Virtue*. Louisville, KY: Westminster/John Knox Press, 1990.

———. "The Search for a Global Ethic." *Theological Studies* 62/1 (2001): 105–21.

Porter, Stanley E. "Literary Approaches to the New Testament: From Formalism to Deconstruction and Back." In *Approaches to New Testament Study*, edited by Stanley E. Porter and David Tombs, *Journal for the Study of the New Testament and Supplementary Series* 120, 77–128. Sheffield: Sheffield Academic Press, 1995.

Post, Stephen G. *More Lasting Unions: Christianity, the Family, and Society*. Grand Rapids, MI: Eerdmans, 2000.

Powell, Mark Allan. *What Is Narrative Criticism?* Minneapolis: Fortress Press, 1990.

Preston, Ronald H. "*Centesimus Annus*: An Appraisal." *Theology* 95 (1992): 405–16.

Rahner, Karl. "The Abiding Significance of Vatican II." *Theological Investigations*, vol. 20, *Concern for the Church*. Translated by Edward Quinn, 90–102. New York: Crossroad, 1981.

———. "Dialogue with God." *Theological Investigations*, vol. 18, *God and Revelation*. Translated by Edward Quinn, 122–31. New York: Crossroad, 1983.

———. *The Dynamic Element in the Church*. Montreal: Palm, 1964.

———. "The Experience of God Today." *Theological Investigations*, vol. 11, *Confrontations*. Translated by David Bourke, 149–65. New York: Seabury Press, 1974.

———. *Foundations of Christian Faith: An Introduction to the Idea of Christianity*. Translated by William V. Dych. New York: Crossroad, 1984.

———. *Hearer of the Word: Laying the Foundation for a Philosophy of Religion*. Edited by Andrew Tallon. Translated by Joseph Donceel. New York: Continuum, 1994.

————. "The Human Question of Meaning in the Face of the Absolute Mystery of God." *Theological Investigations*, vol. 18, *God and Revelation*. Translated by Edward Quinn, 89–104. New York: Crossroad, 1983.

————. "The Logic of Concrete Individual Knowledge in Ignatius Loyola." In *The Dynamic Element in the Church (Quaestiones Disputatae 12)*, translated by W. J. O'Hara, 115–70. New York: Herder and Herder, 1964.

————. "Poetry and the Christian." *Theological Investigations*, vol. 4, *More Recent Writings*, 357–67. Translated by Kevin Smyth. Baltimore: Helicon, 1966.

————. *The Practice of Faith: A Handbook of Contemporary Spirituality.* New York: Crossroad, 1983.

————. "Reflections on the Experience of Grace." *Theological Investigations*, vol. 3, *The Theology of the Spiritual Life*. Translated by Karl-H. and Boniface Kruger, 86–90. London: Darton, Longman and Todd, 1967.

————. "Some Thoughts on Good Intention." *Theological Investigations*, vol. 3, *The Theology of the Spiritual Life*. Translated by Karl-H. and Boniface Kruger, 105–28. Baltimore: Helicon, 1967.

————. "Theology and Anthropology." *Theological Investigations*, vol. 9, *Writings of 1965–67*. Translated by Graham Harrison, 28–45. London: Darton, Longman, and Todd, 1972.

————. "On the Theology of the Incarnation." *Theological Investigations*, vol. 11, *Confrontations*. Translated by David Bourke, 105–20. New York: Seabury Press, 1974.

Ratzinger, Joseph. *Dogmatic Theology: Eschatology: Death and Eternal Life.* Translated by Michael Waldstein and Aidan Nichols. Washington, DC: Catholic University of America Press, 1988.

Rawls, John. *A Theory of Justice.* Oxford: Oxford University Press, 1971.

Reumann, John Henry. "After Historical Criticism, What? Trends in Biblical Interpretation and Ecumenical, Interfaith Dialogues." *Journal of Ecumenical Studies* 29 (1992): 55–86.

Rhonheimer, Martin. "Vital Conflicts, Direct Killing, and Justice: A Response to Rev. Benedict Guevin and Other Critics." *The National Catholic Bioethics Quarterly* 11/3 (Autumn 2011): 519–40.

Ricouer, Paul. *Hermeneutics and the Human Sciences: Essays on Language, Action and Interpretation.* Cambridge: Cambridge University Press, 1981.

Riga, Peter. *John XXII and the City of Man.* Westminster, MD: Newman, 1966.

Ross, Susan A. "Feminist Theology: A Review of Literature: The Physical and Social Context for Feminist Theology and Spirituality." *Theological Studies* 56/2 (1995): 327–41.

Rourke, Nancy. "Where Is the Wrong? A Comparison of Two Accounts of the Principle of Double Effect." *Irish Theological Quarterly* 76/2 (2011): 150–63.

Ruether, Rosemary Radford. *To Change the World: Christology and Cultural Criticism*. New York: Crossroad, 1981.

———. "Christology and Feminism: Can a Male Saviour Save Women?" In *To Change the World: Christology and Cultural Criticism*. New York: Crossroad, 1981.

———. "The Female Nature of God: A Problem in Contemporary Religious Life." Concilium 143, *God as Father?*, edited by Johannes Baptist Metz, Edward Schillebeeckx, Marcus Lefébure, 61–68. Edinburgh: T and T Clark, 1981.

———. *Gaia and God: An Ecofeminist Theology of Earth Healing*. San Francisco: Harper San Francisco, 1992.

———. *New Woman, New Earth*. San Francisco: Harper and Row, 1975.

———. *Sexism and God-Talk: Toward a Feminist Theology*. Boston: Beacon Press, 1983.

———. ed. *Women Healing Earth: Third World Women on Ecology, Feminism, and Religion*. Maryknoll, NY: Orbis Books, 1996.

Russell, Letty M. *Church in the Round: Feminist Interpretation of the Church*. Louisville, KY: Westminster/John Knox, 1993.

Sachs, John R. "Current Eschatology: Universal Salvation and the Problem of Evil." *Theological Studies* 52/2 (1991): 227–54.

Salzman, Todd A. *What Are They Saying About Catholic Ethical Method?* New York: Paulist Press, 2003.

Sansom, Dennis. "Does Morality Need God? A Kierkegaardian Critique of Kant's Moral Philosophy." *Perspectives in Religious Studies* 26/1 (Spring 1999): 17–33.

Schaab, Gloria L. "Feminist Theological Methodology: Toward A Kaleidoscopic Model." *Theological Studies* 62/2 (2001): 341–65.

Scheffler, Samuel. *The Rejection of Consequentialism: A Philosophical Investigation of the Considerations Underlying Rival Conceptions*. Rev. ed. Oxford: Clarendon Press, 1982.

Schneiders, Sandra M. *Beyond Patching: Faith and Feminism in the Catholic Church*. New York: Paulist Press, 2004.

———. "The Bible and Feminism." In *Freeing Theology: The Essentials of Theology in Feminist Perspective*, edited by Catherine Mowry La Cugna, 31–57. San Francisco: Harper Collins, 1993.

———. "Feminist Ideology Criticism and Biblical Hermeneutics." *Biblical Theology Bulletin* 19/1 (February 1989): 3–10.

———. *The Revelatory Text: Interpreting the New Testament as Sacred Scripture*. 2nd ed. Collegeville, MN: Liturgical Press, 1999.

———. "Spirituality in the Academy." *Theological Studies* 50/4 (1989): 676–97.

———. *Women and Word: 1986 Madaleva Lecture in Spirituality*. New York: Paulist Press, 1986.

Schubeck, Thomas L. "Ethics and Liberation Theology." *Theological Studies* 56/1 (1995): 107–22.

———. "The Reconstruction of Natural Law Reasoning: Liberation Theology as a Case Study." *The Journal of Religious Ethics* 20/1 (1992): 149–78.

Schuck, Michael J. "Early Modern Roman Catholic Social Thought, 1740–1890." In *Modern Catholic Social Teaching: Commentaries and Interpretations*, edited by Kenneth R. Himes, 99–124. Washington, DC: Georgetown University Press, 2004.

———. *That They Be One: The Social Teaching of the Papal Encyclicals, 1740–1989.* Washington, DC: Georgetown University Press, 1991.

Schüller, Bruno. "The Double Effect in Catholic Thought: A Reevaluation." In *Doing Evil to Achieve Good*, edited by Richard A. McCormick and Paul Ramsey, 165–92. Chicago: Loyola University Press, 1978.

———. "Various Type of Grounding for Ethical Norms." In *Readings in Moral Theology*, no. 1, *Moral Norms and Catholic Traditions*, edited by Charles E. Curran and Richard A. McCormick, 184–98. New York: Paulist Press, 1979.

Schüssler Fiorenza, Elisabeth. "Breaking the Silence—Becoming Visible." Concilium 182, *Women: Invisible in Church and Theology*, edited by Mary Collins and Elisabeth Schüssler Fiorenza, 3–16. Edinburgh: T. and T. Clark, 1984.

Segovia, Fernando F. *Decolonizing Biblical Studies: A View from the Margins.* Maryknoll, NY: Orbis Books, 2000.

Selling, Joseph A. "Distinct But Not Separate: The Subject-Object Relation in Contemporary Moral Theology." *Studia Moralia* 44 (2006): 15–40.

———. "*Gaudium et Spes*: A Manifesto for Contemporary Moral Theology." In *Vatican II and Its Legacy*, edited by Mathijs Lamberigts and Leo Kenis, 145–62. Leuven: Leuven University, 2002.

Shannon, Thomas A. "Commentary on *Rerum Novarum*: The Condition of Labor." In *Modern Catholic Social Teaching: Commentaries and Interpretations*, edited by Kenneth R. Himes, 127–50. Washington, DC: Georgetown University Press, 2004.

Simpson, Michael. "Philosophical Certitude and the Ignatian Election." *The Way Supplement* 24 (Spring 1975): 58–66.

Sirico, Robert A. "The Pope, Liberty, and Capitalism: Essays on *Centesimus Annus*." *National Review* 43/11 (June 24, 1991): 12–13.

Sobrino, Jon. *Christology at the Crossroads: A Latin American Approach.* Maryknoll, NY: Orbis Books, 1978.

Spielthenner, Georg. "Lesser Evil Reasoning and Its Pitfalls." *Argumentation* 24 (2010): 139–52.

Spohn, William C. "Jesus and Christian Ethics." *Theological Studies* 56/1 (1995): 92–107.

———. "Passion and Principles." *Theological Studies* 52/1 (March 1991): 69–87.

———. "The Reasoning Heart: An American Approach to Christian Discernment." *Theological Studies* 44/1 (1983): 30–44.

———. "The Return of Virtue Ethics." *Theological Studies* 53/1 (1992): 60–75.

———. "Spirituality and Ethics: Exploring the Connections." *Theological Studies* 58/1 (1997): 109–23.

Sugirtharajah, R. S. "The Bible and Its Asian Readers." *Biblical Interpretation* 1 (1993): 54–66.

———. ed. *Commitment, Context, and Text: Examples of Asian Hermeneutics, Special Issue of Biblical Interpretation* 2 (1993): 251–376.

———. ed. *Voices from the Margins: Interpreting the Bible in the Third World.* Maryknoll, NY: Orbis Books, 2006.

Swidler, Leonard. "Jesus Was a Feminist." *New Catholic World* 214 (1971): 771–73.

Tanner, Kathryn E. *Theories of Culture: A New Agenda for Theology.* Minneapolis: Fortress Press, 1997.

Tillich, Paul. *Dynamics of Faith.* New York: Harper and Row, 1958.

———. *Ultimate Concern: Tillich in Dialogue.* New York: Harper and Row, 1965.

———. *What Is Religion?* New York: Harper, 1969.

Tolbert, Mary Ann. *Perspectives on the Parables: An Approach to Multiple Interpretations.* Philadelphia: Fortress Press, 1979.

Toner, Jules J. *A Commentary on Saint Ignatius' Rules for the Discernment of Spirits.* St. Louis: The Institute of Jesuit Sources, 1982.

———. *Discerning God's Will: Ignatius of Loyola's Teaching on Christian Decision Making.* St. Louis: Institute of Jesuit Sources, 1991.

———. *The Experience of Love.* Washington, DC: Corpus Books, 1968.

Trianosky, Gregory. "What Is Virtue Ethics All About?" *American Philosophical Quarterly* 27 (October 1990): 335–44.

Twiss, Sumner, and Bruce Grelle, eds. *Explorations in Global Ethics: Comparative Interreligious Dialogue.* Boulder, CO: Westview, 2000.

Vacek, Edward Collins. "Divine-Command, Natural-Law, and Mutual-Love Ethics." *Theological Studies* 57/1 (1996): 633–53.

———. *Love, Human and Divine: The Heart of Christian Ethics.* Washington, DC: Georgetown University Press, 1994.

———. "Proportionalism: One View of the Debate." *Theological Studies* 46/2 (1985): 287–314.

Verhey, Allen. "Scripture and Ethics: Practices, Performance, and Prescription." In *Christian Ethics: Problems and Prospects,* edited by Lisa Sowle Cahill and James F. Childress, 18–44. Cleveland: Pilgrim Press, 1996.

Von Balthasar, Hans Urs. *Dare We Hope "That All Men Be Saved"?* Translated by David Kipp and Lothar Krauth. San Francisco: Ignatius, 1988.

Werhane, Patricia. "The Obligatory Nature of Stewardship in *Rerum Novarum* and Its Relevance to the American Economy." In *Celebrating*

One Hundred Years of Catholic Social Thought, edited by Ronald F. Duska. Lewiston, NY: Edwin Mellen, 1991.

Westberg, Daniel. *Right Practical Reason: Aristotle, Action, and Prudence in Aquinas.* Oxford: Clarendon Press, 1994.

Whitmore, Todd David. "John Paul II, Michael Novak, and the Differences Between Them." *Annual Volume of the Society of Christian Ethics* 21 (2001): 215–32.

Wicker, Kathleen O'Brien. "Teaching Feminist Biblical Studies in a Post-colonial Context." In *Searching the Scriptures*, vol. 1, *A Feminist Introduction*, edited by Elisabeth Schüssler Fiorenza, 367–80. New York: Crossroad, 1993.

Wiley, Tatha. *Original Sin: Origins, Developments, Contemporary Meanings.* New York: Paulist Press, 2002.

Williams, Delores S. "A Womanist Perspective on Sin." In *A Troubling in My Soul: Womanist Perspectives on Evil and Suffering*, edited by Emilie M. Townes, 130–49. Maryknoll, NY: Orbis Books, 1993.

Wolfe, Regina Wentzel, and Christine E. Gudorf, eds. *Ethics and World Religions: Cross-Cultural Case Studies.* Maryknoll, NY: Orbis Books, 1999.

Wookey, Charles. "Making Christian Choices in the Political World." *The Way Supplement* 64 (Spring 1989): 103–14.

Yearley, Lee H. *Mencius and Aquinas: Theories of Virtue and Conceptions of Courage.* Albany: State University of New York Press, 1990.

Zappone, Katherine. *The Hope for Wholeness: A Spirituality for Feminists.* Mystic, CT: Twenty-Third Publications, 1991.

Index

Gregory of Nyssa, 180
Grelle, Bruce, 61
Grisez, Germain, 42, 45, 51, 400–401,
    407, 409, 417, 418
Gudorf, Christine E., 61, 62, 198,
    338–39
guild system, 258, 260–61, 343
Gula, Richard, 399
Gustafson, James, xx, 43–44, 434
Gutiérrez, Gustavo, 190, 230–31, 344,
    502

Haight, Roger, 16–17, 201–4,
    219n146, 470
Hales, E.E.Y., 275
Hallett, Garth, 29
Häring, Bernhard, xv–xvi, xxii, 3, 5–6,
    7
Hauerwas, Stanley, 24–25, 29, 49, 118,
    425
healthcare, justice concerns about, 34
heaven, 220
Hebrew scriptures, 165
hegemony, 157
Hehir, Brian, 505
hell
    Christ's descent into, 220
    possibility of, 220, 221
Hellwig, Monika, 230
Henriot, Peter, 79–80, 466
hermeneutical-contextual   approach,
    151n110
hermeneutical privilege of the op-
    pressed, 162, 501
hermeneutics, task of, 13–14
Herzog, William R., 193–96
Heschel, Abraham, 75
hierarchy, 257, 268, 332, 453
Hill, William J., 458–59
Himes, Kenneth, 385
Hines, Mary, 224
historical context, 235
historical-critical method. See histori-
    cal criticism
historical criticism, xvi, 11, 13, 107,
    108, 120, 142, 145, 160–61,
    500, 501
    collapse of, 111
    conjectural nature of, 143
    contributions of, 166

cultural criticism and, 116
distinct from literary criticism,
    113–14
limits of, 166
orientation of, 161
scholarly approach of, 137
sterility of, 112
studying texts as process of accre-
    tion and redaction, 111
tending toward universal meaning,
    145
theological orientation of, 110
working with narrative criticism,
    143
historical movements, 315
Hittinger, Russell, 386
holism, 406
holistic ethical reasoning. See ethics of
    holistic reasoning
holistic reasoning, ethics of. See ethics
    of holistic reasoning
Holland, Joe, 104, 272
Hollenbach, David, 31–32, 33, 101,
    102, 364
Holocaust, 358
holy, encountering, 498–99
Holy Spirit, 212–14, 326
    active in textual interpretation, 138
    Christian doctrine of, 138
Homeric culture, virtues and, 428
homosexuality, 404
hope, 211, 424
    eschatological, 220, 221–22, 230
hospitality, 54, 210
Humanae Vitae (Paul VI), 40–41, 337
human-divine encounter. See divine-
    human encounter
human ecology, 372
humane treatment, as common ethic
    among religions, 58
human goods, 42
humanity
    common, 231
    unity and peace of, 275
human liberation, theology of, 356
human nature
    changing aspect of, 41
    moral significance of, 42–44
humans
    agency of, 453

intrinsic evil, 49, 51, 402, 404
intuitionism, 438, 511
irony, 126
Isasi-Diaz, Ada María, 73
Iser, Wolfgang, 143, 501
Israel, faith of, 175
Italy, unification of, 240, 241
iterative narration, 132–33

Janssens, Louis, 400
Jeremias, Joachim, 193
Jesuits, manuals of, 50
Jesus. *See also* Christ
    attitude of, toward women, 189, 192
    belief in, 15–16
    birth of, read from disenfranchised perspective, 148–49
    blackness of, 208–9
    challenging patriarchal perspectives, 152–54, 184–85
    compassion of, 30
    death of, reasons for, 197–200
    divinity of, 16
    doctrine of, xvii
    execution of, 194
    as God's fullest revelation, 164
    historical, 15, 16–17
    humanity of, 224
    idealistic empathy for, 130
    images of, in Asian context, 206–7
    inclusiveness of, 193
    as Jesus Liberator, 190
    maleness of, 188–90
    as master storyteller, 118
    meaning of, in people's lives, 206–9
    ministry of, linked with economic and political realities, 196–97
    moral significance of, 16
    mystery of, 209–10
    parables of, 191, 193–97
    physical appearance of, 205
    political ministry of, 190–91
    portrayal of, 127
    poverty of, 148–49
    public life of, 194
    reign of God and, 222
    reinterpreting Hebrew scriptures, 165

    religiosity of, and politics, 191
    religious pluralism and, 229–30
    resurrection of, 201–4
    as round character, 127
    self-emptying of, 187
    solidarity of, with the poor, 190
    spirituality of, 197
    submission of, 198
    subversiveness of, 191–97
    table fellowship of, 191–92, 193
    womanist view of, 154–55
Jesus: The Complete Story (Discovery Channel/BBC), 205
Jesus Christ Liberator (Boff), 200–201
Job, narrator's voice in, 124
John XXIII, 330. See also *Mater et Magistra*; *Pacem in Terris*
    agenda of, 274–75
    defining "common good," 280–81
    election of, 275
    envisioning renewed Catholic Church, 274
    methodology of, 279
    optimism of, 276, 279, 282, 294, 296, 300
    papacy of, 273–75, 277, 278–79
    shortsightedness of, 300
    spirit of, 273
    spirituality of, 296
    theology of, 296
    vision of, for Vatican II, 275
    worldview of, 282, 284
John Paul II, 9, 104, 108–9, 227, 339. See also *Centesimus Annus*; *Evangelium Vitae*; *Laborem Exercens*; *Mulieris Dignitatem*; *Sollicitudo Rei Socialis*; *Veritatis Splendor*
    antiwar statement of, 359
    appealing to business leaders, 386–87
    calling for conflict resolution, 381
    and the failure of *Octogesima Adveniens*, 335
    influence of, on collapse of communism, 352–53
    misinterpretation of, 383–84
    on religious representatives meeting, 229

Satan
  belief in, 460, 461, 463–67, 476
  demythologizing, 464
  ways of, 488
satellites, 131
satisfaction-atonement, 197–99
Scent of a Woman (Brest, dir.), 426
Schaab, Gloria, 53, 54
Schillebeeckx, Edward, 34–35, 102, 170, 224–25, 230
Schneiders, Sandra, 13n43, 52, 151n110, 184–85, 188
Scholastics, 44–45
Schoonenberg, Peter J., 462–63
Schoonenberg, Piet, 215, 219
Schubeck, Thomas, 38–39
Schuck, Michael, 272, 278
Schüller, Bruno, 26, 407
Schüssler Fiorenza, Elisabeth, 54, 151n111, 191, 192, 198–99
Schüssler Fiorenza, Francis, 169
science, 290, 291, 318–19, 332
  access to, 384–85
  limitations of, 434–35
scripture
  authority of, 164–65
  as basis for moral theology, 107
  character descriptions in, related to plot, 127
  creation accounts in, 174–76, 177
  ever-renewing, 162
  exegesis of, 11
  feminist reading of, 150–56, 160
  God's evaluative point of view in, 123–24
  historical-critical approach to, 11
  illuminative aspect of, 119–20
  illuminative use of, 107
  interpretation of, 500
  language of, 10–11
  as lens, 17, 502
  liberating from patriarchal perspective, 151
  liberationist approach to, 149–50
  literary approach to, 120–21. See *also* literary criticism
  literary quality of, 109
  minorities' reading of, 158
  morality in, 11
  moral theology and, 14, 65

  narrative criticism of, 107–8. See *also* narrative criticism
  prescriptive use of, 107
  reading from call of Jesus, 165
  reading through call to abundant life, 165
  as soul of theology, 2, 500
  as source of moral theology, 10–14
  as story, 112, 500
  story lines in, 134–35
  strangeness of, dealing with, 143
  use of, 14, 69, 117, 119–20, 500
  written within different social locations, 164–65
Second Vatican Council. See Vatican II
Segovia, Fernando, 111, 158
Segundo, Juan Luis, 190–91
self, 180
  character and, 24
  gift of, 351
  preoccupation with, 65
self-care, 425, 426, 436, 509–10
self-transcendence, 76, 103, 104
Selling, Joseph, 6, 51
Semaines Sociales de France, 298
sentir, 486
sexual ethics, 34, 35, 41, 43, 336–37
sexuality, procreative purpose of, 290
Shannon, Thomas A., 237, 245, 246, 247, 273, 305, 341
signs, discernment of, 327
Simon, William, 383
sin, 174
  central reality of, 22
  doctrine of, xvii
  evil assuming human face in, 466
  feminist perspectives on, 216–17
  focus of, reoriented, 65
  freedom exercised in, 489
  grace and, 173
  institutionalized, 219
  liberation theology and, 217–19
  manuals preoccupied with, 23
  meaning of, and disposition of self, 22
  moral life and, 21–22
  moral theology fixated on, 2–3
  mortal, 21, 22
  original, 173, 215–16, 219
  personal, 218–19, 466